INTELLECTUAL PROPERTY TITLES FROM WILEY LAW PUBLICATIONS

ELECTRONIC CONTRACTING, PUBLISHING, AND EDI LAW
   Michael S. Baum and Henry H. Perritt, Jr.
HOW TO LICENSE TECHNOLOGY
   Robert C. Megantz
INTELLECTUAL PROPERTY INFRINGEMENT DAMAGES: A LITIGATION SUPPORT
   HANDBOOK
   Russell L. Parr
INTELLECTUAL PROPERTY: LICENSING AND JOINT VENTURE PROFIT STRATEGIES
   Gordon V. Smith and Russell L. Parr
LAW AND THE INFORMATION SUPERHIGHWAY: PRIVACY • ACCESS • INTELLECTUAL
   PROPERTY • COMMERCE • LIABILITY
   Henry H. Perritt, Jr.
MANAGING INTELLECTUAL PROPERTY RIGHTS
   Lewis C. Lee and J. Scott Davidson
MULTIMEDIA LEGAL HANDBOOK: A GUIDE FROM THE SOFTWARE PUBLISHER'S
   ASSOCIATION
   Thomas J. Smedinghoff
THE NEW ROLE OF INTELLECTUAL PROPERTY IN COMMERCIAL TRANSACTIONS
   Melvin Simensky and Lanning G. Bryer
1996 WILEY INTELLECTUAL PROPERTY LAW UPDATE
   Anthony B. Askew and Elizabeth C. Jacobs
PROTECTING TRADE TRESS
   Robert C. Dorr and Christopher H. Munch
PROTECTING TRADE SECRETS, PATENTS, COPYRIGHTS, AND TRADEMARKS, 2E
   Robert C. Dorr and Christopher H. Munch
SOFTWARE INDUSTRY ACCOUNTING
   Joseph M. Morris
SOFTWARE PATENTS
   Gregory A. Stobbs
TECHNOLOGY LICENSING STRATEGIES
   Russell L. Parr and Patrick H. Sullivan
VALUATION OF INTELLECTUAL PROPERTY AND INTANGIBLE ASSETS, 2E
   Gordon V. Smith and Russell L. Parr

LAW AND THE INFORMATION SUPERHIGHWAY

PRIVACY • ACCESS • INTELLECTUAL PROPERTY • COMMERCE • LIABILITY

SUBSCRIPTION NOTICE

This Wiley product is updated on a periodic basis with supplements to reflect important changes in the subject matter. If you purchased this product directly from John Wiley & Sons, Inc., we have already recorded your subscription for this update service.

If, however, you purchased this product from a bookstore and wish to receive (1) the current update at no additional charge, and (2) future updates and revised or related volumes billed separately with a 30-day examination review, please send your name, company name (if applicable), address, and the title of the product to:

Supplement Department
John Wiley & Sons, Inc.
One Wiley Drive
Somerset, NJ 08875
1-800-225-5945

For customers outside the United States, please contact the Wiley office nearest you.

Professional and Reference Division
John Wiley & Sons Canada, Ltd.
22 Worcester Road
Rexdale, Ontario M9W 1L1
CANADA
(416) 675-3580
1-800-567-4797
Fax: (416) 675-6599

John Wiley & Sons, Ltd.
Baffins Lane
Chichester
West Sussex, PO19 1UD
UNITED KINGDOM
Phone: (44) (243) 779777

Jacaranda Wiley Ltd.
PRT Division
P.O. Box 174
North Ryde, NSW 2113
AUSTRALIA
Phone: (02) 805-1100
Fax: (02) 805-1597

John Wiley & Sons (SEA)
Pte. Ltd.
37 Jalan Pemimpin
Block B # 05-04
Union Industrial Building
SINGAPORE 2057
Phone: (65) 258-1157

LAW AND THE INFORMATION SUPERHIGHWAY
PRIVACY • ACCESS • INTELLECTUAL PROPERTY • COMMERCE • LIABILITY

HENRY H. PERRITT, JR.

Professor of Law
Villanova University
School of Law

Wiley Law Publications
JOHN WILEY & SONS, INC.
New York • Chichester • Brisbane • Toronto • Singapore

Copyright © 1996 by John Wiley & Sons, Inc..

Library of Congress Cataloging-in-Publication Data

Perritt, Henry H.
    Law and the information superhighway / Henry H. Perritt, Jr.
      p.   cm. — (Business practice library)
    Includes bibliographical references.
    ISBN 0-471-12624-1 (cloth : alk. paper)
     1. Telecommunication—Law and legislation—United States.
    2. Data transmission systems—Law and legislation—United
    States.   3. Information superhighway—United States. I. Title.
    II. Series.
    KF2765.P47   1996
    343.7309'944—dc20   95-38871
    [347.3039944   CIP

Printed in the United States of America

10 9 8 7 6 5 4

PREFACE

This book is about the information superhighway, more formally known as the National Information Infrastructure (NII), and the "infobahn" or Global Information Infrastructure (GII) in Europe. The infobahn comprises the Internet, proprietary electronic information services like America Online and CompuServe, basic and enhanced telephone services, and television broadcast distribution using digital technologies and new networking concepts. Following the example of its metaphoric counterpart, a physical superhighway carrying automobiles, buses, and trucks, the NII must have legal systems for handling the electronic equivalent of tolls for use of the highway, payments for bus rides and purchases or rentals of automobiles and trucks. It must have rules for determining who gets to use which lanes when, rules for assigning responsibility for clearing up traffic jams and potholes, rules for dealing with the use of public and private property, rules to constrain police and other searches of vehicles, rules for allocating the risk of loss in the event of accidents and collisions, civil and criminal procedures, and customs and immigration checkpoints.

Chapter 1 introduces the infobahn, explaining the relationship of the different computer and communications technologies and the convergence of traditional legal categories.

Chapter 2 considers legal rights to use the infobahn. It recognizes that the need for access rights and the likely resort to them will be determined by failure of market forces to open up the various parts of the infrastructure. Economics theory says that in those parts of the infrastructure where competitive market conditions exist, self-interest should induce those that control access to make it available to anyone who is willing to pay a price close to marginal costs. But markets do not always work perfectly, and **Chapter 2** surveys the types of access claims that can be asserted under existing legal doctrine.

Chapter 3 addresses privacy. It considers the degree to which information traveling on the infobahn is subject to search and seizure by public authorities or private intruders.

Chapter 4 addresses the computer and digital network equivalent of personal injury and vehicle accident law, inventorying the kinds of legal claims that might arise from information or information practices that harm third parties, ranging from defamation to false and misleading advertising. Because intermediaries and information and communication conduits are likely to play an even more important role in the NII than they play in today's communications and information networks, the chapter pays special attention to the legal position of intermediaries when these claims are asserted because of the conduct of those originating content that traverses intermediary facilities or services.

Chapter 5 considers the responsibility of service providers when things break down. Who bears the loss if there is a traffic jam or potholes or barricades, or signage that results in misrouting? This chapter considers warranties and fraudulent misrepresentation claims against service providers and offers model disclaimer language.

Chapter 6 reviews the impact of the United States Constitution on legal regulation of the infobahn, concentrating on First Amendment and private property protections.

Chapter 7 considers traditional common carrier and broadcast regulation by the FCC, highlights new regulatory doctrines such as price cap regulation and open network architecture, and considers what role regulation by administrative agencies is likely to play with respect to new services and configurations. **Chapter 7** also considers the possibilities for "self-regulation" or "self-governance" of cyberspace.

Chapter 8 explains that standardization is important in this as in any infrastructure. The meaning of roadsigns and lane markings must be immediately clear and cannot vary too much from road to road and vendor to vendor. The ends of surface streets must meet the beginning of entry ramps without impassable differences in level, surface, or width. For computers to "talk" to each other, the interfaces must be more precise than they need be for roads to be passable. The chapter explains that most communications and information standards in the United States are set, not by the government, but by private entities functioning through formalities dictated by the antitrust laws. It also explores particular regulatory techniques used by the Congress and administrative agencies to set or encourage private persons to set standards and assure compatibility and interoperability.

Chapter 9 considers payment systems, technological and legal systems so that vendors of NII services and information content can get paid without having to make arrangements independently through the mail, face-to-face contact, or telephone calls. More generally, it explores how contracts can be made directly through electronic messages, with or without human involvement. Electronic Data Interchange (EDI) is a prominent subject of this chapter.

Intellectual property—copyright, trade secret, patent, and trademark—is the subject of **Chapter 10**. It explains why NII technologies pose even greater threats to the security of property interests in information than proprietary information services like LEXIS, Westlaw, and America Online. It recapitulates the basic principles in the major cases in each of the four areas of intellectual property law and explains how those doctrines are being adapted to the NII. It reviews major proposals for changes in intellectual property law, summarizes the visions of the recently concluded Uruguay Round of amendments to the General Agreement on Tariffs and Trade, which emphasized intellectual property protection, and explains how NII entrepreneurs and their counsel can design products and delivery and payments systems to complement legal protections.

One of the first types of valuable information actually to be traded on the NII was public information—statutes and judicial opinions, weather information, and geographic data. **Chapter 11** presents a policy and legal framework within which the incentives for public agencies to set up monopolies over valuable public information can be channeled to encourage the evolution of a competitive environment within which public and private producers of information value can complement each other to make all types of public information available at reasonable cost. It reviews the Freedom of Information Act and explores how copyright law and antitrust law are applied to public entities.

Chapter 12 considers civil procedure and private dispute resolution, recognizing that one of the challenges presented by the global information infrastructure is that its technologies do not respect the geographic boundaries that historically have limited the jurisdiction of courts and enforcement authorities. This chapter also considers acceptability of electronic formats as evidence in administrative and judicial proceedings.

Chapter 13 addresses information crimes. It explains the substantive crimes most likely to be involved in the NII and explores procedural issues including the efficacy of search warrants across state and national boundaries as well as explaining how search authorization works under the Electronic Communications Privacy Act when law enforcement authorities want to inspect stored electronic records or to intercept electronic messages.

Chapter 14 reinforces material in all of the other chapters on international dimensions of GII law. It explains the major international institutions, including not only governmental institutions like those of the European Union, but also essentially private institutions like the International Chamber of Commerce and the American Arbitration Association, which facilitate the use of arbitration as a dispute resolution mechanism for international disputes.

I have had the privilege of involvement in a number of private lawsuits involving claims over information and computer practices, have been centrally involved in the formulation of federal government information policy for electronic filing and dissemination through the Administrative Conference of the United States and the President's Office of Management and Budget, have drafted recommendations on public information policy adopted by the Board of Governors of the American Bar Association, have advised the European Commission and other international bodies on information law, and have written and participated in academic and bar symposia extensively on these subjects. These experiences and my teaching of law school courses in computer and information law reinforces my conclusion as a lawyer that the information superhighway does not necessitate scrapping legal principles and procedures that have been worked out over a couple of centuries in our legal tradition. The core concepts of torts, contracts, property, crimes, regulation, and procedure continue to be valid. Sound NII law requires knowledge of the technology by counselors, litigants, and judges and an appreciation of how old legal concepts may need to be expressed in new ways to accommodate the real functioning of these technologies.

This book is intended to refresh basic principles in the new contexts, and to further such an appreciation.

Villanova, Pennsylvania   HENRY H. PERRITT, JR.
November 1995

ACKNOWLEDGMENTS

I appreciate tangible and intangible support from Steven P. Frankino, Dean of Villanova University School of Law, and from Susan Rexford Coady and Lori Hallman for cheerful and efficient administrative and word processing support. Villanova Law students Paul Boltz, Ryan Bornstein, Brian B. Crowner, Kevin Ehrlich, William Harrington, Thomas Kessler, Cara Leheny, Sean Lugg, Martin Noonan, Michael Quarles, Eugene Schriver IV, Thomas Thistle, and Andrew Vella did good work in organizing research and checking sources.

More generally, I want to thank David R. Johnson for many stimulating conversations about the role of law in cyberspace, my colleagues James E. Maule, Richard L. Turkington, Joseph E. Dellapenna, and Howard R. Lurie for probing discussions of various legal doctrines, Ronald L. Plesser for his policy and legal leadership in reconceptualizing communications and information law, Ronald L. Staudt for his visions of legal automation, Bruce McConnell and Peter N. Weiss for their stewardship of federal information policy, James Love for his aggressive pursuit of the public interest with respect to public information policy, to Prudence Adler and Thomas Susman for helping to solve policy problems, and to Mitchell T. Bergmann for his support.

H.H.P.

ABOUT THE AUTHOR

Henry H. Perritt, Jr., is a professor of law at Villanova University School of Law and is the author of more than 35 law review articles and 10 books, including the 850-page *Electronic Contracting, Publishing and EDI Law,* published by John Wiley & Sons in 1991. His recent law review articles have addressed "Tort Liability, the First Amendment, and Equal Access to Electronic Networks," copyright-law impediments to standardization and compatibility, and access rights in the National Information Infrastructure. Professor Perritt has prepared reports for the President's Office of Management and Budget on federal electronic information policy, and for the Administrative Conference of the United States on electronic filing and dissemination policies for federal agencies, on Electronic Records Management and Archives, and on electronic dockets regarding the use of information technology in rulemaking and adjudication. He has advised the European Commission and the OECD on the implications of information technology for European administrative agency practice and public information law and policy and organized a major conference on electronic publishing for the National Center for Automated Information Research. Professor Perritt is now chairman of the Committee on Regulatory Initiatives and Information Technology of the ABA Section on Administrative Law and Regulatory Practice, is vice president and a member of the board of directors of the Center for Computer Aided Legal Instruction, and serves as a member of the Advisory Committee on Internet Dissemination of SEC EDGAR data under a NSF Grant to NYU. He received his S.B. and S.M. degrees from M.I.T. and his J.D. degree from Georgetown. He is a member of the bars of Virginia, Pennsylvania, District of Columbia, Maryland, and the United States Supreme Court.

SUMMARY CONTENTS

DETAILED CONTENTS

SHORT REFERENCE LIST

Short Reference	Full Reference
CMRS	commercial mobile radio service system
ECPA	Electronic Communications Privacy Act (codified at scattered sections of 18 U.S.C.)
ftp	file transfer protocol
GII	Global Information Infrastructure
GILS	Government Information Locator System
http	hyper text transfer protocol: the standard for the World Wide Web
IBOS	Inter Bank On-line Systems
IP	Internet protocol
IVDS	interactive video and data service
LAN	local area network
LEC	local exchange carrier
NII	National Information Infrastructure
NIST	National Institute of Standards and Technology
PCS	personal communications system
UNCITRAL	United Nations Commission on International Trade Law 1966
UNIDROIT	The International Institute for the Unification of Private Law
URL	universal resource locator
VAN	value-added network
WAIS	Wide Area Information Service

CHAPTER 1

NII AS A SOURCE OF LEGAL ISSUES

§ 1.1 Introduction and Nature of Problems

The production, modification, dissemination, and use of information is an important economic activity in the developed world. Some information is valuable, and the law must allocate property rights to that information and adjudicate disputes over those rights. It also must facilitate contract and other commercial systems so that valuable information can be exchanged for money. The law also must adjudicate competing claims for access to distribution channels for information so that producers can reach markets, and so that consumers can have access to competing sources. Information also is an essential ingredient of representative democracy, and public law must determine who has rights to obtain and sell government information.

But information also does harm. It ruins reputations, exposes personal secrets, inflicts emotional injury, and misleads people into mistaken purchases and investments. The law must determine who bears the risk of loss from such harm—not only between originators and victims, but also among originators, victims, and all the intermediaries who handle injurious information.

While the law long has subjected communications to some of its most detailed regulation, it also has protected information under the First Amendment from governmentally imposed burdens. This sets up a tension that regularly must be readdressed as information and communication technology evolve.

The Anglo-American legal tradition is strongly based on geographically defined sovereigns; yet, information flows freely across sovereign boundaries. This presents problems for determining the jurisdiction of civil and criminal legal institutions, challenges that must be addressed anew as information technology changes.

This book proceeds from two premises. First, technological change always has been a major source of human problems that the law must address. This was so when the industrial revolution and improved railroad and marine transportation changed markets and employment relationships. It was so when the automobile changed the nature of personal injury claims. It is certainly so as information technology has become important to human activity and economic transactions. Changing information technology also changes dispute resolution. New types of disputes arise, while the feasibility of traditional methods for detecting illegal conduct and enforcing legal decisions diminishes. At the same time, the new technology makes possible new kinds of dispute resolution institutions and procedures that may have lower costs than traditional institutions and procedures. The law therefore must be responsive to changes in information technology. Legal architects and advocates must understand the changes in technology in order to define and apply legal principles appropriately.

Second, law lags technology. An important part of the ethos of market economics, and of the common-law tradition even as statutes and agency regulations have become far more important than pure case law, says that the legal system should not predetermine the course of technology application and product development. Rather, the law should remain in the background available to resolve disputes that cannot be worked out through private accommodation and market mechanisms.

If this is the law's role, then the shape of the technology and the direction of its changes are fundamental to sound legal analysis. Accordingly, this chapter begins by exploring the nature of the National Information Infrastructure and the changes that are occurring in it, especially changes in the four traditional legal compartments for publishers, common carriers, broadcasters, and cable operators.

§ 1.2 Basic Technological Terms and Concepts

This section introduces technological concepts and terminology that are useful in understanding the legal issues arising from the use of computers and computer networks. While one can practice computer law competently without being a technical expert on computer science, good lawyering requires a basic understanding of how the technology works. All too frequently a perceived gap in the law or a perceived mismatch between basic legal concepts and new applications of technology disappears when one understands how a particular computer system actually works and sees obvious analogies between its functions and those of older technologies around which existing legal categories and doctrines arose. This section seeks to provide a starting point for that basic understanding. The section considers six basic subjects: computers, networks, communications, software, compatibility and standards, and the World Wide Web.

Computers come in all types and sizes. Lawyers are most familiar with general purpose computers that perform functions like accounting, word processing, and database management. While general purpose computers can be classified in many ways, a useful distinction for purposes of this book distinguishes *servers* from *clients*. *Servers* store and process information for a multiplicity of clients. Servers are usually more powerful than clients and range in size from slightly souped-up desktop computers using 386, 486, or Pentium Chips, to clusters of the largest mainframe computers. *Client computers* conceptually can be of any size, but in most configurations familiar to practicing lawyers, the client computer is the computer with which a human being directly interacts, for example a notebook or desktop computer. In a typical LEXIS session, the computer on the lawyer's desktop or the terminal in the library is the client, and the array of mainframe computers in Dayton is the server.

In the *client-server model* of computer system design, functions can be allocated between server and client to optimize performance. For example, in both the Westlaw and LEXIS systems, the client manages the graphical user interface, presenting the appropriate icons and text on the screen, while the server maintains the data and responds to user requests for particular statutes or cases.

Desktop computers include PCs, IBM compatibles and Macintoshes. A desktop computer typically is intended for one user and sits on top of a desk or table at a fixed location.

Notebook computers, sometimes called *laptops,* are single-user computers intended to be carried around. The usual definition of a notebook is that it weighs no more than 6.5 pounds and that its dimensions are no greater than 9x12x3 inches. Laptops traditionally were much heavier, but the popularity of notebooks has driven larger laptop products from the market.

All of these types of computers have *processors,* and two basic types of storage: primary and secondary. The name or number of the processor is frequently used to identify desktop and notebook computers. For example, desktops or notebooks using the Intel *80486* processor frequently are referred to as *"486 machines."* Desktop computers using the Intel Pentium processor frequently are referred as "pentiums." *Primary storage* is the main computer memory, virtually always implemented in the form of Random Access Memory (RAM). *Secondary storage* includes fixed or hard disk drives, floppy disks or diskettes, and CD-ROM and other forms of optical storage.

Storage capacity is measured in bytes. A *byte* is usually eight data bits, plus two framing bits for a total of 10 bits. Thus a megabyte is 10 million bits. A single character is equivalent to one byte in most systems.

Networks

Networks connect computers to each other. When networked computers communicate with each other they do so through *packets:* standard size bundles of information into which larger files and messages are carved (packetized). A network must have a system for carving information into packets at the sending end (*packetizing*) and reassembling the packets into messages and files at the receiving end (*depacketizing*). There are a variety of systems or protocols for doing this. Two of the most significant are the *TCP/IP* protocol, used in the Internet, and the *IPX* protocol used in Novell local area networks. When computers are networked, there also must be some system for deciding who gets to "talk" next so that simultaneous efforts by different computers to send information does not confuse receiving computers. Deciding who gets to "talk" next is referred to as *arbitration,* or *contention resolution.* The most popular arbitration system is *Ethernet,* followed by *Token Ring.* Different packetizing and depacketizing protocols can run on top of different arbitration protocols. For example, either IPX or TCP/IP can run on top of both Ethernet and Token Ring.

The *architecture* of an network is its basic design. Network architecture refers to the major structural features or *configuration* of the network.

Local area networks are computer networks connecting from two to several hundred computers located in reasonable proximity to each other, such as within a single building or at a single law firm location. *Wide area networks* span larger physical areas up to and including the entire world. Wide area networks may connect individual computers, but they more often connect local area networks. In any type of network the computer system connected to the network is referred to as a *node*. Some nodes are single computers; others are *subnetworks*. For example, a typical node in a wide area network is a local area network. A typical node on a local area network is a single desktop computer. Networks that connect other networks to each other sometimes are referred to as *internets*, a generic term that includes the Internet.

Closed networks limit connections to a predefined population, frequently by using proprietary hardware and/or software. *Open systems*, in contrast, allow connections to be made freely because they use standard methods for achieving functions like arbitration, and/or because they do not predefine the class of potential nodes.

Bandwidth is the rate of information that can be transferred through a communications channel. It thus measures capacity of a network and usually is expressed in kilo (thousands) of bits per second (kbps), or mega (millions) of bits per second (mbps). For example, a 100 megabit per second Ethernet LAN has 10 times the information transfer capacity of a 10 megabit per second Ethernet LAN.

Switches are computers that establish connections between computers that wish to communicate with each other (circuits) or that direct packets through paths in the network appropriate for them to reach their destinations.

Routers are a type of switch specializing in the routing of packets, as distinct from the establishment of circuit-oriented connections.

The *Internet* is an international network of computers and computer networks connected to each other through routers using the TCP/IP protocols and sharing a common name and address space. One can communicate with any computer connected to the Internet simply by establishing a connection to an Internet router or node. The Internet is not a corporation or administrative arrangement; it is a method for connecting computer systems, and the phenomenon of very widespread adherence to that method. There is no such thing as a president or board of directors of the Internet, although there are voluntary cooperative bodies such as the Internet Engineering Task Force (*IETF*) that discuss and formulate standards and protocols through documents called requests for comments (*RFCs*). The Internet began in the 1960s with federally subsidized connections among universities and government research laboratories. An *acceptable use policy* limited traffic unrelated to research and education. By 1990 the Internet's potential as a model for a National Information Infrastructure had been recognized, and the federal government began to reduce the subsidy and to encourage private entities to take over responsibility for basic communication and traffic management functions. By 1995 most of the traffic on the Internet involved unsubsidized facilities and private traffic. The Internet is the archetypal open network.

Widely used Internet applications (in addition to E-mail) include *telnet,* a method of establishing a remote terminal connection to another computer across the Internet; *file transfer protocol* (ftp), a means for transferring files between computers linked together by the Internet; *gopher,* a user-friendly menuing system for making files and text available; *news* and *newsgroups,* a means for electronic discussions in which posted messages and their replies are accessible to anyone connected to an Internet note; and *World Wide Web,* described later in this section.

Host-based networks move all traffic and requests for information through a single host or server. They are thus centralized, in contrast to the Internet, which is distributed. Until consumer preference for graphical user interfaces became obvious, most host-based networks assumed that those using the network did so with *dumb terminals,* devices that have the capability of sending characters from the keyboard and displaying received characters on a video display, but not otherwise possessing storage or processing capabilities. The move to graphical user interfaces led almost all host-based networks to embrace the client-server model of computing, delegating some processing and information storage functions to client computers (such as PCs) under the management of proprietary interface software or *session managers.* In this client-server approach, most of the graphics are prestored on client computers, permitting client and server to communicate by exchanging relatively succinct strings of characters and numbers representing user requests and server instructions to display certain of the prestored graphical images. The client computer takes the responsibility for managing the windows on the user interface. Westlaw, LEXIS, CompuServe, and America Online all employ this host-based approach.

A *backbone* is the central part of a network with the highest capacity. In a law firm LAN, a backbone would connect workgroup network segments. In the Internet, a backbone connects midlevel networks. Typically, a backbone's bandwidth is an order of magnitude greater than the bandwidth of the pieces connected through the backbone. Sophisticated network architectures rely on routers to pass selectively through to the backbone from each segment (subnetwork) only those packets needing to traverse the backbone to reach another segment. Packets addressed to a computer on the same segment are kept within that segment by the router and never reach the backbone.

Midlevel networks are those parts of the Internet that connect customers of the midlevel network with other customers of the same network and that handle traffic between that network and other midlevel networks through one or more backbones. Historically, midlevel networks in the Internet were regionally oriented. For example, PREPnet[1] connects academic institutions in Pennsylvania with each other and with the Internet backbone. NEARnet[2] did the same thing in New England. As the Internet has grown and become more commercial

---

[1] Pennsylvania Research and Economic Partnership Network.

[2] New England Area Regional Network.

and more private, many midlevel networks have expanded beyond their regions and/or have combined with other regional midlevel networks.[3]

Midlevel networks typically also are *Internet connection service providers,* meaning that they offer dial-up or other moderate bandwidth connections to facilitate connecting individuals or small to medium enterprises to the Internet. Internet connection services are distinguished from midlevel network services in that Internet connection services are accompanied by a wider variety of connection protocols suitable for local area networks and small computers and usually have more extensive customer assistance facilities than midlevel network services not involving connection services. Nevertheless, few providers of midlevel network services do not offer some connection services and vice versa.

Communications

Communications concepts significantly overlap network concepts, although it sometimes is useful to consider communications functions as involving less processing and routing than network functions necessarily involve. An important basic distinction can be made between *analog* and *digital* communications. Analog communications involve representing real world intelligence, such as a sound wave, by an electrical signal, with essentially the same characteristics of frequency and amplitude as the real world phenomenon. Analog communication is exemplified by the original method used by Alexander Graham Bell in proving the concepts for the telephone and remained the dominant communication method for telephonic communications until relatively recently. Analog techniques also are used for broadcast and most cable television and radio.

Digital communication techniques take millions of samples of a real world soundwave or video representation per minute and represent the sampled features of the real world signal by arithmetic quantities, ultimately reduced to binary digits or "bits."

Modems convert digital representations of information to analog representations and vice versa. They are used to connect computing systems to analog telephone networks.

Dial-up connections are like those used in ordinary voice telephone communication. The originator of a communication session establishes a connection by dialing the number of another station. Computers, working through modems do exactly the same thing, using the same dialing tones, to establish connections with other computer systems.

Dedicated communications lines are those that are used only for communications between two points. While they theoretically can be used for either voice or data communications, they virtually always are used for data communications,

---

[3] For example, Bolt Baranek and Newman, which provided operations management on a contract basis to NEARnet acquired NEARnet, California's CERFnet, and SURAnet in 1994.

when the volume of communications between two points is sufficiently great to warrant the added expense of the dedicated line. This reduces the transaction costs associated with establishing a new dial-up communication each time information is to be sent or received.

Software

Software is the same thing as a computer program or an interrelated set of computer programs. Software implements the functions of hardware and communications networks. Digital computers require step-by-step instructions to perform their intended functions. Software comprises those instructions. Software can be classified into two categories: that relating to operating systems, and that relating to applications. *Operating system* software is closely related to the hardware. It permits application software to make use of hardware functions like the keyboard and mouse, the video display, and communications devices like modems. *Application software* performs useful functions in conjunction with human input. It runs on top of operating system software in the sense that the operating system software mediates between application software and the hardware. *MS-DOS, Windows, Novell Netware,* and *Unix* are operating systems. *Microsoft Word for Windows, World Wide Web,* and *Westmate* (the session manager for Westlaw) are application programs.

Software also can be classified into server software and client software, representing the client-server model of computer system design, discussed earlier in this section. Thus, World Wide Web application software includes a server application such as httpd that usually runs on top of the Unix operating system and client applications such as Netscape that run on top of desktop computer operating systems such as Microsoft Windows.

Compatibility and Standards

Standards or some more informal convention are necessary for computers to communicate with each other. In order for computer hardware to make use of electrical signals received from computer networking hardware like modems, in order for operating systems to use hardware functions, in order for application programs to run on top of operating systems, in order for networked computers to communicate with each other, the interface between the subelements must be standardized. When both of the adjacent subelements are written and designed by the same supplier, this is not a major problem. The designer and vendor simply make sure the subelements fit together. But when subelements are unbundled, and supplied by different entities, the designers must know in advance how to make the unbundled pieces fit together.

Public standards and protocols constitute the information necessary to fit the pieces together. Such standards may result from the disclosure by a proprietary vendor, as in the case of the basic features of the interface between applications and Microsoft's MS-DOS and Windows and the basic features of the interface between Apple Macintosh applications and the Macintosh operating system. Sometimes, these basic features are called "hooks."

In many important cases, the standards reflect a consensus among multiple designers and vendors articulated through standard setting bodies. The most general example is *Open Systems Interconnection* (OSI) published by the International Standards Organization. OSI is an abstract concept of how different elements of computing systems, including networks of all kinds, fit together based on seven layers of function, ranging from electrical signals and hardware plug specifications at the bottom or level one, up to the relationship between applications and operating systems at level seven. The seven layers are referred to as the *OSI stack.* Level three (the *network* layer) includes standards for packetizing and depacketizing data in packet-switched networks and also includes standards for routing packets. Level four (the *transport* layer) includes information on reassembling packets and checking for errors. These two levels correspond roughly to the IP standard and TCP standard, respectively. TCP and IP are the two standards or protocols that define the Internet.

The *Novell IPX standard* performs these same two functions albeit in a proprietary environment. Novell discloses the basics of the IPX standard to facilitate the development of software that can be used on Novell Network. Other standards, some long established, and some much newer, relate to the performance of much more particularized functions. For example, the *ASCII standard* is universally used for the representation of characters. As the World Wide Web has become popular so also have the *http standard,* used to regulate communication between web servers and other web servers and clients; the *html standard,* used to mark up or tag documents intended to be published through the World Wide Web; and the *URL standard,* aimed at regulating the way in which an html pointer identifies a resource located on another web node on the Internet.

The standard most familiar to most desktop computer users is the American Standard Code for Information Interchange (ASCII) method for representing characters. Transport Control Protocol (TCP) and Internet Protocol (IP), as already explained in this section, define the Internet. *X.25* is a competing standard for packet-switched networks, which, unlike TCP/IP, relies on setting up virtual circuits between routers, which packets follow. Until the Internet became popular, most wide area networking used the X.25 standard. **Chapter 8** considers means by which standards can be established.

World Wide Web

The *World Wide Web* (Web) is a particularly popular application for the Internet. Reflecting the client-server model of computer program design, the World Wide Web makes use of two kinds of software: server software and client or *browser* software. The client and the server work together during a World Wide Web session, communicating with each other through messages and files conforming to the hypertext transfer protocol (http) and hypertext markup language (html) standards. Documents formatted in html are displayed by browser software that presents colors, typeface styles and sizes, and hypertext links as highlighted text, all according to html instructions or tags.

An increasingly popular form of electronic publishing involves taking documents or graphical images or sound files or a combination of them and placing them on a Web server—usually a small or medium-sized Internet server with several directories devoted to World Wide Web files and the server application software. The World Wide Web is a *hypertext* system. This means that a typical Web document has pointers to other html documents that may be located anywhere in the Internet on a Web server or on the same server on which the pointer is located, or to other parts of the same document that contains the pointer.

For example, one could take this chapter and organize it for electronic publishing on a Web server by substituting internal hypertext pointers for all of the cross-references and substituting external hypertext pointers for all of the reference information in the footnotes. When the document is displayed through a Web browser on a client, each of the pointers, internal or external, would appear as highlighted text or simply a small symbol. A user interested in the information pointed to would click on the highlighted text with his mouse, and that would cause the World Wide Web to retrieve the information pointed to and automatically display it on the client screen.

The World Wide Web thus is a method of organizing information distributed across the Internet. It facilitates unbundling because editors or publishers interested in collecting resources related to a particular subject need not obtain or maintain actual copies of the content of the resources; they can make their knowledge available simply by writing a Web document that contains pointers to the identified references and information about the significance of the resources. The clearest example is a typical law review footnote or citation in a legal brief. One can make the case or statute cited available simply by pointing to it in the brief or law review article, and a user reading the brief or law review article can retrieve the full text pointed to simply by clicking on the footnote or citation.

World Wide Web pointers are formatted in a standard called *Universal Resource Locator* (URL), which identifies the Internet node containing the resource and the file name on that node. For example, the following URL,

http://www.law.vill.edu/vls/student_home,

points to the student home page on the Villanova Law School Internet Server. This URL,

http://www.law.vill.edu/vill.info.l.chron/news/higgarel.htm, points to a brief filed by the author of this book in a case subsequently decided by the New Jersey Supreme Court.

Persons in control of a Web server have absolute control over what information is made available through the Web. Only those files placed on directories associated with the World Wide Web server on that Internet node are reachable by a URL. It also is possible to limit the accessibility of certain files or groups of files to persons who have established an account on that machine and who give a password when they request a file. Absent such protection, however, a Web server has no way of knowing, nor need it prearrange, who points to its resources. In that sense, publishing through a Web server is like broadcasting; an originator does not know who is listening or watching. That feature makes the Web an extremely powerful technique for publishing because the publisher need not make any particular distribution arrangements to reach anybody in the world, and someone who wishes to obtain a particular piece of information located on a particular Web server only need establish a connection to the Internet and point to that resource or server with a URL. The same features, of course, make it difficult for publishers to get paid, as discussed in § **1.11** and **Chapter 10.**

The most popular Web browsers are Netscape and Mosaic, although the nonproprietary nature of the http, URL, and html standards make it possible for anyone to write and sell or give away a Web browser. New browsers are appearing on the market every month.

§ 1.3   What Is the NII?

Although the Internet was the stimulus for public discussion of the National Information Infrastructure (NII) or "information superhighway," the NII contains much more than the Internet. It includes conduits for information like the public-switched telephone network, video rental outlets, movie theaters, cable television systems, and broadcast radio and television networks as well as the Internet. It includes information-content producers and publishers, such as book and newspaper publishers,[4] television and film production studios, radio talk show hosts, and the people who call in to talk show radio programs. It includes information finders and brokers—entities that facilitate identification and retrieval of information desired by particular consumers—such as critics and reviewers, libraries, bookstores, and newsstands. Some of these activities are highly automated, and some are not automated at all, relying primarily on human interaction, human voice, and physical transfer of tangible objects containing information value.

---

[4] Newspaper publishers also run their conduits in the form of the distribution networks.

In a more general and slightly more formal sense, the NII is the collection of complementary and competing subsystems that perform 10 value-adding functions, each associated with its own value-added output. The 10 elements of added value are considered further in § **1.6.**

§ 1.4 —Changing Information Architectures

The most interesting and difficult legal issues that arise in the NII are influenced by the new technical architectures in the NII.[5] Accordingly, it is appropriate to begin NII legal analysis with a recapitulation of the most important new architectural features of the NII and an explanation of why the Internet is a compelling model for future architectures.

For the last 50 years, the growing power, widening availability, and rapidly diminishing costs of computers have caused some important convergences among technologies through which information has been produced and distributed. Office automation, especially word processing, computerization of editorial and pre-press operations in book and newspaper publishing, and the availability of low-cost open architecture computer networks have drawn an increasing portion of the production of information value into computer technologies and away from purely paper and ink–based technologies. The PC revolution and the rapidly increasing proportion of the population having desktop computers and access to digital communications through modems have made it attractive to disseminate information electronically.

Already, of course, much information was produced and disseminated electronically through broadcast and cable television, radio, and telephone conversations. But these were analog systems, sharply demarcated from text production and distribution, which historically had occurred on paper and now are increasingly occurring through digital computer and communications technologies. As improvements were made in the speed of communications networks and in the power of switching in such networks, together with growing sophistication of other aspects of digital network technology, it became feasible to conceive of the voice and video content of television, radio, and telephone being digitized and produced and distributed through digital networks that no longer would be distinct from the networks used for text-based information.

By 1980 it had become reasonably clear to some observers[6] that distinct categories of information production and distribution were becoming less distinct and, indeed, were likely to merge altogether. The old categories had been defined by technology, but they also had distinct positions in the law. Erosion of the boundaries between categories would challenge the law to evolve

---

[5] A computer "architecture" is a particular configuration.

[6] The most prominent and prophetic was Ithiel de Solo Pool at MIT. *See* Ithiel de Solo Pool, Technologies of Freedom (1983).

appropriately. Those distinct categories and the law applicable to them are considered in § **1.7** and **Chapter 6.**

§ 1.5 —Internet as Model for the NII

Shortly after taking office, the Clinton administration announced an initiative aimed at promoting a National Information Infrastructure (NII), frequently known as the initiative for an "information superhighway." The NII quickly captured the imagination of producers and consumers of information and communications services. While book publishers, telephone companies, broadcasters, cable and conventional broadcast companies, and electronic database services were quick to point out that the country already had an extensive information infrastructure,[7] there was something new about the Clinton administration idea. The new flavor to the NII, and indeed the characterization as an information superhighway, was born with Vice President Gore when he was in the Senate and developing legislation for opening up the Internet.

Historically, the Internet had been a little-known set of connections among university and research lab computers. Now it emerged as the model for the entire National Information Infrastructure, including the public-switched telephone network, the cable and conventional telephone systems, and much of publishing and public libraries.

The Internet is the model of convergence. The Internet facilitates electronic publishing of text, images, and voice with the same communication protocols and applications being used for all three.[8] Another aspect of the Internet is as important as its accommodation of historically distinct technological categories. The Internet is an open architecture; indeed, that is all it is. Many people are surprised to find out that the Internet is not an entity. There is no chief executive officer of the Internet nor any board of directors nor any central network administrative apparatus. The Internet is defined as a collection of several million computer networks connected to each other through routers that use the TCP/IP protocol suite (described in § **1.2**) and share a common name and address space.

A connection to the Internet thus is a kind of digital dial tone. Importantly, it is the kind of digital dial tone to which one can connect any kind of computer and run software from any vendor who has written for the Internet. In other words, it is nonproprietary. One can hook up anything to it that respects the TCP/IP protocols. That has enormous implications in terms of the scope of the resulting network. No longer can one exchange E-mail only with other

---

[7] See § **1.3** for an overview of the parts of the NII.

[8] Full motion video is not yet a reality on the Internet, but a variety of interesting research and development focuses on full motion video through the Internet.

subscribers of the same proprietary network like CompuServe or America Online. No longer can one publish electronically only to those who look at particular conferences or file libraries on a proprietary service. Now, one can make something available to the whole world by putting it on a computer connected to the Internet, and one can exchange messages with anyone in the world connected to the Internet.

This kind of open, distributed digital dial tone service presents completely novel challenges for the law of access. If no one owns the infrastructure, how can the law address complaints that access is not available? Open, distributed service also presents new difficulties in allocating the risk of loss from harmful information. It makes the sources of information more difficult to trace and introduces a rich variety of new kinds of intermediaries who may be attractive deep pockets for claims of injury, but who may have relatively little fault in the traditional sense. The distributed nature of the infrastructure means that almost every transaction involves the bundling of pieces contributed by different producers, placing new stress on intellectual property law, which must decide who owns what and what constitutes a trespass and what is privileged for entry. Then, this open infrastructure is oblivious to state and national boundaries, raising new problems for determining jurisdiction of rule makers and adjudicators.

§ 1.6 —New Forms of Electronic Publishing

Publications, paper or electronic, have distinct attributes of value for users. At the core is raw *content*. This is the basic message or data, with nothing added to help users find, retrieve, keep, or browse for particular pieces of information.[9] Virtually all information products have something added to the raw content. Most products have at least some *chunking and tagging* value added. In the print technologies, chunking and tagging value comprises page breaks, running headers and footers, and headlines and subtitles. With digital computer technologies, chunking and tagging value includes things like record and file boundaries, paragraph breaks, and computer-readable tags that can be pointed to from somewhere else. In databases, the database schema and record definitions represent chunking and tagging value. In addition, more sophisticated products have *pointers,* either pointers to other parts of the same document, as in a table of contents, index, or cross-reference;[10] or pointers to another document, as in a conventional footnote reference; or an *html* reference to another resource on the Internet in the World Wide Web.[11] Beyond that are less tangible kinds of

---

[9] An example would be an ASCII file (a raw text file readable by a desktop computer word processing program) of a statute.

[10] These are *internal pointers.*

[11] These are *external pointers.*

value-added features, like an extra copy (*duplication* value),[12] availability at another location (*distribution* value),[13] *integrity assurance, billing and collection* value,[14] and *promotion.*[15]

With print publishing technologies, the publisher bundles most of these attributes of value and the consumer buys the entire bundle from that publisher. Digital computer technologies, particularly as they are implemented on distributed, open systems like the Internet, permit unbundling of the attributes of value so that one supplier may supply only raw content, and another may make available one or more other value-added attributes such as pointers that the user combines with the raw content on demand.[16] Still other suppliers might make available billing and collection[17] and promotion value.

This new architecture makes it easier for owners and creators of content to provide end users and intermediaries with their products and also makes it possible for new types of intermediaries to enter the market and begin adding value to information of all kinds. The same advantage is available to all suppliers of information content, private as well as public.

Figure 1–1 shows how the Internet and similar architectures permit value-added products to be unbundled, with different elements of the bundle being supplied by different entities, and the bundling of these elements occurring according to the desires of a particular user at the time the user wants the complete value-added information product. In this architecture, suppliers of information content, shown in the figure by the circles above the solid line, supply their content to anyone who wants it simply by putting files more or less as they have been generated and used internally on computers connected to the Internet, called servers or "content servers." These suppliers need not worry about adding value-added features like indexes, tables of contents, user-friendly

---

[12] An extra copy exemplifies *duplication* value.

[13] This exemplifies *distribution* value.

[14] Billing and collection value might seem to shift points of view because it seems more valuable to the seller than to the purchaser. On the other hand, the presence of billing and collection value makes it easier for the purchaser to buy something on the spot and therefore can be a form of value to purchaser as well as seller.

[15] Marketing represents *promotion* value. The array of added-value elements is developed more fully in Henry H. Perritt, Jr., *Unbundling Value in Electronic Information Products: Intellectual Property Protection for Machine Readable Interfaces,* 20 Rutgers Computer & Tech. L.J. 415 (1994).

[16] A page on a World Wide Web server and a cluster of Gopher menu items are examples of pure pointers value. World Wide Web and Gopher are applications for information organization and retrieval on the Internet.

[17] Marvin A. Sirbu and other researchers at Carnegie Mellon University have proposed a billing and collection server that would use public key encryption to facilitate charging for resources obtained through the Internet. *See* Marvin A. Sirbu, *Internet Billing Service Design and Prototype Implementation, in* Proceedings, Technological Strategies for Protecting Intellectual Property in the Networked Multimedia Environment (Harvard Kennedy School of Government & MIT Program on Digital Open High-Resolution Systems), Jan. 1994 at 67.

Internet is a market for disaggregating value production

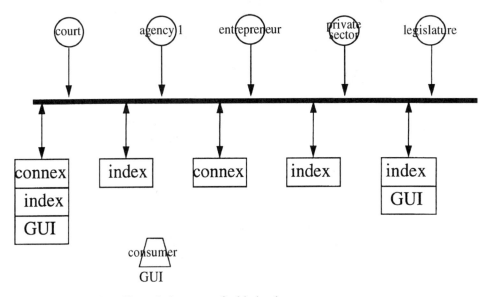

Figure 1–1. Unbundling of elements of added value.

retrieval software, or modems and telephone lines to permit public access. Those value-added features are supplied by others, mostly in the private sector, although one of the advantages of the architecture is that almost anyone— public, private, for profit, nonprofit—can add value to the same stock of information content. These suppliers of value-added features are represented in the figure by rectangles below the solid line. It is entirely possible with Internet applications like the World Wide Web for an entity to supply only index or table of contents value in the form of pointers to content. The pointers are implemented through World Wide Web pages and lists or Gopher menus on an Internet server that offers no other kinds of value. Someone else can provide user-friendly interface software through another server. Still someone else can provide connection services that permit connections through dial-up telephone lines or through higher speed dedicated links.

When a user (consumer) wishes to identify and obtain particular content, the user interacts with several Internet servers operated by different entities. First, the user establishes a connection to the Internet through a connection services provider, then establishes a connection to an index provider. From the lists, tables, and menus provided by that server, the user identifies one or more judicial opinions of interest. The index server downloads the pointers (not the content because the index server does not have the content) through the Internet to the user's client computer. The user's client computer executes the pointers, which automatically causes the information content pointed to be downloaded directly from the content server into the client computer.

This is a kind of assembly line for pieces of information value. It produces product just in time rather than producing it in bulk according to someone else's design just in case someone might want that particular bundle. It lets the user design the product on an ad hoc basis. Most important for the economics of access to information, the user can be either an end user or an information intermediary—Westlaw, LEXIS, or a new competitor.

This is an attractive vision because everyone's costs of obtaining access to information are reduced. Content suppliers' costs are reduced because they need not establish and operate dial-up bulletin boards with attendant telecommunications expenditures and operational demands. They need not make new commitments to organize and index large quantities of material. They can avoid the costs of typesetting, printing, warehousing, and distributing paper products.

This architecture enormously reduces the cost to some intermediaries. Consider legal publishers. No longer must they go from court to court physically and obtain paper copies of opinions or electronic versions on magnetic tape. No longer must they convert paper formats to electronic formats. No longer must they have computers that can maintain the full content that they want their customers to access. Because the costs to intermediaries are reduced, the economic barriers to new entry are reduced, and the market can be more competitive. The combination of lower cost and more competitive market structure drives down prices to consumers who have the benefits of intermediary-provided value-added features at much lower cost as well as seamless access to the content of all the judicial opinions.

There can be, of course, a variety of product concepts in this architecture. That is one of the advantages of competitive markets: they allow entrepreneurs to try out different ways of satisfying customer need. Indeed, some vendors may elect to assemble and sell relatively complete product bundles themselves because of the greater control they can exercise over the way the pieces fit together.

The possibility of unbundling and the emergence of new bundles in the NII portend major challenges for the law. Each of the types of value has unique intellectual property, contractual, access-rights, tort liability, and service quality concerns. As their production is organized differently, the law must cope with these concerns differently.

§ 1.7 Legal Status of the Four Traditional Categories

The different parts of the NII that now find themselves converging have different technological and market cultures. They also have very different legal traditions. Broadcasting and telephone common carriage have been heavily regulated, while newspapers and other publishers have enjoyed broad First Amendment immunity from regulation. Participants in the desktop computer marketplace have been more or less oblivious to both the First Amendment and detailed regulation. This section provides an overview of the legal regimes that have influenced the evolution of broadcasting, telephone and telegraph, cable, and publishing.

Publishing is the least regulated of the four traditional legal compartments. The First Amendment of the United States Constitution was aimed at protecting newspaper publishers and publishers of flyers and handbills.

Because of this central focus of the First Amendment, and the absence of countervailing characteristics justifying regulation as in radio broadcasting, legislators and administrative agencies largely have left traditional publishing alone. When the common law has intruded too far into content-related decision making by traditional publishers, the First Amendment has trimmed it back, as **Chapter 6** explains.

Telephone and telegraph communication are at the opposite end of the legal spectrum from newspaper publishing. Providers of telephone and telegraph service to the public were categorized as common carriers from the earliest days of telegraph service.[18] The basic concept of common carriage obligates a carrier to accept all traffic presented within its physical capacity to handle it.[19] Few controversies arose in which carriers claimed a First Amendment privilege against being required to handle traffic with which they disagreed. Some carriers preferred not to be publishers because of the reduced tort and criminal liability they enjoyed as common carriers.[20] Other carriers and their lawyers no doubt assumed that common carriers simply did not enjoy First Amendment privileges perhaps because they waived First Amendment entitlements by becoming common carriers.[21] In any event, the kind of control over content that is the hallmark

---

[18] Interstate Commerce Act, ch. 104, 24 Stat. 379 (1887) (current version at 49 U.S.C. ch. 1, §§ 1–26 (1995)); Interstate Commerce Act, ch. 382, 25 Stat. 855 (1889) (current version at 49 U.S.C. ch. 1, §§ 1–26 (1995)); Interstate Commerce Act, ch. 28, 26 Stat. 743 (1891) (current version at 49 U.S.C. ch. 1, §§ 1–26 (1995)).

[19] Some concepts, such as those embodied in the communications act, also obligate the carrier to provide sufficient physical facilities. Communications Act of 1934, ch. 652, 48 Stat. 1064 (1934) (current version at 47 U.S.C. § 151 (1995)).

[20] Restatement (Second) of Torts § 581(1) cmt. 6 on subsec. 1 (1976).

[21] *See* Elias Magil, *Liability of Telegraph Companies for the Transmission of Libelous Matter,* 78 U. Pa. L. Rev. 252–57 (1929); William M. Martin, *Telegraphs and Telephones—Qualified Privilege of Telegraph Company to Transmit Defamatory Message Where Sender Is Not Privileged,* 2 Wash. & Lee L. Rev. 141–48 (1940); Robert K. Rodibaugh, *Telephones and Telegraphs—Liability of a Telegraph Company for Transmitting a Defamatory Message,* 16 Notre Dame Law. 150–52 (1941); Young B. Smith, *Liability of a Telegraph Company for Transmitting a Defamatory Message,* 20 Colum. L. Rev. 369 (1920); Vernon Swanson, *Libel*

of a publisher's First Amendment privileges was inconsistent with regulated common carriage.

In some ways broadcast radio and television looks more like newspaper publishing than it does telephone or telegraph service. It is a one-to-many operation, aimed at disseminating content, rather than providing channels for interactive communication on a one-to-one basis. People expect broadcasters to select and organize content that they, the users, receive more or less passively; they do not view broadcasting as a simple channel for them to use in originating communications with someone else. Nevertheless, broadcasting is more heavily regulated than print publishing.

From the earliest days of the radio broadcast industry, use of radio spectrum was the critical feature, economically and in terms of legal status. Spectrum use is the foundation for broadcast regulation. When broadcasters asserted First Amendment privileges to be free from FCC or state or common-law restrictions on broadcast content, their First Amendment arguments usually were deflected by the rationale that scarcity of spectrum justified government regulation of content. The high-water mark of this judicial doctrine was *Red Lion Broadcasting,*[22] considered more extensively in **Chapter 6.**

Cable broadcasting began as a relatively weak substitute for local broadcast outlets for network programming. It was, thus, natural to suppose that cable occupied a niche in the legal framework identical to that occupied by television broadcasting. By 1994, however, it dawned on the cable operators, their lawyers, and the judges hearing their cases that the spectrum-scarcity assumption is unwarranted with respect to cable technology; the cable operator makes its own spectrum as it builds its cable plant. This greatly weakened the constitutional justification for regulation directly aimed at or significantly affecting content, and the Supreme Court in *Turner Broadcasting System, Inc. v. Federal Communications Commission,*[23] analyzed in **Chapter 6,** required regulators to come up with a completely different justification looking more like that required by antitrust law[24] than communications law.[25]

---

and Slander—Liability of a Telegram Company for Transmission of Libelous Message in Course of Business, 5 Wis. L. Rev. 297–300 (1929); Libel and Slander—Privilege: Qualified—Liability of Telegraph Company for Transmission of Libellous Message, 43 Harv. L. Rev. 144 (1929); Libel and Slander—Privileged Communications—Liability of Telegraph Company, 15 Iowa L. Rev. 106 (1929); Must the Telephone Company Censor to Avoid Liability for Libel: Anderson v. New York Telephone Company, 38 Alb. L. Rev. 317–31 (1974).

[22] Red Lion Broadcasting Co. v. FCC, 395 U.S. 367 (1969).

[23] 114 S. Ct. 2445, 2457 (1994).

[24] *Id.* at 2458 (noting government's argument that must-carry provisions are "nothing more than industry-specific anti-trust legislation and thus warrant rational basis scrutiny because aimed at correcting market failure").

[25] *Turner Broadcasting* is discussed more extensively in **Ch. 6.**

§ 1.8   Effect of Digital Phenomena

The four traditional legal categories are converging because technologies used by entities occupying the four categories are converging. The move from analog to digital technologies for storing and transmitting information is the foundational shift in technology.

The movement of most forms of electronic communications to digital representation rather than analog representation makes a difference to technology configurations, economics, and law for the following reasons. Digital technology makes it easier to use packet communication techniques, which improve utilization of existing capacity. Packets, even those associated with a single message, can be distributed across a multiplicity of communication channels depending on the degree to which they are being utilized at the time.

Digital technologies permit routing and addressing to be based on the message itself rather than, as in analog telephone communication, requiring a separate process to set up a channel that remains intact for the duration of a communication session. Digital communication facilitates computer processing of content. An increasing proportion of content exists in digital form before it is transmitted, and recipients would like the option of computer processing after they receive it. Avoiding the conversions necessary to convert from digital to analog and back to digital again saves both sender and receiver time and cost. Digital representation also permits random access to parts of a document or message rather than, like analog representation, requiring review of an entire record from the beginning in order to find a particular segment. This results from computer processability of the digital formats.

Digital technology makes it much easier to combine different kinds of information representations—text, single images, audio, and full motion video. Digital communication does not increase the capacity of communication circuits, although it does permit available capacity to be used more efficiently by facilitating compression.

§ 1.9   —Fast Replication

A central feature of digital information technology is the speed with which pieces of information can be replicated. Each copy is as good as the "original," and there is virtually no difference technologically between making one copy on an ad hoc basis to permit human perception and making a large number of copies for distribution to a large number of recipients.[26]

---

[26] Of course, making a hundred copies takes one hundred times as long as making one copy, but the times involved are very small and the basic technology used to copy the bits is the same for mass duplication as for individual presentation.

This characteristic, not found in analog technologies or in print and paper technologies, presents enormous challenges for adapting intellectual property law and the law of evidence. With respect to intellectual property, the traditional basic distinction between reading something, never within the monopoly granted by the copyright laws, and reproducing it, always within the copyright monopoly, vanishes. Efforts to enforce a copyright holder's reproduction right collide with the traditional privilege of anyone to read a copyrighted work when one possesses it.

Not only that, it is difficult, absent special arrangements, to tell where the copy came from. This opens up a variety of possibilities for forgery—and thus bedevils evidence and commercial law and makes it difficult to track down pirates of intellectual property.

§ 1.10 —Computer Networks

Digital computing crosses organizational boundaries, increasing the number of legal controversies because of two technologies: local area networks (LANs) of desktop computers and wide area networks linking geographically dispersed LANs. LANs permit users of desktop computers to enjoy the performance and autonomy advantages of running software directly on their own computers, while being able to share files and certain other resources with other users through the local area network and its associated "servers."[27] Such an architecture invites work groups to perform sequential steps, such as data entry, editing, and final production, by accessing files through a local area network. The latest generation of desktop computers, using the Intel Pentium microprocessor chip and the Power PC 601 and 604 chips in Apple Macintosh computers, has made it feasible to exchange fairly large files, including graphical images, through local area networks even when the exchange involves simultaneous access by a multiplicity of users.

Wide area networking permits local area networks to be joined electronically regardless of their geographic proximity to each other. Thus, a LAN in Louisiana can exchange information with a LAN in Luxembourg through a wide area network. Advances in modem speeds and wide area networking protocols began to make it realistic in about 1994 for significant quantities of graphical information and large text files to be exchanged over wide area networks.

---

[27] A *server* is a computer attached to a network that performs functions for more than one user. Some servers on small local area networks differ little if at all from individual desktop computers but specialize in access to files stored on their hard disks through the LAN. Other servers, such as those typically connected to wide area networks including the Internet, have greater performance and capacity than individual computers they support and may run specialized applications such as electronic mail, World Wide Web servers, or GOPHER servers.

Sufficient bandwidth is available through the public-switched telephone network to perform these types of information exchange routinely.[28]

Until the Internet became popular, however, most wide area networks were proprietary. The networks were organized around mainframe computers at one end of a connection running proprietary applications and desktop computers or dumb terminals at the other end of a connection running proprietary interface software. Sometimes these proprietary networks utilized international data communications standards such as X.25 for the communications link itself.

The Internet has accelerated an independent tendency toward two important technological phenomena: client-server computing and distributed database management. The client-server model permits software developers to allocate tasks between server and client connected to each other through a network so as to maximize performance, security, and other design criteria. For example, the client-server model permits the client, such as an individual user's desktop computer, to perform most or all of the tasks associated with graphical image management and screen displays. This makes it easier to implement Windows-based and highly graphical computing sessions without burdening the communications link with large quantities of data necessary to describe all the features of a particular screen image. Using this model, the individual user works with a Microsoft Windows or Macintosh display, communicating data and instructions to the server by pointing and clicking with the mouse. The client sends much abbreviated messages of one or a few characters across the communications link based on its "mediation" between the graphical interface and the communications link. The server can cause a particular image or change in the user display to be presented by sending a similarly abbreviated character or character string based on its "knowledge" of the graphical images the client already has and on its "knowledge" of the operational details of the client's interface software.

The second important phenomenon is distributed database management. This concept allows a user to combine data actually stored on a multiplicity of computers. For example, a client interested in a particular submission in notice and comment rule making could retrieve the docket kept on computer A, select a particular item from the docket, which would cause the desired document to be retrieved from computer B. Another document, for example, an opposing party's response, might be retrieved from computer C. Depending on the quality of the user's client software, the user might retrieve all of this material and have it presented to her as an integrated set with no indication that the elements of the

---

[28] *Bandwidth* is a measure of the capacity of a communications link, frequently measured in bits per second. The typical bandwidth over a dial-up telephone connection in 1988 was 1,200 bits per second, limited by the speed of low-cost modems. In mid-1995 the typical dial-up connection bandwidth connection is moving to 288 kilo bits per second because of newly available international standards operating at that speed. Typical dedicated data lines leased from local exchange telephone companies operate at either 56 kilobits per second or "T1"(1.45 megabits per second).

set came from different computers. The flexibility and power of the client-server and distributed database models are enhanced when the protocols for implementing them are nonproprietary and "open." With open protocols, a multiplicity of designers and vendors can make up the pieces that can be combined into a distributed database or a client-server application.

The Internet has a particular role to play in facilitating public access to government agencies and to public information. The Internet is a useful framework for providing public access to agency materials of all kinds, including rule making and adjudication dockets. It is nonproprietary: it permits value-added features to be added by different entities in public and private sectors and it facilitates competition among vendors. Access is available at low cost to members of the public. With respect to electronic filings, the Internet is also attractive because it provides a universally available, standard, and nonproprietary way for lawyers and other members of the public to obtain information on agency proposals and to submit comments and documents.

The growing use of networking, especially wide area networking, complicates legal jurisdiction and choice of law questions because complementary events making up one legal transaction may occur in geographically separated areas.[29] Open networking complicates protection of intellectual property because it breaks up the traditional product bundles to which owners and users of intellectual property have become accustomed.[30] It complicates tort law because responsibility for harmful information is more difficult to assign.[31] To realize its potential, open networking begs for reliable electronic payment and electronic systems.[32]

§ 1.11   Commercializing the Internet

Commercialization of the Internet more generally involves development and acceptance of appropriate payment mechanisms and intellectual property concepts. It is of course much easier to protect intellectual property and to assure payment for information and infrastructure services in closed rather than open systems like the Internet. Commercialization was manifested in Westlaw, LEXIS, CompuServe and America Online (AOL) before it became a reality in the Internet. Now, the Internet and these proprietary services are merging technologically. An America Online subscriber may not immediately know the difference between an information item available directly from AOL and one through AOL's interface to the Internet. Subscribers to Westlaw and LEXIS needing access from a point outside the United States may elect access through

---

[29] See **Ch. 12.**

[30] See **Ch. 10.**

[31] See **Chs. 4** and **5.**

[32] See **Ch. 9.**

the Internet rather than through the public-switched telephone network in another country. At the intersection of purely commercial and commercial value-added additions to public information, more and more of the raw material for commercial legal databases is made available from the originating agencies through the Internet.

This technological convergence puts pressure on traditional institutional arrangements for selling things, collecting money, and preventing piracy. Basic legal concepts are being adopted to the new architectures.

Commercializing new parts of the NII, such as the Internet, involves new concepts of commerce in information. For example, traditional book publishing relies on selling content along with various value-added features bundled with the content in a book. Traditional newspaper publishing depends on drawing consumers to a publication based on its content and then selling advertising space in the same bundle that carries the content so that the advertising reaches the consumers. A portion of the revenue stream for newspapers also is based on subscription revenues, representing consumer payments for content.

Because it was infeasible to obtain payments for content for radio and television broadcasting, that industry grew up selling advertising packaged with the content so it would reach the consumers at whom the content is aimed. Cable television made it feasible to sell content, and thus the original cable model dispensed with advertising and simply relied on subscriber revenues. As cable television has evolved, advertising has reentered the entrepreneurial equation.[33]

The commercial on-line database model looked more like the original cable television model than anything else until the Internet came to the fore. Consumers paid for content by paying for connection time. But unlike the cable television model, commercial database subscriptions were metered by the minute rather than by the month.

The Internet model has perplexed people seeking to commercialize it because its distributed, open architecture makes it difficult for anyone to collect money except an entity providing connection services. A seller of connection services can collect just like the provider of a closed on-line database service such as America Online or CompuServe. Other types of payments necessitate revising Internet applications to allow reliable payment mechanisms to be implemented for viewing or downloading particular information objects, or for establishing connections with particular nodes.[34] All of these approaches no doubt will have a place.

But there is an additional way of making money in the Internet context that is only beginning to be appreciated. Providers of content and value-added features can collect data about the behavior and interests of people who access their

---

[33] See *MTV to lose 10m homes after scrambling signal,* Fin. Times, June 23, 1995, at 16 (MTV hopes scrambling of signal will alter ratio of MTV revenues in Europe from 90% advertising and 10% subscription to 70% advertising and 30% subscription because niche channels not making money in Europe).

[34] *See generally* Internet Engineering Task Force, Proposal for http-ng, available through [URL].

services and then sell the data.[35] The value of such consumer transaction data is in helping product suppliers and marketing personnel to target advertising and direct mail solicitation through conventional media much more narrowly. Obviously, this opportunity for selling data raises major personal privacy concerns, considered in **Chapter 3.**

As the Internet becomes more diverse, with more choices among backbone service providers, access providers, and various intermediaries, the need for mobile addressing will increase. One would like to keep the same Internet address but be able to choose among competing providers more or less on the spot, based on accessibility, congestion, and perhaps price. One would also like to be able to move around the country or the world using the same Internet address. Mobile addressing in the Internet raises the same challenges that mobile addressing in the cellular telephone system and personal communications systems (PCS) raises. Address databases must be dynamic in order to keep track of where all of the devices or nodes are located, they must be able to choose appropriate paths to reach those nodes, and they must make available access to all providers and customers at appropriate prices without inappropriate discrimination. Development of mobile addressing technologies is challenging in and of itself; resolving controversies over the appropriate standard and standards compliance is another level of challenge, more likely to confront the legal system.

§ 1.12   Cellular Telephone

Cellular telephone service is an important transitional phenomenon in the NII. Like the Internet, cellular telephone technologies ("cellular") and market structures are important models for the NII. Aspects of cellular telephones technology represent points of convergence for the traditional four categories discussed in § **1.7.**

While the transition from analog to digital technologies in cellular systems was just beginning in 1995, other well-established aspects of cellular telephone technology were revolutionary in providing proof of the core concepts of what became known as the NII. First, cellular telephone service is the first example of a reversal between the traditional uses of radio and wire. Until cellular, radio generally had been used for broadcasts and wire had been used for point-to-point communications. Cellular reverses this, using radio signals for point-to-point communication (meanwhile cable television demonstrates the use of wire circuits for broadcast communication). This reversal is not only a matter of intellectual interest; it opens the possibility of competition for the last major competitive bottleneck in the NII: local telephone service. Cellular telephone

---

[35] The data is sometimes called the "click-stream." *See* Robert S. Boyd, *On Line Shoppers, Beware: "Free" Forums May Cost You,* Phila. Inquirer, June 20, 1995, at C1 (describing early initiatives to collect click-stream and sell it).

providers not controlled by the telephone company represent a major competitive alternative to traditional telephone local exchange service and thus are entry points to the NII as prices fall and bandwidths rise.

Second, the inherently mobile nature of cellular telephone communications devices presents new challenges for addressing in the NII. When an address is associated with a single device that remains fixed in one place, a network can resolve telephone numbers and addresses more generally through relatively static address tables, changing the routes that messages follow only as appropriate to take advantage of differing levels of utilization of communications channels in different paths. When the communication device moves, addressing cannot work unless the infrastructure has the capability of updating its address databases as each device moves around the physical area covered by the infrastructure.

As long as all stations remain within the reach of a single node or transmitter, each station may be reached simply by broadcasting its address, much as communication occurs on a local area network. But cellular telephone service is based on the concept of cells, each one of which has a transmitter. The mobile telephone instruments move from cell to cell, and some kind of database is necessary to keep track of where they are. As the area within which possible roaming can occur becomes greater, the likelihood becomes greater in a competitive market structure that the databases must cover multiple service providers. This raises shared-resource and equal-access issues not previously encountered in the NII. They are, however, issues that must be dealt with not only as cellular telephone service modernizes and expands, but also with respect to PCS, as explained in § 1.13, and with respect to evolution of the Internet.

§ 1.13   Personal Communications Systems

Personal Communication Systems (PCS) is a term that somewhat vaguely defines a collection of new communications applications naturally evolving from cellular telephone and pager applications. The basic concept of PCS is that each customer would have a number or address assigned to the customer personally, as contrasted to a telephone number or Internet address that is assigned to a particular place. The customer would have one or more devices that would respond to communications sent to that address wherever the device is located. The portability of PCS is roughly equivalent to cellular telephone roaming but would be feasible over much larger geographic areas, perhaps including the entire world. The kinds of messages that PCS customers could receive are expected to include real time voice, voice messaging, text-based similar to E-mail and pager messages, and perhaps graphical images and facsimile as well. Some entrepreneurs contemplate that all these forms of messages would be available on the same device and even perhaps in the same message.

PCS cannot work on a large scale unless mobile addressing is worked out appropriately. **Section 1.12** explains how cellular telephone service requires databases that keep track of where nodes are as they move around the network. As with expanding cellular telephone service, PCS requires dynamic address databases covering many different vendors and large geographic areas, perhaps extending to the entire world. For the services to work as intended, one's PCS device must be able to receive a call or message originating anywhere in the world regardless of whose service area covers the device when the message or call is received.

There are a number of issues to be resolved for this kind of service to be available. The address databases must be accessible technologically and economically by all providers and customers without discrimination. That invites controversy over technical standards and pricing for services. Beyond that, there are decisions that must be made with respect to routing messages and calls. As a competitive infrastructure becomes more diverse, the number of possible routing paths increases and the economic implications of choosing one route over another become more important to more people. The legal system applicable to the NII will be called upon to resolve controversies over access, pricing, and routing choices.

§ 1.14   What's New

The technological environment, and thus the context of law, is influenced by four major phenomena described in the following sections: convergence of technologies that historically defined legal categories, leading to a collapse of the category boundaries; blurring of the distinction between information processing and communications; weakening of the distinctions between basic and enhanced services and between raw content and value-added features; and atomization of production units that now make market transactions through electronic networks.

§ 1.15   —Convergence of Technologies

Specific transmission and channel technologies are no longer a reliable guide to the legal nature of the activity. Radio is used for point-to-point communication as well as broadcast news and entertainment. Wire-based channels are used for broadcasts as well as for point-to-point communication. Both are used for text and still pictures as well as audio and full motion video. Digital and analog no longer are reliable guides to categories; neither are text and voice. Packet switching is migrating from data networks into the full range of infrastructure activities, while certain aspects of circuit switching are influencing the design of the new generation of packet-switching technologies, most prominently in the asynchronous transfer mode (ATM) standard.

§ 1.16 —Collapse of Old Boundaries

The traditional boundaries of communications regulation and of information law were defined in terms of technologies. As distinct technologies have converged, as explained in § 1.7, the legal boundaries have eroded. Cable television networks are entering voice and data communications fields. Telephone companies are entering the broadcast video business. Internet providers are beginning to experiment with voice and audio transmission. Radio licensees are engaging in activities that resemble those of wire-based common carriers. Authors of material on the Internet are indistinguishable from publishers. Intermediaries may function more like reference librarians in terms of their contact with content than like bookstores or newsstands.

§ 1.17 —Communications or Information Processing?

In digital and packet-switched technologies, transmission channels for information must almost always engage in some amount of information processing, if only to switch packets to appropriate routes. More often, it makes sense from a marketing and economic standpoint for the communications provider also to provide certain directory services. Thus, the old distinction between communications and computing that mapped into a distinction between regulated activities and essentially unregulated activities, except for the role of the common law, have become less useful, although the degree to which a particular entity alters and selects content still is an interesting benchmark for determining certain kinds of legal responsibility.

§ 1.18 —Basic or Enhanced Services?

One of the touchstones of regulation of telephone companies in the new environment has been the proposition that basic service should be subjected to traditional common-carrier regulation while enhanced services are not. It is increasingly artificial to maintain and discern the distinction because the digital processing, packet handling, and routing functions associated with basic services are, in many instances, economic to bundle with certain directory services, content-based selections, and pattern matching that would presumably be classified as enhanced services in the earlier 1990 prospective.

§ 1.19 —Raw Information or Value-Added?

In public information policy, the distinction between raw information and value-added information is important. It separates the material traditionally supplied directly by government agencies originating or possessing raw content and the mostly private sector disseminators or redisseminators who provide various value-added enhancements to improve the usability of the raw content. With print or paper technologies the distinction was a fairly clear one. Indexes, topical codes linking particular opinions or decisions to indexes, and definitions of subsets of information collected because of their utility for a particular constituency all rather clearly constituted added value. The basic content of slip opinions or session laws rather clearly constituted raw content.

With information and digital formats and open networks like the Internet, the boundary between adding value and merely supplying raw content becomes more difficult to discern. Full text retrieval permits retrieving information of interest without conventional topical indexes, as long as character-based content representations are available. Subsets of a larger universe of information easily can be assembled simply by identifying an embedded string found in all elements of the subset.

Even the distinct act of publishing becomes less discrete from simply maintaining information as it is used by the agency. With print on paper technologies, to publish agency decisions or regulations or a set of statutes was an obviously distinct undertaking, compared with simply maintaining the slip opinions or the typescript of the session laws in the form they were used in the decisional process. Now, with initiatives like the Government Information Locator System (GILS), and the Internet available as a wholesale marketplace, an agency publishes merely by connecting a server on which its slip opinions and type-script rules and laws exist in word processing files to the Internet.

The blurring of the raw-content/added-value distinction is important for public information policy, considered in **Chapter 11,** and also important for protecting the intellectual property of private sector publishers of public infor-mation who do not normally wish to place their value-added enhancements in the public domain along with the basic content.

§ 1.20 —Atomization

The NII reduces barriers to entry and also reduces transaction costs for exchanges among independent entities. This results in a market structure with many more independent producers, some of small size. No longer is the NII a proposition in which large telephone companies operate in one market segment, large tele-vision networks in another, and a handful of local broadcast stations and newspapers in other market segments. Now a much more diverse collection of providers of information services competes and cooperates in providing complementary pieces of information product bundles.

The fragmentation of production implies loss of control by any single producer, who is much more likely to function at the mercy of market forces. Much smaller transactions, or at least aggregate flows of transactions, mean that entity relations are more anonymous and that relational contract[36] and other legal institutional arrangements that assume ongoing relations between equally powerful firms may no longer be an appropriate model.

The new reality also implies reduced tolerance for transaction costs. That means that most payment mechanisms and enforcement mechanisms must be more efficient so that the costs of arranging for a 50¢ transaction do not dwarf the value of the deal, and that there is some affordable remedy for a $500 deal gone awry. In the current environment, rational businessmen may sue over a $500,000 deal, but not over a $500 one, because the lawsuit costs too much.

Chapter 7 considers where self-governance and self-regulation by electronic network communities fit in the overall scheme of dispute resolution procedure. That subject is important because of the desire of some participants in the NII to have specialized legal machinery and to have greater autonomy from traditional legal institutions. It is also important because the development of specialized dispute resolution techniques with lower transaction costs may be a prerequisite to the effective functioning of NII in which diverse providers of information services and consumers of those services are able to exchange increments of information value of relatively small size without having prior arrangements with each other.

Historically the way of reducing transaction costs has been to empower an administrative agency. That possibility is considered in **Chapter 7.**

§ 1.21 What's Not New

Despite the phenomena that make the NII interesting, it is not revolutionary. It is not necessary to scrap legal doctrines or institutions worked out in the context of other information technologies. Most of the core ideas of the legal subjects discussed in this and subsequent chapters remain sound and can be adapted without much difficulty to the NII. What is needed is a clear understanding of the core legal principles rather than rote application to legal categories that may no longer fit, and a clear understanding of how the various NII technologies actually work.

Many of the concerns expressed about the vulnerability of privacy and intellectual property in open architectures is overblown. If someone infringes intellectual property or initiates other damaging traffic, existing substantive law is mostly adequate to provide remedies. For example, the misrepresentation

---

[36] As **Ch. 2** explains, the relational contract model emphasizes the features of contracts when the relationship is "more like a marriage than a series of one night stands."

that occurs in much abuse and "stalking" is likely to constitute wire fraud. Ordinarily, it is not difficult to trace the origin of Internet traffic, although it is possible to defeat the efficacy of usual tracing mechanisms through things like anonymous servers. But it would be more appropriate to focus legislative initiatives on real problems of tracing rather than on substantive additions to criminalize conduct that already is criminal or to make tortious conduct that already is tortious.

Many of the more dramatic perceptions that national legal systems will become helpless when faced with the global information infrastructure similarly are overblown. Any national legal system can enforce legal obligations against natural persons and physical assets located within its boundaries; that always has been the fundamental basis of legal jurisdiction. Given that leverage, and the preexisting trend toward more international cooperation on civil and criminal proceedings, there is every reason to believe that the law can deal with the NII with no more difficulty that it had dealing with ocean commerce, or international civil aviation, or telecommunications, when they were new.

CHAPTER 2

ACCESS TO NETWORKS AND FACILITIES

§ 2.1   Introduction and Description of the Problem

For the National Information Infrastructure (NII) visions to be realized, a real infrastructure must exist, not an archipelago of electronic islands, none of which is connected with the others. One way for the law to encourage the development of such an infrastructure is for parts of the whole to have legal obligations to provide access to other parts of the whole. Of course the legal intervention is less necessary if market forces effectively induce participants to join together in a universally accessible infrastructure.

So far, the NII has been relatively free of legal claims to access facilities or services provided by another. The only major litigation has involved access to unbundled elements of the local telephone service infrastructure and claims for access to public information and citation systems used to organize public information. The history of communications law and of the law regulating other infrastructure industries like railroads, however, suggests that the NII has more access-right controversies in its future.

Most theories for access rights in the NII focus on communication services, assuming that providers of information and computing services would be exempt from any legally imposed access duties. While distinguishing between communication services and information services has its roots firmly implanted in past distinctions under the Communications Act of 1934[1] and the Modified Final Judgment,[2] such a distinction may be less appropriate for the NII. The Internet, which is the model for the NII, features interoperability not only at the communications level, but also at the application level. One of the features of the Internet that makes it attractive is that virtually any public node can access information on any other public node. This contrasts sharply with the lack of interoperability and access between commercial information providers. While CompuServe has an increasing number of gateways to specialized sources of information, it is not presently possible for one to begin with a CompuServe

---

[1] 47 U.S.C. §§ 151–611. Parts of the analysis in this chapter appeared in an earlier form in Henry H. Perritt, Jr., *Access to the National Information Infrastructure*, 30 Wake Forest L. Rev. 51 (1995).

[2] United States v. American Tel. & Tel. Co., 552 F. Supp. 131 (D.D.C. 1982) (Modified Final Judgment or MFJ), *aff'd,* Maryland v. United States, 460 U.S. 1001 (1983).

connection and go from CompuServe to America Online, Prodigy, or Delphi, nor can one go from America Online to CompuServe.[3]

Interconnections and interoperability are the most basic types of access because they permit end users to access service providers indirectly and thus to experience a system of legally separate service providers as a single network or infrastructure. A rough analogy is the obligation of railroads and airlines to offer through ticketing on connections with other railroads or airlines. In considering legally mandated access duties for the NII, one should consider not only duties that might be imposed on communication services that produce relatively little content, but also on information services. Information services might be obligated to interconnect with other information services through something like today's World Wide Web.

It is important to understand that service providers in the NII span a range from pure communication service providers to almost pure content providers, with some of the most interesting new technology applications in the middle, including Gopher servers and World Wide Web servers. Although the historical dichotomy between information providers and communications providers collapsed under the pressure of new technology, appreciation of the continuum still is valuable. Compatibility is considered in **Chapter 8** as well as in this chapter.

Several sources of access law exist, including contract, statutory and common-law common carriage, and antitrust law. All of these have important limitations, some internal and some externally imposed by constitutional First Amendment and property privileges. They also overlap, sharing two themes: (1) a holding out or offer to serve all comers, and (2) monopoly. *Holding out* is volunteering to serve everyone in a predefined class of customers, without discrimination.[4] The monopoly criterion asks whether customers have alternatives if they are turned away by one provider.

§ 2.2   —Three Kinds of Access Problems

Access can be evaluated in terms of relationships between providers and between providers and markets. Both vertical and horizontal relationships are important. **Figure 2–1** shows an example of each relationship.

---

[3] This relative isolation of the major consumer-oriented commercial information services may change as all of them provide access to the World Wide Web application on the Internet.

[4] Current FCC policy narrowing common carrier regulation de-emphasizes the holding-out theory and emphasizes competitive factors. *See generally* Phil Nichols, Note, *Redefining "Common Carrier": the FCC's Attempt at Deregulation by Definition,* 1987 Duke L.J. 501, 513–14 (FCC redefinition is wrong for three reasons: departure from two centuries of common law; contravenes congressional intent; and unsupported by legislative history). As the FCC observed, the holding-out test lets the regulated define their own duties, it has roots in contract enforcement, and may be the best way to avoid First Amendment and due process blockages to access regulation, considered in **Ch. 6.**

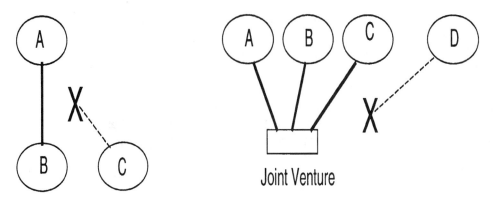

Figure 2–1. Horizontal and vertical relationships between providers and providers and markets.

In the vertical relationship shown in **Figure 2–1,** A supplies communications services and B supplies value-added features, like finding and retrieval aids. The products of the two suppliers are complementary. A and B make a contract, giving B the exclusive right to supply a particular market. Competitors of B get excluded. In the horizontal configuration, A, B, C, and D compete in providing, for example, Internet connection services. A, B, and C jointly operate a router and deny D access to the router, thus disadvantaging D in serving their market. Unilateral action also is conceivable (but not illustrated in the figure). A refuses to handle traffic from B because of political pressure from those opposed to B's point of view.

Access analysis is richer if one assumes an NII architecture much like today's Internet, in which multiple backbones exist (NSFnet, CIX, PSI, Alternet, and MCI); multiple Internet access providers compete with each other to provide basic connection services and also offer some value-added services (AOL, Compu-Serve, CERFnet, NEARnet, BARnet, SURAnet,[5] NetCom, and JVNCnet); a large number of Internet nodes offer pointers and retrieval aids like Gopher and World Wide Web; other Internet nodes offer content through anonymous FTP (file transfer protocol) or through integration with Web or Gopher servers; interexchange and local access telephone companies offer switched digital and analog communications channels both on a dial-up and dedicated line basis, faced with increasing competition from competitive access providers in local markets, competing interexchange carriers in the interexchange market, and traditional X25 (a connection-oriented packet-switching protocol) public data networks like Sprintnet and BT Tymnet. In such an architecture there are many more discrete products than in an older centralized host-based architecture in which elements are more tightly bundled into products spanning a greater range of value-added elements. The larger number of discrete products increases the number of potential markets to be evaluated and the number of interfaces between products representing potential sources of access demands.

---

[5] Bolt, Baranet & Newman bought BARnet, NEARnet, and SURAnet in 1994 and 1995.

§ 2.3 —Access by Suppliers and Consumers

Access rights can be owned by consumers or by suppliers and producers. Access rights in telephone systems refer mostly to access by consumers—universal service. Common carriage in freight transportation means access by suppliers (shippers). In the Internet, every consumer of information is a potential supplier. Thus universal service, traditionally considered in the context of telephone service, now has implications for producer access to channels of distribution because the end users are also potential producers. Producer access to channels of distribution historically was mostly considered in the context of broadcast and cable television,[6] which predominantly is a one-way medium. In distributed, Internet-like architectures, even large producers use the same infrastructure to acquire their raw material as to deliver their product and thus are both consumers and producers through the same network connections. Even if markets distinguish to some degree between end user/consumers and somewhat larger producers,[7] it will be harder for the law to distinguish a priori between producers and consumers.

The convergence of consumer and producer roles has implications for the nature of legal regulation. Compelling a provider to allow someone to put something in potentially influences the obligor's product design and facility control more than letting someone take something out. It represents far less interference with a supermarket, for example, to force it to allow everyone to shop there than it does to mandate shelf space for a particular brand of food. Similarly, it interferes far less with the entrepreneurial prerogatives of an information services provider to force it to allow someone to extract information from a preexisting system than it does to force the same provider to accommodate a new type of information content. The second type of access may force system redesign, while the first type is unlikely to force any such changes. At the most, it would require an increase in capacity. On the other hand, there are supplier-oriented types of access that are less intrusive. Requiring one supplier to be compatible with another—requiring interoperability—does not impose as much on the entity with the duty. If compatibility is not designed into a supplier's facility from the outset, translators always can be written and used, albeit at the cost of some performance penalty. An NII practitioner is as likely to be asked to handle a refusal to allow a client to obtain information, as a refusal to allow a client to send information. Furthermore, the practitioner may be asked to develop arguments against imposition of access duties inconsistent with product concepts.

---

[6] *See, e.g.,* Futurevision Cable Sys., Inc. v. MultiVision Cable TV Corp., 789 F. Supp. 760, 766 (S.D. Miss. 1992) (dispute over access by programming suppliers to cable system).

[7] I am skeptical that significant markets will exist for casual content produced by small consumer/producers. The quality and finding-and-retrieval problems are too great.

§ 2.4   —Common Foci of Major Legal Doctrines

The common concerns of legal doctrines that compel distributors to provide access to suppliers of content and to consumers—holding out and monopoly power—are long-standing. The interaction between common carrier status and antitrust law is particularly evident in the interaction between FCC regulatory policy for the post-divestiture local exchange carriers and the Modified Final Judgment (MFJ).[8] The latter, after all, is an antitrust consent decree. The issues with respect to line-of-business restrictions and access obligations are virtually the same under the MFJ as under the FCC's Computer III inquiry.[9]

The doctrines also share a concern with contract obligations, although this common concern is less evident. Tariffing as a technique of common carrier regulation is the bridge. Common carrier obligations, initially conceived as obligations not to discriminate, were effectuated mainly by requiring covered providers to publish their contract terms called tariffs and then to make contracts only on those terms. The detailed terms of the contract of carriage are not directly specified in a statute or agency rule, but in the privately crafted tariff. The difference between this and a pure implied contract approach to access obligations obviously is that the traditional tariffing arrangement started with an underlying statutory duty to provide nondiscriminatory access. The pure implied contract approach finds that duty only in promissory statements by the covered entity—which becomes a covered entity only because of its own promissory statements.[10]

Figure 2–2 shows how the markets, expectation-based, and public interest dimensions have justified legal imposition of access duties. Holding out is shown on the vertical access, monopoly power is shown on the horizontal access, and public interest is shown on the diagonal access. Statutory common carriage, like common-law common carriage, was justified both by the monopoly power and holding out. Contract obligations are justified entirely by holding out. Universal access and interconnection obligations are justified largely by public interest. The public interest dimension of **Figure 2–2** would justify legal intervention aimed at ensuring interoperability even when the monopoly power and expectations dimensions do not justify it.

---

[8] United States v. American Tel. & Tel. Co., 552 F. Supp. 131 (D.D.C. 1982), *aff'd,* Maryland v. United States, 460 U.S. 1001 (1983).

[9] *In re* Amendment of Section 64.702 of the Commission's Rules and Regulations (Third Computer Inquiry), 104 F.C.C.2d 958 (1986). The FCC's fundamental rethinking of communication regulation took place in three regulatory proceedings, usually called the First Computer Inquiry (Computer I), the Second Computer Inquiry (Computer II), and the Third Computer Inquiry (Computer III).

[10] Implied contract also is closely related to the holding-out element of common carrier status. Holding oneself out as a common carrier is similar in some ways to making a general offer to handle traffic from anyone within a class of potential customers. Making the promise is holding oneself out.

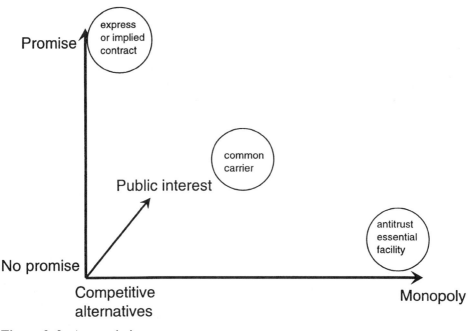

Figure 2–2. Access duties.

§ 2.5 Sources of Right

Universal access can be ensured by market forces, by common-law or statutory common carrier duties, or through application of the antitrust laws. Thus there are a number of legal theories for assuring access to basic infrastructure in addition to statutory common carriage and new statutory "open platform" requirements.[11] One, still mainly speculative, is a common-law common carrier obligation, built on common-law concepts that antedate enactment of the Interstate Commerce Act and that prohibit discriminatory denial of service by entities holding themselves out as serving everyone and possessing certain market power.[12] A second is antitrust essential facilities doctrine and related refusal-to-deal doctrines, which prohibit denial of access to essential facilities by those in competition with the entities denied access. The Supreme Court's decision in *United States v. Terminal Railroad Ass'n*[13] (*TRRA*) sets the basic standards for access by nonparticipating competitors when competitors control an essential facility.[14]

---

[11] *See* H.R. 3636, 103d Cong., 2d Sess., *reprinted in* 140 Cong. Rec. H5216 (daily ed. June 28, 1994) (defining open-platform concept and requiring FCC determinations).

[12] *See* Henry H. Perritt, Jr., *Tort Liability, the First Amendment, and Equal Access to Electronic Networks,* 5 Harv. J.L. & Tech. 65 (1992).

[13] 224 U.S. 383 (1912).

[14] *See generally* John M. Stevens, *Antitrust Law and Open Access to the NREN,* 38 Vill. L. Rev. 571 (1993).

The most attractive doctrine because of its flexibility is express and implied contract. This doctrine obligates a service provider that holds itself out as serving the public from denying access without justification. Contract approaches should include some judicial modification in the historical treatment of credit card arrangements and commercial advertisements in which the representation by the provider is treated not as an offer but rather as a solicitation of offers.[15] The efficacy of a contract-based regime for assuring access could be strengthened legislatively by an approach to tort immunity that extends immunity only to those providers that publish, possibly through some central database, their terms of service and that disavow any intent to screen or censor content.

§ 2.6   FCC Common Carrier Regulation

The best known source of access rights and duties in communications networks is the set of statutory common carrier duties imposed under Title II of the Federal Communications Act of 1934. These duties extend a statutory common carrier scheme expressed in the Interstate Commerce Act, which in turn was derived with little change from common-law common carrier obligations discussed in § 2.6.

Title II access duties are imposed only on communications carriers.[16] The statute defines *communications* as "[interstate][17] transmission [by wire or radio] of writing, signs, signals, pictures, and sounds of all kinds . . . including all instrumentalities, facilities, apparatus, and services (among other things, the receipt, forwarding, and delivery of communications) incidental to such transmission."[18]

The first and historically most important determinant is an undertaking to carry for all potential users, even if the market served is very narrow.[19] This is the "holding-out" criterion. Common carrier status under the statute is determined with respect to particular activities. For example, a cable television system usually is not a common carrier with regard to broadcast retransmission

---

[15] *See* Henry H. Perritt, Jr., *Dispute Resolution in Electronic Network Communities,* 38 Vill. L. Rev. 349, 365–84 (1993) (reviewing cases).

[16] *See* 47 U.S.C. §§ 151, 152 (1988). But even in the area of communications, the regulatory power of the FCC is not absolute. For example, in FCC v. Midwest Video Corp., 440 U.S. 689 (1979), the Supreme Court held that the FCC lacks authority under the Communications Act of 1934, ch. 652 tit. 1, 48 Stat. 1064 (1934), to subject cable television to content-based regulation because the statute indicates that broadcasting is not common carriage. *See* 440 U.S. at 701–02; *see also* 1981 FCC Notice, 46 Fed. Reg. 10,924, 10,933 (1981) (reviewing cases on whether cable television qualifies as common carriage).

[17] The FCC is explicitly denied jurisdiction over intrastate telephone exchange service, 47 U.S.C. § 221(b), and intrastate common carrier obligations, 47 U.S.C. § 152(b) (1988). *See* NARUC v. FCC, 533 F.2d 601, 607 (D.C. Cir. 1976) (overturning FCC preemption of state regulation of intrastate cable two-way, point-to-point communications).

[18] 47 U.S.C. § 153 (1988) (defining covered wire and radio communication in identical language).

[19] NARUC v. FCC, 533 F.2d 601, 608 (D.C. Cir. 1976) (specialized carrier useful only to fraction of population may be a common carrier).

activities,[20] but may be a common carrier when it carries two-way, point-to-point communications.[21]

A further hallmark of common carriage in the communications field, developed by the FCC, is that common carriers leave it to customers to "transmit intelligence of their own design and choosing."[22] One who makes individualized decisions in particular cases whether and on what terms to offer service is not a common carrier.[23] In other words, a common carrier leaves content alone and does not serve or withhold service based on content.

This distinction between communications and information services has proven difficult to implement in practice, and the difficulty, as **Chapter 7** explains, has been responsible in part for the FCC's decisions to contract the scope of common carrier regulation and otherwise to deregulate telecommunications.

The principal implications of common carrier status under the Communications Act[24] historically have been the following:

1. The carrier may not discriminate among customers unjustly or unreasonably or give undue or unreasonable preferences to different classes of users.[25]

2. The carrier must furnish communication service upon reasonable request.

3. The carrier must establish physical connections with other carriers and must establish through routes, charges, and allocation schemes for the charges among participating carriers along with facilities and regulations for through routes.[26]

4. The terms of the contract between the carrier and customer must not differ from those contained in tariffs filed with the FCC.[27]

---

[20] *Id.* at 608 & n.26 (citing cases).

[21] *Id.* at 608–09.

[22] *Id.* at 609 & n.36 (quoting Industrial Radiolocation Serv., 5 F.C.C.2d 197, 202 (1966)); *see also* Frontier Broadcasting Co. v. FCC, 24 F.C.C. 251, 254 (1958) (one-way cable television transmission is not common carrier activity).

[23] NARUC v, FCC, 533 F.2d 601, 608–09 (D.C. Cir. 1976).

[24] Telegraph and telephone carriers originally were regulated by the ICC under the Mann-Elkins Act of 1910, § 7, 36 Stat. 539, 544 (1910) (declaring telephone and telegraph services to be common carriers).

[25] 47 U.S.C. § 202(a) (1988) (defining common carrier obligations). *See* MCI Telecommunications Corp. v. FCC, 765 F.2d 1186, 1192 (D.C. Cir. 1985) (overturning FCC effort to "detariff"; citing 47 U.S.C. §§ 201(b), 202(a)), *aff'd,* 114 S. Ct. 2223 (1994).

[26] 47 U.S.C. § 201(a).

[27] *Id.* § 203; 1981 FCC Notice, 46 Fed. Reg. 10,924, 10,937 (1981) (discussing tariff requirement). *See* MCI Telecommunications Corp. v. FCC, 765 F.2d 1186, 1192 (D.C. Cir. 1985) (overturning FCC effort to "detariff"; citing 47 U.S.C. § 203(a)) *aff'd,* 114 S. Ct. 2223 (1994). A basic concept of common carrier regulation is that the carrier must adhere to filed tariffs and not deviate from these through negotiations with individual customers. *See* Maislin Indus. v. Primary Steel, Inc., 497 U.S. 116 (1990) (reviewing filed rate doctrine and concluding that ICC's negotiated rates doctrine is invalid under statutes governing motor carrier economic regulation). The filed tariff doctrine is considered more fully in **Ch. 5.**

5. Charges, practices, classifications, and regulations must be just and reasonable and may be subject to approval by the FCC.[28]

6. Structural and accounting requirements may be imposed by the FCC in support of its responsibility to eliminate discrimination and to regulate rates.

7. The carrier may be prohibited from entering a market[29] unless the FCC approves the new service in advance.[30]

The fourth through seventh requirements are major reasons for opposition to extending the statutory common carrier concept into parts of the NII not now covered. Yet, the Supreme Court's decision in *MCI,* discussed in § **7.5** suggests that the FCC lacks power to simplify the details of common carrier regulation.[31]

The purest form of access right under the Communication Act is the interconnection obligation imposed on common carriers. The requirement for physical interconnections and through routes is derived from section 1(4) of the Interstate Commerce Act.[32] The Interstate Commerce Act obligation was expanded by the Mann-Elkins Act of 1910,[33] to eliminate a precondition found to exist in *ICC v. Northern Pacific Railway:*[34] that the ICC had no authority to issue such an order in the absence of a finding that no reasonable or satisfactory through route already existed.[35] In the communications context, a number of

---

[28] 47 U.S.C. § 201(a), (b) (requiring just and reasonable charges). *See* 1981 FCC Notice, 46 Fed. Reg. 10,924, 10,926 (1981).

[29] *See generally* 1981 FCC Notice, 46 Fed. Reg. 10,924, 10,946 (1981) (reviewing antitrust cases on market definition) (citing Brown Shoe Co. v. United States, 370 U.S. 294, 325 (1962); United States v. E. I. duPont de Nemours & Co., 351 U.S. 377, 404 (1956)).

[30] 46 U.S.C. § 203 (1988); 1981 FCC Notice, 46 Fed. Reg. 10,924, 10,937 (1981) (discussing tariff requirement); *see* MCI Telecommunications Corp. v. FCC, 765 F.2d 1186, 1192 (D.C. Cir. 1985) (overturning FCC efforts to "detariff"; citing 47 U.S.C. §§ 201(b), 202(a), 214), *aff'd,* 114 S. Ct. 2223 (1994).

[31] *See* 47 U.S.C. §§ 201(b) (charges, practices, classifications, and regulations must be just and reasonable), 203 (tariffs must be filed and no changes may be made without 120 days notice to the commission and the public), 204–205 (hearings and power to prescribe just and reasonable charges), 208 (standing to complain about violations), 214 (prohibiting extensions of line without certificate of convenience and necessity), 215 (commission examination of transactions that might have an impact on services).

[32] Ch. 3591, 34 Stat. 584 (1906).

[33] Ch. 309, 36 Stat. 539, 552 (1910).

[34] 216 U.S. 538 (1910). *See* Kenneth A. Cox & William J. Byrnes, *The Common Carrier Provisions—A Product of Evolutionary Development, in* A Legislative History of the Communications Act of 1934, at 25, 43 (Max D. Paglin ed., 1989) (citing Mann-Elkins Act, 36 Stat. at 552) [hereinafter Cox & Byrnes].

[35] *Id.* at 544 (citing Interstate Commerce Act, 34 Stat. at 589; merely because the public might prefer two routes does not satisfy the condition).

early disputes resulted from the Bell System's policy of refusing to connect with some independent telephone companies from 1894 to 1906. Thirty-four states enacted laws compelling physical connection.[36]

The interconnection obligation under the Federal Communications Act is a reasonableness obligation.[37] The most significant interconnection decision was the FCC's *Carter Phone v. AT&T* decision in 1968, which started the unraveling of the Bell system.[38] The *Carter Phone* decisions were interpreted only to prohibit telephone company refusals of "harmless" interconnections,[39] while allowing refusals based on detriment to the public and adverse effects on the telephone system.[40] In rationalizing regulation of "record carriers," the Congress required then dominant Western Union and RCA to provide unrestricted interconnection to the lines of other record carriers,[41] while exempting from certain of the interconnection requirements carriers that did not control

---

[36] Cox & Byrnes at 42 n.132. *See also* Oklahoma-Ark. Tel. Co. v. Southwestern Bell Tel. Co., 45 F.2d 995, 997 (8th Cir. 1930) (no duty of Bell System to provide physical interconnection with local phone company based on expired contract or at common law (citing cases); state statute required telephone connections for individual customers, but not "the admission of outside rival companies to a proprietary use of its lines" noting that similar statutes in other states have received contrary interpretation). The court also rejected an argument that providing physical connections to other telephone companies while refusing it violated common carrier duties. 45 F.2d at 1000 (citing cases). Finally, the court noted primary jurisdiction of the FCC.

[37] *See* Rogers Radio Communications Servs., Inc. v. FCC, 751 F.2d 408, 415 (D.C. Cir. 1985) (no violation of § 201 for telephone company to deny noncompensatory connection to nonwire line paging service; not reasonable or in the public interest to require telephone company customers to subsidize paging service); Capital Network Sys., Inc. v. FCC, 28 F.3d 201, 203–04 (D.C. Cir. 1994) (describing relationship between major interexchange carriers and pay telephone companies with respect to access to databases of telephone credit card numbers, and noting that pay telephone provider denied access to database could file a complaint with the FCC, but affirming rejection of tariff that would shift costs to AT&T).

[38] 13 F.C.C.2d 420, *reconsideration denied,* 14 F.C.C.2d 571 (1968); *see also* North Carolina Utils. Comm'n v. FCC, 537 F.2d 787, 794 (4th Cir. 1976); North Carolina Utils. Comm'n v. FCC, 552 F.2d 1036 (4th Cir. 1977); Louisiana PSC v. FCC, 476 U.S. 355, 375 n.4 (1986) (explaining and apparently approving decisions approving FCC preemption of CPE interconnection prohibitions by states).

[39] Rogers Radio Communications Servs., Inc. v. FCC, 751 F.2d 408, 415–16 (D.C. Cir. 1985) (applying *Carter Phone*). In the *Hush-A-Phone* decision, Hush-A-Phone Corp. v. United States, 238 F.2d 266 (D.C. Cir. 1956), the D.C. Circuit invalidated an FCC order approving a tariff ban to a consumer device that could be attached to the telephone to enhance privacy in speaking. In *Carter Phone,* the commission invalidated as unreasonable the tariff that prohibited the connection to the telephone system of any device not shown to have a deleterious effect on the system. The *Carter Phone* device itself enabled radio communications to be connected to telephone calls.

[40] Rogers Radio Communications Servs., Inc. v. FCC, 751 F.2d 408, 416 (D.C. Cir. 1985).

[41] 47 U.S.C. § 222 (c)(1)(A)(i); *id.* § 222(c)(1)(B)(ii–iii). The term "record carrier" refers to a carrier like a telegraph or cable carrier that makes a written record of the communication.

significant market share.[42] The distinction between dominant and nondominant carriers in application of common carriage requirements was the one essentially rejected in *Carter Phone*. The difference is that Congress explicitly sanctioned the distinction with respect to record carriers, but remained silent with respect to telephone carriers.

One more recent interconnection controversy arose over access by nonwire line paging services to local access telephone carriers. The telephone companies were concerned that interconnections would be noncompensatory because of short holding times for beeper calls.[43] When the FCC decided to allow competition in the specialized common carrier market, it did so in large part by requiring the telephone companies to allow MCI and others like Southern Pacific Communications to interconnect.[44] The effect of the interconnection decisions is to deny any common-law obligation to allow competing services to interconnect; to impose a burden on common carriers under 47 U.S.C. § 201 to justify interconnection refusals; and to recognize as legitimate those justifications based either on technical harm or noncompensatory rates based on the costs of interconnection.

In the background is the idea that interconnection obligations are easier to rationalize for dominant carriers than for nondominant ones, at least when Congress articulates deferential treatment, as in the record-carrier case.[45] Combined with the decision invalidating on-premises interconnection requirements, discussed in **Chapter 6,** it may be that interconnection requirements can be justified constitutionally only by the existence of monopoly control over a network facility in the absence of acceptable alternatives.

§ 2.7   Who Was a Common-Law Common Carrier?

As noted in § **2.6,** the statutory common carrier obligations are derived, with little change, from common-law common carrier obligations. At common law,

---

[42] *Id.* § 222(c)(1)(B); RCA Global Communications, Inc. v. FCC, 758 F.2d 722, 725–26 (D.C. Cir. 1985) (allowing FCC order that permitted small carrier to offer discounts for customers that use its services without connecting to large carrier; reviewing interconnection requirements under Communications Act).

[43] Most local telephone rates are premised on average call length, and changes and uses can change call length. A typical call to actuate a beeper is much shorter than a typical call for voice conversation. *See generally* Rogers Radio Communications Servs., Inc. v. FCC, 751 F.2d 408, 411 (D.C. Cir. 1985) (explaining basis for claim of noncompensatory character of pager service connections). *See generally* William J. Baumol & J. Gregory Sidak, *The Pricing of Inputs Sold to Competitors,* 11 Yale J. on Reg. 171 (1994) (offering analysis of pricing alternatives to access to components of networks).

[44] Southern Pac. Communications Co. v. American Tel. & Tel. Co., 740 F.2d 980, 985–86 (D.C. Cir. 1984) (reviewing history of specialized common carriage policy).

[45] RCA Global Communications, Inc. v. FCC, 758 F.2d 722, 725–26 (D.C. Cir. 1985) (allowing FCC order that permitted small carrier to offer discounts for customers that use its services without connecting to large carrier; reviewing interconnection requirements under Communications Act).

someone engaged in a public calling, like an innkeeper or a ferry operator, was treated as a common carrier. The early cases are somewhat confused about the determinants of common carrier status, but it seems evident that holding out (a kind of promise to serve all comers), monopoly power, and public interest in having the service performed affordably and fairly were the three important determinants.[46]

One of the most important determinants of common carrier status at common law was holding oneself out as common carrier. Part of the public interest justification, fulfilling the public's expectations, springs from the voluntary undertaking of a service by the business.[47] This voluntary offer creates a kind of implied contract with the public, the terms of which were supplied by the law: to serve all in return for a reasonable compensation.[48]

But explicit statements by the enterprise were not the only indicator of holding out. Whether or not the business intended to be a common carrier, the courts also looked to the nature of the business to determine if it was a common carrier.[49] The clearest example of this analysis is *Dutton v. Strong*,[50] in which wharves were held to be public[51] if "the purpose for which they were built, the uses to which they have been applied, the place located and the nature and character of the structure [were sufficiently public]."[52] In *Bennett v. Dutton* the court similarly looked beyond the defendant's assertions and held that the defendant was a general carrier of passengers.[53]

The second major consideration was the protection of the public from monopoly.[54] Monopoly frustrates regulation by the marketplace and justifies legal control as a substitute. The existence of monopoly power was the most commonly contested issue in the early common-law common carrier cases.

---

[46] Henry H. Perritt, Jr., *Tort Liability, the First Amendment, and Equal Access to Electronic Networks,* 5 Harv. J.L. & Tech. 65 (1992).

[47] Wheeler v. Northern Colo. Irrigation Co., 10 Colo. 582, 589–90, 17 P. 487 (1987); Munn v. Illinois, 94 U.S. 113, 126 (1876); *see also* Nash v. Page, 80 Ky. 539, 544 (1882).

[48] *See* People v. New York Cent. & Hudson River R.R., 35 N.Y. Sup. Ct. (28 Hun.) 543, 550–53 (App. Div. 1883) (railroad business has express contract in charter and implied contract based on the nature of the business).

[49] Dutton v. Strong, 66 U.S. (1 Black) 23, 32 (1861); Barrington v. Commercial Dock Co., 15 Wash. 170, 175 (1896); see Bennett v. Dutton, 10 N.H. 481, 487 (1839).

[50] 66 U.S. (1 Black) 23 (1861).

[51] A finding of public character was tantamount to a finding of common carrier status.

[52] 66 U.S. (1 Black) 23, 33 (1861).

[53] 10 N.H. 481, 487 (1839); *see also* Barrington v. Commercial Dock Co., 15 Wash. 170, 175 (1896) (court looks past defendant's assertions).

[54] *See generally* Bruce Wyman, *The Law of the Public Callings as a Solution of the Trust Problem,* 17 Harv. L. Rev. 156 (1903–04) (urging that trust problem could be solved by extending common carrier (public callings) regulation). Some commentators argue that the monopoly factor does not explain much in the older cases. *See* Edward A. Adler, *Business Jurisprudence,* 28 Harv. L. Rev. 135, 149 (1914–15) (when there is no evidence of differences between market power, monopoly cannot be the deciding factor on which to regulate).

The leading monopoly precedent is the English case of *Allnut v. Ingles,*[55] in which a dock and warehouse were given the exclusive right to collect taxes on imported wines. The court held that the conferring of an exclusive right was a monopoly and therefore the defendant was obliged to take all goods.[56] Identical reasoning is seen in American cases, when other forms of monopoly justified imposition of common carrier duties.[57] These include development of an infrastructure that could not feasibly be challenged by another enterprise[58] and control over a patent.[59]

There is a relationship between the holding-out test and the monopoly test. When someone holds himself out as a common carrier, he discourages other suppliers of the same services from entering the same market, and he also discourages customers from making arrangements for alternative sources of supply,[60] thus increasing the conditions in which a monopoly exists.

The monopoly cases also depend upon other factors, such as holding out, or historical treatment of a particular type of business to support their opinions. The first of these secondary factors is necessity of the service. In each common carrier case the business regulated provided a service that was of great public importance.[61] Nevertheless, trades such as furrier, candle maker, and plumber were all necessary to the public, yet they were never regulated as common carriers regardless of whether monopolies existed. Judge Smith in *Shepard v. Milwaukee Gas Light Co.* suggested that candlestick makers or clothing makers were not regulated because these businesses provided identifiable and transportable goods. The public could protect itself by buying outside of the immediate vicinity of the business.[62]

---

[55] 104 Eng. Rep. 206 (1810).

[56] *Id.* at 211. Chief Justice Ellenbourgh stated, "[A]s long as their warehouses are the only places which can be resorted to for this purpose, they are bound to let the trade have the use of them for a reasonable hire and reward." *Id.*

[57] Nash v. Page, 80 Ky. 539, 547–49 (1882) (citing *Allnut;* tobacco warehouses were common carriers because they controlled trade and thus took on public character); *but cf.* Dutton v. Strong, 66 U.S. 23 (1861); Shepard v. Milwaukee Gas Light Co., 6 Wis. 526, 546–47 (1858) (monopolies must have duties to the public, to justify their continued existence).

[58] State v. Nebraska Tel. Co., 22 N.W. 237, 238 (Neb. 1885) (no two companies will cover same territory once the "plant" is in place); *see also* Bruce Wyman, *The Law of the Public Callings as a Solution of the Trust Problem,* 17 Harv. L. Rev. 156, 170 (1903–04).

[59] Commercial Union Tel. Co. v. New England Tel. & Tel. Co., 17 A. 1071, 1073 (Vt. 1889); Hockett v. State, 5 N.E. 178, 182 (Ind. 1886); Bell Tel. Co. v. Commonwealth, 3 A. 825 (Pa. 1886). But see **Ch. 10,** explaining that owners of intellectual property do not have a duty to license.

[60] There are many counterexamples, of course. One prominent one is the increase in competition in the market for local telephone services.

[61] State v. Citizens' Tel. Co., 39 S.E. 257, 261 (S.C. 1901); State v. Nebraska Tel. Co., 22 N.W. 237, 239 (Neb. 1885); *see generally* 46 Fed. Reg. 10, 924, 10,954 (1981) (FCC finding that "essentiality" was a key at common law).

[62] 6 Wis. 526, 545–46 (1858). *See also* No. 320 (Sub. No. 2), Market Dominance Determinations and Consideration of Product Competition, 365 I.C.C. 118 (1981) (explaining concept of geographic competition, in which competitive conditions are established by providing that a source from a geographically remote location can supply needs).

Modern case law concerned with defining what is meant by the term "common carrier" has developed along two paths. The federal courts, except when they are applying state law in diversity cases, have been primarily concerned with defining a what is meant by "common carrier" for purposes of statutory interpretation and preemption analysis.[63] State courts, in addition to statutory interpretation decisions,[64] deal with the common-law definition of "common carrier" for other purposes such as tort litigation.[65] Both state and federal courts, consistent with the traditional holding-out theory, focus on the undertakings of the entity.[66]

More recently, the common-law definition of "common carrier" has evolved around two inquiries: What is "common"? And what is "carrier"? First, the decisions since 1970 establish three factors to consider when deciding whether an entity is a carrier. Second, the courts have discussed four variables defining what is common.[67]

The first of the three "carrier" variables is whether the entity provides the services on a "for hire" basis.[68] That is, does the entity provide the service for the purpose of strictly generating revenue?[69]

---

[63] *See* FCC v. Midwest Video Corp., 440 U.S. 689 (1979) (deciding whether a cable television station is a common carrier to determine if FCC preemption is appropriate); National Ass'n of Regulatory Util. Comm'rs (NARUC) v. FCC, 533 F.2d 601, 608 (D.C. Cir. 1976) (examining particular activities as to which preemption was asserted to see if qualified as common carriage); *see also* Wold Communications, Inc., v. FCC, 735 F.2d 1465, 1471–73 & n.10 (D.C. Cir. 1984) (FCC validly determined sales of domestic satellite transponders not to be subject to common carrier regulation; rejecting scarcity of supply argument).

[64] North Carolina *ex rel.* Utilities Comm'n v. Simpson, 246 S.E.2d 753 (N.C. 1978) (issue was whether an entity was a radio common carrier within the statutory definition of common carrier).

[65] *See* Alpha Zeta Chapter of Pi Kappa Alpha v. Sullivan, 740 S.W.2d 127 (Ark. 1987) (businessman who rented equipment to students for hayride on an ad hoc basis was not a common carrier and not held to highest standard of care for safety of participants in hayride); Adkins v. Slater, 298 S.E.2d 236 (W. Va. 1982) (to determine appropriate standard of care jury must first determine whether mobile home mover is a common carrier); Summers v. Montgomery Elevator Co., 757 P.2d 1255 (Kan. 1988) (shopping center's private service elevator not a common carrier, therefore, there was not a heightened standard of care).

[66] *See, e.g.,* NARUC v. FCC, 533 F.2d 601, 608 (D.C. Cir. 1976) (cable channels leased for nonvideo point-to-point access were intrastate common carrier services excluded from FCC regulation; test is whether were held out to defined class of consumers indifferently); Kvalheim v. Horace Mann Life Ins. Co., 219 N.W.2d 533, 536 (Iowa 1974) (issue was whether entity was a common carrier for the purposes of determining amount of insurance policy payment, focused analysis upon whether there was a legal undertaking by the entity to provide common carrier services).

[67] These variables are synthesized from the cases, rather than applied explicitly in these cases.

[68] *See, e.g.,* Harper v. Agency Rent-A-Car, Inc., 905 F.2d 71, 73 (5th Cir. 1990) (car rental agency that shuttled customers to a nearby location, as a courtesy, without charge, was not providing services "for hire" and therefore not a common carrier).

[69] *See, e.g.,* Brockway v. Travelers Ins. Co., 321 N.W.2d 332 (Wis. Ct. App. 1982) (bus service provided, without charge, by the National Red Cross, was not a service "for hire" and therefore not a common carrier for the purposes of establishing tort liability).

The second "carrier" variable is whether the entity is primarily engaged in the business in question.[70] Transportation services must be more than an incidental service provided in connection with an entity's other products[71] in order to qualify as carrier services. The analogy in the communications context would be a distinction between a manufacturing company that affords its customers access to an electronic bulletin board versus one that sells electronic bulletin board services.

The third "carrier" factor is whether the entity conducts the service on a regular basis.[72] An entity can receive a significant portion of its income in return for transportation services yet still, because those services are not regularly performed, not be considered a common carrier. For example, a heavy equipment manufacturer may derive significant income from transportation services performed delivering an oversized piece of equipment to a customer's plant. Delivery of the equipment may constitute as much as one-half of the project cost, yet in light of the "regular" test, this entity is not a common carrier.[73]

In addition to the three "carrier" factors, there are four inquiries regarding whether a carrier is "common." The first asks whether an entity holds itself out to the public as willing to serve all who apply: the traditional holding-out test.[74] This inquiry has two components. First, a carrier may only serve a limited number of customers and still be said to hold itself out to the "public."[75] The size of the customer base necessary to meet this test varies depending upon the type of service being provided and the entity's capacity to serve.[76] The second component focuses on activities of the entity designed to promote the entity's transportation services to the public. Endeavors such as advertising, personal

---

[70] *See* Harper v. Agency Rent-A-Car, Inc., 905 F.2d 71, 73 (5th Cir. 1990). The reasoning of transportation cases can be extended to other types of service. Courts have broadly defined transportation to include the electronic transport of information. *See, e.g.,* NARUC v. FCC, 533 F.2d 601, 609 (D.C. Cir. 1976).

[71] Mount Pleasant Indep. Sch. Dist. v. Lindburg, 766 S.W.2d 208, 213 (Tex. 1989) (school district's interest in operating school bus service only "incidental" to primary function of district, therefore not a common carrier).

[72] Harper v. Agency Rent-A-Car, Inc., 905 F.2d 71, 73 (5th Cir. 1990).

[73] Note also that this test is not completely determinative. An entity may conduct regular transportation services and not be considered a common carrier. *See, e.g.,* Mount Pleasant Indep. Sch. Dist. v. Lindburg, 766 S.W.2d 208, 213 (Tex. 1989).

[74] *See, e.g.,* Summers v. Montgomery Elevator Co., 757 P.2d 1255, 1261 (Kan. 1988) (adopting *Black's Law Dictionary* definition of a "common carrier," quoting provision requiring, inter alia, carrier to hold itself out to the public in order to be classified a common carrier).

[75] *See, e.g.,* Straley v. Idaho Nuclear Corp., 500 P.2d 218, 221 (Idaho 1972) (company providing bus service for its employees was common carrier, despite not serving the general public; it need not serve "all" members of public to retain status as common carrier). The focus in *Straley* was upon the bus operation as a separate entity. *Id.* Although, clearly an incidental service in some respects, the bus operation itself met enough of the traditional tests for common carriage to cause the court to impose the higher standard of care. *Id.*

[76] *See, e.g.,* North Carolina *ex rel.* Utilities Comm'n v. Simpson, 246 S.E.2d 753, 755 (N.C. 1978).

solicitation, and keeping in touch with former customers are all evidence that the entity has held itself out to the general public.[77]

The second, somewhat tautological, "common" inquiry is whether the entity serves the public without discrimination.[78] The entity must be willing to serve all those members of the public, as public is defined for the entity, who choose to engage the services of the entity.[79] There is no requirement that the entity be large enough to serve all potential customers.[80] When the entity, however, has the capacity, it must undertake to serve all members of its respective public.[81]

The third "common" variable relates to the traditional monopoly theory of common carrier and also, like the older cases, asks whether the entity is said to be operating in the public interest.[82] Decisions with this focus generally arise when a court is deciding whether an entity is a public utility.[83]

The fourth "common" inquiry focuses on whether the entity has control over the content of the goods being transported. In decisions involving telecommunication carriers, to be a common carrier the entity must not control the content of the message.[84] From the user's point of view, this means that the user must be able to transmit messages of his own design and choosing.[85] Extending the content control variable beyond communications carriage is somewhat artificial, although one can argue that content control is like carriage of physical goods manufactured by the carrier, something that was prohibited during the heyday of railroad regulation.[86]

---

[77] *See* Market Transp., Ltd. v. Maudlin, 725 P.2d 914, 921 (Or. 1986) (quoting F. Kahn, Principles of Motor Carrier Regulation 5 (1958)). The court stated: "Advertising in newspapers and telephone directories, maintaining contacts with old patrons and active personal solicitation—these may constitute a holding out to serve the public generally." *Id.*

[78] *See, e.g.,* Alpha Zeta Chapter of Phi Kappa Alpha v. Sullivan, 740 S.W.2d 127, 131 (Ark. 1987).

[79] *Id.*

[80] *See* Adkins v. Slater, 298 S.E.2d 236, 240 (W. Va. 1982).

[81] Francis X. Welch, Cases and Text on Public Utility Regulation 138–40 (1968) (regulatory orders compelling acquisition of adequate facilities).

[82] North Carolina *ex rel.* Utilities Comm'n v. Simpson, 246 S.E.2d 753, 756 (N.C. 1978); *see, e.g.,* State v. Southwestern Bell, 526 S.W.2d 526, 529 (Tex. 1975) (privately owned entity supplying communication services, which for all intents and purposes enjoyed a monopoly, was a business affected with the public interest and therefore, was under a "common carrier" type obligation as a public utility to provide nondiscriminatory service at reasonable rates).

[83] There is no principled distinction between common carrier and public utility status. *Accord* Joseph J. Spengler, *The Public Utility Problem Viewed Historically, in* A Critique of Administrative Regulation of Public Utilities 165, 171–76 (Warren J. Samuels & Harry M. Trebing eds., 1972) (treating public utilities and common carriers as the same); Francis X. Welch, Cases and Text on Public Utility Regulation 1–4 (1968) (treating common carrier, public utility, and business clothed with public interest the same).

[84] NARUC v. FCC, 533 F.2d at 601, 609–10 (D.C. Cir. 1976).

[85] *Id.*

[86] Interstate Commerce Act § 1(8), recodified, 49 U.S.C. § 10,746 (1988); United States v. Delaware, Lackawana & W. R.R., 238 U.S. 516 (1915) (purpose of "commodities clause" is to prevent dual and inconsistent roles of common carrier and shipper); United States v. South Buffalo Ry., 69 F. Supp. 456, 458 (W.D.N.Y. 1946) (purpose is to avoid tendency to discriminate), *aff'd,* 333 U.S. 771 (1948).

§ 2.8   Common Law Nondiscrimination Obligation

Once someone was determined to be a common carrier, the law imposed a nondiscrimination obligation. Any refusal to serve had to be justified by a legitimate economic interest. Gradually, as alleged discrimination took the form of alleged unreasonable charges, courts applying common carrier duties were drawn into scrutinizing pricing.[87] But the common-law duty not to discriminate apparently extended only to end users and did not mandate interconnections with competitors.[88]

Once a business was classified as a common carrier, it was required to serve all who applied.[89] The carrier was also required to provide service on reasonable terms.[90] This included reasonable price[91] and reasonable regulations for use.[92] Reasonableness was determined on a case-by-case basis.

Later, the common carrier reasonableness standard was enlarged to prohibit discrimination among customers. As described in *McDuffee v. Portland & Rochester Railroad*,[93] "A service or price that would otherwise be reasonable may be made unreasonable by an unreasonable discrimination because such discrimination is a violation of the common right." There is a conflict of authorities as to whether discrimination was actionable in and of itself.[94]

---

[87] Henry H. Perritt, Jr., *Tort Liability, the First Amendment, and Equal Access to Electronic Networks,* 5 Harv. J.L. & Tech. 65, 75–76 (1992). *Cf.* Rogers Radio Communications Servs., Inc. v. FCC, 751 F.2d 408 (D.C. Cir. 1985) (complaint by nonwire line paging services company that interconnections offered by phone company failed to meet statutory requirements because of pricing).

[88] Cox & Byrnes at 42 n.132. *See also* Oklahoma-Ark. Tel. Co. v. Southwestern Bell Tel. Co., 45 F.2d 995, 997 (8th Cir. 1930) (no duty of Bell System to provide physical interconnection with local phone company based on expired contract or at common law (citing cases); state statute required telephone connections for individual customers, but not "the admission of outside rival companies to a proprietary use of its lines" noting that similar statutes in other states have received contrary interpretation). The court also rejected an argument that providing physical connections to other telephone companies while refusing it violated common carrier duties. 45 F.2d at 1000 (citing cases). Finally, the court noted primary jurisdiction of the FCC.

[89] *See* Cook v. Chicago, R.I. & P. Ry., 46 N.W. 1080, 1082 (Iowa 1890); McDuffee v. Portland & Rochester R.R., 52 N.H. 430, 448 (1873); *but see* Bennett v. Dutton, 10 N.H. 481, 486 (1839) (innkeepers and stagecoach owners may refuse service based on character, condition, or purpose of applicant).

[90] Cook v. Chicago, R.I. & P. Ry., 46 N.W. 1080, 1082 (Iowa 1890); Shepard v. Milwaukee Gas Light Co., 6 Wis. 526, 535 (1858).

[91] Cook v. Chicago, R.I. & P. Ry., 46 N.W. 1080, 1082 (Iowa 1890).

[92] Shepard v. Milwaukee Gas Light Co., 6 Wis. 526, 535–36 (1858) (ruling on which regulations were unreasonable).

[93] 52 N.H. 430, 451 (1873).

[94] *Compare* Cowden v. Pacific Coast S.S. Co., 94 Cal. 470, 478 (1892) and (discrimination not sufficient) Johnson v. Pensacola & Perdido R.R., 16 Fla. 623, 667 (1878) (discrimination may be a matter of evidence in determining whether a charge is too much or too little for the service, but the difference between charges cannot be the measure of damages unless it is established

The duty to serve reasonably, both as to terms and as to discrimination, was enforced by actions for mandamus, for damages in trespass, or for unjust enrichment in assumpsit. The carrier was liable for any breach of its common carrier obligations in a mandamus action or an action for trespass.[95] A mandamus action could be brought to compel the business to serve the plaintiff as required by its obligation.[96] The trespass action was available for damages caused by the failure to serve.[97] The trespass action could be maintained for expenditures necessitated by the excessive pricing. The damages would be the difference between the reasonable rate and the price that had to be paid for replacement service.[98] The more common action was in assumpsit. The cause of action was based on the difference between the reasonable price and the amount paid to the defendant.[99]

§ 2.9   Application of Common Carrier Principles to Digital Network Technologies

Development of common-law common carriage was arrested by enactment of the Interstate Commerce Act in 1889, the Federal Communications Act in 1934, and similar statutes in every state, largely preempting the operation of common law with respect to common carriers. Now, however, with deregulation and the pulling back of the scope of statutory common carriage, there is renewed opportunity for the application of common-law concepts, although the cases have not arisen yet.

Properly interpreted and adapted to modern views of competition and emerging network technologies, those common-law principles impose access

---

that the smaller charge is the true and reasonable charge); *with* Scofield v. Lake Shore & M.S. Ry., 43 Ohio St. 571, 598, 3 N.E. 907 (1885) (discrimination sufficient) and Cook v. Chicago, R.I. & P. Ry., 46 N.W. 1080, 1082 (Iowa 1890) (citing treatises stating rights of service are meaningless if the companies can discriminate); New England Express Co. v. Maine Cent. R.R., 57 Me. 188, 196 (1869) (very definition excludes the idea of unequal preferences); Western Union Tel. Co. v. Call Publishing Co., 62 N.W. 506, 510 (Neb. 1895) (terms must be reasonable and nondiscriminatory).

[95] McDuffee v. Portland & Rochester R.R., 52 N.H. 430, 449 (1873); New England Express Co. v. Maine Cent. R.R., 57 Me. 188, 194 (1869).

[96] *See, e.g.,* State v. Citizens' Tel. Co., 39 S.E. 257, 263 (S.C. 1901); State v. Nebraska Tel. Co., 22 N.W. 237 (Neb. 1885) (issuing mandamus to force telephone company to provide service to subscribers complying with established requirements); People v. New York Cent. & Hudson River R.R., 35 N.Y. Sup. Ct. (28 Hun.) 543, 553 (App. Div. 1883) (allowing state to enforce people's rights by mandamus).

[97] *See* Weymouth v. Penobscot Log Driving Co., 71 Me. 29 (1880) (action on the case for damages caused by failure to perform).

[98] *See* Johnson v. Pensacola & Perdido R.R., 16 Fla. 623, 667 (1878); Western Union Tel. Co. v. Call Publishing Co., 62 N.W. 506, 513 (Neb. 1895).

[99] *See* Cook v. Chicago, R.I. & P. Ry., 46 N.W. 1080 (Iowa 1890) (difference was unjust enrichment); Western Union Tel. Co. v. Call Publishing Co., 62 N.W. 506, 513 (Neb. 1895).

obligations only on network service providers who offer to take all comers (the holding-out theory) and when market structures are such that competitive forces are not likely to be effective in ensuring alternative access to ultimate consumers.

When applying common carrier principles to contemporary and potential future digital network technologies, the starting point is to identify the factors that indicate whether the originator or handler of an electronic communication is a common carrier. The factors can be grouped naturally into those relating to the holding-out test and those relating to the market structure test.

The point of the analysis in the following sections is not to suggest that NII service providers meeting the criteria be subjected to statutory common carrier regulation under Title II of the Communications Act. Rather, the purpose is to show how the traditional hallmarks of access obligations fit the technologies and market structures of the NII. The analysis may be pertinent to writing new statutory requirements or to adapting common-law common carriage concepts to NII realities. An entity desiring access to the facilities of an NII service provider and wanting to develop a legal theory supporting its claim to access can use these factors.

It is difficult to draw a line between complete denial of access to facilities and discrimination in price or other services. If, for example, one says that only complete denial of access is justifiable, one then makes it possible for a supplier effectively to deny access by charging an outrageous price. In order to guard against this practice, regulatory bodies may exercise control over a range of prices in the guise of preventing denial access. There is thus a tendency for limited equal access obligations to disintegrate over time into detailed price regulation, accompanied by detailed accounting and reporting requirements. The price regulation usually involves cross-subsidies to serve policy goals, and these cannot be supported without market entry and exit regulation. Thus the full panoply of ICC- and FCC-type economic regulation may be the end result of any kind of equal access regulation. On the other hand, it took approximately a century for limited common-law common carrier regulation to evolve into ICC- and FCC-type regulation, and the long period of gestation may produce desirable results as it is occurring.

§ 2.10   —Holding-Out Factors

The factors determining whether a service provider is holding itself out as a common carrier are as follows:

1. A service provider that engages in mass marketing of its services is more likely to be found to be a common carrier than one that negotiates more privately with individual customers.

2. A service provider that targets its marketing to general populations is more likely to be a common carrier than one that targets its marketing efforts more narrowly to some identifiable group.

3. A service provider that offers standard service to all customers or to customers within broad categories is more likely to be a common carrier than one offering tailor-made services reflecting the needs of a particular customer.

4. A service provider that offers explicitly or impliedly to accept any message tendered is more likely to be a common carrier than one that explicitly announces conditions for acceptance in advance of contracting with a subscriber.

These factors together determine whether the service provider holds itself out as a common carrier. The problem with the holding-out test is that, outside the communications context, almost any modern retailer could be found to be a common carrier.[100] The question of whether "common-carrier-like" non-discrimination obligations should be imposed on mass retailers rarely arises in the consumer context both because retailers have an economic incentive to serve everyone and because state, local, and federal nondiscrimination obligations are imposed on places of public accommodation.[101]

§ 2.11 —Market Structure Factors

The same factors that are important in determining whether a Sherman Act Section 2 violation has been committed, developed in §§ 2.14–2.23, are relevant to determining whether sufficient monopoly power exists to justify common carrier regulation.

The only principled difference between this branch of the common carrier analysis and Sherman Act analysis is the particular market. In common carrier analysis what is relevant is not whether any hypothetical supplier of competing services could enter the market, as in Sherman Act analysis, but rather whether the source itself could start up a parallel service or could induce a third-party supplier to start up a service providing it meaningful access to the same markets. The question for common carrier communication regulation is one of access through competitive communications intermediaries, not only competitive market conditions for their own sake.

---

[100] This is the logical conclusion resulting from applying the four enumerated factors in the text to the usual practices of a mass-market retailer like K-Mart, except that such a retailer selects products to be carried carefully.

[101] *See* 42 U.S.C. §§ 12,181–12,189(1988) (Title III of the ADA); 42 U.S.C. § 2000a (1988) (Title II of the Civil Rights Act of 1964).

§ 2.12 —Narrowed Statutory and Public Contract Duty

The combination of dissatisfaction with the traditional common carrier requirements and continued perceptions that access entitlements are necessary in some parts of the information infrastructure has led the Congress to impose more specialized access requirements, most notably in cable television regulation. The Cable Communications Policy Act of 1994, as subsequently amended,[102] obligates cable television operators to provide access to public, educational, and governmental programming[103] and to unaffiliated commercial programming.[104] In addition, cable operators must carry local television station programming.[105] These entitlements were called into question in *Turner Broadcasting,* decided by the Supreme Court in 1994 and discussed more fully in **Chapter 6** in connection with its First Amendment analysis.[106] More recently, the congressional debate over new communications legislation has viewed sympathetically proposals for open platform obligations, essentially requiring interoperability.

The redesign of the Internet architecture to accommodate the elimination of federal subsidies contemplates that network access providers (NAPs) provide "equitable treatment of various network services providers during routing administration"[107] while allowing NAPs to require payment of both an initial and an annual fee and agreement to adhere to the policies of the NAP manager as preconditions for connections.[108] In addition, connecting networks would be obligated to operate at speeds of 1.5 mbps or greater, be able to switch both IP (Internet protocol) and CLNP (connection-less network protocol) packets, and be able to support video teleconferencing either by packet video or by circuits multiplexed from their total bandwidth.[109] Obviously, these are interoperability

---

[102] 47 U.S.C.A. §§ 521–559 (West Supp. 1995).

[103] *Id.* § 531.

[104] *Id.* § 532.

[105] *Id.* § 534. *See* Adell Broadcasting Corp. v. Cable Vision Indus., 854 F. Supp. 1280, 1290 (E.D. Mich. 1994) (no private right of action to enforce local station must-carry duty under 47 U.S.C. § 534).

[106] Turner Broadcasting Sys., Inc. v. FCC, 114 S. Ct. 2445 (1994).

[107] Request for Public Comment; Solicitation Concept § III(B), 57 Fed. Reg. 26,692 (June 15, 1992). The National Science Foundation Program Solicitation, NSF Solicitation No. 93-52, pursuant to which Internet Network Access Point managers were selected for the five-year period ending in about 1999, requires that "NAP attachment policies should promote fair and equitable pricing for an access to NAP attachment." *Id.* § III(A). NAP managers are charged with developing attachment policies that meet this criterion. *Id.* § III(B). Under the same solicitation, Routing Arbiters (RAs) must "provide for equitable treatment of the various network service providers with regard to routing administration." *Id.* § III(C).

[108] § III(D) 57 Fed. Reg. 26,692.

[109] *Id.* § III(D).

requirements, backed up not by a statutory or regulatory mandate but by "strings" tied to federal support of NAPs.[110]

§ 2.13   —Enforcing Express and Implied Contracts

Contract rights to access may be based on representations or conduct by a service provider to induce users to become or remain customers. Implied contract, more than any statutory or other common-law theory, apparently underlay the claims of an Arizona law firm not to be disconnected from the Internet after it flooded Internet newsgroups with advertisements in 1994.[111] The implied contract theory has a major advantage for persons claiming access rights: it may not require them to make any showing of the absence of alternative sources of supply (except to establish detrimental reliance). Implied contract also offers some advantages to entities denying access: they may negate success- ful contract claims with appropriate disclaimer language.

Several branches of contract law are interesting in the context of informa- tion infrastructure access rights. First, the relationship between the service provider and users of the network may satisfy the conditions of a bargained-for exchange.[112] A service provider unilaterally announces its terms of service. Persons wishing access simply use the network after learning of the service terms.[113] The use may be considered to be an acceptance of the offer represented by the publication of the terms, or it may be considered to be the offer, responding to solicitation of offers represented by the publication of terms.

A second theory is promissory estoppel. Under section 90 of the *Restatement of Contracts,*[114] the person making a promise may be bound to perform the promise if someone else reasonably relies on the promise to the second person's detriment, and it also was reasonable for the first party (the promisor) to anticipate reliance under the circumstances. The detrimental reliance element may be present in the typical network transaction if the customer passes up other network subscription opportunities, or if the customer goes to the trouble to

---

[110] NSF Solicitation No. 93-52 § III(F) at 9 (architectural and policy considerations); *id.* § IV(E)(2) (criteria for evaluating proposals).

[111] *See* Peter H. Lewis, *Arizona Lawyers Form Company for Internet Advertising,* N.Y. Times, May 7, 1994, at Al; Peter H. Lewis, *Sneering at a Virtual Lynch Mob,* N.Y. Times, May 11, 1994, at D1; Laurie Flynn, *"Spamming" on the Internet,* N.Y. Times, Oct. 16, 1994, § 3, at 3.

[112] A *bargained-for exchange* is a traditional express contract. *See* Restatement (Second) of Contracts § 71(2) (1981).

[113] It makes no difference that the provider makes the offer without knowing the identities of the people who may use the network and without any give and take that most people associate with bargaining.

[114] Restatement (Second) of Contracts § 90 (1979).

arrange telecommunication scripts and commits herself to using her E-mail address with the promisor.[115]

The availability of competitive alternatives to a particular facility or service enters into contract analysis by affecting detrimental reliance.[116] If there are many alternatives to a particular provider's service, and the costs of switching are trivial, then someone who expects to use the service in reliance on the provider's statement of concern has suffered little in the way of detrimental reliance if service on those terms is denied. On the other hand, if there are few alternatives or if switching costs are high, the costs of disappointed expectations are higher, increasing the likelihood of enforcement of the promise on a detrimental reliance basis, and increasing the damages likely under the bargain theory.

The utility of contract theories in supporting meaningful access rights may be limited by two lines of cases, one involving advertisements, and the other involving credit card offers. Terms of network access communicated to the general public resemble advertisements, and advertisements have not generally been considered to make advertisers liable for compliance with their terms. Statements in advertisements traditionally were construed as solicitation of offers rather than offers. Thus a refusal to sell on the terms communicated in the advertisement did not breach a contract; it merely was a rejection of the buyer's offer to make a contract. This general rule was not applied when an advertisement manifested a clear intent to make a promise, for example a statement of definite price, accompanied by the phrase, "first come, first served."[117] The most famous case is *Carlill v. Carbolic Smoke Ball Co.,*[118] in which an advertisement promised to pay a £100 reward to anyone contracting a cold after using the advertised smoke ball. Evidencing promissory intent, the advertisement also said that the advertiser had deposited £100 with a bank as a kind of escrow

---

[115] The detrimental reliance pertinent to a promissory estoppel claim may also underpin switching costs pertinent to a monopolization claim under the antitrust laws.

[116] Detrimental reliance is an element of the promissory estoppel theory under § 90, but it also can constitute both the acceptance and the consideration elements of a bargain-theory contract. If the maker of a promise intends that her promise induce reliance, perhaps to increase the prospects of a longer term relationship, the reliance is bargained for.

[117] John E. Murray, Murray on Contracts § 34 at 69 (3d ed. 1990) (citing Lefkowitz v. Great Minneapolis Surplus Store, 86 N.W.2d 689 (Minn. 1957)) [hereinafter Murray on Contracts]. *See* Steinberg v. Chicago Medical Sch., 371 N.E.2d 634 (Ill. 1977). The *Steinberg* court found a cause of action existed for breach of contract when an applicant to medical school submitted an application in response to an invitation expressed in the medical school catalogue, but the medical school failed to evaluate the application according to the criteria set forth in the catalogue. 371 N.E.2d at 638. The *Steinberg* court concluded that the submission of the application and the payment of fee was an offer to apply, which was accepted by receipt of the application and acceptance of the fee. 371 N.E.2d at 641.

[118] 1 Q.B. 256 (1893), *discussed in* Murray on Contracts § 34 at 70.

agent. The nature of the communication evidenced an intent to take the risk of a large number of offers.[119]

The *Restatement* establishes a presumption that advertisements are ordinarily intended as solicitations of offers rather than offers. It nevertheless acknowledges first, that one may make an offer through an advertisement, and second, that an advertisement that is not an offer nevertheless may contain promises or representations that become part of the eventual contract.[120] In the network access context, this rule would allow a network services provider to refuse any particular request for service but would bind it to deliver service according to the published terms once a request for service was accepted.

Terms of access published by a network services provider also are not unlike the terms published by the issuer of a credit card. They are aimed at a very large number of people, who subsequently enter into discrete transactions within the scope of the published terms. The prevailing view is that credit card terms do not give rise to enforceable obligations to allow access to the credit represented by the card.[121] Rather, they are revocable offers of contracts, which are accepted each time the cardholder uses the credit card.[122] "The credit card relationship, properly analyzed, should be viewed as an offer by the issuer to create the opportunity for a series of unilateral contracts which are actually formed when the holder uses the credit card to buy goods or services or to obtain cash."[123]

Followed strictly in the network access context, the credit card cases would permit the service provider to change the terms of the contract virtually continuously. Each request for service would be an offer of a new contract. If the network provided service on that occasion, a contract would be formed only for the duration of that particular transaction on the network. Because no contract

---

[119] One of the rationales for the general reluctance to treat advertisements as offers is a concern about the economic risk that the advertiser will be forced to satisfy an unpredictably large number of responses to the advertisement. The facts of the *Carbolic Smoke Ball* case indicated that the advertiser unequivocally had accepted this risk.

[120] Restatement (Second) of Contracts § 26 cmt. b (1981); *id.* § 2b cmt. f.

[121] *See, e.g.,* Garber v. Harris Trust & Sav. Bank, 432 N.E.2d 1309, 1312 (Ill. App. Ct. 1982) ("prevailing view in this country is that the issuance of a credit card is only an offer to extend credit"); *In re* Ward, 857 F.2d 1082, 1087 (6th Cir. 1988) (Merritt, J., dissenting) ("unilateral contracts are formed each time the card is used"). *But see* Gray v. American Express Co., 743 F.2d 10 (D.C. Cir. 1984) (cardholder whose card was canceled by refusing to authorize a particular charge entitled to statutory procedures; criticizing view that cardholder has no contract rights).

[122] *See* Feder v. Fortunoff, Inc., 494 N.Y.S.2d 42 (App. Div. 1985) (affirming dismissal of complaint). "The issuance of a credit card constitutes an offer of credit which may be withdrawn by the offeror at any time prior to acceptance of the offer through the use of the card by the holder." *Id.* at 42.

[123] *In re* Ward, 857 F.2d 1082, 1087 (6th Cir. 1988) (Merritt, J., dissenting) ("unilateral contracts are formed each time the card is used").

would be in existence, the service provider would remain free to disconnect at almost any time between the end of one transaction and the commencement of the next.

Both the advertising and credit card cases applied in the network access context would leave the service provider free to deny service until a particular request for service is accepted. To understand the implications of this approach, it is crucial to understand what constitutes a "request for service." If each connection request in the TCP protocol constitutes a separate request for service, the obligations of the network service provider remain in effect only until it delivers a particular file or menu item or pointer in response to a World Wide Web or Gopher query or until the termination of a particular FTP or Telnet session. This characterization of request for service imposes little obligation on the service provider and gives the requester legal rights that are of little practical utility. Somewhat greater obligations and entitlements would result from characterizing the first use of a system during any particular billing period as the offer and acceptance, assuming that billing takes place on approximately monthly cycles. But even if the 30 days worth of rights or obligations are of practical significance to service users, it is not likely that the NII will work on 30-day billing cycles. The frequency of billing may be greater and billing may occur as it does between long-distance service providers and individual telephone subscribers, on a per-call basis. The utility of contract-based access entitlements depends on legal recognition of longer term obligations derived from course of dealing.

Assuming recognition of such longer term contractual relationships, the implied contract theory provides much flexibility for market-based definitions of infrastructure. Even when the classical metaphor of two equal parties sitting across a table and explicitly bargaining about their contract terms is silly because it is so remote from reality, the freedom afforded both offeror and offeree when the offeror unilaterally specifies in some detail its terms of service and reserves powers to amend and terminate is considerable. The offeree knows exactly what she is getting into before making an economic commitment. Both bargain theory and promissory estoppel theory allow the maker of the offer or promissory statement the power to limit liability. The maker of an offer can specify how acceptance is to be made,[124] and may define not only the duration of any contract that can be formed by acceptance, but also specify how long the offer will remain in effect.[125] The promissory estoppel theory creates enforceable promises only when detrimental reliance is reasonable.[126] The maker of a promissory statement may circumscribe the range of reasonableness and reliance by the content of the statement.

---

[124] Restatement (Second) of Contracts § 30 (1979).

[125] *Id.* § 35(2).

[126] *Id.* § 90 cmt. b (1979).

The power of suppliers of network services to define and limit their liability may be excessive if consumers of network services lack both the power to bargain for terms that protect them and the power to shop for alternatives.[127] Lack of power may come from disparate size or wealth, or it may come from the transaction costs of bargaining. If a consumer of network services only wants one second of access to a World Wide Web server, the cost of off-line communication about contract terms is too high to be borne. On the other hand, if transaction costs of bargaining can be managed, contract also is an attractive regime for consumers of network services because of the power it gives them to decide what meets their needs. The adverse effects of high transaction costs, like disparate bargaining power, can be mitigated by collective action. Groups of consumers of network services and suppliers of network services can negotiate standard terms of service and then those terms can be incorporated by reference into small transactions.

The prerequisites to a meaningful contract regime are these: First, promissory representations must be treated as such and not treated as mere invitations to make offers. Second, the effect of competitive alternatives is material to the detrimental reliance inquiry. Third, statutes of frauds must not prevent enforcement of contracts made by conduct after publication of the contract terms. Fourth, publication of contract terms should suffice without the offeree having to prove subjective knowledge and detrimental reliance. Fifth, and perhaps most challenging, disclaimers of enforceability and reservations of power to amend or terminate must be circumscribed so they do not swallow up the affirmative theories of contract enforcement. All of these rules can be applied by courts hearing common-law breach-of-contract claims within the general framework established by the *Restatement Second of Contracts* and U.C.C. Article 2.

§ 2.14 Antitrust

The probability of antitrust liability[128] is low for most NII service providers because all of the established and reasonably anticipated markets for infrastructure services are competitive and have low barriers to entry. Nevertheless, certain joint arrangements for packet routing and directory services, and tying arrangements bundling different network and information services, invite

---

[127] The distributed nature of the NII weakens the distinction between suppliers and consumers of network services; everyone is both a supplier and a consumer sometimes. So any ideological preference for supplier interests or consumer interests becomes irrelevant. It is not a consumerism versus business issue; it is an area in which efficient commerce coincides with consumer welfare.

[128] Antitrust cases conceptually involve anticompetitive contracts, which violate § 1 of the Sherman Act, and monopolization claims violative of § 2.

antitrust scrutiny. Also, the antitrust concepts for analyzing market structures enter into any serious analysis of common carrier status or policy-based rationales for imposing new access obligations. Relevant antitrust analysis involves joint ventures, exclusive arrangements constituting vertical and horizontal refusals to deal, and essential facilities. Any of these may involve contracts in restraint of trade violative of section 1 of the Sherman Act,[129] and some of them may involve abuse of monopoly power, violative of section 2 of the Sherman Act.[130]

§ 2.15 —Joint Ventures

A *joint venture* has been defined for antitrust purposes as including the following elements:

> (1) the enterprise is under the joint control of the parent firms, which are not under related control; (2) each parent makes substantial contribution to the joint enterprise; (3) the enterprise exists as a business entity separate from its parents; and (4) the joint venture creates significant new enterprise capability in terms of new productive capacity, new technology, a new product, or entry into a new market.[131]

Joint ventures thus are partnerships to accomplish a particular task or project. In the NII, they are good structures for providing certain common services, for example, routers for exchanging traffic among network service providers. Joint ventures potentially violate the antitrust laws because joint ventures produce goods or services that otherwise would be produced by individual partners in competition with each other. They thus amount to agreements to restrict output because they impliedly involve each partner withholding its own unilateral efforts to produce the good or service that is to be produced by the joint venture. Contracts to restrict output restrain trade and ordinarily are per se violations of section 1. Nevertheless, joint ventures are evaluated under the rule of reason because of the possibility of procompetitive effects.[132] For example, when the joint venture partners sell mostly in exclusive geographic territories, the

---

[129] 15 U.S.C. § 1.

[130] *Id.* § 2. *See* Southern Pac. Communications Co. v. American Tel. & Tel. Co., 740 F.2d 980, 1003 (D.C. Cir. 1984) (need for advertising to overcome reputation of established carrier and establishing carrier's control over local interconnections constitute barriers to entry for purposes of assessing monopoly power, but district court properly found no abuse of monopoly power). *Southern Pacific* is a useful review of the analytical tools for monopolization claims under § 2 of the Sherman Act in the communication context).

[131] Instructional Sys. Dev. Corp. v. Aetna Casualty & Sur. Co., 817 F.2d 639, 643 n.2 (10th Cir. 1987) (quoting J. Brodley, *Joint Ventures and Antitrust Policy,* 95 Harv. L. Rev. 1523, 1526 (1982) and finding criteria not satisfied by agreement in driver simulator market).

[132] Sewell Plastics, Inc. v. Coca-Cola Co., 720 F. Supp. 1186, 1192 (W.D.N.C. 1988) (joint venture to manufacture containers to be evaluated under rule of reason; genuine issue of fact existed regarding effect on competition). *See also* Northwest Wholesale Stationers, Inc.

likelihood of the joint venture violating the antitrust laws is much lower because any negative effect on output is reduced.[133] In general, joint ventures whose procompetitive effects outweigh anticompetitive effects are permissible under section 1.[134] For example, *Broadcast Music, Inc. v. Columbia Broadcasting System, Inc.* approved a copyright collective that had standard license forms for copyrighted music even though it included a standard fee.[135]

On September 15, 1993, the Justice Department issued an enforcement policy statement for joint ventures in the health care industry, which articulates tests useful beyond that industry. The policy statement provides "antitrust safety zones" that immunize joint ventures involving high technology or expensive equipment the cost of which must be shared. The statement suggests a four-step rule of reason analysis. Step one defines the relevant market. Step two evaluates the competitive effects, particularly focusing on the possibility that the joint venture would eliminate an existing or potentially viable competing provider of the service. Step three evaluates the impact of procompetitive efficiencies. Step four evaluates ancillary agreements or conditions that might unreasonably restrict competition and are unlikely to contribute significantly to the legitimate purposes of the joint venture.

The policy statement's approach is consistent with the analytical framework for evaluating joint ventures suggested in the antitrust literature.[136] Analysis begins with an assessment of the restriction on competition, acknowledging that "an inevitable competitive cost occurs when parties who are rivals in a particular area suspend that rivalry in order to cooperate with each other."[137] Then compensating benefits must be identified, including reduction of risk,[138] economies

---

v. Pacific Stationery & Printing Co., 472 U.S. 284 (1985) (procedural protections for enterprise expelled from purchasing cooperative not mandated by § 1 of Sherman Act); J. Brodley, *Joint Ventures and Antitrust Policy,* 95 Harv. L. Rev. 1523 (1982).

[133] Sewell Plastics, Inc. v. Coca-Cola Co., 720 F. Supp. 1186, 1192 (W.D.N.C. 1988).

[134] Broadcast Music, Inc. v. Columbia Broadcasting Sys., Inc., 441 U.S. 1, 23 (1979) ("joint ventures and other cooperative arrangements are also not usually unlawful, at least not as price fixing schemes, where the agreement on price is necessary to market the product at all"). Since agreements to restrict output are no more harmful to competition than agreements on price, the Supreme Court's conclusion applies equally to joint ventures that have the effect of restricting output.

[135] Standard license forms reduce competition over the terms of licenses. *See also* Consolidated Metal Prods., Inc. v. American Petroleum Inst., 846 F.2d 284 (5th Cir. 1988) (affirming summary judgment for trade association that evaluated products and issued opinions; no showing of anticompetitive conduct under rule of reason).

[136] *See* Thomas A. Piraino, Jr., *Reconciling Competition and Cooperation: A New Antitrust Standard for Joint Ventures,* 35 Wm. & Mary L. Rev. 871 (1994) (suggesting evaluation of joint ventures along a continuum reflecting the degree to which the parties have combined their resources, scrutinizing highly integrated joint ventures more sharply than unintegrated ones).

[137] *Id.* at 881.

[138] *Id.* at 885.

of scale,[139] elimination of wasteful redundancies,[140] access to complimentary resources,[141] and making unique products available to consumers.[142]

While the policy statement focuses on health care joint ventures, its analytical approach is applicable to joint ventures in the National Information Infrastructure. For example, a jointly owned and operated router could be subjected to joint venture scrutiny. An agreement among competitors jointly to operate the router is implicitly an agreement for them not to offer their own routers unilaterally. It is thus an agreement to limit supply, like many joint ventures.

The nature of routers, however, makes it impracticable to have a proliferation of routers unilaterally operated. For that architecture to work at all, the degree of cooperation among the unilateral suppliers of routers and routing services would have to be so great as to be equivalent to the cooperation involved in a joint venture router. Thus, the purported supply lost because of the joint arrangement is illusory. Indeed a jointly operated router will in fact enhance consumer access to all of the participants and thus will increase rather than limiting competition among them. Procompetitive justifications figure prominently in the analysis of joint ventures. It is unlikely that the joint router would result in liability for an agreement to limit supply.

§ 2.16 —Tying Arrangements

Tying occurs when a seller bundles components of a system and refuses to sell them separately. An information services provider might bundle content with indexing and searching and retrieval tools, like World Wide Web, and refuse access to the content unless one also buys access to the provider's Web server:

> The essential characteristic of an invalid tying arrangement lies in the seller's exploitation of its control over the tying product [the content] to force the buyer into the purchase of a tied product [the Web server] that the buyer either did not want at all, or might have preferred to purchase elsewhere on different terms. When such "forcing" is present, competition on the merits in the market for the tied item is restrained and the Sherman Act is violated.[143]

---

[139] *Id.* at 886.

[140] *Id.* at 886–87.

[141] *Id.* at 887.

[142] Thomas A. Piraino, Jr., *Reconciling Competition and Cooperation: A New Antitrust Standard for Joint Ventures,* 35 Wm. & Mary L. Rev. 871, 889 (1994) (citing *Broadcast Music*) (suggesting evaluation of joint ventures along a continuum reflecting the degree to which the parties have combined their resources, scrutinizing highly integrated joint ventures more sharply than unintegrated ones).

[143] Eastman Kodak Co. v. Image Technical Servs., Inc., 504 U.S. 451 (1992) (quoting Jefferson Parish Hosp. Dist. No. 2 v. Hyde, 466 U.S. 2, 12 (1984)).

In *Eastman Kodak Co. v. Image Technical Services, Inc.,*[144] the Supreme Court described how antitrust tying doctrine affects product bundles. First, it explained when the elements of a product bundle can be considered to constitute two distinct, albeit tied, products, rather than mere parts of one product. For two functionally linked products to be considered two distinct products, "there must be sufficient consumer demand so that it is efficient for a firm to produce [them separately]."[145] In the case before it, the Court found evidence that service and parts had been sold separately in the past and noted that the development of the service industry, members of which had challenged Kodak, was itself evidence of the efficiency of a separate market for service. In the digital network services area, the analog would be evidence that it is efficient to produce Gopher and World Wide Web servers and sell access to them independently of Internet access, or that it is efficient to produce and sell chunking and tagging value separate from pointers value.[146]

Second, the Supreme Court rejected Kodak's contention that, as a matter of law, a single brand of a product or service can never be a relevant market under the Sherman Act:

> The relevant market for antitrust purposes is determined by the choices available to Kodak equipment owners. Because service and parts for Kodak equipment are not interchangeable with other manufacturer's service and parts, the relevant market from the Kodak-equipment owners perspective is composed of only those companies that service Kodak machines.[147]

Thus the market for PC Internet interface software for CompuServe could be a relevant market for NII antitrust analysis.

Having thus defined the market, the Court proceeded to assess Kodak's behavior. While a firm can refuse to deal with its competitors, it must offer legitimate competitive reasons for the refusal—other than wishing to drive them

---

[144] 504 U.S. 451, 112 S. Ct. 2072 (1992) (remanding as to whether manufacturer unlawfully tied sale of service to sale of parts for line of its micrographic equipment).

[145] *Id.* at 461.

[146] *See* Henry H. Perritt, Jr., *Unbundling Value in Electronic Information Products: Intellectual Property Protection for Machine Readable Interfaces,* 20 Rutgers Computer & Tech. L.J. 415 (1994) (explaining 10 types of value in electronically published products: content, chunking and tagging, internal pointers, external pointers, presentation, duplication, distribution, promotion, billing and collection, and integrity assurance). *See generally* Illinois Bell Tel. Co. v. FCC, 883 F.2d 104, 110–11 (D.C. Cir. 1989) (reviewing rationale for FCC order forcing telephone companies to market competing consumer premises equipment (CPE) along with their own, noting difficulty in unbundling CPE from other parts of the communications package). The service that the Bell companies were forced to provide in *Illinois Bell* was promotion value. In effect the FCC was requiring that hardware be bundled with promotion value.

[147] 504 U.S. 451, 481 (1992).

from the marketplace. Kodak declined to sell parts to its equipment customers unless they also bought its service. Independent service organizations were the plaintiffs in the antitrust action.[148]

Because of the remand for development of factual evidence on the crucial predicates, the *Eastman Kodak* Supreme Court opinion is only an invitation to speculate about the role of antitrust tying doctrine in forcing access to aspects of the National Information Infrastructure. Nevertheless, it does identify one theory for forcing a producer with substantial market power to unbundle[149]—a failure to justify continued bundling on cost or other grounds other than excluding competitors. The theory could be used by an NII service provider offering one type of value, say user interface software, to force a provider of bundled network access and interface software to allow the first provider access to the second provider's network.

§ 2.17 —Exclusive Dealing

Concerted refusals to deal are group boycotts and may be per se violations of the Sherman Act.[150] Concerted refusal to deal claims frequently arise in the context of joint ventures because it is logical for joint venture partners to exclude nonparticipants from the benefits of the venture.

Exclusive dealing arrangements are concerted refusals to deal with anyone outside the arrangement. An exclusive dealing arrangement[151] is potentially violative of the antitrust laws because it reduces competition in either the upstream or downstream markets:

> Exclusive dealing can have adverse economic consequences by allowing one supplier of goods or services unreasonably to deprive other suppliers of a market for their goods, or by allowing one buyer of goods unreasonably to deprive other

---

[148] *Id.* at 483 (liability turns on whether there are valid business reasons for refusing to deal with competitors; citing Aspen Skiing Co. v. Aspen Highlands Skiing Corp., 472 U.S. 585, 605 (1985) and United States v. Aluminum Co. of Am., 148 F.2d 416, 432 (2d Cir. 1945)).

[149] Determination of market power is crucial in tying cases. The restriction on competition in the tied market depends on the export of monopoly power from the tying market into the tied market. If no market power exists in the tying market, there is no source of power to be exported into the tied market. *See generally* Allen-Myland, Inc. v. International Business Machs. Corp., 33 F.3d 194 (3d Cir. 1994) (careful analysis of market definition leading to reversal of district court and conclusion that IBM could have monopoly power in properly defined market for mainframe computer upgrades, sufficient to support tying claim with respect to upgrade consulting services).

[150] Balaklaw v. Lovell, 14 F.3d 793, 800 (2d Cir. 1994) (per se approach generally limited to situations in which firms with market power boycott suppliers or customers to discourage them from doing business with competitors).

[151] A tying arrangement or a refusal to unbundle, like in *Eastman Kodak,* is a form of exclusive dealing arrangement. The refusal to unbundle is an exclusive dealing arrangement with upstream and downstream production facilities in the same enterprise. A tying arrangement is the same thing, but with greater product differentiation between the components, resulting in an express condition in the contract of purchase or sale.

buyers of a needed source of supply. In determining whether an exclusive dealing contract is unreasonable, the proper focus is on the structure of the market for the product or services in question—the number of sellers and buyers in the market, the volume of their business, and the ease with which buyers and sellers can redirect their purchases or sales to others. Exclusive dealing is an unreasonable restraint on trade only when a significant fraction of buyers or sellers are frozen out of a market by the exclusive deal.[152]

Exclusive dealing contracts can violate section 3 of the Clayton Act,[153] and section 1 of the Sherman Act.[154] "The legality of an exclusive dealing arrangement under the Clayton Act depends on whether the competition foreclosed constitutes a substantial share of the relevant market."[155] Not only the absolute percentage of potential market foreclosure is at issue, but also the probable effect of the contract, taking into account the relative strength of the parties and the probable immediate and future effects that preemption of that share of the market might have on effective competition and on the existence of legitimate business justifications for the contracts.[156]

For example, suppose a midlevel network in the Internet (CerfNet) enters into an exclusive dealing arrangement with the Cleveland Freenet, which could be said to provide local Internet access services. This arguably would reduce competition in the local Internet access services market because no other provider of Internet access services would be able to deal with CerfNet. It also could be said to reduce competition in the market for midlevel Internet services because no other midlevel network would be free to deal with Cleveland Freenet. But in order for such an arrangement to violate the antitrust laws, there must be a showing of (1) a reduction of competition, and (2) the absence of procompetitive justification. If the markets for both midlevel network services and network access services are competitive, and if neither exclusive dealing party possesses significant market power, then the exclusive dealing arrangement is permissible.[157] Also, even if competition in either or both markets were reduced, the arrangement still might not produce antitrust liability because it can be justified on the grounds of improving the market position of either Cerfnet or Cleveland Freenet, thus enhancing interbrand competition. The possibility of new entry, even when there are significant barriers to entry, reduces the likelihood of a successful claim in which market power is an element.[158] Thus, for

---

[152] Balaklaw v. Lovell, 14 F.3d 793, 800 (2d Cir. 1994).

[153] 15 U.S.C. § 14 (1988).

[154] *Id.* § 1.

[155] Bar Lab., Inc. v. Abbott Lab., 978 F.2d 98, 110 (3d Cir. 1992) (affirming summary judgment for defendant drug company on several antitrust claims including exclusive dealing).

[156] *Id.* at 111.

[157] *See* Balaklaw v. Lovell, 14 F.3d 793, 798–99 (2d Cir. 1994) (finding no antitrust injury because no change in competitive conditions shown because of exclusive arrangement between one hospital and one provider of anesthesia services).

[158] Bar Lab., Inc. v. Abbott Lab., 978 F.2d 98 113 (3d Cir. 1992) (affirming rejection of attempted monopolization claim because of possibility of entry by new drug producers, despite barriers represented by six-month to two-year waiting period for FDA approval).

example, in a hypothetical claim against West Publishing Company for a hypothetical exclusive dealing arrangement with an Internet services provider, West could probably defeat the element of market power in the market for remotely accessible comprehensive legal databases by demonstrating a high potential for entry by new competitors into that market.[159]

§ 2.18   —Vertical Exclusive Arrangements

Vertical relationships involve suppliers and customers. For example, A supplies communications services and B supplies value-added features, like finding and retrieval aids. A and B make a contract, giving B the exclusive right to supply a particular market. Competitors of B get excluded from the downstream market for A's product, and competitors of A get excluded from B's downstream services. Vertical exclusive arrangements are analyzed more sympathetically under section 1 of the Sherman Act than horizontal exclusive arrangements[160] because vertical arrangements frequently strengthen *interbrand* competition (competition between A and its competitors), even though they may limit *intrabrand* competition (competition between B and its competitors for distribution of A's product).[161] For example, an exclusive arrangement between a legal database provider and an Internet access provider in a particular geographic area, as in the second § 2.17 hypothetical, might strengthen the ability of both partners to compete against other Internet access providers and other database providers, although it would reduce potential intrabrand competition that would occur if multiple Internet access providers competed with each other for customers desiring access to the database.

Futurevision Cable System, Inc. v. MultiVision Cable TV Corp.[162] involved an unsuccessful claim by a new entrant cable network that exclusive contracts between ESPN and the Learning Channel and existing cable networks violated section 1. The court concluded that the plaintiff failed to show market power by ESPN or the Learning Channel or that the exclusive arrangement prevented the plaintiff from entering the market and competing vigorously with other

---

[159] Because market concentration is much higher in the market for comprehensive legal database services, that is the point of greatest vulnerability in the hypothetical case; not in the market structure for network services, where competition is high. *See generally* John M. Stevens, *Antitrust Law and Open Access to the NREN,* 38 Vill. L. Rev. 571 (1993) (exploring hypothetical essential facilities doctrine claim based on concentration in legal database market).

[160] Future Vision Cable Sys., Inc. v. Multivision Cable TV Corp., 789 F. Supp. 760, 766 (S.D. Miss. 1992) (per se rule usually applied to horizontal agreement; rule of reason usually applied to vertical arrangements).

[161] *Id.* at 767–68.

[162] 789 F. Supp. 760 (S.D. Miss. 1992) (granting motion to dismiss).

sources of programming.[163] This case is interesting because it involves exclusive arrangements between content providers (ESPN and the Learning Channel) and a network services provider (the existing cable channels) in which the existence of alternatives (other sources of programming service) nullified an antitrust claim brought by a new entrant in one part of the market. The situation is roughly equivalent to a new network services provider challenging exclusive arrangements between content providers and existing network services providers in the Internet context.

The kinds of vertical arrangements likely to exist in the National Information Infrastructure are unlikely to produce antitrust liability. Although the nature of Internet architectures facilitates technological unbundling,[164] the market for any particular type of value is likely to be quite competitive. Thus a producer excluded from access to any particular type of value by a particular exclusive dealing arrangement can find other alternative sources of that type of value. The relevant adjacent markets for infrastructure services look like the markets for health care services that resulted in rejection of antitrust claims, except that the infrastructure markets are likely to be even more competitive than the health care markets.

The only interesting possibility for liability would be exclusive vertical dealing arrangements relating to public information, like municipal ordinances, state and federal statutes, and judicial and administrative opinions and orders. For these kinds of information, there may not be alternative sources. This is clearly true if the originator—like a legislature, a court, or an agency—asserts copyright or itself enters into an exclusive dealing arrangement.

For example, the Washington State court system has entered into an exclusive arrangement with an electronic publisher for its judicial opinions. Under the arrangement, it denies access to the opinions in their original electronic form to competing distributors and publishers. The Securities and Exchange Commission entered into a similar exclusive arrangement with a dissemination subcontractor, albeit under statutorily mandated conditions that seek to assure equal access to the product of the dissemination subcontractor. Nevertheless, the arrangement excludes those who wish to compete with the dissemination subcontractor during the term of the contract, and has been subjected to criticism by public interest groups.

In this circumstance, the competitive market defense is unavailable with respect to the supply of the information in raw form. Any justification for the arrangement would have to arise from its procompetitive effects or the

---

[163] *Id.* at 769 (failure to show market power); *id.* at 770 (plaintiff's inexperience shows no adverse effect on ability to compete).

[164] Henry H. Perritt, Jr., *Unbundling Value in Electronic Information Products: Intellectual Property Protection for Machine Readable Interfaces,* 20 Rutgers Computer & Tech. L.J. 415 (1994).

unfeasibility of using other less restrictive arrangements. Any procompetitive arguments would track those for essential facilities analysis, summarized in § 2.20.

§ 2.19 —Horizontal Exclusive Dealing Arrangements

Horizontal exclusive arrangements—arrangements between competitors in the same market that exclude other competitors in the same market—are viewed more skeptically than vertical refusals to deal. In *SCFC ILC, Inc. v. VISA U.S.A., Inc.,*[165] a district court approved a jury determination that a decision by the VISA credit card joint venture to exclude Sears Roebuck affiliates from VISA membership because of Sears's competing Discover Card constituted a violation of section 1 of the Sherman Act. The court rejected the argument that the VISA joint venture must be shown to be an essential facility in order to find liability,[166] noting that while *United States v. Terminal Railroad Ass'n* (see § 2.20) involved an essential facility, subsequent cases, like *Associated Press v. United States,*[167] did not involve facts that would meet the essential facilities test.[168] Instead, joint ventures ordinarily are evaluated under rule of reason analysis,[169] which asks whether "the challenge to agreement is one that promotes competition or one that suppresses competition."[170] The court rejected the two legal "screens" that apply rule of reason analysis but keep the case away from the jury. The first such screen involves lack of market power; the second involves plaintiff arguments that make no economic sense.[171] It also rejected VISA's argument that joint ventures are entitled to more deferential section 1 analysis than conduct involving independent entities because of the procompetitive effect of joint ventures.[172]

More particularly, the court found sufficient evidence to support a jury conclusion that VISA bylaw 2.06 had substantial harmful effects on competition, based on evidence that exclusion from highly profitable VISA membership would be a strong disincentive for anyone to introduce a new card if that would

---

[165] 819 F. Supp. 956 (D. Utah 1993).

[166] *Id.* at 980–81 (comparing *Terminal R.R. Ass'n* with *Associated Press*).

[167] 326 U.S. 1 (1945) (invalidating is violative of § 1 bylaws of Associated Press authorizing restrictive conditions on nonmember competitors).

[168] 819 F. Supp. 956, 973–77 (D. Utah 1993).

[169] *Id.* at 969 & n.11.

[170] *Id.* at 968 (citing National Soc'y of Professional Eng'rs v. United States, 435 U.S. 679, 687–88, 691 (1978) (noting that literal construction of language of § 1 would invalidate the entire body of private contract law)).

[171] *Id.* at 970–71.

[172] *Id.* at 978–79.

disqualify it from membership in VISA.[173] It also approved the jury's rejection of VISA's argument that the joint venture enhanced competition at the inter-system level.[174] (It is important to understand that the district court did not reject this procompetitive effects argument as a matter of law; it simply allowed the jury to reject it as a matter of fact.)

Horizontal exclusive arrangements in the NII context could involve agreements with respect to packet routing or to name and address databases that lock out some competitors who are not members of the exclusive club. An agreement among Internet connection services to operate a router might be attacked as a concerted refusal to deal by anyone excluded from use of the router or disadvantaged in the way it operates. Such an attack would succeed if suppliers of relevant network services are excluded from participation in the joint venture even though they are willing to pay and meet other terms satisfied by the joint venturers. On the other hand, if the only entities excluded are those refusing to pay the usual price for membership in the venture and otherwise to comply with the terms of the venture, their claims for a concerted refusal to deal almost certainly will fail. The likely factual argument will center on whether the terms offered are equitable, considering the different situations of different actual and would-be participants.

An essential facilities claim would fail under application of the same standards discussed with respect to a concerted refusal to deal.[175] Neither the concerted refusal to deal nor the essential facilities challenges could succeed unless the challenger could show an absence of competitive alternatives to the jointly operated router.

§ 2.20   —Essential Facilities

Antitrust essential facilities doctrine prohibits discrimination by businesses that control bottlenecks in the market structure. It was antitrust essential facilities doctrine rather than common carrier doctrine that led to the initial restructuring of the voice telephone system.[176]

If an entity that controls essential facilities denies equal access to competitors, it may be violating section 2 of the Sherman Act.[177] The essential facilities

---

[173] *Id.* at 986.

[174] 819 F. Supp. 956, 987 (D. Utah 1993).

[175] In other words, the essential facilities doctrine overlaps concerted refusal to deal analysis so much that essential facilities is more useful as a theory of § 2 monopolization than of § 1 restraint of trade.

[176] United States v. American Tel. & Tel. Co. 41(b) denial, 524 F. Supp. 1336 (D.D.C. 1981).

[177] *Id.* at 1352 (stating general rule); Advanced Health Care Servs., Inc. v. Radford Community Hosp., 910 F.2d 139, 150 (4th Cir. 1990) (setting forth requirements for essential facilities doctrine; reversing dismissal of complaint alleging Sherman Act §§ 1 and 2, and Clayton Act

represent a bottleneck in the market, and the person controlling the bottleneck violates section 2 unless he lets competitors through. There are four elements for essential facilities liability:

1. Control of an essential facility by a monopolist
2. A competitor's inability practically or reasonably to duplicate the essential facility[178]
3. Denial of the use of the facility to a competitor[179]
4. The feasibility of providing access to the facility.[180]

In no event can essential facilities liability exist unless the owner of the essential facility is a competitor of those it excludes.[181] These elements usually are difficult to establish in digital information networks because the availability of

---

§ 3 violations by hospital system that steered durable medical equipment purchases to its own affiliate). A separate inquiry into market power is unnecessary in these circumstances because an "essential" facility by definition represents market power in the market for the services or goods realized through the facility.

[178] Advanced Health Care Servs., Inc. v. Radford Community Hosp., 910 F.2d 139, 150 (4th Cir. 1990); Sun Dun, Inc. v. Coca-Cola Co., 740 F. Supp. 381, 392–93 (D. Md. 1990) (rejecting claim under essential facilities doctrine by vending machine seller challenging territorial restrictions; particular brand names within particular market not appropriate for essential facilities analysis).

[179] Illinois Bell Tel. Co. v. Haines & Co., 744 F. Supp. 815, 823 (N.D. Ill. 1989) (rejecting essential facilities claim by publisher of street address directory; no showing of pricing discrimination in affording access to allegedly essential street address information), aff'd, 905 F.2d 1081 (7th Cir. 1990), vacated on other grounds (copyright), 499 U.S. 944 (1991).

[180] MCI Communications Corp. v. A.T.&T., 708 F.2d 1081, 1132–33 (7th Cir. 1983) (restating elements). Compare Delaware & Hudson Ry. v. Consolidated Rail Corp., 902 F.2d 174, 179–80 (2d Cir. 1990) (reversing summary judgment for defendant under four-factor essential facilities test) with Laurel Sand & Gravel, Inc. v. CSX Transp., Inc., 924 F.2d 539, 544–45 (4th Cir. 1991) (rejecting essential facilities claim under four-factor test); see also Advanced Health Care Servs., Inc. v. Radford Community Hosp., 910 F.2d 139, 150 4th Cir. 1990) (setting forth elements and citing MCI Communications v. American Tel. & Tel. Co., 708 F.2d 1081, 1132–33 (7th Cir. 1983) and Otter Tail Power Co. v. United States, 410 U.S. 366 (1973)). See also Southern Pac. Communications Co. v. American Tel. & Tel. Co., 740 F.2d 980, 1008–10 (D.C. Cir. 1984) (summarizing essential facilities arguments relating to denial of interconnections and concluding that public interest regulation by FCC helps justify the types of interconnections offered; test requires both objective and subjective reasonableness; affirming district court finding of good faith and thus rejection of essential facilities claim); MCI Communications Corp. v. American Tel. & Tel. Co., 708 F.2d 1081, 1133 (7th Cir. 1983) (finding violation of essential facilities doctrine by denial of interconnections).

[181] Advanced Health Care Servs., Inc. v. Radford Community Hosp., 910 F.2d 139, 151 (4th Cir. 1990) (evaluating allegation on whether hospital allegedly constituting an essential facility competed with suppliers of durable medical equipment).

a wide range of alternative paths between any two points tends to negate the first element and the second relating to practical inability of duplicating.[182]

It is relatively rare for a plaintiff to meet the requirements for essential facilities liability. The leading cases involved a group of railroads that formed a partnership to operate the only terminal railroad company in St. Louis, access to which was practically necessary in order to exchange traffic through the St. Louis gateway;[183] denial to MCI by AT&T of access to its long distance network;[184] and denial of access to an electric power grid to customers who purchased power from other sources.[185] On the other hand, the dominant airline reservations systems were found not to constitute essential facilities, although sufficient evidence of market power and predatory conduct was presented to withstand summary judgment.[186]

The Supreme Court's decision in *United States v. Terminal Railroad Ass'n*[187] sets the basic standards for access by nonparticipating competitors when competitors control an essential facility. The case arose after railroads entering St. Louis organized a terminal company (TRRA), which by acquiring two competitors had a monopoly on interchange of traffic in the St. Louis terminal. The Supreme Court recognized that jointly owned terminal facilities can enhance trade. Moreover,

> in ordinary circumstances, a number of independent companies might combine for the purpose of controlling or acquiring terminals for their common but exclusive use. In such cases other companies might be admitted upon terms or excluded altogether. If such terms were too onerous, there would ordinarily remain the right and power to construct their own terminals.[188]

Thus, the court recognized the role that the availability of alternatives plays in applying the antitrust laws to joint ventures of key facilities.

---

[182] John M. Stevens, *Antitrust Law and Open Access to the NREN,* 38 Vill. L. Rev. 571 (1993) (suggesting that some monopolies may exist in NII justifying application of essential facilities doctrine).

[183] United States v. Terminal R.R. Ass'n, 224 U.S. 383 (1912) (requiring terminal association to admit any requesting railroad on equal terms).

[184] MCI Communications Corp. v. American Tel. & Tel. Co., 708 F.2d 1081, 1132–33 (7th Cir. 1983) (affirming jury finding of violation of essential facilities doctrine by AT&T denial of access to MCI).

[185] Otter Tail Power Co. v. United States, 410 U.S. 366 (1973).

[186] *In re* Air Passenger Computer Reservations Sys. Antitrust Litig., 694 F. Supp. 1443 (C.D. Cal. 1988) (computerized reservation systems do not constitute essential facilities; monopoly leveraging theory not available; but triable issues of fact exist on market power and predatory conduct allegations for monopolization and attempted monopolization theories), *aff'd,* 948 F.2d 536 (9th Cir. 1991).

[187] 224 U.S. 383 (1912).

[188] *Id.* at 405.

But in the St. Louis terminal case, physical and topographical conditions prevented the construction of alternative means of access. In those circumstances, "a unified system is an obstacle, a hindrance, and a restriction upon interstate commerce, unless it is the impartial agent of all who, owing to conditions, are under such compulsion, as here exist, to use its facilities."[189] While there was no showing that the terminal company had excluded nonparticipating carriers, there was no guarantee that it would not do so in the future. Moreover, it imposed certain rates that disadvantaged nonparticipating carriers. The government urged that the TRRA be dissolved.[190] The Supreme Court thought that too strong an initial remedy, and instead remanded for entry of a decree directing the parties to submit a plan for the reorganization of contracts among the companies participating in ownership and operation of the TRRA to effect the following, among other things:

> First. By providing for the admission of any existing or future railroad to joint ownership and control of the combined terminal properties, upon such just and reasonable terms as shall place such applying company upon a plane of equality in respect of benefits and burdens with the present proprietary companies.
>
> Second. Such plan of reorganization must also provide definitely for the use of the terminal facilities by any other railroad not electing to become a joint owner, upon such just and reasonable terms and regulations as will, in respect of use, character, and cost of service, place every such company upon as nearly an equal plane as may be with respect to expenses and charges as that occupied by the proprietary companies.
>
> Third. By eliminating from the present agreement between the terminal company and the proprietary companies any provision which restricts any such company to the use of the facilities of the terminal company.[191]

In *MCI Communications Corp. v. American Telephone & Telegraph Co.,*[192] the United States Court of Appeals for the Seventh Circuit affirmed in material part a judgment on a jury verdict against AT&T for denying interconnections to MCI. It found that AT&T controlled an essential facility and that the evidence supported the jury's determination that AT&T denied the essential facilities (interconnections for FX and CCSA service) when it was feasible to provide them.[193] The fact that MCI, the entity desiring interconnection, had not actually built the facilities to make use of the interconnection did not defeat its claim.[194] On the other hand, the court distinguished MCI's claim for multipoint connections. The court of appeals rejected MCI's antitrust challenge to AT&T for

---

[189] *Id.*

[190] *Id.* at 409.

[191] *Id.* at 411 (fourth through seventh terms omitted because pertaining to freight charges and retention of jurisdiction by district court to resolve disputes).

[192] 708 F.2d 1081 (7th Cir. 1983).

[193] *Id.* at 1133.

[194] *Id.* at 1144.

refusing to provide multipoint interconnections that would have given MCI access to AT&T's entire long distance network. The court "concluded that AT&T's refusal to voluntarily assume the extraordinary obligation to fill in the gaps in its competitor's network did not suffice to support a finding that it was trying to maintain its monopoly of long distance telephone service by anticompetitive means."[195]

Interface Group, Inc. v. Gordon Publications, Inc.[196] involved an unsuccessful essential facilities claim by a trade magazine excluded from a computer trade show. The district court distinguished *Terminal Railroad* on the grounds that the trade show was not an essential facility because the market, as the court defined it, included a number of other channels for the plaintiff to communicate its advertising.[197] (The district court treated the product as advertising space.) The analogies between these facts and the possible Internet examples are interesting. Advertising space is like bandwidth that might be sold by a value-added network services provider denied bit services by a conduit.[198] The journal in *Gordon Publications* would be analogous to the network services provider, and the trade show would be analogous to the conduit.

Also of interest in the context of infrastructure access is *Illinois v. Panhandle Eastern Pipe Line Co.*[199] Historically, natural gas pipelines bought gas at the wellhead, transported it, and resold it to customers of the pipeline, bundling the gas with pipeline transportation of it.[200] Panhandle purchased gas at high prices, and wellhead prices for gas subsequently fell.[201] Certain customers of Panhandle bought their own gas, but Panhandle refused to transport it.[202] The Seventh Circuit characterized the contract between Panhandle and its customers as an exclusive dealing contract that required those customers to purchase all of their natural gas requirements from Panhandle.[203] The state of Illinois sued Panhandle both as a natural gas consumer and as *parens patriae* for other consumers.[204] The state pressed both traditional monopolization claims and an essential facilities claim.[205]

Essential facilities liability does not exist if competitors can develop competing facilities and if the owner of the essential facility cannot feasibly provide access to that facility. The court of appeals found that access to Panhandle's

---

[195] Illinois v. Panhandle E. Pipe Line Co., 935 F.2d 1469, 1484 (7th Cir. 1991) (quoting in part *MCI*, 708 F.2d 1081, 1149 (7th Cir. 1983)).

[196] 562 F. Supp. 1235 (D. Mass. 1983).

[197] *Id.* at 1242–43.

[198] *Id.* at 1240 (defining product as advertising space).

[199] 935 F.2d 1469 (7th Cir. 1991).

[200] *Id.* at 1472.

[201] *Id.* at 1472–75.

[202] *Id.* at 1474.

[203] *Id.* at 1480.

[204] *Id.* at 1476.

[205] 935 F.2d 1469, 1482 (7th Cir. 1991).

pipeline was not essential because it would have been economically feasible for competitors to duplicate Panhandle's system by making interconnections between competing pipelines and constructing some new pipelines.[206] Moreover, Panhandle's refusal to carry competing gas on its pipeline was justified by its exposure to extremely large liability for doing so under its long-term contracts.[207]

In most parts of the information infrastructure, status as an essential facility is difficult to establish because of the many alternatives. The only exception might be a central name server or a major router operating as a joint venture. Antitrust essential facilities doctrine also might invalidate exclusive dealing arrangements relating to public information, like municipal ordinances, state and federal statutes, and judicial and administrative opinions and orders. This possibility is considered in **Chapter 11.**

§ 2.21 —Monopolization: The Microsoft Investigations

In 1994 and 1995 the Federal Trade Commission and the Department of Justice launched two investigations of Microsoft Corporation. The first focused on software practices generally, and the second focused on the relationship between Microsoft's dominant position as a provider of operating system software and access to computer networks. In the first investigation, the Justice Department inquiry and complaint was based on a combination of Microsoft's legitimately acquired dominant position in the market for operating systems, combined with a number of practices that were likely to extend Microsoft's monopoly and deny access to that and other markets by competitors. The concern was heightened by the economic characteristics of the software market in which producers confront high fixed costs and virtually zero marginal costs, resulting in high increasing returns to scale[208]—the traditional hallmarks of a natural monopoly.

In the second investigation, the Justice Department scrutinized Microsoft's intention to bundle network and network access features in its Windows 95 operating system but had not filed a complaint by the end of August 1995.

Because the particular practices subjected to scrutiny as potential abuses of monopoly power involved pricing, the details of these investigations are considered in **Chapter 7.**

---

[206] *Id.*

[207] *Id.* at 1483 (contrasting *MCI,* 708 F.2d 1081, 1133 (7th Cir. 1983) (evidence supported jury finding that AT&T could have provided interconnections and no legitimate business or technical reason was shown for denying MCI's requested interconnection)).

[208] United States v. Microsoft Corp., 56 F.3d 1448, 1452 (D.C. Cir. 1995) (describing Kenneth Arrow testimony and market characteristics).

§ 2.22   —Bad-Faith Assertions of
Intellectual Property

Intellectual property can represent a barrier to access in the NII. Bad-faith assertion of intellectual property claims can constitute antitrust violations. In *Christianson v. Colt Industries Operating Corp.,*[209] the Supreme Court addressed the relationship between antitrust and trade secret rights.[210] It noted that a section 2 Sherman Act monopolization claim might arise out of a claim that trade secret misappropriation was asserted falsely either because there were no trade secrets or because the defendant had been authorized to use the trade secrets.[211] A section 1 Sherman Act claim could be based on a purported trade secret confidentiality agreement when there were no trade secrets to protect.[212]

Bad-faith assertion of trade secret misappropriation may constitute a violation of the antitrust laws,[213] by analogy to the doctrine that assertion of an invalid patent in an infringement action can violate section 2 of the Sherman Act.[214] There is a tendency to confuse patent misuse as an element of affirmative liability under the antitrust laws with potential antitrust abuse as a defense in a patent infringement case.[215] Nevertheless, there are cases clearly involving antitrust claims based on earlier patent infringement litigation.[216] The antitrust plaintiff has the burden of proof in showing that the intellectual property position of the defendant was a sham or that the defendant asserted intellectual property with knowledge that legal requirements were not met.[217]

In the NII context, the most likely antitrust claim would involve a baseless assertion of intellectual property protection in underlying factual information. Even though state and local entities are free under the Copyright Act to assert copyrights in information they generate, copyright protection is unavailable for

---

[209] 486 U.S. 800 (1988) (vacating decision by Federal Circuit because antitrust claims did not arise under patent statutes).

[210] The case actually involved a jurisdictional question rather than an antitrust defense to a trade secret misappropriation claim. The case reached the Supreme Court because the 7th Circuit believed that the Federal Circuit had exclusive jurisdiction over an appeal, while the Federal Circuit believed the opposite.

[211] 486 U.S. 800, 811–12 (1988).

[212] *Id.* at 812–13.

[213] CVD, Inc. v. Raytheon, 769 F.2d 842, 851 (1st Cir. 1985).

[214] *See* Walker Process Equip., Inc. v. Food Mach. & Chem. Corp., 382 U.S. 172, 177 (1965) (obtaining and enforcing a patent with actual knowledge that the invention was unpatentable could violate Sherman Act).

[215] *See* Michael D. Oliver, Comment, *Antitrust Liability for Bad Faith Assertion of Trade Secrets,* 18 U. Balt. L. Rev. 544, 552–53 (1989) (discussing antitrust liability and patent infringement defense without clearly distinguishing the two).

[216] *See, e.g.,* Argus Chem. Corp. v. Fibre Glass-Ever Coat Co., 812 F.2d 1381, 1385–86 (Fed. Cir. 1987).

[217] Christianson v. Colt Indus. Operating Corp., 766 F. Supp. 670, 689 (C.D. Ill. 1991).

factual data under *Feist*.[218] The *Feist* case is well-known, and thus one who asserts copyright protection for raw facts or governmental information like federal statutes or judicial opinions, notwithstanding *Feist,* stands a good chance of being found to have asserted copyright in bad faith. Such an actor might face antitrust liability, especially if the arrangements in which it participates create a monopoly or significant monopoly power with respect to access to the public information.

§ 2.23 —Antitrust Requirements for Self-Governance

Chapter 7 explores the possibility of self-governance or self-regulation by NII communities. When such legal autonomy is attempted, the ultimate sanction for violating the self-governing community rules is exclusion from the community, denial of access to community facilities. This section considers whether such denial of access, motivated by a desire to enforce electronic community rules, may violate the antitrust laws.

A variety of antitrust cases have arisen challenging the application and enforcement of rules of associations of competitors. In general, the federal courts have the power under the antitrust laws "to void any significantly restrictive rule of a combination or trade association with significant market power, which lacks competitive justification or whose reach clearly exceeds the combinations legitimate needs."[219]

Scrutiny of private associations of competitors is strengthened when members waive rights to seek judicial relief. That heightened scrutiny can be lessened by transferring antitrust disputes not to a board of directors of a producer's association, but to an arbitrator.[220]

Health care peer review is a particularly pertinent area of antitrust analysis of self-governance because it adapts so easily to NII self-governance. After the Supreme Court denied state-action immunity to physician peer review decisions, the Congress enacted the Federal Health Care Quality Improvement Act,[221] which immunizes from antitrust liability peer review actions meeting

---

[218] Feist Publications, Inc. v. Rural Tel. Serv. Co., 499 U.S. 340 (1991).

[219] Pope v. Mississippi Real Estate Comm'n, 695 F. Supp. 253, 272 (N.D. Miss. 1988) (quoting United States v. Realty Multi-List, Inc., 629 F.2d 1351, 1370 (5th Cir. 1980) in support of conclusion that association of realtors possessed market power); NCAA v. Board of Regents, 468 U.S. 85, 101–02 (1984) (antitrust laws not violated by amateur eligibility rules because they were necessary to preserve the character and quality of "product").

[220] San Juan v. American Bd. of Psychiatry & Neurology, Inc., 40 F.3d 247, 250 (7th Cir. 1994) (Easterbrook, J.) (explaining basis for suspicion that no-suit agreement may be a device for suring up a cartel, but allowing agreements to arbitrate antitrust disputes under Mitsubishi Motors Corp. v. Soler Chrysler-Plymouth, Inc., 473 U.S. 614 (1985)).

[221] 42 U.S.C. § 11,112(a).

certain criteria: being based on a reasonable belief that the action furthered quality health care, appropriate fact gathering, notice and hearing, and reasonable belief resulting from the fact gathering and hearing that the action taken was warranted. The health care peer review act requires the opportunity for a hearing either before an arbitrator or before a hearing officer or panel not in direct competition with the involved physician.[222] The federal act permits states to opt in or opt out.[223]

Even without the statutory immunity, "although revocation of doctors' privileges may, perforce, eliminate competition by decreasing the number of doctors in a given specialty, this alone will not give rise to an antitrust violation."[224] An essential element of a section 1 violation is proof of an unlawful objective, and "corrective action against a physician does not violate the antitrust laws if the physician's peer reviewers had legitimate medical reasons to believe that the physician provided substandard care." That is so because monitoring the competence of physicians through peer review is clearly in the public interest.[225] Actual support for the peer review decision enters into the analysis because if "a peer groups conclusions are so baseless that no reasonable medical practitioner could have reached those conclusions after reviewing the same set of facts," a fact finder may infer the existence of an illegitimate motive.[226]

One commentator notes that the likelihood of a successful antitrust claim based on a peer review decision is extremely small.[227] She suggests three measures to reduce antitrust risk: making sure that no competitor of the physician under review dominates the peer review proceeding especially if the competitor has significant market power; making sure that partners of the same medical group do not act both as complaining witnesses and hearing panel members; and excluding physicians with personal bias or independent personal stake in the outcome from investigative committees or hearing panels, at least without investigating the nature of their potential bias.[228] Further, she suggests that fair hearing procedures, utilization of peer review in a consistent and nondiscriminatory manner, and ensuring that the decision is narrowly focused on professional confidence or conduct will minimize antitrust exposure.[229]

---

[222] *Id.* § 11,112(b)(3)(A)(iii).

[223] *See* Smith v. Our Lady of the Lake Hosp., Inc., 639 So. 2d 730, 742 (La. 1994) (describing federal act). Similar state statutes exist in almost every state. State tort privileges have similar criteria. *Id.* at 743.

[224] Willman v. Heartland Hosp. E., 34 F.3d 605, 610 (8th Cir. 1994).

[225] *Id.* at 610–11.

[226] *Id.* at 611.

[227] Roxanne C. Busey, *Structuring Peer Review to Minimize Antitrust Risk after* Patrick, 3 SPG Antitrust (A.B.A.) 12, 13 (1989).

[228] *Id.* at 15.

[229] *Id.* at 16.

Another respected antitrust commentator agrees, arguing that there is no need for special statutory immunities.[230] He notes that antitrust scrutiny of competitive collaboration to impose and enforce rules should focus on whether any restraints on competition are (1) ancillary, that is, truly necessary for legitimate purposes, and (2) crafted to deminimize the risk of anticompetitive effects.[231] On the other hand, restrictions on competition cannot be defended successfully by mere claims that they are inspired by pure or public-spirited motives; instead, the actions must be justified as not incompatible with maintenance of effective competition.[232] He admits, however, that "coercive boycotts" of unapproved providers are "almost certainly unlawful regardless of their arguably worthy purpose," and that antitrust immunity depends on the peer review organization simply making a report to others like public licensing authorities, hospitals, insurers, referring physicians, and patients themselves who decide for themselves whether to act on the advice provided by the peer reviewers.[233] He suggests that explicit agreements to adhere to ethical or practice standards are problematic.[234] He acknowledges that fee review poses greater problems than review of utilization under published, profession-approved practice standards, but does not endorse anything more than advisory standards.[235]

The case law and commentary on physician peer review is directly applicable to "peer review" by competitors in the NII. The public policy in favor of self-regulation of the NII is no stronger than the public policy in favor of self-regulation in the medical profession. Market structures are similar, and the utility of due process in deflecting claims of anticompetitive motivations is the same in both industries.

§ 2.24   Eminent Domain and Condemnation of Intellectual Property

Denials of access sometimes involve simply the assertion of intellectual property rights. The holder of a copyright in software or information content or the holder of the patent in a computer system or process may deny others the use of the content, software, or system or may charge prices for such use that the entity desiring access finds unaffordable. The copyright and patent clause of the

---

[230] Clark C. Havighurst, *Professional Peer Review and the Antitrust Laws,* 36 Case W. Res. L. Rev. 1117 (1986).

[231] *Id.* at 1119.

[232] *Id.* at 1120.

[233] *Id.* at 1129.

[234] *Id.* at 1144–45.

[235] Clark C. Havighurst, *Professional Peer Review and the Antitrust Laws,* 36 Case W. Res. L. Rev. 1117, 1147 (1986). *See also id.* at 1150–51 (professionally promulgated quality standards, backed by possibility of exclusion from market represent real danger that physician's clinical methods will be centrally determined, contrary to the premises of the antitrust laws).

United States Constitution and the copyright and patent statutes acknowledge the legitimacy of such denials of access in the vast majority of cases.[236] Indeed, there is no duty to license copyrights or patents under the intellectual property laws or antitrust law.[237] The rare circumstance may arise, however, in which legitimate information infrastructure goals cannot be attained without forcing intellectual property owners to grant access. In such circumstances, one source of access right might be partial condemnation, through the exercise of eminent domain powers by the federal government.[238] Indeed, there is a statutory provision in government contract law contemplating condemnation. The condemnation approach, while representing significant intrusion into the prerogatives of the intellectual property owner, nevertheless balances interests of grantor and grantee of access because it envisions judicially determined compensation for the access.

One important limitation on the condemnation approach is that it may be used only for public purposes, while the interests of the entity granted access through condemnation may be largely private.[239] On the other hand, the history of condemnation and eminent domain in the telecommunications industry shows that a mixture of public and private objectives can support the taking of private property, and sufficient public interest certainly could exist to justify condemning strategically situated intellectual property.

A significant disadvantage to the condemnation approach is the uncertainty and cost of determining compensation through a judicial proceeding. On the other hand, infrequent use of the power should make tolerable the transaction costs of compensation setting.

The Congress has imposed compulsory licensing obligations in the limited case of computer chip mask works,[240] and some commentators have proposed compulsory licensing as a useful approach in balancing the interest involved in extending copyright to functional features of computer software.[241]

The controversy over the patents for the RSA encryption algorithm exemplifies one candidate for forcing access through condemnation.[242] Patent holders for the algorithm took the position that certain proposed government encryption standards infringed their patent and that they should be entitled to royalties for use of the government-prescribed standard.

---

[236] See **Ch. 10.**

[237] Data Gen. Corp. v. Grumman Sys. Support Corp., 36 F.3d 1147, 1185 (1st Cir. 1994) (manufacturer's refusal to license its software was not a monopolization violation).

[238] Both copyright and patent statutes broadly preempt state law, and therefore exercise of imminent domain by state governments would interfere with federally granted rights and presumably be preempted.

[239] See **Ch. 6** for a complete analysis of eminent domain and condemnation.

[240] 17 U.S.C. § 903 (1988).

[241] See Wendy J. Gordon, *On Owning Information: Intellectual Property* and the Restitionary Impulse, 78 Va. L. Rev. 149 (1992).

[242] See generally Schafly v. Public Key Partners, 1994 WL 669858 (N.D. Cal. Nov. 22, 1994) (describing patents).

Another possible use for condemnation would be a circumstance in which someone belatedly asserts a copyright interest in basic infrastructure standards like TCP/IP itself, World Wide Web, or Gopher. In such a circumstance, there would be challenging issues with respect to the nature of the intellectual property itself, requiring courts to sort out complex issues of intellectual property law before there would be any need for condemnation. For example, the RSA patent may be invalid. The core Internet standards may represent uncopyrightable functions rather than protectible expression, and even if they represent protectible expression, they may have been placed in the public domain or subject to broad fair use privileges.[243] The condemnation approach might be attractive even when a unilaterally determined royalty arrangement is unattractive, as in the RSA case.[244] Condemnation is a way of forcing an intellectual property owner to grant access when he otherwise would completely refuse access. It also is a way of involving the law in circumscribing pricing for access.

As with the other sources of access rights, the appropriateness of condemnation of intellectual property depends on the availability of alternatives. Alternatives are more likely to be available to copyrighted elements than patented ones. This is so because copyright allows independent creation,[245] and the scope of copyright for functional works is circumscribed when few or no alternatives exist to the copyrighted work.[246] Patent, on the other hand, forecloses independently created inventions within the scope of the patent; therefore, it is much more difficult to avoid a patent in performing the same function as the patented work.

---

[243] *See* Henry H. Perritt, Jr., *Unbundling Value in Electronic Information Products: Intellectual Property Protection for Machine Readable Interfaces,* 20 Rutgers Computer & Tech. L.J. 415 (1994).

[244] *See* Christopher E. Torkelson, Comment, *The Clipper Chip: How Key Escrow Threatens to Undermine the Fourth Amendment,* 25 Seton Hall L. Rev. 1142 (1995) (claims that government-sponsored Clipper Chip infringed RSA patent to public key encryption); *see generally* Schafly v. Public Key Partners, 1994 WL 669858 (N.D. Cal. Nov. 22, 1994) (description of patent).

[245] 17 U.S.C. § 106 reserves to the copyright holder only exclusive rights of reproduction, preparation of derivative works, distribution, public performance, and public display. If someone other than the copyright holder creates something similar or identical to the copyrighted work without engaging in any of these types of conduct with respect to the copyrighted work, there is no infringement.

[246] *See* cases involving need to use copyrighted work in order to achieve compatibility: Sega Enters. Ltd. v. Accolade, Inc., 977 F.2d 1510 (9th Cir. 1992) (Competitor of video game manufacturer permitted to use copyrighted functional requirements to achieve compatibility); Atari Games Corp. v. Nintendo of Am., Inc., Nos. C88-4805 FMS, C89-0027 FMS, 1993 WL 207548 (N.D. Cal. May 18, 1993) ("Program code that is strictly necessary to achieve current compatibility presents a merger problem, almost by definition, and is thus excluded from the scope of any copyright. A defendant may not only make intermediate copies of an entire program to discover the existence of such code, but it may also copy that code into its final product.").

§ 2.25 Privileges and Immunities

Preceding sections of this chapter identify theories supporting rights of users (including suppliers) of the NII to force other NII service providers to give them access to NII facilities. As important as these theories involving rights to access are, two constitutional theories immunize service providers from being forced by common law or statute to give access to those they do not wish to have access. Because NII services involve organization and transfer of information, the First Amendment is potentially involved whenever the law imposes obligations on NII information services. In addition, legally imposed access obligations diminish property rights in many cases and thus must circumvent property-based immunities expressed in the due process and taking clauses of the Fifth Amendment, incorporated into the due process and equal protection clauses of the Fourteenth Amendment.

The recent First and Fifth Amendment cases, discussed in **Chapter 6** suggest that any statutory or regulatory duty to provide access will receive sharp constitutional scrutiny. *Turner Broadcasting*[247] in particular shows the linkage between the availability of competitive alternatives and constitutionally permissible access duties. The First Amendment permits forcing some information conduits to accept content generated by others, but only when such forcing is necessary to permit the content to find its audience. When the entity burdened by the duty has relatively little interest in expression, for example if it is simply a router, the First Amendment allows a broader range of legislative and regulatory discretion to impose a duty because the harm to First Amendment interests is de minimis. No expressive will is involved in operating a router. Conversely, if burdens on First Amendment interests are involved, and there are many competitive alternatives, imposing a duty that does limit First Amendment interests lacks justification because the interest protected by the duty do not need the duty; they can be realized through the alternative channels. Both First Amendment and property-based due process issues are considered more fully in **Chapter 6.**

§ 2.26 Role of Competition

Competition and contract are the two themes of access regulation. Beyond representing an alternative to detailed regulation, competition also shapes the imposition of traditional sources of access duty. The availability of competitive alternatives negates essential facilities obligations under antitrust law. Competitive market conditions make the finding of common carrier status less likely both under communication statutes and at common law. The availability of competitive alternatives with low switching costs lessens detrimental reliance that is a feature of contract enforcement.

---

[247] Turner Broadcasting Sys., Inc. v. FCC, 114 S. Ct. 2445 (1994).

So both from a policy perspective and from a legal analytical perspective, the competitive structure of National Information Infrastructure markets is of central importance. At the leaves of the network, vigorous competition almost certainly will prevail. Internet-like technologies and the existence of a real infrastructure greatly reduce the barriers to entry and thus make it more likely that there will be many more providers of any particular content or service. At the core of the infrastructure, however, there may be some essential facilities pertaining to name and address databases and routers. Similarly, certain white pages and yellow pages services may be natural monopolies. As to these essential facilities, it may be more appropriate to impose specific access duties.

More generally, the competitive conditions that discourage legal intervention will exist only if all of the parts of the system are interoperable. A multiplicity of incompatible systems reduces the available alternatives when markets are defined narrowly, and incompatibility increases switching costs when alternatives exist in more broadly defined markets.

Both sound policy and constitutional law militate against granting access entitlements (beyond those expressly agreed to by both parties) except when competitive alternatives are lacking. In other words, only those with monopoly powers should have legally imposed duties to provide access. The architecture of the NII, assuming it uses the Internet as a starting point, produces monopoly power only with respect to certain backbone routers, name servers, and other "white pages" and "yellow pages" type services with respect to the content of government information as to which exclusive arrangements are established. In those areas, some type of externally imposed access duty may be appropriate.

In order for a competitive market to be relied upon in preference to law, it must exist. It may not exist unless the law intervenes to the limited extent of requiring interoperability.

§ 2.27 Sample Statement of Access Rights

The following statement of access rights could be used either at an associational or interest group level to define good practice by information providers, or it could be adopted by an information service provider.

1. We own the facilities involved in providing access to the Internet through our service arrangements. Accordingly, we have constitutionally protected property and First Amendment privileges that distinguish us from common carriers. We disclaim any intent to be a common carrier.

2. Nevertheless, we will perform our part of the bargain if you perform yours. If you pay our published price, we will allow you to connect to our service under the conditions set forth in our published terms, particularly including the limitations on our liability contained in those published terms. You may obtain an additional copy of our current terms of service from ___.

3.   Just as you reserve the power to take traffic away from our connection at any time and make such other arrangements as you wish, so also do we reserve the power to change our terms of service and adjust our prices. We will not, however, increase your price during the period of time for which you have paid.

4.   If you feel the need to assure a connection through our service for a particular period of time, we are happy to attempt to negotiate such an arrangement with you. Of course part of the negotiation will be an agreement on price and specific terms of service, as well as the length of time during which we will not change terms, adjust the price, or disconnect you.

5.   In the absence of any such negotiated arrangement, our contractual relationship is terminable at will, by either one of us.

§ 2.28   Sample Access Agreement

This is an alternative access agreement, more specific than the one presented in § 2.27.

1.   In exchange for the timely payment of subscription fees under the fee schedule then in effect, provider agrees to make available its services under the following terms and conditions.

2.   Subscriber, in exchange for the services provided by provider, agrees to make timely payment of fees according to the schedule of fees then in effect and to comply with the following terms and conditions.

3.   Provider will make available through dial-up telephone numbers located in the [name of town] area and modems capable of sending and receiving information at least 28,800 bits per second access to its node on the Internet.

4.   Provider will connect its node to the Internet through a dedicated connection capable of speeds of at least 56 kilobits per second to an Internet services provider it reasonably believes to be reliable.

5.   Provider will make available on its Internet node a Gopher server and a World Wide Web server, the contents of which may be determined in the provider's sole discretion.

6.   Provider will keep at least 10 telephone lines and modems available for subscriber use, but does not undertake to ensure against busy signals when all the lines are in use by other subscribers [provider will make available dial-up telephone lines and modems sufficient to maintain the ratio of 60 subscribers per telephone line, but does not undertake to ensure against busy signals when all the lines are in use by other subscribers].

7. Provider will make available to subscriber a telephone number that activates a pager for a duty officer for provider's system. If subscriber finds provider's system unavailable and promptly notifies provider through the telephone number assigned to the pager, provider undertakes to remedy any unavailability caused by problems with its system within six hours or to refund on a pro rata basis the fee attributable to that day.

8. Provider does not accept any responsibility for the accuracy or legality of any content obtained through its facilities; subscriber hereby waives any claim against provider for damages associated with content received through provider service and facilities.

9. Subscriber agrees to indemnify provider against any claim brought by a third party against provider resulting from material subscriber places on or sends through provider service or facilities. Such indemnification shall include the costs of defense including attorneys' fees incurred by provider.

10. [Name of state] law shall be applied to the resolution of any dispute arising under or over the application of this agreement.

11. Any dispute arising under or over the application of this agreement shall be resolved by final and binding arbitration under the rules of the American Arbitration Association, including the international arbitration rules if applicable. Both parties hereby waive any right they otherwise might have to present disputes arising under this agreement to the courts of any state or country except to enforce an arbitration award.

§ 2.29 Sample Electronic Publishing Agreement

[Incorporate indemnification and claim waiver provisions from sample agreement in § 2.28.]

1. Publisher, in exchange for the services provided by provider, and provider, in exchange for the information content provided by publisher, hereby agree to the following terms and conditions.

2. Publisher agrees to pay the electronic publishing fees set forth in the currently effective fee schedule.

3. For so long as publisher pays the publishing fees under the currently applicable fee schedule, provider shall make available through its World Wide Web server connected to the Internet through at least a 56 kbps dedicated line, with all steps taken necessary to make the server reachable

through the Internet address and name resolution system, 10 megabytes of space for publisher works.

4. These works shall be browsable and retrievable through World Wide Web pages maintained on provider's server, along with all of the features available in standard web browsers.

CHAPTER 3

PRIVACY

§ 3.1   Introduction and Description of the Problem

Computer networks spanning organizational and national boundaries raise concerns about personal privacy. Efficiency advantages cause more and more private information to be stored in computer-readable form. Information stored in a networked computer is easy to retrieve unless affirmative steps have been taken to protect it from retrieval. As networks improve and as methods for storing, accessing, and transferring information on widespread networks become standardized, it is easier to assemble individual profiles from bits of information obtained from many different sources.

While these technology changes have focused attention on the relationship between computer technology and personal privacy, they have not caused legislatures to enact comprehensive statutes dealing with computer privacy. There are a variety of laws at the federal and state level that protect certain types of information and that regulate certain kinds of information-intensive industries like the credit reporting industry. Insurance and health care information similarly are subjected to specialized regulation. Common-law and constitutional analysis also afford protection in certain circumstances. The European Union has adopted a comprehensive data privacy protection directive seeking to harmonize national legislation on the subject, and the directive's requirements affect enterprises trading in Europe or exchanging information with enterprises that do business in Europe.

The Electronic Communications Privacy Act (ECPA)[1] is the broadest of the federal statutes. It imposes duties on information service providers and custodians of information as well as imposing duties on intruders and eavesdroppers. The federal Computer Fraud and Abuse Act[2] is narrower in two respects than ECPA. It has a result element, imposing liability only for intrusions that cause certain types of harm enumerated in the statute. Also, it imposes duties only on intruders and eavesdroppers, and not on custodians and service providers. The

---

[1] Pub. L. No. 99-508, 100 Stat. 1848 (1986), codified at 18 U.S.C.A. §§ 2510–2522, 2701–2710, 2711 (West Supp. 1995).

[2] Pub. L. No. 99-474, 100 Stat. 1213 (1986), codified at 18 U.S.C. § 1030.

federal Privacy Act[3] is narrower still. It imposes duties only on federal government agencies, and only then with respect to information items that identify
individuals. Other statutory regimes deal with specialized subject matter: the
Fair Credit Reporting Act[4] relating to credit information, and insurance and
health information statutes dealing with insurance and health information.

The broadest privacy regimes are those provided by common law and the
Constitution. Common law is comprehensive, but uncertain in application. The
Constitution restricts only "state action."

Despite the absence of a comprehensive framework of positive law, virtually
all of the initiatives in privacy law recognize the same conflicting interests and
deal with a set of about a dozen practice elements, which are cogently set forth
in the U.S. information industry's code of good practice (see § 3.4). In dealing
with these elements of practice, it is useful to remember that there are two
important legal dimensions and two conceptually different types of privacy. The
first legal dimension relates to the subject's expectation of privacy; the second
relates to the reasonableness of an intrusion. The first type of privacy is
informational; it concerns the subject's desire to keep information about himself
private. The second type of privacy relates to personal autonomy; it involves the
desire to make independent decisions about oneself.

Throughout this chapter, the rights analyzed belong to the subject or owner of
information. The chapter analyzes the duties of two different kinds of legal
persons with respect to those rights holders. One kind of duty is imposed on
intruders, eavesdroppers, or hackers who obtain information in the custody of
the rights holder or in the custody of someone to whom the rights holder
transferred the information. The second kind of obligor is a person to whom the
rights holder has transferred information: a system operator or service provider.
It is important to keep these two different owers of duties distinct.

§ 3.2 Privacy Audit Checklist

The fragmentation of data privacy law heightens the importance of an orderly
method for information custodians to evaluate their risks of legal liability. The
following checklist for informational privacy analysis is a good starting point
for such an orderly risk assessment.

_____ 1: What computer files or discrete collections of computer-processible
information contain information identifying individuals?

_____ 2. What computer files contain the information pertaining to messages
exchanged between individuals (including both message content and
transactional records)?

---

[3] 5 U.S.C. § 552a.

[4] 15 U.S.C. §§ 1681, 1681a–1681t.

_____ 3. How was this information obtained?

_____ 4. Did the subjects give permission for collection and maintenance of this information? In what form? For what purpose did they consent to have the information used?[5]

_____ 5. Who has access to the information? Is a record made of all disclosures?

_____ 6. Is the information associated with a federal or state agency activity?[6]

_____ 7. Does the information pertain to the subject's creditworthiness or financial accounts?[7]

_____ 8. Are authorizations to use the computer system expressed and communicated in such a way as to provide protection against undesired access under the Computer Fraud and Abuse Act?[8]

§ 3.3 Legal Relationships and Interests

Privacy involves four sometimes conflicting interests:

1. The interests of the subject

2. The interests of custodians of information about the subject

3. The interests of the government in acquiring information and using it for regulatory or prosecutorial purposes

4. The interests of private entities or individuals who want to exploit information about others.

The basic legal framework is this: the common law imposes duties on persons, limiting the acquisition of information and the disclosure of it. The common law gives a concomitant right to subjects to recover damages for violation of the duties. The Constitution gives subjects and custodians a privilege not to disclose information to the government except under certain circumstances, and it imposes a duty on the government not to acquire information except under those same circumstances.[9] It also gives the subjects of information and custodians a right to recover damages or to obtain injunctions against governmental conduct

---

[5] The nature of the consent obtained plays a major role in common-law privacy torts. See § **3.5.**

[6] If the answer to this question is yes, more complete analysis of the possibility of duties under federal or state privacy acts should be done. See § **3.6.**

[7] If the answer to this question is yes, more thorough analysis should be done of the possibility of duties under the Fair Credit Reporting Act. See § **3.17.**

[8] See § **3.14.** The Computer Fraud and Abuse Act prohibits certain accesses to information contrary to authorization.

[9] The Fourth Amendment and search warrant and subpoena procedures are considered in **Ch. 6.**

violating the duties. ECPA reinforces duties of nondisclosure imposed by the common law and channels governmental acquisition requests, thus reinforcing the duties and privileges imposed and granted by the Constitution. It also creates a private right of action for damages for subjects against custodians, governmental actors, and private exploiters. The Fair Credit Reporting Act imposes duties on custodians and exploiters and grants concomitant rights to subjects. The federal Privacy Act and several of the other statutes create a new right for subjects to obtain information about them maintained by custodians and to challenge its accuracy.

§ 3.4   Codes of Good Practice

There is broad agreement in the United States and Europe on the elements of "fair information practices," although there is strong disagreement on whether practice guidelines should be enacted into law. The European Union has done so, as explained in §§ ___. The United States has not. Nevertheless the following practice guidelines provide a good analytical framework within which to analyze statutory, regulatory, and common-law requirements. They also represent standards of conduct to be applied by courts required to make more concrete the *expectation-of-privacy* and *reasonableness* standards that pervade privacy law.

1. No personal data record-keeping system may be maintained in secret.
2. Individuals must have a means of determining what information about them is in a record and how it is used.
3. Individuals must have a means of preventing information about them obtained for one purpose from being used or made available for other purposes without their consent.
4. Individuals must have a means to correct or amend a record of identifiable information about themselves.
5. Limits should be placed on the disclosure of certain personal information to third parties.
6. The individual whose request for correction or amendment is denied may file a statement of disagreement, which must be included in the record and disclosed along with it thereafter.
7. Organizations creating, maintaining, using, or disseminating records of identifiable personal data must assure the reliability of the data for their intended use and must take reasonable precautions to prevent misuses of the data.
8. An individual should have means of seeking review of a denied request or an alleged violation of duty.

Such principles usually focus on data *about* someone. They can be adapted to private communications—data *from* someone—by emphasizing and elaborating items 3 and 7 and recognizing the diminished relevance of the other items to communications privacy.

Such voluntarily developed private practice statements can have significant legal effect through the common law. They are points of reference in deciding standards of care appropriate in a tort lawsuit and the standards of performance and good faith appropriate to a contractual relationship.

Almost any contract dispute requires the court to engage in interpretation of the expressed contract terms. Depending on how general the contract terms are, the interpretation inquiry may be wide-ranging in scope. One of the most legitimate sources of information for interpretation is industry practice. The rationale is, not that the members of the industry are entitled to impose their practices on unwilling contracting parties, but that in the absence of any expression to the contrary, the intent of the contracting parties is supposed to be based on what they are accustomed to seeing in their own industry.[10]

Industry practice is also relevant to common-law tort claims for invasion of privacy. The *Restatement* repeatedly uses the concept of offensiveness to a reasonable person as the standard for limiting liability for invasion of privacy.[11] It also suggests that customs and community standards are the benchmark for determining offensiveness.[12] This derivation of standards of conduct for particular torts is a regular feature of tort law. In negligence, for example, trade or industry custom or practice is not only relevant to the standard for identifying negligent conduct, it may be so probative as to justify a directed verdict.[13]

Thus a plaintiff asserting a common-law claim for invasion of privacy against a provider of communications or information services would offer the statement of fair information practices as an accurate expression of custom and practice in

---

[10] Restatement (Second) of Contracts § 222 (1981) (usage of trade, including system of rules regularly observed, "gives meaning to or supplements or qualifies their agreement" unless otherwise agreed); McCormick on Evidence § 198, at 584 (Edward W. Cleary ed. 1984) (some practices may become so accepted in an industry that they may shape the meaning of most contracts in the field; therefore evidence of third-party conduct and practice can be relevant evidence).

[11] "[H]ighly objectional to a reasonable man," Restatement (Second) of Torts § 652A illus. 1 (1977) (basic invasion-of-privacy concept); "highly offensive to the ordinary reasonable man," *id.* § 652B cmt. d (intrusion tort); "highly offensive to a reasonable person," *id.* § 652D & cmt. c (publicity tort); "highly offensive to a reasonable person," *id.* § 652E & cmt. c (false light).

[12] *Id.* § 652E cmt. c (defendant must know plaintiff as reasonable man would be "justified in the eyes of the community" in feeling seriously offended and aggrieved from false communication); *id.* § 652D cmt. c ("protection [against publicity given to private facts] must be relative to the customs of the time and place").

[13] Restatement (Second) of Torts § 295A & cmts. a & b (1965) (giving as examples marine navigation rules).

the industry, and argue that conduct deviating from the statement is at least prima facie unreasonably offensive. The defendant would be liable unless it could (1) establish that the statement of practices does not represent industry custom, or (2) establish that some special circumstances justified a deviation from the published fair practices in the particular case.

§ 3.5   Common-Law Invasion of Privacy

The common law recognizes a cluster of four invasion-of-privacy torts.[14] Three of these torts embrace a wrongful-conduct view of privacy, and the fourth recognizes a property concept.

The first privacy tort is intrusion upon seclusion.[15] It imposes liability on an actor who unreasonably intrudes into an area or subject as to which the victim has a reasonable expectation of privacy. Telephone wiretaps have been tortious under this theory for decades.[16] If the underlying information is public or if the conduct is not unreasonable, there is no liability under this tort. The intrusion tort category involves the same kind of conduct that is regulated by the Electronic Communications Privacy Act[17] and by the Computer Fraud and Abuse Act,[18] both of which limit unauthorized access to communications and information systems.

Giving publicity to private facts is a second privacy tort.[19] One who publicizes private information widely[20] is prima facie liable under this theory, although the publicity may be privileged.[21] The publicity must be offensive to a reasonable person.[22] The expectation of privacy required for this tort is less than that

---

[14] Restatement (Second) of Torts § 652A (1977) (summarizing four types of invasion of privacy).

[15] *Id.* § 652B.

[16] *See* Rhodes v. Graham, 37 S.W.2d 46 (Ky. 1931) (reversing demurrer on common-law intrusion claim by victims of telephone wiretaps).

[17] See §§ **3.7–3.13.**

[18] See § **3.14.**

[19] Restatement (Second) of Torts § 652D (1977).

[20] The degree of publicity for this tort is greater than that required for defamation. *Id.* § 652D cmt. a (noting that publication for defamation only requires disclosure to one third person; publicity for invasion of privacy requires that the matter become public knowledge). *See* Peacock v. Retail Credit Co., 302 F. Supp. 418, 422–23 (N.D. Ga. 1969) (rejecting claim against credit reporting company on invasion of privacy grounds; no physical intrusion and insufficient publicity because credit report was confidential; and any libel was not claimed within one-year statute of limitation; summary judgment for defendant).

[21] An element of the tort is that the publicized information not be "of legitimate concern to the public," and this is constitutionally required. Restatement (Second) of Torts § 652D(b) (1977).

[22] *Id.* § 652D cmt. c (showing video of surgical procedure to general public though it was meant only for medical students would qualify, but publicizing private wedding would not).

required for the intrusion tort.[23] The publicity tort category involves the same kinds of conduct that are regulated by the federal Privacy Act, by the Fair Credit Reporting Act, by the Financial Records Privacy Act, and by the disclosure limitations of the Electronic Communications Privacy Act.

False-light invasion of privacy[24] is similar to defamation.[25] This theory imposes liability on one who publicizes information in a way that creates false perceptions of the subject of the information. It is not necessary that the original information be private; nor is it necessary that the false impressions in the audience injure reputation in the same way that is necessary for defamation liability.[26] A common example of liability under this tort category is publishing information about a Republican ward leader causing the public to perceive that she is a Democrat. Falsely saying that someone is a Democrat is not defamatory, but such false communication may produce liability under this invasion of privacy tort.[27] Liability is imposed, however, only for publicity that would be offensive to a reasonable person.[28] The false-light privacy tort involves the same kind of conduct involved when the custodian of computer data fails to take appropriate action to ensure its accuracy, conduct addressed by the federal Privacy Act, and by the Fair Credit Reporting Act.

The fourth privacy tort is appropriation of name or likeness.[29] It is the only one of the four privacy categories that has a property flavor. It imposes liability on one who uses the name, image, and possibly other uniquely identifying information about another for the commercial purposes of the actor.[30]

These four privacy torts recognized by the *Restatement (Second) of Torts* originally were suggested by Dean William Prosser's analytical framework for making sense of privacy case law in the first half of the twentieth century under the "invasion of privacy" label.[31] All of them generally are acknowledged as having their genesis in a law review article coauthored in the latter part of the 19th century by Brandeis.[32]

---

[23] *But see id.* § 652D cmt. b (giving as examples of private facts: sexual relations, family quarrels, humiliating illnesses, intimate personal letters, details of home life, past personal history that one would want to forget).

[24] *Id.* § 652E.

[25] *Id.* § 652E cmt. b.

[26] *Id.*

[27] Restatement (Second) of Torts § 652E illus. 4 (1977).

[28] *Id.* § 652E cmt. c (publishing erroneous but not derogatory facts about a musician would not be tortious, but falsely placing one's picture in a police rogues' gallery over protest would be).

[29] *Id.* § 652C.

[30] The Restatement commentary says that liability may be imposed for noncommercial appropriation as long as it is for the purpose and benefit of the actor. *Id.* § 652C cmt. b.

[31] William Prosser, *Privacy,* 48 Cal. L. Rev. 383 (1960).

[32] Warrent & Brandeis, *The Right to Privacy,* 4 Harv. L. Rev. 193 (1890). *But see* Richard C. Turkington, George B. Trubow, & Anita L. Allen, Privacy: Cases and Materials 18 (1992) (characterizing DeMay v. Roberts, 9 N.W. 146 (Mich. 1881), as recognizing right to privacy before Warren and Brandeis article was published).

Liability under one or more of these torts can arise in the NII in the following situations. Liability under the intrusion tort is likely whenever someone intercepts messages or stored information intended to remain private.[33] An expectation of privacy may exist with respect to certain types of monitoring even if it does not exist with certain other types of monitoring.[34] Disclosure is not necessary for liability under this tort category.[35] Its coverage resembles statutory civil or criminal liability for electronic eavesdropping under the Electronic Communications Privacy Act. As under the statute, certain monitoring of transactional information in the ordinary course of business may be privileged.[36]

McDaniel v. Atlanta Coca-Cola Bottling Co.[37] is an interesting early case. The plaintiff claimed she had swallowed broken glass in a Coca-Cola bottle. While she was hospitalized, the Coca-Cola Company caused a remote transmitting device to be placed in her hospital room, and she sued for invasion of privacy. The appellate court held that the allegations stated a claim for invasion of privacy under common law, and rejected the defendant's argument that publication of the information was an element of invasion of privacy.[38] It rejected the argument that invasion of privacy could occur only if the defendant were

---

[33] *See* Bussen v. South Cent. Bell Tel. Co., 682 F. Supp. 319, 325 (S.D. Miss. 1987) (plaintiff alleging common-law invasion of privacy by telephone company employee who made anonymous calls after becoming involved with plaintiff's former husband not attributable to telephone company; intrusion variant); Rhodes v. Graham, 37 S.W.2d 46, 47 (Ky. 1931) (reversing grant of demurrer to complaint alleging telephone wiretap; tap invaded privacy recognized by the common law and was similar to eavesdropping, which was an indictable offense at English common law); Hamberger v. Eastman, 206 A.2d 239 (N.H. 1964) (complaint alleging that landlord placed listening device in bedroom of married couple and monitored it through wires connected to a remote location stated claim for intrusion variant of invasion of privacy under Prosser's framework for invasion of privacy). The *Hamberger* case predated the incorporation of Prosser's privacy analysis into the Restatement (Second) of Torts. *See also* Billings v. Atkinson, 489 S.W.2d 858, 860 (Tex. 1973) (reversing judgment n.o.v. and reinstating jury verdict of $10,000 compensatory and $15,000 exemplary damages on Restatement (First) Invasion of Privacy theory against telephone company and its lineman employee who tapped residential telephone line).

[34] LaCrone v. Ohio Bell Tel. Co., 182 N.E.2d 15, 16 (Ohio Ct. App. 1961) (wiretap by telephone company constituted common-law invasion of privacy even though subscriber had notice that other party-to-party line service might overhear conversations; expectation of privacy remained with respect to other eavesdroppers through other means).

[35] Roach v. Harper, 105 S.E.2d 564, 568 (W. Va. 1958) (complaint stated claim for common-law invasion of privacy by alleging that landlord placed an eavesdropping device in apartment rented to plaintiff and thereby overheard private conversations of plaintiff; no need to allege disclosure or special damages).

[36] Schmukler v. Ohio Bell Tel. Co., 116 N.E.2d 819, 826 (Ohio C.P. 1953) (rejecting common-law invasion of privacy claim against telephone company that first installed pen register and then monitored telephone conversation to determine whether they were business or personal calls; evidence indicated monitoring was terminated as soon as character of call could be determined; opinion not particularly analytical and dominated by moralizing about motive to cheat the telephone company).

[37] 2 S.E.2d 810 (Ga. Ct. App. 1939).

[38] *Id.* at 817.

physically present to engage in the eavesdropping personally; placement and use of an electronic device was enough.[39] It also rejected the defendant's argument that its desire to investigate what it believed to be a fraudulent claim constituted justification for the eavesdropping.[40]

The publicity tort will produce liability in the NII for someone who takes information of limited circulation that pertains to an individual (private facts) and significantly increases its circulation. Thus, if someone takes a message inadvertently left in a public file area of a network server and broadcasts it to the general public or to a community of significant size, liability under this tort is likely.[41]

False-light liability is likely under circumstances similar to those that would produce liability under common-law defamation doctrines or under data-accuracy statutes. If a database provider maintains information about individuals and the information is inaccurate, liability under this tort is probable when the provider disseminates the information. The false-light tort is more interesting in the NII context if the mental state it requires is mere negligence, as opposed to intent to place the victim in a false light. If negligence is enough, then this tort is a source of significant concern for anyone who maintains information about protected entities.[42]

---

[39] *Id.* at 816.

[40] *Id.* at 818.

[41] *See* Houghton v. New Jersey Mfrs.' Ins. Co., 615 F. Supp. 299, 307 (E.D. Pa. 1985) (claim for invasion of privacy/disclosure of private facts for investigative report disclosed to insurance company in support of its litigation position failed because of insufficient publication); Beverly v. Reinert, 606 N.E.2d 621, 626 (Ill. App. Ct. 1992) (affirming dismissal of claim for disclosure of private facts because of possibility that fax message could be intercepted by third parties; although Kentucky law permits disclosure claim to be based on disclosure to one significant person, mere possibility of interception of fax message by unidentified third parties insufficient to state claim).

[42] *Compare* Diamond Shamrock Ref. & Mktg. Co. v. Mendez, 844 S.W.2d 198, 199 (Tex. 1992) (false-light invasion of privacy requires showing of actual malice; reversing $460,000 and quoting jury instruction that did not mention malice) *and* Hope v. Hearst Corp., 770 P.2d 203, 207 (Wash. Ct. App. 1989) (false-light liability to public official without showing of actual malice would violate First Amendment) *with* Wood v. Hustler Magazine, Inc., 736 F.2d 1084, 1092 (5th Cir. 1984) (Texas application of negligence standard would be constitutional) *and* Dresbach v. Doubleday & Co., 518 F. Supp. 1285, 1288 (D.D.C. 1981) (D.C.'s negligence standard for defamation actions should be applied to false-light actions) *and* Crump v. Beckley Newspapers, Inc., 320 S.E.2d 70, 88 (W. Va. 1984) (private individual need show only negligence to recover on false-light theory). Recklessness may suffice. *See also* Colbert v. World Publishing Co., 747 P.2d 286, 289–90 (Okla. 1987) (reversing judgment for plaintiff whose photograph was printed and identified with murderer; negligence not sufficient for false-light liability; knowing or reckless disregard must be proven under constitutional constraints). In a number of cases, claims for false-light invasion of privacy were joined with claims for negligent infliction of emotional distress. *See* Russell v. Thomson Newspapers, Inc., 842 P.2d 896, 906 (Utah 1992) (negligence as to falsity of publication by media defendant can provide liability for infliction of emotional distress; reversing summary judgment for defendant).

Appropriation of name or likeness may be less important in the NII unless it is expanded to overlap significantly with trademark and fair competition concepts. Without expansion, this tort would produce liability in the rare situation in which a wrongdoer misappropriates and uses a digitized image of an individual for the wrongdoer's own commercial purposes.

Conceptually, liability under this tort also should be imposed if an actor takes someone's name and uses that name for commercial purposes. Such an application of the publicity tort would overlap with trademark and unfair competition concepts considered in **Chapter 10.** For example, the victim might have a well-established reputation as a consultant or commentator on computer and information network issues. The wrongdoer might use that person's name, falsely reporting that the victim has endorsed a particular product—or even that the victim authored or designed a particular product. In those circumstances, the underlying concept of this tort would seem to warrant the imposition of liability. The interests protected are similar to those involved when the actor appropriates another's trademark or business goodwill and falsely represents products as coming from the victim.[43]

There are a number of reasons why a plaintiff might prefer to litigate under one of these common-law concepts rather than under a related statutory concept.[44] These are intentional torts and therefore compensatory damages for mental suffering and punitive damages usually are available. Damages under data privacy and eavesdropping statutes may be more limited, but even if the statute does not foreclose these traditional tort damages, it is always conceivable that a court applying the statute in a case of first impression will limit the kinds of damages available.

Apart from damages differences between the common-law theories and statutory theories, the common-law categories also might cover situations that are outside the scope of a particular statute. For example, ECPA exempts most internal electronic mail systems, but such mail systems are covered by the

---

[43] *See generally* Candebat v. Flanagan, 487 So. 2d 207, 210 (Miss. 1986) (appropriation involves a kind of trademark in likeness; reversing directed verdict for defendant on claim that automobile association used plaintiff's automobile accident and name for promotional purposes); People for the Ethical Treatment of Animals v. Berosini, 867 P.2d 1121 (Nev. 1994) (reversing $4.2 million judgment for plaintiff; distinguishing appropriation tort, which involves the unwanted and unpermitted use of the name or likeness of an ordinary person for advertising or other commercial purposes, and right-of-publicity tort, which involves appropriation of celebrity's identity for commercial purposes; analogizing right of publicity to "unfair competition"); Maheu v. CBS, Inc., 247 Cal. Rptr. 304, 310 (Ct. App. 1988) (comparing appropriation tort to unfair competition in analyzing copyright preemption); Lugosi v. Universal Pictures, 25 Cal. 3d 813, 603 P.2d 425, 427 (Cal. 1979) (unfair-competition claim related to appropriation of movie actor's name or likeness).

[44] *But see* Fowler v. Southern Bell Tel. & Tel. Co., 343 F.2d 150, 156 (5th Cir. 1965) (allegation of telephone wiretap stated common-law invasion of privacy claim, but federal officers acting within their authority would have an absolute privilege against liability; remanding because of failure sufficiently to establish facts of authority of federal officers).

intrusion tort. Similarly, there might be circumstances not covered by a particular data-accuracy statute that nevertheless would be covered by the false-light tort theory.

One of the major uncertainties with respect to all four invasion-of-privacy torts is whether corporations enjoy protectible privacy interests.[45] The Fourth Amendment cases suggest that corporations and other business entities have only limited privacy interests recognized by the Fourth Amendment. It is not, of course, necessarily true that the common-law privacy torts would be interpreted like the Fourth Amendment, but the Fourth Amendment cases surely would be used by a defendant claiming that privacy tort protection is available only to individuals.

§ 3.6   Comparison of Federal Privacy Statutes

Federal privacy statutes are summarized in **Table 3–1** according to the variables they address.

§ 3.7   Electronic Communications Privacy Act: Background and Structure

The Electronic Communications Privacy Act (ECPA) codifies warrant requirements for the interception of electronic communications and also creates privacy protections for stored electronic messages. The provisions of ECPA authorizing access, use, and disclosure of covered communications by government officials pursuant to judicial process and otherwise are considered in **Chapter 13.** This chapter considers only the duties imposed, rights granted, and privileges recognized with respect to conduits and custodians of information.

Title I of ECPA[46] covers acquisition and disclosure of communications streams.[47] Title II[48] covers acquisition and disclosure of stored information. Both

---

[45] *Compare* Fibreboard Corp. v. Hartford Accident & Indem. Co., 20 Cal. Rptr. 2d 376, 391 (Ct. App. 1993) (citing Restatement (Second) of Torts § 652I in support of proposition that corporations and partnerships have no protectible interest in privacy) *and* N.O.C., Inc. v. Schaefer, 484 A.2d 729, 730 (N.J. Super. Ct. 1984) (following Restatement and denying invasion of privacy cause of action to corporation except for appropriation claim) *and* Wadman v. State, 510 N.W.2d 426 (Neb. Ct. App. 1993) (quoting Nebraska Rev. Stat. § 20-204, which protects only natural persons against false-light invasion of privacy).

[46] Title I is codified at 18 U.S.C. §§ 2510–2521.

[47] *See* United States v. Meriwether, 917 F.2d 955, 960 (6th Cir. 1990) (acquiring telephone number from digital pager did not constitute interception within Title I of ECPA because no use of separate device and because transmission over this system had ceased and number was stored).

[48] Title II is codified at 18 U.S.C. §§ 2701–2710.

Title I and Title II regulate both voice and "electronic communications."[49] Title III[50] covers acquisition and disclosure of transactional information.[51] Subsequent amendments add protection for videotape rental records[52] and regulate transponders (mobile tracking devices).[53]

ECPA, enacted in 1986, was built on the foundation laid by Title III of the Omnibus Crime Control and Safe Streets Act of 1968.[54] Title III responded to *Katz v. United States*[55] and *Berger v. New York*[56] by authorizing government eavesdropping pursuant to court order. It prohibited unauthorized interceptions, but covered only aural interception of communications that can be overheard or understood by the human ear,[57] and applied only to interceptions of communications sent via common carriers.[58] Title III was held constitutional under *Berger* soon after its enactment.[59]

ECPA was intended to expand coverage of the basic concept of Title III to electronic mail operations, computer-to-computer data transmissions, cellular and cordless telephones, paging devices, video conferencing, communications carried by microwave or fiber optics, and digitized voice or video. It also was intended to extend coverage to private networks and thus not limit the protections to common carriage.[60] ECPA also addresses unauthorized interception of

---

[49] Here is how the Senate Report explains the coverage of the phrase "electronic communication":

> As a general rule, a communication is an electronic communication protected by the federal wiretap law if it is not carried by sound waves and cannot fairly be characterized as containing the human voice. Communications consisting solely of data, for example, and all communications transmitted only by radio are electronic communications. This term also includes electronic mail, digitized transmissions, and video teleconferences. Although radio communications are within the scope of the act, the provisions of the Electronic Communications Privacy Act directed specifically to radio do not affect the applicability of § 705 of the Communications Act of 1934, as amended, to actions by members of the public.

S. Rep. No. 541, 99th Cong., 2d Sess. (1986), *reprinted in* 1986 U.S.C.C.A.N. 3555 [hereinafter Senate Report].

[50] Title III is codified at 18 U.S.C. §§ 3121–3126.

[51] Title I, 18 U.S.C. § 2510(8), defines *contents* to exclude the identity of the parties or the existence of the communications, thus distinguishing between transactional records about a communication from the substance, purport, or meaning of the communication itself.

[52] 18 U.S.C. § 2710.

[53] *Id.* § 3117.

[54] Pub. L. No. 90-351, 82 Stat. 213 (June 19, 1968).

[55] 389 U.S. 347 (1967) (Fourth Amendment covers interception of telephone conversations by government).

[56] 388 U.S. 41 (1967) (Fourth Amendment covers electronic eavesdropping on oral conversations).

[57] Senate Report (citing United States v. New York Tel. Co., 434 U.S. 159, 167, 98 S. Ct. 364 (1977)).

[58] Senate Report at 2.

[59] *See* United States v. Cafero, 473 F.2d 489, 501 & n.9 (3d Cir. 1973) (rejecting arguments that Title III failed to satisfy the requirements of *Berger* and citing cases from other circuits).

[60] Senate Report at 3.

Table 3–1

Federal Privacy Statutes

Source of Duty	Privacy Act	Fair Credit Reporting Act	Right to Financial Privacy Act	Computer Fraud and Abuse Act	ECPA
subject matter	records about individuals		financial records	no limitation	no limitation
actors with duties	federal agencies	credit reporting entities	banks and credit card companies	anyone	providers and potential interceptors
means of interception	no limitation	no limitation	no limitation	electronic access	electronic access
the type of information obtained (whether content or transaction)	content	content	content	both	different duties depending on whether content or transaction
whether the information comes from a stream or from storage	no distinction	no distinction	no distinction	no distinction??	Title I—streams; Title II—storage
duty to obtain consent to acquire or maintain data	no	no	no	no	no

Source of Duty	Privacy Act	Fair Credit Reporting Act	Right to Financial Privacy Act	Computer Fraud and Abuse Act	ECPA
data quality duty, including a duty not to engage in negligent processing of data	yes	yes			
advance notice of intent to collect and maintain data on an individual	no, but encouraged to acquire from subject	only investigations	subject provides		
duty to disclose data to the subject upon request	yes	yes	no		
duty to notify subjects of adverse decisions based on data		yes	no		
duty to correct inaccurate data	yes	yes	no		
duty to maintain reasonable security	yes				yes
duty to notify the data authority of certain acts	no	no	no	no	no
duty not to disclose	yes				
duty to notify subjects of disclosure to third parties		yes	yes		yes

satellite transmissions. That material is addressed in **Chapter 10** dealing with intellectual property.

The legislative history emphasizes that a transaction may be partly an electronic communication and partly a wire or aural communication. For example, a telephone call involving some voice communication and some data communication over the same circuit would be an electronic communication for the data portion, and a wire communication for the voice portion.[61] Also, if someone transmits a closed-circuit television picture of a meeting using wires, microwaves, or another method of transmission, the transmission itself would be an electronic communication.

> By contrast, if law enforcement officials were to install their own camera and create their own closed circuit television picture of a meeting, the capturing of the video images would not be an interception under the statute because there would be no interception of the contents of an electronic communication. Intercepting the audio portion of the meeting would be an interception of an oral communication, and the statute would apply to that portion.[62]

According to the legislative history of ECPA, paging technology may result in three different levels of protection. The Justice Department proposed that "tone only" pagers be subject to monitoring without court order because there is no expectation of privacy. Display pager information, however, is within the ambit of Title III, as are "voice pagers," which should be treated as a continuation of the original wire communication.[63]

§ 3.8   —Interception, Use, and Disclosure of Communications Streams

Title I of ECPA protects communications streams (communications while in transit), both voice and data.[64] Its coverage of wire communication is limited to aural transfers made through wire, cable, and similar transmission media maintained by persons engaged in the business of providing or operating facilities for interstate or foreign communications, and includes storage incidental to transmission.[65] Acquisition of telex communications was held not to be aural acquisition because it did not involve hearing sounds of voice.[66] Title I also protects

---

[61] Senate Report at 11–12, 16.

[62] *Id.* at 16.

[63] Report of the Committee of the Judiciary on the Electronic Communications Privacy Act, H.R. Rep. No. 647, 99th Cong., 2d Sess., 24–25 (1986).

[64] The things protected from various kinds of conduct under Title I are "wire, oral, or electronic communications."

[65] 18 U.S.C. § 2510(1) (defining *wire communication*). Oral is limited to oral communications other than electronic communications uttered by a person exhibiting an expectation that the communication will not be intercepted. *Id.* § 2510(2).

[66] United States v. Gregg, 829 F.2d 1430, 1433 (8th Cir. 1987) (obtaining printouts of telex communications from trash did not violate predecessor of ECPA Title I).

electronic communication. *Electronic communication* "means any transfer of signs, signals, writing, images, sounds, data, or intelligence of any nature transmitted in whole or in part by a wire, radio, electromagnetic, photo electronic or photo optical system that affects interstate or foreign commerce."[67] The distinction between wire and electronic communication is that wire communication is limited to voice (aural) and does not include transmission by microwave or other radio media.

Title I makes it a crime and a statutory tort[68] to engage in several different types of conduct. The broadest of prohibitions imposes duties on the class of "any person."[69] It prohibits interception[70] of any of the covered types of communication,[71] disclosure of intercepted communications,[72] use of an intercepted communication,[73] and intentional use of interception devices but only those related to oral communications.[74] Title I imposes a broader nondisclosure duty on a more limited class.[75] It prohibits public electronic communication services from intentionally divulging the contents of a communication to anyone other than the addressee or intended recipient.[76] Title I of ECPA thus imposes duties on third-party intruders and eavesdroppers not to intercept, and a limited

---

[67] 18 U.S.C. § 2510(12).

[68] 18 U.S.C. § 2511(1) ("shall be punished . . . or shall be subject to suit").

[69] *Id.*

[70] The prohibition of Title I is expressed in terms of "interception." *Id.* § 2511(1)(a). *Intercept* is defined to include aural and other means of acquisition to make it clear that it is illegal to intercept the nonvoice portion of communications. *See* Senate Report at 13. *See also* Forsyth v. Barr, 19 F.3d 1527, 1535 (5th Cir. 1994) (no civil liability under § 2511 for independent interception by unrelated third parties; affirming summary judgment for defendants). The plaintiffs earlier had settled with the third-party interceptors. 19 F.3d at 1541 n.29. The defendants still in the case on appeal also were not liable for disclosure accompanied with knowledge of illegal interception under §§ 2511(1)(c) and (d) because their use was permissible under ECPA, being connected with an internal law enforcement agency investigation. 19 F.3d at 1542.

[71] 18 U.S.C. § 2511(1)(a) ("intentionally intercepts, endeavors to intercept, or procures another person to intercept or endeavor to intercept, any wire, oral, or electronic communication"). In Steve Jackson Games, Inc. v. United States Secret Serv., 816 F. Supp. 432, 441–42 (W.D. Tex. 1993), the district court held that "interception" should be construed broadly to include any activity engaged in at the time of the oral communication that causes such communication to be overheard by uninvited listeners, but declined to find that the replaying of a recorded communication constitutes an interception.

[72] 18 U.S.C. § 2511(1)(c) ("intentionally discloses, or endeavors to disclose, to any other person the contents of any wire, oral or electronic communication, knowing or having reason to know that the information was obtained through the interception of a wire, oral, or electronic communication in violation of this subsection").

[73] 18 U.S.C. § 2511(1)(d) ("intentionally uses, or endeavors to use, the contents of any wire, oral, or electronic communication, knowing or having reason to know that the information was obtained through the interception of a wire, oral, or electronic communication in violation of this subsection").

[74] 18 U.S.C. § 2511(1)(b).

[75] *Id.* § 2511(3)(a) ("Person or entity providing an electronic communication service to the public").

[76] *Id.* § 2511(3)(a). *Electronic communication service* is defined as "any service which provides to users thereof the ability to send or receive wire or electronic communication." *Id.* § 2510(15).

nondisclosure duty on a more limited set of service providers—those providing an electronic communication service to the public.[77]

Title I also recognizes certain privileges. It permits system operators to intercept, disclose, and use communications in conjunction with activities that are necessary incidents "to the rendition of [the operator's] service to the protection of the rights or property of the provider of that service," with some limitations.[78] System operators also are granted a privilege to assist law enforcement authorities and others authorized under the act to intercept communications or engage in electronic surveillance.[79] Interception privileges are granted to persons acting under color of law[80] and persons engaged in authorized foreign intelligence surveillance activities.[81] Other persons party to communications or with consent of a party to communications[82] may intercept "unless such communication is intercepted for the purpose of committing a crime or a tort."[83] Anyone has the following privileges:

1. To intercept or access public communications[84]
2. To intercept wire or electronic communications to the extent necessary to identify the source of harmful interference to "any lawfully operating station or consumer electronic equipment"[85]

---

[77] This limitation on the class burdened with a nondisclosure duty leaves intact any privilege a private communication service, like an internal E-mail system, might have to disclose communications. Such a privilege would be determined by the common law of tort and contract and any state statute.

[78] 18 U.S.C. § 2511(2)(a)(i) (limiting "service observing or random monitoring" to mechanical or service quality control checks).

[79] *Id.* § 2511(2)(a)(ii).

[80] *Id.* § 2511(2)(c).

[81] *Id.* § 2511(2)(e).

[82] *See* Manufacturas Internationale, LTDA v. Manufactures Hanover Trust Co., 792 F. Supp. 180, 192 (E.D.N.Y. 1992) (turning over electronic funds transfer orders was no violation of § 2511(2)(c) or stored communication limitations because bank was party to transaction and thus could consent and also because of good-faith compliance with court order). *But see* Deal v. Spears, 980 F.2d 1153, 1156–57 (8th Cir. 1992) (consent to interception under 18 U.S.C. § 2511(2)(d) can be implied from circumstances, but mere notice that monitoring of employee use of business telephone "might" be required in the future and mere existence of extension were insufficient to support an inference of consent).

[83] 18 U.S.C. § 2511(2)(d).

[84] *Id.* § 2511(2)(g)(i) (electronic communication systems configured to be readily accessible to the general public); *id.* § 2511(2)(g)(ii) (certain public radio communications, including subcarrier and UBI communications transmitted for the general public, aeronautical marine and distress communications, amateur radio communications, and police and fire communications readily accessible to the general public). "Readily accessible to the general public" was amended by § 203 of the Digital Telephony Act of 1994 to exclude from that term an electronic communication. Communications Assistance for Law Enforcement Act, Pub. L. No. 103-414, 108 Stat. 4279 (Oct. 25, 1994) (amending 18 U.S.C. § 2511(16) to add subparagraph (f) "or an electronic communication").

[85] 18 U.S.C. § 2511(2)(g)(iv). It is not clear whether "operating station" or "consumer electronic equipment" could be construed broadly enough to permit under this paragraph interception incident to detecting intruders into electronic mail or electronic publishing systems on systems like the Internet.

3. To intercept radio communications made on the same frequency unless the intercepted communications are scrambled or encrypted[86]

4. To use pen registers or trap devices.[87]

Providers of electronic communication services may record the fact that a wire or electronic communication was initiated or completed to prevent fraudulent, unlawful, or abusive use of such service.[88] This paragraph should permit the making of log files identifying senders, addressees, time, and destination within a system for protective purposes. It does not, however, authorize disclosure of the log because it grants a privilege "to record."[89] Title I grants public communication services a privilege to disclose communication contents necessary to the rendition of the service or the protection of rights or property of the provider,[90] with the consent of either the addressee or originator,[91] to forwarders of communications,[92] or communications inadvertently obtained by the service provider and that appear to pertain to the commission of a crime if the disclosure is made to a law enforcement agency.[93]

The prohibition against interception of wire communications does not apply when one party consents to the interception unless the purpose of the consented-to interception is for the purpose of committing a criminal or tortious act in violation of the Constitution or laws of the United States or of any state. The legislative history makes it clear that the exclusion of the phrase "any other injurious act" from this section is meant to overrule *Boddie v. American Broadcasting Co.*[94] In *Boddie* a journalist who recorded the conversation was exposed to liability because his purpose was to embarrass the subject, and this, the Sixth Circuit thought, might constitute an "other injurious act."[95] The phrase tort, however, does include defamation.[96]

Interceptions occurring via a telephone extension also are not prohibited. The business extension exception shields eavesdropping effectuated only by listening on a conventional extension telephone instrument, not by affixing a tap to such an extension.[97] The consent exception is inapplicable unless employees

---

[86] *Id.* § 2511(2)(g)(v).

[87] *Id.* § 2511(2)(h)(i).

[88] *Id.* § 2511(2)(h)(ii).

[89] *Id.*

[90] *Id.* § 2511(3)(b)(i).

[91] 18 U.S.C. § 2511(3)(b)(ii).

[92] *Id.* § 2511(3)(b)(iii).

[93] *Id.* § 2511(3)(b)(iv).

[94] 731 F.2d 333 (6th Cir. 1984).

[95] Senate Report at 17.

[96] *Id.*

[97] Williams v. Poulos, 11 F.3d 271, 279–80 (1st Cir. 1993) (rejecting district court requirement that exception only shields extensions installed by a regular communication service provider, but "we are at a loss to see how . . . alligator clips attached to a microphone cable at one end" and recording device at other end could be considered to be a telephone instrument; reviewing other cases construing the phrase).

who were alleged to have consented impliedly were fully informed as to the manner in which monitoring would occur and that they themselves would be subject to monitoring.[98]

The scope of Title I is determined by the phrase "wire, oral, or electronic communication."[99] *Wire communication* is defined to include "any aural transfer made in whole or in part through the use of facilities for the transmission of communications by the aid of wire, cable, or other like connection between the point of origin and the point of reception (including the use of such connection in a switching station)."[100] Such communications are covered whenever they are "furnished or operated by any person engaged in providing or operating such facilities for the transmission of interstate or foreign communications for communications affecting interstate or foreign commerce."[101] The wire communication definition thus is not limited to communications handled by common carriers.[102] Private networks and intracompany communication systems are intended to be within its scope,[103] but not interceptions made outside the territorial United States.[104] The definition includes electronic storage of such communications,[105] so if an aural transfer were stored in a buffer incident to the communication system, access to the buffer would be covered. In particular, voice mail is covered.[106] Only human voice communications are covered, but conversion of the analog voice signal to digital form does not take it outside the scope of Title I.[107]

Some voice communications are excluded, however. Cordless telephone communications expressly are excluded from the definition.[108] Legislative history

---

[98] *Id.* at 281–82 (insufficient evidence of detailed disclosure of possible monitoring to justify application of consent exception; telephone monitor of officer in corporation).

[99] 18 U.S.C. § 2510(1)(a) (1992). Oral communication is defined circularly but includes only those oral communications "uttered by a person exhibiting an expectation that such communication is not subject to interception under circumstances justifying such expectation." *Id.* § 2510(2). Thus, the oral communication definition is more limited than wire communication and includes both the subjective and reasonableness prongs of *Katz*. This definition excludes radio communications, under 18 U.S.C. § 2510(2) "but such term does not include any electronic communication." *See also* Senate Report at 12 (oral communication is one carried by sound waves, not by an electronic medium).

[100] 18 U.S.C. § 2510(1). The definition of aural transfer in § 2510(18) does not include computer-generated or other artificial voices, but they are electronic communications. Senate Report at 16.

[101] 18 U.S.C. § 2510(1).

[102] Senate Report at 12 (also making it clear that the definition extends to cellular communications). Cellular communications are covered because they necessarily involve the use of wire cable or other like connection at switching stations.

[103] *Id.*

[104] *Id.*

[105] 18 U.S.C. § 2510(1).

[106] Senate Report at 12.

[107] *Id.*

[108] 18 U.S.C. § 2510(1).

excludes communications when wire is used only in terminal equipment at either end of the conversation. Thus, wire communication does not include communications amplified by means of electronic equipment, nor does it include oral communications that are being recorded merely because the recorder contains wires.[109]

Title I at 18 U.S.C. § 2510(16) defines radio communications that are not protected from interception. It excludes from the definition—and thus leaves protected from interception—scrambled or encrypted communications, communications transmitted using modulation techniques withheld from the general public in order to protect the privacy of the communications, communications carried on subcarriers, common carrier transmissions, and broadcast auxiliary services.[110] The legislative history says that conversion of form, for example, from analog to digital, does not provide encryption, and neither does the use of a word code "no matter how sophisticated."[111] The modulation technique exception refers to spread spectrum radio communications.[112] The common carrier exception covers alphanumeric paging signals, but not tone-only paging systems.[113] The exclusion referring to subparts of the FCC rules excludes satellite communications, auxiliary broadcast services, and private microwave services, but not two-way voice radio communications made on frequencies shared with services outside 47 C.F.R. part 74.[114]

Under a Seventh Circuit opinion written by Judge Posner,[115] Title I does not cover video surveillance because such surveillance is not aimed at intercepting communication. There is no interception under the statute because video surveillance is not aural, and video cameras do not qualify as a surveillance device under the statute.[116] The court contrasted the Foreign Intelligence Surveillance Act, which it found to cover video monitoring.[117] Nevertheless, the court found authority to issue a warrant for video surveillance under the general search warrant authority in the Federal Rules of Criminal Procedure[118] and in the inherent power of a court to issue warrants.[119] It rejected the defendant's arguments that video surveillance per se violates the Fourth Amendment and held that a video warrant that satisfies the basic requirements of ECPA Title I

---

[109] Senate Report at 12.

[110] *See* 47 C.F.R. pt. 73 (1994) (FCC rules defining broadcast services); *id.* pt. 94 (FCC rules defining microwave common carrier communications).

[111] Senate Report at 15.

[112] *Id.*

[113] *Id.*

[114] *Id.*

[115] United States v. Torres, 751 F.2d 875 (7th Cir. 1984) (reversing suppression of videotapes of Puerto Rican terrorist bomb factory).

[116] *Id.* at 880.

[117] *Id.* at 881. The Foreign Intelligence Surveillance Act is codified at 50 U.S.C. § 1801(f)(4).

[118] Fed. R. Crim. P. 41. *See* United States v. Torres, 751 F.2d 875, 877–78 (7th Cir. 1984).

[119] 751 F.2d at 878–80.

also satisfies the Fourth Amendment.[120] Conversely, a video warrant failing to satisfy the requirements of ECPA Title I would not satisfy the Fourth Amendment.[121]

§ 3.9 —Interception Devices

Title I of ECPA prevents the manufacture, distribution, possession, and advertising of devices designed to be "primarily useful for the purpose of the surreptitious interception of wire, oral, or electronic communications."[122] The use of the term "device" may confine it to hardware, but it is conceivable that a computer program written to intercept data communications would be within the scope of this section.

Pen registers and trap and trace devices are expressly excluded from regulation under Title I of ECPA[123] and instead are covered by Title III.[124] In the 1970s, large numbers of telephone toll record subpoenas were issued.[125] Significantly for new types of NII providers:

> it shall not be unlawful, for a provider of electronic communication service to record the fact that a wire or electronic communication was initiated or completed in order to protect such provider, another provider furnishing service toward the completion of the wire or electronic communication, or a user of that service, from fraudulent, unlawful or abusive use of such service.[126]

Title I at 18 U.S.C. § 2511(2)(g)(iii) eliminates the overlap between ECPA and the Communications Act cable piracy provisions. Conduct that is prohibited by section 633 of the Communications Act[127] or permitted by section 705(b) of the Communications Act[128] is not also a violation of ECPA.

---

[120] *Id.* at 884–85.

[121] *Id.* at 885.

[122] 18 U.S.C. § 2512.

[123] Ch. 119 of 18 U.S.C.

[124] Ch. 206 of 18 U.S.C.

[125] *See* Reporters Comm. for Freedom of the Press v. American Tel. & Tel. Co., 593 F.2d 1030, 1039 & n.20 (D.C. Cir. 1978) (100,000 to 150,000 toll record subpoenas issued during four-year period beginning Mar. 1974).

[126] 18 U.S.C. § 2511(2)(h)(ii).

[127] 18 U.S.C. § 2511(2)(g)(iii)(I) (referring to § 633 of the Communications Act, 47 U.S.C. § 553 (1988) (unauthorized reception of cable television signals)).

[128] 18 U.S.C. § 2511(2)(g)(iii)(II) (referring to § 705(b) of the Communications Act, 47 U.S.C. § 605(b) (exceptions to general prohibition on divulging contents of interstate wire and radio communications)).

§ 3.10   —Stored Communications

Title II of ECPA[129] protects "stored wire and electronic communications and transactional records."[130] Title I at 18 U.S.C. § 2510(17) contains a definition of *electronic storage* that includes random access memory of a computer, magnetic tapes, disks, other magnetic media, and optical media.[131] Title II's prohibitions include unlawful access[132] and certain disclosures of contents.[133] The unlawful access prohibition, "to engage in unauthorized access[134] to a "facility through which an electronic communication service is provided" and thereby to obtain access or to prevent access to a wire or electronic communication while it is being stored in that facility,"[135] involves a *means element* and a *result element*. The *means element* is intentional access without authorization or in excess of an authorization of "a facility through which an electronic communication service is provided."[136] Title I at 18 U.S.C. § 2510(15) defines electronic communication service so as to include existing telephone companies, electronic mail companies, and remote computing services.[137] The *result element* is "to obtain access, alter, or prevent authorized access to a wire or electronic communication while it is in electronic storage."[138] The unlawful access prohibition extends only to third parties; it does not apply to the service provider or to a user of the service with respect to a communication from or to the user.[139] The third-party

---

[129] Beyond extending the wiretap protection to keep pace with technology, ECPA also was intended to protect information stored and processed electronically by third parties. In this respect, it was meant to repudiate the principle of United States v. Miller, 425 U.S. 435 (1976), declining to apply the Fourth Amendment to records kept by third parties. Senate Report at 3.

[130] Codified at 18 U.S.C. §§ 2701–2710. A separate title addresses pen registers and tracing technologies, which are among the means used to create transactional records.

[131] Storage includes any temporary, intermediate storage of a wire or electronic communication incidental to the electronic transmission thereof. 18 U.S.C. § 2510(17)(A).

[132] *Id.* § 2701.

[133] *Id.* § 2702.

[134] Unauthorized access includes intentionally exceeding an authorization. 18 U.S.C. § 2701(a)(2). *See also* American Computer Trust Leasing v. Jack Farrell Implement Co., 763 F. Supp. 1473, 1494–95 (D. Minn. 1991) (counterclaims for ECPA violations against computer leasing company that exercised authorized access to computer data were not meritorious because access was consented to under computer leasing contract).

[135] 18 U.S.C. § 2701.

[136] *Id.* § 2701(a)(1) (intentional access without authorization"); *id.* § 2701(a)(2) ("intentionally exceeds an authorization to access").

[137] " '[E]lectronic communication service' means any service which provides to users thereof the ability to send or receive wire or electronic communications." *See* Senate Report at 14.

[138] 18 U.S.C. § 2701(a).

[139] *Id.* § 2701(c).

database and computer processing protections were modeled on the Right to Financial Privacy Act.[140]

In addition, public electronic communications services and providers of remote public computing services may not divulge the contents of stored communications received electronically from their subscribers or customers when the service provided is merely a storage or computer processing service.[141] Exceptions are provided for disclosure to addressees or intended recipients, to forwarding facilities, and "as may be necessarily incident to the rendition of the service or to the protection of the rights or property of the provider."[142]

Because the nondisclosure duties of Title II at 18 U.S.C. § 2702 are imposed only on providers of electronic communication service and remote computing services "to the public,"[143] they do not prohibit disclosure by operators of private communications or computing services, nor do they prohibit disclosure of messages and files from purely internal communication systems.[144] The legislative history says that § 2701 does not make it a crime to access electronic bulletin boards because they are readily accessible; therefore, access by members of the public is authorized. On the other hand, intentionally exceeding an authorization to access even an electronic bulletin board is prohibited, as is accessing areas not intended to be open to the particular actor.[145]

Title II of ECPA at 18 U.S.C. § 2702 covers the service providers themselves. The legislative history makes it clear that disclosure of only contents is prohibited, and that reckless or negligent disclosure is not prohibited.[146] The legislative history makes it clear that when a service provider is also covered by some other federal statute regulating disclosure, like the Fair Credit Reporting Act, those statutory provisions apply as well as ECPA.[147]

---

[140] Senate Report at 3 (citing 12 U.S.C. §§ 3401–3422). The financial privacy act is considered in § **3.18** of this chapter.

[141] 18 U.S.C. § 2702.

[142] *Id.* § 2702(b).

[143] *See id.* § 2702(a)(1), (2).

[144] An open question is whether a private system becomes one provided to the public when it connects to the Internet and offers E-mail and other message exchange facilities to the Internet. It seems appropriate for a private service that provides electronic publishing, like anonymous FTP access or Gopher or World Wide Web service, to be treated as a provider of a communications or computing service to the public. On the other hand, since § 2702 grants a privilege to divulge contents to an addressee or intended recipient, all of the messages moving in the public part of such a facility would be exempt from the duty anyway. The problems arise with respect to simple E-mail exchange possibly giving rise to a duty not to disclose any E-mail messages regardless of whether they were received from outside the entity; and whether the entire communications network is burdened with the § 2702 nondisclosure duty merely because a part of it provides World Wide Web or Gopher or anonymous FTP service open to the public.

[145] Senate Report at 36.

[146] *Id.* at 36–37.

[147] *Id.* at 37.

§ 3.11   —Pen Registers and Trap and Trace Devices

Title III of ECPA prohibits use of pen registers and trap and trace devices except for operational management of communications systems[148] and pursuant to the procedures of ECPA.[149]

The definition of pen register and trap or trace device[150] may be broad enough to cover digital file access and retrieval logs such as are routinely maintained on multiuser computing systems and script files or other programs specially written to record the origin and destination of E-mail messages to or from certain subjects. Such a log or script, like a pen register, "records or decodes electronic or other impulses which identify the numbers dialed or otherwise transmitted on the telephone line."[151] Like a trap or trace device, it "captures the incoming electronic or other impulses which identify the originating number of an instrument or device from which a wire or electronic communication was transmitted."[152] On the other hand, logs and scripts or programs are not "devices," which also appears in the definition of both pen register and trap or trace device. Also, the definitions are phrased in terms of identifying "numbers." One could argue that logs and scripts identify "addresses" rather than "numbers," although a telephone number is an address and is functionally equivalent to the address of a computer network node.

§ 3.12   ECPA Hypotheticals

Suppose a law firm maintains an electronic bulletin board for the use of one of its clients. An industrial spy obtains access to the telephone number and client password for the bulletin board system by going through the client's trash. The spy accesses the bulletin board and copies certain confidential information. Does this violate ECPA? The actor is covered by Title II at 18 U.S.C. § 2701, and the actor's conduct—obtaining access to the confidential information—is also covered by § 2701. The question is whether the electronic bulletin board constitutes the kind of system protected by § 2701. Section 2701 protects an "electronic communication while it is in electronic storage in such system." *Such system* must refer to "a facility through which an electronic communication service is provided," which in turn is defined as "any service which provides to users thereof the ability to send or receive wire or electronic communications."[153] *Electronic communication* is defined as a transfer of intelligence of

---

[148] 18 U.S.C. § 3121(b).

[149] *Id.* § 3121(a).

[150] *Id.* § 2127.

[151] *Id.* § 2127(3) (defining pen register).

[152] *Id.* § 2127(4) (defining trap or trace device).

[153] 18 U.S.C. § 2510(15).

any nature transmitted in whole or in part by a wire, radio, electromagnetic, photo electronic or photo optical system that affects interstate or foreign commerce."[154] The "while it is in electronic storage" phrase in § 2701 makes it clear that the transfer component of the definition of electronic communication does not render the broad definition inapplicable to stored information. There is little question that the unauthorized access in this hypothetical would violate § 2701.

Suppose a start-up electronic publishing company maintains a World Wide Web server using software that permits certain information to be released only in exchange for electronic payment commitments. Someone circumvents the electronic payment system and obtains access to the information without paying. Does this violate ECPA? The answer almost certainly is yes because the actor is covered by § 2701; she obtained access, which is the prohibited conduct under § 2701; and the system almost certainly is an electronic communication service covered by § 2701. The only questions are whether the access was unauthorized or in excess of authorization, and whether the conduct was privileged because the material obtained was intended for the public. The answer to the first question almost certainly is yes. Access was authorized only for those making electronic payment commitments. The second question telescopes into the first because Title II of ECPA, unlike Title I, does not grant a separate privilege with respect to information intended for the public. Rather, it prohibits unauthorized access, thus impliedly recognizing a privilege for authorized access.

Suppose a graduate student assisting in the operation of a World Wide Web server writes a program that traps all of the keystrokes of a particular user. By putting together the file of trapped keystrokes with knowledge of the directory and file structure of the Web server, the graduate student can reconstruct all of the information resources viewed by the user. The graduate student tells a number of his friends about what particular users are looking at. Does this violate ECPA?

This hypothetical involves Title I rather than Title II because the information being obtained is a stream rather than a file in storage. The keystrokes surely qualify as an electronic communication because they constitute signals, data, or "intelligence of any nature." The directory and file structure may not be protected under Title II because the graduate student almost certainly would be authorized to access the directory and file structure, although he might exceed his authorization and thereby violate § 2701 by using it for a purpose not contemplated or desired by the system operator. Then, the question is whether there are two unlawful acts under Title I: the interception of the key strokes, and the disclosure of them. Prima facie, the answer is yes, and thus the only question is whether the acquisition or the disclosure is privileged.

The acquisition may be privileged under Title I at 18 U.S.C. § 2511(2)(a)(i) if the original purpose was to support system accounting and billing or system maintenance. These purposes qualify as "a necessary incident to the rendition of his service or to the protection of the rights or property of the provider of that

---

[154] *Id.* § 2510(12).

service." But even if this were the purpose of the acquisition, the disclosure exceeds any privilege and therefore is a violation. Moreover, the trapping of the keystrokes probably is "service observing or random monitoring" and the privilege for administrative interception under § 2511(2)(a)(i) expressly excludes service observing or random monitoring except for mechanical or service quality control checks. If the acquisition were to satisfy the curiosity of the graduate student, that would be unprivileged as well and thus would constitute a violation. Of course, if the purpose of the keystroke trapping and matching with directory and file structure is to detect system misuse or fraud, it is privileged under Title I at 18 U.S.C. § 2511(2)(h)(ii) because the keystroke trapping does little more than "record[ing] the fact that a wire or electronic communication was initiated or completed."

There is a remote possibility that the software routine used to trap the keystrokes constitutes the use of the pen register or trap or trace device and thus potentially falls within the prohibition of Title III of ECPA.[155] Although that section recognizes a privilege for system operators to use such devices for system administration purposes, the hypothetical involves a purpose other than the privileged purpose. The most appropriate construction of this prohibition would limit it to hardware and exclude software routines entirely. The only problem with this interpretation is that as communication systems become fully digital, the customary means for performing the function of a pen register or trap or trace device will be simply to write or activate a software routine in a switch. Thus, trapping keystrokes may be indistinguishable from the activity of trapping setup signals in a voice telephone system, and thus similarity justifies construing Title III at 18 U.S.C. § 3121 to cover keystroke trapping.

Suppose the same circumstances as in the preceding keystroke-capture hypothetical except that the keystrokes were captured for the purpose of collecting statistics about system usage, and they were disclosed in aggregate form without disclosing the identity of any particular user. Does this violate ECPA? Unlike the Privacy Act, the subject matter protected by ECPA is not limited to records disclosing the identity of individuals. Therefore, while the acquisition is privileged because it supports legitimate system administration purposes, a disclosure may not be privileged, unless one can say that the aggregation of the information caused it to change its identity and no longer to qualify as an "electronic communication" under Title I at 18 U.S.C. § 2510 (12). That is unlikely because electronic communication is defined so broadly. The only possibility is to argue that disclosure of the aggregate statistics no longer constitute "divulging the contents" of the individual session keystrokes. Only content disclosure is prohibited by Title I at 18 U.S.C. § 2511(3). There also exists a relatively weak argument that the keystrokes involved in retrieving material from a Gopher or World Wide Web server are not "contents," but they are all that is necessary to constitute a request for certain information and thus most appropriately should be treated exactly the same as an E-mail message that says, "Please send me a copy of document X."

---

[155] *Id.* § 3121 (general prohibition on pen register and trap and trace device use).

§ 3.13 —ECPA Remedies

At 18 U.S.C. § 2520, civil remedies are authorized against anyone who violates Title I of ECPA.[156] However, Title I immunizes providers of wire and electronic communication services, their officers, employees, agents, landlords, custodians, and other persons who are providers either with a court order directing assistance to law enforcement authorities by disclosing covered wire or electronic communications or by attorney general certifications under 18 U.S.C. § 2518(7).

§ 3.14 Computer Fraud and Abuse Act

The Computer Fraud and Abuse Act[157] makes it a crime to access a "federal interest computer" under certain circumstances. *Federal interest computer* is defined to include computers used by or for the benefit of financial institutions or federal government agencies and computers accessed across state lines.[158] Prohibited acts include the following:

1.   Obtaining national security information with intent or reason to believe that the information will be used to the injury of the United States or to the advantage of any foreign nation[159]

2.   Intentional access resulting in the obtaining of information contained in a financial institution's records or of a credit card issuer or of a consumer reporting agency[160]

3.   Intentional access to a government computer affecting the government's operation of such computer[161]

4.   Knowing, unauthorized access to a federal interest computer resulting in the obtaining of anything of value beyond the mere use of the computer, with intent to defraud[162]

5.   Alteration, damage, or destruction of information

---

[156] *See* Epps v. St. Mary's Hosp., 802 F.2d 412, 417 (11th Cir. 1986) (monitoring of emergency dispatch center employee telephone call criticizing supervisors, which monitoring occurred on regular dispatched terminal recording equipment fell within business extension exception to Title I of ECPA and involved ordinary course of business because call was not personal); Dunn v. Blue Ridge Tel. Co., 868 F.2d 1578, 1582–83 (11th Cir. 1989) (affirming liquidated damages of $1,000 and punitive damages of $50,000 for telephone company wiretaps on business telephones under § 2520).

[157] 18 U.S.C. § 1030 (1988).

[158] *Id.* § 1030(e)(2).

[159] *Id.* § 1030(a)(1).

[160] *Id.* § 1030(a)(2).

[161] *Id.* § 1030(a)(3).

[162] *Id.* § 1030(a)(4).

6.   Intentional access to a federal interest computer and prevention of authorized use of any information or computer services when the loss amounts
to more than $1,000 in a one-year period, or involves medical treatment

7.   Traffic in passwords.[163]

Attempts also are punishable.[164]

In a case arising out of the implantation of a "worm" into the Internet, the
Second Circuit determined, first, that using electronic mail access to implant the
worm exceeded the implied authorization represented by E-mail access, and
thus implicated the unauthorized access element of the statute.[165] In the same
case, the court also decided that the reduced performance caused by the worm
prevented authorized access to the extent required by the $1,000 damage
minimum and that the government need not prove intent to cause that loss.[166]

One of the problems with the statute is that the term *computer* is defined
extremely broadly:

> an electronic, magnetic, optical, electro chemical, or other high speed data process-
> ing device performing logical, arithmetic, or storage functions, and includes any
> data storage facility or communications facility directly related to or operating in
> conjunction with such device but such term does not include an automated type-
> writer or typesetter, a portable hand held calculator, or other similar device.[167]

Computer has even been defined as microwave ovens with microprocessors and
advanced telephone systems.[168]

§ 3.15   State Data Protection Laws

Most states have information practices statutes covering essentially the same
subject matter as the Uniform Information Practices Code.[169] Such statutes

---

[163] 18 U.S.C. § 1030(a)(5), (6).

[164] *Id.* § 1030(b).

[165] United States v. Morris, 928 F.2d 504, 509 (2d Cir. 1991).

[166] *Id.* at 506–07.

[167] 18 U.S.C. § 1030(e)(1).

[168] Presentation by Scott Charney, Chief, Computer Crime Unit, Criminal Division, United States
Department of Justice, & Hal Hendershot, Supervisory Special Agent, Economic Crime Unit,
Federal Bureau of Investigation, before Council of A.B.A. Section on Administrative Law
and Regulatory Practice, in Kansas City, Mo. (Feb. 5, 1994).

[169] Unif. Information Practices Code, 13 U.L.A. 277 (1986). *See also* Cal. Penal Code § 502
(West) (making it a crime knowingly to access and without permission to alter, damage,
delete, destroy, or otherwise use any data, computer, computer system, or computer network
in order to either devise or execute any scheme or artifice to defraud, deceive or distort, or
wrongfully control or obtain money, property or data; or knowingly to access and without
permission to take, copy, or use any data; or knowingly and without permission to use
computer services; or knowingly to add damage, delete, or destroy data, or disrupt the
operation of computer services).

establish a general policy in favor of public access to governmental records, while limiting disclosure of records containing private information about individuals. Thus, they cover the same territory as the Federal Freedom of Information Act (FOIA) and the federal Privacy Act. The basic disclosure obligation is expressed in section 2-102 of the Uniform Act: "Each agency upon request by any person shall make government records available for inspection and copying during regular business hours."[170] Like the FOIA, the act contains a number of exceptions.[171] The privacy exception is expressed as follows: "An agency may not disclose or authorize the disclosure of an individually identifiable record to any person other than the individual to whom the record pertains," subject to exceptions.[172] The commentary notes that this establishes a statutory framework similar to the federal Privacy Act.[173]

Other states have statutes similar to ECPA.[174] Such statutes prohibit disclosure by persons providing electronic communication services, with certain exceptions,[175] and also prohibit unauthorized access similar to the federal Computer Fraud and Abuse Act. For example, *Commonwealth v. Gerulis*,[176] held that breaking into a voice mail message system to obtain a credit card number was illegal because the voice mailbox systems were computers and the defendant acted with intent to interrupt the normal functioning of the systems. **Table 3–2** summarizes state statutes relating to unauthorized access to computer systems and information in transit or stored therein.[177]

---

[170] 13 U.L.A. at 277.

[171] Unif. Info. Practices Act § 2-103, 13 U.L.A. at 289.

[172] Unif. Info. Practices Act § 3-101, 13 U.L.A. at 295.

[173] Unif. Info. Practices Act § 3-101 cmt. (also drawing analogy to Minn. Stat. § 15-162).

[174] *See, e.g.,* 18 Pa. Cons. Stat. Ann. § 5741 (making it a criminal offense "to obtain, alter or prevent authorized access to a wire or electronic communication while it is in electronic storage by intentionally accessing without authorization a facility through which electronic communication services provided; or exceeding the scope of one's authorization to access the facility"). *See also* Md. Code Ann., Cts. & Jud. Proc. §§ 10-4A-01 to -08 (1993) (access to stored communications regulated similarly to the ECPA); Cal. Penal Code § 629 (West 1994) (procedure for orders to intercept wire communications); Colo. Rev. Stat. Ann. § 16-15-102 (West 1994) (ex parte orders for interception of wire, oral, or electronic communication; similar to ECPA Title 1); N.Y. Crim. Proc. Law art. 700 (McKinney 1988 & 1994 Supp.) (based on ECPA). Section 700.10 explicitly authorizes orders for video surveillance.

[175] See 18 Pa. Cons. Stat. Ann. § 5742.

[176] 616 A.2d 686 (Pa. Super. Ct. 1992) (affirming conviction for unlawful use of computer under 18 Pa. Cons. Stat. Ann. § 3933, but reversing conviction for theft of services under 18 Pa. Cons. Stat. Ann. § 3926 because voice mail services were not sold).

[177] Thomas Thistle, Villanova Law School Class of 1996, law clerk to the author, researched statutes used in the table.

Table 3–2

State Statutes Relating to Unauthorized Access to Computer Systems

State	Statute	Brief Description
Alaska	Alaska Stat. § 11.46.484	Unauthorized access is criminal mischief in third degree
Arizona	Ariz. Rev. Stat. Ann. § 41-1750	Unauthorized access to criminal record history
California	Cal. Penal Code § 502 (West)	Unauthorized access to computer system—variety of fines depending on seriousness
California	Cal. Gov't Code § 11771	Chief executive officer of each state agency responsible for policy regarding unauthorized access
Connecticut	Conn. Gen. Stat. § 53a-251	Defines computer crimes of unauthorized access, theft of computer services, interruption of computer services, misuse of computer system information, destruction of computer equipment
Connecticut	Conn. Gen. Stat. § 54-142i	Unauthorized access to criminal history records
Delaware	Del. Code Ann. tit. 11, § 933	Theft of computer services with intent to obtain unauthorized computer services
Delaware	Del. Code Ann. tit. 11, § 932	Unauthorized access to computer system
Delaware	Del. Code Ann. tit. 11, § 8606	Unauthorized access to criminal history records
Delaware	Del. Code Ann. tit. 11, § 935	Without authorization, copies data, damages information, interrupts data, uses or discloses such data—misuse of computer system information
Hawaii	Haw. Rev. Stat. §§ 708-890 to 708-896	Unauthorized computer use—class C felony

Table 3–2
(continued)

State	Statute	Brief Description
Iowa	Iowa Code § 716A.1	Definitions
Iowa	Iowa Code § 716A.2	Unauthorized access to computer system
Maine	Me. Rev. Stat. Ann. tit. 17, § 431 (West)	Definitions of computer crimes
Maryland	Maryland Ann. Code of 1957 art. 27, § 146	Without authorization, accesses computer system to cause malfunction, damage—identifies access codes and publishes them
Minnesota	Minn. Stat. § 609.891	Risk of death—felony—up to 10 years imprisonment or up to $20,000 fine; second grade misdemeanor—same; public health risk—misdemeanor—up to one-year imprisonment or up to $3,000 fine; misdemeanor—up to 90 days imprisonment or up to $700 fine
Minnesota	Minn. Stat. § 609.87	Definitions
Minnesota	Minn. Stat. § 270B.18	Unauthorized computer data access is a gross misdemeanor
Nebraska	Neb. Rev. Stat. § 28-1343.01	Risk of death—class IV felony; risk to public health—class I misdemeanor; compromise security data—class II misdemeanor
Nebraska	Neb. Rev. Stat. § 29-3519	Unauthorized access to criminal history record
Nebraska	Neb. Rev. Stat. § 28-1343	Definitions

Table 3–2

(continued)

State	Statute	Brief Description
Nebraska	Neb. Rev. Stat. § 29-3518	Limiting access to criminal history information
Nevada	Nev. Rev. Stat. § 242.111	Unauthorized access for the information systems of executive branch of government
New Hampshire	N.H. Rev. Stat. Ann. § 638:17	Computer crime of unauthorized access, theft of computer services, interruption of computer services, misuse of computer system information
New Jersey	N.J. Stat. Ann. § 2A:38A-3 (West)	Provides for compensatory and punitive damages if person or business damaged
New Mexico	N.M. Stat. Ann. § 30-45-5 (Michie)	Unauthorized computer system use; variety of fines depending on severity
New Mexico	N.M. Stat. Ann. § 15-1-9 (Michie)	Unauthorized access to computer database that is public record is a misdemeanor, imprisonment up to 1 year or up to $5,000 fine, and not employed by state for 5 years after conviction
New York	N.Y. Penal Law § 156.05 (McKinney)	Unauthorized use if knowingly used with coding system; class A misdemeanor
Ohio	Ohio Rev. Code Ann. § 2913.04 (Anderson)	If unauthorized access to defraud and loss is greater than $100,000, felony of second degree; if not, and previously convicted of theft, felony of third degree; if neither of two above, felony of fourth degree
Oklahoma	Okla. Stat. Ann. tit. 21, § 1958 (West)	Use of computer system data for violation of any statute will result in fine up to $5,000 or five years imprisonment

Table 3–2

(continued)

State	Statute	Brief Description
Oklahoma	Okla. Stat. Ann. tit. 21, § 1953 (West)	Unauthorized access of computer system will be felony or misdemeanor depending on severity of act
South Carolina	S.C. Code Ann. § 16-16-20 (Law. Co-op.)	Unauthorized access guilty of computer crime in first degree—if loss is greater than $25,000, crime is a felony and fine is up to $125,000 or up to 10 years; second degree—if loss is less than $25,000 but more than $1,000; other acts can cause second degree crime, it is a misdemeanor and fined up to $50,000 or up to three years
Utah	Utah Code Ann. § 53-5-214 (1953)	Unauthorized access to criminal history records
West Virginia	W. Va. Code § 61-3C-5	Unauthorized access to computer system is misdemeanor—will be fined not less than $200 or more than $1,000 or one-year imprisonment
Wisconsin	Wis. Stat. § 943.70	Modifies, destroys, accesses, takes possession, copies, or discloses data without authorization

§ 3.16   Privacy Act

The federal Privacy Act covers federal agency records. The scope of the Privacy Act is determined in large part by its definition of *record:*

> any item, collection, or grouping of information about an individual that is maintained by an agency, including, but not limited to, his education, financial transactions, medical history, and criminal or employment history and that contains his name, or the identifying number, symbol, or other identifying particular assigned to the individual, such as finger or voice print or a photograph.[178]

---

[178] 5 U.S.C. § 552a(a)(4).

Because records are covered only if they contain a specific identifying element, a mere aggregation of information about transactions or environmental conditions is not covered even though it may substantially identify an individual.[179]

The Privacy Act forbids disclosure of any record without the written consent of an individual to whom the record pertains[180] unless the disclosure is for the purpose that is compatible with the purpose for which the data was collected.[181] It mandates disclosure to the subject of a record upon his request.[182] It mandates an accurate accounting of all disclosures and corrections[183] and requires the agency to accept "statements of disagreement" from subjects challenging a refusal to amend a record to correct an alleged inaccuracy.[184] The statute also prohibits agencies from maintaining records other than those "relevant and necessary to accomplish a purpose of the agency required to be accomplished by statute or by executive order of the president."[185] It obligates agencies to maintain records with "such accuracy, relevance, timeliness, and completeness as is reasonably necessary to assure fairness to the individual"[186] in determinations made based on the records.[187] Agencies must make reasonable efforts to notify subjects when records about them are disclosed under compulsory process.[188]

Finally, agencies must establish appropriate administrative, technical, and physical safeguards to ensure security and confidentiality and to protect records against anticipated threats to their integrity.[189] The only element from the "fair

---

[179] In theory, one could establish a record with detailed geographic information and temporal information that would identify an individual because she was the only one standing in a particular place at a particular time.

[180] 5 U.S.C. § 552a(b).

[181] Subsection (b)(3) is an exception to the general prohibition against disclosure without written permission and is linked to the definition of *routine use* in subsection (a)(7), where it is defined with respect to the purpose for which the record data was collected.

[182] 5 U.S.C. § 552a(d).

[183] *Id.* § 552a(c). The accounting must be made available to subjects upon their request. *Id.* § 552a(c)(3)

[184] *Id.* § 552a(d)(2)–(4).

[185] *Id.* § 552a(e)(1).

[186] *Compare* Sellers v. Bureau of Prisons, 959 F.2d 307, 312 (D.C. Cir. 1992) (adverse determinations supported by unchecked information result in civil liability if agency could have verified accuracy; reversing district court) *with* Johnston v. Horne, 875 F.2d 1415, 1422 (9th Cir. 1989) (inaccurate background briefing supporting involuntary retirement was grossly negligent but did not violate Privacy Act, which imposes liability only for willful or intentional conduct).

[187] 5 U.S.C. § 552a(e)(5).

[188] *Id.* § 552a(e)(8).

[189] *Id.* § 552a(e)(10).

information practices" list summarized in § **3.4** missing from this array is a requirement of routine notification of subjects upon every disclosure (recalling that disclosures under the statute are defined as not pertaining to the original purpose for which the information was collected). There is some dispute as to whether the Privacy Act provides the exclusive remedies for disclosure of false information.[190]

In *Albright v. United States*,[191] the court of appeals found that a videotape made of an employee protest of personnel changes constituted a Privacy Act record even though it was not indexed and made a part of a system of records. The court concluded that the Act's explicit prohibition against making or maintaining records of individual exercises of rights guaranteed by the First Amendment[192] prohibits the collection of such a record independent of any agency's maintenance, use, or dissemination of it thereafter. Thus, to exempt such a record from coverage of the Act would negate the obvious purpose of the subsection. The legislative history reveals that the unwarranted collection of information is a distinct harm.[193] Of broader significance is the court's conclusion that a videotape is a record under the Privacy Act: "As long as the tape contains a means of identifying an individual by picture or voice, it falls within the definition of a 'record' under the Privacy Act."[194]

Federal contractors as well as federal agencies may be subject to obligations imposed by the Privacy Act. The Act provides that, "when an agency provides by contract for the operation by or on behalf of the agency of a system of records to accomplish an agency function, the agency shall, consistent with its authority, cause the requirements of this section to be applied to such system."[195] This effectively obligates the agency to impose contractual obligations on its contractors when they operate "systems of records." In addition, the same subsection continues, "for purposes of subsection (i) of this section any such contractor and any employee of such contractor, if such contract is agreed to on or after the effective date of this section, shall be considered to be an employee of an agency."[196] This directly imposes statutory obligations and affords statutory remedies with respect to contractor conduct within the scope of subsection

---

[190] *Compare* Mittleman v. United States Treasury, 773 F. Supp. 442, 452 (D.D.C. 1991) (constitutional claims precluded by Privacy Act because it provides a comprehensive scheme for protection; applying Bush v. Lucas, 462 U.S. 367, 378 (1983)) *with* Doe v. United States Civil Serv. Comm'n, 483 F. Supp. 539, 563 (S.D.N.Y. 1980) (section not intended to be exclusive remedy for claims arising out of administrative investigations because does not provide for injunctive relief).

[191] 631 F.2d 915 (D.C. Cir. 1980).

[192] 5 U.S.C. § 552(a)(e)(7).

[193] Albright v. United States, 631 F.2d 915, 919 (D.C. Cir. 1980).

[194] *Id.* at 920 (citing Save the Dolphins v. United States Dep't of Commerce, 404 F. Supp. 407, 410–11 (N.D. Cal. 1975) (motion picture film is FOIA record)).

[195] 5 U.S.C. § 552a(m)(1).

[196] *Id.*

(i). Subsection (i) imposes criminal penalties on agency employees (and by virtue of subsection (m) on contractors and their employees) who, knowing of the Privacy Act prohibitions on disclosure of specific material, nevertheless willfully disclose it to someone not entitled to receive it.[197]

An actual example of the application of this section may be helpful. The author was a member of the advisory committee for a project to disseminate SEC EDGAR[198] data on the Internet, supported by the National Science Foundation (NSF). The question arose whether it would be permissible under the Privacy Act for the grantees to use UNIX TCP/IP transaction records to generate survey forms that would be sent to persons shown by the transaction records to have accessed the Internet server sponsored by the NSF grant and whether it would be permissible to disclose publicly the transaction records. A typical transaction record shows that a particular Internet address accessed a particular file on such and such a date at such and such a time. When the Internet address is associated with a specific individual, the record containing that Internet address as a data element qualifies as a "record" under the Privacy Act. The systematic maintenance of these transaction records qualifies as a system of records.

But is the grantee a government contractor within subsection (m)? Maybe. The phrase "when an agency provides by contract for the operation . . . of a system of records" would be satisfied, but the omitted language in that quotation "by or on behalf of the agency . . . to accomplish an agency function" may not be satisfied. The agency is the NSF. The agency's function is the sponsorship of research and development. Arguably, the grantee's operation of the system of access records is too attenuated from the NSF function to fall within this limitation. Moreover, it is not clear that the grantee is operating the EDGAR data retrieval system "on behalf of" the NSF. The NSF surely would not operate an EDGAR data retrieval system on its own. The best interpretation of subsection (m) is that it is aimed at ensuring that agencies cannot evade their obligations under the Privacy Act by delegating internal agency functions to private contractors. That is not what the NSF has done when it sponsors applied research in demonstration programs, and therefore the research or demonstration grantees should not be within the ambit of subsection (m).

§ 3.17 Fair Credit Reporting Act

The Fair Credit Reporting Act (FCRA) imposes duties on *consumer reporting agencies,*—persons who regularly engage in assembling or evaluating consumer credit information for the purpose of furnishing consumer reports to third

---

[197] *Id.* § 552a(i).

[198] The Securities and Exchange Commission (SEC) Electronic Data Gathering Analysis and Retrieval (EDGAR) system receives all required corporate filings, manages them within the SEC, and disseminates them in electronic form.

parties.[199] FTC Policy Guidance on the FCRA says that commercial credit reports are not covered,[200] nor are insurance claims reports prepared by claims investigation services.[201] Although FCRA is not intended to address business credit data and reporting, it can be implicated when credit reports are prepared that indirectly relate to a business purpose.[202]

FCRA addresses data quality in several ways. It limits the persons to whom information may be disclosed by consumer reporting agencies,[203] although a catchall in the limitation allows disclosure "to a person which [the reporting agency] has reason to believe - (E) otherwise has a legitimate business need for the information in connection with a business transaction involving the consumer."[204] The catchall has been limited to some extent in the case law, however.[205] Also, certain types of information may not be included in a report, principally involving information more than seven to ten years old.[206] "Investigative consumer reports, those involving personal interviews with persons other than creditors, may not be made unless the fact of the preparation of the report is made to the subject."[207] Quality, in the sense of data integrity and accuracy, is promoted by subjecting a credit reporting agency to civil liability unless it follows "reasonable procedures to assure maximum possible accuracy."[208]

---

[199] 15 U.S.C. § 1681a(f) (1988). *See* Hoke v. Retail Credit Corp., 521 F.2d 1079, 1084 (4th Cir. 1975) (report furnished to physician licensing agency, resulting in denial of practice privileges, constituted "consumer report" under § 1681a(d) because it would be used for "employment purposes" as defined in §§ 1681a(h) and 1681b(3)(B) and because determination of eligibility for a license brought it under § 1681b(3)(D)).

[200] 16 C.F.R. pt. 600, app. § 603.1 (1995).

[201] *Id.*

[202] *See, e.g.,* Rasor v. Retail Credit Co., 554 P.2d 1041, 1047 (Wash. 1976) (credit report prepared in connection with life insurance application which was necessary in order to obtain small business administration loan qualified as "consumer report").

[203] 15 U.S.C. § 1681b (1988 & Supp. III 1991).

[204] *Id.* § 1681b(3)(E).

[205] *Compare* Houghton v. New Jersey Mfrs.' Ins. Co., 795 F.2d 1144 (3d Cir. 1986) (legitimate business need proviso not unlimited in scope, but personal injury accident report was not "investigative consumer report") *and* Mathews v. Worthen Bank & Trust Co., 741 F.2d 217, 219 (8th Cir. 1984) (report to bank providing financing to subject of report was business report not covered by FCRA) *with* Russell v. Shelter Fin. Servs., 604 F. Supp. 201 (W.D. Mo. 1984) (report to former employer so former employer could determine if former employee had been embezzling funds was not permissible) *and* Mone v. Dranow, 945 F.2d 306, 307 (9th Cir. 1991) (report to employer to determine whether former employee could satisfy judgment in planned lawsuit against him violated FCRA).

[206] 15 U.S.C. § 1681c.

[207] *Id.* § 1681d.

[208] *Id.* § 1681e(b). *See* Koropoulos v. Credit Bureau, Inc., 734 F.2d 37, 40 (D.C. Cir. 1984) (factually correct information that nevertheless misleads readers does not satisfy requirement of FCRA); Collins v. Retail Credit Co., 410 F. Supp. 924, 931 (E.D. Mich. 1976) (allowing, but reducing, punitive damages for haphazard investigatory techniques); Millstone v. O'Hanlon Reports, Inc., 383 F. Supp. 269, 276 (E.D. Mo. 1974) (information collected from neighbors without verification, and withholding file from subject, justified mental suffering and punitive damages for willful violation of accuracy and disclosure duties), *aff'd,* 528 F.2d

FCRA imposes broad duties to disclose information to the subjects of the information. Consumer reporting agencies must disclose, upon request, the following:

1.   The nature and substance of all information in their files
2.   The sources of the information except for sources of investigative reports, unless litigation is involved
3.   Recipients of any consumer report within the preceding six months (two years in the case of employment recipients).[209]

FCRA allows subjects to challenge the accuracy of information.[210] When such a challenge is made by the subject, the consumer reporting agency must reinvestigate and record the current status of the challenged information, and the agency must delete it if it can no longer be verified or is found to be inaccurate. If the information is not deleted, the subject is entitled to file a statement of not more than 100 words setting forth the nature of the dispute, and the consumer's statement or a summary of it must be provided in any future reports.[211]

Users of credit reports must notify the subjects of such reports when they make adverse decisions based on the report. In addition, the users of the reports must, upon request, disclose any other basis for adverse credit decisions not involved in the credit reports.[212]

Compliance with FCRA is assured by a private right of action in which punitive and compensatory damages and attorneys' fees may be recovered.[213]

---

829 (8th Cir. 1976); Cahlin v. General Motors Acceptance Corp., 936 F.2d 1151, 1156 (11th Cir. 1991) (agency may escape liability if it shows that inaccurate report was prepared by following appropriate procedures; not strictly liable for inaccuracies).

[209] 15 U.S.C. § 1681g. *See* Collins v. Retail Credit Co., 410 F. Supp. 924, 931 (E.D. Mich. 1976) (allowing, but reducing, punitive damages for refusal to disclose all material elements in file, resulting in incomplete rebuttal statement).

[210] 15 U.S.C. § 1681i.

[211] *Id.* § 1681i(b) (subject's statement of dispute); *id.* § 1681i(c) communication of subject's statement in future reports). *See* Stevenson v. TRW, Inc., 987 F.2d 288, 292 (5th Cir. 1993) (reporting agency negligently failed to meet its duty of reinvestigation and deletion when disputed items remained after eight weeks). *But see* Williams v. Colonial Bank, 826 F. Supp. 415, 418 (M.D. Ala. 1993) (reporting agency had no duty to reinvestigate because of reasonable belief that challenge was frivolous).

[212] 15 U.S.C. § 1681m (1994).

[213] *Id.* § 1681n (1988) (allowing damages for willful violations). *See* Houghton v. New Jersey Mfrs.' Ins. Co., 615 F. Supp. 299, 305 (E.D. Pa. 1985) (awarding $3,500 compensatory, $3,500 punitive damages, and $7,770 in attorneys' fees against insurance company that caused investigative report to be prepared in conjunction with defense of automobile accident lawsuit; report constituted a credit report although for improper purpose); Thorton v. Equifax, Inc., 467 F. Supp. 1008, 1009 (E.D. Ark. 1979) (approving $250,000 exemplary damages award), *reversed on other grounds,* 619 F.2d 700 (8th Cir. 1980) (jury instruction erroneous on qualified privilege and on common-law standards); Rasor v. Retail Credit Co., 554 P.2d 1041, 1049 (Wash. 1976) (FCRA damages are not limited to out-of-pocket losses, but may not be presumed; there must be some proof); Jones v. Credit Bureau, 399 S.E.2d 694, 700 (W. Va. 1990) (statute allows humiliation and mental distress damages even when no out-of-pocket expenses are proven; affirming compensatory award of $4,000 and punitive award of $42,500).

When noncompliance is merely negligent rather than willful, punitive damages are not available, but attorneys' fees and compensatory damages for mental distress are available.[214] Civil actions may be brought in either state or federal court, and there is some controversy over whether actions brought in state court are removable to federal court.[215]

In addition, criminal penalties are imposed for obtaining information from credit reporting agencies under false pretenses.[216] Criminal penalties are imposed on individual employees of credit reporting agencies who willfully disclose information to persons not authorized under FCRA to receive it.[217] Supplementary enforcement powers are given to the Federal Trade Commission, which may proceed against violators of the Fair Credit Reporting Act under the Federal Trade Commission Act.[218]

State laws explicitly are preserved from preemption.[219] An intermediate court in California held that a state statute that prohibits credit reporting agencies from disclosing information about tenant involvement in tenant rights litigation violated the First Amendment.[220]

The definitions of the Fair Credit Reporting Act make it clear that credit reporting activities carried on through the NII would be fully covered by the Act. For example, *consumer report* includes any "other communication of any information [on certain subject],"[221] and the term *file* includes information recorded and retained by a reporting agency "regardless of how the information is stored."[222] Thus, both storage and disclosure in computer networks are covered.

---

[214] 15 U.S.C. § 1681o. *See* Stevenson v. TRW, Inc., 987 F.2d 288, 296–97 (5th Cir. 1993) (mental distress and humiliation damages recoverable even when fault is no greater than negligence).

[215] *Compare* Haun v. Retail Credit Co., 420 F. Supp. 859, 862 (W.D. Pa. 1976) (action brought in state court is removable) *and* Broom v. TRW Credit Data, 732 F. Supp. 66, 68 (E.D. Mich. 1990) (action brought in state court is removable) *with* Ruth v. Westinghouse Credit Co., 373 F. Supp. 468, 469 (W.D. Okla. 1974) (action brought in state court not removable).

[216] 15 U.S.C. § 1681q.

[217] *Id.* § 1681r.

[218] *Id.* § 1681s (Supp. IV 1992).

[219] *Id.* § 1681t. *See* Credit Data v. State of Ariz., 602 F.2d 195, 197 (9th Cir. 1979) (FCRA did not preempt state law); Retail Credit Co. v. Dade County, 393 F. Supp. 577, 579 (S.D. Fla. 1975) (municipal regulation also not preempted).

[220] U.D. Registry, Inc. v. California, 40 Cal. Rptr. 228 (Ct. App. 1995) (information as to which publication is prohibited was lawfully obtained through examination of court records open to the public and is truthful; under Florida Star v. BJF, 491 U.S. 524 (1989) (invalidating statute to protect the privacy of sexual offense victims), these characteristics gave credit reporting agency First Amendment right to release it).

[221] 15 U.S.C. § 1681a(d).

[222] *Id.* § 1681a(g).

§ 3.18   Financial Records Privacy Act

The Financial Records Privacy Act prohibits access to financial records by government authorities except under certain circumstances.[223] Exceptions are provided for agencies supervising banks,[224] and for the Internal Revenue Service.[225] *Financial records* are defined as information derived from "any record held by a financial institution pertaining to a customer's relationship with the financial institution."[226] Only individual customer records are covered.[227] A *financial institution* is defined to include banks, savings banks, savings and loan associations, credit unions, consumer finance institutions, and credit card issuers.[228] *Government authority* means "any agency or department of the United States, or any officer, employer agent thereof."[229]

Customers may consent to disclosure,[230] but they may not be required to do so as a condition of doing business.[231] Absent a judicial order to the contrary, a customer may obtain copies of records that the financial institution must keep of instances in which a customer's record is disclosed to a government authority.[232]

Records may be disclosed pursuant to administrative subpoenas or summons otherwise authorized by law, but only if

---

[223] 12 U.S.C. § 3402 (1988). *See* Neece v. Internal Revenue Serv., No. 88-C1320-E, 1993 WL 305963 (N.D. Okla. May 21, 1993) (on remand from court of appeals, awarding $100 statutory damages and modest compensatory damages for property damage, but denying pain and suffering and punitive damages against bank and IRS in case in which bank voluntarily disclosed financial records of tax evader).

[224] *See* Adams v. Board of Governors, 855 F.2d 1336, 1341–42 (8th Cir. 1988) (12 U.S.C. § 3412(d) permitted Federal Reserve Board of Governors to access information pertaining to purchases of stock connected with ownership of supervised banks; no subpoena necessary; no violation to transfer information between comptroller of currency and Federal Reserve Board).

[225] Raikos v. Bloomfield State Bank, 703 F. Supp. 1365, 1369–70 (S.D. Ind. 1989) (Right to Financial Privacy Act does not prevent informal access to bank records by IRS, because of exception in 12 U.S.C. § 3413(c) which permits access authorized by I.R.C. § 7602(a)).

[226] 12 U.S.C. § 3401(2).

[227] *See* Manheim BMW, Inc. v. Hamilton Bank, No. 84-2561, 1985 WL 2638 (E.D. Pa. Sept. 10, 1985) (dismissing Right to Financial Privacy Act claim because it does not protect corporations' records); Ridgley v. Merchants State Bank, 699 F. Supp. 100, 101 (N.D. Tex. 1988) (Right to Financial Privacy Act did not protect records of nonprofit political association despite arguments that it merely represented interests of individual members).

[228] 12 U.S.C. § 3401(1).

[229] *Id.* § 3401(3).

[230] Duncan v. Belcher, 813 F.2d 1335, 1338–39 (4th Cir. 1987) (reversing district court and holding that Right to Financial Privacy Act prevented Army from accessing American Express credit card records of individual covert operatives despite purported consent by the cover company employing them).

[231] 12 U.S.C. § 3401(a) (consent); *id.* § 3404(b) (no authorization as a condition of doing business).

[232] *Id.* § 3404(c).

(1) there is reason to believe that the records sought are relevant to a legitimate law enforcement inquiry;

(2) a copy of the subpoena or summons has been served upon the customer or mailed to his last known address on or before the date on which the subpoena or summons was served on the financial institution.[233]

Alternatively, records may be obtained pursuant to a search warrant under the Federal Rules of Criminal Procedure, in which case notice is given to the customer only after execution of the search warrant.[234] Notice may be delayed upon finding that there is a need for such delay in terms of protecting witnesses, protecting life or physical safety, or preventing evidence tampering or flight from prosecution.[235]

Records also may be obtained pursuant to judicial subpoenas and simple formal written request by the authority, but only when the formal written request procedure is authorized by regulations promulgated by the head of the requesting agency.[236] Disclosures must not exceed the scope of the subpoena or other formal request.[237] The statute expressly authorizes customer motions to quash or applications to enjoin disclosure of financial records.[238] Records disclosed under the statute may not be passed on to another agency absent written certification that the other agency has a legitimate law enforcement need for the records.[239] Civil penalties are provided for against an agency or department of the United

---

[233] *Id.* § 3405.

[234] *Id.* § 3406.

[235] *Id.* § 3409(a).

[236] 12 U.S.C. § 3407 (judicial subpoena); *id.* § 3408 (formal written request).

[237] Liffiton v. Keuker, 850 F.2d 73, 79 (2d Cir. 1988) (claim stated under Right to Financial Privacy Act for disclosure of records outside scope of subpoena, but no damages against individual defendants); *In re* Grand Jury Proceedings, 587 F. Supp. 1210, 1212 (E.D. Cal. 1984) (financial institution was required to respond to Grand Jury subpoena but was not required to comply with instructions in subpoena to deliver records to serving agent rather than producing them before Grand Jury and also was not bound by instruction not to inform subject of subpoenaed records; subpoena in Financial Records Privacy Act should be harmonized).

[238] 12 U.S.C. § 3410. The Right to Financial Privacy Act gives the subject standing to move to quash a subpoena directed to a bank for the subject's financial records. *In re* Grand Jury Proceedings, 587 F. Supp. 1210, 1215 (E.D. Cal. 1984) (cases to the contrary preceded enactment of Right to Financial Privacy Act); *In re* Vescovo Special Grand Jury, 473 F. Supp. 1335 (E.D. Cal. 1979) (grand jury subpoena secrecy obligation could not override disclosure obligation under Right to Financial Privacy Act); United States v. Wilson, 571 F. Supp. 1417, 1420 (S.D.N.Y. 1983) (subpoena in criminal case seeking financial records met requirements of Right to Financial Privacy Act and therefore should not be quashed).

See also In re Request for Int'l Judicial Assistance, 700 F. Supp. 723, 726 (S.D.N.Y. 1988) (propriety of Brazilian letter rogatory evaluated under Right to Financial Privacy Act).

[239] 12 U.S.C. § 3412(a).

States or financial institution violating the statute.[240] The Act does not limit ordinary civil discovery of financial records.[241]

§ 3.19   Constitutional Protection

Constitutional privacy cases are worth analyzing in some detail, not only because they are important limitations on governmental invasions of electronic privacy, but because they embrace the same analytical framework as common-law privacy cases.[242] They also articulate the analytical frameworks that have been imposed by statute to protect electronic communications more broadly then the Constitution would protect them. In particular, the analytical framework developed in the constitutional cases is now imposed by statute to protect against private invasions while the Constitution only protects against governmental invasions. Constitutional privacy cases are considered in **Chapter 6** in connection with search warrant procedures.

§ 3.20   State Statutes Limiting Insurance Information Disclosure

Insurance information privacy is of growing importance as insurers collect growing amounts of information about lifestyles and other risk factors of applicants for insurance. Increasingly such information is shared between insurers, and as the NII matures it will be easier for such sharing to occur. In analyzing state information disclosure statutes, there are several issues that must be addressed.[243] First, it is important to examine the entities that gather information as well as those that disclose information. It is also necessary to see the various kinds of information that are made available to information-gathering organizations. This analysis gives a clearer picture as to what types of information may or may not be disclosed. Finally, there are several privacy issues that emerge when structuring an information disclosure statute. These issues are used to frame the various rights and duties of the subject of the information and the custodian of the information respectively.

---

[240] *Id.* § 3417(a) (authorizing actual and punitive damages, costs, and $100 regardless of the volume of records involved).

[241] Sneirson v. Chemical Bank, 108 F.R.D. 159 (D. Del. 1985) (Right to Financial Privacy Act does not limit civil discovery under Fed. R. Civ. P.).

[242] Richard C. Turkington, *Legacy of the Warren and Brandeis Article: The Emerging Unencumbered Constitutional Right to Informational Privacy,* 10 N. Ill. U. L. Rev. 479, 490–91 (1990) (arguing that constitutional privacy and common-law privacy protection has as a core value the nature of the injury regardless of different actors).

[243] Andrew J.Vella, law clerk to the author assisted with research and drafting of this section.

Statutes in Massachusetts and Connecticut exemplify state limitations on insurance information disclosure. There are a variety of organizations enumerated in both the Connecticut and Massachusetts insurance information disclosure statutes that collect personal information. They fall into four broad categories, each having some distinguishing characteristics but performing essentially the same statutorily defined functions.

Consumer Reporting Agencies. A consumer reporting agency is defined as a person that generally prepares consumer reports[244] and furnishes them to other persons for a fee. The information used in the preparation of these reports is obtained primarily from sources other than insurance institutions.[245]

Institutional Sources. An institutional source is "any person or governmental entity that provides information about an individual to an [insurance] agent, insurance institution, or insurance support organization." However, the definition of institutional source does not extend to an insurance agent, the subject of the information, or an individual acting in a personal capacity when providing the information.[246]

Insurance Support Organizations. An insurance support organization assembles or collects "information concerning individuals for the primary purpose of providing the information to an insurance institution or agent for insurance transactions."[247] Not included in the definition of insurance support organization are "[insurance] agents, government institutions, medical care institutions and medical professionals."[248]

---

[244] " 'Consumer report' means any written, oral or other communication of information bearing on an individual's creditworthiness, credit standing, credit capacity, character, general reputation, personal characteristics, or mode of living which is used or expected to be used in connection with an insurance transaction." Conn. Gen. Stat. Ann. § 38a-976(f) (West 1987); *see* Mass. Gen. Laws Ann. ch. 175I, § 2 (West Supp. 1994) (the Massachusetts statute tracks the language of the Connecticut statute closely).

[245] Conn. Gen. Stat. Ann. § 38a-976(g) (West 1987); *see also* Mass. Gen. Laws Ann. ch. 175I, § 2 (West Supp. 1994).

[246] Conn. Gen. Stat. Ann. § 38a-976(k) (West 1987); *see also* Mass. Gen. Laws Ann. ch. 175I, § 2 (West Supp. 1994).

[247] Conn. Gen. Stat. Ann. § 38a-976(m)(1) (West 1987); *see also* Mass. Gen. Laws Ann. ch. 175I, § 2 (West Supp. 1994). This information includes "[t]he furnishing of consumer reports or investigative consumer reports to an insurance institution or agent for use in connection with an insurance transaction, or . . . the collection of personal information from insurance institutions, agents or other insurance-support organizations for the purpose of detecting or preventing fraud, material misrepresentation or material nondisclosure in connection with insurance underwriting or insurance claim activity." Conn. Gen. Stat. Ann. § 38a-976(m)(1) (West 1987).

[248] Conn. Gen. Stat. Ann. § 38a-976(m)(2) (West 1987); *see also* Mass. Gen. Laws Ann. ch. 175I, § 2 (West Supp. 1994).

Other Organizations.   Both the Connecticut and Massachusetts statutes identify other collectors of personal information. Generally speaking, there are three
other groups that collect personal information. They are distinguished from the
first three groups of information gatherers mentioned in that their primary
purpose is not collecting personal information. First, there are *medical care
institutions.* These are defined as "any facility or institution that is licensed to
provide health care services to individuals."[249] Second, there are *medical professionals,* defined as "any person licensed or certified to provide health care
services" to individuals.[250] Finally, there are insurance institutions themselves.
Generally, an *insurance institution* is defined as a corporation or association
engaged in the business of insurance.[251] Of necessity, each of these organizations must gather personal information to conduct their respective businesses.

An insurance information disclosure statute must define covered information.
Both the Connecticut and Massachusetts statutes define three different categories of information. Each category confers special rights on the individual,
and there are statutorily imposed duties on the custodian of the information with
respect to each category.

Personal information is defined as "any individually identifiable information
gathered in connection with an insurance transaction from which judgments
can be gathered about an individual's character, habits, avocations, finances,
occupation, general reputation, credit, health or any other personal characteristics."[252] Personal information includes medical record information.

Medical record information is information that "[r]elates to an individual's
physical or mental condition, medical history or medical treatment . . . [that] is
obtained from a medical professional or medical-care institution, from the
individual, or from the individual's spouse, parent or legal guardian."[253]

Privileged information is "any individually identifiable information that . . .
[r]elates to a claim for insurance benefits or a civil or criminal proceeding
involving an individual, and . . . is collected in connection with or in reasonable
anticipation of a claim for insurance benefits or a civil or criminal proceeding
involving an individual."[254]

---

[249] Conn. Gen. Stat. Ann. § 38a-976(p) (West 1987); *see also* Mass. Gen. Laws Ann. ch. 175I,
§ 2 (West Supp. 1994).

[250] Conn. Gen. Stat. Ann. § 38a-976(q) (West 1987); *see also* Mass. Gen. Laws Ann. ch. 175I,
§ 2 (West Supp. 1994).

[251] Conn. Gen. Stat. Ann. § 38a-976(*l*) (West 1987); Mass. Gen. Laws Ann. ch. 175I, § 2 (West
Supp. 1994).

[252] Conn. Gen. Stat. Ann. § 38a-976(t) (West 1987); *see also* Mass. Gen. Laws Ann. ch. 175I,
§ 2 (West Supp. 1994).

[253] Conn. Gen. Stat. Ann. § 38a-976(r) (West 1987); *see also* Mass. Gen. Laws Ann. ch. 175I,
§ 2 (West Supp. 1994).

[254] Conn. Gen. Stat. Ann. § 38a-976(w) (West 1987); *see also* Mass. Gen. Laws Ann. ch. 175I,
§ 2 (West Supp. 1994).

There are several privacy issues that must be addressed when structuring an information disclosure statute, generally framed by the information practices principles summarized in § 3.4. First, the subject of the information is entitled to know what may be disclosed about him and to whom it will be disclosed. Closely paired with this right is the duty of the custodian of the information to give notice of disclosure to the subject when it makes a disclosure. Second, the subject is entitled to have access to personal information and submit a request for the correction of erroneous information. The custodian of the information then has the duty to correct the information that it possesses if the information is in fact erroneous. Additionally, the custodian has the duty not to disclose the erroneous information. Third, the custodian has the duty to disclose information about the subject only for purposes for which it was gathered. Finally, the custodian of the information has the duty to disclose to only certain persons or organizations. This aspect of information disclosure is also closely tied with the notion of giving the individual notice of disclosure. Each of these various aspects of privacy is addressed in both the Connecticut and Massachusetts statutes dealing with disclosure of policyholder information by insurance companies and other related organizations.

Both the Connecticut and Massachusetts statutes provide that insurers must furnish all applicants or policyholders with a notice of information practices in connection with insurance transactions.[255] The notice must be in writing.[256] The notice must state "whether personal information may be collected from persons other than the individual proposed for coverage." Additionally, the notice must indicate the type of personal information that may be collected and the investigative techniques that may be used to collect such information. The notice must also list the types of disclosure permitted by the information disclosure statute and the circumstances under which those disclosures may be made without prior authorization by the applicant or policyholder. The notice must have a description of the rights that the statute entitles the applicant or policyholder to and the manner in which the rights may be exercised.[257] Finally, the notice must state "that information obtained from a report prepared by an insurance-support organization may be retained by the insurance-support organization and disclosed to other persons."[258] However, in lieu of such notice, the insurer may furnish the applicant or policyholder with an abbreviated notice.[259]

---

[255] Conn. Gen. Stat. Ann. § 38a-979(a) (West 1987); Mass. Gen. Laws Ann. ch. 175I, § 4(a) (West Supp. 1994).

[256] Conn. Gen. Stat. Ann. § 38a-979(b) (West 1987); Mass. Gen. Laws Ann. ch. 175I, § 4(b) (West Supp. 1994).

[257] Conn. Gen. Stat. Ann. § 38a-979(b)(4) (West 1987); Mass. Gen. Laws Ann. ch. 175I, § 4(b)(4) (West Supp. 1994).

[258] Conn. Gen. Stat. Ann. § 38a-979(b)(5) (West 1987); see also Mass. Gen. Laws Ann. ch. 175I, § 4(b)(5) (West Supp. 1994).

[259] Conn. Gen. Stat. Ann. § 38a-979(b)(5) (West 1987); Mass. Gen. Laws Ann. ch. 175I, § 4(b)(5) (West Supp. 1994) (the abbreviated notice must inform "the applicant or policy

An insurance company or other insurance information-gathering organization must make available to the individual "any personal information maintained in connection with an insurance transaction in its possession or control.[260] In terms of enforcement of this entitlement, the individual may submit a written request to the insurance company or other insurance information-gathering organization for access to the recorded personal information requested. The insurance company or other insurance information-gathering organization usually has 30 days to respond to the request.[261] There are a variety of ways that the insurance company or insurance information-gathering organization may respond, each depending upon the nature of the request.[262] If an individual requests medical care information from a medical care institution, the information is usually sent directly to the individual or to a designated medical professional.[263]

When requesting personal information, the applicant or policyholder can request that certain information be corrected, amended, or deleted from the records of the insurance company or insurance information-gathering organization. The insurance company or insurance information-gathering organization must respond to the individual's request within 30 days. The insurance company or insurance information-gathering organization may or may not agree to the request of the individual.[264]

If the insurance company or insurance information-gathering organization does correct, amend, or delete any information, it must notify the individual in writing. The insurance company or insurance information-gathering

---

holder that (1) personal information may be collected from a person other than the individual proposed for coverage; (2) such information as well as other personal or privileged information subsequently collected by the insurance institution or insurance representative may in certain circumstances be disclosed to a third party without authorization; (3) a right of access and correction exists with respect to all personal information collected; and (4) "The notice . . . shall be furnished to the applicant or policyholder upon request.").

[260] Conn. Gen. Stat. Ann. § 38a-979(b)(5) (West 1987); *see also* Mass. Gen. Laws Ann. ch. 175I, § 4(b)(5) (West Supp. 1994).

[261] Conn. Gen. Stat. Ann. § 38a-983(a) (West 1987); Mass. Gen. Laws Ann. ch. 175I, § 8(b) (West Supp. 1994).

[262] Conn. Gen. Stat. Ann. § 38a-983(a) (West 1987); Mass. Gen. Laws Ann. ch. 175I, § 8(b) (West Supp. 1994). The insurance company or insurance information-gathering organization may inform the individual of the substance of the recorded information through writing, telephone, or some other form of oral communication; permit the individual to see and copy the recorded information requested; inform the individual as to whom the information has been disclosed in the past two years; and provide the individual with a summary of procedures by which the individual may request a correction, amendment, or deletion of recorded personal information.

[263] Conn. Gen. Stat. Ann. § 38a-983(c) (West 1987); Mass. Gen. Laws Ann. ch. 175I, § 8(d) (West Supp. 1994).

[264] Conn. Gen. Stat. Ann. § 38a-984 (West 1987); Mass. Gen. Laws Ann. ch. 175I, § 9(a) (West Supp. 1994).

organization must also furnish the correction, amendment, or deletion to a number of parties who have received this information in prior years.[265]

If the insurance company or insurance information-gathering organization denies the individual's request, it must notify the individual of its refusal, the reason for such refusal, the individual's right to make a statement, and the individual's right to request review.[266] When there has been a dispute between the individual and the insurance company or insurance information-gathering organization, the individual is entitled to file a statement concerning that particular information. The statement specifies what the individual believes to be the correct information and states reasons why the individual disagrees with the insurance company's or insurance information-gathering organization's decision. That statement is filed with the insurance company or insurance information-gathering organization.[267] Once the insurance company or insurance information-gathering organization receives the statement from the individual, it must file the statement with the disputed personal information contained in their own records and provide a means by which anyone reviewing the file will be cognizant of the individual's statement and have access to it.[268] In any subsequent disclosure of the disputed information, the insurance company or insurance information-gathering organization must clearly identify the matter in dispute and provide the individual's statement along with the information being disclosed. Additionally, the insurance company or insurance information-gathering organization must also furnish the statement to certain persons or organizations that have received information about the individual in

---

[265] Conn. Gen. Stat. Ann. § 38a-984(b) (West 1987). Mass. Gen. Laws Ann. ch. 175I, § 9(c) (West Supp. 1994). The correction, amendment, or deletion must be furnished to

(1)   any person who, . . . has within the preceding two years received such recorded personal information from the insurance institution, insurance representative, or insurance-support organization, and any person specifically designated by the individual who may have, within the preceding two years, received such recorded information; provided, however, that this subsection shall apply only to information which is medical record information or which relates to the individual's character, general reputation, personal characteristics or mode of living;

(2)   any insurance-support organization whose primary source of personal information is insurance institutions if the insurance-support organization has systematically received such recorded personal information from the insurance institution within the preceding seven years; provided, however, that the correction, amendment or fact of deletion need not be furnished if the insurance-support organization no longer maintains recorded personal information about the individual; and

(3)   any insurance-support organization that furnished the personal information that has been corrected, amended or deleted.

[266] Conn. Gen. Stat. Ann. § 38a-984(a) (West 1987); Mass. Gen. Laws Ann. ch. 175I, § 9(b)(2) (West Supp. 1994).

[267] Conn. Gen. Stat. Ann. § 38a-984(c) (West 1987); Mass. Gen. Laws Ann. ch. 175I, § 9(d) (West Supp. 1994).

[268] Conn. Gen. Stat. Ann. § 38a-984(d) (West 1987); Mass. Gen. Laws Ann. ch. 175I, § 9(e) (West Supp. 1994).

prior years from the insurance company or insurance information-gathering organization.[269]

Closely related to the issue of information correction is the duty of the insurance company or insurance information-gathering organization to disclose only information that it knows to be correct. The statutory corollary to this duty is that the insurance company or insurance information-gathering organization is not permitted knowingly to disclose any information about the individual that it knows to be false.[270]

Generally, an insurance company or insurance information-gathering organization may not disclose any personal or privileged information concerning an individual collected or received in connection with an insurance transaction.[271] This rule, however, is subject to a great many exceptions, and there are also specific limitations set forth in both the Connecticut and Massachusetts statutes. These limitations specify the permissible recipients of the information and for what purposes the information may be disclosed.

Information disclosure by the insurance company or insurance information-gathering organization is first limited by the practices described in the notice of information practices furnished to the individual.[272] The notice of information practices generally informs the individual of the persons that the information will be furnished to and the circumstances under which the information will be disclosed.[273]

The second limitation on disclosure is authorization by the individual. Generally, an insurance company or insurance information-gathering organization may disclose only that information that has been authorized to be disclosed by the individual. One way that insurance companies and insurance information-gathering organizations are able to collect and disclose information is through a disclosure agreement made between the applicant or policyholder and the insurance company or insurance information-gathering organization. The disclosure form[274] authorizes the insurance company or insurance information-gathering

---

[269] Conn. Gen. Stat. Ann. § 38a-984(a) (West 1987); Mass. Gen. Laws Ann. ch. 175I, § 9(c) (West Supp. 1994). The statement must be furnished to the same persons or entities entitled to receive the correction or amendment if one were made.

[270] Conn. Gen. Stat. Ann. § 38a-966 (West 1987); Mass. Gen. Laws Ann. ch. 175I, § 21 (West Supp. 1994) (both the Connecticut and Massachusetts statutes require that the false information be disclosed with malice or willful intent to injure).

[271] Conn. Gen. Stat. Ann. § 38a-988 (West 1987); Mass. Gen. Laws Ann. ch. 175I, § 13 (West Supp. 1994).

[272] Conn. Gen. Stat. Ann. § 38a-988 (West 1987); Mass. Gen. Laws Ann. ch. 175I, § 4(e) (West Supp. 1994) (it is interesting to note that the Connecticut statute does not specifically spell out this limitation).

[273] Conn. Gen. Stat. Ann. § 38a-979 (West 1987); Mass. Gen. Laws Ann. ch. 175I, § 4 (West Supp. 1994).

[274] Conn. Gen. Stat. Ann. § 38a-981 (West 1987); Mass. Gen. Laws Ann. ch. 175I, § 6 (West Supp. 1994). For the disclosure form to be valid it must comply with several statutory formalities. Generally, the form must be written in plain language, must be dated, must specify

organization to furnish information about the applicant or policyholder to a third party.[275] In the case of marketing and research questions, the insurance company or insurance information-gathering organization must clearly specify that purpose of the questions when obtaining such information from the individual.[276]

The Massachusetts statute authorizes enforcement by the insurance commissioner[277] and by individuals adversely affected by violations.[278] The statute preempts actions for defamation, invasion of privacy, or negligence for disclosure except for false disclosures accompanied by malice or willful intent to injure and for disclosures involving misidentification of an individual.[279]

§ 3.21   Effect of Unintended Disclosure

It is inevitable that confidential communications occasionally will be disclosed inadvertently or in violation of policies and procedures of the custodian. It is useful to evaluate the legal implications of such disclosure in the context of lawyer-client communications, familiar to most lawyers. The analysis can be generalized to any type of confidential communications.

The most notable issues result from situations in which an intruder has intercepted a client's confidential information. Such instances present the following two issues:

1. Whether a lawyer is liable for breaching the client's confidentiality; and

2. Whether a client is deemed to have waived her attorney-client privilege.

Although limited case law exists involving these precise issues, some insight can be obtained from a survey of cases that do not involve electronic communications and/or attorney-client privileges.[280]

---

the type of persons authorized to disclose information about the individual, must specify the nature of the information authorized to be disclosed, must name the third party that individual is authorizing the information be disclosed to, must specify the purposes for which the information is collected, and must specify the length of time such authorization shall be valid.

[275] Conn. Gen. Stat. Ann. § 38a-988(a) (West 1987); Mass. Gen. Laws Ann. ch. 175I, § 13 (West Supp. 1994).

[276] Conn. Gen. Stat. Ann. § 38a-980(a) (West 1987); Mass. Gen. Laws Ann. ch. 175I, § 5 (West Supp. 1994).

[277] Mass. Gen. Laws Ann. ch 175I, §§ 14–19 (West Supp. 1994).

[278] *Id.* § 20.

[279] *Id.* § 21.

[280] Case law involving a breach of confidentiality can be divided into two lines of cases, one involving physicians and the other involving banks. Mark D. Schneider, Note, *Breach of Confidence: An Emerging Tort,* 82 Colum. L. Rev. 1426, 1428 (1982). There does not appear to be any explanation for the low incidence of cases involving breaches of other confidential relationships, such as attorney-client. *Id.* at 1431. Nevertheless, the principles for imposing liability on doctors apply equally to the attorney-client relationship. *Id.* at 1431–32.

§ 3.22   —Breach of Confidentiality

To avoid liability for a breach of confidentiality, an attorney and his law firm must take all reasonable precautions to safeguard the integrity of a client's electronic communication. Two recent cases have applied an analogous standard to the medical profession. In *Martin v. Baehler*[281] and *Behringer v. Medical Center at Princeton,*[282] both courts held that a physician and/or hospital could be liable for breaching a patient's confidentiality if the physician and/or hospital failed to implement reasonable procedures to ensure that a patient's medical condition was not disclosed without the patient's consent.

In *Martin,* a physician's employee, without the patient's consent, disclosed a patient's pregnancy to several of the patient's family members.[283] Although the physician did not disclose the information herself, the patient sued the physician on two theories. The patient argued that the physician was liable either under respondeat superior or for failing to train and/or supervise her employees properly and adequately with regard to the confidentiality of a patient's information. The court reasoned that the duty to keep confidential matters confidential was recognized by the medical profession,[284] the legislature,[285] and the courts.[286] The court took judicial notice of the fact that patients themselves are aware of this duty. The court, therefore, held that a duty of confidentiality exists and a breach of that duty constitutes a tort with damages recoverable at law. The court did not address the patient's respondeat superior argument because it held that

---

[281] Civ. A. No. 91C-11-008, 1993 WL 258843 (Del. Super. Ct. May 20, 1993). This opinion resulted from a pretrial conference. *Id.* at *1. The court based its decision on facts taken from the pleadings and pretrial motions.

[282] 592 A.2d 1251 (N.J. Super. Ct. Law Div. 1991).

[283] 1993 WL 258843 at *1 (Del. Super. Ct. May 20, 1993). The employee, without any justification, informed the patient's grandmother, mother and stepfather.

[284] *Id.* at *3. The medical profession imposes a duty of confidentiality on physicians, which is embodied in the Hippocratic Oath. Relevant portions of the Hippocratic Oath are as follows: "Whatever, in connection with my professional practice, or not in connection with it, I see or hear in the life of men, which ought not to be spoken of abroad, I will not divulge as reckoning that all such should be kept secret." In addition, the American Medical Association has incorporated this duty in the Principles of Medical Ethics as "A physician shall respect the rights of patients, . . . and shall safeguard patient confidences within the constraints of the law." 1992 Code of Medical Ethics: Current Opinions of the Council on Ethical and Judicial Affairs of the American Medical Association (Principle IV).

[285] Delaware enacted legislation that also recognizes a physician's duty to maintain a patient's confidence. Martin v. Baehler, Civ. A. No. 91C-11-008, 1993 WL 258843 at *3 (Del. Super. Ct. May 20, 1993). According to the legislation, unprofessional conduct by a physician includes "[w]illful violation of the confidential relations and communications of a patient." Del. Code Ann. tit. 24, § 1731(b)(12).

[286] 1993 WL 258843 at *3. The Delaware courts adopted a privilege that recognizes the confidentiality of the physician-patient relationship. Del. R. Evid. 503.

the physician was liable for failing to implement reasonable office procedures to prevent a disclosure of confidential information.[287]

The court's reasoning applies equally to the legal profession. A duty of confidentiality is recognized by the legal profession, the legislature, and the courts. Therefore, attorneys would also be liable for a breach of confidentiality if they fail to make adequate safeguards to protect a client's confidential communications. Such safeguards could include adequately training all attorneys in security procedures, developing a system for encrypting electronic communications, and implementing procedures to ensure that attorneys are using the established procedures.

The lack of foreseeability that electronic communications could be intercepted is no defense for a breach of confidentiality. In *Behringer v. Medical Center at Princeton (MCP)*, the court also held that reasonable procedures must be followed to maintain the confidentiality of a patient's medical records.[288] The *Behringer* court, however, held that the failure to recognize the potential for a breach of confidentiality provides no defense.[289] In *Behringer*, a staff surgeon at MCP was admitted to MCP and was later diagnosed with AIDS. Within days of his diagnosis, knowledge of his condition became public not only within the hospital but within his community. The patient sued MCP for failing to maintain the confidentiality of his diagnosis. The court agreed with the patient and stated that MCP's failure to take reasonable measures to ensure the patient's confidentiality was negligence. As a result, the court held that MCP violated its duty and obligation to maintain the patient's confidentiality.[290]

Two consequences could result if the *Behringer* decision is applied to the legal profession. First, law firms as well as individual lawyers could be held liable for breaches in a client's confidentiality. Second, as technology progresses, lawyers are under a duty to upgrade their security precautions. The *Behringer* decision removed unforseeability as a defense to a breach of confidentiality. Therefore, law firms must continue to upgrade their security procedures to stay ahead of any rapid developments in computer technology. For example, if an encryption technique is "broken," a law firm cannot argue that it was not foreseeable that the encryption algorithm would be deciphered.

---

[287] 1993 WL 258843 at *4.

[288] 592 A.2d 1251, 1274 (N.J. Super. Ct. Law Div. 1991).

[289] *Id.* at 1272. In support of its position, the court cited the Restatement of Torts § 449 (1965) which states:

> If the likelihood that a third person may act in a particular manner is the hazard or one of the hazards which makes the actor negligent, such an act whether innocent, negligent, intentionally tortious, or criminal does not prevent the actor from being liable for harm caused thereby.

[290] The court rejected MCP's argument that the disclosure resulted from a decision by an attending physician to include the patient's AIDS diagnosis on his chart. The court stated that MCP failed to restrict access to the patient's chart or provide any procedures to prevent a breach of confidentiality from occurring. The court, therefore, concluded that MCP was also liable for breaching the patient's confidentiality.

§ 3.23 —Waiver of Attorney-Client Privilege

If an electronic confidential communication is intercepted by an intruder, a client may have waived her attorney-client privilege. Although no cases have been found involving the interception of an attorney-client communication, there is a line of cases involving intercepted communications between spouses. An analogy between the two privileges can be drawn because, as one commentator notes, the rules concerning the loss of the privilege respecting documents intercepted by a third party are much the same for the attorney-client privilege and the marital communication privilege.[291] The general rule holds that the privilege ceases if the communication was intercepted or obtained without the addressee's consent.[292]

Many courts analogize intercepted letters to statements overheard by a third person. Once a statement is overheard, it is no longer confidential and therefore not entitled to a privilege.[293]

§ 3.24 European Initiatives

In October 1992, the European Commission issued a revised proposal for a directive from the council of Europe on data protection.[294] The 1992 proposal requires the members of the European Community to enact data protection statutes meeting minimum requirements. It precludes restrictions on movement of data within the community, but restricts the movement of data to countries that do not provide equivalent data protection to that provided under its terms. Member states were expected to come into compliance by July 1994.[295] The European Parliament reacted adversely to the proposed ban on transfer of personal data from member states with high levels of protection to those with less protection, and requested changes in the Commission

---

[291] 8 Wigmore on Evidence § 2325, at 62 (John T. McNaughton ed., 1961).

[292] Michigan v. Fisher, 503 N.W.2d 50, 71 (Mich. 1993). This also agrees with McCormick who states that the majority of case law supports the view that the privilege does not protect against the testimony of a third person who has learned of the contents of a letter by interception, or through loss or misdelivery by the custodian. 1 McCormick on Evidence § 82, at 304 (John Strong ed., 1992). This conclusion is based on the theory that the sender assumes the risk that the message may be lost or misdelivered.

[293] Michigan v. Fisher, 503 N.W.2d 50, 71 (Mich. 1993).

[294] Amended Proposal for a Council Directive on the Protection of Individuals with Regard to the Processing of Personal Data and on the Free Movement of Such Data, Eur. Comm. Doc. COM(92) 422, final-SYN 287, art. 6(1)(b) (Oct. 15, 1992) [hereinafter 1992 Proposal].

[295] 1992 proposal, art. 35, § 1. *See generally* Patrick E. Cole, *New Challenges to the U.S. Multinational Corporation in the European Economic Community: Data Protection Laws,* 17 N.Y.U. J. Int'l L. & Pol. 893 (1985) (surveying law in member states and comparing with EC directive).

proposal.[296] In August 1995, the Commission issued a revised data protection directive.[297]

The 1992 European proposal envisions establishment of a data protection supervisory institution, similar to that established in Great Britain.[298] The European Commission proposal contemplates eight duties:

1. A data quality duty,[299] including a duty not to engage in negligent processing of data[300]

2. An advance notice of an intent to collect and maintain data on an individual[301]

3. A duty to disclose data to the subjects upon request[302]

4. A duty to notify subjects of adverse decisions based on data[303]

5. A duty to notify subjects of disclosure to third parties[304]

6. A duty to correct inaccurate data[305]

7. A duty to maintain reasonable security[306]

8. A duty to notify the data authority of certain acts.[307]

The duties have counterparts in American law, most notably the Fair Credit Reporting Act.[308] Many state personnel records statutes contain similar provisions.[309] The most novel feature of the European approach is its institutional arrangements, especially a central data authority. Also, the security duties are somewhat broader under the European approach, as is the prohibition, as a part of the data quality duty, of surreptitious collections.

The 1992 European Community proposal is important to U.S. companies for two reasons. First, it affects companies that do business in Europe.[310] Second, it

---

[296] *See Less Stringent EC Data Protection Requested,* 4 J. Proprietary Rts., No. 5, at 31 (Apr. 1992).

[297] *See* Steve Gold, European Commission Adopts Privacy Directive, Newsbytes News Network, 1995 WL 9986303 (Aug. 11, 1995).

[298] See § **3.25.**

[299] 1992 Proposal art. 6.

[300] *Id.* art. 23(1).

[301] *Id.* art. 11, § 1.

[302] *Id.* art. 10, § 1.

[303] *Id.* art. 13, § 5.

[304] *Id.* art. 12, § 1.

[305] 1992 Proposal art. 13, § 3.

[306] *Id.* art. 17.

[307] *Id.* art. 18, § 1.

[308] 15 U.S.C. §§ 1681–1681t (1988 & Supp. II 1990).

[309] *See, e.g.,* Pennsylvania and other state statutes. See also **Table 3–1** in § **3.6** of this chapter, comparing federal statutory privacy rights and duties.

[310] *See* Patrick E. Cole, *New Challenges to the U.S. Multinational Corporation in the European Economic Community: Data Protection Laws,* 17 N.Y.U. J. Int'l L. & Pol. 893 (1985); George B. Trubow, *The European Harmonization of Data Protection Laws Threatens U.S. Participation in Trans-Border Data Flow,* 13 Nw. J. Int'l L. & Bus. 159 (1992).

is likely to stimulate enactment of expanded data protection in the United States so that data flows from Europe to the United States will not be restricted under European Community law. **Sections 3.26** and **3.29** in this chapter discuss congressional reactions to this possibility.

Many privacy advocates oppose the British and Swedish models.[311] A big problem for the European Community licensing approach is how it should treat the press. Most newspapers and other press publications keep databases organized by people, and thus under the literal terms of the draft directive these databases would require licensing. Even if the press were exempt, there would be problems in defining the press in order to apply the exemption. Such an approach would encounter huge First Amendment problems in the United States. In Europe, many countries require the press to be licensed anyway, and thus the regulatory regime is more comfortable.

§ 3.25   English Data Protection Act of 1984

The 1984 British Data Protection Act is exemplary of data protection legislation of broad scope. It forbids the holding of data within its scope unless the holder is registered with a data protection registrar and requires that personal data be handled in accordance with enumerated principles. *Personal data,* and therefore the scope of the statute, is defined as "data consisting of information which relates to a living individual who can be identified from that information (or from that and other information in the possession of the data user), including any expression of opinion about the individual but not any indication of the intentions of the data user in respect of that individual."[312] The secretary of state is authorized to issue regulations to provide additional safeguards with respect to personal data consisting of information on race, political opinions or religious beliefs, physical or mental health or sexual life, or criminal convictions.[313]

No person may hold personal data unless the person is registered with the data protection registrar.[314] A registered data user may not hold personal data not specified in its registration, hold any data or use any data held for any purpose other than the purposes described in the registration, obtain data from any source not described in the registration, disclose data to any person not described in the registration, or directly or indirectly transfer data outside the United Kingdom

---

[311] *See Data Protection, Computers, and Changing Information Practices: Hearing Before the Government Information, Justice, and Agriculture Subcomm. of the House Comm. on Government Operations,* 101st Cong., 2d Sess. 6, 8 (May 16, 1990) (statement of David H. Flaherty, Professor of History and Law, University of Western Ontario) (French, British, Swedish data protection schemes are heavily bureaucratic because they require the registration of information systems; British registrar has 292 bags of unopened mail containing registrations in 1984; West German and Canadian advisory models are better).

[312] Data Protection Act 1984 § 1(3), 6 Halbury's Statutes 899, 901 (4th ed. 1992) [hereinafter Data Protection Act].

[313] Data Protection Act § 2(3).

[314] *Id.* § 5(1).

to any country not named in the registration.[315] Criminal penalties are provided for violation.[316] The Act articulates data protection principles in an appendix:

1. The information to be contained in personal data shall be obtained, and personal data shall be processed, fairly and lawfully.

2. Personal data should be held only for one or more specified and lawful purposes.

3. Personal data held for any purpose or purposes shall not be used or disclosed in any manner incompatible with that purpose or those purposes.

4. Personal data held for any purpose or purposes shall be adequate, relevant and not excessive in relation to that purpose or those purposes.

5. Personal data shall be accurate and, where necessary, kept up to date.

6. Personal data held for any purpose or purposes shall not be kept for longer than is necessary for that purpose or those purposes.

7. An individual shall be entitled—

(a) at reasonable intervals and without undue delay or expense—

(i) to be informed by any data user whether he holds personal data of which that individual is the subject; and

(ii) to access to any such data held by a data user; and

(b) where appropriate, to have such data corrected or erased.[317]

Additional principles are imposed on computer bureaus:

8. Appropriate security measures shall be taken against unauthorized access to, or alteration, disclosure or destruction of, personal data and against accidental loss or destruction of personal data.[318]

The registrar may refuse registration when it believes that violation of the principles is likely.[319] Then, having been denied registration, the entity is forbidden to handle the data, thus indirectly being sanctioned for violating the data protection principles.

When the registrar is satisfied that a registrant has contravened any of the data protection principles, the registrar may serve a notice containing proposed compliance measures.[320] Failing to comply with the remedial measures specified in a notice constitutes a criminal offense.[321] This is a parallel enforcement provision to deregistration.[322] Separate enforcement provisions are provided for

---

[315] *Id.* § 5(2).

[316] *Id.* § 5(5).

[317] Data Protection Act sched. 1, 6 Halbury's Statutes 899, 940 (4th ed. 1992).

[318] Data Protection Act sched. 1.

[319] Data Protection Act § 2n.

[320] *Id.* § 10.

[321] *Id.* § 10(9).

[322] *Id.* § 11 (reregistration notices).

data transfers to countries not bound by the European Convention. Such transfers may be prohibited if the data registrar is convinced that the transfer is likely to lead to a contravention of any of the data protection principles.[323] The European Convention is the "convention for the protection of individuals with regard to automatic processing of personal data," prepared by the council of Europe and open for signature on 28 January 1981.[324]

Enforcement notices from the registrar may be appealed to a data protection tribunal also established by the Act.[325] The tribunal may overturn the registrar's decision if it is not in accordance with the law or if the tribunal determines that the registrar should have exercised his discretion differently.[326] Subsequent review on points of law are available to the regular courts.[327]

Subjects about whom data is maintained have the right under the statute to be informed of any personal data held and to be supplied with a copy in response to a written request and payment of fees.[328] Judicial orders compelling compliance are provided for.[329] In addition, subjects may recover damages, including mental distress damages for inaccurate data maintained by a data user.[330] An immunity from damages is provided to a data user who receives information from the subject or a third party and does not change it and who includes any statement of inaccuracy provided by the subject and accompanies any disclosure with the statement.[331] A privilege also is provided to data users who show that they took "such care as in all the circumstances was reasonably required to insure the accuracy of the data at the material time."[332] Courts are authorized to order the correction of the erasure of inaccurate data.[333]

Payroll and related accounting information is excluded from the operative provisions of the Act.[334] Also excluded are personal data held and used only for the management of personal, family, and household affairs or for recreational purposes; data held by private clubs with the permission of the subjects; and

---

[323] *Id.* § 12(2).

[324] *Id.* § 12n. The Convention for the Protection of Individuals with Regard to Automatic Data Processing of Personal Data (1981) is reprinted in *Data Protection, Computers, and Changing Information Practices: Hearing Before the Government Information, Justice, and Agriculture Subcomm. of the House Comm. on Government Operations,* 101st Cong., 2d Sess. 205 (May 16, 1990).

[325] Data Protection Act § 13.

[326] *Id.* § 14(1). The tribunal thus has de novo review authority.

[327] *Id.* § 14(5).

[328] *Id.* § 21(1)(2).

[329] *Id.* § 21(8).

[330] *Id.* § 22(1). Data are inaccurate if "incorrect or misleading as to any matter of fact." Data Protection Act § 22(4).

[331] Data Protection Act § 22(2).

[332] *Id.* § 22(3).

[333] *Id.* § 24.

[334] *Id.* § 32.

personal data held only for the purpose of distributing or recording the distribution of articles and information to the data subject and consisting only of their names, addresses, and other particulars.[335] Thus, direct mail solicitation information apparently is excluded from the Act. Nevertheless, the exclusion is available only if the data user has been asked whether he objects to the holding of the data and the user has not objected, and if no further disclosure is made or use for purposes other than for which the data was collected is made without the consent of the data subject.[336] Government departments and police generally are subject to the same obligations as private entities.[337]

Data held outside the United Kingdom is not subject to the Act.[338] Conversely, nonresidents of the United Kingdom are subject to the Act when they exercise control or perform enumerated acts within the United Kingdom through a servant or agent.[339] Data is treated as held where the data user exercises control.

§ 3.26 Future U.S. Legal Initiatives

The United States Congress probably will enact comprehensive data privacy legislation in the 1990s, driven by pressure from firms trading in Europe, by others desiring preemption of conflicting state requirements, and by privacy advocates. As such legislation is framed, its drafters will have to choose between a property and a tort approach; they will have to decide how to deal with transactional records, increasingly valuable because they show shopping patterns and product preferences; and they will have to confront real issues of practicable enforcement.

§ 3.27 —Basic Approaches: Property or Tort?

The most fundamental choice with respect to legal protection of informational privacy is a choice between treating private information as property and protecting it only against certain defined wrongful acts. Approaches that entitle the subject of data to opt out of a database embrace property approaches. The property approach in theory provides much broader protection because it prevents any use or other conduct relating to information about an individual without that individual's permission.

The difficulty with the property approach is its impracticability. Property approaches, for example, are fundamentally inconsistent with the First Amendment

---

[335] *Id.* § 33.

[336] *Id.* § 33(3)(5).

[337] Data Protection Act § 38.

[338] *Id.* § 39(1).

[339] *Id.* § 39(3).

because much communication involves use of information about individuals. Moreover, even outside the ambit of First Amendment privileges, commerce requires exchanging information that presumably would be within the scope of privacy protection. A property-based approach would frustrate much of this commercial activity. Most commentators, courts, and legislators have rejected the property approach and individual waiver or grants of permission in favor of a wrongful-conduct approach.[340]

The wrongful-conduct approach, like tort law generally, identifies certain types of conduct that either are especially likely to harm legitimate interests of the subject of information, or are particularly devoid of the legitimate justification or both. These types of conduct are forbidden. Thus, negligent processing of information or maintaining erroneous information is particularly likely to harm the subject and is not justifiable. Similarly, a failure to notify the subject of adverse decisions based on information about her is not justifiable.

Prohibiting uses of information inconsistent with the purpose for which it was obtained has a hybrid rationale. Focusing on purpose conceptually is associated with a property approach because an individual may consent to the acquisition and storage and use of information about him for some purposes but not for others, and a use inconsistent with the original purpose is, in that sense, outside the permission granted by the "owner." Such a limitation also, however, can be justified on prohibited conduct grounds. Use for other than the original purpose is more likely to harm legitimate interests of the subject because the loss of context impairs accuracy. Use for other purposes also is likely to evade the other duties like notification. Justification more easily can be weighed against risk when justification must be articulated for a particular purpose and the use of the data limited to that purpose unless further precautions are followed.

Models for legal regulation of the use of information can be drawn from other areas of law. One of the most general is the prohibition against employment discrimination. While most lawyers do not think of Title VII of the Civil Rights Act or the Americans with Disabilities Act as being information statutes, they do prohibit the use of certain information about a person's race, gender, religion, or disability to make certain kinds of decisions—those adversely affecting employment status. Some interest group representatives acknowledge that the ADA gives important basic protection against the misuse of health data for adverse employment decision makings, but would go further and prohibit the collection of certain medical information by employers.[341]

---

[340] *See* Spiros Simitis, *Reviewing Privacy in an Information Society,* 135 U. Pa. L. Rev. 707 (1987).

[341] *Domestic and International Data Protection Issues: Hearings Before the Government Information, Justice, and Agricultural Subcomm. of the House Comm. on Government Operations,* 102d Cong., 1st Sess. 218–19 (Apr. 10 & Oct. 17, 1991) (prepared statement of Nancy S. Wexler, Chairperson, Joint NIH/DOE Working Group on the Ethical, Legal, and Social Issues of the Human Genome Project); President, Heredity Disease Foundation; Columbia University, Departments of Neurology and Psychiatry.

There also is long-standing legal regulation of private information pertaining to business activity, under the tort of misappropriation of trade secrets. The core idea is that a person is entitled to maintain the secrecy of certain information that confers an economic advantage. Anyone who frustrates this secrecy with knowledge, actual or imputed, of the secret status of the information is subject to liability. Most of the cases involve persons in special confidential relationships with the holder of the trade secret. Recent restatements of trade secret law, however, including the Uniform Trade Secrets Act, impose liability on third parties with no prior relationship with the trade secret owner when they have certain mental states.

Within the basic tort approach are two ways for the law to protect privacy interests and personal data. It can regulate harmful acts based on use of data, or it can regulate the collection and maintenance of data. In particular, the use of certain personal data in making economically significant decisions can be made illegal. Thus, trafficking in data about an HIV condition would not be addressed, but denying employment or a loan or insurance based on that information would be illegal. The two approaches overlap to some extent. For example, a legal prohibition on making decisions based on data about HIV status, which was originally collected for another purpose, arguably is both a restriction on collection and maintenance and a restriction on a use. Regulatory regimes involving licensing of databases like the European approach clearly seek to regulate the collection and maintenance. Some tort-based approaches, such as those under the invasion of privacy tort,[342] also clearly fall into this category, focusing on disclosure and use. While regulation focused on wrongful decisions might seem to present less risk of interfering with legitimate data collection and maintenance activities, such approaches are ineffective unless wrongful decisions based on personal data can be detected, unless the transaction costs of asserting claims are commensurate with the stakes involved, and unless any required mental state element can be proven without undue difficulty.

Decision-based data privacy for ordinary citizens encounters problems on each of these criteria. Transaction costs of litigating a common-law tort claim are high and completely disproportionate to the injury involved in most data privacy controversies. Proving the mental element can be difficult because most disclosures of data are not accompanied by an intent to injure the subject, but rather to serve business interests that but for the involvement with personal data are entirely legitimate. Moreover, detecting any particular disclosure is extremely difficult absent large-scale discovery once litigation has begun.

All of those institutional factors drive policy makers and commentators to prefer an approach that

---

[342] See § **3.5.**

1. Utilizes a data protection agency to distribute the transaction costs of investigating and litigating
2. Redefines wrongful conduct to reduce the problem in proving legal responsibility
3. Focuses on bottleneck institutions such as credit reporting agencies and others that specialize in collecting, organizing, and releasing personal data.

Therefore, enforcement of the regulatory norms can be shifted to a private institution that internalizes them to reduce its liability.[343]

§ 3.28   —Transactional Records versus Content: Data Aggregation

Transactional records—like those captured by pen registers and those captured by remotely accessible database logs—and arguably financial records are protected not because the subject has a subjective expectation in the secrecy of the content, but under an aggregation theory. The idea was considered, but not actually adopted in *Nader v. General Motors*.[344] In that case, Judge Breitel in his concurrence said, "although acts performed in 'public,' especially if taken singly or in small numbers, may not be confidential, at least arguably a right to privacy may nevertheless be invaded through extensive or exhaustive monitoring and cataloguing of acts normally disconnected and anonymous."[345] In other words, some sets of data by themselves may not be clothed with a reasonable expectation of privacy. When they are combined or aggregated with other sets of data, however, they may become private.[346] This is the same basic idea embedded in the Privacy Act's restriction of combining data sets.[347]

The possibility that some enterprises in Internet-like architectures in the NII may make money by collecting consumer transaction data and selling the "click stream"[348] implicates major personal privacy concerns. One possibility for responding to these concerns, of course, is to expose collectors of such data to

---

[343] A clear example of this internalization is the requirement, more or less honored by most credit reporting agencies, that the reporting agencies establish internal procedures to protect against actions that violate the Fair Credit Reporting Act. See § **3.17**.

[344] 25 N.Y.2d 560, 255 N.E.2d 765 (1970).

[345] 255 N.E.2d at 772.

[346] *See also* Pinkerton Nat'l Detective Agency, Inc. v. Stevens, 132 S.E.2d 119 (Ga. Ct. App. 1963) (imposing liability for invasion of privacy for extensive shadowing and surveillance).

[347] The Computer Matching and Privacy Protection Act of 1988 is codified at 5 U.S.C. § 552a(o).

[348] *See* Robert S. Boyd, *On Line Shoppers, Beware: "Free" Forums May Cost You*, Phila. Inquirer, June 20, 1995, at C1 (describing phenomenon).

liability unless they give notice of the intended use and obtain consent as a precondition for the subscriber's proceeding further in their services. Another possibility is to regulate the activity, much as some have proposed to regulate collection and use of consumer transaction data in other contexts.[349]

§ 3.29 —Federal Proposals

Typical of the proposals considered by recent sessions of Congress is Representative Wise's proposed Data Protection Act of 1991.[350] The motive for the legislation in part was the concern that the draft European Community directive would block data flows to and from American companies who need to transfer personal data to and from Europe. The bill focused on data protection—the "control of the collection, use, and dissemination of personal information"—rather than privacy more generally. The bill would establish a Data Protection Board, recommended by the Privacy Protection Study Commission in 1977. Unlike the English data registrar, the board would not have regulatory authority, but would only facilitate the development and adoption of voluntary data protection codes.[351] Congressman Wise argued that "as an alternative to a regulatory apparatus controlled in Brussels," a new American system of data protection could be built around new industry codes, existing legislation, and activities by a nonregulatory Data Protection Board.[352]

In the 1991 hearings before the House Government Operations Committee,[353] David F. Linowes, former chairman of the U.S. Privacy Protection Study Commission, testified.[354] He reiterated the following principles for privacy protection legislation:

1. Only information that is relevant to a particular decision should be collected. The information collected should be used only for that purpose.

2. No information should be transferred to a third person without the subject's approval, or at least notification.

3. The subject should be informed how information will be collected, how it will be used, and to whom it will be disclosed.

4. The subject should have the right to see and copy records about himself.

---

[349] Proposals have been made to regulate the use of data collected by credit card and telephone companies and by retailers like grocery stores.

[350] 137 Cong. Rec. H755 (daily ed. Jan. 29, 1991).

[351] *Id.* at H756.

[352] *Id.* at H757.

[353] *Domestic and International Data Protection Issues: Hearings Before the Government Information, Justice, and Agriculture Subcomm. of the House Comm. on Government Operations,* 102d Cong., 1st Sess. (Apr. 10 & Oct. 17, 1991) [hereinafter 1991 House Hearings].

[354] 1991 House Hearings at 84 (statement of David F. Linowes, Professor of Political Economy and Public Policy, University of Ill. at Urbana-Champaign).

5. He should be entitled to question its accuracy and to correct the record. If there is a dispute, the subject's statement should be made a part of the permanent file.

6. Government officials desiring access to individual records, should be required to "present proper authorization before being permitted to access the information, and the subjects should be notified of any such access.

Significantly, Mr. Linowes did not propose creating an enforcement agency, but instead would rely on private rights of action, reinforced by "general damages."[355]

The subcommittee chairman summarized the concerns about data privacy in the following way:

> [I]n the not too distant future, consumers face the prospect that a computer somewhere will compile a record about everything they purchased, every place they go, and everything they do. The information may be used to send targeted mail, to make telephone solicitations, to create consumer profiles, and for other purposes.[356]

Other privacy advocates are particularly concerned about the privacy-invading potential of transactional information like retail purchase data, credit card purchase data, and telephone records.[357]

Of particular concern is the growing availability of genetic information:

> The standard privacy remedies of notice, access, and other fair information practices will be needed to protect the rights of individuals. But these traditional solutions will not be enough to address the broader problems that arise. We have to recognize in advance that the availability of identifiable genetic information may force us to find new ways of looking at privacy and at the relationship between individuals and society. . . . One of the most serious and most immediate concerns is that genetic information may be used to create a new genetic under class. People may be unable to obtain jobs and insurance, or participate in other routine activities, because of the stigma of having an undesirable gene.[358]

One novel question posed by genetic data is the possibility of conflict over "ownership" of genetic information.

---

[355] *Id.* at 95–96.

[356] *Id.* at 138 (statement by Robert E. Wise).

[357] *Data Protection, Computers, and Changing Information Practices: Hearing Before the Government Information, Justice, and Agriculture Subcomm. of the House Comm. on Government Operations,* 101st Cong., 2d Sess. 105, 106 (May 16, 1990) (statement of Mark Rotenberg, Director, Washington Office, Computer Professionals for Social Responsibility, expressing concerns and characterizing establishment of a data protection board under H.R. 3669 as a "modest first step").

[358] 1991 House Hearings at 138.

In that regard, Chairman Wise thought H.R. 2045, a bill introduced in 1991 by Representative Conyers,[359] a useful starting point. It established rules governing use of genetic information by the federal government.[360] It would require federal agencies maintaining genetic information about individuals to disclose that fact to individuals and would prohibit the agencies from using the information for any purpose except that for which it was collected. Subsequently, the House Committee on Government Operations adopted a report recommending the establishment of a temporary advisory commission to address privacy issues arising out of the Human Genome Project.[361]

§ 3.30 —Compliance Procedures

One of the most difficult problems confronting any legal system for protecting data privacy in automated information systems is the difficulty of detecting violations. Accordingly, it is appealing for privacy protection law to force covered systems to implement technological policing mechanisms, that at least detect—or seek to detect—attempts to make unpermitted uses or access of information and that prevent certain activities. If this is to be effective, an external audit mechanism of these technical subsystems must exist. One possibility is to allow the subject of data to demand disclosure of the protection subsystem. Another is to require that the protection subsystems notify the subject when unauthorized access occurs.

The Fair Credit Reporting Act offers an example of this approach. The Act requires covered entities to "maintain reasonable procedures designed to avoid violations, and to "limit the furnishing of consumer reports to the purposes listed."[362] The internal procedures must require prospective users of information to identify themselves, to certify the purposes for which the information is sought, and to certify that the information will be used for no other purpose.

> Every consumer reporting agency shall make a reasonable effort to verify the identity of a new prospective user in the uses certified by such prospective user prior to furnishing such user a consumer report. No consumer reporting agency may furnish a consumer report to any person if it has reasonable grounds for believing that the consumer report will not be used for a purpose listed in § 1681b of this Title.[363]

The remainder of the section requires covered entities to follow reasonable procedures to assure "maximum possible accuracy" of information in its

---

[359] H.R. 2045, 102d Cong., 1st Sess. (introduced Apr. 24, 1991).

[360] 1191 House Hearings at 139.

[361] Robert M. Gellman, *Fragmented, Incomplete, and Discontinuous: The Failure of Federal Privacy Regulatory Proposals and Institutions,* 6 Software L.J. 199, nn. 47–54 (Apr. 1993) (tracing the history of federal privacy initiatives).

[362] 15 U.S.C. § 1681e(a).

[363] *Id.*

reports.[364] There are a number of cases applying the accuracy procedural provisions, but none applying the purpose and use procedural provisions.

It is not altogether clear what legal effect the "certification" by a user has. The basic FCRA approach could be strengthened by requiring prospective users to obligate themselves contractually to the holder of the data and then to require the holder of the data to take reasonable contract enforcement measures against users breaching their contractual undertakings.

Detecting violations also requires that someone with an interest in forcing compliance knows about transactions that may involve violation. Notifying subjects is one way of doing this. FCRA also provides a strong example of mandatory notification of a subject when certain information is requested or released. FCRA at 15 U.S.C. § 1681d requires automatic disclosure to the subject the fact of a request for an investigative consumer report not later than three days after the request is made. The notification must inform the subject of her right to seek disclosure of the contents of the report.[365]

§ 3.31 Different Types of Service Providers and Their Potential Liability

This section considers different types of service providers in the NII and summarizes the duties and privileges they may have under the privacy law regimes explained in this chapter, based on analogies drawn to traditional categories of information services. Taking the perspective of the service provider does not mean that the section considers only the interests of potential defendants. To understand the duties of service providers is to understand the rights of their customers; thus, this section considers the interests of plaintiffs as well as defendants.

Two types of NII service provider fit comfortably within established legal categories. The first of these is providers of telecommunication services with little or no content alteration. These are "conduits." The second type is providers of content owned by the provider. These are "content providers." Conduits look like telephone and telegraph companies, which historically have had common carrier obligations and specially favored treatment under the law of torts either because of their common carrier duties,[366] or on the fiction that they merely provide facilities and do not actually republish information.[367] Conduits are the ones typically asked to implement electronic eavesdropping, and they continue to have such obligations under ECPA. They have nondisclosure obligations

---

[364] *Id.* § 1681e(b).

[365] *Id.* § 1681d(a) ("disclosure of fact of preparation").

[366] Restatement (Second) of Torts § 612 & cmt. g (1977) (limiting liability of common carriers for defamatory communications carried).

[367] *Id.* § 581 cmt. b, § 612 cmt. g (telephone companies merely provide facilities and are not republishers).

under Title I of ECPA and the common law. They also may have obligations to provide reasonable security to prevent third-party interception, as under the European directive.

Store-and-forward services, including news servers and mail servers, are squarely within the stored message provisions of ECPA. They perform services like conduits[368] but through a different technology, and their privacy duties appropriately are quite similar: a duty not to disclose absent a supervening privilege created by a court order, and an associated duty to cooperate with authorities executing a warrant or other compulsory process.

Content providers are most like publishers. Publishers' First Amendment rights traditionally have limited their liability under tort and criminal regimes with respect to content they publish,[369] while leaving them with considerably more liability than conduits. Also, liability of content providers for invasion of privacy ordinarily is limited as a practical matter because their content typically is intended for public consumption and therefore enjoys no expectation of privacy. On the other hand, if a content provider disseminates private facts or is used by a third person to publicize information obtained by unlawful intrusion, the disseminating content provider may be liable at common law and under ECPA, FCRA, and state ECPA analogues.

New kinds of NII service providers do not have clear analogies in the nonelectronic context. For example, a provider may simply provide pointers to content provided by somebody else. Such providers proliferate in the Internet community in the form of World Wide Web and Gopher servers. Increasingly, commercial services provide gateways to other services, and these gateways are forms of pointers. A good government example is the Commerce Department FedWorld electronic bulletin board. This service provides a single point of access through a multiplicity of separate agencies who offer on-line access to their electronic information products. CompuServe is a long-standing private example.

Classification of such NII services for privacy law purposes is uncertain. Under general tort law concepts, it may be most appropriate to treat them more or less like newsstands and bookstores, giving them a conditional privilege because the absence of such a privilege would chill the socially desirable offering of such pointer services.[370] On the other hand, it is conceivable that a pointers service would establish a pointer to private information and therefore become the instrumentality of an invasion of privacy. It would seem appropriate to impose a duty on pointers providers to ascertain that the information

---

[368] One could argue that they are like content providers because they do more than handle information in transit. Nevertheless, the crucial similarity to conduits is the crucial difference from content providers: they handle other people's information and they do not select what they handle based on content.

[369] See the discussion in **Ch. 6.**

[370] *See* Restatement (Second) of Torts § 581 cmt. d (1977) (news dealers); *id.* cmt. e (bookstores and libraries).

pointed to is intended to be available to the public, or at least to the community expected to use the pointers. Thus, a pointers provider that points to a digitized movie that invades someone's privacy should not be liable absent a showing of knowledge of the privacy intrusion by the provider. But a pointers provider that establishes a pointer to someone's private E-mail box should be liable unless the provider affirmatively can establish that it lacked knowledge of the private nature of the E-mail box.

Routers as independent entities are new phenomena. Of course, routing takes place in conduit services, but in the Internet, an entity entirely independent from the conduit may engage in routing to someone else on the network. Because such routers ordinarily do not alter or filter content, they should be treated like conduits. The technology, however, does permit routers to filter packets, and when they do so, it may be more appropriate to subject them to higher levels of liability. It is unlikely that a router would filter packets so as to invade privacy interests except by selecting particular communications and disclosing them, which would violate privacy duties even if the routers were treated as conduits.

Conversation managers include moderated conferences and similar activities in which the provider selects, and may edit or comment on, contents submitted by others participating in the conference. This activity clearly involves a high degree of editorial participation, justifying classification as content providers. Major privacy issues are not likely to be involved in such activities because all participants expect their communications will be relatively public. If privacy invasion claims are made, however, basic principles of obligation and privilege developed in the context of defamatory electronic communications are appropriate.[371]

§ 3.32 Procedural Issues

The nature of the NII raises a number of procedural issues that are addressed in greater depth in **Chapter 12.** For example, identifying the sovereign with jurisdiction over privacy-invading conduct may be difficult. Typically in the nonelectronic network environment, alleged invasions of privacy under the common-law theories occur within the confines of a single jurisdiction. The information originally resides unambiguously in a particular state, and the harm—the intrusion, the false impression, or the publicity—also is likely to occur in that particular state . Such limited geographic connection is unlikely in the NII. First, it is likely to be ambiguous where the original information actually resides. Does it reside on the computer where it usually is stored (the

---

[371] *See* Cubby, Inc. v. Compuserve, Inc., 776 F. Supp. 135 (S.D.N.Y. 1991) (electronic information services provider not liable for allegedly defamatory communication in specialized conference because no control exercised over content; applying republisher and new distributory concepts).

server)? Does it reside on the computer to which it was moved when accessed or copied (the client)? Regardless of where the original information resides, the actor's conduct may well occur in a completely different jurisdiction, and regardless of where the actor's conduct occurs, the harm may result in yet a third place. These possibilities greatly intensify the importance of personal jurisdiction and choice-of-law questions considered in **Chapter 12.**

Standing also can be important in intrusion or eavesdropping cases. The person from whom information is obtained usually is not the subject of the information.[372]

§ 3.33 Anonymity

The spread of Internet use has made anonymous communication a prominent feature of the National Information Infrastructure. Participants in electronic discussion groups regularly use pseudonyms that conceal their real identities.[373] Consumers of electronically published information frequently obtain it through "anonymous ftp," Gopher, or World Wide Web servers, none of which ordinarily require user information before permitting access.

As anonymous participation in this part of the information infrastructure has become more visible and common, a number of analysts and commentators have concluded that anonymity plays an important role in protecting personal privacy.[374] Indeed, the United States Supreme Court has noted that anonymity can play an important role in realizing First Amendment values.[375] An anonymous sender of information protects his privacy because the content of the information is not associated with the individual who sent it. Of greater importance, engaging in electronic transactions anonymously frustrates collectors of transactional data who seek to construct profiles of the participant. Anonymity thus shields the participant from marketing activities targeted at that individual or law enforcement activities targeted at the individual based on the transactional data profiles. These and other relationships between anonymity and privacy have led privacy advocates to insist on the preservation of anonymity in legal and technological systems.[376]

---

[372] *See* Alderman v. United States, 394 U.S. 165, 89 S. Ct. 961 (1968) (disallowing Fourth Amendment challenge by codefendant or coconspirator).

[373] Newsgroups within the Usenet framework of the Internet.

[374] *See* Reid Kanaley, *On the Internet, Anonymity Is Serving the Twisted Too,* Phila. Inquirer, Feb. 1, 1995, at 1 (reviewing arguments favoring and opposing anonymity).

[375] McIntyre v. Ohio Elections Commn., 115 S. Ct. 1511 (1995) (Ohio election law prohibiting all anonymous campaign literature violated First Amendment); Talley v. California, 362 U.S. 60 (1960) (invalidating city ordinance prohibiting the distribution of handbills without names and addresses of authors or sponsors).

[376] *See* George P. Long, *Who Are You?: Identity and Anonymity in Cyberspace,* 55 U. Pitt. L. Rev. 1177 (1994) (evaluating arguments for and against anonymity).

This position raises particular problems in connection with allocating responsibility for harmful communication. Intermediaries seek to avoid criminal and tort liability for harmful or offensive communications passing through their electronic hands on the grounds that the originator of such communications is a more appropriate target for liability. This argument looses its force when the originator cannot be identified. As legal and technological systems for protecting intermediaries from tort and criminal liability mature, the clash between anonymity advocates and other participants in the National Information Infrastructure will intensify.

§ 3.34 Encryption as a Solution

Encrypting electronic messages greatly increases privacy. Only those with a key or those who successfully break the encryption can read an encrypted message. There are, however, two problems with this means of assuring privacy in the NII. The first problem is that encryption is infeasible unless all those wishing to communicate with each other use the same encryption and decryption techniques. This requires the existence of technical standards for encryption and also may require a certain degree of specialized infrastructure for key management. The second problem is that widespread use of encryption frustrates governmental efforts to obtain evidence of criminal conduct. Two major policy battles were fought in the first two years of the Clinton administration about the second of these two problems: the battle over the clipper chip, and the battle over digital telephony legislation. The clipper chip battle ended in more or less of a draw. The digital telephony battle resulted in legislation.

The clipper chip initiative, announced by the White House press secretary on April 16, 1993,[377] proposed widespread use of a microprocessor chip that would encrypt and decrypt electronic messages using a public key encryption algorithm. The algorithm used in the clipper chip was classified.[378] Use of a chip would increase performance, compared with software encryption techniques. The government developed specifications for the chip for two reasons: first to make it easy for encryption to become standard, and second to enable government eavesdropping on encrypted messages in appropriate circumstances. The eavesdropping part of the initiative was to be accomplished by "escrowed" keys—a copy of private keys held by two government escrow agents, who would make then available for use only at the request of the key owner, for example, to replace a lost key; and pursuant to appropriate judicial process.

---

[377] *See* 58 Fed. Reg. 40,791 (July 30, 1993) (National Institute of Standards and Technology (NIST) proposed federal information processing standard for escrowed encryption standard; referring to White House press release).

[378] *Id.* at 40,792.

The key component escrow agents provide the key components to a "grantee" (i.e., a government agency) only upon fulfillment of the condition that the grantee properly demonstrates legal authorization to conduct electronic surveillance of communications which are encrypted using the specific device whose key component is requested. The key components obtained through this process are then used by the grantee to reconstruct the device unique key and obtain the session key (contained in the LEAF) which is used to decrypt the communications that are encrypted with that device.[379]

In July 1994, the administration abandoned its original clipper proposal. The vice president announced that the original clipper chip technology would be used for telephone communications, but that the administration would launch a five-month study to develop a new encryption initiative for computer use. The new proposal would be voluntary, would not rely on a classified algorithm, and would be exportable.[380]

The Digital Telephony Act was signed by the president on October 25, 1994.[381] The Act imposes a general duty on common carriers to facilitate government eavesdropping.[382] While the FCC may extend the definition of common carrier for the purposes of the act, it may not include providers of information services.[383] Such carriers must enable the government when properly authorized to isolate and intercept call-identifying information and the actual wire and electronic communications carried by the carrier.[384] The covered carriers also must be able to transmit intercepted communications and call-identifying information to the government off-site.[385] The duties do not apply to information services,[386] nor do they cover transport or switching of communications for

---

[379] *Id.* at 40,791.

[380] Holly Bass, *U.S. Scales Back Encryption Plan for Computers,* Wall St. J., July 22, 1994, at B7 (reporting on letter from vice president to Representative Maria Cantwell).

[381] Communications Assistance for Law Enforcement Act, Pub. L. No. 103-414, 108 Stat. 4279 (Oct. 25, 1994).

[382] The duty imposed by § 103 of the Communications Assistance for Law Enforcement Act, amending 47 U.S.C. § 1002, is imposed on "a telecommunications carrier." *Telecommunications carrier* is defined in § 102, amending 47 U.S.C. § 1001, to mean "a person or entity engaged in the transmission or switching of wire or electronic communications as a common carrier for hire."

[383] *See id.* § 102(8)(B)(ii) (authorizing commission extension of term); *but see* § 102(8)(C)(ii) (amending 47 U.S.C. § 1001(8)(C)(i)).

[384] *Id.* § 103(a) (amending 47 U.S.C. § 1002(a)).

[385] *Id.* § 103(a)(3) (amending 47 U.S.C. § 1002(a)(3)).

[386] *Id.* § 103(b)(2)(A) (amending 47 U.S.C. § 1002(b)(2)(A)). *Information services* is defined as offering of a capability or generating, acquiring, storing, transforming, processing, retrieving, utilizing, or making available information via telecommunications, and includes a service that permits a customer to retrieve stored information from, or file information for storage in, information storage facilities; electronic publishing; and electronic messaging service; but does not include any capability for a telecommunication carrier's internal management, control, or operation of its telecommunications network. *Id.* § 101(6) (to be codified at 47 U.S.C. § 1001(6)).

private networks or for the sole purpose of interconnecting telecommunications carriers.[387] In addition, the Act does not require carriers to decrypt or ensure the government's ability to decrypt subscriber-encrypted information unless the encryption was provided by the carrier and the carrier possesses the ability to decrypt.[388]

Covered entities are obligated to develop the capability to permit required interceptions, and the FCC is authorized to impose requirements if they are not achieved voluntarily.[389] Costs of compliance must be paid by the government,[390] and failure to make payment suspends the technical compliance obligation until equipment is upgraded.[391] Carriers must publish in the *Federal Register* notices of their interception capacity.[392]

§ 3.35   Model Statement of Privacy Rights

The following model statement is intended to be disseminated to employees who use an internal E-mail system. It easily could be adapted for publication to other groups, like students and faculty, who use an institutional E-mail system:

As a general rule, your E-mail communications to other employees are private. Unless we get a report or complaint as described later in this statement, we do not generally monitor E-mail messages.[393]

You must keep your username and password to yourself, and change it frequently. You should use passwords conforming to the guidelines issued by the information services department to make it harder for an intruder to guess. If you use an easy-to-guess password, or if you allow your username and password to be discovered by others, the privacy of your E-mail and that of others is compromised.

You must not seek access to mailboxes other than your own or seek to read E-mail traffic not directed to you.

We reserve the privilege of accessing the content of your E-mail messages if we receive a complaint or report of misuse of the E-mail system or harmful messages or messages that intrude into another's privacy or property rights.

---

[387] Communications Assistance for Law Enforcement Act § 103(b)(2)(B) (to be codified at 47 U.S.C. § 1002(b)(2)(B)).

[388] *Id.* § 103(b)(3) (to be codified at 47 U.S.C. § 1002(b)(3)).

[389] *Id.* § 107 (to be codified at 47 U.S.C. § 1006).

[390] *Id.* § 109 (to be codified at 47 U.S.C. § 1008).

[391] *Id.* § 109(d).

[392] *Id.* § 104 (to be codified at 47 U.S.C. § 1003).

[393] This may seem like too broad a commitment of privacy to make, but it serves the institution because it makes it clear that the institution does not undertake to screen E-mail messages for harmful content.

We reserve the privilege of monitoring information about your use of the E-mail system, other than the content of messages, on a routine basis and disclosing this information as we believe appropriate in the management of the business. You thus should understand that the people to whom you send messages and from whom you receive messages, the dates and times you exchange messages, and the volume of messages are not private.

You should be aware that when you exchange E-mail with persons outside this organization, through the Internet or otherwise, the privacy of your messages depends on policies and practices of service providers and network managers not within the control of this organization.

§ 3.36   Sample E-mail and File Storage Agreement Provisos

This is a somewhat more formal and detailed statement, intended to have contractual effect.

1. Provider agrees to provide E-mail services and file storage and exchange services, totalling up to ___ megabytes, for so long as subscriber adheres to its obligations under this agreement, including prompt payments of subscription fees according to the fee schedule as it may be revised from time to time.

2. In exchange for the services provided by provider to subscriber [student/faculty member/employee], subscriber agrees as follows:

    (a) Provider may access files stored on provider's system by subscriber in order to determine that subscriber is not storing illegal information or information likely to infringe the rights of third parties on provider's system.

    (b) Provider may access subscriber's E-mail mailbox and check the contents of messages contained therein in order to determine that subscriber is not sending or receiving E-mail messages likely to violate federal or state law or to infringe the rights of third parties.

    (c) Provider may disclose the contents obtained under paragraphs (a) or (b) as it reasonably deems appropriate to report violations of federal or state law or to permit third parties to assert their rights in appropriate forums.

(d) Provider may delete files or messages it reasonably believes violate federal or state law or infringe the rights of third parties.

(e) If provider deletes files or messages under paragraph (d), it will notify subscriber and, if feasible, considering the content of the files or messages, provide subscriber with an opportunity to make archival copies of the files or messages before they are deleted.

CHAPTER 4

LIABILITY FOR HARMFUL COMMUNICATIONS

§ 4.1   Introduction and Description of the Problem

The NII may enhance the supply of all forms of information value because it reduces barriers to entry for any particular level of the overall production chain.[1] It also, however, diminishes the control available over content by entities engaged in later stages in the production process. An entity that produces only pointers to information content maintained by someone else has much less control over that content than its generator. This diminished control naturally raises concerns about liability for errors, defects, or other harmful characteristics in the information that may have been introduced at earlier stages in the production process. For example, the vendor of a value-added information product like a graphical interface for using geographic data might be subjected to liability for errors in the underlying data actually generated by a governmental entity. Or an electronic bulletin board or a World Wide Web (WWW) server might be held liable for a defamatory message passing through its facilities, or for a file reachable through its facilities that infringes intellectual property rights or contains child pornography.

This chapter explores the possibility of such liability. It concentrates on the liability of intermediaries because originators of electronic information content stay in essentially the same legal position they would if their content were on paper. The chapter concentrates on intentional tort, negligence, misrepresentation, derivative intellectual property infringement, and product liability theories, explaining how First Amendment considerations militate against imposing liability without fault on channels for the distribution of information.[2] It also considers the possibility that the distinction between manufacturers and retailers

---

[1] See Henry H. Perritt, Jr., *Unbundling Value in Electronic Information Products: Intellectual Property Protection for Machine Readable Interfaces,* 20 Rutgers Computer & Tech. L.J. 415 (1994); Henry H. Perritt, Jr., *Commercialization of Government Information: Comparisons between the European Community and the United States,* 4 Internet Research 7 (Meckler Summer 1994) (both explaining how unbundling of different types of value in public information enhances dissemination and improves competitiveness and how use of the Internet and Internet-like architectures can enhance unbundling).

[2] Criminal liability is addressed primarily in **Ch. 13,** although some of the issues relating to intermediary liability in tort extend to the criminal context as well.

might result in reduced liability for mere "conduits" of information. The chapter also evaluates the possibility that sovereign immunity of the originating entity might be delegated to or otherwise enjoyed by a private sector intermediary.

Special attention is given to information systems involving geographic data, useful in vehicle navigation,[3] and systems involving medical data, useful in diagnosis and treatment. Defects in such products may support claims for strict products liability. Such products are becoming more numerous and increasingly rely on the NII.[4]

This chapter focuses predominantly on liability to third parties, and **Chapter 5** considers liability of information service providers to their own customers for failure of their products to perform as promised. There is some overlap, as when a product used by a customer causes physical injury to the customer.

§ 4.2 Legal Position of Intermediaries

The National Information Infrastructure of the future will be more diverse, more multidirectional, more decentralized, more distributed, and less proprietary in important respects than today's converging but still separate telephone, broadcast, cable, and computer database markets. In other words, the NII will have important features of today's Internet. In that kind of infrastructure, intermediaries play an even more important role than do interexchange networks in today's telephone system; local broadcast stations in today's network television system; local cable franchises in today's cable television system; libraries, newsstands, and bookstores in today's print distribution chain. Already, small and large bulletin board operators make it possible for individual citizens and small companies to exchange E-mail with each other and to engage in electronic discussions by posting messages. Larger information services enterprises like America Online, CompuServe, and Prodigy serve similar information-brokering functions.

Importantly, it is in Internet architectures where intermediaries really flourish. Virtually all of the new Internet applications that have engendered so much excitement, such as Gopher, World Wide Web, and Wide Area Information Services under the international Z39.50 standard, rely on a web of intermediaries to make it possible for users and publishers to find resources scattered around the worldwide information infrastructure. The provider of a Gopher or World Wide Web service aids in the dissemination of information by

---

[3] Purposes include not only traditional aviation and maritime mapping and charting functions, but also "911" emergency response systems.

[4] Some of the first geographic information systems (GIS) were distributed on CD-ROM or other physical media. The growing use of satellite navigation systems increases the attractiveness of using the NII as a market or virtual assembly line in which preexisting geographic information can be combined with satellite and real-time vehicle data.

establishing pointers to information resources located on other computers connected to the Internet. In most cases the other computers are controlled by someone else. Assembling collections of pointers that are expected to meet the needs of a particular user population is an important way of adding information value because it reduces search costs.

Such an infrastructure is multilayered. In many cases a pointer points, not directly to the full information resource, but to another collection of pointers, which may point to still other collections of pointers and so on, collectively marking a trail to the complete resource. The computer programs involved assemble a trail from the pointers and then retrieve the desired content from wherever it resides, sometimes directly into the computer of the requester without the content having to traverse all the intermediary computers, and sometimes through intermediate processors. Whether an intermediary points directly or indirectly to the desired resource is inherently an engineering decision driven by performance considerations. In many cases, the decision to maintain copies of a particular information resource is made entirely automatically without any human intervention.

If this infrastructure is to function anywhere close to its potential as a mechanism for disseminating information, the intermediaries must not be inhibited from performing their dissemination function by fears of vicarious liability for the wrongdoing of others. The Supreme Court and the legal literature long have recognized that the privilege of publishing and speaking is meaningless unless distribution channels are available. Thus, prior restraint of a disseminator harms First Amendment interests just as much as prior restraint of publisher.

In most areas of potential intermediary liability, fault-based concepts protect intermediaries from major liability. Although there are not many cases involving electronic services and formats, there is support for the idea that a pure conduit or intermediary who lacks control over content and who does not vouch for it may have a reduced exposure to liability. This conclusion is reinforced by the First Amendment, which disfavors no-fault liability. In copyright law, however, fault-based concepts do not operate with respect to liability.

Defamation law says that conduits for harmful information products produced by others escape liability unless they are at fault, usually based on knowledge of the harmful tendency.[5] Products liability retailer and lessor rules are moving toward a similar standard of fault-based liability under the *"sealed container"* *doctrine.* An exception is when an upstream producer is unavailable to pay a judgment; in which case, even a faultless conduit may be liable in order to avoid placing loss on an innocent consumer.

There are a handful of cases involving computer technology suggesting that conduits have diminished responsibility for harmful content flowing through intermediary electronic hands but that they must be concerned especially about

---

[5] *See* Cubby, Inc. v. CompuServe, 776 F. Supp. 135 (S.D.N.Y. 1991).

the possibility of contributory infringement of intellectual property rights. In *Cubby, Inc. v. CompuServe,*[6] the district court, influenced by the First Amendment interests in the free flow of information,[7] held that a conduit is not liable for defamation in the absence of evidence that it knew or should have known about the harmful tendency of the information flowing through its service.[8] This accords with general principles of tort law.[9] In *Playboy Enterprises v. Frena,*[10] however, the district court held a conduit (a dial-up electronic bulletin board service) liable for copyright and trademark infringement for material available through its service without clear proof that the intermediaries knew of the infringing nature of the content.[11]

Cubby suggests that electronic conduits, like retail bookstores and newsstands, should not be strictly liable for harmful material they make available. On the other hand, if the intermediaries have knowledge of harmful tendencies or if they vouch for the quality or edit the underlying material, they face the same liability as an author or original publisher.

First Amendment considerations also play a role in applying products liability theories. As in the defamation claim in *Cubby,* the Ninth Circuit was concerned about the chilling effect on First Amendment interests if the publisher of *The Encyclopedia of Mushrooms* were held strictly liable (the book erroneously named edible mushrooms) in *Winter v. G.P. Putnam's Sons.*[12] Without this First Amendment influence, however, the traditional products liability doctrine held conduits liable even though they had no responsibility for product defects.

Copyright liability poses special problems. The problem with present copyright law as applied to computer networks is that de facto prior restraint will occur because of the combination of the rules of intermediary liability for copyright infringement and the economics of intermediaries in the information infrastructure. The intermediary is likely to impose prior restraint at the first hint of a controversy over mutual property. Such a low threshold for restraint certainly would not pass muster under either First Amendment prior restraint law outside the intellectual property context or under due process standards that require some kind of finding by a judicial officer. The point is not only that the intermediary may be subjected to an injunction or criminal prosecution in advance of the dissemination; the point is that the possibility of a damages

---

[6] *Id.* (granting summary judgment to defendants).

[7] *Id.* at 139–40.

[8] *Id.* at 141.

[9] Restatement (Second) of Torts § 12 cmt. a (1965).

[10] 839 F. Supp. 1552 (M.D. Fla. 1993) (granting partial summary judgment to plaintiff).

[11] In another district court case, Sega Enters., Ltd. v. Maphia, 857 F. Supp. 679 (N.D. Cal. 1994), the plaintiff showed knowledge by the conduit of the copyright-infringing activity by others and thus the district court did not have occasion to test the standard for imposing liability on a conduit. *Id.* at 683 (finding of fact No. 16); *id.* at 686 (conclusion of law No. 9).

[12] 938 F.2d 1033 (9th Cir. 1991).

judgment effectively works to shut down the dissemination just as effectively as an injunction or incarceration of the intermediary would.

What is needed is to give the intermediary more certain guidance as to what exposes it to liability and what does not. The law should insulate an intermediary from damages exposure unless and until it is presented a neutral determination that a particular item is infringing.

But because information technology permits the elements of value-added information products to be unbundled and produced by independent suppliers, it increases the likelihood that a supplier of particular types of value to information supplied by another might be subjected to liability even though it is a mere conduit for harmful characteristics resulting from another's authorship or design or manufacturing defects.

§ 4.3   Early Questions of Intermediary Liability

The question of intermediary liability for harmful or offensive messages passing through intermediary facilities arose relatively early in the development of commercial telegraph and telephone services. The literature at the time recognized that putting a telegraph company at peril if it transmitted defamatory material would present a serious impediment to the free movement of traffic.[13] How is the operator to determine quickly and with certainty whether the sender is acting in good faith[14] or is moved by some improper motive?[15] The delay necessary for an investigation would defeat the purpose of a telegram."[16] The concern about delay applies equally to an intermediary in the NII, such as a World Wide Web server that points to content contained on another node. On the other hand, "an immunity so broad as to encourage indifference on the part of telegraph operators as to whether the message is a proper one to be sent is not to be desired."[17]

Another commentator said, "because of the importance and high public accountability of the telegraph company, it should be granted [a] privilege in cases of non-intentional defamation."[18] Otherwise, "even expert legal opinion

---

[13] Note, *Liability of a Telegraph Company for Transmitting a Defamatory Message* (pt. 2): *Privilege,* 20 Colum. L. Rev. 369, 374 (1920) (analyzing hypotheticals and pointing out difficulty is that telegraph operator had to determine whether message was defamatory and thus decide whether to send it or not).

[14] Young v. Smith, 47 N.E. 265 (1897) (giving printer of libel authored by attorney same privilege that attorney had, based on good faith).

[15] Note, *Liability of a Telegraph Company for Transmitting a Defamatory Message* (pt. 2): *Privilege,* 20 Colum L. Rev. 369, 378–79 (1920).

[16] *Id.* at 379.

[17] *Id.* at 392.

[18] Elias McGil, Note, *Liability of Telegraph Companies for the Transmission of Libelous Matter,* 78 U. Pa. L. Rev. 252, 255.

upon the validity of a message would not ensure the company against liability."[19] Because the telegraph company was not in a good position to ascertain the facts, it was suggested it would "seem fairer to require the plaintiff to sue the sender of the message."[20] Other commentators agreed with the basic thrust: "It seems best to rest the privilege . . . on the interest of the public in an efficient telegraph service; to hold otherwise would force the company's agents to be learned in the law of defamation, with the possibility of liability for refusing to accept messages."[21]

By 1940 a commentator had this to say about the nature of telegraph service, which would seem to apply to entities like World Wide Web servers in the NII:

> the difficulty and inconvenience of requiring the operators to analyze either the message or the senders from either a factual or legal standpoint is manifest. The indispensability of the telegraph, on the other hand, is as unchallenged as the realization that speed is the essence of its worth. Telegraph companies operate under statutes subjecting them to penalties and fines for discrimination and negligent transmission. The pressure and responsibility thrust upon the companies by these statutes are unbearable unless the companies can comply without subjecting themselves to a libel action.[22]

A major difference, of course, is that a World Wide Web server does not operate under statutes compelling timely transmission. Thus, one could argue that the strong privilege for telegraph companies depended logically on reconciling a tension between defamation law and the legal duties of a common carrier. Absent common carrier status or similar such duties, responsibility for screening messages might occupy a higher place in the equation.

The purely technical justification for immunizing intermediaries for tort liability is stronger in the case of telephone companies than telegraph services:

> Telephone service, once established, is essentially passive. The telephone company does not know the contents of each and every call, and it does not have an opportunity to question each subscriber when a call is made as to the truth of the message. In fact, only their machinery is even aware that any given subscriber's phone is being used. The telegraph company, on the other hand, plays an active part in the dissemination and communication of all messages. Its clerks hear or see all

---

[19] *Id.*

[20] *Id.* at 256 (reacting in large part to Flynn v. Reinke, 225 N.W. 742 (Wis. 1929)). *Id.* at 252.

[21] Note, *Libel and Slander—Privilege: Qualified—Liability of Telegraph Company for Transmission of Libelous Message,* 43 Harv. L. Rev. 144 (1929) (reporting on Flynn v. Reinke, 225 N.W. 742 (Wis. 1929), and other cases).

[22] William M. Martin, Note, *Telegraphs and Telephones—Qualify a Privilege of Telegraph Company to Transmit Defamatory Message Where Sender Is Not Privileged,* 2 Wash. & Lee L. Rev. 141, 147 (1940) (analyzing with approval O'Brien v. Western Union Tel. Co., 113 F.2d 539 (1st Cir. 1940) (telegraph company not liable for transmitting defamatory message except in rare instances when company's agent had actual knowledge that message was false or sender was not privileged)).

messages before or at the time of communication and have the opportunity to question those who wish to have messages sent.[23]

This commentator emphasized the telephone company's common carrier duty, in eliminating culpability in transmitting a harmful message.[24] Significantly, he recognized that failing to immunize the telephone company would have the same effect as prior restraint in the form of an injunction.[25] Given the likely inefficacy of an investigation by the carrier, the commentator thought an absolute privilege for the carrier the most practicable solution.[26] Alternatively, and interestingly, he suggested that an adaptation of the action for interpleader might be appropriate, under which the carrier could present the question of the competing rights of the sender to transmission services and of the subject of the message to prevent or obtain remedies for defamation.[27] The problem with the interpleader approach for NII intermediaries is that the absence of a right to continued service or to transmission of a particular message would negate the existence of a res as the subject matter of the interpleader action.[28] Of course, any source of legal right to transmission, including one based on contract, could support the res element of interpleader.

While these cases and commentaries support some degree of immunity or privilege for NII intermediaries based entirely on the public interest in expeditious transmission of messages and on the absence of prior restraint, they also are supported by the notion of intermediary obligation. To the extent that intermediaries disavow any such obligation and actually exercise the power to screen messages, they not only negate that basis for immunity, they also undermine the safe and expeditious and prior restraint arguments because they are in fact screening and delaying and are in fact exercising prior restraint.

---

[23] J.S., Note, *Must the Telephone Company Censor to Avoid Liability for Libel:* Anderson v. New York Telephone Company, 38 Alb. L. Rev. 316, 318–19 (1974) (analyzing Anderson v. New York Tel. Co., 345 N.Y.S.2d 740 (App. Div. 1973) (telephone company liable for defamatory material made available on recorded message because tariff gave company sufficient authority to terminate service and not an unreasonable burden for telephone company to make investigation)). The New York Court of Appeals subsequently reversed, on the ground that the telephone company did not publish the defamatory material, being instead merely a passive conduit. Anderson v. New York Tel. Co., 35 N.Y.2d 746, 320 N.E.2d 647 (1974). Indeed, an earlier lower court case suggested that tariffed privileges for the telephone carrier to censor might violate the First Amendment. *See* Figari v. New York Tel. Co., 32 A.D.2d 434, 303 N.Y.S.2d 245, 253 (1969).

[24] *Id.* at 324.

[25] *Id.* at 328.

[26] *Id.* at 330.

[27] *Id.* at 331 (suggesting that the right to telephone service would be the disputed res for the interpleader action).

[28] *See* 28 U.S.C. § 1335 (1992) (jurisdiction over interpleader depends on value of property).

§ 4.4   Types of Information Torts

The most obvious legal theories for imposing liability on vendors of information products are defamation, invasion of privacy, copyright or trademark infringement, intentional or negligent infliction of emotional distress, misrepresentation, negligence, strict products liability, and breach of warranty (considered in **Chapter 5**).

§ 4.5   Defamation

Defamation is defined as publication of a false statement tending to injure the reputation of another.[29] In order for the injured person to establish liability, she must show that the actor acted with fault regarding both the falsity of the statement and its publication.[30] The level of fault that must be established depends on the identity of the victim. When a public figure is the victim, the First Amendment requires that the plaintiff establish that the defendant either knew that the statement was false or that he recklessly disregarded whether it was true or false.[31] When the plaintiff/victim is not a public figure, she must establish only that the defendant was at least negligent with respect to truth or falsity.[32] Fault also must be established with respect to publication.[33] Writing a defamatory note to oneself does not give rise to tort liability if a thief steals it and posts it on an electronic bulletin board.

In *Cubby, Inc. v. CompuServe,*[34] the district court held that an electronic intermediary was not liable for a defamatory communication carried through its service in the absence of proof that it knew or should have known about the defamatory character of the communication. In *Stratton Oakmont, Inc. v. Prodigy Services Co.,*[35] the plaintiff alleged that Prodigy faced greater exposure than CompuServe because Prodigy undertook to screen and censor messages to assure that they met certain standards of acceptability, but nevertheless allowed a message to be posted alleging criminal fraud by the plaintiff. The trial court granted partial summary judgment, holding that Prodigy qualified as a publisher and that the person retained under contract by Prodigy to supervise the conference on which the offending message appeared was Prodigy's agent.[36] The

---

[29] Restatement (Second) of Torts § 559 (1976).

[30] *Id.* § 558; *id.* §§ 580B, 581A (public figure).

[31] New York Times v. Sullivan, 376 U.S. 254, 279–80 (1964).

[32] Gertz v. Welch, Inc., 418 U.S. 323, 345 (1974).

[33] Restatement (Second) of Torts § 580B (1976).

[34] 776 F. Supp. 135 (S.D.N.Y. 1991).

[35] ___ N.Y.S.2d ___, Index No. 31063/94, 1995 WL 323710 (Trial/IAS Part 34 Nassau County, entered May 26, 1995).

[36] *Id.* slip op. at 1–4 (distinguishing CompuServe).

difference between the two cases is that CompuServe did not undertake to edit material appearing on its service and had a relatively remote relationship with the organizer and operator of the particular conference on which the offensive message appeared. Prodigy, however, did undertake to edit material appearing through its service and had a direct supervisory relationship over the person operating the conference on which the offending message appeared.

The CompuServe and Prodigy cases define the appropriate standard for intermediary liability when tortuous messages are involved and are not limited by their reasoning to defamation.

§ 4.6   Intentional or Negligent Infliction of Emotional Distress

Intentional infliction of emotional distress involves outrageous conduct engaged in with intent or substantial certainty that it will inflict emotional distress on another, coupled with unusually severe distress resulting from the conduct.[37] A few states have recognized the possibility of negligent infliction of emotional distress, although there is concern that relaxing the intent requirement opens the door too wide to insubstantial claims unless some sort of physical contact is involved as well as the emotional distress itself.[38] A claim for intentional or negligent infliction of emotional distress could arise in the NII against one who sends a message or publishes a file intended to shock or upset another. For example, such a claim could arise from sending obscene or pornographic materials to one not desiring to see such materials. As with other tort claims, there is a possibility that intermediaries could be liable for material passing through their facilities, although the likelihood of an intermediary being liable for *intentional* infliction of emotional distress is low; rather, intermediary liability would arise if at all under the negligent infliction theory.

Intentional infliction of emotional distress claims involving publishers are far from unknown,[39] but the characteristics of electronic publishing and conferencing reduce the probability of liability. Consider a situation in which someone

---

[37] Restatement (Second) of Torts § 46 (1965).

[38] *Compare* Bass v. Nooney Co., 646 S.W.2d 765 (Mo. 1983) (en banc) (abandoning the impact rule) *with* Towns v. Anderson, 579 P.2d 1163, 1164 (Colo. 1978) (upholding the impact rule).

[39] *See* Vail v. Plain Dealer Publishing Co., 649 N.E.2d 182, 186 (Ohio 1995) (reversing and reinstating dismissal of complaint for defamation and intentional infliction of emotional distress because statement in column was constitutionally protected); Raskin v. Swann, 454 S.E.2d 809, 811 (Ga. Ct. App. 1995) (no claim for intentional infliction of emotional distress for truthful article); Andrews v. Stallings, 892 P.2d 611, 624 (N.M. Ct. App. 1995) (mere insults in published stories about political controversy cannot support claim for intentional infliction of emotional distress; observing that Hustler Magazine, Inc. v. Falwell, 485 U.S. 46 (1988), limited increasingly frequent efforts by plaintiffs to use intentional infliction of emotional distress to circumvent constitutional limitations on defamation actions).

sends an obscene message or image to another intending that the other be shocked and offended by it. The likelihood of liability being imposed under this tort on the sender is remote. Although the sender's conduct may satisfy the outrageousness requirement, it is hard to imagine that the distress experienced by the recipient would satisfy the severity requirement. Even under extreme circumstances (for example, if someone sent an abusive message to the parents of a child victim of the 1995 Oklahoma City disaster, or in the case of unusually extreme sexual harassment) likely to produce liability against the sender,[40] intermediary liability is quite unlikely. Under the *Cubby* standard, such an intermediary would not be liable. If the message were posted on a conference or newsgroup, the intermediary might have greater reason to know about it, but also would have the additional defense that the reader and plaintiff voluntarily subjected herself to the injury.[41]

§ 4.7   Invasion of Privacy

Liability for common-law invasion of privacy can result from any one of four "subtorts": intrusion upon seclusion, giving publicity to private facts, placing the plaintiff in a false light, and appropriating name or likeness.[42] Any of the four can be committed by using the facilities of an information services provider. For example, a wrongdoer could use the facilities of an Internet server to obtain access to private files of another, thus intruding upon seclusion.[43] Or, a wrong-doer could use facilities of an information services provider to publish private information, thus committing the publicity to private facts subtort. Just as defamation can be committed through an information services intermediary, so also may the similar subtort of false light. Finally, a wrongdoer can appropriate the name or likeness of another by using an information service providers facilities.

In all of these instances, the liability of the intermediary should depend, as it does with other intentional torts, on a showing that it knew or should have

---

[40] Retherford v. AT&T Communications, 844 P.2d 949, 978 (Mont. 1992); Davis v. Black, 591 N.E.2d 11 (Ohio Ct. App. 1991) (giving plaintiff the benefit of the construction of evidence of sexual harassment and other factors to support a claim of intentional infliction of emotional distress); McDaniel v. Gile, 230 Cal. App. 3d 363, 281 Cal. Rptr. 242 (1991) (finding that sexual harassment may culminate in intentional infliction of emotional distress when there is an abuse of a position that gives actual or apparent authority). *See also* Restatement (Second) of Torts § 46 cmt. d (1965) (stating that liability is found when conduct goes "beyond all bounds of decency" and is "utterly intolerable in a civilized community); Garcia v. Andrews, 867 S.W.2d 409, 412 (Tex. Ct. App. 1993).

[41] Murphy v. Steeplechase Amusement Co., 250 N.Y. 479, 166 N.E. 173 (1929) (rejecting claim for personal injury by amusement park patron who volunteered for risk that he would fall).

[42] Restatement (Second) of Torts §§ 652B–652E (1976).

[43] *Id.* § 652B.

known of the use of its facilities for the tortuous conduct. The intrusion and publicity to private facts are likely to involve security violations on the computer system in which the private information is stored. While merely negligent failure to maintain adequate security would not expose an intermediary to liability for invasion of privacy—an intentional tort—failure to act on specific reports of security violations might give rise to intermediary liability. For example, suppose a victim reported to an intermediary, say the service through which an intruder gains access to the Internet, that the intruder has broken into the victim's E-mail box twice. If the intermediary declines to take any action whatsoever, the chance of liability for invasion of privacy is significantly greater if a third intrusion occurs otherwise constituting invasion of privacy by the intruder himself. The victim would argue that the failure to act is tantamount to intending the intrusion. But if the intermediary lacks the practical capability of doing anything about the problem, its failure to remedy it hardly can be said to amount to intentional or reckless conduct meeting the mental state required for intentional tort liability.[44]

§ 4.8   Negligence

The law of negligence imposes liability on one who fails to exercise reasonable care to prevent foreseeable harm to the legally protected interests of another.[45] Negligence imposes a duty to act carefully only with respect to those to whom one has a duty. One has a duty to act reasonably so as to avoid foreseeable risks of physical injury to persons or property of anyone, but the duty to avoid foreseeable economic injury is more narrowly circumscribed and runs only to persons with whom the actor has a special relationship.[46]

The most difficult barrier to negligence recovery is the traditional unavailability of recovery for economic loss in the absence of a traumatic injury to person or property.[47] Such recovery is not allowed by the majority rule,[48] but

---

[44] Garratt v. Dailey, 279 P.2d 1091 (Wash. 1955); Restatement (Second) of Torts § 8A (1964) (describing mental state necessary to satisfy intent requirement).

[45] Restatement (Second) of Torts § 281 & cmts. 3, 11, 12 (1964).

[46] Aikens v. Baltimore & O.R.R., 501 A.2d 277, 278 (Pa. Super. Ct. 1985) (stating general rule; denying claim by employees who lost wages because plant was damaged by defendant); People Express Airline, Inc. v. Consolidated Rail Corp., 495 A.2d 107, 112 (N.J. 1985) (giving examples of special relationships necessary to produce liability for negligence causing economic injury).

[47] Negligence damages categories traditionally are divided into personal injury, economic loss, and property damage. *See* Kelly M. Hnatt, Note, *Purely Economic Loss: A Standard For Recovery,* 73 Iowa L. Rev. 1181, 1187 & n.21 (1988).

[48] Basham v. General Shale, 377 S.E.2d 830, 834 (W. Va. 1988) (tort recovery not permitted for pure economic injury); Utah Int'l, Inc. v. Caterpillar Tractor Co., 108 N.M. 539, 775 P.2d 741, 744 (Ct. App. 1989) (product injuring itself not actionable in tort); Ora Fred Harris & Alphonse M. Squillante Warranty Law in Tort and Contract Actions § 3.10, at 93–94 (John Wiley & Sons, Inc., 1989) (discussing Seely v. White Motor Co., 63 Cal. 2d 9, 403 P.2d 145, 45 Cal.

there are significant minority rule cases in California and Washington,[49] with a special set of rules for defendants likely to be relied on for special expertise.[50] Some commentators perceive a trend to allow recovery for economic loss, at least economic loss suffered by commercial plaintiffs.[51]

Accordingly, while negligence concepts may play a role in determining liability of suppliers of NII services to their own customers, as considered in **Chapter 5,** the tort of negligence is likely to be a fruitful theory for third-party claimants only in the unusual case involving personal injury or property damage, considered in conjunction with the analysis of strict liability in this chapter.

Nevertheless, a situation might arise in which an NII service provider, say the operator of a router, having contractual relationships only with connection services sending packets through that router and not with end users, might carelessly misprogram the router and fail to monitor its operation so that significant data loss occurs before the problem is detected and corrected. In such a circumstance, a claim brought by the third party whose data is lost against the operator of the router for negligence would encourage modification or adaptation of the general rule against allowing negligence claims to be supported only by economic injury. The victim would have no contract arguments because the victim lacks privity of contract with the wrongdoer. There is no physical damage or personal injury and thus no liability on traditional negligence theories. There is no intentional conduct by the router operator and thus no intentional tort claim. So unless the law is to leave the loss with the innocent victim, it must adapt negligence to cover the victim. The special relationship theory in negligence law is a possible starting point. Negligent operation of law enforcement computer systems may implicate search-and-seizure exclusionary rules, as considered in **Chapter 13.**

Rptr. 17. (1965) and Santor v. A.&M. Karagheusian, Inc., 44 N.J. 52, 207 A.2d 305 (1965) as the leading cases denying recovery for economic loss) [hereinafter Harris & Squillante].

[49] *See* Harris & Squillante § 3.10, at 91–94 (discussing Biakanja v. Irving, 49 Cal. 2d 647, 320 P.2d 16 (1958) (allowing recovery for loss of inheritance resulting from negligent preparation of will); Ales-Peratis Foods Int'l v. American Can Co., 164 Cal. App. 3d 277, 290, 209 Cal. Rptr. 917, 925 (1985) (canner's loss due to defective cans); Berg v. General Motors Corp., 87 Wash. 2d 584, 555 P.2d 818 (1976) (commercial fisherman's lost profits resulting from defective diesel engine and clutch)).

[50] First Fla. Bank, N.A. v. Max Mitchell & Co., 558 So. 2d 9, 12 (Fla. 1990) (reviewing different approaches; adopting Restatement § 552 "known third party" rule); Raritan River Steel Co. v. Cherry, Bekaert & Holland, 322 N.C. 200, 367 S.E.2d 609, 615, 617 (1988) (rejecting privity requirement as too narrow and reasonably foreseeable test and *Biakanja* balancing test as too broad; adopting Restatement "known third party" test for public accounting firm defendant); Thayer v. Hicks, 793 P.2d 784 (Mont. 1990) (reversing dismissal of complaint against public accounting firm; adopting Restatement "known third party" rule).

[51] Harris & Squillante § 3.10, at 94 (general negligence rules should apply to claims for economic loss); Note, *Purely Economic Loss: A Standard For Recovery,* 73 Iowa L. Rev. 1181 (1988) (reviewing near per se rule against recovering economic loss when unaccompanied by physical damage or injury in negligence cases, but endorsing trend toward allowing recovery; suggesting guidelines).

§ 4.9   Third-Party Beneficiary of Contract

A third-party beneficiary of a contract is one intended to receive the benefits of a contract made between two others. An intended third-party beneficiary is one who expressly is identified as the intended recipient of benefits in the contract itself. An incidental third-party beneficiary is one who is not expressly identified but who receives benefits under circumstances indicating that the flow of benefits to him was one of the purposes of the contract. Third-party beneficiaries are entitled to enforce contracts and to sue for breach as though they were parties.[52] In other words, third-party beneficiary theory is a way of avoiding the limits imposed by the privity of contract requirement which ordinarily limits recovery on contract theories to those actually parties.

In the example given in § 4.8, relating to negligence, the victim of the failure of the router operator to program his router correctly might be able to maintain a third-party beneficiary action for breach of contract between the router operator and the connection service provider through whose service the victim's packets flowed. The argument would be that the contract between the connection service and the router operator had as its only purpose the accommodation of customers of the connection service, thus making them incidental third-party beneficiaries.

§ 4.10   Direct Infringement of Intellectual Property Rights

Chapter 10 explains that copyright, patent, and trademark infringement are no-fault concepts. Thus, an intermediary whose computer systems copy a copyrighted item or distribute it, or publish a trademark belonging to another, or use patented software potentially is liable for direct infringement.[53]

There is, however, the theory developed mostly in the defamation context, considered in §§ 4.5 and 4.21, that the First Amendment immunizes from liability intermediaries lacking knowledge or reason to know of harmful materials passing through their hands in order to keep the channels open. Under First Amendment protections internalized into certain intellectual property privileges, primarily the fair use privilege in copyright law, it is appropriate to require that fault be shown before an intermediary is liable for intellectual property infringement.

Here is how intermediary liability might arise. An intermediary would disseminate an infringing work and would, because of the architecture of its system, commit direct infringement. The direct infringement could occur either because the intermediary permits the posting of copies on the intermediary

---

[52] Restatement (Second) of Contracts § 304 (1979).

[53] *See* Playboy Enters. v. Frena, 839 F. Supp. 1552, 1555–57 (M.D. Fla. 1993).

computer by third parties, because its caching algorithm makes an intermediate copy to improve system performance, or because establishing pointers executable by the user might be found to violate the distribution, display, or performance right exclusively reserved to the copyright holder. What happens here is not that the intermediary accesses the copyright holder's material without permission, but that the intermediary unwittingly aids in the dissemination of an infringement committed by someone else.

The likelihood of direct infringement depends on the particular technology application used by the intermediary. Because of the way certain Internet applications like World Wide Web and Gopher work, liability for direct infringement by intermediaries in these technologies is low. Many Web and Gopher intermediaries do not ever actually copy the content; they simply transmit pointers. For electronic bulletin board operators, however, distribution and publishing usually involve reproduction, which makes direct infringement liability far more likely. It is nonsensical for intermediary liability to depend on the particular technology used to perform essentially the same function.

Caching presents an especially difficult problem in shaping intermediary liability for copyright infringement. Consider how caching works in currently popular software for World Wide Web applications on the Internet. Suppose the supplier of information content has made it available on the World Wide Web through a "content server," a web server from which the content may be retrieved. Suppose further that this content supplier has imposed restrictions on the content thus published, permitting access for purposes of browsing and viewing, but not copying.[54]

Suppose there are three others involved in a World Wide Web transaction: an ultimate consumer (C); another Internet server (PS) which provides pointers on its web pages to the content server (CS); a firewall computer (F). (A firewall computer isolates an internal computer system from the Internet for security reasons.) Suppose C initially establishes a session with PS to locate material of interest. C finds on PS a pointer to an item on CS. C clicks on this pointer. As a result, PS automatically uploads to C's computer the selected pointer (in the form of a URL).[55] Now, the web browser software running on C's computer automatically establishes a connection with CS and retrieves the web file pointed to by the pointer. C's web browser caches the file thus retrieved so that if C requests it again, the cache copy can be loaded in the browser rather than the browser having to fetch the file again over the Internet.

In the transaction just described, PS never had the requested file either before or after C requested it. Any downloading and caching occurred on C's web browser application running on C's client computer.

---

[54] The content supplier might be tempted to permit viewing and browsing but not "downloading." The difficulty with this distinction is that downloading is necessary to permit browsing and viewing on the client computer.

[55] Actually, the page containing the pointer already had been uploaded into C's computer.

As a second example, suppose that C's computer is connected through a Local Area Network that in turn is connected to the Internet through a firewall computer. While there are a variety of firewall configurations, one common one would cause the firewall to serve as a "proxy" for C. The popular web browser software has a proxy option to accommodate such a firewall role. The proxy function is best defined by describing how it works in a World Wide Web transaction. Similar to the one used on Example 1. C seeks to establish a connection to PS. The connection request is forwarded to F, which duplicates the request. Any information returned by PS, including the pointer, is transferred to F, which then caches it and sends a copy along to C. When C's computer activates the pointer to CS, CS returns the requested file to F, which caches it, and sends a copy along to C, which also caches it because it is running the same web browser as in Example 1.

Some web browsers, such as Netscape, keep the cached material even after the browser is exited. The next time the browser is run, the cached files are available to it. How long a browser uses a cached version rather than reloading from the server from which the material originated is determined by an expiration date included in the files sent by CS and thus kept in the cached version. This expiration date is set by CS and is modifiable by C. It thus is not factually correct to conceive of the browser's—and the firewall's—caching as being ephemeral or transitory.

As a third example, consider an information services provider such as CompuServe, Prodigy, or America Online. Such a service provider might want to provide World Wide Web access to its customers so that information retrieved through the web would be more or less indistinguishable from material retrieved from the provider's host computer. It would be natural for the provider to design its client software to include a web browser function that would work somewhat differently than the web browser software described in Examples 1 and 2. The provider's World Wide Web access system, while it might call for its client software to cache material whether retrieved through the web or from the provider host, almost certainly also would provide for the caching of material retrieved through the web on the provider's host so that if another subscriber wished to retrieve the same material, the second subscriber could do so directly from the provider's host computer, without the host having to go out and fetch the material again across the Internet.

In all three examples, it seems appropriate to classify the caching as consistent with the assumed restrictions on use of the content. In other words, the caching described should not be considered to be prohibited copying. The problems are first to associate a privilege with an established copyright law doctrine,[56] and second, to determine how to describe such privileged caching.

---

[56] The approach discussed in this section involves defining the duplication rights so that it does not cover caching; an alternative approach would be to define a new privilege, or to amend the fair use privilege so that it covers caching.

Defining the privileged caching is problematic. Limiting the privilege to ephemeral copies would be too narrow because of the way Netscape caches to disk and preserves cached files after a Netscape session is terminated. Extending the privilege to copies made merely to facilitate performance in retrieving the same material in the future might be overbroad because such a privilege could frustrate a content supplier's legitimate interest in restricting secondary copying. For example, the provider in the third example might find it convenient to allow its customers to obtain material from its host without paying for access to the material from CS. Or, C might pay once for an access to CS, but then obtain another copy from the cached version on the provider's host and make prohibited copies of that second cached copy, arguing that the restrictions applicable to the original accessed material do not apply to material accessed from the provider's host. It might be appropriate to condition any privilege on the cached version not being used intentionally or foreseeably to frustrate the restrictions imposed by the content supplier with respect to third parties.

As the caching issue illustrates, *Cubby*'s fault-based standard, if adapted to the copyright context, perhaps through the fair use privilege, would say that an intermediary is liable for direct copyright infringement (contributory infringement depends on other factors) if the intermediary "knows or has reason to know" that information is infringing. The problem with this standard is that it forces an intermediary to be the judge of a copyright infringement allegation. A mere allegation or rumor that certain content is infringing may constitute "knowledge," thus exposing the intermediary to increasing exposure to damages the longer it permits the content to be disseminated through its service. Investigation and adjudication of copyright cases is expensive and requires legal expertise. Because intermediaries face almost no liability if they remove a particular item or a pointer to that item, the economics of intermediary services dictate in almost all cases that the intermediary simply will stop disseminating an item merely on accusation or rumor of infringement.

§ 4.11   —Contributory Infringement of Intellectual Property Rights

One is liable for contributory infringement of a patent or copyright, and conceivably, of a trademark, if one provides an instrumentality whose predominant use is infringement.[57] For example, one who provided an unauthorized key to a copy protection system might be liable for contributory infringement by those using the key to make infringing copies. If the instrumentality has legitimate uses, contributory infringement liability is inappropriate. Accordingly, unless an

---

[57] *See* Sony Corp. of Am. v. Universal City Studios, Inc., 464 U.S. 417 (1984).

intermediary organizes a service for the purpose of facilitating intellectual property infringement, it is unlikely to face liability for contributory infringement.

Nevertheless, there is significant uncertainty. Even in those instances in which particular configurations of technology reduce the risk of no-fault direct infringement, intermediaries potentially are exposed to liability as contributory infringers. For example, a request to suppress certain material might give them sufficient knowledge to make them liable for contributory infringement, although mere knowledge of infringement through one's system ordinarily would not give rise to contributory infringement liability when the system is capable of substantial noninfringing uses.

The nature of increasingly complex intermediation technologies makes it infeasible for many intermediaries to check out the bona fides of the information they assist in disseminating. It may be more or less feasible for a service provider actually maintaining copies of files and messages on its own computer to screen for certain offensive words or identifiable files, but it certainly is not feasible to automate screening for copyright or trademark infringement, especially for one who merely points to information resources created and maintained by others or who merely uploads textual files. Any attempt at such screening would so clog up the functioning of the dissemination technologies that their power largely would dissipate. Arguments about "fair use," for example, are subtle and cannot be decided by a computer algorithm, much less an automated filter that cannot possibly "know" enough about the surrounding circumstances to spot material that infringes copyright. The volume of messages is such that inquiry into detailed factual circumstances would impose a major burden on providers.

Communications law, written into the Copyright Act, offers a useful model for statutory protection of intermediaries in its specialized privileges for broadcast intermediaries. Section 111(a)(3)[58] provides that it is not an infringement of copyright if a secondary transmission embodying a performance or display of a work is made by

> any carrier who has no direct or indirect control over the content or selection of the primary transmission or over the particular recipients of the secondary transmission, and whose activities with respect to the secondary transmission consists solely of providing wires, cables, or other communications channels for the use of others.[59]

The legislative history notes that clause (3) intends to grant a privilege to "passive carriers."[60] A similar privilege is given for secondary transmissions to

---

[58] 17 U.S.C. § 111(a)(3).

[59] *Id.*

[60] *Id.* § 111 note.

parts of a hotel, apartment house, or similar establishment, but only so long as no alterations are made.[61]

Intermediaries in the NII play a somewhat different role from transmission facilities in broadcast media. Intermediary protection must recognize the necessity of a system operator's selection of classes of communications to conform to its entrepreneurial definition of its product or service niche. It also must recognize the appropriateness of certain transformations and alterations that occur as part of normal digital processing. One could adapt the language of § 111 to the position of other kinds of intermediaries in the NII in the following way:

> the forwarding or transferring of a work infringing the copyright of another is not itself an infringement of copyright if the forwarding or transferring is made or facilitated by an electronic service provider who has no direct or indirect control over the content of the infringing work and whose activities with respect to the forwarding consist solely of providing communications channels, pointers, and intermediate copying at the request of another or for the use of others: provided that the exemption provided by this section shall not extend to sponsoring, soliciting, promoting or adopting infringement as the provider's own.

§ 4.12 Strict Products Liability

Strict products liability,[62] unlikely to be a concern to intermediaries (or originators) who face claims for defamatory, privacy-invading, or copyright-infringing files or messages, is a concern for producers of geographic information systems, emergency communications systems, and health care information systems. Strict liability is imposed on manufacturers of defective products for public policy reasons, essentially to ease the plaintiff's burden of proof by eliminating the necessity of proving the manufacturer's negligence.[63] The idea of liability for the harm caused by a defectively designed or manufactured good originated in *Greenman v. Yuba Power Products, Inc.*[64] In that case, the plaintiff was injured by a piece of wood that shot out of a home lathe manufactured by the defendant. The plaintiff alleged that the lathe lacked proper screws to hold wood being cut and was therefore defectively designed. The Supreme Court of

---

[61] *Id.* § 111(a)(1).

[62] Law student Paul Boltz did the research for this section.

[63] Restatement (Second) of Torts § 402A cmt. a (1965). *See also* Ellen Wertheimer, *Unknowable Dangers and the Death of Strict Products Liability: The Empire Strikes Back,* 60 U. Cin. L. Rev. 1183 (1992); Ellen Wertheimer, *The Smoke Gets in Their Eyes,* 61 Tenn. L. Rev. 1429 (1994) (critique of *Third Restatement*); Ellen Wertheimer, *Azzarello Agonistes: Bucking the Strict Products Liability Tide,* 66 Temp. L. Rev. 419 (1993).

[64] 59 Cal. 2d 57, 377 P.2d 897 (1963).

California allowed recovery for the plaintiff even though the plaintiff could prove no fault on the defendant's part in the design of the lathe. It was sufficient that the "plaintiff proved that he was injured while using the [lathe] . . . as a result of a defect . . . of which plaintiff was not aware."[65]

This strict liability for defective products was then classified in the *Restatement (Second) of Torts.*[66] It says in part:

> (1) One who sells any product in defective condition unreasonably dangerous to the user or consumer or to his property is subject to liability for the physical harm thereby caused to the ultimate user or consumer, if
>
> (a) the seller is engaged in the business of selling such a product, and
>
> (b) it is expected to and does reach the user or consumer without substantial change in the condition in which it is sold.
>
> (2) The rule stated in Subsection (1) applies although
>
> (a) the seller has exercised all possible care in the preparation and sale of his product, and
>
> (b) the user has not bought the product from or entered into any contractual relation with the seller.

The *Restatement* explains that justification for strict liability relies on the "special relationship" the seller has assumed toward any member of the public who may be injured by the good.[67] Furthermore, the *Restatement* notes that since no fault by the manufacturer or seller is required, no disclaimer is effective against strict liability.[68] A majority of states have now adopted § 402A in one form or another (in fact, a significant number of states have adopted it verbatim).

The threshold test of "unreasonably dangerous" is applied through a risk-benefit analysis. A product is "unreasonable" if the probability and seriousness of harm outweigh the cost to the seller or manufacturer of taking precautions. If the cost of precaution is small relative to the risk posed, then knowledge of the favorable cost-benefit ratio is imputed to the seller.[69] It is irrelevant that the seller "neither knew nor could have known . . . that the unreasonable risk actually existed."[70] Employing the same underlying logic as the risk-benefit analysis, some courts look to the "reasonable expectations of the ordinary consumer concerning the characteristics" of the good to determine if the good was unreasonably dangerous.[71] This is an objective test, so the court imputes

---

[65] *Id.* at 64, 377 P.2d at 901.

[66] § 402A (1965).

[67] *Id.* cmt. c.

[68] *Id.* cmt. m.

[69] Favorable in the sense that the ratio favors designing the product to reduce the danger.

[70] Robert Keeton, *Products Liability—Inadequacy of Information,* 48 Tex. L. Rev. 398, 404 (1970).

[71] Vincer v. Esther Williams All-Aluminum Swimming Pool Co., 230 N.W.2d 794 (Wis. 1975).

"ordinary knowledge" to the consumer. Assessing the expectations of the ordinary consumer requires weighing "the gravity of the potential harm . . . and the cost and feasibility of eliminating" the risk.[72]

Although plaintiffs need not prove fault on the part of the manufacturer, they still must prove that a defect existed. As the court in *Caterpillar Tractor Co. v. Beck*[73] noted, "a product must be defective as marketed if liability is to attach, and 'defective' must mean something more than a condition causing physical injury." The mere existence of the injury is insufficient to prove the existence of a defect in the product; there must be proximate cause between a defect and the injury. If proof of injury sufficed to impose liability, then the causation factor is eliminated and absolute liability would exist. No authority exists for absolute products liability.[74]

Strict products liability does not award damages for purely economic injury. The *Restatement*[75] refers to "liability for the physical harm" caused by a defective product. This excludes economic injury. A draft European Commission "directive on the liability of suppliers of services"[76] provides that the supplier of a service shall be liable for damage to the health and physical integrity of persons or the physical integrity of moveable or immoveable property caused by a fault committed by him in the performance of this service, with the burden of proving the absence of fault falling upon the supplier of the service.[77] As under American law, economic injury is not covered.

Therefore, strict liability as a legal theory is pertinent only to the activities of suppliers of NII services or information that present a risk of physical injury to personal property if it malfunctions, is inaccurate, or is misused. Such a risk exists with products used to navigate, to make medical treatment decisions, and to protect hardware and software.[78]

§ 4.13   —Publishers and Strict Liability

Relying on the intangible nature of defects in publications, the courts have uniformly refused to hold publishers of written material liable for user injury

---

[72] Seattle First Nat'l Bank v. Tabert, 542 P.2d 774, 779 (Wash. 1975).

[73] 593 P.2d 871 (Alaska 1979).

[74] *Id.* (producers are not absolute insurers of their products so causation must be established).

[75] Restatement (Second) of Torts § 402A (1965).

[76] Michael A. Jones, *Defective Services: A New Dimension for Medical Malpractice?, in* Legal Visions of the New Europe 311 (B.S. Jackson & D. McGoldrick eds., 1993) (citing Draft Directive on the Liability of Suppliers of Services, 1991 O.J. (C12) 8).

[77] Jones v. J.B. Lippincot Co., 694 F. Supp. 1216, 1217 (D. Md. 1988).

[78] For example, a remote service designed to protect power problems for computer systems and to shut them down or take other protective action would confront the risk that its malfunction could cause physical injury to the computer systems.

under a theory of strict liability, with the pronounced exception of publishers of maritime and aeronautical charts. For example, the Ninth Circuit in *Winter v. G.P. Putnam's Sons* held that a publisher of *The Encyclopedia of Mushrooms* was not strictly liable for its book's defect (identifying poisonous mushrooms as delicious mushrooms).[79] *Restatement* § 402A was inapplicable because products liability covers only the "tangible world," rather than the world of "ideas and expressions." This distinction between tangible and intangible goods was reinforced by the public policy in favor of "the unfettered exchange of ideas." The court concluded that society can withstand the stifling of innovation in the production of tangible goods, but would be damaged by the deprivation of the latest ideas and theories. Thus, strict liability is inappropriate for published items.

The United States District Court in Maryland explicitly linked the Ninth Circuit's emphasis on the inherent value of the exchange of ideas with the constitutionally protected privilege of free speech. Invoking the language of a leading free speech and defamation case, *Gertz v. Welch, Inc.*,[80] the court noted that extending *Restatement* § 402A to cover "ideas or knowledge" could "chill" expression in contravention of "fundamental free speech principles."[81] Likewise, the imposition of strict liability on publishers of credit rating reports was found to be inappropriate in *L. Cohen & Co. v. Dun & Bradstreet, Inc.*[82] Although credit reports do not enjoy the same degree of First Amendment protection that matters of public concern enjoy, imposition of liability without fault on any publisher is "just a short step" from nullifying the constitutional constraints on the common law of defamation as enunciated in *New York Times v. Sullivan.*[83]

§ 4.14 —Application of Strict Products Liability to Charts and Maps

Because charts and maps are technical data rather than "ideas," most courts have allowed the imposition of strict liability on publishers of these goods. One of the cases most widely cited for the proposition that charts should be considered goods, *Brocklesby v. United States*,[84] distinguishes charts from other publications because charts have distinct uses from other types of publications. Books and magazines cannot be dangerous for their intended use because their intended use is always limited to "being read." To this court, the act of reading

---

[79] 938 F.2d 1033, 1034 (9th Cir. 1991).

[80] 418 U.S. 323 (1974).

[81] Jones v. J.B. Lippincot Co., 694 F. Supp. 1216, 1217 (D. Md. 1988).

[82] 629 F. Supp. 1425, 1431 (D. Conn. 1986).

[83] 376 U.S. 254 (1964). *See* Herceg v. Hustler Magazine, 565 F. Supp. 802, 804 (S.D. Tex. 1983).

[84] 753 F.2d 794, 800 (9th Cir. 1985).

is not dangerous. Conversely, charts are designed to be "used" by pilots landing aircraft, and so a defective chart can be dangerous. While giving no specific reason why how-to books are not similarly "used," the court noted as determinative the technical nature of a chart and its lack of any other function than for landing an airplane. This court apparently ignored the observation in its previous decision in *Winter,* that ideas in how-to books are "often intimately linked with the proposed action."

To demonstrate that a chart's use and a book's use are substantively different, most courts analogize a chart to a compass. For example, in *Winter* the court observed that both a chart and a compass are technical in nature (as opposed to abstract) and both items have only one purpose, to guide. Thus, they are both tools. Because a defective compass is assumed to warrant strict liability, a defective chart must also be subject to the same treatment. In contrast, a how-to book is "pure thought and expression."[85]

Adding to this doctrinal caprice, no court has explained why the shifting of cost from the user to the seller justifies strict liability on charts,[86] while not justifying the same shift with respect to how-to books and other practical publications. The *Winter* court merely acknowledged that the cost-spreading reasoning has "some appeal." Nonetheless, the value of the exchange of ideas overwhelms this public policy concern. This conclusion presupposes that "ideas" are distinct from information that merely serves to guide and that guiding information is inherently less valuable to society than these "ideas."

The idea/technical tool distinction is not a reliable guide. The reasoning and analogies used to support this treatment of charts is couched in conclusory language that provides little analytical meat into which courts can sink their judicial teeth. A chart resembles a cookbook as much as it resembles a compass.

There is in the distinction between ideas and tools a hint of the traditional distinction in copyright law between creative and practical works. This distinction has given rise to the idea that copyright law affords only "thin" protection for factual works and works constituting compendia of public domain information. But the result of the distinction is the opposite in the two legal domains. This protection for practical works and copyright law is justified by the need for wide dissemination and uninhibited use, while thin protection from tort liability for practical works inhibits their production. Of course, there is another distinction that makes sense. Practical works are more likely to cause physical injury, and the public policies behind tort law in general justify greater risk of liability to the producer.

---

[85] *Winter v. G.P. Putnam's Sons,* 938 F.2d 1033, 1035 (9th Cir. 1991). *See* Way v. Boy Scouts, 856 S.W.2d 230, 238 (Tex. Ct. App. 1993); *but cf.* Lewin v. McCreight & Davis Publications, 655 F. Supp. 282, 283 (E.D. Mich. 1987) (ignoring the "use" analysis, court called charts "goods" because they were created by the publisher rather than merely reprinted work from a separate author).

[86] *See* Brocklesby v. United States, 753 F.2d 794, 796 (9th Cir. 1985) (quoting cost-shifting passage from comments of § 402A).

§ 4.15 —Design and Manufacturing Defects

Product liability cases involve two types of defects—manufacturing defects and design defects. To prove a product is defective, the plaintiff is required to prove three elements:

1. The product has a defect
2. The defect existed when the product left the hands of the manufacturer
3. The defect caused injury to a reasonably foreseeable user.[87]

"The defect in the product . . . distinguishes strict liability from absolute liability and thus prevents the manufacturer from becoming the insurer of the product."[88]

A product that has a manufacturing defect is a product that is not in its intended condition when it leaves the plant.[89] The product fails to conform to the manufacturer's own production standards.[90] For example, if an automobile manufacturer mass-produces cars, and one of these cars comes off the assembly line missing a brake line, that specific car has a manufacturing defect because it fails to conform to the standard of other like cars produced by the manufacturer.

Products with design defects are manufactured as designed, but they fail to conform to some external standard.[91] Courts are called upon to supply this standard.[92] Courts have come to varying conclusions of what constitutes a defect because defining the term "defect" essentially is a policy judgment.[93]

The law is more conservative in assessing liability in design defect cases than in manufacturing defect cases.[94] In a design defect case the law imposes a standard for product design. Manufacturing defect cases involve less legal intrusion because manufacturing defects are measured against clear objective standards set by the product manufacturer himself.[95]

---

[87] Michalko v. Cooke & Chem. Corp., 451 A.2d 179, 183 (N.J. 1982) (holding a contractor strictly liable for rebuilding a transfer press without safety devices, even though the rebuilt press conformed to the design the company gave the contractor).

[88] O'Brien v. Muskin Corp., 463 A.2d 298, 303 (N.J. 1983) (remanding the case for a new trial because the lower courts did not factor into the risk utility analysis state-of-the-art evidence when evaluating the design of an above-ground swimming pool).

[89] Prentis v. Yale Mfg. Co., 365 N.W.2d 176, 182 (Mich. 1984).

[90] Id.

[91] O'Brien v. Muskin Corp., 463 A.2d 298, 304 (N.J. 1983).

[92] Prentis v. Yale Mfg. Co., 365 N.W.2d 176, 182 (Mich. 1984).

[93] Cepeda v. Cumberland Eng'g Co., 386 A.2d 816, 824 (N.J. 1978).

[94] See Prentis v. Yale Mfg. Co., 365 N.W.2d 176, 185 (Mich. 1984) (considering the reasons proposed by the drafters of the Model Uniform Products Liability Act for adopting a negligence standard).

[95] O'Brien v. Muskin Corp., 463 A.2d 298, 304 (N.J. 1983).

Most courts in design defect cases use a risk-utility analysis to evaluate whether a product has been designed defectively.[96] But risk-utility analysis can mean different things. Some courts have adopted a pure negligence standard,[97] others a state-of-the-art analysis,[98] and others a consumer expectations analysis.[99]

Design defect cases are distinguishable from negligence cases because they focus on the condition of the product as opposed to the conduct of the manufacturer.[100] But some courts characterize this distinction as purely formal; decisions in products liability cases are based on the same analysis as in negligence cases.[101] Courts adopting a pure negligence standard cite public policy and clarity under the law as validating reasons for employing this approach. In *Prentis v. Yale Manufacturing Co.,* Prentis alleged that his injury was caused by a defectively designed hand forklift.[102] The court noted that a pure negligence standard would be easier to apply and was essentially the standard most courts were following anyway.[103] Also, the court found a fault-based test to be better policy because using a fault-based system as opposed to a no-fault system would encourage manufacturers to design safe products by rewarding the careful manufacturer and penalizing the careless manufacturer.[104] The *Prentis* court then applied Judge Learned Hand's negligence calculus, which compares the risk of harm inherent in a particular design with the social utility of that particular design.[105]

---

[96] There is a proper place in the evaluation of a design defect through risk-utility analysis for both the judge and the jury. If reasonable men cannot agree when evaluating whether the risk of a product outweighs its utility then the court should decide the case as a matter of law. If it is a question of fact whether the risks of a product outweigh its utility, then the decision rests on the jury's determination.

    Id. at 307.

[97] Prentis v. Yale Mfg. Co., 365 N.W.2d 176 (Mich. 1984).

[98] Suter v. San Angelo Foundry & Mach. Co., 406 A.2d 140 (N.J. 1979).

[99] Barker v. Lull Eng'g Co., 20 Cal. 2d 413, 573 P.2d 443 (1978).

[100] *Id.*

[101] Prentis v. Yale Mfg. Co., 365 N.W.2d 176 (Mich. 1984).

[102] *Id.*

[103] *Id.*

[104] *Id.*

[105] *See also* John W. Wade, *On the Nature of Strict Liability for Products,* 44 Miss. L.J. 825 (1973) (suggesting use of the following seven factors when applying risk-utility analysis:

1. The usefulness and desirability of the product
2. The likelihood the product will cause injury
3. The availability of a substitute product
4. The ability to eliminate the unsafe characteristic of the product without impairing its usefulness
5. The user's ability to avoid danger by exercising due care
6. The user's anticipated awareness of the danger inherent in the product
7. The feasibility of the manufacturer spreading the loss by carrying insurance or in setting the price of the product.)

Other courts have used a risk-analysis employing a state-of-the-art analysis to evaluate whether a design is defective based on the current level of technology. "State of the art relates to both components of the risk-utility equation."[106] In evaluating the risk, state-of-the-art analysis considers the reasonableness of the manufacturer's conduct in putting the product on the market, including the feasibility of modifying the design such that the accident could have been avoided.[107] On the utility side of the equation, the need for the product is evaluated against the possibility of alternate designs.[108] "Although state of the art evidence may be dispositive on the facts of a particular case it does not constitute an absolute defense apart from risk-utility analysis."[109] Most courts use state-of-the-art analysis not as a dispositive standard independently, but as just one of the risk-utility factors in evaluating a product.[110] A drug used in the treatment of cancer, for example, may be known to be unsafe at the current level of technology, but the need for the drug may be great. Therefore the utility is very high, but one still needs to evaluate the risk.

Finally, other courts have used a consumer expectations test, in which liability is based on the failure of the product to perform safely as measured by the reasonable expectations of the consumer. *Barker v. Lull Engineering Co.,*[111] used this approach when evaluating a plaintiff's claim that a high-lift loader was defectively designed. The consumer expectations test involves two inquiries: (1) whether the failure of the product to perform safely is inconsistent with reasonable expectations of the consumer, and (2) whether the danger inherent in the challenged design outweighs the benefits of such design.[112] The first prong of this test is met when the product fails to perform as an ordinary consumer would expect it to perform when it is used in its intended manner.[113] The second test is necessary because most consumers have no idea how safe a product could be made.[114]

---

[106] O'Brien v. Muskin Corp., 463 A.2d 298 (N.J. 1983) (citing Suter v. San Angelo Foundry & Mach. Co., 406 A.2d 140 (N.J. 1979)).

[107] Suter v. San Angelo Foundry & Mach. Co., 406 A.2d 140, 150 (N.J. 1979).

[108] O'Brien v. Muskin Corp., 463 A.2d 298 (N.J. 1983).

[109] *Id.* at 305 (citing Beshada v. Johns-Manville Prods. Corp., 447 A.2d 539 (N.J. 1982)). In Caterpillar Tractor Co. v. Beck, 593 P.2d 871 (Alaska 1979), the court rejected the state-of-the-art defense in design defect cases, stating that it was no defense in a strict liability case for a manufacturer to claim his product was within the state of the art.

[110] *See* Gerald F. Tietz, *Strict Products Liability, Design Defects and Corporate Decisionmaking: Greater Deterrence Through Stricter Process,* 38 Vill. L. Rev. 1361, 1432–35 (1993) (discussing Boatland of Houston, Inc. v. Bailey, 609 S.W.2d 743 (Tex. 1980), as illustration of how introduction of evidence that recreational boats did not have automatic shutoff devices to prevent injury from propellers potentially prejudiced a case in which the existence of such devices on racing boats clearly indicated their feasibility).

[111] 20 Cal. 2d 413, 573 P.2d 443 (1978).

[112] 20 Cal. 2d 413, 573 P.2d 443 (1978).

[113] Caterpillar Tractor Co. v. Beck, 593 P.2d 871, 885 (Alaska 1979).

[114] Barker v. Lull Eng'g Co., 20 Cal. 2d 413, 573 P.2d 443 (1978).

The distinction between design defect and manufacturing defect cases might arise in the following type of NII situation. Suppose a router operator has misprogrammed the router, causing medical diagnostic information to fail to reach its destination in a timely way, in turn resulting in death or worsening of injury or illness to a patient. That would be an example of a design defect: a defect in the design of the computer program. Alternatively, suppose the same mishap occurred except that the cause was not misprogramming, but an unanticipated condition in the operation of the router that could have been detected by appropriate monitoring; however it was not detected because of the failure of the router operator to have an appropriate staffing and quality control arrangement. That arguably would be analogous to a manufacturing defect. The analogy would be strengthened if the router operator had specified the kind of quality control and monitoring appropriate for a router of that type and then failed to live up to her own standards. That is almost exactly like a manufacturer who has a product design but fails to manufacture in accordance with the design.

§ 4.16   —Strict Products Liability of Retailers

Retailers in product markets are intermediaries for the products they handle, and thus in some sense are analogous to intermediaries in the NII. Because of this similarity, the legal position of retailers confronted with products liability claims is helpful in considering treatment of NII intermediaries under strict product liability law. Absent legislative enactments to the contrary, faultless retailers are liable for damages their products cause as long as a plaintiff proves the existence of a defect at the time of the accident. And even in jurisdictions that statutorily absolve retailers of strict liability, retailer immunity is usually forfeited if the plaintiff cannot recover from any other party in the "market enterprise" which dealt with the product.[115]

§ 4.17   —Origins of Retailer Strict Products Liability

The California Supreme Court, which first pronounced the rule of strict products liability in *Greenman v. Yuba Power Products, Inc.,*[116] later established the rule that retailers as well as manufacturers can be liable for defective products without a finding of fault. In *Vandermark v. Ford Motor Co.,*[117] the defendant, a

---

[115] This notion of making the liability of an enterprise in the product distribution chain depend on the availability of other defendants is potentially useful precedent for the proposal to make the liability of an electronic information intermediary turn on the ability of a victim to identify the originator of a harmful message or file.

[116] 59 Cal. 2d 57, 377 P.2d 897 (1963).

[117] 61 Cal. 2d 256, 391 P.2d 168 (1964).

car dealer, was held liable for the defective condition of a Ford sedan, even though the sedan arrived in its defective condition from the manufacturer. Justice Traynor observed that retailers "are an integral part of the overall producing and marketing enterprise that should bear the cost of injuries resulting from defective products."[118] Thus, the policy-based rationale for products liability in general also justifies its application to conduits.

This "marketing enterprise" concept of the scope of strict products liability was further sharpened in *Kasel v. Remington Arms Co.*[119] That court concluded that "no precise legal relationship to the member of the enterprise causing the defect . . . is required before the courts will impose strict liability. It is the defendant's participatory connection, for his personal profit or other benefit, with the injury-producing product" that justifies the imposition of strict liability. In *Kasel,* an American hunter successfully sued the manufacturer's licensed seller and the licensor for overpacking a shotgun shell which partially blew his hand off. The appellate court held that all members of the corporate family were permissible defendants. Thus, any entity with a financial interest in the product, however tangential, appears to be liable for the defect.

The *Vandermark* court cited two public policy concerns to support the conclusion that retailers could be strictly liable. First, the retailer "may be the only member of that enterprise reasonably available to the injured plaintiff."[120] This language echoes the court's justification for the earlier *Greenman* decision, "[t]he purpose of such [strict] liability is to insure that the costs in injuries . . . are borne by the manufacturers . . . rather than by the injured persons who are powerless to protect themselves." Thus, injured product users have a greater chance of shifting the burden of the injury to another party when all parties in the market enterprise, not just manufacturers, are available for a strict liability action.[121] Second, overall consumer safety is enhanced by holding both retailers and manufacturers liable. That is, retailers will know that they can be liable for the manufacturer's defective design or production so they will "exert pressure on the manufacturer" to ensure the product is safe.[122]

The *Vandermark* court's conclusion was then codified in *Restatement (Second) of Torts* § 402A. That section states: "1) One who *sells* any product in a defective condition unreasonably dangerous to the user or consumer or to his

---

[118] 391 P.2d at 171.

[119] 24 Cal. App. 3d 711, 101 Cal. Rptr. 314 (1972).

[120] 391 P.2d at 171.

[121] *See* Mead v. Warner Pruyn Div., 57 A.D.2d 340 (N.Y. 1977) (though the manufacturer here was apparently available for suit, court in dicta noted that strict retailer liability is justified by the fact that retailer may be the only member of enterprise reasonably available).

[122] Vandermark v. Ford Motor Co., 391 P.2d 168, 172 (Cal. 1964). *See* Blackburn v. Johnson Chem. Co., 490 N.Y.S.2d 452 (Sup. Ct. 1985) (Spreading the burden equally on all parties in the enterprise will "pressure and encourage the party responsible for the defect to turn out a safer and more attractive product." Here, can of Raid insecticide exploded in user's hand.)

property is subject to liability."[123] Any doubt that the restatement drafters did not intend the word "sells" to include retailers within this provision was then firmly dispelled by Comment f, which states in part: "The rule stated in this Section applies to any person engaged in the business of selling products for use or consumption. It therefore applies to any manufacturer of such a product, to any wholesale or retail dealer or distributor."[124]

It is important to note, however, that retailers are not being subjected to absolute liability under the *Restatement*. The plaintiff must still prove that a defect existed in the product at the time of the accident and that there were damages as a result (that is, causation). Also, § 402A does not apply to "occasional sellers" who are not engaged in the particular activity as part of the defendant's business.

Though § 402A has been widely adopted, a few courts have held that retailers are not strictly liable. In one of the leading cases expressing this minority view, *Same Shainberg Co. v. Barlow,*[125] the court held that a shoe store was not liable for the defective condition of a shoe it sold since the shoes were never taken out of the manufacturer's box until a customer bought them and the defect was not readily discoverable by the retailer. This limitation of the strict products liability doctrine relies on the presumptions that retailers rarely create the defect in the product and that forcing retailers to be insurers of every product they sell is inherently destructive to our commerce system.[126]

§ 4.18 —Indemnification: Fault Returns

The general rule is that a retailer who has been found liable for strict products liability action may gain indemnity from any enterprise upstream in the marketing enterprise, unless the retailer was interveningly negligent. For example, a drugstore was allowed to seek indemnity from the manufacturer of defective crutches in *Welkener v. Kirkwood Drug Store Co.*[127] After a thorough review of prior Missouri precedent, the court concluded that a seller at the end of the distribution chain is entitled to indemnity from an entity higher in the chain if (1) the retailer sold the product without actual or constructive knowledge of the defect, and (2) the retailer had no duty to inspect the product.

---

[123] (1965) (emphasis added).

[124] Restatement (Second) of Torts § 402A cmt. f (1965).

[125] 258 So. 2d 242, 244–45 (Miss. 1972).

[126] *See* Frank J. Cavico, Jr., *The Strict Tort Liability of Retailers, Wholesalers, and Distributors of Defective Products,* 12 Nova L. Rev. 213, 226 (1987).

[127] 734 S.W.2d 233, 242 (Mo. Ct. App. 1987) (crutches spontaneously disintegrated under a customer while he was creeping up a staircase).

In addition, many retailers must show that they did not alter the product significantly once it came into their possession. Consequently, any entity in the chain of distribution (a phrase used much like the marketing enterprise language of other courts) may be directly liable to the plaintiff without a showing of fault, yet each faultless judgment debtor then may indemnify himself by showing fault on the part of another entity in the chain.[128]

The allowance of indemnification between parties in the same marketing enterprise according to fault represents an equitable means of accommodating both fault-based allocation of loss within the selling chain and faultless strict liability to shift the loss away from consumers. Consumers need protection and almost any party besides the consumer is preferable for shouldering the burden of the defect; retailers need not shoulder the burden because they can seek indemnity from the manufacturer. For example, the court in *Embs v. Pepsi-Cola Bottling Co.*[129] justified imposition of strict liability throughout the "marketing chain" because the members of the chain, not the user, should as a matter of policy bear the loss from defective products. This strict liability is reasonable for retailers because they can always recoup this liability from the other market enterprises.

Of course, this rationale for imposing no-fault liability on conduits may not apply when the upstream supplier is a governmental entity with sovereign immunity.[130] The policy justification for shifting risk away from the consumer may still be appropriate, but the reinforcing justification that a faultless conduit can shift the loss upstream is not present. Conversely, of course, the possible immunity of the upstream supplier may mean that the conduit is the only potential defendant and therefore may justify posing no-fault liability on the conduit in order to shift the loss away from the consumer.

§ 4.19 —Statutory Reform

Despite the availability of indemnity for retailers against manufacturers, political pressure exists to ease strict liability.[131] The Federal Interagency Task Force on Product Liability reported to Congress in 1977.[132] It identified two major problems with the current scope of § 402A:

---

[128] *But cf.* Koehering Mfg. Co. v. Earthmovers of Fairbanks, Inc., 763 P.2d 499 (Alaska 1988) ("The manufacturer indemnifies not because of its culpability, but because of its position at the head of the product distribution chain.").

[129] 528 S.W.2d 703, 705 (Ky. Ct. App. 1975).

[130] As noted in many other places in this chapter, government entities are frequently the original source of information with economic value in the NII.

[131] *See* Frank J. Cavico, Jr., *The Strict Liability of Retailers, Wholesalers, and Distributors of Defective Products,* 12 Nova. L. Rev. 213 (1987).

[132] *See* Home Warranty Corp. v. Caldwell, 777 F.2d 1455, 1463 (11th Cir. 1985) (describing task force and report).

1.   Product liability insurance premiums were so prohibitively expensive that many retailers were operating without it (thus, public policy of having entities that could best afford the loss bear the loss of the consumer was being foiled), and

2.   There was a lack of uniformity in court application of § 402A and the available remedies.

Two years later, the Task Force published the Model Uniform Product Liability Act to deal with this problem.[133] The most dramatic departure from the common-law application of § 402A appears in section 105(a). It states:

> product sellers shall not be subject to liability in circumstances in which they did not have a reasonable opportunity to inspect the product in a manner which would or should, in the exercise of reasonable care, reveal the existence of the defective condition.

Since liability only attached if the retailer acted without "reasonable care," retailers were effectively returned to a negligence, fault-based standard. In adopting the Model Act, many states have labeled this "lack of opportunity to inspect" exception as the "sealed container defense." Expanding on the Model Act, the Delaware Code provides that a retailer may defend by asserting that the product was received and sent out again in a sealed container, the retailer had no knowledge of the defect, the retailer could not have discovered the defect with the use of reasonable care, the retailer did not alter the product, and the retailer had no notice of the defect from prior purchasers.[134]

This sounds remarkably like the First Amendment–driven rule for recovery against conduits articulated in *Cubby*. Under the Model Act, however, the retailer can still be subject to the same standard of product liability as the manufacturer if

1.   The manufacturer is not subject to service of process in the plaintiff's domicile

2.   The manufacturer has been declared insolvent, or

3.   The court determines that it is highly probable that the plaintiff will not be able to enforce a judgment against the manufacturer.

Thus, the Model Act generally protects retailers from faultless liability, but by imposing strict liability if the manufacturer is unable to pay off any possible judgment, the act still promotes the *Vandermark* public policy that retailers should pay for damages when they are the only party available to pay the injured user.

---

[133] *See* Koch v. Shell Oil Co., 525 F.3d 878, 884 n.5 (10th Cir. 1995).

[134] Del. Code Ann. tit. 18, § 7001 (1974), *See* Kan. Stat. Ann. § 60-3306 (1987) (near verbatim copy of Delaware's "sealed container defense").

Section 4.12 noted that strict products liability is a plausible legal theory only with respect to certain information products, including those that facilitate navigation. Such products almost always rely on basic data received from the government. On-line publishers of charts and maps could successfully argue that the maps they receive from the FAA are virtually sealed, by nature of their enormous detail and complexity. Although the maps would not be physically hidden in a box, they would be of such a technical nature that, as the Delaware Code definition section states, "it would be unreasonable to expect a seller to detect or discover the existence of a . . . defective condition in the product." Furthermore, the publisher would have no reason to know of the defect unless there had been a crash using one of the maps or the map mistake was so significant that anyone should notice, say leaving out a Great Lake.

Unfortunately for publishers of navigational products confronting strict liability claims, the "manufacturer"—the original source—is a government entity and is likely to be immune from a product liability suit. Section 18-7001 of the Delaware Code, and nearly every other state code in one wording or another, states that the sealed container defense is not available if the manufacturer is "immune from suit."

Electronic publishers and software producers would find solace in South Dakota,[135] where strict liability for retailers is absolutely barred. The South Dakota statute does not condition the sealed container defense on a showing of manufacturer availability, so the plaintiff can only reach the retailer under a theory of negligence or of breach of warranty. Elsewhere publishers are held to a strict liability standard.

Intermediaries handling other types of information products likely to support strict liability, such as products involved in medical treatment and diagnosis, do not confront this difficulty because the original source of the information involved in such products is not likely to enjoy sovereign immunity.

§ 4.20 —Leases

As **Chapter 5** explains, users of computer software and other NII services usually do not take title to the processes they use; rather, they are licensees. Licensees are legally similar to lessees, and accordingly the position of lessees in strict liability law is a useful guide for assessing the exposure to products liability of licensees to computer works and services. Moreover, the fact that a licensor does not sell the product does not suggest that the licensor would escape strict liability if the product causes injury.

That a lessee does not take title to the product he is paying for does not distinguish lessors from retailers, manufacturers, or any other part of the market enterprise so long as the lessor is in the business of leasing such products. Evaluating a claim by a worker who was injured when the brakes on the

---

[135] S.D. Codified Laws Ann. § 20-9-9 (1995).

defendant's truck failed, the New Jersey Supreme Court held that the defendant, a truck lessor, could be strictly liable for the defective condition of its trucks because the same public polices are involved whether merely possessionary rights or full ownership rights are transferred between plaintiff and defendant.[136] A truck leasing business, by definition, puts its product out on the roads in the "stream of commerce [acting] not unlike a manufacturer or retailer." Indeed, the truck leasing business is such that its defective products will expose the public to an even greater "quantum of danger" than would arise from an ordinary retailer. Because strict liability derives from the need to protect the public above all over commercial concerns, it would be anomalous to allow leases to escape the same liability retailers and manufacturers face.[137]

Only those leases that are "casual" on the part of the lessor, and not part of the lessor's primary business, are not subject to § 402A. For example, the defendant in *Nastasi v. Hochman*[138] was a lingerie company that had a single lease for a single airplane (which crashed). It was considered not to be in the business of leasing airplanes. Consequently, this lease for the plane was "casual," and § 402A provided an inappropriate standard for the lingerie company. Typically, however, this casual lessor exception to § 402A would not be relevant to on-line publishers because their main source of potential liability, publication, is not an isolated or casual activity of their business.

§ 4.21 —Strict Liability and First Amendment Considerations

When dissemination of any form of public information is involved, First Amendment interests are implicated. When the potential for liability may discourage publishers from making the information widely available, First Amendment arguments are available to constrain the liability rules, at least to the point of allowing the imposition of liability only when fault can be shown. This is the strongest argument in favor of producers and distributors of value-added information products.

On the other hand, some GIS, emergency communications, and health care information services products are intended to be used in ways that would create considerable hazards if they are defective. This is obviously the case with aircraft navigation systems, medical telemetry systems, ocean navigation systems, and 911 emergency response databases. In these cases, policy arguments for strict liability exist. An ordinary consumer as an injured party has no real capacity to determine defects or even to shop around for the safest GIS or

---

[136] Cintrone v. Hertz Truck Leasing, 212 A.2d 769 (N.J. 1965).

[137] *Id.; see* Kemp v. Budget Rent-A-Car, 453 N.W.2d 872, 878 (Wis. 1990) ("the policy considerations which support the imposition of strict liability on manufacturers or sellers . . . apply with greater force in the case of commercial lessors").

[138] 58 A.D. 564, 396 N.Y.S.2d 216 (1977).

medical telemetry system. By offering such systems on the market, the producer is impliedly vouching for their safety. There is not much point in buying a navigation system for an aircraft except to enable one to fly the aircraft safely. It is hard to conceive of someone buying a GIS system for aircraft navigation intending that there might be defects that would render the use of the system unsafe.

Thus, when GIS, emergency communications, or medical systems are intended to be used in safety-critical applications, strict liability is appropriate, and conduits should not be able to escape liability on the grounds that a defect originated with a potentially immune governmental agency. Conduits can protect themselves by indemnification agreements and insurance.

On the other hand, when GIS systems are used to facilitate knowledge of governmental rules and participation in governmental processes, as with planning and zoning applications, liability should be fault-based because the arguments for strict liability are weaker and the First Amendment arguments based on effective operation of the political process are stronger.

New York Times v. Sullivan[139] and its progeny[140] broadly support the proposition that states may not impose strict liability on either originators or intermediaries for tortious information.[141] While this should limit the liability of intermediaries who do not hold themselves out as publishers and for whom it would be impracticable to screen all the material reachable through their services, regardless of whether the theory for imposing liability is defamation, other intentional torts, or intellectual property infringement, the premise supporting this conditional privilege is the need to keep channels of communication open.

If the product does not involve information in the communicative sense, relevant to political debate, but rather involves utilitarian data involved in making operational computations, the First Amendment connection is much more tenuous. Thus the intermediary of navigational or medical diagnosis systems has a much weaker First Amendment defense. Indeed one could reason more generally that if the product has insufficient original expression to qualify for copyright protection,[142] there also is insufficient expression for privileges based on the First Amendment.[143]

---

[139] 376 U.S. 254 (1964).

[140] Dun & Bradstreet, Inc. v. Greenmoss Builders, Inc., 472 U.S. 749, 753 (1985) (referring to "*New York Times* and its progeny" and discussing cases).

[141] United States v. X-Citement Video, 115 S. Ct. 464 (1994) (First Amendment conditioned public expectations so that scienter requirement in statute regulating pornographic publications was strictly applied).

[142] See **Ch. 10** discussing the *Feist* limitation on copyright protection for compilations.

[143] The weakness in this equation is that the First Amendment and the copyright statute have subtly different purposes, even though both aim at enhancing the flow of information.

§ 4.22   Fair Credit Reporting Act Obligations

One of the earliest and most important parts of the global information infra-structure comprised databases of consumer credit information. Liability of maintainers of such databases to the third parties on whom they maintain information long has been a matter of concern both to the database maintainers and to the consumers in the database. The Fair Credit Reporting Act (FCRA)[144] imposes accuracy duties, but only on "consumer reporting agencies"—persons who regularly engage in assembling or evaluating consumer credit information for the purpose of furnishing consumer reports to third parties.[145] FTC Policy Guidance on the FCRA says that commercial credit reports are not covered,[146] nor are insurance claims reports prepared by claims investigation services.[147] Although FCRA is not intended to address business credit data and reporting, it can be implicated when credit reports are prepared that indirectly relate to a business purpose.[148]

FCRA promotes quality, in the sense of data integrity and accuracy, by subjecting a credit reporting agency to civil liability unless it follows "reasonable procedures to assure maximum possible accuracy."[149]

Compliance with FCRA is assured by a private right of action in which punitive and compensatory damages and attorneys' fees may be recovered.[150]

---

[144] **Chapter 3** considers the privacy protective provisions of FCPA.

[145] 15 U.S.C. § 1681a(f) (1988). *See* Hoke v. Retail Credit Corp., 521 F.2d 1079, 1084 (4th Cir. 1975) (report furnished to physician licensing agency resulting in denial of practice privileges constituted "consumer report" under § 1681(a)(d), because it would be used for "employment purposes" as defined in §§ 1681(a)(h) and 1681(b)(3)(B) and because determination of eligibility for a license brought it under § 1681(b)(3)(D)).

[146] 16 C.F.R. pt. 600, at n.1 (1995).

[147] *Id.* § 600(6)(C).

[148] *See, e.g.,* Rasor v. Retail Credit Co., 554 P.2d 1041, 1047 (Wash. 1976) (credit report prepared in connection with life insurance application that was necessary in order to obtain small business administration loan qualified as "consumer report").

[149] 15 U.S.C. § 1681e(b). *See* Koropoulos v. Credit Bureau, Inc., 734 F.2d 37, 40 (D.C. Cir. 1984) (factually correct information that nevertheless misleads readers does not satisfy requirement of FCRA); Collins v. Retail Credit Co., 410 F. Supp. 924, 931 (E.D. Mich. 1976) (allowing, but reducing, punitive damages for haphazard investigatory techniques); Millstone v. O'Hanlon Reports, Inc., 383 F. Supp. 269, 276 (E.D. Mo. 1974) (information collected from neighbors without verification, and withholding file from subject, justified mental suffering and punitive damages for willful violation of accuracy and disclosure duties), *aff'd,* 528 F.2d 829 (8th Cir. 1976); Cahlin v. General Motors Acceptance Corp., 936 F.2d 1151, 1156 (11th Cir. 1991) (agency may escape liability if it shows that inaccurate report was prepared by following appropriate procedures; not strictly liable for inaccuracies).

[150] 15 U.S.C. § 1681n (allowing damages for willful violations). *See* Houghton v. New Jersey Mfrs.' Ins. Co., 615 F. Supp. 299, 305 (E.D. Pa. 1985) (awarding $3,500 compensatory, $3,500 punitive damages, and $7,770 in attorneys' fees against insurance company that caused

When noncompliance is merely negligent rather than willful, punitive damages are not available, but attorneys' fees and compensatory damages for mental distress are available.[151] Civil actions may be brought in either state or federal court, and there is some controversy over whether actions brought in state court are removable to federal court.[152]

§ 4.23   False Advertising

Problems that confront consumers, publishers of advertisements, and advertisers themselves regarding false and misleading advertising must be addressed in the newer technologies of the NII. For example, the Federal Trade Commission filed a complaint regarding false advertising by Chase Consulting on America Online. Chase Consulting advertised a "credit repair" plan for $99 that actually advised consumers to take illegal steps to repair their credit records. Although the promotional material claimed the program was "100% legal," it actually counseled a number of violations of federal law. The FTC entered into a consent decree that prohibited Chase Consulting from "misrepresenting, either directly or indirectly, in writing, via a computer communications network, or by any other means, the legality of any credit repair program"[153] and it also required him to pay the FTC the total amount of money received from consumers.[154] The FTC did not seek relief against America Online, but the possibility of intermediary liability exists with respect to harmful advertisements as much as with defamatory messages and files that infringe copyrights.

---

investigative report to be prepared in conjunction with defense of automobile accident lawsuit; report constituted a credit report though for improper purpose); Thorton v. Equifax, Inc., 467 F. Supp. 1008, 1009 (E.D. Ark. 1979) (approving $250,000 exemplary damages award), *reversed on other grounds,* 619 F.2d 700 (8th Cir. 1980) (jury instruction erroneous on qualified privilege and on common-law standards); Rasor v. Retail Credit Co., 554 P.2d 1041, 1049 (Wash. 1976) (FCRA damages are not limited to out-of-pocket losses, but may not be presumed; there must be some proof); Jones v. Credit Bureau, 399 S.E.2d 694, 700 (W. Va. 1990) (statute allows humiliation and mental distress damages even when no out-of-pocket expenses are proven; affirming compensatory award of $4,000 and punitive award of $42,500).

[151] 15 U.S.C. § 1681o. *See* Stevenson v. TRW, Inc., 987 F.2d 288, 296–97 (5th Cir. 1993) (mental distress and humiliation damages recoverable even when fault is no greater than negligence).

[152] *Compare* Haun v. Retail Credit Co., 420 F. Supp. 859, 862 (W.D. Pa. 1976) (action brought in state court is removable) *and* Broom v. TRW Credit Data, 732 F. Supp. 66, 68 (E.D. Mich. 1990) (action brought in state court is removable) *with* Ruth v. Westinghouse Credit Co., 373 F. Supp. 468, 469 (W.D. Okla. 1974) (action brought in state court not removable).

[153] Federal Trade Comm'n v. Brian Corzine, CIV-S-94-1446 DFL-JFM (E.D. Cal. Consent Decree, filed Nov. 28, 1994), ¶ I(A).

[154] *Id.* ¶ II.

The Lanham Act's false advertising provisions specifically exempt publishers, radio broadcasters, and other media and agencies from liability for any false advertisement unless the intermediary refused on request of the FTC to furnish the name and post office address of the originator of the advertisement.[155] Some state false advertising statutes have similar provisions.[156] The case law avoids a standard that would in effect impose a duty on publishers and intermediaries to investigate the nature of products or services advertised.[157] For example, in *Commonwealth v. Monumental Properties, Inc.,*[158] the Supreme Court of Pennsylvania held that neither typesetters nor distributors of forms that violated state prohibition on false and deceptive advertising could be liable, because they were performing purely mechanical acts.[159] The court's analysis suggested that liability might be imposed upon proof of actual knowledge of the falsity of the content.[160]

---

[155] 15 U.S.C. § 54(b).

[156] *See, e.g.,* Cal. Bus. & Prof. Code § 17,502 (West 1995) (exempting publisher or broadcaster "who broadcasts or publishes an advertisement in good faith, without knowledge of its false, deceptive, or misleading character"); Tex. Bus. & Com. Code Ann. § 17.49 (West 1993), which exempts from deceptive trade practices liability

> owner or employees of a regularly published newspaper, magazine, or telephone directory, or broadcast station, or billboard, where in any advertisement in violation of this subchapter is published or disseminated, unless it is established that the owner or employees of the advertising medium have knowledge of the false, deceptive, or misleading acts or practices declared to be unlawful by subchapter, or had a direct or substantial financial interest in the sale or distribution of the unlawfully advertised good or service.

[157] *See* Suarez v. Underwood, 426 N.Y.S.2d 208 (Sup. Ct. 1980) (general rule is no duty to investigate, but proof of recklessness could support liability; granting summary judgment for newspaper); *see also* Pittman v. Dow Jones & Co., 662 F. Supp. 921, 922 (E.D. La. 1987) (granting newspaper's motion for summary judgment; newspaper has no duty to investigate accuracy of advertisements unless it undertakes to guarantee soundness of products advertised; fraudulent advertisement with respect to interest rates on deposits in Texas financial institution, causing loss to plaintiff). *Compare* Braun v. Soldier of Fortune Magazine, Inc., 968 F.2d 1110, 1119–20 (11th Cir. 1992) (affirming judgment on jury verdict against publisher of advertisement that on its face indicated danger that advertiser might commit murder for hire; adequately met First Amendment standard and did not impose duty to investigate) *with* Eimann v. Soldier of Fortune Magazine, Inc., 880 F.2d 830, 836 (5th Cir. 1989) (reversing judgment on jury verdict against magazine; advertisement for ex-Marines willing to take "high risk assignments" were facially innocuous and magazine had no duty to investigate possibility that murder for hire would result). *See also* Consuelo Lauda Kertz & Roobina Ohanian, *Recent Trends in the Law of Endorsement Advertising: Infomercials, Celebrity Endorsers and Non-Traditional Defendants in Deceptive Advertising Cases,* 19 Hofstra L. Rev. 603, 640 (1991) (reviewing handful of cases limiting publisher liability, but noting that publisher endorsement increases publisher exposure).

[158] 329 A.2d 812 (Pa. 1974).

[159] *Id.* at 827.

[160] *Id.*

One of the more interesting cases under this standard is *Thomas v. Times Mirror Magazines, Inc.*[161] In that case, the intermediate California court reversed summary judgment in favor of the publisher of *Popular Science* magazine upon allegations that *Popular Science* continued to run an advertisement by a disbarred patent lawyer after it received a number of letters of complaint and knew that the advertisements were misleading.[162] The court held that the allegations raised triable issues of fact with respect to the privilege granted by the California statute for publishers and intermediaries.[163] On the other hand, in *First Equity Corp. v. Standard & Poor's Corp.,*[164] the district court granted summary judgment in favor of a publisher of information about securities because the publisher did not know that the published information was erroneous. The district court emphasized First Amendment considerations as applied by *New York Times v. Sullivan* and concluded that publishers cannot be liable for any false material, regardless of the legal theory, absent proof of knowledge of falsity or reckless disregard of the truth.[165]

Under these cases and the typical statutory provisions, an NII intermediary does not face liability for false and misleading advertising passing through its service when it is without fault. On the other hand, if it does anything that vouches for the product or service advertised, or if it receives complaints likely to put a reasonable person on notice of the character of the advertisements and nevertheless continues to handle them, its potential liability increases considerably.

The best course of action is to have a general notice that the intermediary does not vouch for goods or products advertised. If complaints are received, the intermediary either should remove or suppress the offending material or accompany the link to the advertisement with a notice that complaints have been received. The latter course raises the possibility of liability for defamation unless disclosure of the complaints is handled carefully.

If it is not feasible to suppress transmission of the advertisements, the disclaimer notice should say that. Such infeasibility should reduce the likelihood of liability because of the consistent theme in all of the case law that the First Amendment does not allow statutory or common law to impose no-fault liability on publishers or intermediaries. The infeasibility of removing or suppressing an advertisement eliminates any fault element in continuing to disseminate the advertisement.

§ 4.24   Liability Resulting from Self-Help Remedies

Chapter 7 explains that much regulation of the NII is and will continue to be self-regulation. When electronic communities in the NII engage in

---

[161] 159 Cal. Rptr. 711 (Ct. App. 1979).

[162] *Id.* at 715–16.

[163] *Id.*

[164] 690 F. Supp. 256 (S.D.N.Y. 1988).

[165] *Id.* at 258.

self-regulation, they frequently use self-help as a remedy for violation of their rules. The use of self-help creates incentives for the entity against whom self-help is used to challenge the legality of that self-help in regular legal forums. This section and the two that follow it explore the substantive legal theories that might be asserted by a challenger to self-help, including challenges to a particular instance of self-help as well as challenges to the overall scheme of self-regulation.

§ 4.25   —Tort

To facilitate the legal analysis, suppose a participant in an electronic community, for example an Internet newsgroup, has had her postings erased and has been denied access to the newsgroup because she violated content-based rules, perhaps by posting anti-Semitic messages. She now is a third party, outside any contractual relationship binding the electronic community together, and seeks to challenge the erasing of her messages and her exclusion from the group. She may have breach of contract claims against anyone with whom she has a contractual relationship, but she may have difficulty arguing that a contractual relationship exists between her and the newsgroup to which she posted.[166] Thus, establishing a prima facie case probably depends on being able to identify tort or statutory claims.

Successful claims under the Federal Civil Rights Act are unlikely. Section 1983[167] affords relief only against state actors or persons acting in concert with state actors.[168] The whole point of the self-government activity is to arrange remedies not involving state enforcement. If the electronic community used judicial process to enforce its rules it might be a state actor. The conspiracy section, § 1985,[169] is unavailable because the action almost certainly does not involve "going in disguise on the highway or on the premises of another,"[170] because the motive of the actors did not involve racial or other class-based discrimination, and because the interest protected by the section primarily includes only those, such as free speech and assembly, protected against government but not private interference.[171] Section 1981 only protects the privilege of making and enjoying the benefits of contracts in the context of racial or other

---

[166] This possibility is explored in **Chs. 5, 7, and 9.**

[167] 42 U.S.C. § 1983 (1988).

[168] *Compare* Lugar v. Edmondson Oil Co., 457 U.S. 922 (1982) *with* Flagg Bros. v. Brooks, 436 U.S. 149 (1978) *and* Wyatt v. Cole, 504 U.S. 158 (1992) (businessman who obtained writ of replevin and cooperated with sheriff to seize cattle subject to liability under § 1983, but did not enjoy immunity afforded public officials).

[169] 42 U.S.C. § 1985 (1988).

[170] *Id.* § 1985(3).

[171] Scott v. Carpenters, 463 U.S. 825 (1983) (reversing court of appeals because nonunion construction workers injured by mob of union workers were not victims of racial animus and First Amendment interests are protected only against state action).

class-based animus. There may, of course, be statutory claims if members of the self-governing community committed technical violations of 18 U.S.C. § 1030, the Computer Fraud and Abuse Act,[172] or—less likely—the Electronic Communications Privacy Act.[173]

Otherwise, the plaintiff must establish one or more tort claims. The problem here is in establishing legal injury. If she can establish legal injury, she at least can plead a prima facie tort.[174] Establishing that legal injury element for prima facie tort recovery most often brings the claim within one or more traditional tort categories, such as intentional interference with contractual relations, trespass to chattel, conversion, nuisance, fraudulent misrepresentation, intentional infliction of emotional distress, or invasion of privacy.[175]

Of these, private nuisance can be ruled out because this tort only protects interests in the use and enjoyment of land.[176] Liability for conversion and trespass to chattels depends on the plaintiff being able to establish the proposition that the messages containing the advertisement constituted chattels.[177] Fraudulent misrepresentation depends on some misstatement of fact coupled with the intent that the plaintiff rely on it.[178] Those elements are unlikely to be satisfied in the factual context. Negligence is unlikely because only economic injury is involved.[179]

That leaves intentional interference with contractual relations, which is a strong prima facie theory. This tort[180] extends to prospective economic relations

---

[172] This statute is analyzed in **Chs. 3** and **13.**

[173] See **Chs. 3, 13.**

[174] Restatement (Second) of Torts § 870 (1979) allows tort damages to be recovered for any intentional, unjustifiable injury to another, but only when the harm is to a legally protected interest of the plaintiff. *Id.* cmt. e.

[175] *See generally* Restatement (Second) of Torts § 870 cmt. d (1979) (established intentional torts and their established legal privileges amount to crystallizations of general principles dated in § 870).

[176] *See* Restatement (Second) of Torts § 821D ("a private nuisance is a non-trespassory invasion of another's interest in a private use and enjoyment of land").

[177] See Restatement (Second) of Torts § 217 (1964) (ways of committing trespass to chattel); *id.* § 223 (ways of committing conversion). Both Restatement sections are written in terms of interferences with "chattels." *See* Star Contracting Co. v. McDonald's Corp., 608 N.Y.S.2d 327 (App. Div. 1994) (no cause of action for conversion of intangibles under New York law); United Leasing Corp. v. Thrift Ins. Corp., 440 S.E.2d 902, 906 (Va. 1994) (generally conversion applies only to tangible property although some cases extended to intangible rights integrated with a document such as a stock certificate, promissory note, or bond) (citing cases); Equity Group, Ltd. v. PaineWebber, Inc., 839 F. Supp. 930, 933 (D.D.C. 1993) (traditionally conversion did not extend to intangible property interests; any liberalization has stopped with documentary interests; citing cases involving business relationships, partnership interests).

[178] Restatement (Second) of Torts § 525 (1976) (summarizing elements).

[179] See **§ 4.8** explaining that negligence liability depends on physical injury to persons or property, outside the context of a special relationship.

[180] Restatement (Second) of Torts §§ 766–766C (1977) (summarizing elements of variations of intentional interference tort).

as well as expectations under enforceable contracts.[181] The commentary to the *Restatement* emphasizes that this tort protects interests generally in commercial relationships.[182] It should encompass the plaintiff's lost business opportunities resulting from being unable to post (this argument might be stronger if the facts involved advertisements rather than hate postings) as well as injury to more concrete interests represented by any contracts the plaintiff may have with service providers who were prevented from or induced to refuse to handle the plaintiff's messages.[183] Typically, successful plaintiffs are able to identify at least some potential customers.[184]

Regardless of the tort theory used to establish prima facie liability, important issues of privilege and immunity almost certainly will be involved. For example, when such tort and statutory claims are asserted against public officials, sovereign immunity is a frequent defense.[185] Beyond immunity arguments is the common-law privilege of "authority of law."[186] The very nature of private enforcement suggests that these privileges would not be available, but the prima facie tort, the intentional interference tort, and the nuisance concept all admit a general justification defense, which involves balancing the interests of the actor against those of the plaintiff.[187] This opens up the possibility of a fairly

---

[181] *Compare id.* § 766B (intentional interference with prospective contractual relations) *with id.* § 766 cmt. d (types of contract).

[182] *Id.* § 766D cmt. c.

[183] *See generally* Ervin v. Amoco Oil Co., 885 P.2d 246, 253 (Colo. Ct. App. 1984) (affirming judgment on jury verdict against oil company on intentional interference and other tort grounds; no need for plaintiff to identify specific contracts that were interfered with; approving jury instruction, "for plaintiffs to prove Count VI they must prove . . . Amoco intentionally and improperly interfered with plaintiff's prospective contractual relations by: (a) inducing or otherwise causing actual or potential gasoline customers not to enter into or continue the prospective relationship with the plaintiff, or (b) preventing the plaintiff from acquiring or continuing the prospective relations with actual or potential gasoline customers."). *But see* Fineman v. Armstrong World Indus., Inc., 980 F.2d 171, 195 (3d Cir. 1992) (plaintiff may be required to prove the likelihood of economic relations with which interference is claimed).

[184] *See, e.g.,* Kelly-Springfield Tire Co. v. D'Ambro, 596 A.2d 867, 871 (Pa. Super. Ct. 1991) (referring to identification of one potential buyer).

[185] *See* Wiatt v. Cole, 112 S. Ct. 1827 (1992) (private actor sued under 42 U.S.C. § 1983 for seizing cattles under unconstitutional replevin statute did not enjoy sovereign immunity that would be available to public official; reviewing history of immunity claims).

[186] *See* Restatement (Second) of Torts § 145 (1964) (privilege to use amount of force reasonably necessary to execute order of court or other public authority that is valid on its face); *id.* § 146 (orders of military or naval superiors); *id.* § 118 (privilege of arrest when certain preconditions are satisfied).

[187] Restatement (Second) of Torts § 870 cmt. e (1977) (explaining balancing process for prima facie tort liability); *id.* § 767 (factors in determining whether interference with contractual relations is improper and less actionable include the nature of the actor's conduct, the actor's motive, the interests of the victim, the interests thought to be advanced by the actor, the social interests of protecting the freedom of action of the actor and the economic interest of the victim, and the relations between parties); *id.* § 828 (liability for private nuisance depends on utility of actor's conduct).

freewheeling judicial inquiry into the appropriateness of the plaintiff's conduct, in light of the interests protected by electronic community self-governance. In this inquiry, the trade custom of Usenet would be relevant, as would the fairness of the methods used by the particular community. Procedural due process concepts would enter into the analysis in assessing the methods used by the particular group. The reasonableness and representative character of rules developed by the particular community as accurate statements of trade custom also could enter into the analysis.

§ 4.26 —Antitrust

A variety of antitrust claims might be brought by someone excluded from a self-governing electronic community. These would proceed like any other anti-trust claim by someone confronted with a refusal to deal, and thus implicates the analysis of refusals to deal under the antitrust laws presented in **Chapters 2** (access) and **5** (licensing). The analysis of physician peer review under the antitrust laws is particularly interesting in conjunction with self-government by electronic communities because the peer review cases involve self-government by a nonelectronic professional community.

§ 4.27 Availability of Sovereign Immunity

Sovereign immunity is significant in considering liability for many NII products because the underlying data comes from a government agency. Sovereign immunity has receded in importance, particularly at state and local levels of government, but it still must be considered because of a possibility that it would shield originators of data from liability and because its existence for those in the supply chain might intensify exposure of downstream private sector entities, as explained in § **4.18.**

§ 4.28 —Sovereign Immunity in General

The defense of sovereign immunity[188] initially arose from the old English concept that a king had a divine right to rule (the "king can do no wrong") and so should not be subject to suit.[189] Later, the absolute rule gave way, through common-law erosion[190] and legislative enactments such as the Federal

---

[188] Paul Boltz, law clerk to the author, did the research for this section.

[189] *See* Carley v. Wheeled Coach, 991 F.2d 1117 (3d Cir. 1993) (detailed history of early sovereign immunity theories).

[190] *See* Restatement (Second) of Torts § 8a introductory note (1964) (erosion of sovereign immunity).

Tort Claims Act (1946) (FTCA).[191] The FTCA provides that damages may be recovered from the federal government "for injury or loss . . . caused by the negligent or wrongful act or omission of any employee of the Government while acting within the scope of his office or employment."[192]

This seemingly broad waiver of federal sovereign immunity is greatly limited by an FTCA exception. Section 2680(a) of title 28 states that there is no liability when the act is "based upon the exercise or performance or the failure to exercise or perform a discretionary function or duty on the part of a federal agency or an employee of the Government, whether or not the discretion involved be abused" [emphasis added]. This discretionary exception is broad, under the principle of *Dalehite v. United States*.[193] The Court there held that federal decisions as to how fertilizer should be bagged, labeled, and transported were discretionary decisions so the government could not be liable. Only purely ministerial decisions or those activities that are merely a rubber stamping qualify for the FTCA immunity waiver. Given this broad interpretation of section 2680, it is likely that some government information dissemination, such as publication of maps and charts, is discretionary in nature, although one could argue that physical reality leaves little room for discretion in placement of basic information and the value of certain variables like latitude, longitude, and elevation. Other design features, however, like cultural detail representation, clearly is discretionary. Whether a map or chart feature is sufficiently expressive to qualify for copyright protection[194] may be a useful starting point for deciding whether it is sufficiently discretionary to be outside the scope of the FTCA.

§ 4.29 —Derivative Sovereign Immunity for Government Contractors

Even when the government enjoys immunity for its actions, the government's contractors cannot directly access this same immunity. The definition section of the FTCA establishes that the term "federal agency . . . does not include any contractor with the United States."[195] A contractor is not subject to section 2671's exclusion, however, if (1) the government itself has immunity for the act (that is, it involves discretionary government actions), and (2) the contractor was acting as an agent of the government. The rationale behind allowing contractors to access the government's immunity in these circumstances rests on two public policy arguments. The first argument is commonsensical: if the government has the power to have certain work done (for example, have a helicopter built for it),

---

[191] Title IV Legislative Reorganization Act, Pub. L. No. 79-601 (1946), codified at 28 U.S.C. §§ 1346(b), 2401(b), 2671–2680.

[192] 28 U.S.C. § 1346(b).

[193] 346 U.S. 15 (1953).

[194] See **Ch.10.**

[195] 28 U.S.C. § 2674.

then "it [can] employ servants to do the work."[196] Secondly, the pragmatic concern that allowing liability for contractors will ultimately increase the over-all price level of government bids reinforces this expansion of immunity. In *Boyle v. United Technologies Corp.,*[197] the Supreme Court acknowledged that "the imposition of liability on Government contractors will directly affect the terms of Government contracts: either the contractor will decline to manufacture the design specified by the Government, or it will raise its price." In that case, the plaintiff sued the manufacturer of a military helicopter for negligently making an escape hatch that could not be blown if the helicopter were under water. The Court determined that the contractor may be entitled to derivative sovereign immunity because the government had a substantial interest in con-tinuing its contracting out of military goods.[198]

The test for whether the contractor is an agent of the government rests on slight variations in standard agency doctrine. A contractor is an agent and eligible for the sovereign immunity defense, rather than an independent contrac-tor and fully liable for all torts, if the principal maintained control over the physical details of the project. For example, the Fourth Circuit applied this precise test to a contract between the government (FAA) and Arrow General, an airport janitorial service. That contractor was found to be an independent one because the government's supervision of the contract was perfunctory at best.[199]

In examining military procurement contracts (certainly the most prolific area of derivative sovereign immunity cases), courts have developed a more detailed, but substantively similar test to the traditional physical control test. Liability cannot be imposed on a contractor if

1. The government approved reasonably precise specifications, *and*
2. The good produced met those specifications, *and*
3. The supplier warned the government of the dangers.

The first two conditions ensure that the government was engaged in a discretionary act and is immune itself for the given tort. The third condition prevents a circumvention of the public policy that the contractors should enjoy immunity to promote the government's interest in contracting out various projects. By requiring the contractor to report any dangers it discovers, the court ensures that contractors do not profit from concealing information that the government would use in making its discretionary decisions.[200]

---

[196] Green v. ICI Am., Inc., 362 F. Supp. 1263, 1266 (E.D. Tenn. 1973).

[197] 487 U.S. 500, 507 (1988).

[198] *See* Carley v. Wheeled Coach, 991 F.2d 1117, 1119 (3d Cir. 1993) (citing *Boyle,* the court observed that "there is a unique federal interest in all contracts in which the government procures equipment").

[199] Berkman v. Arrow Gen., Inc., 957 F.2d 108, 113 (4th Cir. 1992) ("the FAA took [no] control over the actual performance of the janitorial services . . . on a day-to-day basis").

[200] Boyle v. United Technologies Corp., 487 U.S. 500, 512 (1988).

§ 4.30   —Privity of Contract

What is common to all judicial extensions of sovereign immunity to contractors is that the contractors were in an actual contractual relationship with the government. While there is little explicit authority that a contract with the government is a prerequisite for derivative immunity,[201] the rationale behind the contractor immunity suggests that a contract is essential.

Because contractor immunity is based on the idea that the contractor is controlled by the government and is thus an extension of the government, an entity that has no contract with the government logically could not be under such a contractual obligation. Thus, a publisher that unilaterally takes public records and publishes them would be under no compulsion to follow the government's specifications. In fact, it would be very likely that the government would not have the slightest idea that its records were being used for this particular purpose. The lack of contractual burden on the publishers eliminates any likelihood that they are under any control apart from the influence the government exerts over any normal business operating in this country.

The only sovereign immunity argument that a publisher of public records could pursue with any possible chance of success would be to argue that the public policy for derivative immunity, promotion of governmental interest in contracting out procurement, is implicated even when no contract is present. That is, even though the government has no contract with the publisher, it still has a very real interest in the dissemination of the information it makes available. To deny sovereign immunity to these publishers would "chill" the government's efforts to make, say, maps and charts widely available. And without any chance of immunity, publishers will have no incentive to report any defects in the public records to the government as entities with contracts are required to do under the courts' three-prong test.[202] Therefore, publishers could make a viable public policy argument to include them in the immunized class of contractors, yet this argument would be up against a Sisyphusean quantity of decisions that either implicitly or directly refute immunity when a contractual relationship is absent.

---

[201] One court did conclude that a construction subcontractor, which had a contract with the general contractor and not with the government directly, could not invoke sovereign immunity. United States v. Small Business Admin., 807 F. Supp. 675, 677 (D. Colo. 1992) ("The requirement that there be privity of contract between a [contractor] and the United States is firmly established.").

[202] The arguments in favor of eliminating a privity requirement to permit the extension of sovereign immunity are the opposite of the arguments in favor of eliminating the privity requirement between plaintiff and the products liability defendant, accepted in MacPherson v. Buick Motor Co., 111 N.E. 1050 (N.Y. 1916). In *MacPherson*, elimination of privity enabled a consumer to shift the loss to a manufacturer of a defective product. In contract immunity controversies, eliminating the privity requirement would prevent a consumer from recovering from anyone.

§ 4.31   Model Disclaimer Language

Disclaimers are mainly contract terms, negating duties that otherwise might be implied by the contract. They deflect liability to third parties who do not have privity of contract and thus are not bound in a formal sense by a disclaimer. By giving the customer notice, a disclaimer can change the range of conduct that is reasonable for the customer. Unreasonable customer conduct may give rise to defenses to tort claims influenced by plaintiff expectations, as in the products liability area and in the invasion of privacy area. In addition to the following disclaimer language, one can find additional language in **Chapter 5.**

Transmitted: 95-02-21 10:43:16 EST

American Online Rules of the Road

Purchasing Products and Services through the AOL Service

Please remember that AOL Inc. does not endorse, warrant or guarantee any product or service offered through the AOL Service and will not be a party to any transaction between you and third-party providers of products or services. As with the purchase of a product or service through any medium or in any environment, you should use your best judgment and exercise caution where appropriate. Blind opportunity ads and "get rich quick" schemes should be approached with ample skepticism. The AOL Service cannot mediate disputes and cannot assume responsibility for any outcome. Be careful, be smart, have fun!

§ 4.32   Notice of Lack of Control of Third Parties

The following is the notice provided by CompuServe with respect to its Internet gateway:

"Welcome to the CompuServe FTP service!

"There are several facts to keep in mind as you are using the FTP Internet service.

"By proceeding, you indicate that you understand and agree to the following:

"When using the Internet, you are using a completely different physical network than the CompuServe network. The CompuServe network is centralized and uniformly managed. The Internet is maintained independently at thousands of sites around the world. The reliability, availability and performance of resources accessed via the Internet are beyond CompuServe's control and are not warranted or supported by CompuServe in any way. If many people access a site at the same time, performance will deteriorate. Be prepared to wait for the remote system to respond to your requests if you are using it during periods of peak demand. Files you download from

Internet file library archives may not have been pre-checked by any content manager. It is your responsibility to determine that a file contains information or programs you want, that it will work on your equipment, that you have rights to copy and use the information, and that it does not contain any virus or other potentially damaging side effects. It is prudent to run a virus checking program on any file you download from the Internet.

"Since CompuServe exercises no control over the content of the information passing through the FTP interface, please be sensitive to the rights of ownership and assure compliance with copyright law and the CompuServe Agreement and Operating Rules before redistributing any information obtained through this FTP interface.

"Thank you for using the CompuServe FTP service.

"telnet warning:

You are about to establish a connection to an Internet host. The performance, reliability, availability and content of Internet hosts is beyond CompuServe's control. You may return to CompuServe at any time by holding down the Control key and pressing ']'."[203]

§ 4.33 Language Disclaiming Third-Party Beneficiaries

As § 4.9 explains, third-party beneficiary status can arise from the inference that a contract between two others are intended to benefit the third party. One way to prevent third-party beneficiary suits for breach of contract is to disclaim the intent to benefit third parties. The following language does that:

This contract is intended for the sole benefit of the two parties whose signatures appear at the end. It is not their intent to create contractual benefits running to any third party and they specifically desire not to create third-party beneficiary status in any other person or entity.

The same basic language could be used in an on-line contracting situation by deleting reference to the signatures at the end of the document.

---

[203] Communicated to the author by CompuServe 10:00 A.M., 22 June 1995.

CHAPTER 5

LIABILITY FOR SERVICE FAILURES

§ 5.1 Introduction and Description of the Problem

Information technology does not work perfectly, and many persons—those with a sophisticated understanding as well as those with an incomplete understanding of technology's capability—are frequently disappointed by the performance of systems they buy or use. E-mail messages get lost or are delayed. Network routers fail to route traffic to intended destinations and sometimes send it to unintended destinations; firewalls fail to exclude damaging intrusions. Data communication systems intended to be used for critical communications are unavailable at the desired time; representations that a legal or medical information base contains all of the relevant material on a particular subject turn out to be false.

In these circumstances, the disappointed purchaser or user of the technology may assert legal claims against the technology provider. Such claims, unlike third-party claims considered in **Chapter 4,** can be based on contractual duties of the defendant, because plaintiff and defendant usually have some kind of contractual relationship. Whether license or other type of contract encompasses the relationship, warranty frequently is a basis for the claim. In addition, many plaintiffs seek to assert tort claims, either to broaden the types of duties they allege their defendants breached, or to expand the kind of damages available. On occasion, they also assert misrepresentation claims seeking punitive damages for this intentional tort. Finally, antitrust enters the picture when contracts impose limitations on entrepreneurial activity by one of the parties.

This chapter focuses on liability by a service provider to someone who obtains goods or services from that service provider. It explains the role of contract and license, considering coverage of the Uniform Commercial Code. Then, it analyzes warranties and explores the boundaries between tort and contract in evaluating duties and damages.

This chapter concentrates on contract obligations running between NII service providers and their own customers, centered in contract law. **Chapter 4** concentrates on obligations running to third parties, based mostly on tort law. **Chapter 9** focuses on the use of information technology to make contracts. It and this chapter are closely related. The contracts made under the techniques and theories considered in **Chapter 9** may give rise to liabilities considered in this chapter. Conversely, disclaimers of warranties and other contract obligations considered in this chapter may be effected through the techniques and under the theories considered in **Chapter 9.**

§ 5.2 Breach of Contract

A variety of contractual relations may bind service providers and their customers, including contracts for the sale of goods covered by Article 2 of the Uniform Commercial Code, contracts for the performance of services, arguably covered by the common law of contract but not by Article 2, and licenses for the use of goods with or without accompanying services. Within all of these forms of contract, specific provider obligations may be labeled warranties and may be express or implied by law. Within all of these forms of contract, the user of the goods or services may waive certain rights, and the provider may disclaim certain duties.

§ 5.3   Coverage by U.C.C. Article 2

The Uniform Commercial Code (UCC) and *Restatement (Second) of Contracts* both address the sale of goods,[1] and both deal with breach of contract arising in the sale of goods context.[2] *Goods* are defined in the UCC as "all things which are moveable at the time of identification to the contract for sale other than money in which the price is to be paid, investment securities and things in action."[3] In most jurisdictions computer software falls within the UCC definition of a good.[4]

§ 5.4   Warranty Concepts

In contract law, a *warranty* is defined as "an undertaking or stipulation, in writing, or verbally [sic], that a certain fact in relation to the subject of a contract is or shall be as it is stated or promised to be."[5] In sales of personal property, a *warranty* is defined as "a statement or representation made by the seller of goods, contemporaneously with and as a part of the contract of sale, though collateral to the express object of it, having reference to the character, quality, or title of the goods, by which he promises or undertakes that certain facts are or shall be as he then represents them . . . a statement of fact respecting the quality or character of goods sold, made by the seller to induce the sale, and relied on by the buyer."[6] Professor Corbin explained that some warranties are representations of fact rather than promises, "the truth of which is a condition precedent to the duty of the other party."[7] In other instances, however, proper interpretation shows warranties to be promises, in which case the promisor is

---

[1] *See generally* Raymond T. Nimmer, *Intangible Contracts: Thoughts of Hubs, Spokes, and Reinvigorating Article 2,* 35 Wm. & Mary L. Rev. 1337 (1994) (overview of revision of Article 2 of UCC, in symposium on same subject). *See also* Raymond T. Nimmer, *License Articles Under Article 2 of the UCC: A Proposal,* 19 Rutgers Computer & Tech. L.J. 281 (1993); Raymond T. Nimmer, *Services Contracts: The Forgotten Sector of Commercial Law,* 26 Loy. L.A. L. Rev. 725 (1993); Andrew Roudau, *Computer Software: Does Article 2 of the Uniform Commercial Code Apply?,* 35 Emory L.J. 853, 920 (1986) (suggesting that commentators' views have shifted on whether software licenses are covered by Article 2).

[2] Research and initial drafting for this section was done by Andrew J. Vella and William Harrington, Villanova Law School Class of 1996, law clerks to the author.

[3] U.C.C. § 2-105 (1977).

[4] *See* Advent Sys. v. Unisys Corp., 925 F.2d 670 (3d Cir. 1991) (both hardware and software are goods under UCC); Douglas E. Phillips, *When Software Fails: Emerging Standards of Vendor Liability Under the Uniform Commercial Code,* 50 Bus. Law. 151, 158–59 (1994) (explaining that software qualifies as a "good" under Article II of UCC because Article II focuses on moveability not tangibility, and software is not intangible even though intellectual property rights embodied in it may be).

[5] Black's Law Dictionary 1758 (rev. 4th ed. 1968).

[6] *Id.*

[7] Arthur L. Corbin, Corbin on Contracts § 14, at 21 (1952).

obligated to indemnify the promisee against loss.[8] For purposes of this chapter it is simpler and more useful to consider warranties as promises, recognizing the theoretical possibility of treatment instead as conditions precedent.

Generally, there are two types of warranties in the sale of goods context: express and implied.[9] Express warranties by a seller can be created as follows:

(a) Any affirmation of fact or promise made by the seller to the buyer which relates to the goods and becomes part of the basis of the bargain creates an express warranty that the goods shall conform to the affirmation or promise.

(b) Any description of the goods which is made part of the basis of the bargain creates an express warranty that the goods shall conform to the description.

(c) Any sample or model which is made part of the basis of the bargain creates an express warranty that the whole of the goods shall conform to the sample or model.[10]

The word *warranty* need not be used to create an express warranty,[11] but the statement that creates the express warranty "must be a statement of fact as contrasted with a statement of the seller's opinion or recommendation of the goods."[12]

The second type of warranties is implied warranties. There are two classes of implied warranties: implied warranty of merchantability[13] and implied warranty of fitness for a particular purpose.[14] The basic concept behind implied warranty of merchantability is that "[g]oods delivered under an agreement made by a merchant in a given line of trade must be of a quality comparable to that generally acceptable in that line of trade under the description or designation of the goods used in the agreement."[15] Under this warranty the goods must be "of fair average quality within the description and . . . fit for the ordinary purposes for which such goods are used."[16]

The implied warranty of fitness for a particular purpose requires that the seller have knowledge of the buyer's particular purpose required for the good.[17] Further, the buyer must rely on the seller's knowledge when selecting the good.[18] An implied warranty for a particular purpose arises in the situation when

---

[8] *Id.*

[9] Warranties also arise in licensing arrangements as well as in "sales" contracts. As § **5.6** explains, licenses usually are covered by U.C.C. Article 2.

[10] U.C.C. § 2-313 (1977).

[11] *Id.* § 2-313(2).

[12] John Edward Murray, Jr., Murray on Contracts § 100B (3d ed. 1990).

[13] U.C.C. § 2-314 (1977).

[14] *Id.* § 2-315.

[15] *Id.* § 2-314 cmt. 2.

[16] *Id.* § 2-314(2)(b)–(c).

[17] *Id.* § 2-315.

[18] *Id.*

"[a] product [that] may be suitable for ordinary purposes [is] unsuitable for the special or particular purpose of the buyer."[19] If the seller is aware of the particular needs of the buyer, he is subject to a higher standard of quality.[20] Whether the seller is aware of the particular needs of the buyer is a question of fact that is determined by the surrounding circumstances.[21] Under the UCC,

> the buyer need not bring home to the seller actual knowledge of the particular purpose for which the goods are intended or of his reliance on the seller's skill and judgment, if the circumstances are such that the seller has reason to realize the purpose intended or that the reliance exists.[22]

The second element of warranty of fitness for a particular purpose is the particular purpose for which the goods will be used. A particular purpose is distinguished from an ordinary purpose in that a particular purpose "envisages a specific use by the buyer which is peculiar to the nature of his business."[23] For example, shoes are normally used for walking upon ordinary ground, but a seller may know that a buyer has selected a pair for climbing mountains.[24] The seller is aware that the buyer is going to use the shoes for mountain climbing and is held to the standard of supplying the buyer with a pair of shoes that are suitable for mountain climbing. There are some limited situations, however, when warranty of fitness for a particular purpose would not apply. In the previous example, if the buyer insists on a pair of Nike shoes, there is no resulting implied warranty of fitness for a particular purpose. When a buyer insists on a particular brand, "he is not relying on the seller's skill and judgment . . . so no warranty results."[25] Similarly, a warranty of fitness for a particular purpose may arise if the purchaser of a computer system, intended to connect several simultaneous users to the Internet, makes it clear that simultaneous access is required. While an MS-DOS® system might be more appropriate for single-user access, the vendor's knowledge of the particular requirements would give rise to an implied warranty of fitness for multiuser use, unless the customer particularly insists on the MS-DOS system.

The UCC contains a special provision that addresses inconsistent warranties and sets up what is essentially a hierarchy of warranties.[26] Generally, all

---

[19] John Edward Murray, Jr., Murray on Contracts § 100D (3d ed. 1990). *See* U.C.C. § 2-315 (1977) (implied warranty for a particular purpose where "seller . . . has reason to know any particular purpose for which the goods are required and that the buyer is relying on the seller's skill or judgment to select or furnish suitable goods").

[20] *See* John Edward Murray, Jr., Murray on Contracts § 100D (3d ed. 1990) (when seller knows buyer has relied on seller's skill, buyer's reliance justifies imposition of higher standard of quality).

[21] U.C.C. § 2-315 cmt. 1 (1977).

[22] *Id.*

[23] *Id.* cmt. 2.

[24] *Id.*

[25] *Id.* cmt. 5.

[26] U.C.C. § 2-317 (1977).

warranties are construed as being consistent with each other or as cumulative.[27] When consistent construction is unreasonable, the intent of the parties determines which warranty is dominant.[28] The application of this general rule is subject to a hierarchy of warranties.[29] Under the UCC, "[e]xpress warranties displace any inconsistent implied warranties of merchantability."[30] Nevertheless, an express warranty does not displace any warranty for fitness for a particular purpose.[31]

§ 5.5 Disclaimer of Warranties

Implied warranties can be disclaimed but express warranties cannot.[32] To disclaim an implied warranty of merchantability, the disclaimer must be conspicuous,[33] mention the word merchantability, and be in writing.[34] Under the UCC, a disclaimer is conspicuous if the writing is one that a reasonable person against whom it is to operate ought to have noticed it.[35] This is accomplished by printing the disclaimer in capital letters, varying the print color of the disclaimer, or using boldfaced type for the clause containing the disclaimer.[36]

Disclaimers limiting the purchaser's recovery by excluding consequential damages are valid under the UCC unless they are unconscionable.[37] Limitations on consequential damages are not unconscionable and do not fail in their essential purpose if the parties negotiate to allocate the risk in advance, and if the transaction occurs in a commercial setting between two experienced business enterprises.

Achieving sufficient prominence with respect to disclaimers for products and services offered through the NII is challenging. The problem also is considered in **Chapter 9,** relating to electronic commerce. The prevailing practice is similar

---

[27] *Id.*

[28] *Id.*

[29] *Id.*

[30] *Id.* § 2-317(c).

[31] *Id.*

[32] *Id.* § 2-316.

[33] *See generally* Page M. Kaufman, *The Enforceability of State "Shrink Wrap" License Statutes in Light of* Vault Corp. v. Quaid Software, Ltd., 74 Cornell L. Rev. 222 (1988); Deborah Kemp, *Mass Marketed Software: The Legality of the Form License Agreement,* 48 La. L. Rev. 87 (1987).

[34] U.C.C. § 2-316 & cmts. 3 & 4 (1977).

[35] American Computer Trust Leasing v. Jack Farrell Implement Co., 763 F. Supp. 1473 (D. Minn. 1991), *aff'd sub nom.* American Computer Trust Leasing v. Boerboom, 967 F.2d 1208 (8th Cir. 1992).

[36] *Id.*

[37] U.C.C. § 2-719(3) (1977).

to that used by America Online, some of whose disclaimers are quoted in §§ **5.18** and **5.19.** When a user originally signs up for service, AOL, like most of its competitors, transmits a notice that the service is subject to the terms and conditions expressed in a terms of service document, which is readily available to the user, although not automatically displayed in full text on the user's screen.

World Wide Web technologies in the Internet make it relatively easy to do the same kind of thing on any Web server. The first time an identified user[38] uses a Web page, a particular notice can be displayed. The same general approach can be used by Gopher servers, although it is difficult to display as much text at any particular level. Even anonymous FTP servers can be programmed to display a small amount of text automatically when a connection is established.

When a connection is completely automatic, the values of certain variables in the transaction set, as defined by a trading partner agreement or trade practice,[39] may signify either an express warranty or a disclaimer. The prominence requirement must be interpreted with respect to the unambiguous nature of the value of the variable. In recent cases involving the sale of hardware and software, sellers have successfully disclaimed express and implied warranties on their goods.[40]

§ 5.6   Licensing

A *license* is a grant of a privilege to use the grantor's property. A license of a patent, for example, permits the licensee to engage in conduct that otherwise would be patent infringement. A license also may convey rights of the grantor. For example, the patent licensee may be able to bring its own infringement actions against third parties. Licenses also may grant powers. For example, license of A's copyright to B may also grant B the power to sublicense or to transfer the license.

Licenses may be exclusive or nonexclusive. If A grants an exclusive license to B to use A's copyrighted computer program, and A subsequently grants another license to C, B has a breach of contract action against A for granting the

---

[38] Anonymous users are more of a problem. They can be handled by causing the disclaimer notice to be displayed at the beginning of every transaction in which the user cannot be identified, disclaiming warranties and expressing other limitations on express or implied contract rights against the provider of the service.

[39] See **Ch. 9.**

[40] *See* Transport Corp. v. IBM, 30 F.3d 953, 958–59 (8th Cir. 1994) (transferred lease of computer hardware retained initial disclaimer and bound third party); LS Heath & Son, Inc. v. AT&T Info. Sys., Inc., 9 F.3d 561, 569–70 (7th Cir. 1993) (merger clause did not reflect parties' actual intent and therefore proposal language that computer network would "satisfy all of user's stated objectives" constituted express warranty that could not be disclaimed by master agreement); Ritchie Enters. v. Honeywell Bull, Inc., 730 F. Supp. 1041 (D. Kan. 1990) (negligent misrepresentation claim dismissed due to integration clause and clear disclaimer of all other remedies).

second license.[41] B also may have a claim against C for intentional interference with contractual relations (B's exclusive license from A) and possibly for infringement of the copyright licensed to B.

Licenses clearly are contracts and are covered by Article 2 of the U.C.C. in most jurisdictions.[42] They also may be conveyances of property.

Characterization of a legal relationship as a license does not make as much difference in the event of bankruptcy of the grantor as it did after the United States Court of Appeals for the Fourth Circuit decided *Lubrizol Enterprises, Inc. v. Richmond Metal Finishers, Inc.*[43] In *Lubrizol* the court held that the trustee or debtor in possession could exercise its power under § 365 of the Bankruptcy Code unilaterally to reject a license agreement, thereby eliminating the right of the licensee to use intellectual property covered by the license.[44] The Congress reacted by adopting § 365(n) of the Bankruptcy Code.[45] Now, a licensee of intellectual property may elect to retain the intellectual property covered by the license when the trustee in bankruptcy initially exercises the option of disaffirmance.[46]

Of course, licenses, like other contracts, are subject to statutes of frauds requirements.[47] The special requirement for a "note or memorandum of a transfer agreement," required by § 101 of the Copyright Act[48] can be satisfied by a license, but it must be in writing either when it is initiated or later.[49]

---

[41] *See* Levi Case Co. v. ATS Prods., Inc., 788 F. Supp. 428, 431–32 (N.D. Cal. 1992) (grant of exclusive license covering patent excludes even patent holder from exercising rights conveyed by license).

[42] For example, the New Hampshire version of U.C.C. § 2-202 provides that Article 2 is applicable to any "transaction in goods," and this statement of scope generally is construed to extend Article 2 to licenses as well as sales involving transfer of title. *See* Colonial Life Ins. Co. v. Electronic Data Sys. Corp., 817 F. Supp. 235, 238 (D.N.H. 1993) (quoting N.H. Rev. Stat. Ann. § 382-A: 2-202 (1991) and citing cases). *See also* Step-Saver Data Sys., Inc. v. Wyse Technology, 939 F.2d 91 (3d Cir. 1991) (treating license for computer software as covered by Article 2); Harper Tax Servs., Inc. v. Quick Tax Ltd., 686 F. Supp. 109 (D. Md. 1988) (same); *cf.* Neilson Business Equip. Ctr., Inc. v. Italo V. Monteleone, PA., 524 A.2d 1172, 1173 (Del. 1987) (lease of computer hardware, software, and related services covered by UCC Article 2 because effectively was sale although structured as lease).

[43] 756 F.2d 1043 (4th Cir. 1985).

[44] *Id.* at 1048.

[45] 11 U.S.C. § 365(n); *see also* H.R. Rep. No. 1012, 100th Cong., 2d Sess. (1988), *reprinted in* 1988 U.S.C.C.A.N. 3200.

[46] *See generally* David S. Kupetz, *Intellectual Property Issues in Chapter 11 Bankruptcy Reorganization Cases,* 42 J. Copyright Soc'y USA 68 (1994).

[47] Musim Boutique Intercontinental, Ltd. v. Picasso, 880 F. Supp. 153 (S.D.N.Y. 1995) (applying statute of frauds to oral license subsequently memorialized by writing; citing cases). *See also id.;* Genin Trudeau & Co. v. Integra Dev. Int'l, 845 F. Supp. 611, 616 (N.D. Ill. 1994) (promissory estoppel avoided statute of frauds defense to oral contract).

[48] 17 U.S.C. § 204(a) (1988).

[49] Playboy Enters., Inc. v. Dumas, 53 F.3d 549 (2d Cir. 1995) (acceptance clauses added to payment checks insufficient for express writing).

§ 5.7 —Licenses and the First Sale Doctrine

The first sale doctrine originated in antitrust law, but has implications for intellectual property more generally.[50] The doctrine prevents the exercise of control by a seller over a product once it is sold.

Now, the first sale doctrine is codified in the Copyright Act.[51] It allows the owner of a copy of a copyrighted work to sell or otherwise dispose of the possession of that copy, thus guaranteeing freedom of alienation. Much computer program licensing seeks to defeat the operation of the first sale doctrine,[52] although there are questions about the efficacy of licensing to achieve this objective.[53] Moreover, special requirements apply in foreign markets, leading some software vendors to prefer annual licenses and actual signatures on a license agreement in order to preserve the license characterization under the EC directive for copyright protection of software.[54]

§ 5.8 —Licensing and Antitrust

Important restrictions on the content of licenses arise from the antitrust laws in the United States and procompetitive principles in the European Union. These restrictions on licensing arrangements are important to customers of NII service suppliers because they circumscribe the potential protections for the parties, and they provide the customer with a way of avoiding the contract and challenging certain supplier conduct. They also, of course, have implications beyond protection of customer interests in a contractual setting. The interaction between licensing and antitrust involves the interplay of three attributes of a particular license: the procompetitive effect of the rights, privileges, and powers granted by the license; the anticompetitive effect of restrictions imposed by the license; and the justification for the restrictions.

---

[50] *See* United States v. Wise, 550 F.2d 1180, 1187 (9th Cir. 1977) (explaining first sale doctrine); Red Baron-Franklin Park, Inc. v. Taito Corp., 883 F.2d 275, 280–81 (4th Cir. 1989) (describing first sale doctrine and concluding it does not apply to performance right).

[51] 17 U.S.C. § 109(a) (1988).

[52] Microsoft Corp. v. Harmony Computers & Elects., Inc., 846 F. Supp. 208, 212–13 (E.D.N.Y. 1994) (license for software was not a sale under the first sale doctrine); Intel Corp. v. ULSI Sys. Technology, Inc., 995 F.2d 1566 (9th Cir. 1993) (computer chip transfer was a first sale because of permission under licensing agreement); Step-Saver Data Sys., Inc. v. Wyse Technology, 939 F.2d 91, 96 n.7 (3d Cir. 1991) (explaining motivation and uncertainty in using licensing to evade first sale doctrine).

[53] David A. Rice, *Licensing the Use of Computer Program Copies and the Copyright Act First Sale Doctrine,* 30 Jurimetrics J. 157 (1990).

[54] *See* Council Directive 91/250 EEC of 14 May 1991 on Legal Protection of Computer Programs, Doc. No. 391L0250, 1991 O.J. (L 122) 42 (providing in art. 4 for exhaustion of distribution right upon first sale).

There is nothing inherent in a license agreement that implicates the antitrust laws. A license is a grant of capacity to enter a particular market and thus enhances competition rather than restricting it.[55] But most license agreements also contain restrictions limiting the duration of the license, limiting the geographic area within which it grants privileges, or limiting the uses of the licensed subject matter. In some cases, a license also limits what the licensee may do with subject matter outside the licensed subject matter.

When such restrictions exist, section 1 of the Sherman Act potentially is implicated. That section prohibits agreements in restraint of trade; however, it allows contracts that restrain trade when they are justified by other interests and when their procompetitive effects outweigh their anticompetitive effects.[56] Thus, licenses of intellectual property may impose restrictions consistent with the Sherman Act because the grantor has a legitimate interest in protecting its intellectual property—for example, preventing a trade secret from being disclosed to the world and thus being destroyed.[57] Additionally, the grant of a license with respect to intellectual property increases by at least one the number of producers offering that particular intellectual property in the marketplace, thus creating procompetitive effects.

Justice Department Guidelines recognize that licensing of intellectual property facilitates its integration with complementary factors of production.[58] Moreover, "sometimes the use of one item of intellectual property requires access to another." An item of intellectual property "blocks" another when the second cannot be practiced without using the first. For example, an improvement on a patented machine can be blocked by the patent on the machine. Licensing promotes the coordinated development of technologies that are in a "blocking relationship."[59] An example of this kind of procompetitive effect of licensing intellectual property is the cross-licensing between the owners of the

---

[55] Draft Guidelines for the Licensing and Acquisition of Intellectual Property, 59 Fed. Reg. 41,339, 41,340 (Aug. 11, 1994) ("the Department recognizes that intellectual property licensing allowing firms to combine complementary factors of production is generally procompetitive"). The guidelines were finalized on April 6, 1995. *See* 49 Pat. Trademark & Copyright J. (BNA) 703, 714 (1995). The final guidelines differ from the August 1994 draft by stating more definitely that anticompetitive effects are not likely to arise from nonexclusive licensing arrangements and by providing more detail on how technology and innovation markets should be defined.

[56] *See* Orson, Inc. v. Miramax Film Corp., 862 F. Supp. 1378, 1385–86 (E.D. Pa. 1994) (exclusive license by film distributor to exhibitor was vertical restraint subject to rule of reason analysis, was reasonable, and did not violate antitrust laws because promotion of interbrand competition outweighed adverse affects on intrabrand competition); Futurevision Cable Sys., Inc. v. Multivision Cable TV Corp., 789 F. Supp. 760, 768 (S.D. Miss. 1992) (vertical exclusive license over popular television programming did not violate antitrust laws because it promoted interbrand competition more than it restricted intrabrand competition).

[57] See **Ch. 10.**

[58] Justice Department Guidelines § 3.4, 59 Fed. Reg. at 41,343 (Aug. 11, 1994).

[59] Request for Comments on Draft Antitrust Guidelines for the Licensing and Acquisition of Intellectual Property, 59 Fed. Reg. 41,339, 41,341 (Aug. 11, 1994).

public key algorithm and the Diffie Hellman algorithm, used in most commercial versions of public key encryption.[60]

On the other hand, when an intellectual property license imposes broad restraints on licensee activities beyond those "ancillary" to the intellectual property protection, such restrictions potentially violate the antitrust laws. For example, A grants to B a license to use A's computer program, useful in presenting material in the World Wide Web. As a condition of the license, A requires B to withdraw from the market its computer program that facilitates connections to the Internet. The restrictions on B's Internet-access software would be greater than those necessary to protect A's intellectual property, and the license probably would be found to violate the antitrust laws.

Conversely, if the license covers a trade secret in a World Wide Web browser caching algorithm, and the license imposes no restrictions except for restricting the licensee from disclosing the trade secret to anyone else, the restriction almost certainly does not violate the antitrust laws. The restrictions are no greater than necessary to protect the legitimate interest in the trade secret belonging to the licensor.

Antitrust and contract analysis of license restrictions is similar to antitrust and public policy analysis of convenants not to compete. Contract law reinforces antitrust law by invalidating certain contracts in restraint of trade.[61] The general rule in contract law is that "a promise is unenforceable on grounds of public policy if it is unreasonably in restraint of trade."[62] Promises to refrain from competition that are not ancillary to otherwise valid transactions or relationships are unreasonable restraints on trade.[63] Ancillary restraints are permissible as long as they are no greater than that needed to protect the promisee's legitimate interest, and the promisee's need is not outweighed by the hardship to the promisor and the likely injury to the public.[64]

Geographic restrictions are permissible as long as they can be shown to have a reasonable relationship to the licensor's legitimate interest.[65] Geographic restrictions are evaluated under the antitrust rule of reason standard,[66] allowing restrictions that have a reasonable relationship to the legitimate interests of

---

[60] Public key encryption is considered extensively in **Ch. 9.**

[61] Restatement (Second) of Contracts § 186, Topic 2 preliminary note preceding section (1981).

[62] *Id.* § 186.

[63] *Id.*

[64] *Id.* § 188.

[65] *See* Levi Case Co. v. ATS Prods., Inc., 788 F. Supp. 428, 431–32 (N.D. Cal. 1992) (grant of exclusive license covering patent excludes even patent holder from exercising rights conveyed by license; exclusive license by itself cannot constitute illegal restraint under antitrust laws).

[66] Justice Department Guidelines § 3.4, 59 Fed. Reg. at 41,343 (Aug. 11, 1994) (restraints in intellectual property licensing arrangements usually evaluated under rule of reason). Per se treatment would apply only to naked price fixing, output restraints, and market division among horizontal competitors, although some group boycotts and resale price maintenance provisions might also be per se illegal. *Id.* (citing National Soc'y of Professional Eng'rs v. United States, 435 U.S. 679, 692 (1978)).

the licensor.[67] Use restrictions are particularly appropriate in connection with trademark licensing because the idea of a trademark is to permit control over the quality of a product associated with a particular source.[68] The Justice Department Guidelines give the following example:

> Conversely, licenses raise antitrust questions when they limit competition that would have taken place in the absence of the license. The following kinds of restrictions or arrangements are particularly suspect:
>
> Restrictions on goods, services, or technologies other than the licensed technology. Penalties on licensees for dealing with suppliers of substitute technologies.
>
> Licenses that transfer little intellectual property but impose restrictions on competitive entities.
>
> Combination of research and development activities of most of the entities in a particular field licensing between potential competitors that reduce competition in markets where they are likely to compete.
>
> Restrictions with respect to one market that reduce competition in another market, for example, by foreclosing access to or raising the price of an important input.
>
> Delta, Inc. develops a new software program for inventory management. The program has wide application in the health field. Delta licenses the program in an arrangement that imposes both field of use and territorial limitations. Some of Delta's licenses permit use only in hospitals; others permit use only in group medical practices. Delta charges different royalties for the different uses. All of Delta's licenses permit use only in specified geographic areas. The license contains no provisions that would prevent or discourage licensees from developing, using, or selling any other program. None of the licensees are actual competitors of Delta in the sale of inventory management programs.
>
> Discussion: The key competitive issue raised by the licensing arrangement is whether it harms competition that would likely have taken place in its absence. (See section 3.) Such harm could occur if the licenses foreclose access to competing technologies (in this case, most likely competing computer programs), prevent licensees from developing their own competing technologies (again, in this

---

The guidelines suggest the first look analysis and rule of reason treatment of a license that contributes to efficiency by integrating economic activity. On the other hand if a putative integration is a sham or if there is an insufficient relationship between the restraint and an efficiency-producing integration, per se treatment is a possibility. Justice Department Guidelines § 3.4, 59 Fed. Reg. at 41,343 (Aug. 11, 1994).

[67] Continental TV, Inc. v. GTE Sylvania, Inc., 433 U.S. 36, 45–46 (1977) (restrictions placed on retailers are not per se illegal but should be evaluated under a reasonableness standard to accommodate legitimate manufacturer interests).

[68] *See* Susser v. Carvel Corp., 206 F. Supp. 636 (S.D.N.Y. 1962), *aff'd*, 332 F.2d 505 (2d Cir. 1965) (protecting right to insist on production according to secret formula because of unique nature of item); Instructional Sys., Inc. v. Computer Curriculum Corp., 614 A.2d 124, 126 (N.J. 1992) (noting importance of trademark name in context of franchise); Neptune T.V. & Appliance Serv., Inc. v. Litton Microwave Cooking Prods. Div., 462 A.2d 595, 598 (N.J. Super. Ct. App. Div. 1983) (franchise license provides authorized use of trade name).

case most likely computer programs), structure royalties to impose an effective requirements contract upon licensees, or facilitate market allocation or price-fixing for any product or service supplied by the licensees. If the license agreements contained such provisions, the Department would analyze their competitive effects as described in sections 3–5 of these Guidelines. In this hypothetical, there are no such provisions, and there is no apparent harm to competition. The arrangement appears to do no more than increase the value of the licensed technology by subdividing it among different fields of use and territories and charging royalties that differ among licensees. The Department therefore would be unlikely to object to this arrangement. The result would be the same whether the technology was protected by copyright, patent, or trade secret. The Department's conclusion as to competitive effects could differ if, for example, the license barred licensees from using any other inventory management program.[69]

Although horizontal licensing arrangements are not inherently suspect, they raise more possibilities for anticompetitive effects than vertical licenses.[70] Horizontal arrangements involve rights for technologies that are economic substitutes for technologies that a licensee owns or controls.[71] Vertical arrangements involve complementary technologies.

The Justice Department Guidelines create an antitrust "safety zone" within which the Justice Department will not challenge a restraint in a licensing arrangement "absent extraordinary circumstances."[72] The *safety zone* is defined as including restraints not of a type normally warranting condemnation under the per se rule, in which the licensor and its licensees collectively account for no more than 20 percent of each relevant market affected by the restraint.[73] Outside this safety zone, anticompetitive effects worthy of concern include the following:

1. Vertical relationships that foreclose access or increase competitors' costs to critical technologies, taking into account concentration, difficulty of entry, and the elasticities of supply and demand[74]

2. Exclusive arrangements restricting licensor rights to license others when the licensor and licensees are actual or potential competitors, or when they restrict the licensee from using competing technologies, depending on the

---

[69] Request for Comments on Draft Antitrust Guidelines for Licensing and Acquisition of Intellectual Property, 59 Fed.Reg. 41,339, 41,341 (Aug. 11, 1994).

[70] Vertical arrangements affect activities that occur in a complementary relationship.

[71] Justice Department Guidelines § 3.3, 59 Fed. Reg. at 41,342–43 (Aug. 11, 1994) (distinguishing vertical and horizontal license components but noting that horizontal relationship between licensor and licensees is not inherently suspect).

[72] *Id.* § 4.1, 59 Fed. Reg. at 41,344.

[73] *Id.* § 4.1.

[74] *Id.* § 4.3, 59 Fed. Reg. at 41,344–45.

availability of other outlets for competitive viable exploitation of rival technologies[75]

3. Package licensing that constitutes suspect tying arrangements because the related licenses involve separate products.[76]

Licenses of trade secrets may provide for an indefinite stream of royalties, but licenses of patents are different; they may not require payment of royalties beyond the end of the patent.[77]

A license restriction that seeks to suppress independent inventive or creative effort is impermissible as monopolization under section 2 of the Sherman Act.[78] A license restriction that simply seeks to reinforce prohibitions on infringement is permissible.[79] Other considerations also may be legitimate justifications for license arrangements that tend to exclude some producers, especially when alternative markets and sources of supply exist.[80] Blanket license arrangements frequently are attacked under the antitrust laws, but rule of reason analysis accommodates the pragmatism of such an approach because it reduces transaction costs to everyone.[81] Refusals to license intellectual property are

---

[75] *Id.* § 4.3.2, 59 Fed. Reg. at 41,345.

[76] *Id.* § 5.3, 59 Fed. Reg. at 41,347.

[77] *Compare* Brulotte v. Thys Co., 379 U.S. 29 (1964) (obligation to pay royalties does not extend beyond patent life) *with* Aronson v. Quickpoint Pencil Co., 440 U.S. 257 (1979) (permissible for license to provide for negotiated reduced royalty payments after patent application rejected).

[78] See **Ch. 2** (discussing antitrust challenges to Microsoft). License restrictions almost always can be § 1 as well as § 2 violations because they are contracts. Monopolization conduct provided for in a contract violates § 2 because it is monopolization and § 1 because it is a contract that restrains competition.

[79] *See* Advance Computer Servs. v. MAI Sys. Corp., 845 F. Supp. 356, 370 (E.D. Va. 1994) (allowing license restrictions on use of copyrighted software; distinguishing Laser Comb Am., Inc. v. Reynolds, 911 F.2d 970, 978 (4th Cir. 1990) (finding that restrictions on independent creative effort were copyright "misuse")).

[80] Northeastern Educ. Television v. Educational Television Ass'n, 758 F. Supp. 1568, 1574–75 (N.D. Ohio 1990) (vertical exclusive license for educational television program survived rule of reason analysis because of alternative sources of competing programming, increased inter-brand competition resulting from license terms, and absence of evidence of intent to achieve unlawful objective).

[81] *See generally* National Cable Television Ass'n, Inc. v. Broadcast Music, Inc., 772 F. Supp. 614, 629–30 (D.D.C. 1991) (reviewing history of antitrust litigation involving Broadcast Music and its blanket license arrangements; finding that blanket licensing arrangements either did not restrain trade because of available alternatives or survive rule of reason scrutiny; but found certain split blanket licensing practices violated previous antitrust consent decree). *But see* Broadcast Music, Inc. v. Hearst/ABC Viacom Entertainment Serv., 746 F. Supp. 320, 326 (S.D.N.Y. 1990) (denying motion to dismiss antitrust § 1 claim against blanket license arrangements that allegedly suppressed competition represented by independent licensing by copyright holders under rule of reason standard).

not antitrust violations.[82] The European Commission has issued guidelines creating a kind of safe harbor for license agreements containing territorial restrictions.[83]

§ 5.9 —Relationship among Contract, Warranty, and Tort Theories

It is important to understand the law's reluctance to give tort damages for breaches of contract. It involves a reluctance to allow negligence claims to be premised on duties created by contract and an even greater reluctance to allow negligence or products liability claims to proceed when the only injury is economic rather than physical damage to person or property. Warranty is a contract theory, with tort overtones. Negligence and strict products liability are tort concepts.

Implied warranty claims are contractual and carry with them contractual defenses, such as lack of privity, notice of the defect, and disclaimer of warranty.[84] In product liability claims these defenses made it too easy for suppliers to shift the loss occasioned by injury to consumers.[85] "Products liability grew out of a public policy judgment that people need more protection from dangerous products than is afforded by the law of warranty."[86] Because

---

[82] *See* Dawson Chem. Co. v. Rohm & Haas Co., 448 U.S. 176, 215 (1980) (compulsory license of patents has often been proposed but never has been enacted; compulsory license requirements are a rarity in U.S. patent system; declining to impose indirect requirement to license in order not to forfeit protection against contributory infringement of patent); United States v. Studien Gesellshaft Kohle, 670 F.2d 1122, 1127 (D.C. Cir. 1981) (upholding patent holders' placing limits on use by licensed parties); United States v. Westinghouse Elec. Corp., 648 F.2d 642 (9th Cir. 1981) (allowing parties to agree to limit use of patent and thus to evade governmental antitrust concerns); LucasArts Entertainment Co. v. Humongous Entertainment Co., 870 F. Supp. 285, 290 (N.D. Cal. 1993) (noting intellectual property is controlled exclusively by owner).

[83] *See generally* Commission Regulation 556/89 of 30 November 1988 on the application of art. 85(3) of the EEC Treaty to certain categories of know-how licensing agreements, Doc. No. 389R0556, 1989 O.J. (L 061). *See id.* art. 1 (permissible terms of different types of license agreements, ranging from five to ten years); *id.* ¶ 7 (rationale for limiting term of restrictive license agreements). In mid-1995, the Commission was revising its licensing guidelines.

[84] The research for this section was done by William Harrington, law clerk to the author.

[85] *See* Sterner Aero AB v. Page Airmotive, Inc., 499 F.2d 709 (10th Cir. 1974) (reversing summary judgment; disclaimers are not effective in strict liability cases); Commonwealth Bank & Trust v. Spectrum Leasing, 719 F. Supp. 346 (M.D. Pa. 1989) (denying defendant's motion for summary judgment; if given the opportunity, manufacturers would use disclaimers to nullify their responsibility).

[86] East River S.S. Corp. v. Transamerica Delaval, Inc., 476 U.S. 858, 866 (1986) (citing Seely v. White Motor Co., 63 Cal. 2d 9, 403 P.2d 145, 149 (1965)).

of this policy judgment, most of the cases involving choice between contract and tort theories have involved strict products liability claims. Such claims can be made by customers, or they can be made by third parties. Strict liability third-party claims are considered in **Chapter 4;** this section focuses on the analysis applicable to claims by one in a contractual relationship with the supplier.

Whether a victim can recover under warranty (contract) or strict liability (tort) depends on two factors: the damages the aggrieved party is seeking, and the relationship between the parties. Recovery for personal injuries and physical property damage is covered under strict liability and the law of tort; economic losses are covered under the law of warranty and contract. The distinction between implied warranty claims and strict liability claims also is important because warranties, whether arising under the common law or the Uniform Commercial Code, can be disclaimed, but disclaimers are not effective for strict liability based on tort.

Contract law seeks to give aggrieved parties the benefit of their bargain, putting them in the position they would have been in had the promises made to them been fulfilled.[87] Tort law seeks to protect everyone from unreasonable risk of injury arising from a duty imposed by law on actors in general, regardless of whether they ever dealt with the victims.[88] The difference in the remedies means that choosing between contract and tort recovery effectively determines whether benefit of the bargain or traditional tort compensation for pecuniary, nonpecuniary emotional injury, and punitive damages is available. Ultimately, the choice between theories represents a policy choice of risk allocations.

As discussed in **Chapter 4,** products liability claims for NII products and services are viable only when personal injury or property damage is involved. Although certain computer and information systems may result in personal injury, such as geographic information systems (GIS) and health care information systems, a wider range of NII systems might cause property damage if they malfunction.[89]

The Supreme Court in *East River Steamship Corp. v. Transamerica Delaval, Inc.,*[90] examined three approaches that bracket the possibilities for answering the property damage question:

---

[87] John W. Wade, *Is Section 402A of the Second Restatement of Torts Preempted by the UCC and Therefore Unconstitutional?,* 42 Tenn. L. Rev. 123 (1974).

[88] *Id.*

[89] *See* Elsken v. Network Multi-Family Sec. Corp., 49 F.3d 1470 (10th Cir. 1995) (unsuccessful suit by estate of woman murdered when remotely monitored burglar alarm system failed to produce timely response to alarm).

[90] 476 U.S. 858 (1986) (ruling on a products liability claim brought in admiralty by evaluating land-based theories of strict liability).

1. The law of warranty prevails if a defective product causes purely mone-
    tary injury (the *Seely* approach)[91]
2. Strict liability prevails because even purely economic losses are protected
    under strict liability (the *Santor* approach),[92]
3. The distinction is based upon the degree of risk imposed by the defect.[93]

The *Seely* approach refers to an often quoted opinion, in which Justice
Traynor clarified a policy-based distinction between contract and tort theories,
grouping property damage and personal injury together, and distinguishing both
from monetary injury:

> The distinction that the law has drawn between tort recovery for physical
> injuries and warranty recovery for economic loss is not arbitrary and does not
> rest on the "luck" of one plaintiff in having an accident causing physical injury.
> The distinction rests rather on an understanding of the nature of responsibility a
> manufacturer must undertake in distributing his products. He can appropriately
> be held liable for physical injuries caused by defects requiring his goods to
> match a standard of safety defined in terms of conditions that create unreason-
> able risks of harm. He cannot be held for the level of performance of his prod-
> ucts in the consumer's business unless he agrees that the product was designed
> to meet the consumer's demands. A consumer should not be charged at the will
> of the manufacturer with bearing the risk of physical injury when he buys a
> product on the market. He can, however, be fairly charged with the risk that the
> product will not match his economic expectations unless the manufacturer agrees
> that it will.[94]

The law of warranty prevails if the defect causes only monetary harm.[95] Physical
injury to property is governed by strict liability because it is so akin to personal
injury.[96]

---

[91] Seely v. White Motor Co., 63 Cal. 2d 9, 403 P.2d 145 45 Cal. Rptr. 17 (1965) (holding that the
law of warranty governs economic damages arising from a defect in the truck sold to the
plaintiff by the defendant).

[92] Santor v. A&M Karagheusian, Inc., 207 A.2d 305, 312 (N.J. 1965) (holding defendant liable
for selling defective carpet and remanding the case to the district court on the question of
damages, instructing the district court to use a benefit of the bargain calculation when assessing damages).

[93] Pennsylvania Glass & Sand Corp. v. Caterpillar Tractor Co., 652 F.2d 1165 (3d Cir. 1981)
(reversing the district court's ruling for summary judgment in the case of fire damage to a
front-end loader caused by a defect in the machine).

[94] Seely v. White Motor Co., 63 Cal. 2d 9, 403 P.2d 145, 151, 45 Cal. Rptr. 17 (1965).

[95] 403 P.2d at 151.

[96] *Id.*

The *Santor* approach holds that the responsibility of the manufacturer is no different in the case of damage to a person's property or her person.[97] The *Santor* court disallowed the contract defense of lack of privity and held a manufacturer liable for a defective carpet sold to the plaintiff. Strict liability was imposed for a product's mere presence on the market, and the proper method for calculating damages was the plaintiff's loss on the bargain.[98] "[T]hey [courts following this approach] believe that recovery for economic loss would not lead to unlimited liability because they think a manufacturer can predict and insure against product failure."[99]

Under the third approach evaluated in *East River*, courts choose between contract and tort theories on a case-by-case basis depending on the type of risk created by the defect. The court in *Pennsylvania Glass & Sand Corp. v. Caterpillar Tractor Co.* stated that the guiding factors distinguishing tort and contract claims are the nature of the defect and the type of risk it imposes.[100] A fire in a front-end loader constituted a serious safety hazard and thus fell within the ambit of tort law.

After evaluating the three approaches, the *East River* court adopted the *Seely* approach. The court held that a manufacturer has no duty under a strict liability theory to prevent a product from damaging itself.[101] It rejected the *Santor* argument as unpersuasive, and dismissed the intermediate approach because of its failure to distinguish contract and tort theories.

Other courts have chosen between contract and tort theories based on the relationship between the parties. Private consumers do not possess equal bargaining power and thus have, on public policy grounds, less power to bargain away their right to recovery. In strict liability cases involving the "garden variety" consumer, sound public policy prohibits the disclaimer of *Restatement* § 402A benefits.[102] Commercial entities with equal bargaining power, however, are allowed to disclaim liability through negotiated agreements.[103] This allows the buyer the flexibility in a commercial setting to use his business judgment to

---

[97] Santor v. A&M Karagheusian, Inc., 207 A.2d 305, 312 (N.J. 1965); *see* Spring Motors Distribs., Inc. v. Ford Motor Co., 489 A.2d 660, 672 (N.J. 1985) (limiting *Santor* by holding that it does not apply in the commercial context).

[98] 207 A.2d 305, 312 (N.J. 1965).

[99] East River S.S. Corp., 476 U.S. 858 (1986) (citing Emerson G.M. Diesel, Inc. v. Alaskan Enter., 732 F.2d 1468 (9th Cir. 1984)).

[100] 652 F.2d 1165 (3d Cir. 1981).

[101] East River S.S. v. Transamerica Delaval Inc., 476 U.S. 858 (1986).

[102] Garden variety consumers have included commercial entities. *See* Sterner Aero AB v. Page Airmotive, Inc., 499 F.2d 709 (10th Cir. 1974) (stating that a commercial entity with no expertise in the manufacturing of airplanes may be considered an ordinary consumer when purchasing a refurbished airplane). Restatement (Second) of Torts § 402(A) cmt. m (1965).

[103] Idaho Power Co. v. Westinghouse Elec. Corp., 596 F.2d 924, 928 (9th Cir. 1978) (holding defendant's disclaimer of tort liabilities an effective defense to strict liability action).

forgo claims of liability in exchange for receiving a lower price from the seller. The social policies involved in protecting the ordinary consumer are not applicable to commercial transactions involving two knowledgeable corporations that have conspicuously negotiated the terms of the agreement.[104]

Thus, policy considerations affect the choice between warranty and tort when consumers are the plaintiffs, allowing only warranty when commercial entities with significant bargaining power are the plaintiffs. The choice between warranty and tort determines whether damages for noneconomic injury are available and whether liability can be disclaimed or waived.

Products liability does not exhaust the tort possibilities. Negligence also is a tort. Rarely, however, is a disappointed contract promisee entitled to maintain a parallel negligence action for breach of the duties established by the contract. The traditional test to determine whether a negligence cause of action is supportable by a breach of contract was whether there was an improper performance of a contractual obligation (misfeasance) rather than a mere failure to perform (nonfeasance).[105] Another way that the general rule is often stated is to say that

> when the only loss or damage is to the subject matter of the contract, a plaintiff's action is ordinarily on the contract—rather than in tort. . . . [M]isfeasance, or negligent affirmative conduct in the performance of a promise, generally subjects an actor to tort liability as well as contract liability for physical harm to persons and tangible things; [but] recovery of intangible economic losses is ordinarily determined by contract law; and there is no tort liability for nonfeasance, i.e., for failing to do what one has promised to do in the absence of a duty to act apart from the promise made.[106]

"A tort claim may be maintained only when the wrong ascribed to the defendant is the gist of the action, the contract being collateral."[107]

There are circumstances in which a duty independent of the contractual duty arises from the nature of the relationship between the plaintiff and the defendant. In such "special relationship" cases,[108] a plaintiff may maintain both a breach of

---

[104] Keystone Aeronautics Corp. v. R.J. Enstrom Corp., 499 F.2d 146 (10th Cir. 1974) (the court remanded the case to the district court for a clearer evaluation of the exculpatory language in the disclaimer; however, the court stated that disclaimers of strict liability were valid when the transaction involved commercial entities and only property damage was at issue.)

[105] Valhal Corp. v. Sullivan Assocs., Inc., 44 F.3d 195, 228 (3d Cir. 1995) (stating general rule; comparing with more modern rule, and vacating judgment in claim against architect for breach of contract and negligence in failing to honor building height limitations).

[106] Janicek v. Kikk, Inc., 853 S.W.2d 780, 781 (Tex. Ct. App. 1993) (radio station's cancellation of advertising contract did not give rise to tort claim, but only breach of contract claim).

[107] Grode v. Mutual Fire, Marine, & Inland Ins. Co., 623 A.2d 933, 935 (Pa. Commw. Ct. 1993) (allowing tort and contract claims against contractor providing administrative, investigative, and adjustment services to insurance company).

[108] These claims sometimes are called *professional malpractice claims*.

contract action and a negligence claim.[109] In the NII context, a plaintiff might be able to argue that certain service providers are involved in a special relationship. For example, a relatively unsophisticated plaintiff who relies upon a systems integrator to select and evaluate software and hardware for a specific purpose might be able to show a special relationship, supporting negligence as well as warranty-based theories if a system component selected fails. Also, the user of a system designed to handle especially sensitive data, perhaps data involving medical diagnosis, could show a special relationship. In evaluating the existence of a special relationship, not only the relative unsophistication of the plaintiff and dependence by the plaintiff on the defendant's expertise is necessary, but also a holding out by the defendant of special expertise. In other words, the typical medical or architectural malpractice is a good model for testing NII special relationships.[110]

The interplay between negligence and contract as the basis for liability has been explored recently in the employment context. The cases rejecting negligence claims based on contractual duties should be understood primarily as rejecting the idea of extra-contractual damages for breach of contract; they logically do not reject the idea that a duty independent from the contract may exist, based on the relationship of the parties. Indeed, authority abounds for the proposition that a negligence duty can arise out of an essentially contractual relationship.[111] Outside the employment-at-will context, there is more authority

---

[109] *See* Kaiser Aluminum & Chem. Corp. v. Ingersoll-Rand Co., 519 F. Supp. 60, 68 (S.D. Ga. 1981) (absent special relationship, misfeasance/nonfeasance distinction governs; owner-operator of plant could not maintain negligence action against contractor who built air compressor that failed); Red Lobster Inns v. Lawyers Title Ins. Co., 492 F. Supp. 933, 939 n.1 (E.D. Ark. 1980) (allowing damages for negligent failure by title company to discover use restriction, based in part on special relationship; because basic recovery was in tort, consequential damages were recoverable, including lost profits); Southwestern Bell Tel. Co. v. DeLanney, 809 S.W.2d 493, 494 n.1 (Tex. 1991) (stating general rule and giving professional malpractice cases as example, but denying tort claim against telephone company for negligent omission of directory advertising).

[110] *See generally* Jay M. Feinman, Economic Negligence: Liability of Professionals and Businesses to Third Parties for Economic Loss (1995) (suggesting new tort theory to cover claims against accountants, attorneys, evaluators of business issues, real estate brokers, bankers, construction contractors, and owners of property, but not addressing suppliers of computers or communication services).

[111] *See generally* Kaiser Aluminum & Chem. Corp. v. Ingersoll-Rand Co., 519 F. Supp. 60, 68–70 (S.D. Ga. 1981) (breach of contract may result in tort liability if (1) conduct violates independent tort duty, or (2) if contract itself gives rise to tort duty as in common carrier, principal and agent, bailor and bailee, attorney and client, physician and patient, master and servant, engineer and client; usually only special relationship contracts such as those involving professional responsibility give rise to tort duties); *see* Brewster v. Martin Marietta Aluminum Sales, Inc., 145 Mich. App. 641, 668, 378 N.W.2d 558, 569 (1985) (no cause of action for "negligent breach of contract" when no breach of duty other than breach of contract); Haas v. Montgomery Ward & Co., 812 F.2d 1015, 1016 (6th Cir. 1987) (no negligent evaluation action because no duty independent of duty arising from employment contract; split panel); Struble v. Lacks Indus., Inc., 157 Mich. App. 169, 403 N.W.2d 71, 74 (1986) (same); Budd v. American Sav. & Loan Ass'n, 89 Or. App. 609, 750 P.2d 513, 515 (1988) (claim for negligence limited when it arises in a "special relationship" like employment, the terms of which circumscribe generalized duty to avoid foreseeable risks of harm).

for the proposition that a negligence duty can arise out of an essentially contractual relationship.[112]

The most difficult part of negligence recovery, overlapping somewhat with the establishment of a duty, is in convincing the court to allow recovery for economic loss in the absence of a traumatic injury to person or property.[113] Such recovery is not allowed by the majority rule,[114] but there are significant minority rule cases in California and Washington,[115] with a special set of rules for professionals likely to be relied on for special expertise.[116] Some commentators believe the trend is to allow recovery for economic loss, at least to commercial plaintiffs.[117]

---

[112] *See generally* Walker v. Rowe, 535 F. Supp. 55, 59 (N.D. Ill. 1982) (master has duty to servant, arising out of special relationship, to protect servant against foreseeable risks of harm by acts of third parties; wrongful death action against state officials for failure to protect from inmate riot), *rev'd,* 791 F.2d 507 (7th Cir. 1986) (reversed on grounds that due process clause does not guarantee safe working conditions; no common-law negligence analysis) (Easterbrook, J.); Kaiser Aluminum & Chem. Corp. v. Ingersoll-Rand Co., 519 F. Supp. 60, 68–70 (S.D. Ga. 1981) (breach of contract may result in tort liability (1) if conduct violates independent tort duty, or (2) if contract itself gives rise to tort duty as in common carrier, principal and agent, bailor and bailee, attorney and client, physician and patient, master and servant, engineer and client; usually only special relationship contracts such as those involving professional reponsibility give rise to tort duties) (non employment case).

[113] Negligence damages categories traditionally are divided into personal injury, economic loss, and property damage. Kelly M. Hnatt, Note, *Purely Economic Loss: A Standard For Recovery,* 73 Iowa L. Rev. 1181 nn.12 & 21 (1988).

[114] Basham v. General Shale, 377 S.E.2d 830, 834 (W. Va. 1988) (tort recovery not permitted for pure economic injury); Utah Int'l, Inc. v. Caterpillar Tractor Co., 108 N.M. 539, 775 P.2d 741, 744 (Ct. App. 1989) (product injurying itself not actionable in tort); Ora Fred Harris & Alphonse M. Squillante Warranty Law in Tort and Contract Actions, § 3.10, at 93–94 (John Wiley & Sons, Inc., 1989) (discussing Seely v. White Motor Co., 63 Cal. 2d 9, 403 P.2d 145, 45 Cal. Rptr. 17 (1965), and Santor v. A&M Karagheusian, Inc., 44 N.J. 52, 207 A.2d 305 (1965), as the leading cases denying recovery for economic loss) [hereinafter Harris & Squillante].

[115] *See* Harris & Squillante § 3.10, at 91–94 (discussing Biakanja v. Irving, 49 Cal. 2d 647, 320 P.2d 16 (1958) (allowing recovery for loss of inheritance resulting from negligent preparation of will); Ales-Peratis Foods Int'l v. American Can Co., 164 Cal. App. 3d 277, 290, 209 Cal. Rptr. 917, 925 (1985) (canner's loss due to defective cans); Berg v. General Motors Corp., 87 Wash. 2d 584, 555 P.2d 818 (1976) (commercial fisherman's lost profits resulting from defective diesel engine and clutch)).

[116] First Fla. Bank, N.A. v. Max Mitchell & Co., 558 So. 2d 9, 12 (Fla. 1990) (reviewing different approaches; adopting Restatement § 552 "known third party" rule); Raritan River Steel Co. v. Cherry, Bekaert & Holland, 322 N.C. 200, 367 S.E.2d 609, 615, 617 (1988) (rejecting privity requirement as too narrow and reasonably foreseeable test and *Biakanja* balancing test as too broad; adopting Restatement "known third party" test for public accounting firm defendant); Thayer v. Hicks, 793 P.2d 784 (Mont. 1990) (reversing dismissal of complaint against public accounting firm; adopting Restatement "known third party" rule).

[117] Harris & Squillante § 3.10, at 94 (general negligence rules should apply to claims for economic loss); Note, *Purely Economic Loss: A Standard For Recovery,* 73 Iowa L. Rev. 1181 (1988) (reviewing near per se rule against recovering economic loss when unaccompanied by physical damage or injury in negligence cases, but endorsing trend toward allowing recovery; suggesting guidelines).

Once a plaintiff is past the duty and economic-injury hurdles, the usual categories of tort damages are available for negligence,[118] including amounts for loss of earning capacity,[119] and emotional distress,[120] which may include fear and anxiety.[121] The measure of recovery for emotional distress includes the length of time during which the distress was or will be experienced and the intensity of the distress.[122] Damages for emotional distress and punitive damages can be substantial.[123]

Some negligence claims in the contract context are barred by the filed tariff rule, considered in § **5.17.** Negligence concepts also enter the equation in evaluating a promisor's performance under a contract. The standards for evaluating contractual performance are considered in § **5.11** of this chapter.

§ 5.10 —Checklist for License Agreement

License agreements for NII services should include terms addressing the following matters.

_____ 1. Names and addresses of parties

_____ 2. Purpose of agreement

_____ 3. Subject matter (description of product or service)

_____ 4. Site license or individual license

_____ 5. Exclusivity, transferability

_____ 6. Successorship

_____ 7. Specifications for performance of product or service

_____ 8. Payment amounts and schedule

_____ 9. Confidentiality obligations

_____ 10. Warranties and disclaimers

_____ 11. Form and delivery of notices

_____ 12. Power to terminate

_____ 13. Posttermination rights

_____ 14. Indemnification

---

[118] Restatement (Second) of Torts § 917 & cmts. b, e (1965) (generally making Restatement damages provisions applicable to negligent actor).

[119] *Id.* § 906B.

[120] *Id.* § 905 illus. 3 (damages for humiliation for negligently causing bodily disfigurement).

[121] *Id.* § 905 cmt. e (fear and anxiety compensable if expectable result of defendant's conduct).

[122] *Id.* § 905I.

[123] *See* Brown v. Burlington Indus., Inc., 93 N.C. App. 431, 378 S.E.2d 232 (1989) ($10,000 compensatory and $50,000 punitive damages judgment on jury verdict affirmed on negligence and intentional infliction theories), *review dismissed,* 326 N.C. 356, 388 S.E.2d 769 (1990).

§ 5.11   Negligence Standards in Evaluating Breach

It is tempting to suppose that many breach of contract claims would begin with an assertion that the defendant is liable for breach of contract because the defendant acted negligently. The customer of an Internet connection service provider might argue that the service provider negligently operated the service, resulting in interruptions. The occasion for making such an argument arises less frequently than one might suppose. Contract liability is not based on fault. The plaintiff recovers simply by proving that the defendant did not perform as promised. The defendant's mental state is irrelevant. The Internet access service provider either did or did not promise uninterrupted service. If it promised uninterrupted service, an interruption constitutes a breach, regardless of whether the operation was negligent. If the provider did not promise uninterrupted service, the interruption is not a breach, even if the provider was negligent. Thus, evaluating a breach of contract claim does not involve the decision maker in considering the defendant's understanding of risk and comparing the defendant's actions to forestall the risk with those of a reasonable person.

Another negligence concept does come into play in determining contract damages. Foreseeability is a central concept of negligence.[124] As § 5.16 in this chapter explains, contract defendants are liable for consequential damages only when such damages are foreseeable. There is one further point of comparison between contract analysis and negligence analysis: reference to the standards of particular communities in determining the defendants' duty. Negligence allows such a reference to give meaning to the reasonable person standard for the duty of care; contract law allows such a reference to interpret the meaning of particular contract duties, especially certain standard warranties, as discussed in § 5.12.

§ 5.12   Warranties and Usage of Trade

Evidence of custom in the trade regularly is employed to flesh out contractual duties, especially in the warranty context. Trade custom evidence is used frequently to limit or negate certain warranty claims. Conceptually, the same kinds of evidence can be used to expand warranty concepts, thus assisting in the interpretation of the scope of contractual duties.

---

[124] See **Ch. 4.**

Uniform Commercial Code § 2-316(3)(c) allows an implied warranty to be modified or excluded by course of dealing, course of performance, or usage of trade.[125] A good example of how this works is *Torstenson v. Melcher*,[126] in which the buyer of a bull bought for breeding purposes lost a lawsuit against the seller based on its catalogue guarantee that the bull was suitable for breeding purposes. The dispute was over what percentage of available cows the bull should be able to impregnate. There was testimony by the plaintiff and a representative of a trade association that the terminology used in the catalogue was standard in the industry. The defendants had pleaded in their answer that trade usage in the cattle industry excluded any implied warranty of fitness for a particular purpose.[127] The Nebraska Supreme Court found that this satisfied the requirements of U.C.C. § 1-205(6), excluding evidence of usage of trade until opposing parties were given sufficient notice to prevent unfair surprise.[128] The court also approved, as supported by the evidence, the trial court's instruction:

> The jury is instructed that under the facts in this case an implied warranty of fitness for breeding purposes may be excluded by the usage of the trade in question, and that before the jury shall consider whether or not the implied warranty of fitness stated in instruction no. 13 is breached, the jury shall consider and determine whether or not the implied warranty of fitness has been excluded by the usage of the purebred Hereford cattle trade. In the event the jury shall find the implied warranty of fitness has been excluded, then the jury shall disregard all instructions with respect to damages, for breach of the alleged and implied warranty of fitness for breeding purposes.[129]

Whether a warranty is excluded by trade custom can be indistinguishable from a question whether a duty is implied by trade custom.[130] The central concept of the implied warranty of merchantability is based on trade usage.[131]

---

[125] *See* ITT Corp. v. LTX Corp., 926 F.2d 1258, 1267–68 (1st Cir. 1991) (reversing district court; even if contract for cable assemblies was covered by U.C.C. Article 2, the course of dealing between buyer and seller excluded implied warranty against breakage under usage encountered by buyer).

[126] 241 N.W.2d 103 (Neb. 1976). *See also* Alphert v. Thomas, 643 F. Supp. 1406, 1415 (D. Vt. 1986) (custom and usage in horse trade indicated that implied warranty of merchantability included warranty that stallion was fertile and capable of getting a mare in foal).

[127] 241 N.W.2d at 107.

[128] *Id.* at 106 (characterizing § 1-205(6)).

[129] *Id.* (quoting and approving jury instruction).

[130] *See* Alfred C. Toepfer, Inc. v. Federal Barge Lines, Inc., 466 F. Supp. 40, 43 (S.D.N.Y. 1978) (judgment for seller; language in meal trading rules and bill of lading appropriately interpreted to require barge owners to provide insurance for meal shipped on barge, based on testimony of marine insurance adjuster and corporate risk manager as to trade custom).

[131] John E. Murray, Murray on Contracts § 100(C), at 546 (3d ed. 1990) (implied warranty of merchantability is most important UCC warranty, and it is written in terms of ordinary purposes for which goods are used; giving example of trade usage evidence).

Particularly significant in the NII context is *Wilson v. Marquette Electronics, Inc.*[132] A physician sued the seller of computer-assisted electrocardiographic equipment for excessive downtime. The district court found certain oral express warranties and implied warranties of merchant ability and fitness applicable and that they had been breached. The seller claimed that trade usage excluded or modified the warranties, but the court of appeals agreed with the district court that the buyer was not the type of party who was or should be aware of those trade customs. The buyer was purchasing his first computer system and was entering a market in which he was relying on the seller's expertise.[133] This reasoning would operate to bar the exclusion of implied warranties in a wide variety of NII services because when most new technologies are introduced, the provider of the service is relied upon by most users of the service for expertise and most users lack much knowledge of trade usage with respect to the new technology.[134]

On the other hand, express warranties usually cannot be negated by custom or usage or trade,[135] although trade custom evidence should be admissible to help interpret language in express warranties. Because trade usage is admissible generally to construe the terms of a contract under U.C.C. Article 2, it is admissible to construe the terms of an express warranty.

§ 5.13 Disclaimers of Warranties in Computer Cases

Since 1990, several purchasers of computer hardware and software have brought claims alleging that the hardware and software they purchased failed to perform as advertised and marketed.[136] Generally, the purchasers have

---

[132] 630 F.2d 575 (8th Cir. 1980) (modifying and affirming judgment for buyer on warranty claim).

[133] *Id.* at 582.

[134] *See also* Diversified Human Resources Group, Inc. v. PB-KBB, Inc., 671 S.W.2d 634, 637 (Tex. Ct. App. 1984) (custom in employment agency business was not admissible to negate implied warranty that applicant's academic credentials were valid because employer receiving referral was not shown to have known of custom in employment agency business).

[135] Bodine Sewer, Inc. v. Eastern Ill. Precast, Inc., 493 N.E.2d 705, 710 (Ill. App. Ct. 1986) (rejecting usage of trade argument with respect to express warranty); Southern States Coop., Inc. v. Townsend Grain & Feed Co., 163 B.R. 709, 720 (Bankr. D. Del. 1994) (trade usage was not the standard against which a breach is determined; rather it was the affirmation or promise that set the standard for determining a claim with respect to a herbicide that resulted in crop damage).

[136] Step-Saver Data Sys., Inc. v. Wyse Technology, 939 F.2d 91 (3d Cir. 1991) (breach of warranty action based on agreement printed on software package); Walter Raczynski Prod. Design v. International Business Mach. Corp., No. 92C6423, 1993 WL 282722 (N.D. Ill. July 21, 1993) (negligent misrepresentation of hardware and software performance); American

attempted to recover on two theories: in contract for a breach of express and implied warranties, and in tort for misrepresentation or fraud. The sellers have successfully thwarted these claims by employing effective disclaimers and by not blatantly misrepresenting the capabilities of their products.[137]

In *Ritchie Enterprises v. Honeywell Bull, Inc.,*[138] the purchaser of a mainframe computer brought an action for breach of warranty and fraud. The plaintiff, Ritchie Enterprises, purchased several computers from the defendant, Honeywell Bull, to automate its order entry system. The plaintiff then sued the defendant for breach of warranty and fraud when the computers did not perform as expected. The court granted the defendant's motion for partial summary judgment on the plaintiff's warranty claims, the plaintiff's request for consequential damages, and the plaintiff's negligent misrepresentation claim.

On the warranty claim, the court concluded that the written purchase agreement entered into by the parties was a fully integrated contract. Therefore, the court held that the disclaimers of the express and implied warranties in that agreement were effective, limiting the plaintiff's recovery to the express warranties in the basic agreement.

The plaintiff argued that the limited remedies granted in the basic agreement failed of their essential purpose. The court held that the agreement did not fail of its essential purpose because the provision in the agreement excluding consequential damages was valid. The provision was valid because the disclaimer was a freely negotiated allocation of risk between two sophisticated commercial enterprises.

In *American Computer Trust Leasing v. Jack Farrell Implement Co.,*[139] the plaintiff, American Computer Trust Leasing (hereinafter ACTL), brought an action against the defendant, Jack Farrell, an agricultural equipment dealer, for its failure to make payments on hardware leased from ACTL. The defendant counterclaimed, alleging fraud, breach of contract, and breach of express and implied warranties.

The agreement between ACTL and Farrell limited express warranties to direct damages and excluded any recovery for consequential damages. The court concluded that this provision was effective and not unconscionable because the provision allocated the risk in advance and was negotiated in a commercial

---

Computer Trust Leasing v. Jack Farrell Implement Co., 763 F. Supp. 1473 (D. Minn. 1991) (alleging fraud and breach of contract under hardware lease); Ritchie Enters. v. Honeywell Bull, Inc. 730 F. Supp. 1041 (D. Kan. 1990) (alleging fraud, breach of warranty, negligent misrepresentation, breach of implied covenant of good faith, and breach of fiduciary duty after purchase of mainframe computer).

[137] American Computer Trust Leasing v. Jack Farrell Implement Co., 763 F. Supp. 1473 (D. Minn. 1991); Ritchie Enters. v. Honeywell Bull, Inc., 730 F. Supp. 1041 (D. Kan. 1990); Walter Raczynski Prod. Design v. International Business Mach. Corp., 1993 WL 282722, (N.D. Ill. 1993); Step-Saver Data Sys., Inc. v. Wyse Technology, 939 F.2d 91 (3d Cir. 1991).

[138] 730 F. Supp. 1041 (D. Kan. 1990).

[139] 763 F. Supp. 1473 (D. Minn. 1991).

setting between two business enterprises. Therefore, the court limited Farrell's recovery to direct damages on the breach of warranty claim.

In *Walter Raczynski Product Design v. International Business Machine Corp.,*[140] an engineering and design firm sued IBM for breach of contract, breach of warranty, and fraudulent misrepresentation. The plaintiff, Walter Raczynski, a sole proprietor, alleged that the hardware sold by IBM and the software recommended by IBM did not function as represented.

On plaintiff's breach of contract claim, the court concluded that the System-Plan agreement signed by both Raczynski and IBM governed all of the parties' dealings. Noting that the parol evidence rule operated to exclude evidence of any prior agreements, the court concluded that the SystemPlan was a valid contract because of the unambiguous integration clause contained in the SystemPlan. Therefore, the SystemPlan with its references to other agreements could only be modified by future writings between the parties, not by future oral representations by the parties.

Because the SystemPlan explicitly excluded the implied warranties of merchantability and fitness for a particular purpose, the plaintiff's claim for breach of implied warranties was dismissed. The court ruled that these disclaimers were valid because they contained the pertinent language, they were in writing, and they were conspicuous. The court also upheld IBM's disclaimer limiting the express warranties between the parties. This disclaimer was upheld because there was no suggestion of high-pressure sales tactics and the clause was specifically referred to in bold on the front of the contract. Therefore, the plaintiff's remedy was limited to the express warranty in the contract.

In *Step-Saver Data Systems, Inc. v. Wyse Technology,*[141] Step-Saver, a value-added retailer, brought suit against TSL Industries, the producer of the operating system purchased by Step-Saver, and Wyse Technology, the producer of computer terminals used by Step-Saver. The plaintiff, Step-Saver, was marketing a multiuser system for small professional offices that would allow multiple terminals to operate from only one computer. Step-Saver sued Wyse and TSL in contract for breach of warranties and sued TSL in tort for intentional misrepresentation.

The district court granted a directed verdict in favor of TSL on the intentional misrepresentation and on the breach of warranty claims. On the warranty claim, the court granted a directed verdict holding that the license employed by TSL became part of the contract. In Step-Saver's action against Wyse, the district court instructed the jury on the issues of express warranty and implied warranty for a particular purpose but refused to instruct the jury on the issue of the implied warranty of merchantability. The jury returned a verdict in favor of Wyse on these issues. Step-Saver appealed on four points:

---

[140] 1993 WL 282722 (N.D. Ill. 1993).

[141] 939 F.2d 91 (3d Cir. 1991).

1. Step-Saver and Wyse did not intend the box top license[142] to be a complete and final expression of the terms of their agreement

2. There was sufficient evidence to support Step-Saver's intentional misrepresentation claim

3. There was sufficient evidence to submit Step-Saver's breach of warranty claim of merchantability to the jury

4. The trial court abused its discretion by excluding from evidence a letter from Wyse to Step-Saver.

The appellate court examined each issue separately. The first issue was whether the box top license became part of the contract.[143] The court decided that the box top license was to be treated as written confirmation under the U.C.C. § 2-207, because the court noted that the dispute was not over whether there was a contract but over what terms were in the agreement. The court concluded that this was a classic case of the battle of the forms because the terms in the offer did not match the terms in the acceptance.

The defendant, TSL, argued that the parties intended the box top license to be part of the contract because without the box top license the contract would not have been sufficiently definite. TSL based its theory on the fact that without the box top license the parties would not be able to distinguish whether the contract was for a license to use a copy of the program or whether the contract was for the sale of a copy of the program. The court ruled that this was immaterial to the case because both parties agreed that Step-Saver was allowed to transfer copies of the program. The court noted that power to transfer was the only significant difference between a license to use and the sale of a copy of the program. Therefore, the court found that the contract was sufficiently definite.

Evaluating the box top license under U.C.C. § 2-207(1), the court ruled that the box top license did not constitute a conditional acceptance. The court concluded that because the transferability provision in the box top license was not intended to be part of the agreement, it would be unreasonable to conclude that the offeror would assume some terms of the box top license were essential to the contract such as the disclaimers of warranties but others such as transferability were not.

Further, TSL industries employed a course of dealing argument, stating that even if the terms of the agreement did not become part of the contract for each individual transaction, the actions of the parties over time incorporated the terms of the box top license. The court rejected this argument for two reasons: first, repeated sendings only imply a desire if the terms are not agreed to by the parties, and second, a failure to negotiate specific terms into an agreement cannot be cured by repeated sending of the license.

---

[142] A "box top" license is one printed on the packaging for a product.

[143] 939 F.2d 91 (3d Cir. 1991) (evaluating whether the license was an integrated writing under U.C.C. § 202 or a proposed modification and under the U.C.C. § 209 or a written confirmation under U.C.C. § 2-207).

The court continued its U.C.C. § 2-207 analysis, ruling that under U.C.C. § 2-207(b)2 the box top license did not become part of the agreement because it included additional terms that materially altered the agreement. The court held that the box top license materially altered the agreement because TSL included express and implied warranties in the original agreement and then attempted to disclaim them in the box top license. This was a material alteration of the original agreement.

TSL argued that this holding would have grave consequences on the software industry. The court disagreed stating "that requiring software companies to stand behind their representations will [not] inevitably destroy the software industry."[144]

Next, the court evaluated the trial court's decision to direct a verdict on the intentional misrepresentation claim. Step-Saver alleged that TSL's cofounder made representations about the compatibility of TSL products intended to deceive Step-Saver. The court held that the statements were merely expressions of technical facts explaining the concepts of complete compatibility and practical compatibility. The court concluded that they were not an admission of deceit. Therefore, the court affirmed the trial court's ruling on the misrepresentation issue because Step-Saver failed to allege a misstatement of fact.

The third point raised on appeal was whether there was sufficient evidence in the record to prove that Wyse terminals were not merchantable. The court ruled that just because a terminal is not compatible with one computer does not mean it is of unacceptable quality when compared to like goods. Because the Wyse terminal conformed to industry standards, the court held that there was no evidence that Wyse breached the implied warranty of merchantability.

State courts generally have engaged in the same analysis as federal courts, both applying state law. Since 1990, several purchasers of computer hardware and software have brought claims in state court alleging that the hardware and software they purchased failed to perform as marketed.[145] As in federal court, purchasers of hardware and software have attempted to recover on two theories: in contract, for a breach of express and implied warranties, and in tort, for misrepresentation or fraud.[146]

In *McCrimmon v. Tandy Corp.*,[147] McCrimmon, a lawyer, purchased computer equipment from Tandy for his law office. Subsequently, McCrimmon sued Tandy, alleging fraud and breach of warranty, claiming that the equipment was

---

[144] *Id.* at 104.

[145] Latham & Assocs., Inc. v. William Raveis Real Estate, Inc., 589 A.2d 337 (Conn. 1991); McCrimmon v. Tandy Corp., 414 S.E.2d 15 (Ga. Ct. App. 1991); VMark Software, Inc. v. EMC Corp., 642 N.E.2d 587 (Mass. App. Ct. 1994); Delorise Brown, M.D., Inc. v. Allio, 620 N.E.2d 1020 (Ohio. Ct. App. 1993).

[146] Latham & Assocs., Inc. v. William Raveis Real Estate, Inc., 589 A.2d 337 (Conn. 1991); McCrimmon v. Tandy Corp., 414 S.E.2d 15 (Ga. Ct. App. 1991); VMark Software, Inc. v. EMC Corp., 642 N.E.2d 587 (Mass. App. Ct. 1994); Delorise Brown, M.D., Inc. v. Allio, 620 N.E.2d 1020 (Ohio. Ct. App. 1993).

[147] 414 S.E.2d 15 (Ga. Ct. App. 1991).

unsuitable for his needs. McCrimmon also claimed that Tandy had falsely represented the equipment as suitable for his needs. The court affirmed the trial court's grant of summary judgment on both the contract and the tort claim.

The court dismissed the contract action because it held that the limited warranty was valid and that all implied warranties were validly disclaimed by Tandy. The court upheld Tandy's 30-day limited warranty because the purchaser was or should have been aware that the limited warranty was the exclusive remedy in the event of a defect. The court noted that this was clearly marked on the sales receipt. Further, the court stated that it was the purchaser's responsibility to read the sales receipt. Next, the court upheld Tandy's implied warranty disclaimers because they were conspicuous, they were properly worded, and they were in writing. Therefore, the court affirmed the trial court's grant of summary judgment for breach of warranty.

In *Latham & Associates v. William Raveis Real Estate, Inc.,*[148] Latham & Associates filed suit to recover the unpaid purchase price of hardware and software delivered to Raveis Real Estate. Raveis counterclaimed, alleging breach of warranty and misrepresentation. The trial court awarded damages in favor of the purchaser, noting that the vendor never provided software that reliably delivered the information sought by the purchaser. On appeal, the issue presented was whether a purchaser may recover for breach of an express warranty without providing expert testimony to identify the cause of the system's failure.

The court held that expert testimony is not required in every case when there is dissatisfaction with the output produced by a computer system. The court concluded, given the trial court's unchallenged finding that the software did not perform as expected, the purchaser had produced sufficient evidence without expert testimony.

In *Delorise Brown, M.D., Inc. v. Allio,*[149] the plaintiff, Dr. Delorise Brown, purchased a computer system from the defendant, William Allio. Dr. Brown purchased the system to automate her billing and to hold patient files. Dr. Brown relied on Allio for selecting an appropriate system to meet these specific needs. The issue before the court was whether this invoked the implied warranty of fitness for a particular purpose and whether it was breached.

The court held that the implied warranty of fitness for a particular purpose was invoked but that it was not breached. The court concluded that the plaintiff did not satisfy the burden of proving that the cause of the problem was the condition of the computer system. Therefore, the court held that the plaintiff was not entitled to damages on the breach of warranty claim.

§ 5.14 Fraudulent Misrepresentation

Fraudulent misrepresentation is an important theory in claims by customers against suppliers of computer hardware, software, and services and suppliers of

---

[148] 589 A.2d 337 (Conn. 1991).

[149] 620 N.E.2d 1020 (Ohio Ct. App. 1993).

communication services. Most of the warranty claims discussed in § 5.13 were accompanied by fraudulent misrepresentation claims. The elements of fraudulent misrepresentation are these:

1. Fraudulent intent
2. Misrepresentation of fact, opinion, intention, or law
3. Made for the purpose of inducing conduct in reliance on the statement
4. Justifiable reliance on the statement
5. Pecuniary loss caused by the reliance.[150]

Negligent misrepresentation claims require the plaintiff to establish that

1. The defendant owed a duty of care to the plaintiff[151]
2. The defendant negligently asserted a false statement
3. The defendant knew that the plaintiff would rely on the statement
4. The plaintiff justifiably relied on the statement, and
5. The plaintiff suffered damages.[152]

The interests protected by the fraudulent misrepresentation theory, sometimes referred to as *deceit* or *fraud,* are essentially the same interests protected by breach of contract: reasonable plaintiff expectations induced by verbal or other conduct by the defendant. The culpability involved in fraudulent misrepresentation and breach of contract is different, however. Breach of contract is a strict liability concept; a breaching defendant is liable regardless of intent or degree of care involved. A fraudulent misrepresentation defendant is liable only on evidence of intent to mislead.[153] This fault requirement for fraudulent misrepresentation justifies tort damages in excess of the usual out-of-pocket contract damages.

The modern law of fraudulent misrepresentation is only subtlely different from the modern law of breach of contract. In many factual situations the factors determining whether recovery is available under fraudulent misrepresentation determine whether recovery is available under a breach of contract theory. For example, a general statement about success in implementing automation plans may be insufficiently specific to support a claim for breach of contract, and the same lack of specificity defeats either the misstatement or the reasonable reliance elements of fraudulent misrepresentation, or both. Or, a customer may lack evidence of reliant conduct, induced by a service provider statement. This

---

[150] Restatement (Second) of Torts § 525 (1976).

[151] As § 5.9 explains, establishing the duty is a difficult problem with any type of negligence claim in a contract setting.

[152] Foundation Software Lab., Inc. v. Digital Equip. Corp., 807 F. Supp. 1195, 1200 (D. Md. 1992) (restating elements and concluding no genuine question of fact regarding issue of reasonable reliance in decision to buy MicroVAX computer).

[153] *See* Restatement (Second) of Torts § 531 (1976) (expectation of influencing conduct).

defeats both breach of contract (depending on the nature of consideration or detrimental reliance alleged) and fraudulent misrepresentation.

Two traditional distinctions between the contract and fraud theories are still useful rules of thumb, but honored less under modern interpretations of fraudulent misrepresentation. Traditionally, a prima facie case of fraudulent misrepresentation required proving a misstatement of fact. Proving a promise to act in the future was not enough. Conversely, establishing a breach of contract required proving a promise to act in the future. This distinction is fading. In some states, no tort liability could be established under any theory based on duties arising from the contract promises themselves; tort liability, including fraudulent misrepresentation liability, required showing breach of a duty independent from breach of contract.[154]

Now controversy exists over whether statements about future conduct or present intentions regarding future conduct can satisfy the misstatement requirement. The controversy arises because it becomes difficult to distinguish the factual misrepresentation element from a promise, which traditionally did not satisfy the misstatement element of fraudulent misrepresentation.

The *Restatement (Second) of Torts*[155] endorses recovery for misrepresentations as to the actor's intent. Despite the distinction drawn in many of the cases, the Restatement gives authority for finding fraudulent misrepresentation when the defendant's verbal conduct is promissory in character. Comment to the *Restatement*[156] says that a promise that implies the promisor knows of no facts that would prevent performance of the promise satisfies the misstatement element of fraudulent misrepresentation. The *Restatement*[157] says that representations about past events implying that future events will be similar satisfy the misrepresentation element of fraudulent misrepresentation. The distinction between the factual statements and promises is even more artificial when one recalls that warranties, commonly thought of as promises, as explained in § 5.4, are defined as statements of fact and definitionally distinguished from promises; yet warranties are more often characterized as relating to contract law than tort law, as explained in § 5.9.

The second traditional distinction between fraud and breach of contract is that the traditional measure of damages for misrepresentation was reliance, while the traditional measure of damages for breach of contract was expection. Now, however, the *Restatement* permits expectation damages for fraudulent misrepresentation[158] and the *Restatement of Contracts* permits reliance damages for breach of contract.[159]

---

[154] *See* Bernoudy v. Dura-Bond Concrete Restoration, Inc., 828 F.2d 1316, 1318 (8th Cir. 1987) (finding requirement satisfied because representations about eight years of employment were part of negotiations over accepting job; not one of the terms of employment).

[155] Restatement (Second) of Torts § 530 (1976).

[156] *Id.* § 525 cmt. f.

[157] *Id.* cmt. g.

[158] *See id.* § 549(2) cmt. l (benefit of the bargain damages available if proven with reasonable certainty).

[159] *See* Restatement (Second) of Contracts § 90 (1979).

Nevertheless, despite the imperfections in the doctrinal basis for distinguishing contract and fraud, the courts regularly draw the distinction, usually, but not always, denying claims for fraudulent misrepresentation that arise in a contract setting. In *Ritchie Enterprises v. Honeywell Bull, Inc.,*[160] the court dismissed the plaintiff's negligent misrepresentation claim. The court concluded that the plaintiff's claim was simply a disguised breach of warranty claim. In a product sales context in which the integrated purchase contract disclaims prior representations and warranties, it is easier to reject negligent misrepresentation claims.[161]

In *American Computer Trust Leasing v. Jack Farrell Implement Co.,*[162] the plaintiff, American Computer Trust Leasing (ACTL), brought an action against the defendant, Jack Farrell, an agricultural equipment dealer, for its failure to make payments on hardware leased from ACTL. The defendant counterclaimed, alleging fraud, breach of contract, and breach of express and implied warranties.[163] The defendant based its claim of fraud on the fact that the plaintiff failed to disclose royalty payments it was paying its clients for endorsing its products.[164] The court ruled that because no fiduciary relationship existed between the parties, the plaintiff had no duty to disclose its financial arrangements to the defendant. When there is no legal duty, nondisclosure does not constitute fraud. Further, the court noted that the defendant's statements were either true, ordinary sales talk, puffing, or opinion. They were not, therefore, the kind of statements contemplated by a cause of action for fraud.

In *Walter Raczynski Product Design v. International Business Machine Corp.,*[165] an engineering and design firm sued IBM for breach of contract, breach of warranty, and fraudulent misrepresentation. The plaintiff, Walter Raczynski, a sole proprietor, alleged that the hardware sold by IBM and the software recommended by IBM did not function as represented. The plaintiff's first count alleged that IBM fraudulently misrepresented the capabilities of its computer hardware and software.[166] Although the court concluded that the plaintiff adequately identified false statements of fact, which formed the basis

---

[160] 730 F. Supp. 1041 (D. Kan. 1990).

[161] *Id.* (citing Isler v. Texas Oil & Gas Corp., 749 F.2d 22 (10th Cir. 1984) and United States Welding, Inc. v. Burroughs Corp., 640 F. Supp. 350 (D. Colo. 1985)).

[162] 763 F. Supp. 1473 (D. Minn. 1991).

[163] *Id.* The contract and warranty claims are considered in § **5.13.**

[164] (The court noted that the representation must be false and made with knowledge of its falsity, or held out as true although made without knowledge of its truth or falsity. Moreover, the party making the representation must intend that the other party rely on it, the statement must be material and must concern a past or present fact rather than a promise of future performance.

[165] No. 92C6423, 1993 WL 282722 (N.D. Ill. July 21, 1993).

[166] *Id.* (concluding that to allege a claim of fraud plaintiff must plead the following: (1) that there was a false statement of material fact rather than a promise or opinion, (2) that the statement was known by the speaker, (3) that it was made to induce the plaintiff to act affirmatively, (4) that the plaintiff reasonably relied on the truth of the statement, (5) that the plaintiff suffered damage as the result of such reliance).

for a claim of fraudulent misrepresentation, the court dismissed the fraudulent misrepresentation claim because the plaintiff failed to allege either that IBM knew its representations were false or that IBM intended to induce the plaintiff's reliance by these representations.

In *Step-Saver Data Systems, Inc. v. Wyse Technology,*[167] Step-Saver, a value-added retailer, brought suit against TSL, the producer of the operating system purchased by Step-Saver, and Wyse Technology, the producer of computer terminals used by Step-Saver. The plaintiff, Step-Saver, was marketing a multi-user system for small professional offices that would allow multiple terminals to operate from only one computer. Step-Saver sued Wyse and TSL for breach of warranty and sued TSL in tort for intentional misrepresentation. The district court granted a directed verdict in favor of TSL on the intentional misrepresentation and on the breach of warranty claims. The court held that as a matter of law the evidence presented by Step-Saver was insufficient to establish two[168] of the five elements[169] necessary to establish a prima facie case for misrepresentation.

In *Foundation Software Laboratories, Inc. v. Digital Equipment Corp.,*[170] the district court held that the purchaser of a MicroVAX computer failed to establish reasonable reliance on the vendor's statements concerning the ease with which certain software would run on the computer system. Rather, the plaintiff/purchaser based its decision to purchase the MicroVAX on its own feasibility study and the conclusions of its own computer staff person.[171] The computer staff person admitted in his deposition that he was well aware of the possibility that the critical software might not port easily onto the MicroVAX, and the plaintiff conceded at oral argument that it never provided detailed information to the vendor about its software. Thus, any reliance on the vendor's general statements about the performance of the plaintiff's software on the hardware was unreasonable.[172] Alleged vendor promises about technical support and marketing similarly did not support the negligent misrepresentation claim because the plaintiff failed to show that any communications made were at variance with the vendor's true intentions or that they were false.[173]

In *VMark Software, Inc. v. EMC Corp.,*[174] VMark Software sued EMC to recover its lease fee. EMC counterclaimed, alleging breach of warranty and

---

[167] 939 F.2d 91 (3d Cir. 1991).

[168] (1) fraudulent intent by TSL; (2) reasonable reliance by Step-Saver.

[169] Step-Saver Data Sys., Inc. v. Wyse Technology, 752 F. Supp. 181, 189 (E.D. Pa. 1989) (five elements are (1) material misrepresentation, (2) intended to deceive, (3) made with intention of inducing reliance, (4) justifiably relied upon, (5) resulting in damage), *aff'd in part, rev'd in part,* 939 F.2d 91 (3d Cir. 1991).

[170] 807 F. Supp. 1195 (D. Md. 1992) (granting defendant's motion for summary judgment).

[171] *Id.* at 1200–01.

[172] *Id.* at 1201.

[173] *Id.* at 1202.

[174] 642 N.E.2d 587 (Mass. App. Ct. 1994).

intentional misrepresentation. In June 1990 Vmark Software granted a license to EMC to use its UniVerse software. The UniVerse product was written to translate old software applications, making them compatible with new, more advanced hardware. The UniVerse software was supposed to make EMC's old software compatible with the new hardware EMC had purchased. The software failed to function as expected. Subsequently, EMC refused to pay the license fee. The court ruled in favor of EMC, predicating its decision on the misrepresentation claim. EMC was entitled to all damages it suffered as a proximate result of VMark's misleading representations.[175] VMark representatives made glowing representations of the UniVerse product's ability to make EMC's software compatible with the specific hardware purchased by EMC. Vmark employees knew at the time of the sale that the UniVerse product did not perform as represented and did not disclose this knowledge to EMC. VMark representatives knew EMC was materially relying on these representations. Further, EMC did materially rely on these representations to its detriment. In light of these facts, the court held that EMC had successfully sustained an actionable claim for misrepresentation.

In *McCrimmon v. Tandy Corp.,*[176] McCrimmon, a lawyer, purchased computer equipment from Tandy for his law office. Subsequently, McCrimmon sued Tandy, alleging fraud and breach of warranty. McCrimmon claimed that Tandy had falsely represented the equipment as suitable for his needs. The court affirmed summary judgment on both the contract and the tort claim. It held that there was no evidence of fraud. "The tort of fraud has five elements: a false representation by a defendant, scienter, intention to induce the plaintiff to act, justifiable reliance by the plaintiff, and damage to the plaintiff."[177] There was no false representation by the defendant, and further there was no evidence that the representations were knowingly false.

§ 5.15   —Fraud in the Inducement

The difficulties with overlapping fraud and breach of contract claims can be avoided by asserting fraud in the inducement. The theory succeeded in *Triangle Underwriters, Inc. v. Honeywell, Inc.,*[178] which involved a proposal by Honeywell to a general insurance agent to replace its existing computer system with a new hardware and software system, including custom application software

---

[175] *Id.* (holding EMC entitled to damages including hours spent by employee trying to make the defective system work).

[176] 414 S.E.2d 15 (Ga. Ct. App. 1991).

[177] *Id.* at 17 (quoting Crawford v. Williams, 375 S.E.2d 223 (1989)).

[178] 604 F.2d 737 (2d Cir. 1979). Although the court addressed only a statute of limitations issue rather than the merits of the claim, it reversed the district court and held that the plaintiff had pleaded fraud in the inducement, entitling it to a 6-year statute of limitations rather than a 4-year limitation for contract claims.

specifically designed for Triangle's needs. Triangle accepted the proposal, but the system as delivered did not perform its intended function. Among other things, Triangle sued Honeywell with fraud for falsely representing that it was ready to install a fully tested and operative system, claiming fraud in the inducement.[179] Fraudulent inducement

> does not involve [an] attempt to dress up a contract claim in a fraud suit of clothes. The fraud Triangle alleged in Count I consisted of independent false representations, made before there ever was a contract between the parties, which led Triangle to enter into it. In other words, Triangle clearly alleged fraud that was extraneous to the contract rather than a fraudulent non-performance of the contract itself.[180]

While the distinctions expressed by the Triangle Underwriters court are logical, they may be subtle in practice. The gist of fraud in the inducement is making a fraudulent statement in order to induce the other party to enter into a contract.[181] But that can be said of many promises that become part of the contract, inasmuch as the bargain theory of contract contemplates that promises are the inducement for the exchange. Therefore, success in maintaining a fraudulent inducement claim frequently depends on persuasiveness in explaining how the fraudulent statement is properly understood as being extrinsic to the contract and inducing conduct that antedated the formation of the contract.

In *Accusystems, Inc. v. Honeywell Information Systems, Inc.,*[182] the plaintiffs succeeded in establishing fraudulent inducement at trial based on evidence that Honeywell had represented that a computer system had been tested and could perform multitasking and multiprocessing functions for up to 24 terminals. In fact no testing had occurred and the delivered system bogged down with more than three terminals.[183] The court found that the two-year contractual limitations period did not apply to the fraud in the inducement claim.[184] It further found that the plaintiffs were entitled to damages for their actual pecuniary loss sustained as a result of entering into the computer contract.[185] The plaintiffs were not,

---

[179] *Id.* at 740.

[180] *Id.* at 747.

[181] *See* Furniture Consultants, Inc. v. Datatel Mini Computer Co., No. 85 Civ. 8518 (R.L.C.), 1986 WL 7792 (S.D.N.Y. July 10, 1986) (accepting possibility of fraud in the inducement claim based on statements as to computer system's ability to perform functions in furniture industry before contract was entered into, but dismissing with leave to amend because fraud was not pleaded with sufficient specificity); *see also* Financial Timing Publications, Inc. v. Compugraphic Corp., 893 F.2d 936, 943–44 (8th Cir. 1990) (fraud in the inducement based on statements by marketing personnel about capabilities of computerized typesetting system can be pursued independently of contract claims, thus supporting denial of summary judgment).

[182] 580 F. Supp. 474 (S.D.N.Y. 1984).

[183] *Id.* at 481–82 (reviewing evidence).

[184] *Id.* at 482–83.

[185] *Id.* at 483.

however, entitled to damages for lost profits nor for damages incurred after the point in time when they failed to mitigate.[186]

§ 5.16 Damages Generally

Several types of damages potentially are available when a contact for NII goods or services is breached, including expectation damages, incidental damages, and consequential damages. Generally, "[t]he injured party has a right to damages based on his expectation interest as measured by . . . the loss in the value to him of the other party's performance caused by its failure or deficiency," plus any incidental or consequential damages.[187]

Incidental damages are those expenses that the purchaser has reasonably incurred due to the seller's breach.[188] Incidental damages frequently are quantifiable without much difficulty because the costs incurred by the purchaser are likely to have an exact dollar figure. Incidental damages would include the cost of a cable to connect a newly purchased printer to one's computer.

Consequential damages are defined in the UCC as "[a]ny loss resulting from general or particular requirements and needs of which the seller at the time of contracting had reason to know and which could not reasonably be prevented by cover or otherwise."[189] Consequential damages frequently are more difficult to quantify than incidental or expectation damages. The definition of consequential damages is a codification of language in the classic case, *Hadley v. Baxendale.*[190]

Conceptually, damages—both contract and tort—usually are limited to those that are foreseeable.[191] But, under *Hadley v. Baxendale,*

> [t]he extent of the recovery is to be measured, not by what the defendant actually foresaw when he made the contract, but by what a hypothetical, reasonable person in the position of the defendant, with the defendant's knowledge of the

---

[186] *Id.* at 484.

[187] Restatement (Second) of Contracts § 347 (1979).

[188] *See* U.C.C. § 2-715(1) (1977) (list of expenses includes expenses incurred in inspection, receipt, transportation, and care and custody of goods rightfully rejected).

[189] U.C.C. § 2-715(2) (1977). "After a breach . . . the buyer may 'cover' by making in good faith and without unreasonable delay any reasonable purchase or contract to purchase goods in substitution for those due from the seller." *Id.* § 2-712(1).

[190] 9 Ex. 341, 156 Eng. Rep. 145 (1854).

[191] *See* Restatement (Second) of Contracts § 351 (1979) ("[d]amages are not recoverable for loss that the party in breach did not have reason to foresee as a probable result of the breach when the contract was made"); John Edward Murray, Jr., Murray on Contracts § 120 (3d ed. 1990). Under the Restatement, limiting a plaintiff's recovery may be directly placed in the hands of the court: "[a] court may limit damages for foreseeable loss by excluding recovery for loss of profits, by allowing recovery only for loss incurred in reliance, or otherwise if it concludes that in the circumstances justice so requires in order to avoid disproportionate compensation." Restatement (Second) of Contracts § 351(3) (1979).

circumstances surrounding the transaction, could reasonably have been expected to foresee, had he directed his attention to a consideration of the matter.[192]

Additionally, only foreseeability from the perspective of the breaching party is relevant.[193] There is no requirement of foreseeability placed on the injured party.[194] Also, foreseeability of probable consequences is determined at the time of contract formation: "If additional knowledge comes to the promisor subsequent to that time, it is irrelevant."[195] Finally, the foreseeability test is objective: "the defaulting promisor is liable not only for those consequences which he actually thought were probable but also those which a reasonable person should have considered probable."[196]

Hadley v. Baxendale articulates an objective test for foreseeability. The overall foreseeability test contains two distinct tests within it. The first is the imputed foreseeability test defined as "that which any reasonable person should have foreseen."[197] The question asked is whether a reasonable person would have foreseen the damages that the purchaser encountered. The second test is the actual foreseeability test, which is defined as "what the reasonable person with particular knowledge should have foreseen."[198] The question asked in this test is whether the seller, with his particular knowledge, would have foreseen the damages encountered by the purchaser.

When determining foreseeability, it is necessary to determine what kind of knowledge the seller is presumed to have. Broadly stated, a purchaser's "general needs must rarely be made known to charge the seller with knowledge."[199] However, the purchaser must notify the seller of his particular needs to charge the seller with particular knowledge.[200] In other words, the "ordinary" needs of a purchaser need not be explicitly stated for a seller to have reason to know what those needs are, but if the purchaser has particular needs, he must put the seller on notice of them. Once the seller knows what the purchaser's needs are, he is liable for any consequential damages resulting from a breach of contract when performance was within the parameters of those needs.

---

[192] John Edward Murray, Jr., Murray on Contracts § 120 (3d ed. 1990). Under the UCC "the burden of proving the extent of loss incurred by way of consequential damage is on the buyer." U.C.C. § 2-715 cmt. 4 (1977).

[193] U.C.C. § 2-715(2) (1977) refers to loss of which the "seller" had reason to know.

[194] Restatement (Second) of Contracts § 351 cmt. a (1979).

[195] John Edward Murray, Jr., Murray on Contracts § 120A (3d ed. 1990). *See also* U.C.C. § 2-715(2)(a) (1977) (consequential damages assessed as of the time of formation); Restatement (Second) of Contracts § 351 (1979) (foreseeability measured from time of contracting).

[196] John Edward Murray, Jr., Murray on Contracts § 120A (3d ed. 1990).

[197] *Id.*

[198] *Id.*

[199] U.C.C. § 2-715 cmt. 3 (1977).

[200] *Id.*

Once it has been determined that consequential damages were foreseeable, the next issue that arises is how to measure those damages in terms of a dollar figure. "The burden of proving the extent of loss incurred by way of consequential damage is on the buyer."[201] Generally, the purchaser must show with "reasonable certainty" the amount of damages suffered.[202] The purchaser does not have to be mathematically precise in proving the loss.[203] Both the UCC and *Restatement (Second) of Contracts* allow a purchaser great leeway in determining the amount of consequential damages.[204]

The only real difficulties arise when the issue of proving loss of profits enters into the picture. "Where a business has been established and earning profits for some time, there is little difficulty in establishing lost profits for such a business assuming that the prior and subsequent experiences are comparable."[205] However, if the business is a new one the purchaser will have greater difficulty in establishing a basis for profits.[206] Traditionally, courts did not allow a new business to recover anticipated profits.[207] That rule has slowly been eroded and now "there is no per se rule precluding [proof of lost profits] so long as reasonably certain data are provided as the basis for recovery."[208]

§ 5.17   Tariff Limitations

Many claims for NII service failures will be brought against common carriers. The filed tariff doctrine or "filed rate doctrine" insulates a common carrier from claims by customers for negligent or intentional misquotation of a tariffed

---

[201] *Id.* § 2-715 cmt. 4.

[202] *See id.* § 1-106 cmt. 1 (damages need not be calculable within mathematical certainty); Restatement (Second) of Contracts § 352 (1979) ("[d]amages are not recoverable for loss beyond an amount that the evidence permits to be established with reasonable certainty").

[203] U.C.C. § 2-715 cmt. 4 (1977).

[204] The UCC states that "the section on liberal administration of remedies (U.C.C. § 1-106) rejects any doctrine which requires almost mathematical precision in the proof of loss. Loss may be determined in any manner which is reasonable under the circumstances." U.C.C. § 2-715 cmt. 4 (1977). The Restatement (Second) of Contracts explains the certainty limitation as "exclud[ing] those elements of loss that cannot be proved with reasonable certainty." Restatement (Second) of Contracts § 352 cmt. a (1979).

[205] John Edward Murray, Jr., Murray on Contracts § 120B (3d ed. 1990). The Restatement (Second) of Contracts supports this view by stating "[e]vidence of past performance will form the basis for a reasonable prediction as to the future." Restatement (Second) of Contracts § 352 cmt. b (1979).

[206] *See* Restatement (Second) of Contracts § 352 cmt. b (1979) (stating that "if the business is a new one or if it is a speculative one that is subject to great fluctuations in volume, costs or prices, proof will be more difficult").

[207] John Edward Murray, Jr., Murray on Contracts § 121B (3d ed. 1990).

[208] *Id.*

service. The doctrine conclusively presumes that both the utility and its customers know the contents and effects of published tariffs.[209] The basis for the filed tariff doctrine is that a carrier may not charge or receive a different compensation from the rate specified in its tariff: "At least since 1915, [the Supreme Court] has held that the doctrine entitles the carrier to collect the rate on file . . . despite a contract, negotiated between [customer] and carrier, setting a lower price."[210] For example, in *Marco Supply Co. v. AT&T Communications*,[211] AT&T charged Marco twice as much for installation charges and three times as much for the monthly service charges as the prices quoted to Marco by AT&T. Marco filed suit for breach of contract and negligent and willful misrepresentation. The district court dismissed the complaint, and the court of appeals affirmed.

The court held that a regulated carrier such as AT&T must charge the tariff rate established with the appropriate regulatory agency, even if different from the quoted rate to the customer.[212] To do otherwise would discriminate in favor of the customer.[213] The customers are presumed to know the applicable tariff, and there is no claim for relief even if the misrepresentation is fraudulent.[214]

In an opinion critical of *Marco Supply, MCI Telecommunications v. TCI Mail*[215] noted that the filed tariff doctrine determined the terms of the contract between the parties.[216] Accidental or intentional misquotation of a rate governed by a tariff cannot alter the terms of a binding contract based on the tariff.[217] On the other hand, the court held that the MCI tariff does not limit MCI's liability if judicial or administrative proceedings establish that MCI committed willful misconduct.[218] The entire tariff must be controlling, not just the rates.[219]

The MCI tariff itself did not clearly preclude a contract or tort claim against MCI based on its alleged willful misconduct.[220] Analysis of the Communications

---

[209] Teleconnect Co. v. U.S. W. Communications, Inc., 508 N.W.2d 644, 647 (Iowa 1993) (reversing denial of common carrier's motion for summary judgment on tort and contract claims based on telephone company's refusal to sell services to reseller, based on filed tariff doctrine).

[210] Security Servs., Inc. v. Kmart Corp., 114 S. Ct. 1702, 1716 (1994) (Ginsberg, J., dissenting; explaining filed rate doctrine).

[211] 875 F.2d 434 (4th Cir. 1989).

[212] *Id.* at 436.

[213] *Id.*

[214] *Id.*

[215] 772 F. Supp. 64 (D.R.I. 1991).

[216] *Id.* at 66.

[217] *Id.*

[218] *Id.* at 67.

[219] *Id.; see* Stand Buys, Ltd. v. Michigan Bell Tel. Co., 646 F. Supp. 36, 37–38 (E.D. Mich. 1986) (applying willful misconduct clause of carrier's tariff, but concluding that no evidence of willful misconduct existed at summary judgment stage).

[220] 772 F. Supp. at 68.

Act of 1934 supports this conclusion. The Act prohibits unjust or unreasonable discrimination in a carrier's rates, and it prevents making or giving any undue or unreasonable preference or advantage to any customer.[221] The court stated that the adjectives "unjust," "undue," and "unreasonable" suggest that some kind of just and reasonable price discrimination and preferences are not unlawful; thus, a preference that is not "undue" or "unreasonable" need not violate the statute.[222] The *TCI Mail* court was aware that its holding contradicts *Marco Supply*,[223] but thought the *Marco Supply* court blindly applied the Interstate Commerce Act tariff doctrines without analyzing the history of the Communications Act of 1934.[224]

In *Cooperative Communications, Inc. (CCI) v. AT&T Corp.*,[225] the filed tariff doctrine did not bar CCI's claims. AT&T pointed out that the Communication Act of 1934 requires filing of tariffs not only as to the rates to be charged, but also with regard to the classifications, regulations, and practices affecting such charges.[226] AT&T argued that CCI's claims pertained to its business practices, and those claims thus were protected by the filed tariff doctrine.[227] The court declined to interpret the word "practices" so broadly and found no case law in support of such a reading.[228]

CCI also distinguished *Marco Supply* because it was not seeking to enforce the misrepresentations.[229] CCI claimed that AT&T made fraudulent representations to CCI's customers regarding rates, and CCI was seeking damages for intentional interference with prospective economic relations and business disparagement resulting from those alleged misrepresentations.[230] Therefore, the filed tariff doctrine did not bar CCI's state law claims against AT&T.

One court[231] identified two principles at the core of the filed rate doctrine: (1) uniform rates (antidiscrimination strand), and (2) the relative institutional incompetence of courts to engage in retroactive rate setting (nonjusticiability strand).[232]

In the typical discrimination case, the regulated carrier must charge the tariff rate established with the regulatory agency, even if a lower rate was quoted to

---

[221] *Id.* (citing 47 U.S.C. § 202(a) (1988)).

[222] *Id.*

[223] *Id.* (citing Marco Supply v. AT&T Communications, 875 F.2d 434, 436 (4th Cir. 1989)).

[224] *Id.*

[225] 867 F. Supp. 1511 (D. Utah 1994).

[226] *Id.* at 1518.

[227] *Id.*

[228] *Id.* at 1518–19, n.3.

[229] *Id.* at 1519.

[230] *Id.*

[231] Wegoland Ltd. v. NYNEX Corp., 806 F. Supp. 1112, 1115 (S.D.N.Y. 1992).

[232] US Wats, Inc. v. American Tel. & Tel. Co., No. Civ. A. 93-1038, 1994 WL 116009, at *3 (E.D. Pa. Apr. 5, 1994) (citing *Wegoland*, 806 F. Supp. at 1115).

the customer.[233] Courts have adhered to this antidiscrimination principle even when carriers have made fraudulent representations to customers regarding rates.[234]

In a typical justiciability case, the tariff rate is unreasonably high because of alleged wrongdoing on the part of the carrier. The court is asked to determine a reasonable rate retroactively by assessing how much the defendants had inflated the rate through their alleged wrongdoing.[235] The filed tariff doctrine prohibits a party from recovering damages measured by comparing the filed rate and the rate that might have been approved absent the conduct in issue.[236]

In *US Wats, Inc. v. American Telephone & Telegraph Co.*, AT&T claimed that the filed tariff doctrine precluded US Wats' breach of implied-in-fact contract claim because AT&T cannot owe US Wats any nontariff obligation; only the filed tariff doctrine governs the relationship between AT&T and US Wats. If the obligation is not in the tariff, it cannot be implied in fact or in law.[237]

The court disagreed. US Wats neither challenged its liability for charges associated with the tariff nor attacked the reasonableness of the applicable tariff, thus implicating neither the antidiscrimination strand nor the nonjusticiability strand of the filed tariff doctrine.[238] Adjudication of US Wats' claim would neither result in rate discrimination nor embroil the court in a dispute over the reasonableness of AT&T's charges.[239] Because the court's decision would have little effect on agency procedures and rate determinations, the filed tariff doctrine did not bar determination of US Wats' breach of implied-in-fact contract claim.[240]

§ 5.18   Model Disclaimer Language

Section 5.13 presented a number of cases in which warranties successfully were disclaimed by providers of NII services. This section presents model language regularly used by two major suppliers of NII services: one an on-line information services and Internet access provider; the other a software supplier.

---

[233] *Id.*

[234] *Id.* at *4; *see* Marco Supply v. AT&T Communications, 875 F.2d 434, 436 (4th Cir. 1989).

[235] U.S. Wats, Inc. v. American Tel. & Tel. Co., 1994 WL 116009, at *4 (E.D. Pa. ___), (citing *Wegoland,* 806 F. Supp. at 1115).

[236] *Id.* (citing H.J., Inc. v. Northwestern Bell Tel. Co., 954 F.2d 485, 488 (8th Cir.), *cert. denied,* 113 S. Ct. 657 (1992)).

[237] *Id.*

[238] *Id.* at *5.

[239] *Id.*

[240] *Id.*

America Online Terms of Service

3. Third-Party Sales and Services

3.1 Member may order and purchase merchandise or services from other Members and users of the AOL Service, who are not affiliated with AOL Inc. All transactions concerning third-party ("Merchant") goods or services, including, but not limited to, purchase terms, payment terms, warranties, guarantees, maintenance and delivery, are solely between Merchant and Member. AOL Inc. makes no warranties or representations whatsoever with regard to any good or service provided or offered by any Merchant. AOL Inc. shall not be a party to a transaction between Member and Merchant, or be liable for any cost or damage arising either directly or indirectly from any action or inaction of any Merchant.[241]

LIMITATION OF LIABILITY AND DISCLAIMER OF WARRANTY

5.1 MEMBER EXPRESSLY AGREES THAT USE OF THE AOL SERVICE IS AT MEMBER'S SOLE RISK. NEITHER AOL INC., ITS EMPLOYEES, AFFILIATES, AGENTS, THIRD-PARTY INFORMATION PROVIDERS, MERCHANTS, LICENSORS OR THE LIKE, WARRANT THAT THE AOL SERVICE WILL BE UNINTERRUPTED OR ERROR FREE; NOR DO THEY MAKE ANY WARRANTY AS TO THE RESULTS THAT MAY BE OBTAINED FROM THE USE OF THE AOL SERVICE, OR AS TO THE ACCURACY, RELIABILITY OR CONTENT OF ANY INFORMATION, SERVICE, OR MERCHANDISE PROVIDED THROUGH THE AOL SERVICE. NEITHER AOL INC. NOR ANY OF ITS INDEPENDENT NETWORK SERVICE PROVIDERS MAKE ANY REPRESENTATIONS OR WARRANTIES, EITHER EXPRESSED OR IMPLIED, THAT ANY AVAILABLE ACCESS NUMBER WILL BE A LOCAL CALL FROM YOUR AREA CODE AND EXCHANGE.

5.2 THE AOL SERVICE IS PROVIDED ON AN "AS IS," "AS AVAILABLE" BASIS WITHOUT WARRANTIES OF ANY KIND, EITHER EXPRESSED OR IMPLIED, INCLUDING, BUT NOT LIMITED TO, WARRANTIES OF TITLE OR IMPLIED WARRANTIES OF MERCHANTABILITY OR FITNESS FOR A PARTICULAR PURPOSE, OTHER THAN THOSE WARRANTIES WHICH ARE IMPLIED BY AND INCAPABLE OF EXCLUSION, RESTRICTION OR MODIFICATION UNDER THE LAWS APPLICABLE TO THIS AGREEMENT. NO ORAL ADVICE OR WRITTEN INFORMATION GIVEN BY AOL INC., ITS EMPLOYEES, AGENTS (INCLUDING MEMBER REPRESENTATIVES OR GUIDES), THIRD-PARTY INFORMATION PROVIDERS, MERCHANTS, LICENSORS OR THE LIKE, SHALL CREATE A WARRANTY; NOR SHALL MEMBER RELY ON ANY SUCH INFORMATION OR ADVICE.

5.3 UNDER NO CIRCUMSTANCES, INCLUDING NEGLIGENCE, SHALL AOL INC., OR ANYONE ELSE INVOLVED IN CREATING, PRODUCING OR DISTRIBUTING THE AOL SERVICE OR THE AOL SOFTWARE, BE LIABLE FOR ANY DIRECT,

---

[241] American Online Terms of Service, Transmitted: 95-02-16 19:48:08 EST. Copyright 1995 America Online, Inc. All Rights Reserved.

INDIRECT, INCIDENTAL, SPECIAL OR CONSEQUENTIAL DAMAGES THAT RESULT FROM THE USE OF OR INABILITY TO USE THE AOL SERVICE INCLUDING, BUT NOT LIMITED TO, RELIANCE BY A MEMBER ON ANY INFORMATION OBTAINED ON THE AOL SERVICE; OR THAT RESULT FROM MISTAKES, OMISSIONS, INTER-RUPTIONS, DELETION OF FILES OR E-MAIL, ERRORS, DEFECTS, VIRUSES, DELAYS IN OPERATION, OR TRANSMISSION, OR ANY FAILURE OF PERFOR-MANCE,WHETHER OR NOT LIMITED TO ACTS OF GOD, COMMUNICATIONS FAILURE, THEFT, DESTRUCTION OR UNAUTHORIZED ACCESS TO AOL INC.'S RECORDS, PROGRAMS OR SERVICES. MEMBER HEREBY ACKNOWLEDGES THAT THIS PARAGRAPH 5.3 SHALL APPLY TO ALL CONTENT, MERCHANDISE OR SERVICES AVAILABLE THROUGH THE AOL SERVICE. BECAUSE SOME STATES DO NOT ALLOW THE EXCLUSION OR LIMITATION OF LIABILITY FOR CONSEQUEN-TIAL OR INCIDENTAL DAMAGES, IN SUCH STATES AOL'S LIABILITY IS LIMITED TO THE GREATEST EXTENT PERMITTED BY LAW.

5.4 NOTWITHSTANDING THE FOREGOING, IN NO EVENT SHALL THE TOTAL LIABILITY OF AOL INC., OR ITS EMPLOYEES, AFFILIATES, AGENTS, THIRD-PARTY INFORMATION PROVIDERS, MERCHANTS OR LICENSORS, FOR ALL DAMAGES, LOSSES AND CAUSES OF ACTION WHETHER IN CONTRACT, TORT, INCLUDING NEGLIGENCE, OR OTHERWISE, EITHER JOINTLY OR SEVERALLY, EXCEED THE AGGREGATE DOLLAR AMOUNT PAID BY MEMBER TO AOL INC. IN THE TWELVE (12) MONTHS PRIOR TO THE CLAIMED INJURY OR DAMAGE. The foregoing provisions of this Section 5 are for the benefit of AOL Inc., its employees, directors, affiliates, agents, Information Providers, Merchants and Licensors, and each shall have the right to assert and enforce the provisions directly on their own behalf.[242]

Purchasing Products and Services through the AOL Service

Please remember that AOL Inc. does not endorse, warrant or guarantee any product or service offered through the AOL Service and will not be a party to any transaction between you and third-party providers of products or services. As with the purchase of a product or service through any medium or in any environment, you should use your best judgment and exercise caution where appropriate. Blind opportunity ads and "get rich quick" schemes should be approached with ample skepticism. The AOL Service cannot mediate disputes and cannot assume responsibility for any outcome. Be careful, be smart, have fun![243]

Public and Private Communication

The AOL Service offers Members the capability to communicate in Public Areas generally accessible to other Members or to communicate privately with another Member. Public Areas are those features that are generally accessible to other Members, such as, but not limited to, chat rooms, online forums, and message boards. Private Communication is electronic correspondence sent or received by you to

---

[242] American Online Rules of the Road, Transmitted: 95-02-21 10:43:16 EST. Copyright 1995 America Online, Inc. All Rights Reserved.

[243] American Online Rules of the Road, Transmitted: 95-02-16 20:55:27 EST. Copyright 1995 America Online, Inc. All Rights Reserved.

particular individuals. AOL Inc. will maintain the AOL Service Public Areas as an open forum for discussion of a wide range of issues and expression of diverse viewpoints. AOL Inc. will administer standards of online conduct according to its TOS for the enjoyment of all its Members. While we will endeavor to monitor the Public Areas to ensure that online standards are being maintained, AOL Inc. has neither the practical capability, nor does it intend, to act in the role of "Big Brother" by screening public communication in advance.

It is AOL Inc.'s policy to respect the privacy of personal electronic communication. AOL Inc. will not intentionally inspect the contents of an electronic message ("E-Mail" or "Instant Message") sent by one Member to another individual, monitor discussions in private rooms, or disclose the contents of any personal electronic communication to an unauthorized third party, except as required or permitted to do so by law. AOL Inc. reserves the right to cooperate fully with local, state, or federal officials in any investigation relating to any Content, including private electronic communication, transmitted on the AOL Service or the unlawful activities of any Member.

AOL Inc. reserves the right to remove any Content that it deems in its sole discretion to be a violation of its Terms of Service. AOL Inc. may terminate immediately any Member who misuses or fails to abide by its Terms of Service. AOL Inc.'s current general practice is that (i) E-Mail is retained on the AOL Service for five (5) days after the date it is read and then permanently deleted, and (ii) unread E-Mail is kept on the AOL Service for approximately thirty (30) days; however, AOL Inc. makes no warranties of any kind with respect to its E-Mail service and is not responsible for any message which may be misprocessed by AOL Inc. AOL Inc. reserves the right to change its general E-Mail practice at any time without notice. If a screen name is deleted, any unread E-Mail sent prior to that deletion will also be removed, as a deleted screen name cannot be reinstated.[244]

America Online Warning with respect to Internet Newsgroups

IMPORTANT: PLEASE READ

Newsgroup discussions are among the most fascinating and diverse sources of content to be found on the Internet. Newsgroups offer America Online members the unique opportunity to participate in discussions on a wide range of subjects with millions of people all around the world.

Since the content of the Newsgroups area comes from OUTSIDE of America Online, the thousands of Newsgroup messages that you see in this area are NOT subject to America Online's Terms of Service. Everything you see in this area is exactly as it appears on the Internet.

How will this affect your experience with Newsgroups?

---

[244] Transmitted: 95-02-16 20:55:27 EST. Copyright 1995 America Online, Inc. All Rights Reserved.

You may find that in certain Newsgroups, the participants use language and discuss subject matter that would not be acceptable on America Online. Although this is the exception rather than the rule, you may choose to avoid certain Newsgroups if you are uncomfortable with the discussion that takes place in them.

If you are a parent, you may wish to supervise your child's use of this area.

SENDING MESSAGES AND RESPONSES

One of the most exciting aspects of being a part of the Internet Community is personal participation in the wide-ranging discussions that take place in Newsgroups.

Through America Online, you can post your own messages to the Newsgroups that you are following, and respond to messages from other participants. When you respond to posted messages, you can even elect to copy your response via electronic mail to the author of the original message.

In any social interaction, certain rules of etiquette can lead to more enjoyable and productive communication. The Internet is no different—in fact, there's even a special word for it: "Netiquette!"

The following tips for posting messages and responses to Newsgroups are adapted from guidelines originally compiled by 'Net citizens Chuq Von Rospach and Gene Spafford. They are good rules of thumb for any online communication, but are particularly appropriate on the Internet (so many people, and so much volume).

1. Never forget that the person on the other side is a human being.

Even though you are using a computer to communicate, and your words are going outside of the familiar America Online community, don't forget that other people are on the receiving end. Millions of people all over the world are reading your words. Avoid personal attacks. Don't speak (type) hastily—try not to say anything to others that you would not say to them in a room full of people. Remember that you are playing an important role in building an online community—and we all want this community to be a good, friendly place.

2. Be brief.

With millions of people participating, you'll find that Newsgroups generate LOTS and LOTS of words. Other participants will appreciate your ability to stay on topic. If you say what you want to say succinctly, it will have greater impact. Likewise, don't post the same message on more than one Newsgroup unless you are sure it is appropriate.

3. Your messages reflect on YOU—be proud of them.

Although you will meet thousands of people through the Internet, chances are you won't meet many of them in person. Most people will only know you by what you say, and how well you say it. Take time to make sure that you are proud of the messages you send. Take time to make sure your messages are easy to read and understand.

4. Use descriptive Subject headings in your messages.

The subject line of your message is there to help people decide whether or not they want to read it. Use the subject line to tell people what your message is about. For example, if you are sending a message to an Automobiles Newsgroup, a subject like "66 MG Midget for Sale: Oregon" is much more informative than "Car for Sale."

5. Think about your audience.

Stay on topic. Post your messages in the appropriate Newsgroup. By reading a number of the messages before sending one yourself, you will be able to get a sense of the ongoing conventions and themes of the Newsgroup.

6. Be careful with humor and sarcasm.

Without the voice inflections and body language of personal communications, it is easy for a remark meant to be funny to be misinterpreted. You can convey the emotions that words alone cannot express by using such online conventions as "smileys" :)

7. Summarize what you are following up.

When you are making a follow-up comment to someone else's message, be sure to summarize the parts of the message to which you are responding. Summarization is best done by including appropriate quotes from the original message. Don't include the entire message, since this could be irritating to people who have already read it.

8. Give back to the Community

If you send a message to a Newsgroup requesting information, and you get lots of responses via electronic mail, it's a nice courtesy to prepare an edited message compiling your responses to the Newsgroup where you originally posted your question. Take the time to strip headers, combine duplicate information, and write a short summary. Credit the information to the people who sent it to you.

Likewise, be a "giver" as well as a "taker" in this online community. If you have good and valuable information to share, please do so in the appropriate Newsgroups.

9. Try not to repeat what has already been said.

Read responses to messages before you chime in, so that you are not needlessly repetitive. And make sure your responses have substance—answers like "Yup" and "I agree" probably won't be widely appreciated.

10. Cite appropriate references.

If you are using facts to support a cause, state where they came from.

(Again, thanks to Chuq Von Rospach and Gene Spafford for originally outlining these useful points.)

AMERICA ONLINE NEWSGROUP TERMS OF SERVICE

Last updated on 1 September 1994

INTRODUCTION

This document explains how America Online's Terms of Service are applied to Newsgroups. It outlines the procedures that America Online members or other Newsgroups participants can use to handle Newsgroup abuses. It also gives pointers to other resources available to learn about Newsgroups' culture.

GUIDELINES

It is important for members to make themselves aware of the various conventions, guidelines and local culture in Newsgroups before becoming an active participant. Read the document titled "IMPORTANT: Please Read" for general guidelines, as well as the articles posted to aol.motd. news.answers and news.newusers.questions.

NEWSGROUPS TERMS OF SERVICE VIOLATIONS

Participating successfully in Newsgroups is a matter of common sense and common courtesy. Most AOL members are able to use their own sense of what is appropriate to guide their behavior. There will, however, always be innocent, inadvertent postings and there will also always be malicious, intentional postings. While it is not always clear which case is which, certain activities will result in an America Online member receiving a Terms of Service warning or more severe action. Postings that will result in Terms of Service actions include the following:

CHAIN LETTERS. Chain letters are prohibited on America Online and the Internet. Posting a chain letter to Newsgroups (or via e-mail on the Internet) is an inappropriate thing to do and can result in your account being terminated or your access to Newsgroups being restricted. If you receive a chain letter from an America Online member, report it to postmaster@aol.com immediately. If you receive a chain letter from someone on the Internet, contact the postmaster at their site (using postmaster@their.domain.name; for example, postmaster@umd.edu).

COMMERCIAL ARTICLES. The vast majority of Newsgroups are NOT commercial and participants in those Newsgroups will usually object strongly to commercial traffic. If you have any questions about a commercial article, contact NewsMaster, one of the America Online Cyberjockeys (identifiable by their screen name beginning with "CJ") or PMDAtropos for clarification.

INAPPROPRIATE POSTS. Each Newsgroup focuses on a particular set of topics. Posts not related to these topics are not appreciated by the participants. It is important that America Online members become familiar with the culture and guidelines of a particular Newsgroup BEFORE posting. Doing so will make your experience with Newsgroups much more pleasant.

TERMS OF SERVICE ACTIONS

Most valid complaints against a member will result in the offending article(s) being canceled and the America Online member receiving a Terms of Service warning.

Second instances of abuse will result in your account and all screen names associated with it being restricted from Newsgroups access.

Third instances of abuse will result in your termination from America Online.

America Online also reserves the right to either restrict access to Newsgroups or terminate accounts for severe cases of Newsgroup abuse. This would include what is known as "spamming"—posting large numbers of articles to many Newsgroups.

SUBMITTING COMPLAINTS

To report a violation of America Online's Newsgroup Terms of Service, send a complete copy of the article or e-mail message to postmaster@aol.com.

CANCELING NEWSGROUP ARTICLES

Inappropriate posts to Newsgroups can be deleted if action is taken in time. When the postmaster, working in conjunction with Terms of Service staff, determines that a complaint is valid and that the violation occurred on Newsgroups, a special message will be sent out which will cancel (delete) the original article. While members should always do their best to post appropriately in a Newsgroup, it is possible that they may need to have an article they posted canceled. An article can be canceled by sending the following information in e-mail to NewsMaster:

1. The date the article was posted.

2. The subject of the article.

3. The Message-ID of the article.

Each article sent to Newsgroups has a unique identifier called the Message-ID. The America Online Newsgroup administrative staff use Message-IDs to issue cancel messages. You can find the Message-ID of an article by looking in the headers section of the article (located at the bottom). You will see a line which is similar to the following:

Message-ID: <287bdqf$g7u@search01.news.aol.com>

The information inside the '<' and '>' characters is what we need to cancel the article.

NewsMaster can cancel a Newsgroup article up to four days after it was originally posted. Due to the nature of Newsgroups, it is important that cancels be issued as soon after the original posting as possible—preferably within 48 hours.

QUESTIONS

If you have questions about Newsgroups or an article you'd like to post, you have several avenues you can pursue, including:

— Reading and posting in aol.newsgroups.help.

— Reading news.newusers.questions.

— Reading the *.answers Newsgroups (soc.answers, alt.answers, news.answers, etc.).

— Checking for FAQs and Charters in a given Newsgroup.

— Asking one of America Online's Cyberjockeys.

— Asking NewsMaster.

— Calling America Online Technical Support at 1-800-827-3338

§ 5.19 Alternative Model Disclaimer Language

Net Manage, Inc.—Shrink Wrap License Agreement

"Notice read this before opening this package (disk packet)

"Opening this package (disk packet) indicates your acceptance of these terms and conditions. Read all of the terms and conditions of this license agreement prior to opening. If you do not accept these terms, you must return the unopened package (packet and all other materials) within 5 days of obtaining the package, with your receipt, and your money will be returned.

"License: this software program and documentation are licensed, not sold, to you. You have a nonexclusive and nontransferable right to use the enclosed program and documentation. This program can only be used on a single computer located in the United States and its territories or in any other country to which this software is legally exported. You may physically transfer the program from one computer to another provided that the program is used on only one computer at a time. This software is considered to be in use on a computer when it is loaded into the temporary memory (i.e. RAM) or installed into the permanent memory (e.g. hard drive) of that computer, except that a copy installed on a network server for the sole purpose of distribution to other computers is not "in use." You may merge it into another program for your use on a single machine. You agree that the program and documentation belong to Net Manage. You agree to use your best efforts to prevent and protect the contents of the program and documentation from unauthorized disclosure or use. Net Manage reserves all rights not expressly granted to you.

***

Limited warranty. Net Manage warrants the media on which the program is furnished to be free from defects and materials and workmanship under normal use for thirty days from the date that you obtained the program. EXCEPT FOR THIS LIMITED WARRANTY, THE PROGRAM AND THE DOCUMENTATION ARE PRO-VIDED 'AS IS' WITHOUT WARRANTY OF ANY KIND EITHER EXPRESSED, IMPLIED OR STATUTORY, INCLUDING BUT NOT LIMITED TO THE IMPLIED WARRANTIES OF MERCHANTABILITY AND FITNESS FOR A PARTICULAR PURPOSE.

"Some states do not allow the exclusion of implied warranties, so the above exclusion may not apply to you. This warranty gives you specific legal rights and you may also have other rights which vary from state to state.

"Limitation of remedies. Net Manage's entire liability and your exclusive remedy in connection with the program and the documentation shall be that you are entitled to return the defective media containing the program together with the documentation to the merchant. At the option of the merchant, you may receive replacement media containing the program and documentation that conforms with the limited warranty or a refund of the amount paid by you. IN NO EVENT WILL NET MANAGE BE LIABLE FOR ANY INDIRECT DAMAGES OR OTHER RELIEF ARISING OUT OF YOUR USE OR INABILITY TO USE THE PROGRAM INCLUDING, BY WAY OF ILLUSTRATION AND NOT LIMITATION, LOST PROFITS, LOST BUSINESS OR LOST OPPORTUNITY, OR ANY SPECIAL, INCIDENTAL OR CONSEQUENTIAL DAMAGES ARISING OUT OF SUCH USE OR INABILITY TO USE THE PROGRAM, EVEN IF NET MANAGE OR AN AUTHORIZED NET MANAGE DEALER, DISTRIBUTOR OR SUPPLIER HAS BEEN ADVISED OF THE POSSIBILITY OF SUCH DAMAGES, OR FOR ANY CLAIM BY ANY OTHER PARTY.

"Some states do not allow the exclusion or limitation of incidental or consequential damages so the above limitation or exclusion may not apply to you.

"This license will be governed by the laws of the state of California, as applied to transactions taking place wholly within California between California residents."[245]

---

[245] Net Manage, 10725 North DeAnza Blvd., Cupertino, CA 95014, (408) 973-7171. Accom-panying version of Chameleon sent to the author on March 29, 1995, under PO number S016721. Reprinted with permission of NetManage, Inc.

CHAPTER 6

CONSTITUTIONAL CONSIDERATIONS

§ 6.1 Overview of Constitutional Concepts

The United States Constitution shapes and limits the law of the National Information Infrastructure, just as it shapes and limits all other American law. The First Amendment is particularly important because its core goal is to promote the free flow of information content, and the NII transports information. When states or the federal government establishes penalties for handling certain kinds of content, such as child pornography, the First Amendment obviously comes into play. Less obvious is the role of the First Amendment in limiting access duties, but it protects the right of publishers not to express certain viewpoints as well as their right to express the views they favor. Thus, when the Congress forces cable providers to carry programming they do not wish to carry, the First Amendment is implicated. Also, when an alleged copyright infringer or intermediary carrying his traffic is confronted with an action for damages or a suit for an injunction, First Amendment interests of the alleged infringer are implicated. Indeed, whenever liability is imposed on an intermediary for traffic it handles, the First Amendment may affect the standard against which liability should be determined.

As Ithiel de Solo Pool observed more than a decade ago, in each of the three parts of the American communication system—print, common carriers, and broadcasting—the law has rested on a perception of technology that is sometimes accurate and often inaccurate, and which changes slowly as technology changes fast.[1] "Convergence of delivery mechanisms for news and information raises anew some critical First Amendment questions."[2] The essential problem is that newspapers historically enjoyed a high degree of First Amendment protection against any regulation of their editorial choices,[3] while common carriers enjoyed almost no First Amendment protection and were readily forced to carry whatever was presented to them and broadcasters were somewhere in the middle, not entirely without First Amendment protections, but subject to certain content regulation such as the fairness doctrine and various must-carry and indecency rules. Now, the old broadcasts, common carrier, and publishing boundaries are collapsing. That was Pool's seminal observation.[4]

But the First Amendment is not the only provision of the Constitution that affects NII law. Constitutional protections of private property also limit regulation, including eminent domain, exercised expressly as such, and certain kinds of access requirements involving physical access to switches.

This chapter collects the basic constitutional analysis in one place. Other chapters touch on constitutional issues as they relate to particular subjects addressed in those chapters.

---

[1] Technologies of Freedom 7 (1983).

[2] *Id.* at 1.

[3] When the Florida legislature tried to require newspapers to allow a right of reply by political candidates, the United States Supreme Court said no. In Miami Herald Publishing Co. v. Tornillo, 418 U.S. 241 (1974), the Supreme Court held that such a statute invalidated the First Amendment. The Court acknowledged that many newspapers enjoy a monopoly in their markets. *Id.* at 249, and that entry into the marketplace served by the print media is "almost impossible." *Id.* at 251. Nevertheless, the Court thought the collision between establishing an enforceable right of access collides too strongly with the First Amendment and that "liberty of the press is in peril as soon as the government tries to compel what is to go into a newspaper." *Id.* at 258 (quoting 2 Z. Chaffee, Government and Mass Communications 633 (1947)). This contrasts sharply with the rule allowing the FCC to require broadcasters to give free time for reply, justified by spectrum scarcity in Red Lion Broadcasting Co. v. FCC, 395 U.S. 367 (1969) (affording broadcasters less First Amendment protection against content regulation).

[4] **Ch. 1** explores the blurring of the traditional boundaries.

§ 6.2 First Amendment: Introduction

First Amendment considerations pervade NII law. This is so because the economic value that moves through the NII involves information, and the free flow of information is the central purpose of the First Amendment. The First Amendment limits liability on tort theories like defamation, considered in **Chapter 4.** It limits efforts by state, local, and federal government entities to restrict access to public information, considered in **Chapter 11.** It protects electronic publishers against governmental efforts either to prohibit certain content or to force those publishers to carry certain content, as considered in **Chapter 2.**

The particularized First Amendment applications are analyzed in those chapters. This chapter takes a broader view of the First Amendment, reviewing its development and explaining how it comes into play in the NII. Particular emphasis is given in this chapter to the limitations imposed by the First Amendment on government regulation of offensive material.

The First Amendment to the United States Constitution reads, in pertinent part, as follows: "Congress shall make no law . . . abridging the freedom of speech, or of the press."[5] Literally, this restricts only congressional power to enact federal legislation. It is interpreted, however, to limit states as well as the federal government[6] and to limit judicial application of common-law principles as well as statutory law.[7] Purely private conduct is not covered by the First Amendment, however, no matter how adverse an effect it has on free speech.[8] Thus only state (governmental) action is circumscribed by the First Amendment.[9]

There are several variables that affect the level of constitutional scrutiny applied to regulation of communicative activity. First is whether the regulation is content neutral or whether it singles out particular content for regulation. Strict scrutiny is applicable to regulation that discriminates based on content.[10] Content neutral regulation, which nevertheless imposes a significant burden on expressive activity, is judged under an "intermediate standard," under *United States v. O'Brien.*[11] There also is authority for the proposition that regulations

---

[5] U.S. Const. amend. I.

[6] City of Ladue v. Gilleo, 114 S. Ct. 2038, 2040 n.1 (1994) (citing Gitlow v. New York, 268 U.S. 652 (1925) (applicable to states), and Lovell v. Griffin, 303 U.S. 444 (1938) (applicable to political subdivisions of states)).

[7] *See* New York Times v. Sullivan, 376 U.S. 254 (1964).

[8] *But see* Novosel v. Nationwide Ins. Co., 721 F.2d 894 (3d Cir. 1984) (acknowledging general rule that First Amendment has not reached private conduct but its principles can be used as a source of public policy to impose tort liability on employers that use power of dismissal to chill testimony to state legislative committee).

[9] See § **6.3.**

[10] Turner Broadcasting Sys., Inc. v. Federal Communications Comm'n, 114 S. Ct. 2445, 2459 (1994) (restating standard for discrimination based on content).

[11] 391 U.S. 367 (1968).

that focus on the "press," including newer news-carrying technologies, are subject to some degree of heightened First Amendment scrutiny.[12]

Under *O'Brien,* content neutral regulation is constitutional

> if it furthers an important or substantial governmental interest; if the governmental interest is unrelated to the suppression of free expression; and if the incidental restriction on alleged First Amendment freedoms is no greater than is essential to the furtherance of that interest. To satisfy this standard, a regulation need not be the least speech-restrictive means of advancing the government's interests. Rather the requirement of narrowed tailoring is satisfied so long as the regulation promotes a substantial government interest that would be achieved less effectively absent the regulation.[13]

In addition, stronger presumptions of validity are accorded congressional judgments, as contrasted with judgments of individual government officials or regulatory agencies.[14] Moreover, advance statutory or regulatory bans on entire classes of expressive conduct are scrutinized more closely than post hoc analysis of speech.[15]

When legislatures or administrative agencies regulate in a way that has an adverse effect on expression and communication, the regulation nevertheless may be justified if it serves a compelling state interest.[16] But a mere connection between the regulatory strategy and a compelling state interest is not enough; there is a proportionality requirement.[17] Overbreadth (overinclusiveness) is a fatal flaw in speech-affecting regulation; if the regulation has a broader effect on speech than is strictly necessary in order to serve the compelling state interest that justifies the regulation in the first place, it is invalid under the First Amendment to the extent of the overbreadth.[18] Underbreadth (underinclusiveness)

---

[12] Turner Broadcasting Sys., Inc. v. Federal Communications Comm'n, 114 S. Ct. 2445, 2458 (1994).

[13] *Id.* at 2469 (citing and quoting United States v. O'Brien, 391 U.S. 367, 377 (1968) and Ward v. Rock Against Racism, 491 U.S. 781, 799 (1989)) (internal citations, quotes, and ellipsis omitted).

[14] United States v. National Treasury Employees Union, 63 U.S.L.W. 4133 (1995) [hereinafter NTEU]; Turner Broadcasting Sys., Inc. v. Federal Communications Comm'n, 114 S. Ct. 2445, 2473 (1994) (Stevens, J., concurring; emphasizing deference to congressional judgments).

[15] NTEU § III. The Court was referring to post hoc analysis of a government employee's speech, to determine whether it adversely affected the employee's public responsibilities. Nevertheless, the rationale for the distinction—the greater chilling effect of an across-the-board ban in advance, than a post hoc determination on a case-by-case basis—is pertinent more generally.

[16] United States v. O'Brien, 391 U.S. 367, 376 (1968) (sufficiently important government interest in regulating nonspeech elements can justify incidental effect on speech); NAACP v. Button, 371 U.S. 415, 438 (1963) (asserted state interests insufficiently compelling to justify limitations on expression by NAACP).

[17] United States v. O'Brien, 391 U.S. 367, 376 (1968).

[18] NAACP v. Button, 371 U.S. 415, 438–39 (1963); *see also* Broadrick v. Oklahoma, 413 U.S. 601 (1973) (criterion for statute is "substantial overbreadth").

also can be a problem because allowing some of the harm to remain by only removing a portion of it undercuts the argument that speech must give way in order for the state to serve its interests; if the state is willing to allow some of the harmful speech to remain, it appears arbitrary to restrict some of it.[19] Thus, if the compelling state interest is avoiding exposure of children to offensive material, a regulation prohibiting the offensive material altogether would be overbroad and thus invalid.[20] One prohibiting only offensive material broadcast by NBC would be suspect because it is underinclusive. On the other hand, a prohibition against transmitting and distributing the offensive material during the hours the children ordinarily used the medium may be permissible.[21]

Significantly for traditional Internet practices, the Supreme Court in 1995 held that the First Amendment protects the right to publish anonymously.[22] First Amendment privileges can be waived, and this sometimes is a powerful argument for regulators who condition the grant of a license on consent to limitations on expressive conduct.[23]

§ 6.3   —State Action Requirement

Conduct restricting speech is not affected by the First Amendment unless the conduct constitutes state action. There are at least three ways that apparently private conduct may nevertheless constitute state action:

1.   When a private entity is performing an inherently public function[24]
2.   When the private entity is in a symbiotic relationship with the government and its conduct is effectively mandated by the government[25]

---

[19] Ginsburg v. New York, 390 U.S. 629, 634–35 (1968) (upholding regulation of obscenity targetted at minors).

[20] Upper Midwest Booksellers v. City of Minneapolis, 780 F.2d 1389, 1391–92 (8th Cir. 1985) (exempting certain entities from liability for displaying sexually explicit materials was unconstitutional).

[21] Ginsburg v. New York, 390 U.S. 629, 634–35 (1968).

[22] McIntyre v. Ohio Elections Comm'n, 115 S. Ct. 1511 (1995). *Accord* Figari v. New York Tel. Co., 303 N.Y.S.2d 245 (App. Div. 1969) (tariff requiring subscribers to recorded announcement service to give name and address violated First Amendment).

[23] Paragold Cable Vision, Inc. v. City of Paragold, 930 F.2d 1310, 1315 (8th Cir. 1991) (rejecting First Amendment argument by cable television franchisee confronted with competition from franchising municipality, in part because any First Amendment privileges had been bargained away in the franchise agreement).

[24] *See* Marsh v. Alabama, 326 U.S. 501 (1946).

[25] *See* Jackson v. Metropolitan Edison Co., 419 U.S. 345 (1974) (state not sufficiently involved to make private decisions equivalent to state action); Burton v. Wilmington Parking Auth., 365 U.S. 715 (1961) (state sufficiently involved to make decisions as state action).

3.   When private entities make use of state coercive powers to serve their own interests.[26]

In the NII context, electronic communication service providers such as telephone companies have been found to be engaged in state action. This occurs when they simply carry out orders of regulatory authorities, such as orders to exclude offensive material, but not when they exercise essentially private discretion within powers allowed to them by regulatory agencies or other legal regimes.[27] **Section 6.12,** considering the use of the First Amendment as a "sword," probes the state action requirement more deeply.

§ 6.4   —Commercial Speech

Until 1976, commercial speech was unprotected by the First Amendment.[28] In *Virginia State Board of Pharmacy v. Virginia Citizens Consumer Council, Inc.,*[29] the Supreme Court concluded that commercial speech is protected by the First Amendment because of the essential role that the free flow of commercial information plays in the operation of a market economy.[30] Indeed, the Court observed that a particular consumer may be more interested in commercial information than political debate.[31] Nevertheless, *Virginia Board of Pharmacy* itself acknowledged that commercial speech might be subjected to restrictions that would be suspect if applied to noncommercial speech. Later cases, like *Central Hudson Gas & Electric Corp. v. Public Service Commission,*[32] gradually evolved a "commonsense" distinction between "speech proposing a commercial transaction, which occurs in an area traditionally subject to government regulation, and other varieties of speech." The basic test for government regulation of commercial speech is

---

[26] *See* Lugar v. Edmondson Oil Co., 457 U.S. 922 (1982) (use of court system may constitute state action); *but see* Flagg Bros. v. Brooks, 436 U.S. 149 (1978) (self-help creditors remedies under authority of state statute did not constitute state action).

[27] Alliance for Community Media v. Federal Communications Comm'n, 56 F.3d 105, 113 (D.C. Cir. 1995) (en banc) (stripping cable operator of editorial control over access channels, but then reinstating control with respect to indecent material did not mean that exercise of that exceptional power constitutes state action).

[28] Valentine v. Chrestensen, 316 U.S. 52 (1942) (upholding constitutionality of municipal ordinance forbidding distribution of commercial handbills in streets).

[29] 425 U.S. 748 (1976) (invalidating statute making it unprofessional conduct to advertise prescription drug prices).

[30] *Id.* at 765.

[31] *Id.* at 763.

[32] 447 U.S. 557, 562 (1980) (noting "commonsense" distinction but finding complete ban on advertising by electric utility was unconstitutional despite commercial nature of speech).

For commercial speech to come within the First Amendment, it at least must concern lawful activity and not be misleading. Next, we asked whether the asserted governmental interest is substantial. If both inquiries yield positive answers, we must determine whether the regulation directly advances the governmental interest asserted, and whether it is not more extensive then is necessary to serve that interest.[33]

In *Rubin v. Coors Brewing Co.,*[34] the government proposed that the *Central Hudson* test should be modified so that legislatures have broader latitude to regulate speech that promotes socially harmful activities, such as alcohol consumption.[35] The Supreme Court impliedly rejected the argument by applying the traditional *Central Hudson* test. It found that the government's interest in preventing competition over alcohol levels in beer and the desire of discouraging alcohol consumption were insufficiently substantial to meet the *Central Hudson* requirements.[36] The Court further concluded that the ban on alcohol content labels could not materially advance the asserted interests "because of the overall irrationality of the government's regulatory scheme."[37] The application of the federal regulation applied unevenly to states depending on their own approaches and did not apply to distilled spirits or wine. Moreover, the government's evidence about the existence of the problem sought to be remedied by the regulation was thin, at best.[38] Justice Stevens, concurring in the judgment, expressed his view that the most appropriate approach for regulation of commercial speech is to ask whether the particular regulation passes muster under two typical justifications: whether it prohibits misleading speech, and whether it requires affirmative disclosures that the speaker might not make voluntarily.[39] Moreover, he thought that a rigid distinction between commercial and non-commercial speech usually is not helpful.[40]

In *United States v. Edge Broadcasting Co.,*[41] the Supreme Court applied the formula for regulation of commercial speech to uphold a prohibition on the broadcast of lottery advertising by radio or television stations licensed in states

---

[33] Rubin v. Coors Brewing Co., 115 S. Ct. 1585, 1589 (1995) (quoting Central Hudson, 447 U.S. 557, 566 (1980)).

[34] 115 S. Ct. 1585 (1995) (statutory requirement that beer labels display alcohol content violated First Amendment).

[35] *Id.* at 1589 n.2.

[36] *Id.* at 1591 (noting that states have ample authority to accomplish the needed regulation).

[37] *Id.* at 1592.

[38] *Id.* at 1592–93.

[39] *Id.* at 1594 (Stevens, J., concurring).

[40] 115 S. Ct. 1585, 1595 (1995) (Stevens, J., concurring) ("economic motivation or impact alone cannot make speech less deserving of constitutional protection, or else all authors and artists who sell their works would be correspondingly disadvantaged").

[41] 113 S. Ct. 2696 (1993) (reversing court of appeals and finding federal statute constitutional).

that prohibit such advertising, even though the prohibition had the effect of blocking the flow of advertising information into a nearby state that permitted it.[42] Conversely, in *City of Cincinnati v. Discovery Network, Inc.*,[43] the Court overturned a local ban on news racks containing commercial handbills that did not apply to news racks containing newspapers because it did not relate sufficiently closely to the city's legitimate interest in safety and aesthetics.[44] In part, the city unsuccessfully sought to justify its differential treatment of the two types of news racks based on a distinction between commercial and noncommercial speech.[45]

In *Destination Ventures, Ltd. v. Federal Communications Commission*,[46] the court of appeals found that a ban on unsolicited fax messages containing advertising constituted a reasonable fit with the objective of shifting the cost of advertising to consumers.[47] The cost shift occurs because the recipient of a faxed advertisement must pay for the paper and toner used to print the fax. The court of appeals found that arguments over the magnitude of the cost shifting were outside the record.[48] Conversely, an intermediate court in California held that a state statute that prohibits credit reporting agencies from disclosing information about tenant involvement in tenant rights litigation (a form of commercial speech) violated the First Amendment.[49]

§ 6.5   First Amendment as a Shield: Blocking Access Duties

The First Amendment entitles one to refrain from speaking as well as to speak. Imposing access duties on a provider of infrastructure services potentially offends this guarantee.

---

[42] *Id.* at 2705.

[43] 113 S. Ct. 1505 (1993).

[44] *Id.* at 1510.

[45] *Id.* at 1511 ("the city's argument attaches more importance to the distinction between commercial and noncommercial speech than our cases warrant and seriously underestimates the value of commercial speech"). *See also* Moser v. Federal Communications Comm'n, 46 F.3d 970, 973 (9th Cir. 1995) (rejecting invitation to distinguish between commercial and noncommercial speech in upholding ban on prerecorded telephone solicitation calls).

[46] 46 F.3d 54 (9th Cir. 1995).

[47] *Id.* at 56.

[48] *Id.*

[49] U.D. Registry, Inc. v. California, 40 Cal. Rptr. 228 (Ct. App. 1995) (information as to which publication is prohibited was lawfully obtained through examination of court records open to the public and is truthful; under Florida Star v. BJF, 491 U.S. 524 (1989) (invalidating statute to protect the privacy of sexual offense victims), these characteristics gave credit reporting agency First Amendment right to release it).

In *Turner Broadcasting System, Inc. v. Federal Communications Commission*,[50] the United States Supreme Court invalidated a lower court's decision upholding cable television must-carry rules. The case was remanded to the lower court for development of a better record on whether local television's survival was jeopardized by unrestricted cable television activity and whether there were less restrictive means of achieving governmental interests in assuring an outlet for local broadcasting.[51] The *Turner Broadcasting* analysis was based on First Amendment privileges and immunities rather than the Fifth Amendment takings or due process clauses.[52]

Turner Broadcasting resulted in five opinions among majority, concurring, and dissenting justices. The diversity of their views illustrates how First Amendment interests can support both sides of information infrastructure access controversies. The case arose when cable programmers and cable operators challenged new statutory requirements that cable television systems devote some of their channels to the transmission of local broadcast television station signals.[53] The rationale for this must-carry requirement was a congressional concern that without the requirement the economic viability of free local broadcast television and its ability to originate quality local programming would be seriously jeopardized.[54] In a sense, the Congress was enacting industry-specific antitrust and fair trade practice regulatory legislation to cure market imperfections.[55] The cable companies on whom the obligations were imposed represented bottlenecks in the distribution channels for content originated by local broadcast stations.[56]

A key part[57] of Justice Kennedy's opinion commanded only a plurality of the Court. In that part, Justice Kennedy concluded that there was insufficient evidence in the record to support the proposition that broadcast television is in jeopardy—the principal market failure argument advanced by the government— and to support the actual effects of must-carry rules on the speech of cable operators and cable programmers. Without such evidence, the analysis commanded by O'Brien could not be undertaken, "for unless we know the extent to

---

[50] 114 S. Ct. 2445 (1994).

[51] *Id.* at 2471–72.

[52] *Id.* at 2451 ("this case presents the question whether these provisions [the must-carry provisions for local broadcast television signal] abridge the Freedom of Speech or of the press in violation of the First Amendment").

[53] Sections 4 and 5 of the Cable Television Consumer Protection and Competition Act of 1992, Pub. L. No. 102-385, 106 Stat. 1416, (codified at 47 U.S.C. §§ 534(b)(1)(B)(h)(1)(A), 535 (Supp. IV 1992)).

[54] 114 S. Ct. 2445, 2455 (1994) (quoting congressional findings).

[55] *Id.* at 2455 (summarizing lower court description of congressional approach).

[56] *Id.* at 2473 (Stevens, J., concurring) (cable operator's control of essential facilities provides basis for intrusive regulation that would be impermissible for other communicative media).

[57] Pt. III(B).

which the must carry provisions in fact interfere with protected speech, we cannot say whether they suppress 'substantially more speech than . . . necessary' to ensure the viability of broadcast television."[58] Justice Stevens would have deferred to congressional judgments about market structure and the effect of the must-carry provision.[59] Justice O'Connor wrote a separate opinion, joined by Justices Scalia and Ginsburg and joined in part by Justice Thomas,[60] concluding that "cable programmers and operators stand in the same position under the First Amendment as do the more traditional media."[61] She disagreed that the government interest in diversity or in access to a multiplicity of diverse and antagonistic sources is content neutral for First Amendment analysis purposes.[62] She thought that interests in preserving local broadcast viewpoints were insufficiently compelling to justify the content regulation. "It is for private speakers and listeners, not for the government, to decide what fraction of their news and entertainment ought to be of a local character and what fraction ought to be of a national (or international) one."[63] She would have found the must-carry rules prohibited by the *Tornillo* concept.[64] While she thought the restrictions also failed content neutral analysis, she noted that Congress does have the power under the First Amendment to act to relieve the "danger in having a single cable operator decide what millions of subscribers can or cannot watch."[65]

She suggested that Congress might foster competition among cable systems, encourage the creation of new media, such as inexpensive satellite broadcasting or fiber-optic networks or simple devices to let people switch easily from cable to over-the-air broadcasting.[66] She also thought Congress

> might also conceivably obligate cable operators to act as common carriers for some of their channels, with those channels being open to all through some sort of lottery system or time sharing arrangement. Setting aside any possible takings clause issues, it stands to reason that if Congress may demand that telephone companies operate as common carriers, it can ask the same of cable companies; such an approach would not suffer from the defect of preferring one speaker to another.[67]

---

[58] 114 S. Ct. at 2472.

[59] *Id.* at 2473 (Stevens, J., concurring in part and concurring in the judgment). He concurred in the judgment in order to have a majority. *Id.* at 2475 (Stevens, J., concurring and concurring in the judgment).

[60] *Id.* at 2475 (O'Connor, J., concurring in part and dissenting in part).

[61] *Id.* at 2476.

[62] *Id.* at 2477.

[63] 114 S. Ct. at 2478 (O'Connor, J., concurring and dissenting).

[64] *Id.* at 2479 ("squarely within" Pacific Gas & Elec. Co. v, Public Utils. Comm'n, 475 U.S. 1, 14–15 (1986) (plurality); citing also Miami Herald Publishing Co. v. Tornillo, 418 U.S. 241 (1974).

[65] *Id.* at 2480 (O'Connor, J., concurring and dissenting).

[66] *Id.*

[67] *Id.* (O'Connor, J., concurring and dissenting).

In terms of the analysis, the Court seems about evenly divided with Justices O'Connor, Scalia, Ginsburg, and Thomas recognizing the legitimacy of possible common carrier obligations imposed on the cable industry for part of its capacity, and everyone else except Justice Kennedy concluding that a factual record can be made of market failure sufficient to justify compelling cable companies to carry the signals of disadvantaged sources such as local broadcast stations.

The dissenters acknowledged the central dispute is who should have control of who gets to speak over cable—the Congress or the cable operator. They acknowledged that there is a danger in having a single cable operator, most of whom occupy monopoly positions, decide what millions of subscribers can or cannot watch.[68]

§ 6.6 First Amendment as Limitation on Private Rights and Remedies

New York Times v. Sullivan,[69] clearly establishes the principle that private legal actions can in some circumstances be limited by the First Amendment.[70] That case involved a damages action for defamation, and the Supreme Court held that it violates the First Amendment, incorporated through the Fourteenth Amendment, to subject a newspaper to no-fault liability for publishing an allegedly defamatory advertisement. The principle has been extended to common-law actions for invasion of privacy, but not, oddly enough, to copyright infringement actions even when injunctive relief is sought and granted. The operation of these principles in the NII is illustrated by comparing *Cubby, Inc. v. CompuServe,*[71] in which CompuServe was held not to be subject to no-fault liability for an allegedly defamatory message appearing on one of its conferences, largely due to First Amendment concerns, with *Playboy Enterprises v. Frena,*[72] in which an electronic bulletin board operator was held liable for files appearing on its service that allegedly infringed copyright and trademark, without proof of fault and without any analysis of the First Amendment. *Cubby* is mainstream law, and therefore sets the standard applicable to NII actors when defamation[73] and

---

[68] *Id.*

[69] 376 U.S. 254 (1964).

[70] Lugar v. Edmondson Oil Co., 457 U.S. 922 (1982) (use of court system may constitute state action); *but see* Flagg Bros. v. Brooks, 436 U.S. 149 (1978) (self-help creditors remedies under authority of state statute did not constitute state action).

[71] 776 F. Supp. 135 (S.D.N.Y. 1991).

[72] 839 F. Supp. 1552 (M.D. Fla. 1993).

[73] Stratton Oakmont, Inc. v. Prodigy Servs. Co., Index No. 31063/94, 1995 WL 323710 (Trial/IAS pt. 34 Nassau County, N.Y. May 26, 1995)) (the *Cubby* standard was applied to find Prodigy to be a publisher, because it affirmatively undertook to screen and censor material on its service).

invasion of privacy are involved.[74] When other kinds of counts are involved, such as sexual harassment or "stalking," it is less certain that *Cubby* is the appropriate standard. If, for example, the victim of such harassment or stalking were to sue an intermediary for intentional or negligent infliction of emotional distress, the plaintiff might successfully avoid *Cubby* and *New York Times v. Sullivan* by claiming that conduct rather than speech was involved. It long has been recognized that when conduct and speech are coupled, the state, through common law or otherwise, has a broader ambit of action to regulate the conduct component than it would have to regulate pure speech.[75]

It is the copyright area that is the most troubling analytically. The relatively automatic availability of injunctions for copyright and trademark infringement without serious consideration of countervailing First Amendment interests is unprincipled, as considered more fully in § **6.10.**

§ 6.7 —Indecent Content

Obscene material is not protected by the First Amendment at all, but indecent material is. A good example of the different treatment of these two classes of content is the Supreme Court's decision in *Sable Communications v. Federal Communications Commission.*[76] Sable Communications offered sexually oriented prerecorded telephone messages, popularly known as "dial a porn," through the Pacific Bell Telephone Network. It began doing this in 1983. When § 223(b) of the Communications Act of 1934 was amended in 1988 to impose an outright ban on indecent as well as obscene interstate commercial telephone messages,[77] Sable sued to enjoin the FCC and the Justice Department from enforcing the ban.[78] The Supreme Court upheld the district court's validation of the ban on obscene telephone messages: "We have repeatedly held that the protection of the First Amendment does not extend to obscene speech."[79] It observed that because of the local community-based test for obscenity, Sable was free to tailor and target its messages so they would be compatible with community standards.[80]

Merely indecent messages are another matter. The Supreme Court agreed with the district court that although the government had a legitimate interest in protecting children from exposure to indecent dial a porn, the statute was not

---

[74] See **Ch. 4** (analyzing application of *Cubby* to tort claims).

[75] Texas v. Johnson, 491 U.S. 397 (1989) (flag burning was protected expressive conduct); Giboney v. Empire Storage & Ice Co., 336 U.S. 490 (1949) (regulation of picketing does not impermissibly infringe free speech).

[76] 492 U.S. 115 (1989).

[77] 47 U.S.C. § 223(b) (1988).

[78] 492 U.S. 115, 118 (1989).

[79] *Id.* at 124.

[80] *Id.* at 125–26.

narrowly enough drawn to serve that purpose and thus violated the First Amendment.[81] Although the government may serve the legitimate interest of shielding minors from the influence of literature that is not obscene by adult standards, "it must do so by narrowly drawn regulations designed to serve those interests without unnecessarily interfering with First Amendment freedoms. It is not enough to show that the government's ends are compelling; the means must be carefully tailored to achieve those ends."[82] The Court distinguished its earlier decision in *FCC v. Pacifica Foundation*,[83] which allowed the FCC to regulate radio broadcasts that were indecent but not obscene. The *Pacifica* opinion relied on the unique attributes of broadcasting—uniquely pervasive and able to intrude on the privacy of the home without prior warning as to program content, and uniquely accessible to children—from the substantially different private commercial telephone communications involved in *Sable*.[84] It also noted that a variety of technological means, including special access codes, credit card preauthorization, and scrambling might be more effective, and certainly narrower, ways of excluding minors from the harmful communications.[85] Thus, the congressional decision to impose an outright across-the-board ban was "another case of burning the house to roast the pig."[86]

The *Sable Communications* analysis is significant not only for its reiteration of the long-established distinction between unprotected obscenity and protected indecent content and the similarly long-established ban against overinclusive regulation of protected speech, but also for its novel recognition of the roles that technological measures might play in First Amendment scrutiny. As the Court suggests,[87] when technological measures potentially protect against the harm that gives rise to the legitimate state interest, broader legal restrictions on communicative activity are overinclusive and therefore should not survive First Amendment scrutiny. This is an extremely powerful idea for the NII, suggesting that when communicative activities endanger legitimate state interest the first resort should be technological rather than broad legal prohibitions.

Another, technological, dimension is important to the analysis. The starting point in *Sable* was a communications medium that must be affirmatively reached for. One must find the telephone number and call a dial-a-porn service. The Court distinguished media that intrude, such as broadcasting. That distinction created difficulty for the United States Court of Appeals for the D.C.

---

[81] *Id.* at 126.

[82] *Id.* at 126 (citations omitted).

[83] 438 U.S. 726 (1978).

[84] 492 U.S. 115, 127 (1989) (no captive audience problem with telephone messages; medium requires listeners to take affirmative steps to receive the communication).

[85] *Id.* at 131 & n.10.

[86] *Id.* at 131.

[87] *Id.* at 131 & n.10.

Circuit in *Alliance for Community Media v. Federal Communications Commission.*[88] The case involved indecent programming on cable "access" channels—those channels the cable operator must set aside for public educational or governmental use, or for use by unaffiliated commercial programmers ("least access"). The FCC sought to regulate indecent programming on those channels, presenting two constitutional questions framed thus by Circuit Judge Wald, writing for the panel:

> First, when the government compels private cable operators to relinquish editorial control over a certain number of "access" channels, making these available for general use by unaffiliated programmers, may it permit cable operators to deny access on those channels to programs that are "indecent," as defined by the FCC?
>
> Second, if the cable operator does not ban "indecent" programs from leased access channels, may the government compel the cable operators to place on a separate channel all leased access programs the programmer as required by law, has identified as "indecent," and to block such channel until the subscriber requests in writing that the block be lifted?[89]

On the first question, the panel held that the First Amendment prevented the government from "deputizing cable operators" with the power to effect a ban on all indecent speech from access channels.[90] On the second question, it found the FCC's approach underinclusive and remanded so the commission could cure that underinclusiveness.[91] The FCC regulations were underinclusive because they singled out leased access channels for segregation and blocking, while leaving commercial channels and public education and government channels wholly unregulated.[92]

Underinclusiveness implicates equal protection as well as the First Amendment.[93] The First Amendment does not absolutely prohibit underinclusiveness, but a restriction on communication may not single out a class of speakers on the basis of criteria that are wholly unrelated to the interest sought to be advanced.[94] The panel decision did not place much emphasis on the difference between cable broadcasting and dial a porn, but the nature of its analysis is consistent with treating cable programming as the same as conventional broadcast television under the earlier case distinguished by *Sable.*

---

[88] 10 F.3d 812 (D.C. Cir. 1993), *superseded,* 56 F.3d 105 (D.C. Cir. 1995) (en banc) (no state action). Despite its being vacated, the panel opinion is illustrative of the analytical difficulty.

[89] *Id.* at 814–15.

[90] See § **6.12** for further analysis of the deputizing argument to deal with the state action requirement.

[91] 10 F.3d 812, 815 (D.C. Cir. 1993) (summarizing conclusions).

[92] *Id.* at 817.

[93] *Id.* at 825 (explaining underinclusiveness concepts).

[94] *Id.* (citing R.A.V. v. City of St. Paul, 112 S. Ct. 2538, 2545 (1992) and City of Cincinnati v. Discovery Network, Inc., 113 S. Ct. 1505, 1509, 1517 (1993) (invalidating prohibition on commercial news racks because noncommercial news racks presenting identical problems remain unregulated)).

A similar challenge in the Ninth Circuit[95] resulted in a preliminary injunction against a cable operator's outright ban on indecent programming, on essentially the same analytical basis relied on by the alliance panel.[96] However, the court found that the plaintiffs had not, at the preliminary injunction stage, raised sufficiently serious questions that the segregation and scrambling requirements imposed by the FCC were not the least restrictive means of regulating indecent material on leased access cable.[97] The court thus granted an injunction against the cable operator imposing an outright ban or utilizing its editorial discretion to regulate indecent material through segregation or otherwise except in strict compliance with § 10(b) and the FCC's implementing regulations.[98] The court was presented with a variety of arguments on the relative merits of various technological means of limiting access to the indecent programming, but elected to wait for development of a fuller record before finding the FCC's approach underinclusive.

§ 6.8   —Telephone Company Video Production for Cable

The First Amendment figured prominently in a series of cases involving relaxation of the traditional ban against allowing telephone companies to enter the cable market. After a number of years of relatively strict enforcement of a telephone-cable cross-ownership prohibition,[99] the FCC by the late 1980s had concluded that allowing the telephone companies into the cable market would be appropriate under certain conditions and that a blanket prohibition on cross-ownership should be repealed.[100] Under the FCC's video dial tone order, telephone companies were allowed to offer conduit services for video programming, but were not allowed to originate programming themselves.[101] The telephone companies challenged the constitutionality of the ban on programming and succeeded in the Fourth and Ninth Circuits and in district court cases in a number of other circuits.[102] The courts were influenced by the Supreme

---

[95] Altmann v. Television Signal Corp., 849 F. Supp. 1335 (N.D. Cal. 1994).

[96] *Id.* at 1341–42.

[97] *Id.* at 1344.

[98] *Id.* at 1346–47.

[99] *See* U.S. West, Inc. v. United States, 48 F.3d 1092, 1095 (9th Cir. 1994) (reviewing history of cross-ownership prohibition, beginning in 1970 FCC rule, codified as § 533(b) in 1984 Cable Act).

[100] Chesapeake & Potomac Tel. Co. v. United States, 42 F.3d 181, 187–88 (4th Cir. 1994) (reviewing history of FCC views).

[101] *Id.* at 188 (describing prohibition and § 533(b)).

[102] Chesapeake & Potomac Tel. Co. v. United States, 42 F.3d 181 (4th Cir. 1994); U.S. West, Inc. v. United States, 48 F.3d 1092 (9th Cir. 1994); Ameritech Corp. v. United States, 867 F. Supp. 721 (N.D. Ill. 1994); Bells. Corp. v. United States, 868 F. Supp. 1335 (N.D. Ala. 1994).

Court's decision in *Turner Broadcasting,* reasoning that if cable companies have free speech rights, so do telephone companies.[103]

The courts rejected opposing arguments that the video programming ban was subject only to rational-basis scrutiny because it constituted economic regulation[104] and arguments by the telephone companies that strict scrutiny was appropriate because the ban was content based.[105] Instead the courts applied intermediate scrutiny under *United States v. O'Brien.*[106] The courts accepted the proposition that the interests promoted by the ban qualified as significant governmental interests: restricting telephone company cross-subsidization of cable services, preventing pole-access discrimination against cable providers, and preserving diversity of ownership in communications outlets and means of electronic access to homes and businesses.[107] But the outright ban failed the narrowly tailored test. There were no congressional findings of fact to which the courts could defer, and the courts noted a variety of less restrictive alternatives to the outright ban, including requirements for telephone company lease of a certain percentage of channels on a common carrier basis to unaffiliated video programmers,[108] enforcement of the Pole Attachment Act of 1978 to prevent discrimination in pole access,[109] and effective enforcement of cost allocation and accounting rules to combat cross-subsidization.[110]

§ 6.9 —Limiting Liability for Harmful Content

The circumstances under which intermediaries can be held liable criminally or civilly for content that passes through their electronic hands is important to First Amendment interests.[111] No-fault liability for intermediaries threatens to chill

---

[103] Chesapeake & Potomac Tel. Co. v. United States, 42 F.3d 181, 190 (4th Cir. 1994); U.S. West, Inc. v. United States, 48 F.3d 1092, 1097 (9th Cir. 1995).

[104] Chesapeake & Potomac Tel. Co. v. United States, 42 F.3d 181, 191 (4th Cir. 1994) (rejecting minimal scrutiny arguments for government); U.S. West, Inc. v. United States, 48 F.3d 1092, 1092 (9th Cir. 1995) (same).

[105] Chesapeake & Potomac Tel. Co. v. United States, 42 F.3d 181, 195–198 (4th Cir. 1994) (reviewing and rejecting strict scrutiny, content-based argument); U.S. West, Inc. v. United States, 48 F.3d 1092, 1098 (9th Cir. 1995) (same).

[106] Chesapeake & Potomac Tel. Co. v. United States, 42 F.3d 181, 198 (4th Cir. 1994) (adopting intermediate scrutiny standard); U.S. West, Inc. v. United States, 48 F.3d 1092, 1100 (9th Cir. 1995) (quoting *O'Brien* test).

[107] Chesapeake & Potomac Tel. Co. v. United States, 42 F.3d 181, 198 (4th Cir. 1994) (following *Turner Broadcasting* and finding those interests to qualify); U.S. West, Inc. v. United States, 48 F.3d 1092, 1101–04 (9th Cir. 1995) (finding interests to qualify).

[108] Chesapeake & Potomac Tel. Co. v. United States, 42 F.3d 181, 202 (4th Cir. 1994); U.S. West, Inc. v. United States, 48 F.3d 1092, 1105 (9th Cir. 1995).

[109] U.S. West, Inc. v. United States, 48 F.3d 1092, 1102–03 (9th Cir. 1995).

[110] *Id.* at 1103–04.

[111] See § **6.6** for more general consideration of the First Amendment as a limit on private lawsuits.

the implementation of the kind of infrastructure that is necessary for a robust dissemination of ideas. *Cubby, Inc. v. CompuServe*[112] recognizes this and uses the First Amendment as a basis for circumscribing liability for the tort of defamation by interposing a fault requirement on intermediaries. The same kind of analytical process occurs in the interpretation of criminal law.

In *Cubby, Inc. v. CompuServe,* the district court, influenced by First Amendment interests in the free flow of information,[113] held that a conduit is not liable for defamation in the absence of evidence that it knew or should have known about the harmful tendency of the information flowing through its service.[114] This accords with general principles of tort law.[115] In *Playboy Enterprises v. Freña,*[116] however, the district court held conduits (electronic bulletin board services) liable for contributory copyright and trademark infringement for material available through their services without clear proof that the intermediaries knew of the infringing nature of the content.[117]

Another district court found *Cubby's* approach appropriate in evaluating a defamation suit against a television network and local broadcast stations carrying the network programming. In *Auvil v. CBS "60 Minutes,"*[118] the district court granted summary judgment in favor of the broadcast stations, while denying it with respect to the network. Although the broadcast stations exercised no editorial control over the broadcast, they did have the power to do so, and in fact they occasionally did censor programming. In the particular case they merely served as conduits.[119] Conduits are not liable in the absence of fault under the relevant state law. While most of the decisions deal with liability, vis-à-vis booksellers, there is no logical basis for imposing a duty of censorship on the visual media that does not likewise attach to the print chain of distribution.[120] The district court found that imposing no-fault liability or a duty to screen on intermediaries not only would be unrealistic, but "it is difficult to imagine a scenario more chilling on the media's right of expression and the public's rights to know."[121] Nor did it think the legitimate need of victims of harmful communication to be compensated would be hurt by insisting that fault be shown with respect to intermediaries: "[p]ersons injured by defamatory material are not impaired by limiting conduit liability to those situations where culpability is

---

[112] 776 F. Supp. 135 (S.D.N.Y. 1991) (granting summary judgment to defendants).

[113] *Id.* at 139–40.

[114] *Id.* at 141.

[115] Restatement (Second) of Torts § 581 (1976).

[116] 839 F. Supp. 1552 (M.D. Fla. 1993) (granting partial summary judgment to plaintiff).

[117] *See* Sega Enters., Ltd. v. Maphia, 857 F. Supp. 679 (N.D. Cal. 1994) (the record showed knowledge by the conduit of the copyright-infringing activity by others, and thus the district court did not have occasion to test the standard for imposing liability on a conduit). *Id.* at 683 (finding of fact No. 16); *id.* at 686 (conclusion of law No. 9).

[118] 800 F. Supp. 928 (E.D. Wash. 1992).

[119] *Id.* at 931.

[120] *Id.* at 932 (citing *Cubby*).

[121] *Id.*

established. The generating source, which in a national broadcast will generally be the deepest of the deep pockets, may still be called upon to defend."[122] Of course, in the NII context more broadly, while it may be appropriate to insist that the victims seek compensation from the source of the harmful communication, it may not be true that the source has deeper pockets than the intermediary.

Cubby suggests that electronic conduits, like retail bookstores and newsstands, should not be strictly liable for harmful material they make available. On the other hand, if the intermediaries have knowledge of harmful tendencies or if they vouch for the quality or edit the underlying material,[123] they face the same liability as an author or original publisher.

§ 6.10   Prior Restraint and Copyright

The First Amendment traditionally was particularly hostile to prior restraints—governmental bans on publication before it occurs.[124] Surprisingly, the constitutional preference for avoiding prior restraints does not operate when intellectual property is involved: "No one denies that a newspaper can properly be enjoined from publishing the copyrighted works of another."[125]

The district court opinion in *New Era Publications International v. Henry Holt & Co.*[126] is an exception. That case involved a suit by a Church of Scientology affiliate to enjoin publication of a critical biography of L. Ron Hubbard, the founder of the Church of Scientology, on the grounds that the biography infringed copyright. The district court, in an opinion written by District Judge Pierre Leval, found some infringement outside the scope of fair use but nevertheless denied an injunction on First Amendment grounds. "Courts should weigh cautiously whether a prior restraint in the form of an injunction is the appropriate remedy."[127] He also suggested that in determining questions of fair use and remedy, courts should consider "whether a copyright action is brought in good faith to preserve the benefits secured by the copyright law or whether it is brought to accomplish a different purpose, such as combating hostile or derogatory publication."[128] More generally, the district judge noted

---

[122] *Id.*

[123] Stratton Oakmont, Inc. v. Prodigy Servs. Co., Index No. 31063/94, 1995 WL 323710 (Trial/IAS pt. 34 Nassau County, N.Y. May 26, 1995) (the *Cubby* standard was applied to find Prodigy to be a publisher because it affirmatively undertook to screen and censor material on its service).

[124] New York Times Co. v. United States, 403 U.S. 713 (1971) (enjoining publication of "Pentagon Papers" was impermissible prior restraint).

[125] *Id.* at 730, 731 (White, J., concurring).

[126] 695 F. Supp. 1493 (S.D.N.Y. 1988), *aff'd,* 873 F.2d 576 (2d Cir. 1989) (disagreeing with district court reasoning on First Amendment).

[127] *Id.* at 1527–28 (quoting 3 M. Nimmer, Nimmer on Copyright §§ 14.06[B], 14-56.1 (1987)).

[128] *Id.* at 1528 n.14.

that § 512 of the Copyright Act does not require a grant of injunctive relief and that "we must therefore focus with a new intensity on the potential conflict between the copyright and freedom of speech, and particularly on the question whether a finding of infringement should ritualistically call forth an injunction."[129]

The court of appeals affirmed denial of an injunction, but only on laches grounds, noting its disagreement with much of the district court's analysis: "We are not persuaded, however, that any First Amendment concerns not accommodated by the Copyright Act are implicated in this action. Our observation that the fair use doctrine encompasses all claims of First Amendment in the copyright field never has been repudiated.[130] Chief Judge Oakes concurred, expressing greater support for District Judge Leval's analysis.[131] He recognized the strong authority against separate consideration of First Amendment matters in a copyright injunction, but nevertheless thought that the grant of injunction in the copyright case is inherently a matter of discretion.[132] The matter did not rest there because Judges Newman, Oakes, Kearse, and Winter issued a rather lengthy dissent from denial of rehearing en banc,[133] urging that the panel majority opinion not be understood as saying that injunctive relief follows as a matter of course once copyright infringement has been found. Rather, equitable discretion remains as to the propriety of an injunction.[134] One New York trial court opinion used a similar approach to that used by Judge Leval.[135]

A minority of the Supreme Court recognized the potential for even contractual restrictions to offend the First Amendment by imposing de facto prior restraint, albeit in a case in which one party to the contract was the United States government.[136] The dissenting views thus support the idea of a de facto prior restraint but do not extend the concern into purely private activities.

---

[129] *Id.* at 1526 (characterizing 17 U.S.C. § 502).

[130] 873 F.2d 576, 584 (2d Cir. 1989) (citing Roy Export Co. Establishment v. Columbia Broadcasting Sys., Inc., 672 F.2d 1095, 1099–100 (2d Cir. 1982) and Harper & Row Publishers, Inc. v. Nation Enters., 471 U.S. 539, 557 (1985).

[131] *Id.* at 585 (Oakes, C.J., concurring).

[132] *Id.* at 595–96 (acknowledging "no circuit that has considered the question has ever held that the First Amendment provides a privilege in the copyright field distinct from the accommodation embodied in the fair use doctrine"; citing Roy Export Co. Establishment v. Columbia Broadcasting Sys., Inc., 672 F.2d 1095, 1099 (2d Cir. 1982) and Harper & Row Publishers, Inc. v. Nation Enters., 471 U.S. 539, 557, 559 (1985)).

[133] 884 F.2d 659, 662 (2d Cir. 1989) (on petition for rehearing and suggestion for rehearing en banc).

[134] *Id.* at 663–64.

[135] Rosemont Enters., Inc. v. McGraw-Hill Book Co., 380 N.Y.S.2d 839, 843 (Sup. Ct. 1975) (denying injunction against allegedly infringing autobiography because injunction against publication would violate First Amendment).

[136] Snepp v. United States, 444 U.S. 507, 516, 520 (1980) (Stevens, J., joined by Brennan & Marshall, JJ., dissenting from holding that CIA agent who published memoirs in violation of contract with CIA validly was subject to constructive trust for all profits he made).

The voice of commentators is nearly unanimous that First Amendment and copyright interests should be balanced more explicitly. It is likely that this pressure from the literature will have some effect on the courts as copyright is used more aggressively to blunt NII activities. The law review literature almost uniformly urges more attention to the First Amendment in copyright injunction cases.[137] The freedom with which injunctions are available is ironic, considering copyright's origins as a government censorship tool.[138] "Having a doctrine in free speech law that severely limits the use of prior restraints, only to throw it all out whenever even a small amount of someone else's expression has been incorporated into the defendant's speech makes no sense."[139]

§ 6.11   Conflict Between First Amendment and Antitrust Principles

Suppose the antitrust analysis developed in **Chapter 2** imposes an obligation on a consortium of information service providers controlling an essential facility. The burdened providers may oppose such an obligation on First Amendment grounds. The Supreme Court long has recognized that the First Amendment constrains application of the antitrust laws.[140] Conversely, in *Associated Press v.*

---

[137] *See also* Wendy J. Gordon, *A Property Right in Self Expression: Equality and Individualism in the Natural Law of Intellectual Property,* 102 Yale L.J. 1533, 1537 (1993) (legions of commentators have deplored tendency of courts to ignore First Amendment privileges when copyright or trademark suits are brought, but "the courts have too often turned a deaf ear to these arguments. The incantation 'property' seems sufficient to render free speech issues invisible."). *See also* articles cited in *id.* n.16; Jessica Litman, *Copyright and Information Policy,* 55-SPG Law & Contempt. Probs. 185 nn.131–37 (1992) (questioning conventional wisdom that First Amendment need not be considered separately in copyright cases); Ralph S. Brown, *Civil Remedies for Intellectual Property Invasions: Themes and Variations,* 55 Law & Contempt. Probs. 45 (1992) (surveying injunctive and damages remedies for intellectual property invasion; observing that injunction for copyright infringement is virtually automatic, despite plausible First Amendment concerns); *see also* James Hall, Comment, *Bare-Faced Mess: Fair Use in the First Amendment,* 70 Or. L. Rev. 211 (1991) (urging evolution of fair use doctrine to give First Amendment considerations more emphasis); Tiffany D. Trunko, Note, *Remedies for Copyright Infringement: Respecting the First Amendment,* 89 Colum. L. Rev. 1940 (1989) (suggesting revised fair use formula better to accommodate First Amendment concerns, including greater reliance on damages).

[138] Diane Leenheer Zimmerman, *Information as Speech, Information as Goods: Some Thoughts on Marketplaces and Bill of Rights,* 33 Wm. & Mary L. Rev. 665, 677 (1992) (reviewing history of British copyright law and role of prior restraints not abolished until 1694).

[139] *Id.* at 737–38 (if primary justification for protecting intellectual property interest is economic, compensatory damages should be primary form of remedy).

[140] *See* Eastern R.Rs. Presidents Conference v. Noerr Motor Freight, Inc., 365 U.S. 127, 138 (1961) (reversing court of appeals for allowing antitrust liability to be imposed on group of railroads that sought enactment of legislation harmful to truckers, based on right to petition government); Federal Trade Comm'n v. Superior Court Trial Lawyers Ass'n, 493 U.S. 411, 426–28 (1990) (antitrust enforcement against trial lawyers who participate in boycott to force increased fees did not violate First Amendment; purpose of concerted action was economic rather than political).

United States,[141] the Supreme Court rejected the argument that newspaper publishers could not be subjected to antitrust liability for a concerted refusal to deal through the Associated Press based on the First Amendment.[142] Indeed, the Court found that First Amendment considerations reinforced antitrust liability because breaking up the bottleneck on freer dissemination of news represented by the Associated Press would enhance a free press—an argument also available in the NII when the antitrust law imposes a duty to allow a new provider to reach a market.[143] The Court, however, noted that nothing in the antitrust decree compelled the defendants to permit publication of anything they did not want to publish.[144] An antitrust-based order compelling the carriage of content would raise more serious First Amendment questions.

These cases involve analysis of two factors. The first is whether the purpose of the allegedly anticompetitive conduct is primarily economic or primarily political. In *Eastern Railroads Presidents Conference v. Noerr Motor Freight, Inc.,* the primarily political purpose of the combination gave it First Amendment immunity from antitrust liability. It did not matter that there were incidental economic benefits (to members of the combination) of the essentially political campaign.[145] Conversely, in *Associated Press* and *Federal Trade Commission v. Superior Court Trial Lawyers Ass'n,* the concerted action had primarily an economic motive, and this justified imposition of antitrust liability because the First Amendment–related political and press effects were incidental and secondary.[146]

The other factor is the impact of the antitrust liability on traditional editorial and content selection activities associated with free speech and press. The *Associated Press* footnote acknowledges the importance of distinguishing between an antitrust inquiry that would circumscribe content selection from one that does not.[147] The *Noerr* court rejected a content-oriented analysis used by the lower courts to justify punishing the allegedly malicious and fraudulent publicity campaign under the antitrust laws.[148]

Associated Press, like the more recent cases culminating in *Turner Broadcasting,* also acknowledges the internal conflict within the First Amendment itself. Some combinations of those exercising First Amendment privileges may be questionable not only under the antitrust laws but also operate to block the free flow of information the First Amendment is aimed at furthering.

---

[141] 326 U.S. 1 (1945) (affirming summary judgment and injunction against Associated Press for prohibiting its members from disseminating news to competing wire services and from giving competitors applications for membership).

[142] *Id.* at 19–20.

[143] *Id.* at 20.

[144] *Id.* at 20 n.18. Rather, the decree simply invalidated limits on the dissemination of things the publishers already have published.

[145] 365 U.S. 127, 138 (1961).

[146] 326 U.S. 1, 40 (1945); 493 U.S. 411, 416 (1990).

[147] 326 U.S. 1, 20 n.18 (1945).

[148] 365 U.S. 127, 138 (1961).

This was the situation in *Citizen Publishing Co. v. United States,*[149] in which the Supreme Court upheld an antitrust challenge to a partial combination of the two newspapers in one city. Antitrust liability involved neither news gathering nor news dissemination; in fact the challenged combination diminished dissemination of information.[150] The same mutual reinforcement of antitrust and First Amendment concerns existed in *Federal Communications Commission v. National Citizens Committee for Broadcasting,*[151] in which the Supreme Court upheld FCC regulations limiting common ownership of radio and television stations and daily newspapers in the same community. It justified its conclusion in part by the traditional susceptibility of broadcasters to regulation, based on limited spectrum,[152] and in part by the mutual reinforcement between antitrust laws and First Amendment interests noted in *Associated Press.*[153]

§ 6.12   First Amendment as a Sword: Source of Private Duty

Section 6.3 explains that the First Amendment ordinarily only operates as a limitation on the exercise of governmental power, embodied in the state action element. There is, however, a narrow range of circumstances in which the First Amendment can operate as a source of private duty, imposing obligations on private entities. One involves the government enlisting private intermediaries as censors of content. The other, more speculative in nature, involves electronic bulletin boards as public forums.

Usually, refusal of access by a private network services provider cannot support a claim for violation of the constitutional rights of the entity desiring access because the refusal is not "state action." *Altmann v. Television Signal Corp.,*[154] however, found that sections 10(a) and (c) of the 1992 Cable Act sufficiently encourage private cable operators to ban constitutionally protected material from leased and public access channels to justify an injunction against an outright ban. The district court made this finding, while acknowledging the general rule that regulation of a private industry usually is not enough to establish state action.[155] The court emphasized that, in general, the statute deprives cable operators of editorial control over constitutionally protected speech,[156] but expressly authorizes them to exclude indecent material from

---

[149] 394 U.S. 131 (1969).

[150] *Id.* at 139–40.

[151] 436 U.S. 775 (1978).

[152] *Id.* at 798.

[153] *Id.* at 800 n.18 (citing *Associated Press* and *Citizen Publishing*).

[154] 849 F. Supp. 1335 (N.D. Cal. 1994) (granting preliminary injunction against complete ban by cable television network on broadcast of allegedly obscene programming).

[155] *Id.* at 1342.

[156] *Id.* (citing 47 U.S.C. §§ 531(e), 532(c)(2)).

leased and public access cable channels. "This solitary government exception focuses the cable operator's attention on the material the government wishes to suppress and gives the operator the authority to ban the material entirely."[157] The case does not say that the First Amendment is a source of right to access or a source of duty on the part of the cable operator. It merely proscribes governmental direction to the cable operator to limit access.

Computer bulletin boards are "public" message areas provided by the operator of an on-line service.[158] They are easily accessible[159] and are widely used by individuals and groups as a means of communicating and as a forum for exchanging ideas. Using bulletin boards as a forum for exchanging ideas is commonplace and has been at the center of controversy in recent years. The controversy extends beyond small dial-up bulletin boards to large information service providers.[160] The remainder of this section explores the possibility that bulletin boards could be considered to be public forums under the First Amendment similar to shopping centers.

The Supreme Court has examined the question of whether private property can be considered a public forum on a number of occasions.[161] An analysis of whether a privately owned and operated computer bulletin board might implicate First Amendment rights of users begins with the question of whether a computer bulletin board is a public space that may be treated as a public forum. The Supreme Court has articulated various criteria that would transform a mere public space into a public forum.

The "principal purpose of [a] traditional public forum is the free exchange of ideas."[162] It is clear that the principal purpose of a computer bulletin board is to

---

[157] *Id.* at 1343.

[158] The analysis of First Amendment treatment of private bulletin boards is the work of Andrew J. Vella, law clerk to the author. This section uses the term "bulletin board" broadly to include many Internet applications, such as newsgroups and listservs as well as independent dial-up services.

[159] Generally, an individual needs to own or have access to a computer and have a user account with an on-line provider. Once the user connects with the on-line provider, he is able to access thousands of bulletin boards.

[160] On two occasions Prodigy, an on-line provider, came under public scrutiny with regard to its bulletin board policy. In November 1990, Prodigy prohibited posting messages on its bulletin boards regarding its E-mail pricing policy. *See* John Markoff, *Home-Computer Network Criticized for Limiting Users,* Wall St. J., Nov. 27, 1990, at D1. In October 1991, Prodigy was criticized for allowing anti-semitic messages to be posted on its bulletin boards and defended its actions stating that the messages "were posted within the policy of free expression on the service." *See* Michael W. Miller, *Prodigy Network Defends Display of Anti-Semitic Notes,* Wall St. J., Oct. 22, 1991, at B1.

[161] Marsh v. Alabama, 326 U.S. 501 (1946) (whether company-owned town assumed the attributes of a municipality); Lloyd Corp. v. Tanner, 407 U.S. 551 (1972) (whether owner of a shopping center could prohibit leafletting on shopping center premises); Hudgens v. National Labor Relations Bd., 424 U.S. 507 (1976) (whether owner of a shopping center could prevent labor union members from picketing on shopping center premises).

[162] Cornelius v. NAACP Legal Defense & Educ. Fund, 473 U.S. 788, 800 (1984).

exchange information and ideas. A large number of people who use computer bulletin boards use them as a means to convey their ideas, messages, and views on a wide array of topics. There are tens of thousands of "mailboxes," "news-groups," and "usergroups" that are solely dedicated to the exchange of information and ideas. Second, is the requirement that the property be "intentionally open[ed] . . . for public discourse."[163] Although access is limited to those who subscribe to many bulletin boards,[164] it is evident that computer bulletin boards have been "intentionally opened for public discourse." One of the main concepts behind the bulletin boards is that they are a way for individuals or groups to communicate their ideas to others. Often bulletin boards act as sounding boards of public opinion with some boards dedicated to discourse on particular issues.

Merely because computer bulletin boards constitute public forums in the factual sense does not mean that the conduct of their operators constitutes state action.[165] There are several arguments that can be made that would support a finding of state action in the privately owned computer bulletin board context, even though computer bulletin boards are unquestionably private property.[166] In assessing these arguments, it is important to remember that certain state constitutions are more expansive in their view of First Amendment protection, and a suit brought in those states would be more likely to succeed.

The first state action argument is that private bulletin board operators have assumed the role of the state in providing a public forum. In *Marsh v. Alabama*,[167] the Court held that Alabama could not constitutionally "impose criminal punishment on a person who undertakes to distribute religious literature on the premises of a company-owned town contrary to the wishes of the town's management."[168] In that case a Jehovah's Witness was distributing religious literature on a sidewalk within the company-owned town of Chickasaw, Alabama. The corporation that owned the town placed a notice prohibiting solicitation in the windows of the town's stores. Marsh was asked to leave and upon her refusal to do so was arrested for violating an Alabama statute that made it illegal to remain on the premises of another after having been warned not to do so. The Court stated that the corporation "built and operated [Chickasaw] primarily to benefit the public" and that the operation was "essentially a public function."[169]

---

[163] *Id.* at 802.

[164] This is not true for most Internet newsgroups. Anyone can access them without any prior subscription arrangements.

[165] *See* Marsh v. Alabama, 326 U.S. 501 (1946); Lloyd Corp. v. Tanner, 407 U.S. 551 (1972). See also § **6.3** for an analysis of the state action requirement.

[166] Edward J. Naughton, *Is Cyberspace A Public Forum? Computer Bulletin Boards, Free Speech, and State Action*, 81 Geo. L.J. 409, 432 (1993). ("Since access to the board is conditioned upon payment of a fee and compliance with the provisions of the subscription agreement, it cannot fairly be said that commercial bulletin boards are held open to the public at large.").

[167] 326 U.S. 501 (1946).

[168] *Id.* at 506.

[169] *Id.*

The Court went on to state that "[t]he more an owner, for his advantage, opens up his property for use by the public in general, the more do his rights become circumscribed by the statutory and constitutional rights of those who use it."[170]

In *Marsh,* the Court concluded that the town of Chickasaw had assumed all the attributes of a state-created municipality.[171] This in essence meant that the conduct of the corporate owner constituted state action.[172] Chickasaw had assumed the role of the state and therefore had the obligation to protect the constitutional guarantees of the First Amendment.[173]

It can be argued that computer bulletin board operators similarly have assumed the role of the state. A computer bulletin board itself can be viewed as a "municipality." Although a computer bulletin board may not possess the physical attributes of a municipality, it can be argued that it is the functional equivalent of one.[174] It is an "area" that is open to the public where public discourse, private conversation, and business transactions occur. It does not, however, undertake any other governmental roles relating to law enforcement, public health, or public works.

The owners of the bulletin boards control the instrumentalities of the municipality. They create the governing bodies, decide what the predominant subject matter of the boards will be, and most importantly, they regulate the users. Regulation of users comes in various forms. First, use of the boards is restricted to those who subscribe to the boards. Second, once users have subscribed to the board, they are further limited by the terms of the subscription agreement.[175] Finally, the owners of the boards can limit the topics available and the content of discourse. Potential subscribers can be refused service by the owners, and existing subscribers can be refused service if they do not comply with the terms of the subscription agreement, which itself may contain prohibitions on certain kinds of speech. Owners exert total control over their own "private municipality."

Once it has been shown that the computer bulletin board operators have assumed the role of the state by creating and controlling a privately owned municipality, under *Marsh* they are under a duty to protect the guarantees of the First Amendment. Under this analysis, the owners could not cancel subscriptions of those users for exercising their First Amendment right to speak, and owners could not deny potential subscribers access to the boards based on their viewpoints.

---

[170] *Id.*

[171] *See id.* at 506–07.

[172] The Court subsequently articulated the test for state action stating "the inquiry must be whether there is a sufficiently close nexus between the State and the challenged action of the regulated entity so that the action of the latter may be fairly treated as that of the State itself." Jackson v. Metropolitan Edison Co., 419 U.S. 345 (1974) (citing Moose Lodge No. 107 v. Irvis, 407 U.S. 163 (1972)).

[173] 326 U.S. 501 (1946).

[174] See **Ch. 7,** regarding self-governance in electronic communities.

[175] See generally America Online "Rules of the Road," reprinted in **Ch. 5.**

Of course, the flaw in this argument is that the government functions performed by bulletin board operators focus almost entirely on expression, unlike the functions performed in *Marsh v. Alabama,* which extended to physical public service and law enforcement functions. The absence of physical state functions means that extending *Marsh v. Alabama* to the private bulletin board context has a kind of bootstrap character: limitation on expression constitutes governmental conduct, which implicates the First Amendment, which prohibits the limitations on expression.

Moreover, the Supreme Court has declined to extend the company town status to ordinary shopping centers. In *Lloyd Corp. Ltd. v. Tanner,*[176] the Supreme Court held that the owner of a private shopping center could prohibit Vietnam War protesters from leafletting on the premises of the shopping center without violating their First Amendment rights.[177] The Court began its analysis by stating, "the First and Fourteenth Amendments safeguard the rights of free speech and assembly by limitations on state action, not on action by the owner of private property used nondiscriminatorily for private property purposes only."[178] The protesters argued that "the property of a large shopping center is 'open to the public' [and] serves the same purposes as a 'business district' of a municipality, and therefore has been dedicated to certain types of public use."[179] The Court rejected this argument stating, "property [does not] lose its private character merely because the public is generally invited to use it for designated purposes."[180] In its holding, the Court stated that "there [was] no dedication of Lloyd's privately owned and operated shopping center to public use as to entitle [the protesters] to exercise therein the asserted First Amendment rights."[181]

The *Lloyd* Court failed to find any state action by Lloyd opening its doors to the public. Lloyd did not "assu[me] or exercise . . . municipal functions or power."[182] Absent a finding of state action, it appears that the Court will not infringe on the property rights of a private owner in this context. Clearly, *Lloyd* is a major barrier to treatment of private bulletin board operators as state actors.

Theoretically, the analysis of state action might be different when legislative or regulatory requirements are imposed. The Supreme Court examined that issue in *Hudgens v. National Labor Relations Board.*[183] The issue in *Hudgens* was whether the owner of a private shopping center could prohibit members of a labor union from picketing on the grounds of the shopping center.[184] The

---

[176] 407 U.S 551 (1972).

[177] *Id.* at 570.

[178] *Id.* at 567.

[179] *Id.* at 568–69.

[180] *Id.* at 569.

[181] *Id.* at 570.

[182] 407 U.S. 551, 569 (1972).

[183] 424 U.S. 507 (1976).

[184] *Id.* at 507.

National Labor Relations Board (Board) acting pursuant to the National Labor Relations Act,[185] would determine the respective rights and liabilities of the parties in this context.[186] "Statutory or common law may in some situations extend protections or provide redress against a private corporation or person who seeks to abridge the free expression of others."[187] Here, the statutory law provided that the role of the Board in such a situation was to "resolve conflicts between § 7 rights and private property rights."[188] The Board determined that "the pickets were within the scope of Hudgens's invitation to members of the public to do business at the shopping center, and that it was, therefore, immaterial whether or not there existed an alternative means of communicating with the customers and employees of the . . . store."[189] The Court remanded the case to the Board for it to consider the case under the National Labor Relations Act alone.[190]

The Supreme Court revisited the issue of whether the owners of private property could prohibit speech on their premises in *Pruneyard Shopping Center v. Robins.*[191] In *Pruneyard,* the owner of a shopping center promulgated regulations prohibiting any visitor or tenant from engaging in any publicly expressive activity that was not directly related to the shopping center's commercial purpose.[192] The appellees set up a card table in the shopping center and began soliciting support for their opposition to a United Nations resolution against Zionism.[193] Soon after the appellees had set up their card table, a security guard informed them that they would have to leave because they were violating Pruneyard's regulations.[194]

The appellees brought an action in the California Superior Court seeking to enjoin Pruneyard from denying access to the shopping center and alleging violations of the California Constitution.[195] The Superior Court held that the "appellees were not entitled under either the federal or California Constitutions to exercise their asserted rights on the shopping center grounds."[196] The

---

[185] 29 U.S.C. §§ 151–206.

[186] 424 U.S. 507, 512 (1976).

[187] *Id.*

[188] *Id.* at 521. Section 7 of the National Labor Relations Act provides: "Employees shall have the right to self organization, to form, join, or assist labor organizations, to bargain collectively through representatives of their own choosing, and to engage in other concerted activities for the purpose of collective bargaining or other mutual aid or protection." 29 U.S.C § 157.

[189] 424 U.S. 507, 511 (1976).

[190] *Id.* at 522.

[191] 447 U.S. 74 (1980).

[192] *Id.* at 77.

[193] *Id.*

[194] *Id.*

[195] *Id.*

[196] *Id.*

California Court of Appeal affirmed.[197] The California Supreme Court reversed, holding that the "California Constitution protect[s] speech and petitioning, reasonably exercised, in shopping centers even when the centers are privately owned."[198] In its analysis, the California Supreme Court embraced shopping centers as public forums, stating "[t]he California Constitution broadly proclaims speech and petition rights. Shopping centers to which the public is invited can provide an essential and invaluable forum for exercising those rights."[199]

On appeal from the California Supreme Court, the Supreme Court of the United States held that "neither [Pruneyard's] federally recognized property rights nor their First Amendment rights ha[d] been infringed by the California Supreme Court's decision recognizing a right of appellees to exercise state-protected rights of expression and petition on appellants' property."[200] The Court noted the differences between state and federal constitutional protection while distinguishing *Lloyd,* stating that "[o]ur reasoning in *Lloyd* . . . does not ex proprio vigore limit the authority of the State to exercise its police power or its sovereign right to adopt in its own Constitution individual liberties more expansive than those conferred by the Federal Constitution."[201]

In *Pruneyard,* the California Supreme Court took an expansive view of the respondents' right to free speech under the California Constitution.[202] The Supreme Court held that a state constitution could offer more protection to individuals than the federal Constitution.[203] States that adopt a more expansive view of the right to free speech may be more inclined to offer users of computer bulletin boards greater protection under a state constitution.

Thus, *Pruneyard* illustrates the possibility that state constitutional entitlements might be implicated in a broader range of private bulletin board operator conduct than the federal First Amendment. On the other hand, proponents of treating private service provider conduct as state action must be mindful of the likelihood that a state constitutional requirement to allow access might conflict with the federal constitutional privilege of denying access under *Turner Broadcasting.*[204]

§ 6.13   Property Rights

Much legal regulation diminishes the privileges and powers associated with ownership of property. This is particularly true when one must allow one's property to be used for some purpose identified by the government or a third party.

---

[197] 447 U.S. 74, 78 (1980).

[198] Robins v. Pruneyard Shopping Ctr., 592 P.2d 341, 347 (Cal. 1979).

[199] *Id.*

[200] 447 U.S. 74, 88 (1980).

[201] *Id.* at 80 (citing Cooper v. California, 386 U.S. 58, 62 (1967)).

[202] 592 P.2d 341, 344 (Cal. 1979).

[203] *Id.* at 342.

[204] Turner Broadcasting Sys., Inc. v. Federal Communications Comm'n, 114 S. Ct. 2445, 2459 (1994). *Turner Broadcasting* is discussed more fully in § 6.5.

Private property is protected by the due process and taking clauses of the United States Constitution.[205] The takings clause requires just compensation for property taken for public use.[206] It thus figures prominently in eminent domain proceedings, considered in § **6.15**. The due process clause has two components. The first component, substantive, requires that there be a rational relationship between any deprivation of property and a legitimate governmental interest.[207] The second component, procedural, requires the use of procedures before or soon after the deprivation of property aimed at assuring accurate fact-finding commensurate with the magnitude of the deprivation and the burden to governmental interests of additional procedural elements.[208]

Substantive due process under the Fourteenth Amendment of the United States immunizes persons from deprivation of life, liberty, or property except when the deprivation is justified by a legitimate state interest. Equal protection analysis is similar.[209] After a long period in which substantive due process based on economic interests was mostly a dead letter, recent emphasis on rationality of regulatory schemes invites greater attention to the doctrine. Now, government regulation that significantly impairs enjoyment of property interests may be unconstitutional unless property owners are compensated for the loss occasioned by the regulation. Particularly focusing on the National Information Infrastructure, the D.C. Circuit in *Bell Atlantic Telephone Co. v. Federal Communications Commission*[210] used constitutional property concerns to construe the Federal Communications Act narrowly and thus excluded the FCC's authority to force telephone companies to allow competitors to connect to the telephone system on telephone company premises.[211]

The court acknowledged that it lacked authority to decide whether the FCC order constituted a taking because exclusive jurisdiction over takings claims exceeding $10,000 in magnitude is given to the United States Claims Court.[212] Nevertheless, it thought itself obligated to construe the FCC's statutory authority so as to reduce constitutional questions: "The Commission's decision

---

[205] U.S. Const. amend. V.

[206] Blanchette v. Connecticut Gen. Ins. Corp. (rail reorganization cases), 419 U.S. 102 (1974); Bauman v. Ross, 167 U.S. 548, 574 (1897); United States v. Gettysburg Elec. Ry., 160 U.S. 668, 681 (1896).

[207] Hawaii Hous. Auth. v. Midkiff, 467 U.S. 229, 239 (1984) (rejecting "public use" challenge, requirement is coterminous with state's police power; scope of judicial review of legislative judgment is very narrow).

[208] *See* Mathews v. Eldridge, 424 U.S. 319 (1976).

[209] Bray v. Alexandria Women's Health Clinic, 113 S. Ct. 753, 773, 777 (1993) (Souter, J., concurring in part and dissenting in part) (noting that civil rights conspiracy claim could be evaluated similarly under substantive due process or equal protection tests). *But see* Nollan v. California Coastal Comm'n, 483 U.S. 825, 835 n.3 (1987) (questioning whether equal protection and substantive due process standards are the same in property taking cases).

[210] 24 F.3d 1441 (D.C. Cir. 1994).

[211] "The orders raise constitutional questions that override our customary deference to the Commission's interpretation of its own authority." *Id.* at 1443.

[212] *Id.* at 1445 n.1 (citing 28 U.S.C. § 1346(a)(2)).

to grant CAPs the right to exclusive use of a portion of the petitioner's central offices directly implicates the just compensation clause of the Fifth Amendment, under which 'a permanent physical occupation authorized by government is a taking without regard to the public interest that it may serve.' "[213] The fact that the telephone companies were allowed by the FCC order to file new tariffs under which they could obtain compensation from the competitive access providers for the reasonable cost of collocation did not defeat the concern.[214] As a matter of statutory construction, the court of appeals contrasted the Communications Act's lack of explicit collocation authority with the explicit authority contained in the Interstate Commerce Act for the Interstate Commerce Commission to force railroads to provide switch connections for shippers and other carriers.[215]

The FCC almost immediately adopted a revised interconnection order that avoided the problems that led the court of appeals to invalidate its physical collocation order. However, the analysis used by the court of appeals, in combination with the regulatory taking concept, raises the possibility that a variety of requirements for interconnection, access, and compatibility, considered in **Chapters 7** and **8** will be subjected to constitutional scrutiny because they interfere with the property interests of those on whom such duties are imposed. Moreover, the analysis suggests the possibility of greater constitutional scrutiny of any judicial or congressional efforts to impose compulsory licensing requirements on owners of intellectual property, considered in **Chapter 10.**

Not all cases support such an approach. In *G.T.E. Northwest v. Public Utility Commission,* subsequently reversed by the Oregon Supreme Court,[216] the Oregon intermediate court rejected a constitutional takings challenge almost identical to that accepted in the D.C. Circuit *Bell Atlantic* case. The Oregon Public Utility Commission (PUC) collocation order was apparently more or less identical to the FCC order invalidated by the D.C. Circuit. Distinguishing the D.C. Circuit case by bare mention of it in a cryptic footnote, perhaps on the grounds that construction of a different statute was involved,[217] the Oregon Court of Appeals found no serious constitutional problem presented by the authority exercised by the Oregon PUC on two grounds. First, the occupation resulting from the collocation was not permanent under *Loretto v. TelePrompTer.*[218] Second, the property enjoyment the telephone companies had after implementation of the order was not materially less than they had

---

[213] *Id.* at 1445 (acknowledging that such a taking nevertheless could be constitutional if compensation is allowed in the claims court or otherwise).

[214] *Id.* at 1445 n.3.

[215] *Id.* at 1446 (characterizing 49 U.S.C. §§ 11104(a), 11103(a)). "Switch connections are to railroads what cable hook ups are to telephone companies." *Id.*

[216] 883 P.2d 255 (Or. Ct. App. 1994), *rev'd,* 321 Or. 458 (1995) (co-location order constitutes taking under state constitution).

[217] *Id.* at 260 n.11.

[218] 458 U.S. 437 (1982).

before issuance of the order because of the PUC's general authority to make inspections and otherwise act in ways that intruded on the telephone company's property rights.[219] The Oregon and D.C. Circuit cases represent contrasting ways to apply essentially the same standards to essentially the same regulatory initiative.

At the very least, this line of constitutional attack reinforces the need for arrangements that compel the connection of one service provider with another to require the party desiring the interconnection to compensate the reluctant party for its reasonable costs. The forum for resolving disputes over reasonable compensation may be administrative, or it may be the forum set up by the particular jurisdiction to adjudicate takings claims, for example the United States Claims Court in the case of federal takings.

§ 6.14   Burdens on Interstate Commerce

Most of the responsibility for legal regulation of conduct in the NII rests with the states. Whenever the states regulate conduct, like the flow of information that inherently crosses state lines, the possibility exists that the state regulation may unconstitutionally burden interstate commerce. Such burdens are permissible, but only when they are justified by pursuit of legitimate state interests.

In evaluating state regulations of activity in the NII, the first step is to identify the burden on interstate commerce. Typically, that is hard to do because of the difficulty of segregating intrastate from interstate communications. Second, one must determine if a legitimate state interest is asserted by the state as justification for the regulation. Then, one must determine whether the regulation furthers that state interest and if it does so in an appropriately narrow way.[220]

The "dormant commerce clause" is a phrase referring to an implied limitation on state power arising from the commerce clause. The underlying issue is whether the grant of power to Congress to control interstate commerce found in Article I, § 8 of the Constitution prevents states from regulating interstate commerce in a subject area not addressed or dealt with explicitly by Congress.

In *Gibbons v. Ogden*,[221] the Supreme Court first addressed this issue. Ogden had an exclusive steamboat operating license from New York State. Gibbons, who had a federal license to operate his vessel between New York and New Jersey, was stopped by New York from entering New York State waters because of Ogden's steamboat monopoly. Gibbons brought suit, arguing that this was a

---

[219] 883 P.2d 255, 260 (Or. Ct. App. 1994) (explaining basis for concluding that no permanent property deprivation had occurred).

[220] Hunt v. Washington Apple Advertising Comm'n, 432 U.S. 333, 353 (1977) (exclusion of out-of-state apples violated dormant commerce clause notwithstanding asserted justifications); Hughes v. Oklahoma, 441 U.S. 322 (1979) (limiting export of minnows was violative of dormant commerce clause notwithstanding asserted justification).

[221] 22 U.S. (1 Wheat.) 1 (1824).

violation of the Constitution and specifically the commerce clause. The Court found that New York's grant of the monopoly was invalid because it interfered with interstate commerce. The Court later found that states could regulate those parts of interstate commerce that are local in nature and need different treatment state to state.[222]

Under *Pike v. Bruce Church, Inc.,* a two-prong test is to be used to determine if state regulation is unconstitutional.[223] First, does the regulation discriminate against interstate commerce? Second, are the burdens on interstate commerce clearly excessive compared to the local benefits to that particular state? This second prong involves a balancing test. If the answer to both of these questions is yes, then the state regulation is unconstitutional and therefore invalid.[224]

In this analysis, it is necessary to see if the state regulation is discriminatory against people from other states or interstate commerce in general. A regulation or law is facially discriminatory if it imposes restrictions or penalties on out-of-state people and not in-state people. If a statute does discriminate, then it is unconstitutional if the state interest does not outweigh the burden on interstate commerce. In *City of Philadelphia v. New Jersey,*[225] a New Jersey statute prohibiting out-of-state waste from being brought into the state was invalid. There was an obvious, legitimate state interest in keeping waste out, yet there was no need to discriminate and burden interstate commerce. A state, in pursuing a legitimate state interest, cannot use a discriminatory method to achieve that interest if there are effective nondiscriminatory procedures that can be used.[226] If a regulation is facially discriminatory, then there must be a legitimate state interest that outweighs the discrimination on interstate commerce, and there must be no alternative nondiscriminatory means to achieve that state interest.

A statute may be discriminatory in effect but not facially discriminatory.[227] This occurs when a state does not explicitly treat out-of-state people differently, but in the application and practical aspects it puts a greater burden on out-of-state people than in-state people.[228] Even if a state statute or regulation is found to be nondiscriminatory, it may violate the dormant commerce clause if it puts

---

[222] Cooley v. Board of Wardens, 53 U.S. (1 How.) 299 (1851).

[223] 397 U.S. 137 (1970).

[224] This modern approach develops a further conflict between what might be good for one state and its citizens and that of the nation as a whole. For example, in Baldwin v. Seelig, 294 U.S. 511 (1935), a New York statute requiring a minimum milk price was unconstitutional since this amounted to economic protectionism and would have a negative effect on the national economy. This result was reached despite the fact that the statute may have helped certain citizens of New York and the New York state economy.

[225] 437 U.S. 617 (1978).

[226] If there is an available alternative that is not used which is nondiscriminatory, then the statute is unconstitutional. Hughes v. Oklahoma, 441 U.S. 322 (1979).

[227] There are some scholars and judges who do not believe in this balancing approach. They argue that if a statute is nondiscriminatory on its face, then the dormant commerce clause does not apply.

[228] *See* Hunt v. Washington State Apple Advertising Comm'n, 432 U.S. 333 (1977).

too great a burden on interstate commerce. Conversely, a state law can burden interstate commerce and be upheld as long as it pertains to local matters and the burden on interstate commerce is not too great.

§ 6.15 —Eminent Domain for Rights-of-Way

Construction of infrastructure frequently requires that the property interests of one group give way to the interests of others. Historically, such conflicting property interests have been resolved in constructing transportation in communications infrastructures by exercise of eminent domain.[229] Often, the eminent domain power is exercised directly by a private entity, not by the government itself. When that occurs, questions arise about whether the eminent domain power may be exercised privately.

Eminent domain is a power granted by the Fifth Amendment of the United States Constitution that allows the taking of private property for public use with just compensation.[230] Public use is a legislative determination that has not been clearly defined.[231] However, "once the object is within the authority of Congress, the right to realize it through the exercise of eminent domain is clear."[232] Congress can attain eminent domain by any means, once it has the authority. Thus, if Congress chooses a private enterprise to carry out its object, this is proper as long as a public purpose has been established. Such a determination is also applicable to state legislation.[233] Whenever eminent domain is rationally related to a public purpose, the Court has never held a compensated taking to be proscribed by the public use clause of the Fifth Amendment.[234]

The fact that property taken by eminent domain is later transferred to private beneficiaries does not necessarily mean the taking only has a private purpose. The Court has stated that, "it is not essential that the entire community, nor even any considerable portion, . . . directly enjoy or participate in any improvement in order [for it] to constitute a public use."[235] The government does not have to take the property, as long as the taking of the property passes scrutiny under the public use clause.[236] However, a purely private taking would serve no legitimate purpose of the government and would not pass the public use scrutiny.[237]

---

[229] The underlying analysis for this section was done by Tom Thistle, law clerk to the author.

[230] Hawaii Hous. Auth. v. Midkiff, 467 U.S. 229 (1984).

[231] *Id.* (citing Berman v. Parker, 348 U.S. 26 (1954)).

[232] *Id.* at 240 (quoting Berman v. Parker, 348 U.S. 26, 33 (1954)).

[233] *Id.* at 243.

[234] *Id.* at 241. *See also* Berman v. Parker, 348 U.S. 26 (1954); Rindge Co. v. Los Angeles, 262 U.S. 700 (1923); Block v. Hirsh, 256 U.S. 135 (1921).

[235] 467 U.S. 229, 244 (1984) (quoting Rindge Co. v. Los Angeles, 262 U.S. 700, 707 (1923)).

[236] *Id.* at 244. *See also* Fallbrook Irrigation Dist. v. Bradley, 164 U.S. 112, 161–62 (1896) (public purpose will not be defeated because it confers an incidental private benefit).

[237] 467 U.S. 229, 245 (1984). *See also* Missouri Pac. Ry. Co. v. State of Neb., 164 U.S. 403 (1896) (property cannot be taken by eminent domain for a predominantly private purpose).

In examples of a telephone company exercising condemnation of property, Utah law "allows the right of eminent domain may be exercised in behalf of . . . all . . . public uses for the benefit of any county, city or incorporated town, or the inhabitants thereof."[238] Providing telephone service is one use for which Utah allows condemnation of private property by eminent domain. Texas law conferred the telephone company's eminent domain power by statute.[239] In a Mississippi case, the legislature granted telephone companies the right to construct their lines and facilities in the highways, roads, streets, and public places of Mississippi.[240]

Private enterprises do not have eminent domain power over private property unless they have a partnership with a state entity or have statutory authority to use the property for a public purpose. Certain private enterprises, telephone companies, have been granted eminent domain power by state legislatures for public purposes.

Eminent domain is the power to take private property for public use by the state or persons authorized to take private property.[241] The process of exercising the power of eminent domain is commonly referred to as *condemnation* or *expropriation. Eminent domain,* or the power of the sovereign to condemn private property for public use, has been recognized by jurists for centuries.[242]

Based on these definitions, condemnation and eminent domain are not independent doctrines. Rather, condemnation is the means of effecting eminent domain. He who condemns the lands has the power of eminent domain.[243] An example of how eminent domain and condemnation work together is through the Tennessee Valley Authority (TVA). The TVA, a corporate agency of the United States, has been vested by an act of Congress with the power of eminent domain.[244] This power is expressly applicable to the taking of easements and rights-of-way for electric power transmission lines. Under the act by which it was created, the TVA can take by condemnation whatever it deems necessary to carry out its functions.

Once eminent domain and condemnation have been determined to be appropriate, virtually every jurisdiction specifies the procedures to be used to effect condemnation. The following procedures are to be used in the condemnation of property under the Federal Rule of Civil Procedure 71A:

1.   The caption of the complaint shall be as provided in Rule 10a except the plaintiffs will name as defendants the property, location of condemned property, and at least one of the owners of the property.

---

[238] Doelle v. Mountain States Tel. & Tel., 872 F.2d 942, 946 (1989).

[239] Gully v. Southwestern Bell Tel. Co., 774 F.2d 1287 (1985).

[240] Davis v. South Cent. Bell Tel. Co., 480 F. Supp. 826, 829 (S.D. Miss. 1979).

[241] Black's Law Dictionary 523 (6th ed. 1990).

[242] Henry E. Mills, A Treatise Upon the Law of Eminent Domain § 1 (1879).

[243] United States v. Miller, 317 U.S. 369, 375–76 (1942).

[244] United States v. Susong, 87 F. Supp. 396 (E.D. Tenn. 1948).

2. The complaint shall contain a short and plain statement of the authority for the taking, the use of the property, a description of the property, the interests acquired, and a designation of the defendants who have been joined as owners for each separate piece of property taken. Prior to the hearing for condemnation, the plaintiff must add all defendants having a claim in the property. Defendants not discovered will be placed under the description "Unknown Owners."

3. Complaints must be filed with the court, at least one copy to the clerk for defendants, and as many more as the clerk or a defendant requests.

4. After filing of the complaint with the clerk, the plaintiff shall deliver to the clerk joint or several notices directed to the defendants named in the complaint.

5. Each notice shall state the court, title of action, name of the defendant, that the action is to condemn the property, description of the property, interest to be taken, authority for the taking, the uses for which the property is to be taken, that the defendant may serve an answer to the plaintiff's attorney within 20 days after service of notice, and that failure to answer constitutes a consent to the taking and to the authority of the court to proceed to hear the action and fix compensation. The notice concludes with the name of the plaintiff's attorney and an address within the district in which the action is brought where the attorney may be served.

6. Personal service of the notice can be served in accordance with Rule 4 upon a defendant who resides in the United States.

7. If a defendant cannot be personally served because the defendant's residence cannot be ascertained or it is beyond the territorial limits of personal service, service can be made by publication in a newspaper published in the county where the property is located once a week for not less than three successive weeks. Prior to the last publication, a copy of the notice shall also be mailed to a defendant who cannot be personally served but whose place of residence is now known. Service by publication is complete upon the date of the last publication. Proof of publication and mailing shall be made by certificate by the plaintiff's attorney, to which shall be attached a printed copy of the published notice on which the name and dates of the newspaper are marked.

8. If there is no objection by the defendant to the taking of the property, the defendant may serve a notice of appearance designating the property in which the defendant claims to be interested. The defendant will receive all notices of proceedings affecting the property, thereafter. The defendant has 20 days to file an objection after service of the notice. The answer identifies the property in which the defendant has an interest, the extent of the interest, and states all objections and defenses to the taking of the property. Any objections or defenses not presented are considered waived. No other pleading or motion asserting any additional defense or objection will be allowed.

§ 6.16 —Condemnation and Eminent Domain in Intellectual Property

Denials of access sometimes involve simply the assertion of intellectual property rights. The holder of a copyright in software or information content or the holder of the patent in a computer system or process may deny others the use of the content, software, or system or may charge prices for such use that the entity desiring access finds unaffordable. The copyright and patent clause of the United States Constitution and the copyright and patent statutes acknowledge the legitimacy of such denials of access in the vast majority of cases. Indeed, there is no duty to license copyrights or patents under the intellectual property laws or antitrust law. The rare circumstance may arise, however, in which legitimate information infrastructure goals cannot be attained without forcing intellectual property owners to grant access. In such circumstances, one source of access right might be partial condemnation through the exercise of eminent domain powers by the federal government.[245] Indeed, there is a statutory provision in government contract law contemplating condemnation by use.[246] The condemnation approach, although representing significant intrusion into the prerogatives of the intellectual property owner, nevertheless balances interests of grantor and grantee of access because it envisions judicially determined compensation for the access.

A significant disadvantage to the condemnation approach is the uncertainty and cost of determining compensation through a judicial proceeding. On the other hand, infrequent use of the power should make the transaction costs of compensation setting tolerable.

The Congress has imposed compulsory licensing obligations in the limited case of computer chip mask works,[247] and some commentators have proposed compulsory licensing as a useful approach in balancing the interest involved in extending copyright to functional features of computer software.[248]

The recent controversy over the patents for the RSA encryption algorithm exemplifies one candidate for forcing access through condemnation. Patent holders for the algorithm took the position that certain proposed government encryption standards infringe their patent and that they should be entitled to royalties for use of the government-prescribed standard.

Another possible use for condemnation would be a circumstance in which someone belatedly asserts a copyright interest in basic infrastructure standards like TCP/IP itself, Worldwide Web, or Gopher. In such a circumstance, there

---

[245] Both copyright and patent statutes broadly preempt state law; therefore, exercise of eminent domain by state governments would interfere with federally granted rights and presumably be preempted.

[246] 28 U.S.C. § 1498.

[247] 17 U.S.C. §§ 901–914.

[248] *See* Wendy J. Gordon, *On Owning Information: Intellectual Property and the Restitutionary Impulse,* 78 Va. L. Rev. 149 (1992).

would challenging issues with respect to the nature of the intellectual property itself, requiring courts to sort out complex issues of intellectual property law before there would be any need for condemnation. For example, the RSA patent may be invalid. The core Internet standards may represent uncopyrightable functions rather than protectible expression, and even if they represent protectible expression, they may have been placed in the public domain or subject to broad fair use privileges.[249] The condemnation approach might be attractive even when a unilaterally determined royalty arrangement is unattractive, as in the RSA case. Condemnation is a way of forcing an intellectual property owner to grant access when he otherwise would completely refuse access. It also is a way of involving the law in circumscribing pricing for access.

As with the other sources of access rights, the appropriateness of condemnation of intellectual property depends on the availability of alternatives. Alternatives are more likely to be available to copyrighted elements than patented ones. This is so because copyright allows independent creation,[250] and the scope of copyright for functional works is circumscribed when few or no alternatives exist to the copyrighted work.[251] Patent on the other hand forecloses independently created inventions within the scope of the patent, and therefore it is much more difficult to avoid a patent in performing the same function as the patented work.

---

[249] Henry H. Perritt, Jr. *Unbundling Value in Electronic Information Products: Intellectual Property Protection for Machine Readable Interfaces,* 20 Rutgers Computer & Tech. L.J. 415 (1994).

[250] 17 U.S.C. § 106 reserves to the copyright holder exclusive rights only of reproduction, preparation of derivative works, distribution, public performance, and public display. If someone other than the copyright holder creates something similar or identical to the copyrighted work without engaging in any of these types of conduct with respect to the copyrighted work, there is no infringement.

[251] *See* Sega Enters., Ltd. v. Accolade, Inc., 977 F.2d 1510, 1524 (9th Cir. 1992).

CHAPTER 7

REGULATION

§ 7.1   Nature of the Problem and Introduction

As **Chapter 1** notes, the NII is emerging from a convergence of three historically distinct legal categories: publishing, broadcasting, and telephone and telegraph service. Two of the three categories were subject to detailed administrative regulation by a federal agency called the Federal Communications Commission under authority given it by the Federal Communications Act of 1934.[1] The Congress, the FCC, and the courts must determine the degree to which continued administrative regulation is appropriate for any part of the NII. If it is appropriate for any part, the same institutions must define workable boundaries between those parts subject to administrative regulation and those parts subject to other kinds of legal or market regulation. For example, as telephone companies have entered the broadcast market by offering their own video programming through communications facilities competing with cable television, they successfully have asserted First Amendment immunities historically associated with publishers. As telephone companies have sought to enter the market for cable television, the FCC and the courts have been called upon to determine whether they need cable television franchises. Similar questions arise as cable television systems seek to enter the point-to-point communications market potentially subject to entry restrictions under Title II of the Communications Act.

In each of these cases, the line-drawing problem is made more difficult by the distinct character of the regulatory compartments. The form of price and entry regulation in the cable television marketplace is dramatically different from the forms those types of regulation take in the telephone industry. Both are dramatically different from the forms they take in the broadcast television and radio industries.

The need to draw lines can be eliminated if competition is sufficient to justify a removal of administrative regulation. Accordingly, this chapter begins by assessing the role of competition as a justification for deregulation and, conversely, the role of a finding of the absence of competition as a justification for administrative regulation.

Competition and several other legal, technological, and economic issues shaping the analysis in this chapter also are important in the analysis of other chapters. This chapter concentrates on administrative agency regulation as a mechanism for the law to shape rights, privileges, power, and immunity in the NII. Other chapters address other forms of regulation. For example, **Chapter 2** considers the relative places of common-law contract, common carrier concepts, and antitrust regulation as means of assuring access to the NII. **Chapter 8** considers the relative places of administration regulation and market forces as ways of assuring compatibility and interoperability of interconnected parts of the NII.

Therefore, this chapter focuses on a particular means of regulation, through an administrative agency, rather than a particular kind of problem. In addition, price regulation, or as it is more often known in connection with the NII, rate regulation, is addressed in this chapter because the existence of price regulation presupposes the existence of administrative regulation. Price regulation in the public mind is associated with detailed regulation by administrative agencies

---

[1] 47 U.S.C. §§ 151–613 (as codified, statute comprises seven subchapters: subchapter I covers FCC composition and scope, subchapter II regulates common carriers of wire or radio service, subchapter III controls radio licenses and operations, subchapter IV describes administrative and procedural provisions, subchapter V covers penalties and forfeitures, subchapter V-A relates to cable communications, and subchapter VI covers miscellaneous provisions).

such as the Federal Communications Commission. In fact, administrative regulation has other purposes in addition to price regulation, including enforcing rights of access to the infrastructure, discussed in **Chapter 2,** and enforcing interoperability and compatibility among different parts of the infrastructure, considered in **Chapter 8.** This chapter provides contextual information on the regulatory apparatus used for price regulation and considers the different types of price regulation used and proposed for the National Information Infrastructure.

As § **7.3** explains, rate regulation almost always is backed up by accounting regulation and restrictions on entry and exit. Accordingly, this chapter also considers accounting regulations such as structural separation requirements and restrictions on cross-subsidization and on regulation of market entry and exit. Antitrust law enters into a variety of legal analyses related to the NII. This chapter considers antitrust law as a basis for government oversight of pricing practices by firms with a dominant position in NII markets.

Significant parts of the NII are self-regulating, and the chapter concludes with a section on legal mechanisms and limitations on self-regulation or "self-governance."

§ 7.2 Competition's Role

A prominent feature of the value system surrounding American law is that market forces are a better choice than detailed legal regulation when competitive market conditions exist. Although the law must provide a basic infrastructure within which markets can operate,[2] the more dramatic forms of nonconsensual regulation are reserved for situations of "market failure," including the following:

1. Inequality of bargaining power[3]
2. "Externalities" that are not taken into account by market transactions[4]
3. Public goods for which the market provides insufficient incentives[5]
4. Imperfect information, which makes it difficult or impossible for consumers to make the rational choices on which market efficiency depends[6]
5. Natural monopolies, in which market forces are blunted by the absence of competition.[7]

---

[2] For example, the law of contract is necessary if market participants are able to make exchanges, at least part of which are to be performed in the future.

[3] Labor and employment regulation is an example.

[4] Environmental regulation is an example.

[5] Intellectual property law is an example.

[6] Consumer product safety regulation is a usual example. Trademark and unfair competition regulation is a plausible additional example.

[7] Later parts of this section explain natural monopoly.

The most important of these in the NII is natural monopoly. Many providers of information infrastructure services enjoy natural or de jure monopolies, for example, local cable television service providers and local telephone service providers. Monopolists have an incentive to set prices higher than they would be in competitive market conditions,[8] and thus monopoly market structures have the potential for inefficient price regulation.[9] This perspective on price regulation suggests government intervention to set maximum prices. In fact, however, much administrative regulation in the communications field, as in other areas, has been aimed at setting minimum prices to protect existing suppliers from competition, frequently to support the generation of revenues for cross-subsidies.

Moreover, a natural monopoly in any part of the NII may distort the operation of competition in other parts of the NII. The clearest example of this is the widespread perception that the natural monopolies of local exchange carriers over local telephone service threaten fair competition in the market for enhanced services, including information services,[10] and threaten appropriate market structures in video production and cable television service.[11]

In a competitive market structure, microeconomic theory says that producers will price at or near marginal costs because they will expand output until their average costs equal marginal costs.[12] In some situations, however, the most efficient producer faces declining marginal costs throughout the full range of expected demand. This situation is known as natural monopoly. Less efficient producers are put out of business by the most efficient producer because there is no point on their cost curves that is as low as the price for which the most efficient producer can sell.[13] A natural monopolist maximizes her revenue if she prices above average costs.[14] The dominant justification for public utility rate regulation is that public utilities are natural monopolies and governmental

---

[8] Dayne B. Matthew, *Doing What Comes Naturally: Antitrust Law and Hospital Mergers*, 31 Hous. L. Rev. 813, 829 (1994) (monopolists charge higher prices for fewer goods than do perfectly competitive firms, resulting in allocative inefficiency).

[9] *Efficient*, as the term is used in the text, means that price regulation could result in an allocation of resources that results in a level of social welfare higher than would exist in the absence of the price regulation.

[10] See § **7.13.**

[11] See § **7.12.**

[12] This condition occurs at the point in the supply function at which the average cost curve intersects the marginal cost curve. This occurs at a production level somewhat higher than the one at which diminishing returns begin. Diminishing returns begin at the minimum of the marginal cost curve where $dMC/dY=0$. *See* Scott Bertschi, *Integrated Resource Planning and Demandside Management in Electric Utility Regulation: Public Utility Panacia or Waste of Energy,* 43 Emory L.J. 815, 820 (1994).

[13] It might seem that the same thing would be true of a competitive market structure. That is not so because the equation of price to average cost in a competitive market structure is with respect to the industry cost function. In a natural monopoly market structure, the reference point is the average cost curve of a single firm—the most efficient producer.

[14] Because a monopolist can control output, she can set output at a level such that marginal revenue equals marginal cost, and this may not be the point of minimum cost, and therefore minimum price. *See* Edwin Mansfield, Microeconomics Theory and Application 270 (2d ed. 1975).

intervention in the form of rate regulation is necessary to prevent the allocative and distributive inefficiencies that would result from allowing the monopolist public utility to keep its monopoly profits.[15]

There are sharp disagreements among economists as to the most appropriate method of price regulation of public utilities.[16] Even the justification for rate regulation can change over time. In an expanding market, demand that once was sufficient only to support a single producer—resulting in the natural monopoly condition—can grow to the point where it supports many producers—a condition approaching a competitive market structure. Or, if a market is shrinking because of changes in consumer preferences or the availability of substitutes,[17] what once was a level of demand sufficient to support a multiplicity of producers now can support at most one.[18] Of course, in the real world a variety of justifications for administrative regulation exists beyond the straightforward natural monopoly justification for rate regulation. The issues before the FCC with respect to video dial tone services by the Regional Bell Operating Companies (RBOCs), considered in § **7.13** is a good example.

Chapter 2 notes the relationship between market structures and the justification for access rights, with competitive market structures vitiating the need for legally imposed access rights. There also is a relationship between market structures and rate regulation. Thus evaluation of market structure is unavoidable as Congress and the FCC shape administrative regulation. The FCC and, to a lesser extent, the Congress, have concluded repeatedly that emerging segments of the NII enjoy actual or potential competition and thus do not need detailed administrative regulation. Information services is an example;[19] long distance

---

[15] *Allocative inefficiency* is a misallocation of resources arising because of a monopoly condition that uses resources instead of permitting them to produce other goods to which society places a higher degree of importance. *See* Robert H. Lande, *Wealth Transfers as the Original and Primary Concern of Antitrust: The Efficiency Interpretation Challenged,* 34 Hastings L.J. 67, 72 (1982). *Distributive inefficiency* is the corresponding wealth and power transfer that accrues to the monopolist instead of to the market competitor filling market demand, and to consumers from lower prices for the monopoly good. *Id.* at 74–75.

[16] *See* Allen Severn, *Price Theory and Telecommunications Regulation: A Dissenting View,* 3 Yale J. on Reg. 53, 58–60 (1985) (noting that most public utility rate regulation has been based on value of service rather than cost of service concepts, while most economists have argued in favor of cost of service basis for pricing; challenging assertion that cost of service rates are either feasible or that they maximize welfare). *Id.* at 58 (noting "insurmountable difficulties" of pricing a multiproduct enterprise with complex cost characteristics "at cost").

[17] The availability of substitutes invites argument that the relevant market is actually one that includes both the market for the product experiencing the shrinking demand and the market for substitute products. See cases litigating the railroad's arguments as to how a dominant carrier should be determined by the ICC: Bessemer & Lake Erie R.R. v. Interstate Commerce Comm'n, 691 F.2d 1104 (3d Cir. 1982) (describing relationship between ICC regulation and market dominance); Conrail Rail Corp. v. United States, 812 F.2d 1444 (3d Cir. 1987) (generally examining ICC regulatory and rate structure and processes).

[18] This is roughly the experience of the daily newspaper market.

[19] Notice of Inquiry, *In re* Reexamination of the Commission's Cross-Interest Policy, MM Docket No. 87-154, FCC 87-188, 2 F.C.C.R. 3699, ¶ 25 (June 5, 1987) (inviting comment on how "highly competitive" nature of information services market may have affected need for certain

service is another;[20] telephone directories is a third;[21] cellular telephone service is another.[22] The same economic analysis that underpins evaluation of the need for access regulations, considered in **Chapter 2** also determines the need for administrative regulation of prices.

§ 7.3   Institutional Mechanisms for Price Regulation

Chapter 2 notes that access regulation tends to turn into price regulation over time, as an increasing number of complaints of illegal denial of access assert that access is allowed only at unreasonable prices. Beyond that, price regulation tends to become more complicated over time.[23] Understanding why this is so illustrates the principal features of any program of price regulation, certainly including rate regulation under the Federal Communications Act. The first feature is the definition of the product or service category to which a particular price specification applies. If the price for product A is limited, one must be able to determine what product A includes. In a market economy, the process of innovation constantly redefines product categories, and when price regulation exists, there are additional incentives to redefine products so as to remove them from regulated categories or to move them from a less favorable price restriction to a more favorable one.

Second, part of the regulation of pricing categories naturally extends to regulation of product quality. A highly reliable network connection is worth more than an unreliable one; it also usually costs more. A regulated entity has an

---

types of regulatory intervention); United States v. Western Elec. Co., 767 F. Supp. 308 (D.D.C. 1991) (lifting information services restriction on LECs pursuant to remand order, despite continued market power). *But see* United States v. NYNEX Corp., 814 F. Supp. 133, 136 (D.D.C. 1993) (criminal contempt judgment against LEC for continuing to provide information services in violation of MFJ).

[20] Report and Order, *In re* Policies and Rules Concerning Unauthorized Changes of Consumers; Long Distance Carriers, CC Docket No. 94-129, FCC 95-225, 1995 WL 358243, ¶ 8 (June 14, 1995) (noting emergence of competition in long distance markets); United States v. Western Elec. Co., 154 F.R.D. 1, 9 (D.D.C. 1994) (noting good results from elimination of monopoly for long distance service, declining to waive limitation on limitations imposed on AT&T).

[21] United States v. Western Elec. Co., 767 F. Supp. 308, 321 & n.60 (D.D.C. 1991) (noting evidence that LECs lack market power with respect to yellow pages, cellular service, and pay phones).

[22] Report and Order, *In re* Petition on Behalf of La. Public Serv. Comm'n, FR Docket No. 94-107, FCC 95-191, 1995 WL 312494, ¶ 12 (May 19, 1995) (noting limited competition in cellular market); United States v. Western Elec. Co., 767 F. Supp. 308, 321 & n.60 (D.D.C. 1991) (noting evidence that LECs lack market power with respect to yellow pages, cellular service, and pay phones).

[23] The author was executive secretary of the cost of living council and involved in simplification and eventual dismantling of the comprehensive wage in price controls of the Nixon administration, 1971–1974.

incentive to evade price regulation by diminishing product quality, and regulators usually get drawn into setting standards for quality.[24]

Third, much price regulation involves cost justification. When cost justification is involved, it is necessary to have a cost accounting system to determine what costs may be counted and what costs may not be counted. There must be a rule to specify when a price is charged so that one can identify the conduct subject to the price regulation.

Fourth, price regulation often is accompanied by restrictions on market exit. Frequently, the perceptions of regulators and entrepreneurs may differ as to whether rates of return on capital resulting from particular prices for particular products or services are appropriate. The entrepreneur may perceive that his capital can earn a higher rate of return if employed elsewhere, while the regulator may conclude that the rate of return resulting from a particular regulated price is "adequate." In such cases the viability of the regulated price depends on a prohibition on market exit. This situation also occurs when revenues for one product line are used to subsidize artificially low prices for another. In such instances the entrepreneur would like to keep the enhanced revenues from the source and stop using them to support the low price in the other product market.

Fifth, there also are situations in which price regulation is accompanied by restrictions on entry. When the legislature or a regulatory agency has concluded that particular levels or quality of service is desirable, free market entry may jeopardize those service goals, either because new entrants will offer lower prices and not give the required service, or because a more dynamic market is difficult for the regulatory agency to police. In other instances, restrictions on regulatory entry are necessary to support an artificially high price in order to generate a cross-subsidy. The clearest example of this was long distance telephone service before the breakup of AT&T. One of the causes of the breakup was the insistence by MCI and non-AT&T providers of customer premises equipment that they be allowed to enter the market. At the lower prices they charged, it was difficult or impossible for AT&T to generate revenues necessary to cross-subsidize local telephone service.

§ 7.4 Legal Overview

The Communications Act of 1934 has seven titles.[25] Title I articulates the policy and establishes the Federal Communications Commission.[26] Title II covers common carriers.[27] Title III covers radio transmissions, including radio and

---

[24] *See* Performance Review, 1995 WL 222130 (Apr. 7, 1995), ¶ 36.

[25] 47 U.S.C. §§ 151–613 (Supp. VI 1994).

[26] *Id.* §§ 151–158.

[27] *Id.* §§ 201–226.

television broadcasting.[28] Title VI covers cable communications.[29] Titles IV, V, and VII contain administrative, penal, and miscellaneous provisions.

Originally, there was little intellectual integrity to combining, in the Act, terrestrial-telecommunications-common-carrier regulation with radio regulation.[30] The two types of regulation had completely different histories; yet the FCC was given both. The common carrier provisions were adopted wholesale from the Interstate Commerce Act, while the radio provisions were adopted wholesale from the Radio Act of 1927.[31] Early regulation of telephone common carriage had been supported by industry because it favored control of market entry and pricing.[32] Radio regulation under the 1927 Act was a reaction to the court of appeals decision holding that the secretary of commerce lacked authority to withhold a license even to protect against interference.[33] The original theme of broadcast regulation was to rationalize spectrum use and also to impose a public service obligation on those licensed to use the public spectrum.[34]

Operation under Title II is controlled by general duties imposed to furnish communication service upon reasonable request, to adhere to contract terms disclosed in tariffs, as discussed in § **7.6,** and not to construct or operate new lines without a certificate of present or future public convenience and necessity from the FCC, when interstate lines are involved.[35]

The basic standard for granting licenses under Title III is a commission finding "that public interest, convenience, and necessity would be served by the granting" of a radio license.[36] The scope of Title III is determined by this prohibition: "no person shall use or operate any apparatus for the transmission of energy or communications or signals by radio ... except under and in accordance with this act and with a license in that behalf granted under the provisions of this act."[37]

---

[28] *Id.* §§ 301–399(b).

[29] *Id.* §§ 521–559.

[30] *See* Glen O. Robinson, *The Federal Communications Act: An Essay on Origins and Regulatory Purpose, in* Legislative History of the Communications Act of 1934, at 3, 4 (Max D. Paglin ed., 1989) [hereinafter Robinson].

[31] Robinson at 4–5 (citing H.R. Rep. No. 1918, 73d Cong., 2d Sess. (1934) (Conference Comm. Rep.); S. Rep. No. 781, 73d Cong., 2d Sess. (1934) (Senate Comm. Rep. on S. 3285); and H.R. Rep. No. 1850, 73d Cong., 2d Sess. (1934) (House Rep. on S. 3285 as amended by House Comm.) as sources for detailed comparison of 1934 Act with predecessor statutes).

[32] *Id.* at 7.

[33] Hoover v. Inter City Radio Co., 286 F. 1003 (D.C. Cir. 1923) (imposing duty to issue license upon satisfaction of requirements and restricting discretion to selection of wave length).

[34] Robinson at 8–13.

[35] 47 U.S.C. § 214(a).

[36] *Id.* § 309(a).

[37] *Id.* § 301.

Title VI (subchapter V-A of title 47 U.S.C.) covers operators of *cable service,* which is defined as providing video programming over a set of closed transmission paths, encompassing also associated signal generation, reception, and control equipment.[38] The federal statute imposes prohibitions on ownership of cable systems by broadcasters and common carriers,[39] and generally obligates cable operators to provide channel space for certain unaffiliated commercial programmers and for public, educational, and governmental use.[40] Otherwise, Title VI imposes a structure within which local franchising authorities directly regulate cable operators. The statute is less an imposition of duties on cable operators than a grant or affirmation of power in local regulatory entities.

§ 7.5   Common Carrier Regulation

Title II of the Federal Communications Act of 1934 authorizes Federal Communications Commission (FCC) regulation of common carriers of communications. The FCC has jurisdiction only over communications carriers.[41] The statute defines *communications* as "transmission [by wire or radio] of writing, signs, signals, pictures, and sounds of all kinds . . . including all instrumentalities, facilities, apparatus, and services (among other things, the receipt, forwarding, and delivery of communications) incidental to such transmission."[42] Whether an entity is a common carrier subject to FCC regulation is decided by a two-prong test: (1) Does the entity's service constitute interstate communications? (2) If so, is this service rendered for hire to the public?[43] **Chapter 2** analyzes the determinants of common carrier status.

---

[38] *Id.* § 522(5), (6).

[39] *Id.* § 533.

[40] *Id.* §§ 531–532. These provisions were invalidated in part in the *Turner Broadcasting* case, considered in **Ch. 6.**

[41] *See* 47 U.S.C. § 151, 152 (1988). But even in the area of communications, the regulatory power of the FCC is not absolute. For example, in FCC v. Midwest Video Corp., 440 U.S. 689 (1979), the Supreme Court held that the FCC lacks authority under the Communications Act of 1934, Pub. L. No. C. 652, 48 Stat. 1064 (1934), to subject cable television to content-based regulation because the statute indicates that broadcasting is not common carriage. *See* 440 U.S. at 701–02; *see also* 1981 FCC Notice, 46 Fed. Reg. 10,924 10,933 (Feb. 5, 1981) (reviewing cases on whether cable television qualifies as common carriage).

[42] 47 U.S.C. § 153 (1988) (defining covered wire and radio communication in identical language).

[43] Graphnet Sys., Inc., 73 F.C.C.2d 283, 288–89 (1979). The FCC is explicitly denied jurisdiction over intrastate telephone exchange service, 47 U.S.C. § 221(b), and intrastate common carrier obligations, 47 U.S.C. § 152(b) (1988). *See* NARUC v. FCC, 533 F.2d 601, 607 (D.C. Cir. 1976) (NARUC II) (overturning FCC preemption of state regulation of intrastate cable two-way, point-to-point communications).

In 1973 the FCC determined that packet-switching network services offered to the general public constituted common carriage,[44] raising the possibility that traditional common carrier regulation might be extended as technology produced new digital communications services. In 1979 the FCC determined that an electronic mail service intended to be offered by the U.S. Postal Service in cooperation with Western Union constituted common carrier service.[45]

While such instances of common carriage were found, other forces encouraged deregulation of common carriers.[46] By the early 1970s, it had become evident that the administrative apparatus erected to apply regulatory requirements was imposing unacceptable costs on the evolution of the communications infrastructure.[47] Accordingly, the FCC began to modify its interpretation of the common carrier category, narrowing it to allow more services to be offered free of common carrier obligations (the "redefinition" initiative). The FCC also exempted some "nondominant" common carriers from most of the detailed tariffing requirements (the "forebearance" initiative).[48]

---

[44] Packet Communications, Inc., 43 F.C.C.2d 922 (1973) (application by PCI—Telenet subsidiary—to offer packet-switching services).

[45] Graphnet Sys., Inc., 73 F.C.C.2d 283, 299 (1979) (USPS must submit application for certificate of public convenience and necessity).

[46] 1981 FCC Notice, 46 Fed. Reg. 10,924, 10,932 (Feb. 5, 1981) (proposed rules for competitive common carrier service, describing NARUC v. FCC, 525 F.2d 630 (D.C. Cir. 1976) (NARUC I)).

[47] Illinois Bell Tel. Co. v. FCC, 883 F.2d 104, 105–06 (D.C. Cir. 1989) (reviewing deregulation of consumer premises equipment and enhanced services, retaining common carrier regulation only for basic transmission service). The FCC's progression regarding deregulation is marked by three major proceedings: First Computer Inquiry (Computer I), Tentative Decision of the Commission, *In re* Regulatory and Policy Problems Presented by the Interdependence of Computer and Communication Services and Facilities (First Computer Inquiry), 28 F.C.C.2d 291 (1970) (Computer I Tentative Decision); Final Decision and Order, *In re* Regulatory and Policy Problems Presented by the Interdependence of Computer and Communication Services and Facilities (First Computer Inquiry), 28 F.C.C.2d 267 (1971) (Computer I Final Decision); the Second Computer Inquiry (Computer II), *In re* Amendment of Section 64.702 of the Commission's Rules and Regulations (Second Computer Inquiry), 77 F.C.C.2d 384, 420 (1980) (Computer II Final Decision); and the Third Computer Inquiry or Computer III, Report and Order, *In re* Amendment of Sections 64.702 of the Commission's Rules and Regulations (Third Computer Inquiry,) Docket No. 85-229, 104 F.C.C.2d 958 (1986) (Phase I Order), *on reconsideration,* 2 F.C.C.R. 3035 (1987) (Phase I Reconsideration), 2 F.C.C.R. 3072 (1987) (Phase II Order). The FCC on Feb. 18, 1988, released an order on further reconsideration of the Phase I Order, Memorandum Opinion and Order on Further Reconsideration, *In re* Amendment of Sections 64.702 of the Commission's Rules and Regulations (Third Computer Inquiry), 3 F.C.C.R. 1135 (1988) (Phase I Further Reconsideration); and an order on reconsideration of Phase II Order, Memorandum Opinion and Order on Reconsideration, *In re* Amendment to Sections 64.702 of the Commission's Rules and Regulations (Third Computer Inquiry), 3 F.C.C.R. 1150 (1988) (Phase II Reconsideration). Each of these proceedings has multiple orders, with names such as "final order," "order on reconsideration," and "phase I recommendation."

[48] *See* Henry H. Perritt, Jr., *Tort Liability, The First Amendment and Equal Access to Electronic Networks,* 5 Harv. J.L. & Tech. 65 (1992).

In 1979 the FCC began deregulating services theretofore considered to be common carriage.[49] Originally, the Commission pursued two means of deregulation: by forbearance (a term signifying a suspension of regulation) to impose the requirements of Title II of the Communications Act on activities traditionally considered common carriage; and by narrowing the scope of the common carrier concept.[50]

In 1981 the FCC determined that the Communications Act of 1934 does not compel the application of the Act's economic regulation regime in Title II to all suppliers of communications services and facilities.[51] The FCC also determined that it had discretion to exempt some common carriers from the "full panoply" of economic regulation.[52] It rejected common-law analysis and its "holding out" criterion, because these made legal treatment turn on the intent of the potential regulatee rather than on a principled analytical framework.[53] In resolving this question, the FCC noted that tariff requirements can be anticompetitive[54] and that rate regulation is unnecessary in competitive markets because competitive carriers would price at cost.[55] It concluded that the statutory duty to serve is unnecessary in competitive markets.[56]

Evolution of the forbearance initiative stopped with the *MCI* case, discussed in § 7.5, invalidating the FCC's "Sixth Report."[57] The redefinition initiative reached its high-water mark in the Third Computer Inquiry (Computer III) followed by its invalidation by the Ninth Circuit.[58] Those cases are considered in this section.

---

[49] Phil Nichols, Note, *Redefining "Common Carrier:" the FCC's Attempt at Deregulation by Definition,* 1987 Duke L.J. 501, 503–04 (1987) (overview of "The FCC's Drive Towards Deregulation").

[50] *Id.* at 504 (explaining forbearance and redefinition); Dean Burch, *Common Carrier Communications by Wire and Radio: A Retrospective,* 37 Fed. Comm. L.J. 85 (1985) (reviewing two deregulation initiatives).

[51] 1981 FCC Notice, 46 Fed. Reg. 10,924 (Feb. 5, 1981) (notice of proposed rule making to exempt from regulation communications common carriers lacking market power). *See also* ALLNET Communications Servs., Inc. v. National Exchange Carrier Ass'n, 741 F. Supp. 983, 984 (D.D.C. 1990) (determining, with little analysis, that tariff filing agent for local exchange carriers established under 47 C.F.R. §§ 69.601–69.612 (1989) was not common carrier subject to Title II of Communications Act).

[52] 1981 FCC Notice, 46 Fed. Reg. 10,924 (Feb. 5, 1981) (notice of proposed rule making to exempt from regulation communications common carriers lacking market power). *But see id.* at 10,933 (reserving the power to continue determining whether a common law obligation should be imposed on a particular firm).

[53] *Id.* at 10,933.

[54] *Id.* at 10,937.

[55] *Id.* at 10,940.

[56] *Id.* (noting that statute facially leaves little discretion to exempt carriers from duty to serve).

[57] 99 F.C.C.2d 1020 (1985).

[58] California v. FCC, 905 F.2d 1217 (9th Cir. 1990).

As the NII evolved over the last two decades, the FCC limited the scope of statutory common carrier obligations by distinguishing between basic services and enhanced services. This was a refinement of an earlier distinction between data processing and communications.[59] Basic services are regulated as common carriers, while enhanced are not.[60] Communications systems (for example, packetizing) are regulated, while those incorporating data processing (for example, protocol conversion) are not.[61] "Basic services, such as 'plain old telephone services' ('POTS'), are regulated as tariffed services under Title II of the Communications Act." Enhanced services are "anything more than basic transmission services."[62] In these services additional, different, or restructured information may be provided the subscriber through various processing applications performed on the transmitted information, or other actions can be taken by either the vendor or subscriber based on the content of the information transmitted through editing, formatting, and so forth. Moreover, in an enhanced service the content of the information need not be changed and may simply involve "subscriber interaction with stored information."[63] "Enhanced services use the existing telephone network to deliver services other than basic transmission, such as voice mail, E-mail, voice store and forward, fax store and forward, data processing, and gateways to on-line databases."[64]

The basic/enhanced distinction originated in the Second Computer Inquiry,[65] in which the Commission abandoned in 1980 the attempt to classify activities as

---

[59] *See generally* Amendment of Section 64.702 of the Commission's Rules and Regulations (Second Computer Inquiry), 84 F.C.C.2d 50 (1980) (Petitions for Reconsideration).

[60] 47 C.F.R. § 64.702(a) (1989) ("Enhanced services are not regulated under Title II of the Act."). Title II contains the common carrier provisions. *See also* Second Computer Inquiry Memorandum and Order, 84 F.C.C.2d 50, 51 (1980) (discussing possible modification of definitional plan). The Commission decided that the plan would be unworkable in any other form, and declined to change the rules. *See generally* Public Service Comm'n v. FCC, 909 F.2d 1510, 1512–17 (D.C. Cir. 1990) (reviewing FCC decision to exercise authority under Title I to deregulate billing and collection services as not involving common carriage, and only "incidental" to statutory communications; denying petition to review FCC preemption of state regulation of rates for disconnect service provided by LECs to IECs).

[61] Amendment of Section 64.702 of the Commission's Rules and Regulations (Second Computer Inquiry), 77 F.C.C.2d 384, 424, 426–27 (1980) (final decision).

[62] *Id.* at 418, ¶ 90. "[T]his structure requires the facilities of the underlying carrier to be transparent to the information transmitted." *Id.*

[63] *Id.* at 420–21, ¶ 97 (discussing demarcation between basic and advanced services); *see generally* Michigan Bell Tel. Co. v. Pacific Ideas, Inc., 733 F. Supp. 1132, 1136 (E.D. Mich. 1990) ("976" billing services for dial-a-porn provider was enhanced service and not common carrier service).

[64] Notice of Proposed Rulemaking, *In re* Computer III Further Remand Proceedings: Bell Operating Company Provision of Enhanced Services, CC Docket No. 95-20, FCC 95-48, 1995 WL 170713 (Feb. 7, 1995).

[65] *See generally* Computer & Communications Indus. Ass'n v. FCC, 693 F.2d 198 (D.C. Cir. 1982) (approving FCC Computer Inquiry II decision); *In re* Policy Rules Concerning Rates for Common Carrier Services and Facilities Authorizations Therefor, 77 F.C.C.2d 308 (1979); *In*

either communications or data processing based on the nature of the processing performed. The respective technologies had become so intertwined, according to the Commission, that it had become impossible to draw an "enduring line of demarcation" between them. In the course of its Second Computer Inquiry, the Commission concluded that the only clear and lasting distinction would be one between basic transmission service on the one hand and enhanced services and consumer premises equipment (CPE) on the other. In that decision, the FCC concluded that enhanced services themselves should not be regulated under Title II of the Communications Act, but it imposed structural separation requirements on former Bell System companies that wished to offer enhanced services.[66]

The Commission found that enhanced services and CPE were not within the scope of its Title II jurisdiction but were within its ancillary jurisdiction. Accordingly, the Commission discontinued Title II regulation of enhanced service, and with the exception of AT&T, relieved common carriers of the maximum separation requirement which constrained enhanced services under Computer I.[67]

Noting that finding enhanced services to be covered by Title II would have required the Commission to reverse its Computer I policy of not regulating data processing services, the United States Court of Appeals for the D.C. Circuit approved the Computer Inquiry II decision not to regulate enhanced services.[68] It approved both rationales offered by the commission: (1) enhanced services are not common carrier services under Title II, and (2) even if they are, the Commission has discretion to abstain from regulating them.[69] The proposition that enhanced services are not common carrier services depends upon acceptance of a key idea: "Inherent in enhanced service offerings is the ability of vendors to tailor their services to meet the particularized needs of individual customers."[70] This conception of enhanced services fails to meet the common carrier criterion of meaning in the communications context, "providing a service whereby customers may transmit intelligence of their own design and choosing."[71] The alternative ground for finding nonregulation appropriate was affirmed essentially on impracticability grounds.[72]

---

re Amendment of Section 64.702 of the Commission's Rules and Regulations (Second Computer Inquiry), 77 F.C.C.2d 384 (1980); *In re* Amendment of Section 64.702 of the Commission's Rules and Regulations (Second Computer Inquiry), 84 F.C.C.2d 50 (1980) (Computer II Reconsidered Decision); Memorandum Opinion and Order on Further Reconsideration, *In re* Amendment of Section 64.70 of the Commission's Rules and Regulations, 88 F.C.C.2d 512 (1981) (Computer II Further Reconsidered Decision).

[66] 1995 WL 170713, ¶ 4 (characterizing Computer II).

[67] Computer & Communications Indus. Ass'n v. FCC, 693 F.2d 198, 204–05 (D.C. Cir. 1982).

[68] *See id.* at 209.

[69] *See id.* at 210.

[70] *Id.* at 210 & n.62.

[71] *Id.* at 210 & n.61.

[72] *See id.* at 210–11.

In its affirmance of Computer Inquiry II, the D.C. Circuit also approved preemption of state regulation of enhanced communication services on the grounds that such regulation would interfere with the market forces the FCC found most appropriate to protect the public interest.[73] Eight years later, however, the Ninth Circuit found invalid as overbroad the FCC conclusion that any kind of state structural separation requirements would frustrate its regulatory strategy for enhanced services.[74] This suggests that a mere determination by the FCC that something should go unregulated does not necessarily preempt state law. However, the Ninth Circuit invalidation of the Computer III preemption decision rested on narrow grounds, namely, specific language in section 2(b)(1) of the Communications Act preserving jurisdiction over intrastate services to the states.[75]

In Computer III, the FCC rejected an approach to protocol conversion (for example, converting digital to analog or converting ASCII to EBCDIC for representing characters) that would have allowed treatment of protocol conversion as either non–common carrier enhanced services, or common carrier basic services depending on which type of underlying service the protocol conversion is integrated with. It accepted the arguments of Tymnet, Telenet, and others opposing relaxation of protocol conversion services provided by RBOCs and AT&T. These unregulated suppliers argued that protocol conversion increasingly includes things like translating word processing file formats and handling electronic mail envelopes, activities more closely associated with data processing than communication services.[76]

In Computer III, the FCC proposed, but later failed to adopt, a definition of *enhanced service* that depends on whether content is affected.[77] This definition proposed that end-to-end "net user conversions" are enhanced services, while protocol conversions associated with call setup and similar basic communications activities are basic services.[78] The FCC also avoided reregulation of value-added networks, something the opponents of further relaxation of protocol conversion services by the RBOCs argued might occur.[79]

---

[73] See 693 F.2d 198, 214–15 (D.C. Cir. 1982).

[74] *See* California v. FCC, 905 F.2d 1217, 1243 (9th Cir. 1990) (vacating and remanding Computer Inquiry III).

[75] *Id.* at 1239 (construing 47 U.S.C. § 152(b)(1)).

[76] *See* Amendment of Section 64.702 of the Commission's Rules and Regulations (Third Computer Inquiry), 2 F.C.C.R. 3072, ¶ 35 (1987) (Report and Order—summarizing Telenet arguments about new applications for "code/protocol/format/language/conversions" including word processing format conversions, EDI, message handling systems, and natural language translation systems) [hereinafter Computer III].

[77] *See* Computer III, ¶¶ 64–68.

[78] *See* Computer III, ¶ 69; *id.* ¶¶ 55, 57 (deciding not to change to new "change-in-information content" test to define the regulatory boundary between enhanced and basic services).

[79] *See generally* Computer III, ¶ 38 (summarizing reregulation fears); *id.* ¶ 46 (fear of reregulation of VANs at the state level is significant).

FCC deregulation of communications services has been complicated by two cases, which affected both the forebearance and the redefinition branches of the deregulation effort. In *MCI Telecommunications Corp. v. FCC,* the Supreme Court blocked the Commission's order to MCI and others to stop filing tariffs, holding that the statute requires that tariffs be filed as to common carrier services.[80] In *California v. FCC,*[81] the Ninth Circuit invalidated major aspects of the FCC's Computer III, including its preemption of state regulation of services by providers of common carrier services.

In *American Telephone & Telegraph Co. v. Federal Communications Commission,*[82] the court of appeals held that the FCC's order exempting nondominant interexchange carriers like MCI from tariff requirements violated the Communications Act. Once common carrier status exists, the court found, the FCC lacks discretion to tailor the requirements of Title II of the Act. This basic decision eventually was affirmed by the Supreme Court in *MCI Telecommunications Corp. v. American Telephone & Telegraph Co.*[83] This decision limits flexibility to adapt the existing Title II common carrier obligations to the particular needs of a digital information infrastructure. Once common carrier status is found, the traditional statutory requirements apply.

The most important implication of the *MCI* case is that, under current law, once a service is determined to be common carriage, the Communications Act requires tariffing and the full panoply of cost-of-service regulatory measures.[84] This implication may lead to modification of the statute and renewed effort by the FCC to change the definition of common carrier in order to narrow its scope to services in which market structures inadequately protect access and other public interests.[85]

§ 7.6   —Tariffs

Under the Communications Act of 1934, all telecommunications service providers must file with the FCC a listing of terms and conditions under which they

---

[80] *See* 765 F.2d 1186, 1195–96 (D.C. Cir. 1985) (overturning FCC effort to "detariff").

[81] 905 F.2d 1217 (9th Cir. 1990); *see also id.* at 1223 n.1 (a complete list of the orders under review).

[82] 978 F.2d 727 (D.C. Cir. 1992).

[83] 114 S. Ct. 2223 (1994) (affirming court of appeals; FCC's authority to modify common carrier requirements, granted by § 203, does not authorize Commission to relieve nondominant telephone carriers of obligation to file tariffs).

[84] *But see* MCI Telecommunications Corp. v. FCC, 765 F.2d 1186, 1196 (D.C. Cir. 1985) (allowing FCC to "streamline" regulation in unspecified ways).

[85] For an example of how one state has extended common carrier status to include video and data transmission, see N.Y. Pub. Serv. Comm'n, Opinion and Order Adopting Regulations Concerning Common Carriage, Opinion No. 0-9, Case 89-C-099 (1990) (adopting Common Carrier Rules, N.Y. Comp. Codes R. & Regs. tit. 16, § 605 (1990)); *see also* the preceding report, N.Y. Pub. Serv. Comm'n, Common Carriage Principles in the New Telecommunications Environment, Case 89-C-099 (discussing the historical role of common carrier regulation and requesting comments from interested parties).

will provide services to their customers.[86] This listing is known as a *tariff* and must set forth the carrier's charges, classifications, practices, and regulations.[87] Under the "filed tariff doctrine," a tariff filed with the FCC supersedes all other agreements between the parties.[88] Thus, the tariff is more than a contract because it exclusively controls the rights and liabilities of the parties as a matter of law.[89] Congress developed the published tariff system as a way of preventing carriers from giving more advantageous prices and terms to favored customers, while customers without a special relationship would be compelled to pay the difference.[90]

In *MCI Telecommunications Corp. (MCI) v. American Telephone & Telegraph Co.* (ATT),[91] the Supreme Court held that the FCC's permissive detariffing policy is not a valid exercise of its Code § 203(b)(2)[92] authority to "modify any requirement." The *MCI* case is important for two reasons. First, it discusses the underlying rationale and nature of tariffs. Second, it makes it clear that the FCC's power to effect deregulation administratively without congressional action is limited.

The Supreme Court characterized the requirements of 47 U.S.C. § 203 that common carriers file tariffs and charge only the rate filed in the tariff as the "centerpiece" of the Federal Communication Act's regulatory scheme.[93] The tariff requirement had "always been considered essential to preventing price discrimination and stabilizing rates"[94] and supporting most of the other particulars of rate regulation, including the prohibition on overcharges and the power for customers and competitors to challenge rates as unreasonable and discriminatory.[95] Indeed, the Court concluded that Congress would be unlikely to leave to an administrative agency whether a part of an industry would be subject to these aspects of rate regulation through the power to modify the tariff requirement.

This case presented the question whether the FCC's decision to make tariff filing optional for all nondominant long distance carriers[96] was a valid exercise

---

[86] MCI Telecommunications Corp. v. Best Tel. Co., No. 93-1581-CIV-MOORE, 1994 WL 397238, at *3 (S.D. Fla. Apr. 26, 1994). The research for this section was done by Tom Thistle.

[87] *Id.* (citing 47 U.S.C. § 203(a) (1988)).

[88] *Id.* (citing 47 U.S.C. § 203(c) (1988)). (The filed tariff doctrine is considered more fully in **Chs. 4** and **5**).

[89] *Id.* (citing Carter v. American Tel. & Tel. Co., 365 F.2d 486, 496 (5th Cir. 1966), *cert. denied.,* 385 U.S. 1008 (1967)).

[90] *Id.* at *4 (citing Maislin Indus. U.S. v. Primary Steel, Inc., 497 U.S. 116 (1990)).

[91] 114 S. Ct. 2223, 2225 (1994).

[92] 47 U.S.C. § 203 (1988 & Supp. IV 1992).

[93] 114 S.Ct. 2223, 2226 (1994).

[94] *Id.* at 2231.

[95] *Id.* at 2231–32.

[96] *See* the First Report and Order, 85 F.C.C.2d 1, 30–49 (1980); the Second Report and Order, 91 F.C.C.2d 59 (1982); the Fourth Report and Order, 95 F.C.C.2d 1191 (1984); the Fifth Report and Order, 98 F.C.C.2d 1191 (1985).

of its modification authority.[97] The outcome turned on the meaning of the phrase "modify any requirement" in § 203(b)(2).[98] The Court ruled that the most relevant time for determining the meaning of a word was at the time the statute was created. At that time "modify" had a narrow definition of connoting moderate change.[99] Thus, the FCC's detariffing policy could be justified only if it made a less than radical change in the Act's tariff filing requirement.[100] The Supreme Court determined that lifting the tariff requirements from MCI hardly could qualify as a mere modification, and thus was invalid.[101]

MCI argued that the FCC's interpretation of § 203 furthered the Communications Act's broad purpose of promoting efficient telephone service,[102] but the Court observed that desirable policy cannot alter the meaning of a statute. For better or worse, the Act establishes a rate-regulation, filed-tariff system for common carrier communications, and the FCC's desire to increase competition could not provide it authority to alter the well-established statutory filed-rate requirements.[103] Such considerations address themselves to Congress, not the courts.[104]

Chapter 5 considers the impact of tariffs on efforts to impose liability based on contract or tort under the "filed tariff doctrine."[105]

§ 7.7   —Price Cap Regulation

The FCC considerably simplified rate regulation through its price cap approach. The price cap approach is intended to reproduce, to the extent possible, the effects of competition.[106] In 1989 the FCC eliminated traditional rate of return regulation for AT&T and implemented a system of price cap regulation.[107] It

---

[97] 114 S. Ct. 2223, 2226 (1994).

[98] *Id.* at 2229.

[99] *Id.* at 2230.

[100] *Id.* at 2231.

[101] *Id.* at 2232.

[102] *Id.* at 2233.

[103] 114 S. Ct. 2223, 2233 (1994) (citing Maislin Indus. U.S. v. Primary Steel, Inc., 497 U.S. 116, 135 (1990)). *See also* Southwestern Bell Corp. v. FCC, 43 F.3d 1515 (D.C. Cir. 1995) (invalidating FCC order permitting nondominant carriers to file tariffs with range of rates rather than detailed schedules of specific rates).

[104] 114 S. Ct. 2223, 2233 (1994) (citing Armour Packing Co. v. United States, 209 U.S. 56, 92 (1908)).

[105] The research and initial drafting of this section was done by Tom Thistle, law clerk to the author.

[106] First Report and Order, *In re* Price Cap Performance Review for Local Exchange Carriers, CC Docket No. 94-1, FCC 95-132, 1995 WL 222130 (adopted Mar. 30, 1995), ¶ 67 [hereinafter Performance Review].

[107] Report and Order, *In re* Revisions to Price Cap Rules for AT&T Corp., CC Docket No. 93-197, FCC 95-18, 1995 WL 15731 (adopted Jan. 12, 1995), ¶ 1 (characterizing history and citing report and order and second further notice, 4 F.C.C.R. 2873 (1989) (AT&T price cap order), erratum, 4 F.C.C.R. 379 (1989)).

substituted price cap regulation for rate of return regulation for local exchange carriers (LECs) in 1990.[108] The LEC price cap plan is mandatory for the seven RBOCs and GTE. It is optional for all other LECs.[109] Under the price cap approach, carrier services are grouped into categories called "baskets." The initial four baskets for LEC interstate services are "traffic sensitive," "trunking," "common line," and "interexchange." For AT&T, the baskets comprise (1) residential and small business services (basket 1); (2) "800" number services (basket 2); and (3) other business services (basket 3).[110] Rates within each basket are capped by an aggregate inflation index—the gross national product price index, minus an X-factor to compensate for productivity improvements.[111]

In contrast to the pure price cap plan adopted for AT&T, the FCC adopted a hybrid plan for LECs, which included a rate of return "backstop" intended to compensate for the possibility of inaccuracy in the calculation of the X-factor.[112] Several modifications occurred during the first five years of this new rate regulation approach. The FCC modified the LEC basket structure and proposed a separate price cap basket for video dial tone services.[113] In addition, the Commission significantly expanded the monitoring of service quality and infrastructure development.[114] In March 1995 the Commission made further technical changes in the price cap formulas and solicited comment on further steps that might be appropriate to relax regulation further.[115] In 1995 the FCC removed commercial services from AT&T price cap regulation while keeping analog private line services and 800 directory assistance services under price cap regulation.[116]

---

[108] Performance Review, 1995 WL 222130, ¶¶ 1–4 (history of LEC price cap regulation).

[109] Performance Review, 1995 WL 222130, ¶ 33.

[110] Report and Order, *In re* Revisions to Price Cap Rules for AT&T Corp., CC Docket No. 93-197, FCC 95-18, 1995 WL 15731, at n.2.

[111] Performance Review, 1995 WL 222130, ¶ 30. For example, one of the issues causing considerable controversy was whether carriers ought to be able to adjust their price levels upward to reflect "exogenous" treatment for costs of retiree health care benefits, when accounting rules required them to show accrued liabilities on their books. *See* Memorandum Opinion and Order, *In re* Bell Atl. Tel. Cos. Tariff, FCC No. 1, D.A. 94-1613, CC Docket No. 94-157, 1994 WL 719752 (adopted Dec. 28, 1994) (denying request for exogenous treatment).

[112] Performance Review, 1995 WL 222130, ¶ 32.

[113] Performance Review, 1995 WL 222130, ¶ 34 (citing transport rate structure and pricing CC Docket No. 91-213 at 9 F.C.C.R. 615, 615–16 (1994) (second transport order) (modifying basket structure). *See also* Further Notice of Proposed Rulemaking, *In re* Price Cap Performance Review for Local Exchange Carriers; Treatment of Video Dialtone Services Under Price Cap Regulation, CC Docket No. 94-1, FCC 95-49, 1995 WL 170744 (adopted Feb. 7, 1995).

[114] Performance Review, 1995 WL 222130, ¶ 36.

[115] Performance Review, 1995 Wl 222130, ¶¶ 406–11.

[116] *In re* Revisions to Price Cap Rules for AT&T Corp., CC Docket No. 93-197, FCC 95-18, 1995 WL 15731 (adopted Jan. 12, 1995) ¶ 5.

Significant to the underpinnings of price cap regulation and its eventual relaxation is FCC assessment of market conditions. The price cap baskets were defined to minimize cross-subsidies between competitive and noncompetitive markets, and the general view is that even price cap regulation is unnecessary in fully competitive markets.[117] The three elements of market structure assessment under the FCC's current approach are market share and concentration, demand elasticity, and supply elasticity.[118] Demand elasticity measures the degree to which customers actually respond to changes in price. Supply elasticity measures the degree to which competitors of a provider with substantial market share accommodate increased demand for their services. Low-concentration, high demand elasticity and high supply elasticity all point toward relaxation of regulatory constraints because they are hallmarks of a competitive market.

§ 7.8   —Interexchange Access Charges

With the breakup of AT&T in 1984, the FCC directly imposed rate regulation on LEC charges for originating and terminating interstate calls.[119] Part 69 of 47 C.F.R. covers rate structure and pricing of interstate access. Under part 69, interstate services that use switching in the local telephone office switch at either the originating or terminating end are subject to "switched access charges," composed of three elements: a common line element, a local switching element, and transport interconnection charge.[120] Common line charges are recovered by a combination of end user monthly charges and per minute charges billed to interexchange carriers.[121] Local switching costs are billed to interexchange carriers on a per minute basis, pursuant to jurisdictional separation allocation rules.[122] The transport interconnection charge is recovered from interexchange carriers on a combination of flat fees and per minute charges depending on the degree to which switching between end office switches and interexchange carrier points of presence is dedicated.[123]

---

[117] See id. ¶ 16 (justifying removal of price cap regulation of commercial services based on competitive nature of market).

[118] Id. ¶ 17 (market share); id. ¶¶ 20–21 (demand responsiveness); id. ¶¶ 22–25 (supply elasticity).

[119] See generally Report and Order, In re Amendment of Part 65 and 69 of the Commission's Rules to Reform the Interstate Rate of Return Represcription and Enforcement Processees, CC Docket No. 92-133, FCC 95-134, 1995 WL 156764 (adopted Mar. 30, 1995), ¶¶ 8–14 (history of rate of return regulation for interstate access charges; part of streamlining rate of return evaluation for those LECs remaining under rate of return regulation rather than price cap regulation).

[120] Memorandum Opinion and Order, In re NYNEX Telephone Company's Petition for Waiver, FCC 95-185, 1995 WL 271737 (adopted May 3, 1995), ¶ 5.

[121] Id. ¶ 6.

[122] Id. ¶ 9.

[123] Id. ¶ 10.

In May 1995 the FCC granted a limited waiver to NYNEX with respect to some of the interstate access charge rules, to permit it to meet growing competition in the interexchange access market.[124]

§ 7.9   Broadcast Regulation

Title III of the Federal Communications Act controls radio and television broadcasts.[125] The Act states that the purpose of the title is to maintain federal control over "all the channels of radio transmission" by the granting of licenses under federal authority.[126] It goes on to state that "[n]o person shall use or operate any apparatus for the transmission of energy or communications or signals by radio . . . except under . . . a license."[127] Further, *radio communication* entails "the transmission by radio of writing, signs, signals, pictures, and sounds of all kinds, including all instrumentalities, facilities, apparatus . . . incidental to such transmission."[128]

Courts have universally held that "radio communication" includes television as well as radio. In a well-reasoned opinion, the Third Circuit found two bases for holding that the Act implicitly covered the emerging technology of television. First, it noted that the definition of radio specifically mentioned the transmission of sounds and pictures.[129] Second, the legislative intent of the Act indicates that Congress wanted to form a commission "with regulatory power over all forms of electrical communication."[130] The court concluded that the Act failed to identify television simply because it had not yet been invented and that Congress clearly wanted the FCC to have authority over unknown forms of transmissions.

The Act gives the FCC wide latitude to require information from and impose prerequisites on potential licensees. It states that "all applications for station licenses . . . shall set forth such facts as the Commission [the FCC] by regulation may prescribe as to the citizenship, character, and financial, technical and other qualifications of the applicant to operate the station."[131] The regulations implementing this section require that applicants provide such diverse information as the location of the station, the hours of operation, and the purpose of the station (that is, commercial, religious, all news, and so forth).[132]

---

[124] *Id.* ¶ 25 (noting changes in market structure resulting from entry of new providers).

[125] This section prepared by Paul Boltz, Villanova University School of Law, Class of 1996, law clerk to the author.

[126] 47 U.S.C. § 301.

[127] *Id.*

[128] *Id.* § 153(b).

[129] Dumont Lab., Inc. v. Carroll, 184 F.2d 153, 154 (3d Cir. 1950).

[130] *Id.*

[131] 47 U.S.C. § 308(b).

[132] 47 C.F.R. § 73.1015 (1994).

The Act directs that the FCC exercise this power over licensing so as to promote the "public convenience, interest, or necessity."[133] The meaning of this "public necessity" standard has been the source of much litigation. In one of the first cases to address this issue, the Supreme Court upheld the standard against a claim by a broadcaster that it was too vague to be used by an administrative agency.[134] Approving the FCC's rule that "chain broadcasting systems" obtain special licenses, the Court found that public necessity was not vague because it was a clear mandate for the FCC to seek effective competition in the industry so as to increase output and lower costs to the consumer. Though employing slightly different language, the Court later affirmed this economic definition of public interest, construing the phrase to include diversity of ownership and the best practicable service to the public.[135] The FCC has been guided by this procompetitive-antimonopoly ideal in much of its regulatory activities under Title III.

Over time, the FCC has alternated among comparative hearings, competitive bidding, and lotteries as methods for awarding licenses to entities that meet the basic qualifications. Currently, the Act allows the FCC to pursue any of the three methods in its discretion, although the Act suggests that licensing of communications of a commercial nature may be better accomplished by competitive bidding.[136]

The Federal Communications Act also grants the FCC a number of powers related to the admission of new market participants. For example, the FCC shall

1.   "[P]rescribe the nature of the service to be rendered by each class of licensed stations and each station within any class"[137]
2.   "[A]ssign frequencies for each station and determine the power which each station shall use and the time during which it may operate"[138]
3.   "[D]etermine the location of classes of stations or individual stations"[139]
4.   "[P]rescribe the qualifications of station operators."[140]

In addition, the Act provides that no license can be granted to any foreign government, alien, or corporation incorporated in a foreign country.[141] This prohibition on foreign ownership has become a contentious issue between the FCC and the owner of 20th Century Fox.[142]

---

[133] 47 U.S.C. §§ 309(a), 303.

[134] National Broadcasting Co. v. United States, 319 U.S. 190 (1943).

[135] FCC v. National Citizens Comm. for Broadcasting, 436 U.S. 775, 780 (1978).

[136] 47 U.S.C. § 309.

[137] Id. § 303(b).

[138] Id. § 303(c).

[139] Id. § 303(d).

[140] Id. § 303(l)(1).

[141] Id. § 310(a), (b).

[142] For an interesting discussion of Rupert Murdoch's attempts to avoid § 310, see Claudia MacLachlan, *NAACP to Murdoch: turn off Murdoch,* Nat'l L.J. (1994), at B1.

The Act regulates the daily operations of licensed stations in both their physical apparatus and their broadcast content. For example, the Act allows the FCC to regulate the equipment employed by stations to encourage "the purity and sharpness of the emissions."[143] The FCC may also require stations to keep certain records concerning program lists, transmission data, and other technical information.[144]

In comparison to apparatus regulation, the Act's policy towards content regulation is literally inconsistent. The Act states that nothing gives the FCC "the power of censorship over the radio communications . . . and no regulations or conditions shall be promulgated . . . [by the FCC] which shall interfere with the right of free speech."[145] However, the FCC may suspend any operator's license if that operator has transmitted "superfluous radio communications . . . or communications containing profane or obscene language."[146] The Constitution resolves the conflict, allowing government content regulation only to the extent that the regulated speech has been held to be unprotected by the Constitution, as considered in **Chapter 6.**

Another provision also conflicts with the Act's noncensoring directive. The Act requires that the FCC make regulations that promote the broadcasting of a certain number of children's programs each day,[147] and advises that license renewal by the FCC should be based in part in the particular station's compliance with that requirement.[148] Despite the Act's protestation to the contrary, this children's programming requirement directly affects the content that stations air, thereby precluding the broadcast of other programs. This "crowding out" of other programs serves as an indirect form of censorship by the government. It is important to note that this part of the Act was added only recently as part of the Television Program Improvement Act of 1990.[149] There is little case law concerning these sections, so it remains uncertain how they will be interpreted by the courts.

Another more established exception to the noninterference-in-content rule is the requirement that candidates for public office be given equal airtime. The Act decrees that "[i]f any licensee shall permit any person who is a legally qualified candidate for any public office to use a broadcasting station, he shall afford equal opportunities to all other such candidates for that office."[150] This equal opportunity rule does not apply to on-the-spot coverage of bona fide news events.[151]

---

[143] 47 U.S.C. § 303(e).

[144] *Id.* § 303(j).

[145] *Id.* § 326.

[146] *Id.* § 303(m)(1)(D).

[147] *Id.* § 303a(a).

[148] *Id.* § 303b.

[149] Title V, § 501, Pub. L. No. 101-650, 104 Stat. 5127 (1990) (codified at 47 U.S.C. § 303(c)).

[150] 47 U.S.C. § 315(a).

[151] *See* Kennedy for President Comm. v. FCC, 636 F.2d 417 (D.C. Cir. 1980) (JFK demanding a chance to respond to a news report about Nixon pursuant to § 315).

Licenses to operate a broadcast station are temporary permits to utilize a certain frequency for a certain purpose. Licensees neither own nor have any property expectation in their frequency. The power to deny license renewal is derived from the FCC's power to grant frequency licenses initially and so is within the FCC's plenary powers.[152]

The Act provides that no television license may last longer than five years and no radio license may last more than seven years.[153] Renewal of the license is given only upon application by the existing license holder, and the FCC may require the licensee to provide "any new or additional facts it deems necessary to make its findings."[154] As with the initial grant of a license, the Act directs the FCC to base its decision to renew on whatever best serves the "public interest, convenience, or necessity."[155] The Act explicitly mentions enhanced children's programming as being part of the public interest that the FCC should consider in making its decision.[156]

In addition to the power to decline to renew licenses, the FCC also has the power to revoke licenses during their five- or seven-year time period. There are four primary bases for revoking an active license. A revocation may occur if

1. The applicant made "false statements knowingly . . . either in the application or in any statement of fact"[157]

2. The licensee willfully or repeatedly failed "to operate substantially as set forth in the license"[158]

3. The licensee willfully or repeatedly failed to provide equal access to political candidates[159]

4. The licensee used his license to distribute any controlled substance.[160]

In any proceeding to revoke a license, the burden of proof rests on the FCC.[161]

To transfer, assign, or dispose of a station license, the licensee must apply to the FCC for permission.[162] The FCC must evaluate the application for ownership transfer by the same standards it granted the license. That is, the transfer must

---

[152] American Broadcasting Co. v. FCC, 191 F.2d 492, 497 (D.C. Cir. 1951) (station license was revoked by FCC because FCC had agreed in a bilateral treaty to assign that frequency for Mexican use).

[153] 47 U.S.C. § 307.

[154] *Id.* § 307(c).

[155] *Id.* § 307(c), (e).

[156] 47 U.S.C. § 303b.

[157] *Id.* § 312(a)(1).

[158] *Id.* § 312(a)(3).

[159] *Id.* § 312(a)(7).

[160] *Id.* § 312(a).

[161] *Id.* § 312(d).

[162] 47 U.S.C. § 310(d)

serve the public interest.[163] The Act contains no specific provision for the abandonment of a frequency.

§ 7.10   —Spectrum Auctions

The Federal Communications Act[164] authorizes the use of competitive bidding for initial licenses for certain communication systems. The statute defines the uses for which competitive bidding is permitted as involving compensation for systems that enable subscribers to receive communication signals and to transmit communication signals utilizing frequencies on which the licensee operates.[165] The competitive bidding authority expires in 1998[166] and is to be exercised under detailed rules developed by the FCC for the actual bidding process.[167] The rules must include appropriate performance requirements;[168] ensure opportunities for small businesses, rural telephone companies, and minority- and female-owned businesses;[169] inhibit trafficking in the auctioned licenses;[170] provide for the development and rapid deployment of new technologies;[171] and avoid excessive concentration of licenses.[172] The rules must also consider nationwide, regional, and local licenses or permits.[173] The Commission explicitly is authorized to grant "pioneer preferences."[174]

The auction system was intended to respond to two deficiencies in other procedures. Comparative license hearings proved inefficient because they were subjected to protracted litigation and resulting delays.[175] The lottery system

---

[163] *Id.*

[164] 47 U.S.C. § 309(j) (Supp. V 1993) (added by Pub. L. No. 103-66 § 6002(a) (1993)).

[165] *Id.* § 309(j)(2).

[166] *Id.* § 309(j)(11).

[167] *Id.* § 309(j)(4). *See* 59 Fed. Reg. 64,159 (Dec. 13, 1994) (final rules modifying three aspects of auction design relating to triggers for close of an auction, timing of auctions for entrepreneur's block, and anticollusion rules); 60 Fed. Reg. 13,102 (Mar. 10, 1995) (proposed rules to meet 18-month deadline for auctioning spectrum transferred from federal government use to private use); 59 Fed. Reg. 63,210 (Dec. 7, 1994) (final rule and resolution of petitions for reconsideration governing certain aspects of auctions, including protections for small businesses, rural telephone companies, and minority- and women-owned businesses and various joint venture and entrepreneur requirements).

[168] 47 U.S.C. § 309(j)(4)(B).

[169] *Id.* § 309(j)(4)(D).

[170] *Id.* § 309(j)(4)(E).

[171] *Id.* § 309(j)(3)(A).

[172] *Id.* § 309(j)(3)(B).

[173] *Id.* § 309(j)(6)(F).

[174] 47 U.S.C. § 309(j)(6)(G). Pioneer preference regulations are subject to particular requirements. *Id.* § 309(j)(13).

[175] H.R. 88, 104th Cong., 1st Sess. (Mar. 23, 1995) (to accompany H.R. 1218, extending authority for auctions through the end of FY2000 and explaining rationale for auction system).

relieved those problems but allowed a number of applicants interested only in speculating in lottery-awarded licenses to participate. These speculators received large amounts of money when they sold their licenses, and Congress thought some of this revenue stream should accrue to the public treasury.[176]

From 1993 to 1995 the FCC conducted four spectrum auctions, two for narrowband personal communication systems (PCS) (considered in **Chapter 1**), one for interactive video and data service (IVDS) licenses, and one for broadband PCS licenses. The four auctions produced a total of $9 billion for the general fund of the United States Treasury.[177]

The Act makes it clear that licensees do not enjoy vested property interests in their licenses won through auction.[178] It has long been established that FCC licensees do not enjoy the constitutionally protected property interest in the renewal of their licenses, which traditionally have had a fixed term.[179]

§ 7.11   —Other Radio Regulation

The prohibition in Title III of the Communications Act against operating radio transmitters without an FCC license covers much more than commercial radio and television radio broadcast transmitters. It also includes common carrier radio communication such as that used by marine telephone service, utility and public safety radio transmissions, and cellular telephone and similar services.[180] Common carrier radio services must comply with basic requirements under Title II of the Communications Act as well as satisfying Title III.[181] The FCC also regulates satellite communications.[182]

---

[176] *Id.* at 2.

[177] *Id.* at 2–3 (H.R. 88 is available on WESTLAW, 1995 WL 131875 (Leg. Hist.)).

[178] *See* 47 U.S.C. § 309(j)(6)(C) (preserving commission authority to regulate or reclaim spectrum licenses); *id.* § 309(j)(6)(D) (disavowing construction to convey any rights including any expectation renewal of a license differing from rights that apply to other licenses not issued through auction).

[179] Brandywine-Main Line Radio, Inc. v. FCC, 473 F.2d 16, 61 (D.C. Cir. 1972); Citizens Communications Ctr. v. FCC, 447 F.2d 1201, 1210 (D.C. Cir. 1971) (explaining 47 U.S.C. § 307(d) (three year term) and 47 U.S.C. § 309(h) (license does not vest any right to use frequencies beyond its term)).

[180] 47 C.F.R. pt. 20 (1994) (commercial mobile radio services, including public safety, industrial, maritime service accept for public host stations, and cellular service); *Id.* § 20.6 (specifically referring to PCS, cellular, and SMR services as within commercial mobile radio services); *Id.* § 22.99 (defining public mobile services to include cellular service and paging service); 47 C.F.R. pt. 24 (personal communication service); *Id.* § 24.5 (defining personal communication service (PCS) as "radio communications that encompass mobile and ancillary fixed communication that provides services to individuals and businesses and can be integrated with a variety of competing networks").

[181] 47 C.F.R. § 20.15.

[182] *See* 47 C.F.R. pt. 25.

All of these aspects of radio regulation are important as the NII integrates the types of communications historically carried by wire with methods of communication historically associated with radio and television broadcasts. Cellular telephone regulation is the most fully developed of the new technologies. Initially, the FCC awarded two licenses in each metropolitan statistical area and rural statistical area. A *B block* license was usually awarded to the local telephone company, while *A block* licenses were generally awarded to firms unaffiliated with telephone companies. In 1986 the FCC allowed telephone companies to purchase interests in A block licenses outside their own operating areas.[183]

Although the FCC has been shrinking coverage of the common carrier definition, its control over radio transmissions and the relatively broad grant of statutory authority to impose conditions on radio licenses does not portend a weaker role for the FCC as the NII emerges.

§ 7.12 Cable Regulation

The Cable Communications Policy Act of 1984[184] added Title VI to the Communications Act of 1934 (codified as subchapter V-A of title 47 U.S.C).[185] With the exception of cable operators who were providing service without a franchise before July 1, 1984, no cable operator can provide cable service without the grant of a franchise from a franchising authority.[186] Title V-A provides that *cable service* is

> (A) the one-way transmission to subscribers of (i) video programming, or (ii) other programming service, and
> (B) subscriber interaction, if any, which is required for the selection of such video programming or other programming service."[187]

A *cable operator* consists of "any person . . . (A) who provides cable service over a cable system and . . . owns a significant interest in such cable system, or (B) who otherwise controls or is responsible for . . . the management and operation of such a cable system."[188] A *cable system* means "a set of closed

---

[183] *See* United States v. Western Elec. Co., 154 F.R.D. 1, 3 (D.D.C. 1994) (reviewing history of cellular regulation by FCC). *See also* United States v. Western Elec. Co., 158 F.R.D. 211 (D.D.C. 1994) (granting limited waiver of Modified Final Judgment to allow AT&T to purchase interest in licenses owned partially by McCall cellular and partially by local telephone companies).

[184] This section was prepared by Paul Boltz.

[185] 47 U.S.C. § 521.

[186] *Id.* § 541.

[187] *Id.* § 521(6).

[188] *Id.* § 522(5).

transmission paths and associated signal generation, reception, and control equipment that is designed to provide . . . video programming . . . which is provided to multiple subscribers within a community."[189]

A cable system does not include any facility which "serves only subscribers in one or more multiple unit dwellings under common ownership" (that is, an apartment building).[190] In addition, Title V-A flatly states that no cable system as defined in the Act is subject to regulation as a common carrier.[191] However, it is important to note that cable operators can bring themselves under common carrier regulation (state or federal) if their activities later deviate from the definition. In New Mexico, a cable operator who had been franchised as such for over a decade became subject to the state's common carrier regulation when it began transmitting digitally compressed communications between corporate offices.[192] The court found that because these transmissions were not listed in 47 U.S.C. § 522, the Cable Act's limitations were no longer applicable and the state could freely regulate the cable company.[193]

Fulfilling Congress's goal of promoting a market-oriented regulatory scheme, the Act is much less specific as to what constitutes a franchise authority than as to what constitutes a cable service, presumably leaving institutional design of such authorities to lower levels of government who can effectively gauge their cable needs. The only definition the Act provides is that a *franchiser* is "any governmental entity empowered by Federal, State, or local law to grant a franchise."[194] Neither the Act nor its regulations[195] give any indication how the states or local governments decide what will be an authority. The end result of this open-ended grant of power from the Act is that virtually any governmental body can establish an authority if the body possesses power to do so.[196]

For example, in *Warner Cable Communications v. Borough of Schuykill Haven*,[197] the court held that a Pennsylvania municipality could not spontaneously transform itself into a franchise authority because it had no grant of power from the state. The court explained that municipalities in that state possessed only those powers that were expressly given by the state or were indispensable to the running of the government. Because the Borough's code

---

[189] *Id.* § 522(7).

[190] *Id.*

[191] 47 U.S.C. § 541(c).

[192] Las Cruces TV Cable, Inc. v. New Mexico State Corp. Comm'n, 707 P.2d 1155 (N.M. 1985).

[193] *Id.*

[194] 47 U.S.C. § 522(10).

[195] 47 C.F.R. pt. 76 (1994).

[196] *See* H.R. Rep. No. 934, 98th Cong., 2d Sess. (1984), *reprinted in* 1984 U.S.C.C.A.N. 4655, 4682 (franchise authority could include state agencies and "any local government body with authority to grant a franchise").

[197] 784 F. Supp. 203 (E.D. Pa. 1992).

provisions contained no grant of cable regulation power (no express grant) and because the Borough had existed for decades without this power (no indispensable need for the power), the Borough was acting ultra vires. In contrast, the court noted in dicta that the Pennsylvania state government did have the power under the state constitution to set up its own franchise authority within the existing Public Utilities Commission.[198] Similarly, the Delaware legislature empowered its Public Utilities Commission to act as the state's exclusive franchising authority.[199] On the other hand, the New York legislature gave that state's utility commission the power to set standards for the grant of franchises but expressly left the administration and evaluation of franchise applications to the state's municipalities.[200] On the federal level, the Eleventh Circuit held that Congress could empower the United States Air Force to act as a franchising authority on military bases.[201]

A single cable operator can be subject to more than one franchise authority. In *Burlington v. Mountain Cable Co.*,[202] a city government attempted to avoid the Act's broad limitations on local rate regulation by arguing that 47 U.S.C. § 543 only disables franchise authorities from rate regulation and in Vermont, the state Public Utility Commission, not the city, was the franchise authority.[203] Thus, the city was not subject to the limitation. The court held that because the city had the initial power to be a franchise authority and had acted like an authority, it had become an authority in tandem with the already existing state authority.[204] Thus, cable operators in that area need to seek approval from both levels of government.

Assuming the franchising authority has been established by an appropriate government entity, the authority has the right to grant any number of franchises. The Act provides that each authority may award "one *or more* franchises within its jurisdiction."[205] In a nod toward free market forces, the Act also specifies that a franchise authority may not "grant an exclusive franchise and may not unreasonably refuse to award a competitive franchise."[206] Monopoly cable operators have been forbidden only since 1992.[207] Indeed, in *City of Los Angeles*

---

[198] *Id.*

[199] Del. Code Ann. tit. 26, § 601 ("No entity shall . . . have the power either express or implied . . . to grant franchises").

[200] N.Y. Exec. Law § 815 (McKinney).

[201] Cox Cable Communications, Inc. v. United States, 992 F.2d 1178 (11th Cir. 1993).

[202] 559 A.2d 153, 155 (Vt. 1988).

[203] *Id.*

[204] *Id.*

[205] 47 U.S.C. § 541(a)(1) (emphasis added).

[206] *Id.*

[207] *See* James Cable Partners v. City of Jamestown, 43 F.3d 277, 279 (6th Cir. 1995) (1992 prohibition on exclusivity did not operate retroactively so as to extinguish exclusive rights of pre-Act franchisee). *But see* Cox Cable Communications, Inc. v. United States, 866 F. Supp. 553 (M.D. Ga. 1994) (giving retroactive effect to prohibition on exclusive franchises).

v. Preferred Communications, Inc.,[208] the Supreme Court suggested that exclusive franchises for cable television operators might violate the First Amendment.[209] Once a franchise has been granted, cable operators are entitled to public rights-of-way (via easements) to construct their systems and, as mentioned earlier, can maintain a cable system in the jurisdiction. In addition to regulating cable operators, a state or franchise authority itself may own a cable system as long as the state or franchising authority does not exercise any editorial control over the content of the cable service.[210]

A franchising authority may at its discretion require its cable operators to assign certain broadcast channels for "public, educational, or governmental use."[211] Yet this control over the assignment of public channels is tempered by an absolute prohibition of any exercise of editorial control by the authority over those same channels. The *Turner Broadcasting* case[212] discussed in **Chapter 6** raises questions about the constitutionality of such set-aside requirements. Courts have enforced the no-censorship requirement quite literally. For example, the Ku Klux Klan of Missouri successfully sued a cable operator for denying it access to the public channel on the system because of the content of the Klan's desired broadcast.[213]

In addition to public channel allocation, the franchising authority may also regulate the cable operator's facilities and equipment pursuant to the franchise agreement.[214] However, this grant of power over physical aspects of the cable operator is wed to a limitation on the authority's ability to regulate the content of cable broadcasts. The Act states that "a franchise . . . may not establish requirements for video programming."[215] The legislative history of the rule indicates that while Congress wanted the franchise authorities to have the power to require certain facilities, it did "not believe it is appropriate for government officials to dictate the specific programming to be provided over a cable system."[216] From this history and the plain language of the rule, the D.C. Circuit determined that any franchise rule that was content-based violated 47 U.S.C. § 544.[217]

---

[208] 476 U.S. 488, 495 (1986).

[209] The Court did not decide that the particular limitation imposed by L.A. violated the First Amendment, but simply affirmed a court of appeals remand order so that more facts could be developed. *Id.* at 495. The lower court subsequently determined that the city's policy did violate the First Amendment. Preferred Communications, Inc. v. City of L.A., 13 F.3d 1327, 1330 (9th Cir. 1994).

[210] 47 U.S.C. § 533(e).

[211] *Id.* § 531(b).

[212] 114 S. Ct. 2445 (1994).

[213] Missouri Knights of the Ku Klux Klan v. Kansas City, 723 F. Supp. 1347 (W.D. Mo. 1989).

[214] 47 U.S.C. § 544.

[215] *Id.*

[216] H.R. Rep. No. 934, 98th Cong., 2d Sess. 26 (1984).

[217] United Video, Inc. v. FCC, 890 F.2d 1173, 1189 (D.C. Cir. 1989).

Nonetheless, the franchise authority may still regulate content that is "obscene or otherwise unprotected by the Constitution."[218] The legislative history of the Act indicates that the "otherwise unprotected" language covers such expressions as fighting words and "clear and present danger" speech.[219] The federal district court for Utah reasoned that the syntactic structure of 47 U.S.C. § 544(d)(1) indicated that regulation of obscene content was valid only if the Constitution failed to protect the specific obscene speech.[220] Determining whether the state's Cable Decency Act was a valid exercise of § 544(d)(1), the court reviewed the forms of speech which typically had been protected by the First Amendment.[221] The court held that obscenity had not been traditionally protected and hence could be regulated by the franchise authority.[222] But, mere indecent speech was protected and could be regulated only in limited circumstances.[223]

Regulation of cable television rates has provoked much controversy. Before 1992, the Act precluded franchise authorities from regulating local cable operator rates.[224] Currently, under the Cable Act of 1992, cable rates are regulated by local franchising authorities under guidelines set by the FCC.[225] Under the FCC rules authorized by this Act, local franchise authorities can regulate rates of cable systems where competitive pressures do not effectively regulate rates.[226] When franchising authorities lack authority under their own legal charters to regulate rates, the Commission itself may regulate them.[227] Provisions in cable franchise agreements that prohibit rate regulation are preempted by the 1992 Act.[228] Franchising authorities seeking to regulate rates must first seek certification from the FCC.[229] The FCC adopted comprehensive rules concerning cable rates[230] and subsequently amended them to allow more flexibility for pricing of

---

[218] 47 U.S.C. § 544(d)(1).

[219] H.R. Rep. No. 934, 98th Cong., 2d Sess. 95 (1984).

[220] Community Television, Inc. v. Wilkinson, 611 F. Supp. 1099 (D. Utah 1985), aff'd, 800 F.2d 989 (10th Cir. 1986).

[221] Id. at 1104 (among other cases, court examined New York Times v. Sullivan, 376 U.S. 254 (1964), and Roth v. United States, 354 U.S. 476 (1957)).

[222] Id.

[223] Id.

[224] "Any Federal agency or State may not regulate the rates for the provision of cable service except to the extent provided under this section." 47 U.S.C. § 543 (1988).

[225] 58 Fed. Reg. 29,736 (May 21, 1993) (FCC final rule).

[226] Id. at 29,737, ¶ 5 (defining effective competition to encompass competition between cable providers or fewer than 30 % of households served by cable system).

[227] Id. at 29,738, ¶ 14. But see id. ¶ 16 (FCC will not regulate where local authority is satisfied with rates).

[228] Id. at 29,738, ¶ 17; 47 U.S.C.A. § 543 (West Supp. 1995).

[229] 58 Fed. Reg. 29,736 29,738, ¶¶ 18–26 (May 21, 1993).

[230] Proposed Rulemaking, In re Implementation of Sections of the Cable Television Consumer Protection and Competition Act of 1992: Rate Regulation, MM Docket No. 92-266, 10 F.C.C.R. 1226, 1994 WL 667966 (adopted Nov. 10, 1994), ¶ 1 (summarizing regulatory history after 1992 Act).

new product tiers, new channels, and certain adjustments that do not undermine the fundamental price structure.[231] Price regulation in the cable industry, like price regulation in other aspects of public utility regulation, is extremely complex.[232]

The Cable Act itself directly regulates cable systems' daily operations by requiring certain channel allocations. It provides that each cable operator must broadcast the signals of a certain number of commercial stations that are unrelated (financially) to the cable operator.[233] The exact number of channels dedicated to airing unrelated commercial stations depends on the total number of channels the system normally carries. Similar to public channels, the cable operator is prohibited from exercising editorial control over any "video programming provided pursuant to" 47 U.S.C. § 532.[234]

The Cable Act also requires that cable operators carry local television broadcasts.[235] A cable system with more than 12 channels must devote up to "one-third of the aggregate number of usable activated channels of such system" to local stations.[236] The Act also empowers the FCC to adjudicate any complaints from local stations and to issue orders to operators who fail to comply with this section.[237] Although *Turner Broadcasting,*[238] discussed in **Chapter 6,** did not completely prohibit must-carry rules, it raised doubts about the constitutionality of these requirements.[239]

A franchised cable operator does not "own" its franchise. A franchise is, in effect, a temporary license to operate a certain business. The cable operator must seek a renewal of the franchise every few years from the franchising authority.[240] The precise length of the franchise depends on the particular franchise agreement. For example, Delaware grants franchises of 15-year terms.[241] Under the Act, the franchiser may grant the renewal summarily, or it may hold public hearings on the suitability of the current operator. Also by request, the operator can require the franchise authority to hold a public hearing. The Act provides that the primary basis for refusal of renewal is failure by the operator to comply substantially with the terms of the existing franchise

---

[231] *Id.* (summarizing 1994 proposed rule making).

[232] *See* Stanley M. Besen & John R. Woodbury, *Rate Regulation, Effective Competition, and the 1992 Cable Act,* 17 Hastings Comm. & Ent. L.J. 203 (1994) (challenging reimposition of rate regulation on cable industry, in terms of flaws and statistical development of benchmark rates by FCC).

[233] 47 U.S.C. § 532.

[234] *Id.*

[235] *Id.* § 534(a) (Supp. IV 1992).

[236] *Id.* § 534 (b)(1)(B).

[237] *Id.* § 534(d).

[238] Turner Broadcasting Sys., Inc. v. Federal Communications Comm'n, 114 S. Ct. 2445 (1994).

[239] *Id.* at 2453–54.

[240] 47 U.S.C. § 546.

[241] Del. Code Ann. tit. 26, § 604.

agreement.[242] Finally, the Act requires that any franchise authority that acquires a cable system due to a denial of franchise renewal shall reimburse the former operator for the fair market value of the system as an on-going concern.[243] The Act requires no payment for the value of the franchise itself.

The franchise authority's decision for renewal is considered a final determination under the Act.[244] Any aggrieved operator may appeal the decision to either state or federal court.[245] The Act directs the court hearing such a grievance to grant appropriate relief if it finds that the authority did not follow the Act's procedural requirements.

Revocation of franchises is regulated by federal law. For example, a franchise authority may not revoke a franchise for refusal to comply with rate regulation not authorized by the federal Act.[246]

The Cable Act directly restricts sale of a franchise: "No cable operator may sell or otherwise transfer ownership in a cable system within a 36-month period following . . . acquisition."[247] This three-year requirement can be avoided if the transfer incurs no federal income tax, the transfer is required by law, or the FCC waives the three-year period in the public interest.[248] Beyond this three-year period, the Act does not preclude additional restrictions on transfers imposed by the franchise authorities. Both Delaware and New York prohibit any transfer of franchise ownership without prior approval from their Public Utilities Commissions.[249] However, 47 U.S.C. § 537(e) requires that such franchise approval be given in 120 days after notification if the three-year limit has passed. If a decision is not rendered in that time, the transfer is deemed approved under the Act. Within the confines of § 537, franchise authorities have the power to regulate any transfer of cable system ownership.

The Act makes no provision for the abandonment of a franchise before or after the three-year limit. Yet because the Act implicitly allows franchise authorities to regulate transfers of ownership after three years, it can be inferred that the related action of abandonment is also under the authorities' purview. Indeed, New York requires six-months written notice to the state authority before a franchiser is permitted to abandon.[250]

---

[242] 47 U.S.C. § 546(c)(1)(A); *see* Del. Ann. Code tit. 26, § 606 (franchise may be revoked "only for failure of the franchisee to comply with the terms of the franchise").

[243] 47 U.S.C. § 547.

[244] *Id.* § 546(f).

[245] *Id.* § 555.

[246] Cable Vision Sys. Corp. v. Town of E. Hampton, 862 F. Supp. 875 (E.D.N.Y. 1994) (private agreement between parties fails to supersede federal law and must conform to rate regulations).

[247] 47 U.S.C. § 537(a).

[248] *Id.*

[249] Del. Code Ann. tit. 26, § 609; N.Y. Exec. Law § 822.

[250] N.Y. Exec. Law 28, § 826.

§ 7.13 Video Dial Tone Services

The convergence of the cable television and telephone industries has excited producers of both types of services and engendered much administrative regulatory activity and litigation. Originally, the two industries were kept separate by the interaction of FCC and statutory "cross-ownership" restrictions.[251] In 1992, however, recognizing that threats of monopolization of the emerging cable industry by the telephone companies were probably a fantasy, the FCC adopted a video dial tone rule permitting local exchange carriers to offer, on a non-discriminatory basis, a basic common carrier video delivery platform capable of accommodating multiple video programmers.[252] Under the 1992 rule, however, the LECs could not offer video programming, a restriction that was overturned in litigation reaching the United States Courts of Appeals for the Fourth and Ninth Circuits and district courts in three other circuits.[253] Because the litigation negated the statutory basis for the Commission's restriction on video programming offered by LECs, it proposed in early 1995 to eliminate the restriction.[254]

But that was not the only matter to be resolved. The Commission also had to decide whether video programming by LECs should be allowed only over video dial tone platforms, a situation that would make the benefits of video common carriage available to competing providers, or whether LECs should be allowed to provide video programming on a non–common carriage basis.[255] In addition, it was necessary to determine whether Title VI of the Communications Act (subchapter V-A of title 47 U.S.C.) restricts entry into the cable market of LECs offering video programming.[256]

---

[251] Fourth Further Notice of Proposed Rulemaking, *In re* Telephone Company-Cable Television Cross-Ownership Rules, CC Docket No. 87-266, FCC 95-20, 1995 WL 170692 (adopted Jan. 12, 1995), at ¶ 3 (reviewing 1970 Commission rule and 1984 Cable Act ban) [hereinafter Fourth Video Dial Tone NPRM].

[252] Fourth Video Dial Tone NPRM, ¶ 5.

[253] *Id.* ¶ 2 (citing Chesapeake & Potomac Tel. Co. v. United States, 42 F.3d 181 (4th Cir. 1994) (providing history of cross-ownership restrictions and finding statute attempted to control content and thus unconstitutional); U.S. West, Inc. v. United States, 48 F.3d 1092 (9th Cir. 1994) (finding restriction preventing telecommunications companies from entering into video transmission market violates First Amendment); Bellsouth Corp. v. United States, 868 F. Supp. 1335 (N.D. Ala. 1994) (finding restraints not narrowly tailored enough to advance government's goals); Ameritech Corp. v. United States, 867 F. Supp. 721 (N.D. Ill. 1994) (finding statute not justified as legitimate time, place, or manner restriction on speech); NYNEX Corp. v. United States, Civ. No. 93-323-P-C, 1994 WL 779761 (D. Me. Dec. 8, 1994) (statutory restrictions not narrowly tailored enough to pass Constitutional muster)).

[254] *Id.* ¶ 10.

[255] *Id.* ¶ 11 (stating basic question); *id.* ¶ 13 (seeking comment on whether FCC has authority under § 214 of the Communications Act to require LEC video programming offerings to be made only over video dial tone common carrier platforms).

[256] *Id.* ¶ 14. The FCC earlier had concluded that the offering of a video dial tone platform without video programming did not trigger Title VI of the Communications Act (requiring

Beyond that, the FCC was confronted with deciding what kind of regulatory regime is appropriate for a market in which telephone companies offer video dial tone services and video programming. The principal concerns were the possibility of anticompetitive behavior and cross-subsidy by the newly entering LECs.[257] Some possible remedies were these:

- To continue prohibitions on telephone companies having more than a 5 percent interest in or exercising direct or indirect control over an entity providing video programming in its telephone service area[258]
- To require an LEC to provide sufficient capacity to serve multiple service providers on a nondiscriminatory basis[259]
- To limit the percentage of its own video dial tone capacity an LEC can use for its own video programming[260]
- To require LECs to share video dial tone capacity with commercial broadcasters, public educational and governmental channels, and nonprofit programmers[261]
- To prohibit discriminatory channel positioning by LECs.[262]

In addition, the FCC stated that restrictions on LEC acquisition of cable facilities for the provision of video dial tone in their own telephone service areas should be continued to reduce the likelihood that the potential for video dial tone service competition between existing LECs and existing cable companies would be blunted by LEC acquisition of existing cable companies.[263]

The commission also was concerned about the potential for cross-subsidization of nonregulated enhanced video dial tone–related services by regulated Title II activities. It tentatively concluded that existing protections against cross-subsidization should be extended to video programming.[264] The particular concern here was that the LECs have market power in the regulated market segments and thus could, if they could get regulatory authorities to agree, increase their prices in those markets to a sufficient level to provide a subsidy for the unregulated cable market, permitting them to undercut prices by other cable providers and to put them out of business.

---

cable franchise as condition of entry under § 621(b) because video dial tone service is not a cable service as defined in the 1984 Cable Act, and LECs are not cable operators as defined in that Act. *Id.* ¶ 4 (characterizing initial video dial tone FCC decision).

[257] Fourth Video Dial Tone NPRM, ¶ 18.

[258] *Id.* ¶ 19.

[259] *Id.* ¶ 20.

[260] *Id.* ¶ 21.

[261] *Id.* ¶ 22.

[262] *Id.* ¶ 23.

[263] Fourth Video Dial Tone NPRM, ¶ 27.

[264] *Id.* ¶ 34.

Finally, the FCC sought comment on whether it should strengthen its requirement that telephone companies seeking to provide video dial tone or video programming services demonstrate that they are making pole attachment rights or conduit space available "at reasonable charges and without undue restrictions on the uses that may be made of the channel by the operator."[265]

The 1995 video dial tone proposal illustrates the several concerns that justify administrative regulation in the NII:

1. The possibility that a firm with a monopoly in one market would extend that monopoly into other markets by cross-subsidizing offerings in the competitive markets

2. That they would have such an abundance of capital and technical resources that they could in effect dominate new markets

3. That capital goods, such as poles or conduits useful for both markets, would be used to the disadvantage of participants in fewer markets than the monopolist.

While identifying the justifications does not suggest that administrative regulation is appropriate, one can count on the use of such justifications by proponents of regulation in order to limit competition—fair or unfair—by telephone companies and others with an actual or perceived monopoly in important parts of the NII.[266]

§ 7.14   Antitrust Limitations on Pricing

The antitrust laws' influences are pertinent to NII activities in many respects. **Chapter 2** considers the antitrust laws as a source of rights to access NII facilities and services. **Chapter 4** considers how antitrust liability might result from efforts at self-regulation or self-governance by NII communities. **Chapter 6** considers the interaction between antitrust liability and constitutional protections. **Chapter 10** considers the relationship between intellectual property and antitrust law. This chapter considers antitrust law as a source of more general regulatory oversight of NII entities, which otherwise might be subject to administrative regulation.

---

[265] *Id.* ¶ 40.

[266] The problems also sometimes are forecast by scholarly commentators. *See* Bruce A. Olcott, *Will they take away my video-phone if I get lousy ratings?*, 94 Colum. L. Rev. 1558 (1994) (suggesting possibility "that massive horizontally and vertically integrated companies could create de facto monopolies over telephone and video distribution systems in large regions of the country," and "could also threaten to dominate the program production industry"). *Id.* at 1560–61. *See also id.* at 1593–616 (proposing statutory video common carrier regulation and statutory structural separation requirement including programming subsidiary requirement).

The clearest example of antitrust law as a source of general regulatory oversight in the communications and information industry is the breakup and continued supervision of the pieces of AT&T under the antitrust laws.[267] More recently, the antitrust laws have been used to limit Microsoft's dominance of the desktop computer software industry and potentially to limit establishment of Internet and other NII connections tightly bundled with its operating system.

After the Federal Trade Commission deadlocked on whether to issue a complaint against Microsoft for monopolization in violation of sections 1 and 2 of the Sherman Act, the Justice Department filed a complaint and a proposed consent decree based in large part on the FTC investigation.[268] The Justice Department inquiry and complaint was based on a combination of Microsoft's legitimately acquired dominant position in the market for operating systems, combined with a number of practices that were likely to extend Microsoft's monopoly and deny access to that and other markets by competitors. The concern was heightened by the economic characteristics of the software market in which producers confront high fixed costs and virtually zero marginal costs, resulting in high increasing returns to scale[269]—the traditional hallmarks of a natural monopoly.

The consent decree prohibited Microsoft from certain actions:

1. Licensing its operating system software to computer sellers on a "per processor basis," under which the licensee must pay a fee to Microsoft for each computer regardless of whether the Microsoft operating system is used on that computer

2. Pricing on a lump sum basis

3. Pricing with minimum commitments

4. Imposing unduly restrictive nondisclosure conditions on licensees that might block them from legitimate and productive discussions with vendors of competing operating systems.[270]

The first three prohibitions were aimed at eliminating the tendency of those pricing arrangements to freeze out competitors; if a licensee used competing operating system software for processors covered by the per processor agreement, a lump sum or minimum price, the licensee in effect would be paying twice for operating system software for that computer. In essence, Microsoft was giving its software away for processors covered under the minimum price

---

[267] *See* United States v. Western Elec., No. 82-0192 (D.D.C. 1983) (modified final judgment in AT&T breakup case, providing for continued supervision of AT&T and "baby bells" by the district court).

[268] United States v. Microsoft Corp., 56 F.3d 1448 (D.C. Cir. 1995) (reversing district court refusal to approve consent decree).

[269] *Id.* at 1452 (describing Kenneth Arrow testimony and market characteristics).

[270] *Id.* (summarizing terms of consent decree).

or per processor umbrella and not originally intended by the licensee to use Microsoft software. This is the ultimate in predatory pricing.

Other restrictions were sought by the district judge who disapproved the consent decree, subsequently reversed by the court of appeals:

1. Prohibition on vaporware
2. Establishment of a "wall" between the Microsoft operating system and application software activities
3. Disclosure of operating system instruction codes so as to permit the easier construction of interoperable and compatible products.[271]

Vaporware is the announcement of future products accompanied by an intent that the announcement undermine consumer intentions to buy a presently available competing product. Vaporware has the effect of diminishing the demand for competing products. A wall between operating system and application software development would be a technique for forcing a limited degree of unbundling of the two types of software, thus making it easier for competing providers of application software to compete with Microsoft in the application software market. Disclosure of instruction codes for the operating system facilitates access by competing operating system software producers and competing application software producers who can, once they know the instruction codes, make their products more compatible and interoperable with Microsoft's products.

The reversal of the district court's refusal to approve the consent decree limited the judicial role and expanded the Justice Department role in tailoring regulatory requirements, including regulation of pricing strategies, under the antitrust laws. In mid-1995, the Justice Department was embarked on a further investigation of Microsoft's intention to bundle network and network access features in its Windows 95 operating system but decided not to file a complaint before the product was released.

§ 7.15   Proposed Federal Legislation

Telecommunications reform legislation almost certainly will relax restrictions on entry into the telephone market by cable operators and entry into the cable market by telephone operators. It also may extend universal service obligations and certain common carriage obligation beyond "plain old telephone service" (POTS) to certain basic aspects of digital nonvoice communication and information services, possibly under the open platform proposal initially submitted by Mitchell Kapor, the developer of Lotus 1-2-3 and the founder of the Electronic Frontier Foundation.

---

[271] *Id.* at 1454 (summarizing additional restrictions desired by district court).

Legislation has been proposed by Senator Exon that would impose broadly on information service intermediaries' legal and civil obligations with respect to pornographic and obscene material.[272] Competing proposals with respect to immunities for intermediaries also is likely to be considered. Many commentators propose enactment of a sui generis statute for intellectual property protection of electronic formats, as noted in **Chapter 10.**

§ 7.16 State Regulation

The interplay between federal, state, and local regulation of cable service is considered in **§ 7.12.** With respect to broadcast, other radio, and common carrier regulation, states also have authority to apply their common and statutory law to fraudulent practices and breaches of contract,[273] at least when the conduct giving rise to the state claim is not covered by a tariff filed by the FCC.[274] State content regulation, most often seen in connection with state obscenity regulation, usually is preempted.[275] Usually, state regulation has been permitted only when it is focused on intrastate communications and has only an incidental effect on interstate communications. Regulating content that originates from outside the state is targeted at intrastate communication.[276]

---

[272] S. 314, 104th Cong., 1st Sess. (introduced by Mr. Exon Feb. 1, 1995).

[273] *Compare* Unimat, Inc. v. MCI Telecommunications Corp., Civ. A. No. 92-5941, 1992 WL 391421 (E.D. Pa. Dec. 16, 1992) (claim against MCI for assigning 800 number that attracted large numbers of hang up calls was preempted because it involved service considerations within FCC's exclusive jurisdiction) *with* U.S. Sprint Communications Co. v. Computer Generation, Inc., 401 S.E.2d 573, 575 (Ga. Ct. App. 1991) (reversing dismissal of state counterclaims for fraud and breach of contract against carrier; claims not preempted) *and* Cooperative Communications, Inc. v. AT&T Corp., 867 F. Supp. 1511, 1516–17 (D. Utah 1994) (claims by telephone communication aggregator for intentional interference with economic relations, interference with contract, business disparagement, breach of covenant of good faith and fair dealing, unfair competition, and violation of state Uniform Trade Secrets Act were not preempted but rather were saved by § 414 savings clause).

[274] *See* Kellerman v. MCI Telecommunications Corp., 479 N.E.2d 1057, 1061 (Ill. Ct. App. 1985) (state fraud and deceptive advertising claims against long distance telephone service provider were not preempted), *aff'd*, 493 N.E.2d 1045 (Ill. 1986) (no preemption because state law claims involve neither quality of provider service nor reasonableness and lawfulness of its rates); American Inmate Phone Sys., Inc. v. U.S. Sprint Communications Co., 787 F. Supp. 852, 856–57 (N.D. Ill. 1992) (state deceptive trade practices claim against Sprint, accompanied by breach of contract claim, was not preempted and thus not removable to federal court); *In re* Long Distance Telecommunications Litig., Kaplin v. ITT-U.S. Transmission Sys., Inc., 831 F.2d 627, 631–34 (6th Cir. 1987) (state claims regarding reasonableness of rates were preempted, but not state claims for fraud and deceit for failure to disclose charges for uncompleted long distance calls).

[275] Sprint Corp. v. Evans, 818 F. Supp. 1447, 1457 (M.D. Ala. 1993) (state antiobscenity regulation of 800 number service was preempted because it imposed reporting duties on interexchange carriers; citing cases).

[276] *Id.*

A broad range of questions regarding the respective roles of state and federal regulatory agencies arose in conjunction with the FCC's effort to preempt state regulation of areas that it had deregulated under the federal act. The broadest of these orders was contained in the Computer III Inquiry and invalidated by the Ninth Circuit in 1990.[277] Invalidated FCC orders precluded state regulators from tariffing enhanced services sold by communications carriers, requiring communications carriers to maintain structural separation between their basic and enhanced service operations, or requiring nonstructural safeguards that were inconsistent with or more stringent than the FCC's nonstructural safeguards. The nonstructural safeguards involve unbundling under the so-called open network architecture philosophy.[278] The court of appeals found that § 2(b)(1) of the Communications Act, preserving state authority to regulate intrastate communication, also included enhanced services provided by common carriers and therefore was outside the FCC's jurisdiction either to regulate or to preempt.[279] Ultimately, the court of appeals approved a modified preemption order.[280] The approved FCC order preempted only that state regulation that imposed structural separation requirements on facilities and personnel used to provide the intrastate portion of jurisdictionally mixed enhanced services while leaving the states alone to impose structural separation requirements on enhanced services offered on a purely intrastate basis. It also preempted state rules requiring disclosure of network changes at a different time from its own disclosure rules.[281]

On August 10, 1993, Congress enacted the Omnibus Budget Reconciliation Act of 1993[282] amending § 332 of title 47 U.S.C.[283] OBRA 93 preempts state and local regulation of rates and entry of Commercial Mobile Radio Services (CMRS), which includes paging services, cellular telephone service, and personal communication systems (PCS). States may, however, petition the FCC for continued or new regulatory authority over intrastate CMRS rates. The FCC adopted rules to guide its review of state requests, which specify the kind of evidence, information, and analysis pertinent to the Commission's examination of market conditions and consumer protection.[284] In May 1995 the FCC rejected continued efforts by seven states, including New York and California, to regulate cellular telephone prices under the requirement of the

---

[277] California v. Federal Communications Comm'n, 905 F.2d 1217 (9th Cir. 1990) (People I).

[278] Id. at 1239 (describing FCC order).

[279] Id. at 1241.

[280] California v. FCC, 39 F.3d 919 (9th Cir. 1994).

[281] Id. at 932–33 (approving narrowly tailored preemption order).

[282] OBRA 93, Pub. L. No. 103-66, § 6002(c)(3), 107 Stat. 312, 394 (1993) (codified at 47 U.S.C. § 332(c)(3)).

[283] 47 U.S.C. § 151 (1988 & Supp. VI 1994).

[284] 47 C.F.R. § 20.13(a) (1995); Second Report in Order, Implementation of §§ 3(n) and 332 of the Communications Act, Gen. Docket No. 93-252, 9 F.C.C.R. 1411, 1504–05 (1994).

1993 legislation that allows states to petition the FCC for continued price regulation.[285]

In the cable and broadcast arenas, states maintain their authority to regulate deceptive advertising and certain physical structures that have zoning implications, and at least to some extent, to develop mandatory access rules affecting property rights.[286] The Cable Act at 47 U.S.C. § 521 leaves the formation of cable franchising authorities to federal, state, or local bodies with little guidance as to how or why one type of franchiser should be chosen over another form.

Title III of the Communications Act identifies the FCC's power over radio and television communication, but it fails explicitly to assign any powers to other levels of government. It is safe to say that states have virtually no power in the area of market entry and market retention. Reasoning that the whole purpose of the Act was to streamline the use of the limited number of frequencies, the Supreme Court held that the allocation of radio frequencies should be left solely to the FCC.[287] The only area where states have typically interfered in market entry is in license fees. For example, Delaware requires that all entities licensed by the FCC pay a $50 fee to start operating.[288] Because revocation and renewal of licenses directly affects any FCC frequency allocation scheme, it can be inferred from the Court's analysis that market retention issues are also solely under the FCC's purview.

Some aspects of content regulation are concurrently regulated by the FCC and state governments. Many states have consumer protection laws that affect what licensees can air and the licensee's potential liability. For example, Illinois imposes liability on station owners for damages caused by false, deceptive, or misleading advertising unless the owner can show that she "did not have knowledge of the false, misleading or deceptive character of the advertising, did not prepare the advertising, and did not have a direct financial interest in the sale . . . of the advertised product."[289] Conversely, the Supreme Court in *Dumont Laboratories, Inc. v. Carroll* held that states have no power to censor programs

---

[285] Edmund L. Andrews, *FCC Rejects States' Efforts to Regulate Cellular Prices,* N.Y. Times, May 12, 1995, at D6.

[286] Amsat Cable, Ltd. v. Cable Vision of Conn. Ltd. Partnership, 6 F.3d 867, 875 (2d Cir. 1993) (rejecting preemption argument against state statute that forced apartment complex to allow franchised cable television operator access); Vote Choice, Inc. v. DeStefano, 4 F.3d 26, 42 (1st Cir. 1993) (state statute requiring free advertising for candidates receiving public finance not preempted by FCC doctrine); State of Texas v. Synchronal Corp., 800 F. Supp. 1456, 1458–59 (W.D. Tex. 1992) (state laws regulating infomercials on cable television not preempted by a cable television act); Johnson v. City of Pleasanton, 982 F.2d 350, 354 (9th Cir. 1992) (reversing preemption of receive-only satellite antenna ordinance and remanding for inquiry into whether ordinance imposes unreasonable limitations or discriminates against them compared with similar structures).

[287] FCC v. Sanders Bros. Radio Station, 309 U.S. 470 (1940).

[288] Del. Code Ann. tit. 20, § 2301(14) (1985).

[289] Ill. Ann. Stat. ch. 815, para. 505/10B (Smith-Hurd 1985).

for their content.[290] In *Dumont*, 47 U.S.C. § 326 barred Pennsylvania's attempt to censor television movies it thought obscene because that federal content regulation scheme was broader and more effective than any state method.

§ 7.17   Network Self-Governance

A significant part of the NII is *self-governing*, meaning that private entities or associations make and enforce rules within a relatively general framework represented by the regular legal system. For example, much of existing electronic payments law is spelled out and administered by private check clearing, credit card, and electronic funds transfer networks.[291] State and federal statutes governing payment systems delegate significant authority to such private institutions.[292] Centralized commercial information services providers such as CompuServe and America Online establish detailed policies and maintain procedures for handling complaints and grievances. Network interconnection and routing ventures such as the Commercial Internet Exchange have their own rule-making and dispute resolution procedures. More generally, there are early signs of integrated rule-making and accusatory, adjudicatory, and enforcement arrangements in the Usenet community.[293]

NII participants and their lawyers must be prepared to shepherd more self-governance, recognizing the limitations and understanding how to structure specialized electronic community self-regulatory schemes. The economics literature recognizes that a major reason for integration—for replacing market transactions with bureaucratic regulation—is reduced transaction costs.[294]

---

[290] 184 F.2d 153, 155 (3d Cir. 1950).

[291] See **Ch. 9.**

[292] *See* 15 U.S.C. § 1693f(a) (requires financial institutions to determine if error has occurred upon consumer notification); *id.* § 1681i(a) (allows consumer reporting agency to disregard disputed consumer file if reasonable grounds to believe complaints frivolous).

[293] This phenomenon is most evident in an Internet newsgroup called alt.current-events.net-abuse. This newsgroup was formed to deal with the widespread outrage over the "spamming phenomenon," triggered when two Arizona attorneys sent out thousands of postings to newsgroups on the Internet advertising their immigration law services, without regard to the subject matter of the newsgroup. In alt.current-events.net-abuse, any person can post a notice constituting an accusation that someone is engaged in spanning. The other participants of the newsgroup discuss the incident and decide whether it violates evolving rules distinguishing spanning from legitimate use. If the discussion supports the belief that spanning is involved, one or more of the participants sends out a specialized message called a "cancel bot" that erases the offending span from all newsgroups to which it has been sent.

[294] *See* Oliver Williamson, *Transaction-Cost Economics: The Government of Contractual Relations,* 22 J.L. & Econ. 233 (1979) (suggesting that market structures are determined by the comparative transaction costs of different organization forms such as different levels of vertical integration); Oliver Williamson, *The Organization of Work: A Comparative Institutional Assessment,* 1 J. Econ. Behav. & Organization 5 (1980) (same).

Transaction costs are made up of many things, including search costs, but they also include dispute resolution costs. Dispute resolution costs are lower when disputes over product characteristics or quality arise within an integrated enterprise than when they arise in the marketplace. It is the difference between taking it up the chain of command, and perhaps having an order issued or someone's career penalized, and taking it to a lawsuit.

But the new information technologies reopen the question whether transaction costs are lower inside or outside. It may be that the costs of resolving disputes in cyberspace are lower than the cost of resolving disputes in traditional markets. Thus, the relative advantage of bringing transactions inside would decrease, compared to leaving them outside. This means that the health of cyberspace depends to a significant degree on the efficiency and fairness of its dispute resolution mechanisms. Importantly, new technologies enlarge the possibility of bringing disputes "inside" a community without bringing them inside a single bureaucratic enterprise.

Many commentators believe that major aspects of the NII should be self-governing because self-government mechanisms will do a better job of rule making and enforcement. Participants understand the problems and potential of the NII better than nonspecialized legal institutions, and the transnational character of the NII makes many efforts by national legal institutions to regulate it ineffective.[295]

Regardless of the merits of NII self-governance, attempts at self-government will provoke disputes in which the party disadvantaged by private decisions will seek recourse in regular legal institutions. Lawyers representing such parties must know how to avoid self-government; lawyers opposing such parties must know how to protect self-regulatory institutions from such outside legal assault. For example, consider a credit card holder whose refusal to pay a merchant has been overturned by the credit card issuer pursuant to dispute resolution procedures under the Fair Credit Reporting Act. The cardholder may seek review of the decision by the issuer in court or file a claim directly against the merchant in court (perhaps as a counter-claim in the merchant's collection action). The court presented with either type of claim must decide how much to defer to the private decision of the issuer. In other instances, the same issue of deference is involved, but the private decision involves not rejection of a claim but acceptance of it. For example, in the newsgroup context, a complaint about an advertisement might result in cancellation of the message containing the advertisement. Then, the advertiser might seek recourse in the regular courts. Or, a private service

---

[295] *See generally* William S. Byassee, *Jurisdiction of Cyberspace: Applying Real World Precedent to the Virtual Community,* 30 Wake Forest L. Rev. 197 (1995); Michael I. Meyerson, *Virtual Constitutions: The Creation of Rules for Governing Private Networks,* 8 Harv. J.L. & Tech. 129 (1994); Henry H. Perritt, Jr., *President Clinton's National Information Infrastructure Initiative: Community Regained?,* 69 Chi.-Kent L. Rev. 991 (1994) (Charles Green Lecture) (exploring role of new computer and communications technologies in undermining traditional communities and facilitating new ones); Henry H. Perritt, Jr., *Dispute Resolution in Electronic Network Communities,* 38 Vill. L. Rev. 349 (1993).

provider like CompuServe might terminate service of a subscriber based on a claim that the subscriber has violated CompuServe policies. (**Chapter 3** reprints some America Online dispute resolution procedures.) The subscriber then seeks recourse in the regular courts. In these circumstances also, the party losing in the private governance mechanisms would argue that the regular courts owe little deference to those mechanisms.

The difference between a lawsuit brought by a disappointed claimant and one brought by a losing respondent is that the losing respondent is more likely to be able to demonstrate a cause of action. The disconnected CompuServe subscriber could claim breach of contract; the disappointed advertiser could claim interference with property interests in the ad, constituting trespass to chattel, or intentional interference with contractual relations. Conversely, the disappointed claimant, such as the credit card holder, would have to establish that the Fair Credit Reporting Act gives him a right to a particular determination rather than merely a right to have the card issuer follow some kind of dispute resolution procedure.[296] This is a more demanding argument.

The basic activities of governance conveniently can be classified as the *Restatement (Third) of Foreign Relations Law* classifies jurisdiction: jurisdiction to prescribe (to make rules), jurisdiction to adjudicate, and jurisdiction to enforce.[297] A fourth type of governance activity relates to accusation.[298] Jurisdiction to prescribe is considered in **§ 12.11,** relating to choice of law. Jurisdiction to adjudicate is considered in **§ 12.14,** relating to arbitration. The remainder of this section considers jurisdiction to enforce.

Assertion of the jurisdiction to enforce by self-governance institutions in the NII is likely to involve a variety of self-help remedies.[299] It potentially implicates the jurisprudence of state action under the Supreme Court's decisions in *Shelley v. Kraemer,*[300] *Flagg Bros. v. Brooks,*[301] *Lugar v. Edmondson Oil Co.,*[302] and *Wyatt v. Cole.*[303] In all of these cases, the Supreme Court struggled to find the boundary between purely private self-help remedies—where judicial review, if available at all, would occur in the context of a tort or breach of contract claim—and instances in which the government is sufficiently involved

---

[296] 15 U.S.C 1681i (1988 & Supp. VI 1994) (entitling cardholder to dispute resolution procedure).

[297] Restatement (Third) of Foreign Relations Law § 401 (1987).

[298] Accusation typically is a role played by private citizens even when the prescription, adjudication, and enforcement functions are performed by public officers.

[299] Blackstone, writing in 1768 identifies the following types of self-help: defense of oneself, recaption of chattels or persons, abatement of nuisances, distraint, seizing of heriots. 3 William Blackstone, Commentaries on the Laws of England 1–15 (1768) (facsimile ed., Univ. of Chicago Press, 1979).

[300] 334 U.S. 1 (1948).

[301] 436 U.S. 149 (1978).

[302] 457 U.S. 922 (1982).

[303] 504 U.S. 158 (1992) (businessman obtained writ of replevin and cooperated with sheriff to seize cattle subject to liability under § 1983, but did not enjoy immunity afforded public officials).

so that judicial review can be obtained under 28 U.S.C. § 1983 or in a *Bivens* action.[304] Constitutional procedural and substantive due process criteria are the standards of review for governmental action, but not for private action (see **Chapter 6**).

If one has a purely contractual framework within which rules are made and enforced, as in the previous CompuServe example, the likelihood of state action is de minimis. The only remedy of someone disadvantaged by the private dispute resolver would be for breach of contract or a related tort claim, such as fraudulent misrepresentation or intentional interference with contractual relations. On the other hand, when the dispute resolution mechanism is sanctioned by statute, as in the Fair Credit Reporting Act, the situation looks more like *Flagg Bros.*,[305] in which the self-help repossession was sanctioned by Article 9 of the UCC, as adopted by the New York legislature. But in *Flagg Bros.,* the Supreme Court held that private conduct within a framework established by statute insufficiently engages the power of the state to represent state action under § 1983. State action occurs only when enforcement powers of the state are used by private entities, as when Edmondson Oil Company obtained a writ from the Virginia circuit court[306] or the Mississippi judgment creditor obtained a writ of execution.[307] One of the strongest examples of private enforcement is the landlord's common-law right of distress: the power and privilege of seizing personal property on leased premises as a remedy for tenant nonpayment of rent. The exercise of the distress remedy generally has not been viewed as constituting state action, unless officers of the state such as deputy sheriffs assist the landlord.[308] Thus, designers of private electronic governmental mechanisms have greater autonomy when their arrangements are purely contractual, and

---

[304] Bivens v. Six Unknown Narcotics Agents, 403 U.S. 388 (1971) (the Supreme Court held that a victim of federal deprivations of constitutional rights may assert a private right of action for damages).

[305] Flagg Bros. v. Brooks, 436 U.S. 149 (1978).

[306] Lugar v. Edmondson Oil Co., 457 U.S. 922 (1982) (the Supreme Court held that use of state procedures to effect prejudgment seizure of property constituted state action).

[307] Wyatt v. Cole, 504 U.S. 158 (1992) (businessman obtained writ of replevin and cooperated with sheriff to seize cattle subject to liability under § 1983, but did not enjoy immunity afforded public officials).

[308] *See* Shane J. Osowski, *Alaska Distress Law in the Commercial Context: Ancient Relic or Functional Remedy?,* 10 Alaska L. Rev. 33 (1993); Douglas Ivor Brandon et al., Special Project, *Self Help: Extra-Judicial Rights, Privileges and Remedies in Contemporary American Society,* 37 Vand. L. Rev. 845, 937, 1040 (1984). *See also* Smith v. Chipman, 348 P.2d 441, 442 (Or. 1960) (quoting 3, 4 William Blackstone, Commentaries 1024 (Lewis ed.)). Landlord distress (*distraint* is a broader term for self-help relief, *see* Davis v. Odell, 729 P.2d 1117, 1121 (Kan. 1986) (*distraint* is any seizure of personalty to enforce a lien, while the stress refers to landlord distraint for past rent)) has been found not to violate due process in the post *Flagg Bros.* context. *See* Luria Bros. & Co. v. Allen, 672 F.2d 347 (3d Cir. 1982); Davis v. Richmond, 512 F.2d 201 (1st Cir. 1975); Anastasia v. Cosmopolitan Nat'l Bank, 527 F.2d 150 (7th Cir. 1975) (statutory hotel keepers lien not state action).

correspondingly less when the last step in the private process is resort to public judicial machinery.[309]

The permissible range of self-governance can be tested by constructing an analytical framework such as a respondent might use to challenge private enforcement actions.[310] It is useful to construct such a framework based essentially on the facts involved in the Usenet newsgroup—alt.current-events.net-abuse, (ACENA)—which has "authorized" an anonymous enforcer known as *cancelmoose* to delete messages violating certain "rules" against advertising adopted by the group. Suppose a would-be advertiser has her advertisement canceled by a member of the ACENA group. If the advertiser wishes to recover damages for this act or to obtain an injunction against a repetition of the act, she first must identify a legal theory that prima facie[311] would entitle her to recover. Those legal theories are considered in **Chapter 4.**

---

[309] Professor Larry Alexander observes that "state action is omni present because all acts take place against a legal background." Larry Alexander, *The Public/Private Distinction and Constitutional Limits on Private Power,* 10 Const. Comment 361, 363–65 & nn.4–12 (1993). Thus there is always state action. This does not mean, however, that the scope for private decision making should be narrowed by subjecting a wider range of private decisions to constitutional standards. *Id.* Even when an act is undeniably state action, it nevertheless may be privileged or clothed with an immunity. *See* Butz v. Economou, 438 U.S. 478 (1978) (Supreme Court decision reaffirming absolute immunity for judicial acts).

[310] The analytical framework is the same one used to challenge public enforcement action. *See generally* Benjamin Woods Labaree, The Boston Tea Party (1964) (describing common-law claims against British soldiers involved in the Boston Massacre); Robert W. Tucker & David C. Hendrickson, The Fall of the First British Empire 130, 262 (1982) (one of the problems of imperial control was jurisdiction of common-law colonial courts over customs officers and army); Henry Paul Monaghan, *State Law Wrongs, State Law Remedies, and the Fourteenth Amendment,* 86 Colum. L. Rev. 979, 999 n.87 (1986) (during much of our history only difference between public officer and private tort feasor was availability of defense of official authorization).

[311] *Prima facie* in this sense means the plaintiff's theory, without regard to possible defenses, privileges, or immunities that the defendant might assert.

CHAPTER 8

INTEROPERABILITY AND COMPATIBILITY

§ 8.1 Description of the Problem and Introduction

The NII involves a relentless evolution towards open systems, and the law of interconnection, interoperability, and compatibility is of greater importance in open systems than in closed systems. Two decades ago, virtually every computer system was complete unto itself. Vendors designed, built, and delivered computing systems that covered every major function needed by a customer. There was no need or expectation that customers would substitute components for those

345

supplied by the primary system vendor or that customers would add components bought from other vendors.

If one bought (or leased) a payroll and financial accounting system from IBM, IBM supplied the CPU, the disk drives, the terminals, the printers, and any networks necessary to tie the terminals to the CPU. If one bought a word processing system from Wang, CPT, or Syntrex, one got a minicomputer, a few terminals, one or more printers, and disk storage from one vendor; it was not feasible to attach a Hewlett Packard Laser Jet printer to the proprietary system. When one wanted connections to the telephone system, one went to the one and only telephone company, subscribed to whatever services were available under tariffs filed with the FCC and the applicable state public utility commission, and got consumer premises equipment and any modems from the same company.

The breakup of the telephone company, the PC revolution, and the Internet have changed all that. Now, customers expect choices; they expect to mix and match hardware and software from different vendors. Mixing and matching is possible only if the different components actually match. That means they must have standard interfaces; in other words they must be compatible and they must interoperate.

It is important to understand that compatibility and interoperability can be achieved without standardization. For example, Microsoft and WordPerfect Corporation have not agreed on a file format for word processing documents. Nevertheless, current versions of both Microsoft Word and WordPerfect accommodate the other vendor's file formats almost transparently because each word processing program translates the other's formats on the fly. So neither agreement on a private standard nor a regulatory mandate is necessary if the technology easily allows simultaneous format translation.

When a vendor makes this difficult, customers are dissatisfied and the vendor loses market share. In addition, suppliers of components that might be attached to the vendor's system are deprived of market opportunities. In many instances, customer dissatisfaction will exert influence through market forces to ensure appropriate types of interconnection, compatibility, and interoperability. It is only when market forces do not achieve this result that the law needs to intervene.

This chapter complements **Chapter 2. Chapter 2** focuses on access duties in general, obligations based on common law and antitrust law, to overcome a refusal to permit access. This chapter focuses on a narrower subset of essentially the same questions; it focuses on agency regulation and private standards agreements as means of assuring interconnection, compatibility, and interoperability at a relatively technical level, more or less at the first four layers of the OSI stack.[1]

---

[1] The Open Systems Interconnection (OSI) is a layered model of standards and conventions for communication between computer systems. Uyless Black, OSI: A Model for Computer Communications Standards (1991). The OSI has seven layers: physical, data link, network, transport, session, presentation, and application, from lowest to highest. The first four levels include defining signals (physical), identifying bits in relation to place in the data unit (data link), switching protocols (network), and quality (transport).

Most compatibility and interoperability in components of the NII are assured, not by adherence to government technical requirements, but by adherence to privately developed standards. Private standards development efforts can accommodate expertise, entrepreneurial preferences, and actual experience better than governmental decision-making processes. It is widely perceived in the United States that the government should defer to private standards whenever possible.[2]

Nevertheless, there are at least three problems that limit the effectiveness of private standard setting. First, the economics of private standard setting suggest that some situations exist in which private parties will not agree voluntarily on a standard, or if a standard is agreed upon, it will not be widely adopted. Second, private standards can be used to inhibit competition, and antitrust doctrine has evolved to impose certain requirements on standard setting activities if they are to avoid antitrust liability. Third, a number of the largest private standards organizations charge very high prices for copies of their standards documents, limiting their availability to smaller entrepreneurs. They generally have not made technical information on standards available through the NII itself, but only in paper form. Nevertheless, in many cases market forces, without any special legal intervention, are adequate to ensure compatibility and interoperability.

This chapter reviews the economics of private standards setting and the legal framework for imposing governmental standards, reviewing some recent standardization proceedings at the FCC that represent good examples of government policy-making. Then it considers how the antitrust laws constrain private standard setting activities, concluding with an evaluation of existing and emerging institutions for NII standard setting.

§ 8.2   Infrastructure and Interoperability Requirements

The public needs an infrastructure, a system in which all the pieces work together rather than a collection of largely independent proprietary communication services. The need for infrastructure justifies government intervention with respect to communications and information because of the existence of network externalities. A consumer who connects to a communication service that is not connected to other communication services enjoys less utility than if there are interconnections. The increase in utility with the larger scope of interconnected networks is *network externality*.[3]

---

[2] Office of Management and Budget, Revision of OMB Circular No. A-119, Notice of Implementation, 58 Fed. Reg. 57,643 (Oct. 26, 1993) (circular revised to foster greater agency use of voluntary standards).

[3] Of course, the same level of network externalities can arise from a single network with the same scope as multiple interconnected networks. In other words, in terms of network externalities, consumers may enjoy as much utility from a single monopoly as from interconnected but independent providers. The point is that consumer utility suffers if the market structure is disconnected multiple providers.

In certain circumstances, the presence of network externalities serves as a sufficient economic incentive for private sector decision makers to make the interconnections on their own. However, the economic literature suggests that there is an important range of circumstances in which private decision making will not lead to compatibility and interconnection, thus depriving consumers of the benefits of network externalities.[4] In other words, network effects sometimes are a public good[5] that suppliers have difficulty internalizing into their preference functions.[6] The literature on standard setting suggests that markets will adopt standards only in certain circumstances of market structure, unlikely to exist uniformly throughout the infrastructure. NII regulatory concepts must assure compatibility and interoperability of various parts of the infrastructure. Regulatory intervention may be appropriate to ensure that the country gets a

---

[4] Michael L. Katz & Carl Shapiro, *Network Externalities, Competition, and Compatibility,* 75 Am. Econ. Rev. 424, 425 (1985) (consumption externalities give rise to demand-side economies of scale; multiple fulfilled expectations equilibrium may exist for given set of cost and utility functions; if consumers expect a seller to be dominant, then consumers are willing to pay for the firm's product and the firm will be dominant; firms' joint incentives for product compatibility are lower than social incentives; firms with good reputations and large existing networks will oppose compatibility even though welfare might be increased by a move to compatibility while firms with small networks or weak reputations will favor compatibility even if social costs of compatibility outweigh benefits); Joseph Farrell & Carl Shapiro, *Dynamic Competition with Switching Costs,* 19 Rand J. Econ. 123 (1988) (when switching costs exist, established firms keep their prices high enough to allow new entrants to serve new customers because of inability by established firms to discriminate between new customers and existing customers; switching costs thus induce more than efficient levels of new entry, unless high economies of scale or network externalities exist—in which case the incumbent tends to serve all buyers); Carmen Matutes & Pierre Regibeau, *"Mix and Match": Product Compatibility Without Network Externalities,* 19 Rand J. Econ. 221 (1988) (product compatibility increases range of consumer choices resulting in generally higher consumer and social surplus when full compatibility prevails); Nicholas Economides, *Desirability of Compatibility in the Absence of Network Externalities,* 79 Am. Econ. Rev. 1165 (1989) (*unbundling* (producing individual components compatible with components of other producers) instead of *bundling* (producing systems with components that are incompatible with components of competing producers) produces higher prices and profits); Michael L. Katz & Carl Shapiro, *Product Introduction with Network Externalities; Symposium on Compatibility,* 40 J. Indus. Econ. 55 (1992) (in general, firms introducing new technologies are biased against compatibility, but if compatibility is a practical prerequisite to entry, existing firms prefer incompatibility, and new entrants prefer compatibility; preference for new firms against compatibility arises from extra design cost to achieve compatibility and may produce a bandwagon effect in favor of the new technology; but sophisticated licensing results in compatibility and raises total surplus); Michael L. Katz & Carl Shapiro, *Network Adoption in the Presence of Network Externalities,* 94 J. Pol. Econ. 822 (1986) (markets are biased toward nonstandardization because consumers ignore effects on other consumers when making consumption decisions; when standardization does occur, the wrong standard may be chosen).

[5] *See* Robert C. Ellickson, *Property in Land,* 102 Yale L.J. 1315, 1384 (1993) (explaining public good characteristic as justification for government owned roads in a regime of private property).

[6] When a producer internalizes a factor into its preference function, the producer makes economic decisions based on that factor, along with others.

national infrastructure and not an electronic archipelago of proprietary islands, navigation among which is extremely difficult.[7]

§ 8.3 Economics of Standard Setting

Private parties agree voluntarily on standards only in certain market structures.[8] When one producer has significant market share, it will not agree on a standard that differs significantly from its own, and it also may be unwilling to give up all proprietary claims to its own standard. Thus, IBM should have been reluctant to agree on a networking standard significantly different from its SNA standard, and Microsoft should be reluctant to agree on a microcomputer operating system standard other than MSDOS and Windows. A market in which there is a single dominant producer is likely to be able to standardize only on terms agreeable to the dominant producer. Whether that is open or proprietary in the intellectual property sense is up to the dominant producer's assessment of its economic interest.[9] Additionally, when there are sharp disagreements about the technical merits of different standards, it is harder to standardize.

Commentators Besen and Saloner[10] have identified two variables that influence the standards setting process and its outcomes. The first variable involves economic incentives for agreement on a standard. Incentives are the difference between the costs and benefits of a standard.[11] Incentives are low when the transaction costs of standards development swamp the benefits, as with weights and measures.[12] Incentives also are low when standardization eliminates a

---

[7] For example, Sweden's new telecommunications law, involving more deregulation than U.S. telecommunications law, imposes a general obligation to interconnect with other carriers. See § 8.15.

[8] *See generally* Stanley Besen & Garth Saloner, *The Economics of Telecommunications Standards* [hereinafter Beson & Saloner], *in* Changing the Rules: Technological Change, International Competition, and Regulation in Communications (R. Crandall & K. Flamm eds., 1989) [hereinafter Changing the Rules]; Michael I. Krauss, *Regulation vs. Markets in the Development of Standards*, 3 S. Cal. Interdisciplinary L.J. 781 (advocacy of reliance on markets rather than regulation to set standards), 784–98 (characterizing standards as public goods and reviewing arguments and theory as to why market may not be able to achieve appropriate standardization) (1994); Joseph Farrell, *Standardization and Intellectual Property*, 30 Jurimetrics J. 35 (mobilizing arguments against affording intellectual property protection to standards; explaining the dynamics of standard setting and acknowledging that the demand for variety may constrain standardization, standardization may retard innovation, sunk cost and training may retard standardization), 40–41 nn.13–17 (vested interests in different standards and antitrust prohibitions on enforcement discourage market participants from agreeing), 44–45 & nn.21–25 (strong intellectual property protection retards formal standardization) (1989).

[9] For example, Microsoft has been relatively open with its architecture for MSDOS and Windows; Apple has not been open with its operating system.

[10] *See generally* Besen & Saloner at 177.

[11] The benefits subelement of the Besen & Saloner incentive variable captures the public goods and network externalities effects.

[12] Besen & Saloner at 178.

competitive advantage, easing entry by new competitors and easing customer shifts to those competitors.[13] The second variable is the intensity of disagreement on the merits of the content of a standard.[14]

Besen and Saloner identify three interesting cases, representing permutations of the values of the two variables. In the first, *pure coordination* case, incentives are high and there is not intense disagreement about the content of the standard. Most standards set by standards-setting organizations involve the pure coordination case.

In the second, *pure public goods* case, incentives are low and disagreement about content of the standard also is low. Establishment of standards for weights and measures, time, and language involve the pure public goods case, in which government mandates are likely.

In the third, *pure private goods* case, incentives are low and disagreement about content of the standard is high.[15] Stalemate in public or private standards setting efforts frequently involves the pure private goods case. Sometimes, a potential de facto standards setter, like Ashton-Tate or Lotus, tries to prevent other firms from using its proprietary technology. When this happens, the supplier with incentives to prevent spread of the standard uses intellectual property concepts to convert what otherwise would be a public good into a private good, excluding others from using the private good. In this case, the disincentive to standardization by certain firms overwhelms the potential incentive of other firms to standardize.

Ultimately, whether consensus can be achieved in private cooperative standards setting depends on whether a small number of participants can prevent an effective standard from emerging, and whether side payments are possible.[16] Conflict can be resolved, of course, frequently by the incentives resulting from the need to be compatible with the market leader—but only when the market leader is willing to provide the basis for a standard. [17]

§ 8.4   Legal Framework for Imposing Standards

The FCC has flexible authority to impose standards as part of its authority to regulate common carriers and to license radio transmissions.[18] As noted in

---

[13] *Id.* at 179.

[14] *Id.* at 180 (citing disagreement about VHS and Beta videocassette standard).

[15] The name comes from the fact that, in this case, an acceptable standard will favor a particular product. Adoption of MSDOS or Postscript as de facto standards involved the pure private goods case.

[16] Besen & Saloner at 185.

[17] Besen and Saloner associate with the fourth case the emergence of the IBM personal computer and the MSDOS operating system as the industry standards for microcomputing from 1984–91. When there is no industry leader in terms of market share, conflict resulting from eager participation by all interested parties in the standardization process can be resolved by side payments and the formation of coalitions, such as has occurred with the emergence of two competing drafters of Unix standards. Besen & Saloner at 183.

[18] **Ch. 7** generally reviews FCC regulatory authority.

§ **8.8,** the FCC also has general authority to require standardization. In addition, interoperability requirements could be imposed under antitrust monopolization and essential facility theories.[19] Interoperability is needed the most when the absence of it represents a barrier to accessing a particular market and that barrier overlaps the bottleneck aspect of essential facilities analysis. Usually, interoperability or at least interconnection imposes only modest barriers on the burdened entity and thus would satisfy the reasonableness-of-access element of essential facilities analysis.[20] Nevertheless, there is little precedent for using essential facilities doctrine to force interconnections, aside from the *Terminal Railroad Association* case itself,[21] so a significant part of the justification for such interpretation of essential facilities doctrine must be based on public policy. Otherwise, interconnection and interoperability requirements must be imposed by statute or administrative agency rule.

The policy and legal issues with respect to interoperability requirements get more difficult the farther one moves along the spectrum from pure conduit to pure content.[22] It is relatively easy to conclude that interoperability in basic transmission and switching should be extended from analog voice communications to digital communications. Internet-like functionality probably could be required at least for the basic E-mail, remote log in, and file transfer functions well known to Internet users. It is less clear that compatibility requirements could be imposed on activities closely related to content. For example, a requirement that one menuing system or retrieval syntax be compatible with all others could erect a significant barrier to innovation, just as requiring all computer programming languages or language compilers to be compatible with all others would represent a huge barrier to innovation in the development of compilers of programming languages.

Moreover, the closer one gets to requiring compatibility in content, the harder it is to justify the requirement under the First Amendment.[23] While content-neutral regulation is permissible under the First Amendment even though it has an impact on communication of content, a mandate for compatibility in content is, in effect, a prohibition on incompatible expression. That raises large First Amendment problems.[24]

---

[19] See **Ch. 2.**

[20] See **Ch. 2.**

[21] United States v. Terminal R.R. Ass'n, 224 U.S. 383 (1912). See **Ch. 2.**

[22] While the distinction between information services and communication services has proved insufficiently clear to remain the organizing premise for telecommunications regulation, it is useful as an aid in discussing regulation. This book uses "content" to describe activities and information having lots of authorship and traditional publisher relationship, and "conduit" to describe activities and information services having almost nothing to do with content.

[23] *See generally* Angela J. Campbell, *Political Campaigning in the Information Age: A Proposal for Protecting Political Candidates' Use of On-Line Computer Services,* 38 Vill. L. Rev. 517, 542–44 (1993) (overview of First Amendment principles relating to must-carry and right-of-reply regulation).

[24] *See* Turner Broadcasting Sys., Inc. v. Federal Communications Comm'n, 114 S. Ct. 2445, 2471–72 (1994) (invalidating a lower court decision upholding cable television must-carry rules and remanding to lower court for development of better record on whether local television's

§ 8.5 —FCC's CEI and ONA Rules

Among the most aggressive legally imposed interconnection and interoperability requirements are the FCC's comparably efficient interconnection (CEI) and open network architecture (ONA) requirements.[25] As a part of the transition from a regulated to a deregulated telecommunications industry, the FCC required local exchange telephone carriers, who still possess market power, to unbundle their services. This made it easier for other firms to compete in offering certain unregulated services. The unbundling requirements have taken the form of comparably efficient interconnection (CEI) and open network architecture (ONA). The two are interrelated and were imposed in a broader context of defining the interface between regulated and monopoly telephone services and unregulated, competitive telecommunication services.[26]

The FCC adopted a two-part approach for regulating enhanced or data processing services[27] over the telecommunications network.[28] First, the FCC developed cost allocation methods to minimize the regional Bell operating companies' (BOCs) ability to shift costs from their unregulated to regulated activities.[29] Second, the FCC developed regulations specifically designed to

---

survival was jeopardized by unrestricted cable television activity and whether there were less restrictive means of achieving governmental interests in assuring an outlet for local broadcasting). The case illustrates First Amendment analysis of justification for regulations that burden communication.

[25] ONA and CEI also are regulatory initiatives imposing access requirements. Access requirements are considered in **Ch. 2.** The research and initial drafting for this section was done by Martin F. Noonan, law clerk to the author.

[26] The Court of Appeals for the Ninth Circuit has recently remanded for reconsideration the FCC's regulatory policy of the enhanced services industry described in this chapter. *See* California v. FCC, 39 F.3d 919, 923 (9th Cir. 1994) [hereinafter California III].

[27] The FCC divides telecommunication services into two categories: basic and enhanced services. The FCC defines *basic service* as the "regulated common carrier communication services, which consists largely of plain old telephone service (POTS)." California v. FCC, 905 F.2d 1217, 1223 n.3 (9th Cir. 1990) [hereinafter California I]. The FCC defines *enhanced services* as "unregulated data processing services which use the telephone network to convey information from remote computers to customers' terminals." *Id.* Enhanced services use computerized data processing to provide an expanding variety of information to users over the telephone communication network. California III, 39 F.3d at 923. Examples of enhanced services include the Dow Jones News, Lexis, and "Dial It" sport scores. California I, 905 F.2d at 1223 n.3.

[28] The regional Bell operating companies monopolize the telephone communications network. California III, 39 F.3d at 923. The Bell operating companies control the local telephone exchanges that provide the only access to the telecommunication network. California I, 905 F.2d at 1224 & n.5.

[29] Report and Order, *In re* Amendment of Section 64.702 of the Commission's Rules and Regulations, Docket No. 85-229, 104 F.C.C.2d 958, 1010–11 (1986) [hereinafter Computer III—Phase I Order]. The FCC was concerned that the BOCs would exploit their monopolies over the telephone network by cross-subsidization. California v. FCC, 4 F.3d 1505, 1508 (9th Cir. 1993) [hereinafter California II]. Cross-subsidization would allow the BOCs to pass the costs of their enhanced services to regular telephone ratepayers who are required to use the BOC because of their monopoly over local telephone service.

prevent BOCs from discriminating against competing providers of enhanced services.[30] To achieve this second objective, the FCC adopted a three-part antidiscrimination policy:[31] First, the FCC endorsed an open network policy, which required the BOCs to provide all enhanced service providers with equal access to the components of the BOCs' telecommunication network.[32] Second, the FCC implemented network disclosure rules that required each BOC to notify competing enhanced service providers of changes in the telephone network that may affect enhanced services.[33] Third, the FCC required each BOC to provide competing enhanced service providers with customer proprietary network information (CPNI).[34]

Open Network Architecture

The FCC proposed the development of new technology that would effectively reduce the risk of BOC access discrimination.[35] This new technology involved two development stages: open network architecture (ONA) and comparably efficient interconnection (CEI).[36] The FCC proposed that ONA would be a

---

The FCC has the authority to regulate interstate telecommunications pursuant to the Communications Act of 1934, 47 U.S.C. §§ 151–613 (1988). Although enhanced services involve the use of communications common carriers, the FCC has rejected the argument that it is statutorily required to regulate the enhanced service industry. *See* California I, 905 F.2d at 1224. Instead the FCC favors a regulatory policy that promotes competition in the enhanced service industry, notwithstanding the fact that enhanced service involves a regulated communication component and an unregulated data processing component. California I, 905 F.2d at 1224.

[30] Computer III—Phase I Order, 104 F.C.C.2d at 1026. The FCC was concerned that the BOCs would use their monopoly of the telecommunication network to prevent telephone carriers from entering the enhanced services industry. California III, 39 F.3d at 923. The FCC wanted to prevent the BOCs from unfairly competing in the enhanced service industry by discriminating against competitors when providing access to telephone transmission facilities. California II, 4 F.3d at 1508.

[31] California I, 905 F.2d at 1229.

[32] California III, 39 F.3d 919, 922 (9th Cir. 1994). The FCC required that the telephone network be as accessible to competitors as it is to the BOCs. California I, 905 F.2d 1217, 1229 (9th Cir. 1990).

[33] California I, 905 F.2d at 1229. The FCC included this notice requirement to permit enhanced service providers to take advantage of the changes. *Id.*

[34] *Id.* at 1229–30. CPNI is information concerning a telephone customer's use of the telephone network. California III, 39 F.3d at 930. CPNI includes "the number of lines ordered, service location, type and class of services purchased, usage levels, and calling patterns." 39 F.3d at 930. This information is valuable to BOCs and competing ESPs in developing and marketing enhanced services, and this information assists ESPs in "identifying potential customers, designing more efficient services, and better meeting customer needs." Nevertheless, customers have proprietary and privacy interests in their CPNI. Therefore, customers may seek to restrict access to their CPNI. 39 F.3d at 930.

[35] California III, 39 F.3d at 925.

[36] *Id.*

long-term safeguard for ensuring equal access to the telecommunication network. The FCC ordered the BOCs to develop ONA plans that would allow enhanced service providers (ESPs) "to achieve maximum flexibility in gaining access to telephone transmission facilities."[37] This would allow ESPs to offer innovative services to consumers.[38] The FCC anticipated technological advances that would allow the BOCs to "unbundle" the basic components of the telecommunication network into "building blocks."[39] The FCC defined these "building blocks" as basic service elements (BSEs).[40] The FCC envisioned that ESPs would be able to purchase only those specific BSEs that were necessary to construct their own innovative services.[41] The FCC subjected all basic network capabilities to the unbundling requirement "including signalling, switching, billing and network management."[42]

The FCC approved an initial plan that divided ONA into three categories:[43] basic service arrangements (BSAs), basic service elements (BSEs), and

---

[37] California III, 39 F.3d 919, 927 (9th Cir. 1994).

[38] Id.

[39] Id. In more technical terms, the FCC required the BOCs to "unbundle" the basic "interconnection arrangements" in the telecommunications network and to provide competitors with the ability to access and use these arrangements without interference from the BOCs. Computer III-Phase I Order, 104 F.C.C.2d 958, 1063–65 (1986).

[40] Computer III-Phase I Order, 104 F.C.C.2d at 1064.

[41] California III, 39 F.3d at 927; Computer III-Phase I Order, 104 F.C.C.2d at 1063–65. The FCC stated that "[s]uch unbundling is essential to give competing enhanced service providers an opportunity to design offerings that utilize network services in a flexible and economical manner. In essence, competitors will pay only for those Basic Service Elements that they use in providing enhanced services." Computer III-Phase I Order, 104 F.C.C.2d at 1040. The FCC intended to allow ESPs to purchase only those elements that are necessary to a specific type of enhanced service. California III, 39 F.3d at 927. The FCC's goal was to prevent the BOCs from limiting access to the telephone network. California III, 39 F.3d at 927. In addition, the unbundled elements were tariffed to prevent overcharges. California III, 39 F.3d at 927.

[42] Computer III-Phase I Order, 104 F.C.C.2d at 1040. To avoid inefficiencies resulting from unnecessary unbundled services, the FCC required the BOCs to collaborate with the enhanced services industry. California II, 4 F.3d 1505, 1509 (9th Cir. 1993). The FCC required the BOCs to develop plans that were justified by expected market demand, were technically and economically feasible, and had "utility as perceived by the enhanced services competitors." California II, 4 F.3d at 1509.

[43] Although these plans did not sufficiently unbundle the BSEs as had been envisioned by the FCC in Computer III-Phase I, the FCC concluded that it did not require "fundamental unbundling . . . at this time." Memorandum Opinion and Order, Filing and Review of Open Network Architecture Plans, Phase I, FCC 88-381, 4 F.C.C.R. 1, 42 (1988) [hereinafter BOC ONA Order]. The FCC emphasized that ONA was a long-term goal and directed the BOCs to amend the initial ONA plans to reflect that ONA would evolve in light of new technological developments. California II, 4 F.3d at 1510.

In 1990 the FCC approved the amended ONA plans submitted by the BOCs. Memorandum Opinion and Order, Filing and Review of Open Network Architecture Plans, Phase I, FCC 90-135, 5 F.C.C.R. 3084, 3104 (1990). Although the amended ONA plans contained limited information on how new technologies will be made available to ESPs, the FCC concluded that the amended ONA plans contained sufficient near-term protection to prevent BOCs from discriminating against ESP competitors. California II, 4 F.3d at 1510.

complementary network services (CNSs).[44] BSAs are the fundamental switching and transport services that allow "an ESP to communicate through the BOC network."[45] An ESP had to purchase some form of BSA to gain access to optional unbundle features, such as BSEs.[46] CNSs were optional unbundled basic service features that end users could obtain to receive an enhanced service.[47]

Comparably Efficient Interconnection

Because ONA required advanced technology to unbundle the basic telephone network services, the FCC established "comparably efficient interconnection" (CEI) plans as an interim development stage that would eventually evolve into ONA.[48] The FCC's policy toward CEI was to ensure that each BOC provided ESPs with connections to the telecommunication network that were substantially equivalent to the interconnections that the BOCs provided for their own enhanced services.[49] In addition, FCC required that each BOC incorporate CEI concepts into its ONA design.[50] In contrast to ONA, CEI entitles ESPs only to the interconnections for enhanced services that the BOCs themselves already provide.[51] CEI plans did not allow competitors to select BSEs to create their own enhanced services.[52]

A major difference between CEI and ONA was that CEI plans had to be approved by the Commission in advance on a service specific basis, while ONA permitted the telephone companies to provide integrated enhanced services without prior Commission approval of service-specific plans. Once ONA plans were approved, the Commission said it would completely lift the Computer II structural separation requirements. They are similar in that both are aimed at allowing enhanced service providers to purchase unbundled elements of BOCs' service.[53]

---

[44] BOC ONA Order, 4 F.C.C.R. at 10.

[45] *Id.*

[46] *Id.*

[47] California II, 4 F.3d 1505, 1510 (9th Cir. 1993).

[48] *Id.* at 1511.

[49] *Id.* The FCC requires BOCs to file a CEI plan for each enhanced service that it provides. *Id.* at 1513.

[50] California I, 905 F.2d 1217, 1233 (9th Cir. 1990).

[51] California III, 39 F.3d 919, 927 (9th Cir. 1994). For a good example, see *In re* Bell Atlantic Company's Offer of Comparably Efficient Interconnection to Providers of Video-Dial Tone-Related Enhanced Services, DA 95-1283, 1995 WL 347960 (June 9, 1995).

[52] *Id.* See California II, 4 F.3d 1505, 1511 (9th Cir. 1993) (stating that ONA applies more broadly to BOC's networks regardless of which enhanced services the BOCs themselves choose to offer). The FCC directed the BOCs to incorporate basic CEI concepts into the overall design of ONA. 4 F.3d at 1511.

[53] *See* Notice of Proposed Rulemaking, *In re* Computer III Further Remand Proceedings: Bell Operating Company Provision of Enhance Services, CC Docket No. 95-20, FCC 95-48, 1995 WL 170713, ¶ 5 (adopted Feb. 7, 1995) (describing CEI); *id.* ¶ 7 (describing ONA and comparing it with CEI); Memorandum Opinion and Order, *In re* Bell Operating Companies Joint Petition for Waiver of Computer II Rules, DA95-36, 1995 WL 11273, ¶ 6 (adopted Jan. 11, 1995) (describing ONA and its relationship to Computer II structural separation requirements).

ONA evolved. In its *Computer III* Phase I Order, the FCC declined to adopt specific network architecture proposals and instead specified certain general criteria for carrier ONA plans. It noted that while it wanted BOCs to provide unbundled service elements, it was "well aware of inefficiencies that might result from unnecessarily unbundled or splintered services, and [it] acknowledged that this unbundling could only occur to the degree that it was technologically feasible."[54] In its *Computer III* Phase I Reconsideration Order, it allowed structural relief for BOCs once they implemented initial ONA services and implemented other nonstructural safeguards, but declined to require "the kind of fundamental unbundling that would allow ESPs to connect their own trunks or loops to BOC's switching facilities."[55] That approach was invalidated in *California III,* which "returns the regulation of BOC enhanced services to a Computer III service-specific CEI plan regime."[56]

§ 8.6 —CMRS Interconnections

Local exchange phone carriers must provide interconnection to cellular and other commercial mobile radio services unless the requested interconnection is not technically feasible or "economically reasonable."[57] Complaints of violation of the requirement may be filed with the FCC under section 208 of the Communications Act.[58] Local exchange carriers and commercial mobile radio service (CMRS) providers must pay each other reasonable compensation for traffic originating on the other.[59]

In April 1995, however, the FCC decided not to impose a general interconnection requirement on CMRS systems, including paging, specialized mobile radio (SMR), personal communication systems (PCS), and cellular providers.[60] The Commission found it premature to propose or adopt rules of general applicability requiring direct interconnection. Although cellular service has become "a staple of modern telecommunication service, many of its competitors are just beginning to emerge."[61] While CMRS providers are designated as common carriers by the Omnibus Budget Reconciliation Act,[62] the imposition

---

[54] Notice of Proposed Rulemaking, 1995 WL 170713, ¶ 15 (describing evolution of ONA).

[55] *Id.*

[56] Memorandum Opinion and Order, 1995 WL 11273, ¶ 29.

[57] 47 C.F.R. § 20.11 (a) (1994).

[58] *Id.*

[59] *Id.*

[60] Second Notice of Proposed Rulemaking, *In re* Interconnection and Resale Obligations Pertaining to Commercial Mobile Radio Services, CC Docket No. 94-54, FCC 95-149, 1995 WL 233051 (Apr. 5, 1995).

[61] *Id.* ¶ 2.

[62] *Id.* ¶ 22.

of interconnection obligations historically has been conditioned on finding bottlenecks—monopoly power—to exist.[63]

In general, the Commission thought "interconnectivity of mobile communications networks promotes the public interest because it enhances access to all networks, provides valuable network redundancy, allows for greater flexibility in communications, and makes communication services more attractive to consumers. It is one further step toward a ubiquitous 'network of networks.'"[64] It tentatively concluded that "efficient interconnection" would serve the public interest; that market power analysis should be the basis for imposing specific interconnection obligations; and that consideration also be given to broader public policies such as ensuring broad access to the networks of the future.[65] It emphasized that while it was not imposing general interconnection obligations, it reserved the power to intervene in the event of a refusal by a CMRS provider of a reasonable request to interconnect.[66] In other words, it made it clear that it would receive and adjudicate complaints of unreasonable refusals of interconnection.

Roaming is a particular form of interconnection in the cellular industry. The Commission expressed the view that roaming capability and connections required to support roaming are "critically important to the development of "network of networks." It expressed the determination to continue to monitor the availability of roaming, expressing the "hope" that all CMRS providers would implement nationwide seamless roaming networks and offer roaming service to interested subscribers at attractive, cost-based rates.[67] On the other hand, it also concluded that no regulatory action was necessary at the time it issued the order.[68]

Another form of interconnection is resale of one carrier's services by another. Historically, carriers opposed resale because it undercut price discrimination.[69] Thereafter, the FCC imposed an obligation on cellular carriers to permit resale, limiting that obligation in order to provide incentives for resellers to build out their networks.[70] Some in the industry also proposed a requirement that cellular providers allow cellular resellers to install their own switching equipment between the cellular networks mobile telephone switching office (MTSO) and

---

[63] *Compare id.* ¶ 16 (arguments of CMRS providers in favor of bottleneck prerequisite) *with id.* ¶ 23 (other contentions that there is no bottleneck requirement).

[64] *Id.* ¶ 28.

[65] Second Notice of Proposed Rulemaking, 1995 WL 233051, ¶ 41.

[66] *Id.* ¶ 43.

[67] *Id.* ¶ 56.

[68] *Id.*

[69] Second Notice of Proposed Rulemaking, *In re* Interconnection and Resale Obligations Pertaining to Commercial Mobile Radio Services, CC Docket No. 94-54, FCC 95-149, 1995 WL 233051, ¶ 60 (Apr. 5, 1995) (history of resale obligations in wireline industry).

[70] *Id.* at ¶¶ 61–62.

the facilities of the LEC and IXC (interexchange carrier).[71] The Commission concluded tentatively that the existing obligation on cellular providers to permit resale should be extended to apply to CMRS providers in general "unless there is a showing that permitting resale would not be technically feasible or economically reasonable for a specific class of CMRS providers."[72] It thought a time limitation on the obligation of one facilities-based CMRS provider to permit another facilities-based CMRS provider to resell its services was appropriate,[73] but did not generally impose a reseller's switch requirement.[74] The FCC noted complaints filed by two cellular resellers against two different cellular licensees, claiming that a cellular licensee's refusal to permit interconnections with the cellular reseller's switches violates sections 332(c)(1)(B) and 201(a) of the Communications Act, expressing its intention to address those complaint proceedings separately.[75]

§ 8.7 —Enhanced Service Provider Obligations under the Communications Act

There are two barriers to FCC-imposed interconnection obligations on enhanced service providers—one legal, and the other policy-based. Legally, Title II of the Communications Act at § 201 imposes interconnection obligations only on common carriers. The CMRS proceeding occurred because the Congress had declared CMRS to be common carriage. Absent such a characterization, Title II does not provide authority for interconnection duties. As noted in **Chapter 7,** the FCC consistently has found enhanced service, including information services,[76] not to be common carriage. Thus, any interconnection obligation would have to have its source in something other than Title II of the present Communications Act. One such source is the general authority to impose conditions on licensees of radio transmitters, necessary for cellular, paging, and PCS systems.[77]

---

[71] *Id.* ¶ 78 (characterizing views of NCRA and CSI/ComTech).

[72] *Id.* ¶ 83.

[73] *Id.* ¶ 90.

[74] *Id.* ¶ 95.

[75] Second Notice of Proposed Rulemaking, *In re* Interconnection and Resale Obligations Pertaining to Commercial Mobile Radio Services, CC Docket No. 94-54, FCC 95-149, 1995 WL 233051, ¶ 97 (citing Cellnet Communications, Inc. v. New Par, Inc., DBA Cellular One, File No. WB/ENF-F-ENF-95-010 (filed Feb. 16, 1995); Nationwide Cellular Serv., Inc. v. Comcast Cellular Communications, Inc., File No. WB/ENF-F-ENF-95-011 (filed Feb. 16, 1995)).

[76] *In re* Amendment of section 64.702 of the Commission Rules and Regulations, (*Computer II*), 77 F.C.C. 2d 384, 428–32 (1980); *Computer III-Phase I Order* Docket No. 85-229, 104 F.C.C. 2d 958, 1123 (1986).

[77] See generally **Ch. 7.**

Even for those aspects of the NII that are statutory common carriage under the Communications Act, the FCC's CMRS general interconnection order,[78] reviewed in § **8.6,** illustrates policy reasons why it might forbear to impose interconnection obligations as a general matter: uncertainty as to technological architectures, and the possibility that market forces will be sufficient to induce whatever degree of interconnection is necessary in the public interest. The FCC posture reflected in that statement is an appropriate one. The Commission remains available to adjudicate specific cases of unreasonable refusals to interconnect, while withholding a regulatory mandate that might distort the evolution of technology.

§ 8.8   —Address Assignment

Address standards are essential to the functioning of a communications and information infrastructure. Not only must there be a standard way of expressing addresses so they can be processed by computers, there must also be a master database (which may be distributed) of addresses of participating human or physical entities. Historically, telephone numbers—the addressing scheme for the voice telephone system—were assigned by Bell Labs, and after the breakup of Bell Labs by Bellcore. By early 1994, Bellcore had advised the FCC it no longer wished to administer the North American numbering plan (NANP), and the FCC issued a notice on how telephone numbers should be assigned. [79] The FCC tentatively concluded that ministerial administration of the NANP should be the responsibility of a new, single, nongovernment entity that it could establish. It sought comment on whether a new board also should be established to help in establishing numbering policy and in resolving disputes.[80]

The FCC noted that number administration actually involves four separate, but related functions: policy making, dispute resolution, maintenance of numbering databases, and processing applications for numbers.[81] The FCC thought it had authority under § 201(a), Title II of the Federal Communications Act, to perform these functions because "telephone numbers are an indispensable part of the 'facilities and regulations' for operating space . . . 'through routes' of physical interconnections between carriers."[82] It nevertheless thought efficiency

---

[78] Second Notice of Proposed Rulemaking, *In re* Interconnection and Resale Obligations Pertaining to Commercial Mobile Radio Services, CC Docket No. 94-54, FCC 95-149, 1995 WL 233051 (Apr. 5, 1995).

[79] Notice of Proposed Rulemaking, *In re* Administration of the North American Numbering Plan, CC Docket No. 92-237, FCC 94-79, 9 F.C.C.R. 2068, 1994 WL 282918 (Apr. 4, 1994) [hereinafter NANPNPRM].

[80] NANPNPRM ¶ 4.

[81] *Id.* ¶ 7.

[82] *Id.* ¶ 8.

would be served better by assigning the responsibility to a new nongovernment entity.[83] Regarding the policy making function, the FCC noted comments from a number of participants in its earlier inquiry proceeding claiming that consensus procedures and private standard setting organizations are cumbersome and that they "favor the parties with the most resources because active participation requires 'incredible stamina and enormous, dedicated resources.' "[84]

The FCC's approach to the assignment of telephone numbers is a reasonable indicator of the issues that arise in the assignment of Internet addresses. With the privatization of the Internet, the National Science Foundation recognized the need to establish one or more new entities to assign Internet addresses and maintain databases of such addresses. As part of its privatization of the Internet backbone services, the NSF established an InterNIC, composed in part of the Internet registration service,[85] which has responsibility for registering Internet domain names.

The FCC's approach to telephone number assignment is useful generally in two respects. First, it recognizes residual FCC authority over the question, authority which might extend beyond common carrier telephone service. Second, it concludes a single private entity is the best way to handle the administration. This approach will, however, become more challenging as mobile communications activities through PCS and mobile Internet connections require more sophisticated databases to keep track of where the physical entity associated with a number or an address is located.

§ 8.9 —Encryption Infrastructure

As **Chapter 9** explains, widespread use of encryption in open systems like the Internet requires the existence of an effective infrastructure for associating public keys with the entities or persons to whom they belong. While not purely a standards setting problem, there is certain standardization that must occur in the form of certificate authorities envisioned by RFC 1422[86] and the Utah digital signature act discussed in **Chapter 9.**

---

[83] *Id.* ¶ 16 ("we seek comment on whether we should establish, subject to our oversight, a new non-government entity to handle future administration of the NANP").

[84] *Id.* ¶ 20.

[85] The registration service initially was run by Network Solutions, Inc., of Herndon, VA, ds.internic.net.

[86] S. Kent, Privacy Enhancement for Internet Electronic Mail: Part II Certificate-Based Key Management: RFC 1422 (1993) (available from Internet Engineering Task Force) (defining architecture and infrastructure for authentication system based on public key encryption techniques). A Request for Comment (RFC) is a standard issued by the Internet Engineering Task Force, the body responsible for Internet technical standards.

§ 8.10   Private Standards Agreements under Sherman Act with Government Involvement

As previously noted, private standard setting must function through mechanisms that do not run afoul of the antitrust laws. This section and §§ **8.11** and **8.12** explore the boundaries of private standard setting resulting from the antitrust laws. The Sherman Antitrust Act conceptually covers organizations adopting standards. It makes a big difference, however, whether the standard-setting body is governmental or private.[87]

The United States Supreme Court has long held that Sherman Act liability is limited to combinations of private individuals or entities and that valid acts of government are not violative despite anticompetitive effects.[88] Government affects trade by virtually all of its legislative, administrative, or judicial actions,[89] and these are not antitrust violations.

Difficulty arises when private individuals or entities urge the government to shape competitive conditions in their favor.[90] If the Sherman Act burdens the private requests, the First Amendment privilege to petition the government

---

[87] A private conspiracy to discourage competition and restrain trade is unlawful under § 1 of the Sherman Act. 15 U.S.C. § 1 (1988). However, "[i]n politics, a successful conspiracy is called a majority." Sandy River Nursing Care Ctr. v. National Council on Compensation Ins., 798 F. Supp. 810, 815 (D. Me. 1992).

[88] Standard Oil Co. v. United States, 221 U.S. 1, 51–62 (1911). *See, e.g.,* Parker v. Brown, 317 U.S. 341, 350–51 (1945) (upholding California's restrictions on competition and prices among raisin growers against Sherman Act challenge); City of Columbia v. Omni Outdoor Advertising, Inc., 499 U.S. 365 (1991) ("unlike private actors acting in combination, disinterested governmental decision-makers who take measures to inhibit competition are accountable politically and procedurally to those affected by the anticompetitive measures"); Sessions Tank Liners, Inc. v. Joor Mfg., Inc., 17 F.3d 295, 300 (9th Cir. 1994) (citing Parker, 317 U.S. at 352). For a discussion of the development of antitrust immunity, see Note, *The Quagmire Thickens: A Post-California Motor View of the Antitrust and Constitutional Ramifications of Petitioning the Government,* 42 U. Cin. L. Rev. 281 (1973) (*Parker* served as basis for decisions in Eastern R.R. Presidents Conference v. Noerr Motor Freight, Inc., 365 U.S. 127 (1961) and California Motor Transp. Co. v. Trucking Unltd., 404 U.S. 508 (1972)).

[89] R. Bork, The Antitrust Paradox: A Policy at War with Itself 347 (1978) [hereinafter Bork]. Bork observes governmental impact not only in the expected areas of legislation and judicial decree, but equally in local government through licensing authorities, planning boards, zoning commissions, health departments, etc., that control and qualify the would-be competitors' access to the marketplace. *See* City of Columbia v. Omni Outdoor Advertising, Inc., 499 U.S. 365 (1991) (state action doctrine immunizes municipality from antitrust liability for billboard regulations that made it difficult for new competitor to enter market).

[90] There is a "fuzzy boundary" in anticompetitive activity between economic exercise by a competing business entity and political conduct by a private interest seeking to gain some favorable action by the government. Sandy River Nursing Care Ctr. v. National Council on Compensation Ins., 798 F. Supp. 810, 814 (D. Me. 1992).

collides with section 1.[91] The *Noerr* Doctrine mediates the collision. The *Noerr* Doctrine immunizes from antitrust liability any efforts to petition the government for anticompetitive actions.[92] The doctrine is framed by three cases. The first, which gives the doctrine its name, is *Eastern Railroad Presidents Conference v. Noerr Motor Freight, Inc.*[93] There the Court extended the *Standard Oil* immunity for government to include any actions taken in an effort to influence governmental actions.[94] In the second case, *United Mine Workers v. Pennington,*[95] the Court added to the doctrine the concept that petitioning activity is immune from antitrust law even if it is part of a larger scheme that constitutes a violation. The illegality of the entire scheme does not preclude protection of the specific actions involving petitioning activity.[96] Administrative

---

[91] "Congress shall make no law respecting an establishment of religion, or prohibiting the free exercise thereof; or abridging the freedom of speech, or of the press; or the right of the people peaceably to assemble, and to petition the government for a redress of grievances." U.S. Const. amend. I. *See generally* Henry H. Perritt, Jr. & James A. Wilkinson, *Economic Pressure and Antitrust,* 23 Am. U. L. Rev. 627 (1974) (developing antitrust theory applicable to boycotts protesting governmental price controls).

[92] Eastern R.R. Presidents Conference v. Noerr Motor Freight, Inc., 365 U.S. 127, 136 (1961). The Noerr Doctrine is referred to by some courts as the Noerr-Pennington Doctrine. See Alvord-Polk, Inc. v. F. Schumacher & Co., 37 F.3d 996 (3d Cir. 1994); Greater Rockford Energy & Technology Corp. v. Shell Oil Co., 998 F.2d 391 (7th Cir. 1993).

[93] 365 U.S. 127 (1965). In *Noerr,* a group of railroad companies conducted a publicity campaign designed to promote legislative action that would be detrimental to the trucking industry. *Id.* at 129.

[94] *Id.* at 136 (citing Standard Oil v. United States, 221 U.S. 1 (1911)). The Court based its holding first on the belief that restricting such influential actions would deny government of the feedback it needs to function properly, as well as infringing on the right to petition the government. *Id.* at 137–38. Secondly, the Court noted that the Sherman Act was drafted to limit business, not political, activity. *Id.* at 140–41. Therefore, regardless of the anticompetitive intent of the publicity campaign, the railroads were immune from antitrust action. *Id.* at 144–45. The Court relied substantially on the original discussions of the Sherman Act. *See* 21 Cong. Rec. 2562 (1980) (statement of Senator Sherman) ("[The Sherman Act] does not interfere in the slightest degree with voluntary associations made to affect public opinion to advance the interests of a particular trade or occupation."). *See also* Sandy River Nursing Care Ctr. v. National Council on Compensation Ins., 798 F. Supp. 810, 817 (D. Me. 1992) (holding that insurance lobby's pressure on state legislature for grant of permission for higher rates was immune from antitrust liability).

[95] 381 U.S. 657 (1965). United Mine Workers Union took action to influence the secretary of labor in setting a minimum wage for employees of TVA coal contractors and in reducing the TVA's spot market purchases of coal, which were not subject to the minimum wage requirement. This made it difficult for smaller suppliers to compete. *Id.* at 660–61.

[96] Although the union's other activities were found to violate the Sherman Act, its efforts to influence the secretary of labor were immune. *Id.* at 670. Thus, the charges could proceed on the antitrust liability, but damages related to the secretary of labor's actions were to be excluded. *Id.* at 671.

agencies and the judiciary were included in the fold of immunity by *California Motor Transportation Co. v. Trucking Unlimited.*[97]

If a standard-setting body is a government agency, the *Noerr* Doctrine immunizes not only the agency, but also private parties in their attempts legitimately to influence the agency. The legitimacy criterion screens out nongovernmental parties whose petitioning efforts are for no other reason than to interfere with a business competitor.[98] Such interference invokes the "sham exception" of *Noerr,*[99] which withdraws immunity from bogus governmental petitions cloaking strictly anticompetitive actions.[100] Therefore, if the government were to set a standard for electronic publishing and the standard were an existing product, the government itself could not be liable under section 1, and attempts by software manufacturers to promote their own products as candidates for the standard would be covered by an immunity from section 1 as well. Furthermore, a plaintiff alleging a violation of section 1 must prove that injury was caused by the action of the private software manufacturers, not as a result of independent governmental action.[101]

When standards are made by nominally private bodies, two different frameworks for section 1 analysis may be used. The first framework treats the private standards-setting body as though it were the government, based on the functions it performs. The second framework treats the private standard-setting body as a joint venture.[102]

District courts have suggested that some private standard-setting organizations receive a quasi-governmental status, and therefore, efforts to influence such organizations are equivalent to efforts to influence the government.[103] The

---

[97] 404 U.S. 508 (1972). Rival highway carriers instituted administrative and judicial proceedings to prevent potential competitors from entering the industry. *Id.* at 509. The Court extended immunity based on the right to petition to all branches of government. *Id.* at 510. *See also* Greater Rockford Energy & Technology Corp. v. Shell Oil Co., 998 F.2d 391, 397 (7th Cir. 1993) (holding that oil trade organization's efforts to lobby government agencies to dissuade them from backing use of gasohol was not violation of § 1).

[98] 404 U.S. 508, 511 (1972). In City of Columbia v. Omni Outdoor Advertising, Inc., 499 U.S. 365 (1991), the Supreme Court rejected the argument that there should be a conspiracy branch to the sham exception, which would encompass conspiracies between private and public parties to establish governmental policies that would limit competition. Rather, said the Court, the sham exception includes only illicit private uses of the petitioning *process* to restrain trade, as opposed to private uses of the *outcome* of the process.

[99] Eastern R.R. Presidents Conference v. Noerr Motor Freight, Inc., 365 U.S. 127, 144 (1965).

[100] *Id.*

[101] Sessions Tank Liners, Inc. v. Joor Mfg., Inc., 17 F.3d 295, 299 (9th Cir. 1994) (rejecting plaintiff's § 1 argument because injuries "flowed directly from governmental action").

[102] See **Chs. 4** and **5** for antitrust analysis of joint ventures.

[103] *See* Wheeling-Pittsburgh Steel Corp. v. Allied Tube & Conduit Corp., 573 F. Supp. 833, 841 (N.D. Ill. 1983) (finding that petitioning a private standard-setting organization was a logical and appropriate step considering the amount of effort necessary to bring about the same result

two key district court cases accepting quasi-legislative authority treated standards setting as an activity that "normally" would be performed by a government entity.[104] But commentators have questioned clothing a private body with quasi-governmental immunity. Their questions include: Must the organization be a voice for the public interest? If so, does this diminish the adequacy of the representation to the members? Which of the more than 420 private standard-setting organizations[105] should be elevated to, or deleted from, quasi-governmental status?[106]

The Supreme Court addressed the more fundamental of these questions in *Allied Tube & Conduit Corp. v. Indian Head, Inc.*[107] There, the Court held that "where . . . an economically interested party exercises decisionmaking authority in formulating a product standard for a private association that comprises market participants, that party enjoys no *Noerr* immunity from any antitrust liability flowing from the effect the standard has of its own force in the marketplace." This limitation on the quasi-governmental immunity focuses on

1. The economic interests of the actors
2. The private context in which the actions took place
3. The decision-making role of the defendants.[108]

The *Indian Head* Court held that antitrust immunity is not available to a party petitioning a private standards organization whose efforts are essentially commercial with secondary political aspects. Instead, antitrust immunity for petitioning a government standards-setting organization shields only efforts to

---

through government processes); Rush-Hampton Indus., Inc. v. Home Ventilating Inst., 419 F. Supp. 19, 24 (M.D. Fla. 1976) (approval by various building code organizations was equivalent to approval by several government entities). *Accord* Sessions Tank Liners v. Joor Mfg., Inc., 827 F.2d 458, 463 (9th Cir. 1987) (treating standards body as governmental).

[104] In *Rush-Hampton,* the private organization determined the building codes that were routinely adopted by many governmental entities. 419 F. Supp. at 22–23. In *Wheeling-Pittsburgh,* the government was not capable of processing the codes efficiently, therefore, needed to defer judgment on codes to the private standard-setting organization. 573 F. Supp. at 841.

[105] National Bureau of Standards, NBS Special Pub. No. 161, Standards Activities of Organizations in the United States 1 (Aug. 1984). These organizations promulgate more than 32,000 standards.

[106] James D. Hurwitz, *Abuse of Government Processes, the First Amendment, and the boundaries of* Noerr, 74 Geo. L.J. 65, 92 (1985) (raising the questions in text, author answers, "[P]rofessional and private standard setting organizations are not governmental within the rationale of *Noerr.* Neither an organization's membership nor its leadership is elected by or answerable to the body politic.").

[107] 486 U.S. 492 (1988) (consortium of steel conduit manufacturers agreed to exclude the polyvinyl conduit of respondent from the 1981 National Electric Code, promulgated by the National Fire Protection Association, a private standard-setting organization).

[108] *Id.* at 509.

influence governmental action.[109] The Court noted that quasi-governmental immunity depends on the source, context, and nature of the petitioning activity.[110] The source of the activity takes into account the economic interests of the actors in their horizontal and vertical business relationships.[111] The context of the activity is compared in its proximity to the natural checks and balances of official government to protect the public interest.[112] The nature of the activity evaluates the extent of petitioning as opposed to the extent of decision making. There is a distinction between *advocating* standards favorable to one's economic interests, and actively *participating* in the decision-making process.[113]

A purely neutral private standards-setting organization, governed by democratic procedures and open to participation by all interested parties, would enjoy the greatest chance of quasi-governmental *Noerr* immunity, at least if it were performing a role that otherwise would be performed by the government. In this situation, the immunity of the standards-setting organization should not be eroded by the anticompetitive motivations of petitioners seeking standards favorable to the petitioners' economic interests. Petitioners under such circumstances similarly should enjoy *Noerr* immunity.

Conversely, if the petitioners also were the standards setters, or if the standards setters otherwise were competitively interested in the standards resulting from the process, the basis for quasi-governmental immunity would diminish because the arrangement would more strongly resemble a private horizontal arrangement. The appropriateness of immunity diminishes further as participation is restricted and procedures are less democratic or less reflective of procedural due process concepts. As the quasi-governmental character of the standard-setting organization erodes, so also does the appropriateness of *Noerr* immunity for the petitioner. Petitioner immunity is based on petitioning the government, not competitors.

Of course immunity under the *Noerr* Doctrine is necessary only if the standards-setting conduct constitutes a prima facie violation of the antitrust laws. Sections 1 and 2 of the Sherman Act are the most likely candidates, as considered in §§ **8.11** and **8.12.**

§ 8.11   Private Standards Setting under Sherman Act

Most purely private standards for exchanging information involve agreement among economic suppliers. Such agreements are suspect under section 1 of the

---

[109] *Id.* at 499–500.

[110] *Id.* at 498.

[111] *Id.* at 500.

[112] *Id.* at 506.

[113] 486 U.S. 492, 507 (1988).

Sherman Act.[114] "People of the same trade seldom meet together, even for merriment and diversion, but the conversation ends in a conspiracy against the public, or in some contrivance to raise prices," noted Adam Smith.[115]

Private standards-setting activities are vulnerable to section 1 liability unless the resulting standards are neutral with respect to actual and potential products, except when the lack of neutrality or disparate impact can be justified in terms of procompetitive objects and effects. A standard that is entirely neutral in terms of its competitive effect cannot be an antitrust violation because it does not restrain trade.[116] Conversely, a "standard" defined in terms of a single product has the greatest adverse effect on competition.

Moreover, the concerted appointment of one supplier by others—which can be the effect of a single-product standard—constitutes a group boycott.[117] Group boycotts can victimize either buyers or sellers.[118] But, as **Chapter 2** explains, *groups boycotts,* or *concerted refusals to deal* as they are sometimes called, are not illegal unless they focus on prices or output restrictions (such agreements would be per se illegal), or unless they fail a rule of reason inquiry.[119] Rule of reason analysis shields from liability agreements whose procompetitive effects outweigh their anticompetitive effects. For example, if a new multimedia

---

[114] "[T]here is one common danger for competition: an exclusive arrangement [such as a standard setting] may 'foreclose' so much of the available supply or outlet capacity that existing competitors or new entrants may be limited or excluded and, under certain circumstances, this may reinforce market power and raise prices for consumers." U.S. Healthcare, Inc. v. Healthsource, Inc., 986 F.2d 589, 595 (1st Cir. 1993).

[115] Malcolm v. Marathon Oil Co., 642 F.2d 845, 847 (5th Cir. 1981) (quoting Adam Smith, Wealth of Nations 232 (Pelican reprint 1980) (1776)).

[116] It is conceivable, however, that if competitors were to agree on a standard, this would limit their competition in the future as to features covered by the standard and could be viewed as a kind of output restriction.

[117] A *boycott* in this case is a horizontal agreement between competitors that has the primary effect (and possible purpose) of excluding some other competitor from the market. Certain group boycotts are per se violations of the Sherman Act, as are price-or output-fixing agreements. U.S. Healthcare, Inc. v. Healthsource, Inc., 986 F.2d 589, 593 (1st Cir. 1993). See also Federal Trade Comm'n v. Superior Court Trial Lawyers Ass'n, 493 U.S. 411 (1990) (concerted effort by competitors to provide goods or services to a buyer is per se unlawful); Fashion Originators' Guild v. Federal Trade Comm'n, 312 U.S. 457 (1941) (agreement among garment and textile manufacturers to exclude competitors from the market held per se unlawful); Alvord-Polk, Inc. v. F. Schumacher & Co., 37 F.3d 996 (3d Cir. 1994) (threatened boycott of certain wallpaper manufacturers by retailers through trade association sufficient event for finding of possible § 1 violation); Wilk v. American Medical Ass'n, 895 F.2d 352 (7th Cir. 1990) (ethical canon effectively prohibiting AMA members from associating with chiropractors held unlawful under rule of reason).

[118] Herbert Hovenkamp, Economics and Federal Antitrust Law §§ 10.1–10.2, at 274–75 (1985) (illustrating agreements among sellers not to sell to certain buyers, and agreements among buyers not to buy from certain sellers).

[119] NCAA v. Board of Regents of Univ. of Okla., 468 U.S. 85 (1984) (NCAA's "television plan" limiting total number of televised intercollegiate football games and number of games any one college may televise held to violate § 1 of Sherman Act).

interface for the Internet were selected as a standard, even though only one product currently embodied the standard, the decision could be justified if it induces delivery of a new product into the marketplace and also leaves other producers free to offer competing products. Uninhibited action based on individual consumer preferences is the value the antitrust laws seek to promote.[120] Any agreed limitations among competitors (*horizontal restraints*) must not have any more anticompetitive effects than are reasonably necessary to achieve their procompetitive purposes.[121] In other words, a kind of overbreadth test operates under the rule of reason.[122] There are many ways to provide for file exchange and interoperability, for example, beyond limiting the market to a single product.

Some private standard-setting organizations have run afoul of these requirements.[123] In *Allied Tube & Conduit Corp. v. Indian Head, Inc.,*[124] the Supreme Court observed, "Agreement on a product standard is, after all, implicitly an agreement not to manufacture, distribute, or purchase certain types of products."[125] Nevertheless, because standards have significant procompetitive advantages, when they are promulgated based on merit and through procedures that limit bias flowing from economic interest, the Court endorsed a rule of reason approach to standards-setting activities, while suggesting more rigorous scrutiny of concerted efforts to enforce standards.[126]

---

[120] *Id.* at 104 (citing Northern Pac. R.R. v. United States, 356 U.S. 1 (1958)).

[121] *Id.* at 103–04 (reasonableness of restraint determined by its impact on competition); Broadcast Music, Inc. v. Columbia Broadcasting Sys., Inc., 441 U.S. 1, 20 (1979) ("inquiry must focus on . . . whether the practice facially appears to be one that would always or almost always tend to restrict competition and decrease output and in what portion of the market, or instead one designed to increase economic efficiency and render markets more, rather than less competitive," quoting United States v. United States Gypsum Co., 438 U.S. 422, 441 n.16 (1978)).

[122] Overbreadth analysis is used to evaluate restrictions on expression under the First Amendment. See **Ch. 6.**

[123] *See* American Soc'y of Mechanical Eng'rs, Inc. v. Hydrolevel Corp., 456 U.S. 556 (1982) (volunteer members of code-drafting committee of ASME drafted statement that was harmful to their employer's competitor). *See also* Continental Ore Co. v. Union Carbide & Carbon Corp., 370 U.S. 690, 707–08 (1962) (*Noerr* does not apply when the conduct in question was "private commercial activity, no element of which involved seeking to procure passage or enforcement of the laws"); Radiant Burners, Inc. v. Peoples Gas Light & Coke Co., 364 U.S. 656 (1961) (affirming refusal to dismiss complaint—alleging that association's refusal to approve manufacturer's burner without objective basis was a Sherman § 1 conspiracy to restrain entry into gas burner market.

[124] 486 U.S. 492 (1988) (consortium of steel conduit manufacturers agreed to exclude the polyvinyl conduit of respondent from the 1981 National Electric Code, promulgated by the National Fire Protection Association, a private standard-setting organization).

[125] *Id.* at 500. The type of competitive injury identified by the Court is in the nature of an output restriction ("not to manufacture, distribute"), as well as a concerted refusal to deal ("not to . . . distribute or purchase").

[126] *Id.* at 501.

Therefore, a purely private standard-setting process would violate section 1 if it excluded from the marketplace particular products either directly, as in *Indian Head,* or indirectly through standards contents that are deliberately framed to harm a competitor, or indirectly under *Radiant Burners* through standards that exclude a product while not being supported by a legitimate purpose.[127] All of this leads naturally into the kind of balancing used for scrutiny of any kind of horizontal arrangements under rule of reason analysis.

§ 8.12 Adoption of Proprietary Standards as Sherman Act Monopolization Violations

Section 8.3 notes that some market structures are dominated by a single producer and that a private standard is likely only if it represents the standard of that dominant producer. Suppose there were no agreement on this standard and thus no potential section 1 violation. Suppose instead the dominant producer encourages the adoption of its copyrighted or patented practice or technology as a standard.[128] Under what circumstances, if any, would the "owner" of the standard be subject to section 2 liability? The questions that must be answered are

1. Whether the producer has a monopoly in the relevant market
2. Whether it has market power in that market
3. Whether it used the market power to gain a "competitive advantage."[129]

To answer these questions, the relevant market must first be established.[130] Determining the relevant market is of paramount importance to the outcome of

---

[127] Radiant Burners, Inc. v. Peoples Gas Light & Coke Co., 364 U.S. 656 (1961). *See also* Greater Rockford Energy & Technology Corp. v. Shell Oil Co., 998 F.2d 391, 396 (7th Cir. 1993) ("failure of a private, standard-setting body to certify a product is not, by itself, a violation of § 1"); ECOS Elecs. Corp. v. Underwriters Lab., 743 F.2d 498 (7th Cir. 1984) (rejecting attack on standard embracing competitor's product; choice not shown to be unreasonable in that challengers failed to use standards-setting organization's procedures); Eliason Corp. v. National Sanitation Found., 614 F.2d 126, 130 & n.6 (6th Cir. 1980) (rejecting Sherman § 1 challenge by manufacturer denied approval by standards-setting organization, noting objective reasonableness of standard, independence of standards setters, lack of intent to exclude plaintiff from market).

[128] Examples might be efforts by the owner of patented encryption technology to have it adopted by the federal government as a digital signature standard, or efforts by a legal publisher to have its citation system, in which it claims copyright, adopted by courts and others as a standard citation system for legal documents.

[129] United States v. Grinnell Corp., 384 U.S. 563, 570–71 (1966).

[130] Establishing the relevant market, however, is not always a simple task. As Judge Boudin of the First Circuit lamented in U.S. Healthcare, Inc. v. Healthsource, Inc., "There is no subject in antitrust law more confusing than market definition." 986 F.2d 589, 598 (1st Cir. 1993).

the hypothetical. If an expansive market definition is used, the potential section 2 problems are greatly diminished because the producer is more likely to have competitors in broader markets. On the other hand, if the market were defined as the market for the particular product clothed with intellectual property protection, the producer would have a monopoly in that market by virtue of the intellectual property laws.[131] Plaintiffs would attempt to narrow an expansive market determination through application of the *Brown Shoe Co. v. United States*[132] submarkets theory, which was applied to section 2 in *United States v. Grinnell Corp.*[133]

Even if a market is defined narrowly, so that the first two criteria are satisfied, it is far from clear that merely "encouraging" adoption of one's product as a standard is impermissible conduct under section 2. If the encouragement is aimed at a governmental standard setter, the *Noerr* Doctrine, discussed in **§ 8.10,** would shield the producer from liability. On the other hand, if it could be shown that the intent was to limit competition, and if there also was bad faith involved, the possibility of section 2 liability is higher. Suppose, for example, that the producer encouraged adoption of its product as a standard without making it clear that it intended to assert its intellectual property rights after adoption. The subsequent assertion of intellectual property rights arguably would be impermissible under section 2.

Nevertheless, the basis of the producer's predominant share of the market is entirely due to and under the control of an independent standard-setting organization.[134] So long as there is no link between the producer and the standard-setting organization, the harm protected against by section 2, namely abuse of market power,[135] does not exist.

The producer would increase the risk of section 2 liability if it differentiates its product from other available systems on the market after the product is picked as a standard, thereby making its product incompatible with other potentially complementary products (that is, removing the interchangeability and cross-elasticity with other products). Or the owner of the standard might refuse to license it on reasonable terms in order to maintain its monopoly in the market.[136] In such situations, a plaintiff would claim that the product differences or the refusal to license is an unlawful exercise of the existing market power

---

[131] To the extent that not all purchasers adhere to the standard, WordPerfect *would* have competitors under this definition, however.

[132] 370 U.S. 294, 325 (1962).

[133] 384 U.S. 563, 573 (1966).

[134] *See* Olympia Equip. Leasing Co. v. Western Union Tel. Co., 797 F.2d 370, 374 (7th Cir. 1986).

[135] *Id. See generally* Berkey Photo, Inc. v. Eastman Kodak Co., 603 F.2d 263, 273–74 (2d Cir. 1979) ("The key to analysis, it must be stressed, is the concept of market power").

[136] Brown Shoe Co. v. United States, 370 U.S. 294, 325 (1962). *But see* United States v. Grinnell Corp., 384 U.S. 563, 570–71 (1966) (permitting "growth or development as a consequence of a superior product, business acumen, or historic accident").

creating barriers to entry into the market for competitors. Such an argument would not succeed unless the original monopoly was due to status as the industry standard.[137] Moreover, this section 2 theory depends on a finding of market power. If there is no market power, there is no section 2 violation.[138]

§ 8.13   Federal Contract Requirements

The federal government is a purchaser with substantial market power. Accordingly, when the federal government requires adherence to a particular standard, it forces acceptance of that standard by the universe of vendors who wish to compete for federal contracts. On the other hand, there are significant limitations on federal prescription of standards through the procurement process.[139] Procurements for government contracts are usually through full and open competition.[140] Acquisitions that specify a make and model do not provide such competition and must be justified and approved in accordance with Federal Acquisition Rules 6.302 to 6.304 (FAR).[141] The statutory authority cited in the FAR is 41 U.S.C. § 253.[142] Supplies and services are considered to be available from only one source if the source has submitted an unsolicited research proposal that:

A) Demonstrates a unique and innovative concept or demonstrates a unique capability of the source to provide the particular research services proposed;

B) Offers a concept or services not otherwise available to the Government; and

C) Does not resemble the substance of a pending competitive acquisition. (See 41 U.S.C. 253(d)(1)(A).)[143]

For an acquisition that uses a brand name description to specify a particular feature of a product, peculiar to one manufacturer, does not provide for full and

---

[137] *But see* United States v. Grinnell Corp., 384 U.S. 563, 570–71 (1966) (permitting "growth or development as a consequence of a superior product, business acumen, or historic accident").

[138] *See id.* at 570 (violator must possess "monopoly power in the relevant market"); *see generally* Herbert Hovenkamp, Economics and Federal Antitrust Law § 5.1 (reviewing Judge Wyzanski's three approaches to establishing § 2 violation in United Shoe Machinery; concluding that third, no-fault approach is not the prevailing rule). Wyzanski's first rule finds a § 2 violation when a monopolist commits a § 1 violation; his second rule finds a § 2 violation when a firm with the power to exclude competition exercises that power. Hovenkamp § 5.1, at 136 (citing United States v. United States Shoe Mach. Corp., 110 F. Supp. 295, 342 (D. Mass. 1953), *aff'd per curiam,* 347 U.S. 521 (1954)). *See also* Hovenkamp § 6.5, at 168–69 (discussing role of market power and noting that substantially lower share will support attempt case).

[139] Thomas Thistle, law clerk to the author, did the research for this section.

[140] 41 U.S.C. § 253.

[141] Federal Acquisition Regulation, 48 C.F.R. ch.1, § 6.302 (1994).

[142] *Id.* § 6.302-1.

[143] *Id.*

open competition regardless of the number of sources solicited.[144] It must be justified and approved in accordance with FAR 6.303 and 6.304.[145] The justification should indicate that the use of such descriptions in the acquisition is essential to the government's requirements, thereby precluding consideration of a product manufactured by another company.[146]

In *Southern Technologies, Inc. v. United States*[147] a disappointed bidder challenged a restrictive specification in a bid solicitation.[148] The government, when faced with such a challenge, must demonstrate that the restriction is reasonably related to the minimum needs of the contracting agency.[149] Once this showing is met, the burden shifts to the plaintiff to show the restrictions are clearly unreasonable.[150] The court found that the sole source procurement was not unreasonable; thus, summary judgment was granted for the government.[151]

Often, suppliers of systems that might be disadvantaged by technical specifications lack standing to challenge the specifications. In *Control Data Corp. v. Baldrige*,[152] the defendants filed an action challenging standards promulgated by the Department of Commerce defining certain specifications for connecting computer peripheral equipment as part of medium and large scale data processing systems.[153] The defendants believed these specifications would require considerable expenditures of time and money to produce suitable equipment,[154] and argued that these increased costs would destroy their competitive positions and their position as the sole realistic alternative to IBM.[155] The court of appeals found that the equipment suppliers lacked standing, concluding that the congressional intent in fostering competition was not for the survival of the competing companies, but for the economic acquisition of automatic data processing (ADP) equipment for the government.[156] Thus, this increased competition between the systems manufacturers was to inure to the benefit of the government, rather than the ADP suppliers.[157] If Congress feels these standards do discourage the competition it was intended to promote, Congress will interject itself into the process and take corrective measures.[158]

---

[144] *Id.*

[145] *Id.*

[146] *Id.*

[147] 755 F. Supp. 19 (D.D.C. 1991).

[148] *Id.* at 20. The challenged requirement related to a duty to provide the agency with adequate references.

[149] *Id.* at 21.

[150] *Id.* (citing Dickey-John Corp. v. Bergland, 444 F. Supp. 451 (D.D.C. 1978)).

[151] *Id.* at 22.

[152] 655 F.2d 283 (D.C. Cir.), *cert. denied,* 454 U.S. 881 (1981).

[153] *Id.*

[154] *Id.* at 295.

[155] *Id.*

[156] *Id.*

[157] *Id.* at 296.

[158] 655 F.2d 283, 296 (D.C. Cir. 1981).

Government requirements for compliance with nonproprietary standards should survive even though such standards impose a competitive disadvantage. For example, the government routinely requires compliance with the OSI standard under its government open systems information protocol (GOSIP) requirement.[159] Conversely, if the government requires characteristics that are available from only source, the specification is treated as though it requires a brand name.[160] When that occurs, a bidder is entitled to satisfy a specification by submitting an equal substitute product.[161]

§ 8.14   Functional versus Technical Standards

Regardless of the source of authority, regulatory mandates for interoperability and compatibility should be functional rather than technical. The government's success rate in picking computer standards is not very good. Defense Department adoption of ALGOL as a computer programming language and adoption by the National Institute of Standards and Technology (NIST) of OSI as an interoperability standard are examples of failures. There have been successes, such as the specification of COBOL as a computer language.

Functionally oriented interoperability and compatibility requirements are another matter. Recent initiatives by the FCC in telephone and radio regulation are good models of a functional approach.[162]

---

[159] *See* HFS, Inc. v. National Archives & Records Admin., GSBCA No. 12,010-P, 93-2 B.C.A. (CCH) ¶¶ 245, 812, 1992 WL 448533 GSBA (Nov. 24, 1992) (contract award challenge based in part on application of GOSIP requirements).

[160] Appeal of Harvey Constr. Co., ASBCA No. 93,310, 92-3 B.C.A. (CCH) ¶¶ 25, 162, ASBCA No. 39,310, 1992 WL 151450 (June 19, 1992) (citing Sherwin v. United States, 436 F.2d 992 (Ct. Cl. 1971)).

[161] *Id.,* ASBCA No. 39,310 (citing Urban Plumbing & Heating Co. v. United States, 408 F.2d 382, 386 n.3 (Ct. Cl. 1969)); *see* Manning Elec. & Repair Co. v. United States, 22 Cl. Ct. 240, 36 Cont. Cas. Fed. (CCH) ¶ 75, 993 (1991).

[162] Report and Order establishing general guideline principles to be used in future deregulation rule making proceedings and amending Parts 15, 73 and 74 of the Rules to eliminate unnecessary technical quality regulations, FCC 84-521, GEN Docket No. 83-114 (noting high priority attached to interoperability in many radio services, but also noting that priority of mandating specific interoperability through regulation varies depending on the service).

Direct Commission regulation of interoperability is useful in several cases such as (1) in systems where instant communications between all stations is critical to safety (e.g. the maritime and aeronautical distress frequencies), (2) in systems where interoperability can be shown to be critical to national security/emergency preparedness concerns (e.g. the Emergency Broadcast Service), and (3) in helping the introduction of new services involving large public participation (e.g. cellular radio telephone service). In non-safety cases where we consider mandatory standards we will consider them on a case by case basis, and we will consider whether the benefits of standards outweighs the costs and time delay involved. We will seek to deregulate standards

§ 8.15 Swedish Approach

Approaches by foreign countries to interconnection and standardization are similar in many ways to those of the United States. For example, the Swedish approach resembles the American approach with respect to common carriage and commercial mobile radio systems. The Swedish Telecommunications Act[163]

---

when (1) it can be determined that they are sufficiently well established to be maintained as voluntary standards and (2) enough equipment is installed to give manufacturers and service providers the incentive to make any new changes compatible with the original equipment. In these non-safety cases, we will also consider alternatives to mandatory standards that endorse or give a preference to a specific standard rather than requiring it. [FN10]

Id. See also In re Amendment of the Commission's Rules to Establish New Personal Communications Services, Second Report and Order, FCC 93-451, GEN Docket No. 90-314, 8 F.C.C.R. 7700, ¶ 195 (1993) (noting importance of interoperability in World Wide communications systems); *In re* Advanced Television Systems and Their Impact Upon the Existing Television Broadcast Service, Second Report and Order/Further Notice Of Proposed Rule Making, FCC 92-174, MM Docket No. 87-268, 7 F.C.C.R. 11, ¶ 71 (1992) (noting that interoperability is one of ten selection criteria for advisory committee selection of advanced television systems); *In re* Advanced Technologies for the Public Safety Radio Services, Further Notice Of Inquiry, FCC 89-326, GEN Docket No. 88-441, 4 F.C.C.R. 8519, ¶ 1 (1989) (initiating inquiry to explore possibility that next generation of digital radios for 800 MHz public safety systems may require some degree of standardization to enable system interoperability, but noting earlier conclusions that mandated standards were unnecessary); *In re* Implementation Of Sections 3(N) and 332 of the Communications Act, Regulatory Treatment of Mobile Services, Further Notice of Proposed Rule Making, FCC 94-100, GN Docket No. 93-252, 9 F.C.C.R. 2863, ¶¶ 56–57 (1994) (noting earlier adoption of interoperability rules that require all cellular telephones to be capable of operating on all cellular channels and to be capable of successfully interacting with the base stations of all cellular radio service providers; seeking comment on whether Part 90 CMRS licensees should be subject to mandatory interoperability requirements similar to those applicable to cellular licensees); *In re* Amendment of the Commission's Rules to Establish New Personal Communications Services, Second Report and Order, FCC 93-451, GEN Docket No. 90-314, 8 F.C.C.R. 7700, ¶ 137 (1993) (recognizing that roaming and interoperability are two important features of PCS and that such features could be fostered through adoption of technical standards); *In re* Expanded Interconnection with Local Telephone Company Facilities, Third Report and Order, CC Docket No. 91-141, Transport Phase II, FCC 94-118, at n.8 (May 19, 1994) (noting decision not to address expanded interconnection for provision of subscriber loops, as well as interoperability of LEC local switches and other parties' switches required for competitive provision of local exchange service); *In re* Policies and Rules Concerning Local Exchange Carrier Validation and Billing Information for Joint Use Calling Cards, Report and Order and Request for Supplemental Comment, FCC 92-168, CC Docket No. 91-115, 7 F.C.C.R. 3528 (1992) (review of local exchange carrier (LEC) calling card practices, requiring that LECs provide nondiscriminatory access to card data, inviting comment on billing name and address (BNA) service requirements, noting possibility that industry standards must be agreed upon to ensure interoperability between multivendor networks).

[163] SFS 1993: 597 (promulgated 10 June 1993 pursuant to govt. bill 1992/93:200, Com. Rep.1992/93:TU30, Parl. Pr. 1992/93:443).

provides that telecommunications service providers[164] must provide on request "interconnections with a corresponding service operated by another license holder or by a 'report-liable party.'" If a license holder establishes interconnections to a report-liable party, the license holder is entitled to interconnection with the corresponding undertaking operated by the report-liable party.[165] Telecommunication service providers not covered by the license requirements under section 5 must "pursue, on market conditions, interconnection with a license holder or a report-liable party providing telecommunication services under this act." A party providing interconnection under this duty is entitled to reciprocal interconnections.[166] On the other hand, "a party who provides telecommunication services within a public telecommunications network is not liable to provide interconnection to the extent that such service would restrict to an essential extent his ability to exploit in his own operation the network capacity at his disposal."[167]

The major question regarding application of this language is interpretive: how is the asymmetric obligation on nonlicensed entities "to pursue on market conditions interconnection" to be applied, and how is the obligation to provide interconnections on request "with a corresponding service" for fair and reasonable compensation "in relation to the performance cost"to be applied?[168]

---

[164] Only those providers holding a license under section 5, which requires licenses of providers of telephony services or mobile telecommunication services, and providers of leased lines with significant market share ("considerable extent").

[165] SFS 1993: 597 § 20.

[166] *Id.* § 20, ¶ 4.

[167] *Id.* § 20, ¶ 5.

[168] *Id.* § 20, ¶ 3.

CHAPTER 9

ELECTRONIC COMMERCE: AUTHENTICATION AND ELECTRONIC CONTRACTING

§ 9.1   Nature of the Problem

The NII is of little interest unless it can handle commerce. Traditional parts of the NII—the public-switched telephone system, broadcast and cable television, and print publications—each worked out their own patterns of contracting and securing payment. Newer, open architectures like the Internet present greater challenges. Users of these open networks must be able to make contracts through the net, and they must be able to arrange for payment for goods and services.

Commercialization of the Internet and the growing use of other parts of the NII for commercial transactions will lead to an increasing number of contracts being entered into electronically. In some cases, this simply means presentation of an offer, including some or all of the contract terms in a message on the user's screen, and purported acceptance of this offer by a human keyboard or a mouse action. For example, a seller might communicate price terms in a message displayed on a user's screen, intending that the user "accept" by pressing a keyboard key to move on to another set of choices on a different screen display.

In other cases, involving electronic data interchange (EDI), contractual offers and acceptances are exchanged without conscious human intervention at the time of the exchange.[1] The offering computer simply sends a message in a prearranged format called a *transaction set,* which the receiving computer is able to process through a program using the same format. If the communicated offer matches terms the receiving computer is programmed to accept, that computer sends an acceptance message in an *acceptance transaction set,* thus completing contract formation.[2]

Electronic means can be used not only to make and accept promises, but also to make warranties, representations, and disclaimers. For example, a supplier of information content or of pointers may disclaim liability for defamation or disclaim warranties of fitness for a particular purpose, either under Article 2 of the U.C.C. or the common law.[3]

The same basic techniques can be used for other legally significant events in contract performance, including submission of invoices, payment orders, and

---

[1] EDI is used for a variety of commercial transactions, in addition to contracting. *See* Edward S. Adams et al., *A Revised Filing System: Recommendations and Innovations,* 79 Minn. L. Rev. 877, 920 (1995) (reviewing approaches for using information technology to automate U.C.C. Article 9 filing systems, and noting existence of EDI transaction set for Article 9 filings).

[2] *See generally* Michael S. Baum & Henry H. Perritt, Jr., Electronic Contracting, Publishing and EDI Law (John Wiley & Sons, Inc., 1991).

[3] Warranties are considered in **Ch. 5.**

orders under a master contract. These techniques also can be used for other commercial transactions, such as securities transfers, negotiable instruments, U.C.C. Article 9 filings, and negotiable bills of lading. They obviously can be used, perhaps with additional features, to arrange for payment through systems resembling those used to arrange credit card charges or those used for negotiation of traveler's checks.

When some human response to an electronic message occurs, an offeree may attempt to deny acceptance on the grounds that he did not read the offer or understand the legal significance of the keyboard or mouse actions. Furthermore, the offeree may challenge whether the acceptance by keyboard or mouse action satisfies signature and writing requirements. The same set of possibilities present themselves in the EDI context, except that the problem is intensified because there is no conscious human involvement at the time of the exchange of communications.

In late 1995, the most urgent problem confronting the Internet was the absence of a widely deployed system for making payments. Most of the technological and administrative problems had been worked out, and it was a matter of diffusing the solutions through the marketplace and ensuring the adequacy of the legal parts of the payments infrastructure. As credit card and "cybermoney" transactions become common in the NII, legal solutions to contract formation and performance issues used in the EDI context may not be adequate because of the involvement of consumers in the credit card and cybermoney transactions.[4] Thus, it is important to understand how the fundamental common law and UCC requirements for making and interpreting contractual obligations intersect with basic computer techniques. With this understanding, it is possible to consider solutions like trading partner agreements (TPAs) frequently used in the EDI context.

This chapter explains how technological means of ensuring reliability of electronic transactions leading to contractual obligations can be combined with the traditional law of contract formalities to provide an infrastructure within which electronic commerce can occur. In particular, the chapter shows how statutory, regulatory, and contract arrangements developed for electronic funds transfers can be combined with public key encryption and common-law contract principles to establish that framework.

§ 9.2 —Repudiation Examples

Repudiation is a continuing concern when contractual obligations are made or disclaimed electronically. In legal terms, *repudiation* is a justification for

---

[4] As § **9.15** explains, EDI as currently practiced, relies greatly on trading partner agreements. Those agreements, and much of the model legislation drafted for use in the international context, assumes that the trading partners are merchants and that consumers are not participants. When consumers are involved, commercial law must address disparate bargaining power and sophistication.

nonperformance of an alleged contractual obligation. A supplier confronted with a demand that he ship goods in response to an order denies a contractual obligation to ship by repudiating (denying) the contract alleged by the ordering party. A customer confronted with a demand for payment for services performed refuses to pay based on repudiation of an alleged contractual undertaking to pay. A disappointed merchant filing a breach of contract claim, by repudiating an alleged waiver agreement, denies that she agreed to waive her claim. In all these examples, the time for performance under an alleged contract has occurred, and thus claims for breach have ripened. The term "repudiation" traditionally was applied mainly to *anticipatory repudiation,* which occurred when the alleged obligor refused to perform in advance of the time that performance was due.[5] In the electronic contracting context, the term has come to be used informally to refer to the possibility that an alleged obligor will deny any contractual obligation to perform, before or after the time performance is due.

In this informal usage, *repudiation* includes any defense to a breach of contract claim, conceptually encompassing not only denials of the requirements of offer and acceptance, but also denials of adequate consideration, claims of incapacity and affirmative defenses such as accord and satisfaction, and impossibility of performance. None of these defenses raises problems particularly associated with information technologies, except for denials of offer and acceptance (denial of contract formation) and closely associated contract-interpretation disputes. It is in this sense, that this chapter considers repudiation. In other words, this chapter considers the situation in which persons charged with contractual obligations deny the obligation by repudiating the message on which the obligations are said to be based. The denial may involve assertion of forgery or denial that a particular message was intended to have legal effect.

Most evaluations of electronic contracting and payment systems readily identify the risk of forgery by the purchaser of goods and services as a major risk that must be addressed before such systems can become a commercial reality. The risk of forgery overlaps the risk of repudiation because repudiation is likely to involve an allegation of forgery when none actually occurred. In an actual forgery, the purported purchaser says, "That is not my signature; it is a forgery." In a repudiation, the purchaser says falsely, "That is not my signature; it is a forgery."[6] Unless a seller who accepts the electronic payment can reduce the risk of either an actual forgery or a falsely alleged forgery, the seller is not assured of payment.[7]

---

[5] John E. Murray, Jr., Murray on Contracts § 109(B), at 609 (3d ed. 1990) (describing origin of *anticipatory* repudiation doctrine). *Accord* Restatement (Second) of Contracts § 250 (1981) (repudiation is statement by obligor to obligee that obligor will not perform when the time for performance is due).

[6] *See* Xanthopolous v. Thomas Cooke, Inc., 629 F. Supp. 164, 169 (S.D.N.Y. 1985) (denying payment of traveler's checks to acceptor who did not insist on counter signature in his presence; rejecting theory that original purchaser of traveler's checks had faked a forgery).

[7] This statement begs the question of who bears the ultimate risk of loss when a forgery occurs or is claimed and cannot be disproven. It assumes the seller, as the first person to accept the electronic payment, bears the risk. The rationale is that the first to accept the allegedly forged payment has the best opportunity to detect the forgery.

§ 9.3 Contract Formation

Contractual obligations do not exist unless certain formalities are satisfied. The coming into existence of a contractual obligation is known as *contract formation:* "[T]he formation of a contract requires a bargain in which there is a manifestation of mutual assent to the exchange and a consideration."[8] There are many ways in which mutual assent can be established,[9] and there also are well-recognized doctrinal mechanisms for enforcing promises even when the elements of a bargain are not present.[10] Nevertheless, traditional contract-formation analysis begins with identification of an offer and an acceptance. The exchange represented by the offer and acceptance constitutes formation of a contract.

In the computer context, an offer is manifested by a communication directed to one or more persons that describes a service to be performed or a good to be delivered if the person receiving the communication engages in some expressly described or implied conduct. The form of this computerized offer may be plain language in a message or posted file; it may be values in the fields making up an EDI transaction set; it may be encrypted; it may be a button that says in effect "click here if you want x." No particular form of communication is required.[11] The electronic offer can be directed at a particular person, a specified group, or anyone who makes a return promise or engages in specified conduct.[12]

Of particular importance in the electronic context, is the idea that the maker of the offer defines how it may be accepted:

(1) An offer may invite or require acceptance to be made by an affirmative answer in words, or by performing or refraining from performing a specified act, or may empower the offeree to make a selection of terms in his acceptance.

(2) Unless otherwise indicated by the language or the circumstances, an offer invites acceptance in any manner and by any medium reasonable in the circumstances.[13]

---

[8] Restatement (Second) of Contracts § 17(1) (1981). The author acknowledges the value of many conversations with his colleague Joseph W. Dellapenna, which illuminated the theories of contract formation.

[9] *See id.* § 18 (promise by each party for beginning or rendering performance can show assent); *id.* § 19 (manifestation of assent can be made by written or spoken words or other acts or by failure to act); *id.* § 22 (manifestation of mutual assent usually made by offer followed by acceptance, but contract formation requirements may be satisfied even though neither offer nor acceptance can be identified and even though the moment of formation cannot be determined).

[10] *See id.* § 17 cmt. e (examples of informal contract without bargain); *id.* § 90 (elements of promissory estoppel in which promise is enforced because of reasonable detrimental reliance).

[11] *See* Restatement (Second) of Contracts § 24 (1981) (defining offer as manifestation of willingness to enter into a bargain justifying an understanding that a bargain is invited).

[12] *Id.* § 29 (intent of offeror dictates who holds the power of acceptance; furthermore, offeror has great latitude in conferring power of acceptance).

[13] *Id.* § 30.

This leaves no significant doubt about the efficacy of an offer that empowers persons to accept it only by sending certain types of electronic messages. There also is no doubt that an offer can be effective when it is communicated through an agent,[14] such as a computer program.[15] On the other hand, the offer and acceptance must relate to each other.[16] For example, if A sends a computerized offer to B, perhaps in the form of an EDI transaction set inviting acceptance by B's sending an acceptance transaction set back to A, and the acceptance transaction set is sent by C instead of B, there is no contract. A's offer is not reasonably interpreted as being directed to C or inviting an acceptance by C. Similarly, if B sends an acceptance transaction set to A without reference to A's offer[17] there is no contract because the acceptance did not refer to the offer.

The most likely controversies relating to contract formation involve (1) interpretation of offers, that is, distinguishing offers from solicitation of offers as in the advertising and credit card contexts, and (2) identification of the persons to whom an offer is addressed. Statements in advertisements traditionally were construed as solicitation of offers rather than offers.[18] Thus a refusal to sell on the terms communicated in the advertisement did not breach a contract; it merely was a rejection of the buyer's offer to make a contract. This general rule did not apply when an advertisement manifested a clear intent to make a promise, for example a statement of definite price, accompanied by the phrase, "first come, first served."[19] The most famous case is *Carlill v. Carbolic Smoke*

---

[14] *Id.* § 23 cmt. a (offer can be communicated through agent).

[15] The Restatement deals with agency in terms of a human acting on behalf of another human. It is possible to extend this idea to the operation of a computer program as programmed by a human. Actually, the computer agency concept is a much more pure example of agency theory due to the elimination of the uncertain "human variable."

[16] Restatement (Second) of Contracts § 23 (1981) ("It is essential to a bargain that each party manifest assent with reference to the manifestation of the other").

[17] "Reference" in the sense that it is used in the text and in the Restatement means relationship; it does not mean explicit mention. The reference to A's offer can exist without subjective intent by B. *See generally* Restatement (Second) of Contracts § 23 (1981) and accompanying illustrations, especially illus. 1(b).

[18] *See* Restatement (Second) of Contracts § 26 cmt. b (1981) (advertisements, while they may possibly stand as offers if language of commitment is present, generally are not sufficient alone to act as offer to sell). *See also* Mesaros v. United States, 845 F.2d 1576 (D.C. Cir. 1988) ("[Advertisements] are mere notices and solicitations for offers which create no power of acceptance in the recipient."); Williston, A Treatise on the Law of Contracts § 27 (3d ed. 1957) ("[I]f goods are advertised for sale at a certain price, it is not an offer, and no contract is formed by the statement of an intending purchaser that he will take a specified quantity of the goods at that price. The construction is rather favored that such an advertisement is a mere invitation to enter into a bargain, rather than an offer.").

[19] *See* Restatement (Second) of Contracts § 26 cmt. b, illus. 1 & 2 (comparing an advertisement as a offer with an advertisement found not to be an offer); John E. Murray, Jr., Murray on Contracts § 34, at 69 (3d ed. 1990) (citing Lefkowitz v. Great Minneapolis Surplus Store, 86 N.W.2d 689 (Minn. 1957)). *See also* Steinberg v. Chicago Medical Sch., 371 N.E.2d 634 (Ill. 1977). The *Steinberg* court found a cause of action existed for breach of contract when an

Ball Co.,[20] in which an advertisement promised to pay a £100 reward to anyone contracting a cold after using the advertised smoke ball.[21] Evidencing promissory intent, the advertisement also said that it had deposited £1000 with a bank as a kind of escrow agent.[22] The court found that the nature of the communication evidenced an intent to take the risk of a large number of offerees,[23] the risk motivating the general rule.

The Restatement[24] establishes a presumption that advertisements are ordinarily intended as solicitations of offers rather than offers. It acknowledges, however, first, that one may make an offer through an advertisement, and second, that an advertisement that is not an offer nevertheless may contain promises or representations that become part of the eventual contract.[25]

Terms of contracts communicated electronically are similar to the terms published by the issuer of a credit card. The electronic messages may be intended to reach a very large number of people who may subsequently enter into discrete transactions, presumably under the published terms. The prevailing view is that credit card terms do not give rise to enforceable obligations to allow access to the credit represented by the card.[26] Rather, they are revocable offers of contracts, which are accepted each time the cardholder uses the credit card.[27]

---

applicant to medical school submitted an application in response to an invitation expressed in the medical school catalogue, but the medical school failed to evaluate the application according to the criteria set forth in the catalogue. 371 N.E.2d at 638. The *Steinberg* court concluded that the submission of the application and the payment of fee was an offer to apply, which was accepted by receipt of the application and acceptance of the fee. 371 N.E.2d at 641.

[20] 1 Q.B. 256 (1893) (discussed in Murray on Contracts § 34, at 70).

[21] *Id.* at 257.

[22] *Id.* ("1000 pounds is deposited with the Alliance Bank, Request Street, Shewing our sincerity in the matter.").

[23] *Id.* at 262. "In point of law this advertisement is an offer to pay 100 pounds to anybody who will perform these conditions, and the performance of these conditions is acceptance of the offer." While acknowledging that the advertisement was vague in some respects, L.J. Lindley concluded that "the defendants must perform their promise, and, if they have been so unwary as to expose themselves to a great many actions, so much the worse for them. *Id.* at 265.

[24] *See* Restatement (Second) of Contracts § 26 cmt. b (1981) ("It is of course possible to make an offer by an advertisement directed to the general public, but there must ordinarily be some language of commitment or some invitation to take action without further communication.").

[25] *Id.; id.* cmt. f; *id.* § 24.

[26] *See, e.g.,* Garber v. Harris Trust & Sav. Bank, 432 N.E.2d 1309, 1312 (Ill. App. Ct. 1982) ("prevailing view in this country is that the issuance of a credit card is only an offer to extend credit"); *In re* Ward, 857 F.2d 1082, 1087 (6th Cir. 1988) (Merritt, J. dissenting) ("unilateral contracts are formed each time the card is used"). *But see* Gray v. American Express Co., 743 F.2d 10 (D.C. Cir. 1984) (cardholder whose card was canceled by refusing to authorize a particular charge entitled to statutory procedures; criticizing view that cardholder has no contract rights).

[27] Feder v. Fortunoff, Inc., 494 N.Y.S.2d 42 (App. Div. 1985) (affirming dismissal of complaint). "The issuance of a credit card constitutes an offer of credit which may be withdrawn by the offeror at any time prior to acceptance of the offer through the use of the card by the holder." *Id.* at 42.

"The credit card relationship, properly analyzed, should be viewed as an offer by the issuer to create the opportunity for a series of unilateral contracts which are actually formed when the holder uses the credit card to buy goods or services or to obtain cash."[28]

The advertising and credit card cases raise a presumption that computer messages describing goods or services to be purchased are solicitations of offers rather than offers themselves. But if they invite the person to whom the communication is made to act by pressing a key, clicking a mouse button, or sending a particular type of message, such act is an offer, and an automated response to it by the author of the communication constitutes acceptance.

It is conceivable that an offering or soliciting computer system would function in unanticipated ways, actually communicating an offer or solicitation to persons not subjectively intended to receive it. In that circumstance, the test of "manifested intention" might be satisfied if it is reasonable for an actual receiver to interpret it as intended for her. Thus, a misdirected offer message received by a participant in an EDI market should be legally effective as an offer if it is expressed in the transaction set defined for offers and if its interpretation by the receiver conforms to the interpretation contemplated by the EDI transaction set.

The advertisement and credit card cases and the misaddressed offer analyses relate to the possibility that a purported offeror will repudiate an alleged contract asserted by a purported offeree. There also are circumstances in which purported offerees repudiate contractual obligations asserted by offerors. In the EDI context, an offeree might deny that an acceptance message was sent or deny that a message actually sent was effective as an acceptance.

In the plain language context, an offer may describe conduct and say that such conduct constitutes acceptance of an offer. The conduct may occur with or without the actor intending that it constitute legally effective acceptance. For example, after the purported offer is communicated, a recipient may engage in the specified conduct and subsequently deny that his conduct constituted an acceptance of an offer either because he had no knowledge of the offer or knew of it but did not mean to accept it. Consider a screen message that says, "If you hit any key you accept the following terms," setting forth terms of a proposed contract either on the same screen or incorporating by reference another screen or document. A user of the computer system on which that message appears hits any key to continue. It may be plausible for the user of the computer system to deny knowledge of the screen message (many people ignore some messages that appear on their computer screens) and to deny that simply proceeding to the next series of screens constituted any intentional acceptance of any offer.[29]

The likelihood of this kind of repudiation of acceptance can be reduced by defining accepting conduct so that it is unusual. For example, instead of inviting acceptance by hitting any key, a plain language offeror might define acceptance

---

[28] *In re* Ward, 857 F.2d 1082, 1087 (6th Cir. 1988) (Merritt, J., dissenting) ("Unilateral contracts are formed each time the card is used").

[29] The offer may be a waiver of the right to assert a claim.

as typing the phrase "I accept the offer made by this screen." An offer to sell for a particular price might define acceptance as the conduct of typing the digits representing the price, preceded by a dollar sign.

Repudiation of purely automated offers and acceptances, as in the EDI context, can be managed by designing EDI systems to reduce the likelihood of misdirected offers being decoded and acted upon by receiving programs and to minimize the risk of unintended generation of acceptance messages. Such program design is equivalent legally to careful instruction of a human agent, considered in § 9.5.

§ 9.4   Contract Interpretation

Contract-interpretation disputes arise when one party says, "You agreed to X," and the other party says, "No, I only agreed to Y." Did the contract mean X or Y? Contractual obligations include within their scope only subject matter that was common to the offer and acceptance. Thus determining the scope of a contractual obligation requires interpreting the offer and acceptance to determine the terms included in the contract.[30] So the contract-formation and contract-interpretation inquiries are not entirely distinct. The two inquiries can be separated, however, first by asking whether a contract of some kind exists because the requisites of contract formation have been satisfied, and second by asking whether a breach has occurred based on resolution of a contract-interpretation dispute to give a particular meaning to the obligation.

Electronic commercial contracting is a likely source of contract-interpretation disputes. Computer messages in the commercial context are terse and have meaning only when connected with context. Moreover, fully automated commercial messages have meaning only by resolving external references to computer program code, values in translation tables, and definitions of data structures like EDI transaction sets. One transaction set attaches one meaning to a coded message; another transaction set attaches another.[31]

Such interpretation ambiguities can be resolved by using three techniques. First, it is necessary to decide what documents or other data nominally external to the offer and acceptance appropriately are incorporated into and should be considered a part of the "four corners" of the contract. The evidence may conflict as to which version of a nominally external document is the appropriate one. For example, an offer may incorporate by reference a table equating certain

---

[30] Restatement (Second) of Contracts ch. 9 (1981) (introductory note preceding § 200) (sets forth the applicable principles for assigning contractual obligations to the parties); *id.* § 200 cmt. a (questions of interpretation arise in determining whether there is a contract).

[31] *See generally* Douglas Robert Morrison, *The Statute of Frauds Online: Can a Computer Sign a Contract for the Sale of Goods?,* 14 Geo. Mason U. L. Rev. 637 (1992) (explaining EDI transaction sets, and concluding that audit trail produced by EDI satisfied purposes of statute of frauds).

codes with certain product numbers or prices. Such a table maintained in a computer system is intended to change from time to time, and information is not necessarily available as to when changes were made or what the preceding value was, unless appropriate audit trails are laid. Even if such a table is determined to be part of a contract, a decision maker still must determine what the relevant values in the table are so they may be associated with the codes in the contracting message.

Second, great weight should be given to the actual conduct of the parties in performing their contractual relationship.[32] This means that if a particular message has always been treated by both parties as justifying certain conduct, it presumptively should be interpreted as contemplating that conduct when it recurs.[33]

Third, obligations can be determined by "usage of trade" or trade practice.[34] Extrinsic reference to trade practice is particularly important when new technologies are used to make and perform contracts, especially because the new technologies use specialized terminology and facilitate communication by the use of computer-readable codes that do not have any natural-language meaning.[35]

§ 9.5   Agency

The law of agency plays a role in many contract transactions because many contracts are entered into and performed through agents rather than directly by principals. As noted in **§ 9.3,** the *Restatement (Second) of Contracts* contemplates the making and acceptance of offers through agents. The law of agency determines when a principal is bound by an agent's acts even though the principal claims those acts were unauthorized. The same basic problem, of deciding when a principal is bound by allegedly unauthorized acts of an intermediary, arises in electronic contracting. When a participant in a fully automatic

---

[32] Restatement (Second) of Contracts § 202(4) (1981) ("Where an agreement involves repeated occasions for performance by either party with knowledge of the nature of the performance and opportunity for objection to it by the other, any course of performance accepted or acquiesced in without objection is given great weight in the interpretation of the agreement").

[33] It should be noted, however, that Restatement § 202(4) refers to "course of performance accepted or acquiesced in without objection." Thus, if actual conduct was not known to the other party, he had no opportunity to object to it, and thus the unknown conduct may have only diminished significance in an interpretation dispute. This obviously could occur when two computer agents are interacting with each other and something happens that one party claims was unintended and unknown. The course of performance between the two computer systems thus might have only diminished weight in solving interpretation problems.

[34] Restatement (Second) of Contracts § 202(5) (1981) ("Whenever reasonable, the manifestations of intention of the parties to a promise or agreement are interpreted as consistent with each other and with any relevant course of performance, course of dealing, or usage of trade").

[35] *Cf. id.* § 202 cmt. e (noting usual importance of general English language usage to resolve interpretation disputes; however, "this rule is a rule of interpretation in the absence of contrary evidence").

electronic contracting system like EDI seeks to escape an alleged contractual obligation or waiver of right, he frequently seeks to do so on the grounds that his computer system did something unanticipated and unauthorized. This is exactly the situation the law of agency addresses. The person confronted with the possibility of undesired contractual obligation is the principal, and the computer system is the agent.

In simplest terms, the law of agency binds a principal to the acts of an agent within the agent's actual or apparent authority.[36] If a principal mistakenly gives an agent actual authority, the principal nevertheless is bound by the agent's acts.[37] So also, if a principal makes a mistake in programming an electronic contracting computer system, the principal actually has authorized the computerized agent and is bound by its commitments.

This conclusion is reinforced by *apparent authority* analysis. The theory of apparent authority is that a principal is bound by the conduct of an agent in situations, created or acquiesced in by the principal, in which others reasonably believe the agent has actual authority.[38] Thus, if a principal connects his computer to an electronic contracting system (or in an open architecture adheres to electronic contracting protocols), he is in effect saying to the other participants in that system, "here is my authorized agent." Then, if the agent enters into a transaction that is not subjectively authorized by the principal, the principal is nevertheless bound because he created the situation in which it was reasonable for the others to believe the agent had authority.[39]

§ 9.6   Formalities: Traditional Solutions to Offer-and-Acceptance and Interpretation Problems

Traditionally, contract law, like the law of wills and the law of property, reduced the universe of likely disputes over offer and acceptance and interpretation by

---

[36] Restatement (Second) of Agency § 7 (1957) ("Authority is the power of the agent to affect the legal relations of the principal by acts done in accordance with the principal's manifestations of consent."; cmts. a–d deal with various authority issues); *id.* § 8 ("Apparent authority is the power to affect the legal relations of another person by transactions with third persons, professedly as agent for the other, arising from and in accordance with the other's manifestations to such third persons."); Authority, or actual authority, and apparent authority follow the same general rules of interpretation, but for apparent authority, the manifestation to the third party is substituted in place of the agent. *Id.* § 8 cmt. a.

[37] *Id.* § 7 cmt. b (while consent of the principal is required for authority to exist, "[t]he agent's conduct is authorized if he is reasonable in drawing an inference that the principal intended him so to act although that was not the principal's intent, and although as to a third person such a manifestation might not bind the principal."). *See also id.* § 44 (allowing agent to act upon reasonable beliefs when instructions from the principal are ambiguous).

[38] *Id.* § 8 cmt. c ("Apparent authority exists only to the extent that it is reasonable for the third person dealing with the agent to believe that the agent is authorized.").

[39] However, as noted previously, to be binding the actions must be reasonable.

defining certain formalities. These formalities are the hallmarks of contract formation. These formalities are embodied in the

1. Requirements for writings and signatures
2. Statute of frauds
3. Parol evidence rule, which limits the universe of communications that can be taken into account in resolving interpretation disputes
4. Requirement that certain contracts be under seal and that contracts under seal have certain effects
5. Requirement that certain contracts be attested
6. Requirement that certain contractual obligations be notarized.

Each type of formality is associated to some degree with particular technologies. Thus, changing the technologies of contracting changes the way the formalities must be understood and applied. For appropriate application of contract law to contracts made and performed through information technology, one must begin by understanding the core purposes of contract formalities. Then, one must consider each formality and determine what it should mean in the new technological contexts.

Commentator Lon Fuller postulated that formalities such as signatures in contract law perform three distinct functions: an evidentiary function, a cautionary function, and a channeling function.[40] Other commentators add protective functions.

Formalities serve an evidentiary purpose by ensuring the availability of artifacts that are likely to be admissible as probative evidence should a dispute arise over whether a legally significant act occurred or, if an act occurred, its content. Formalities serve a channeling function by making clear the line between intent to act in a legally significant way and intent to act otherwise.[41] The channeling function also is a way of routinizing decisions as to whether or not a document has legal effect by reducing the need for evidence on the facts of

---

[40] *Consideration and Form*, 41 Colum. L. Rev. 799 (1941). *See* Swerhun v. General Motors Corp., 812 F. Supp. 1218, 1222 (M.D. Fla. 1993) (standard for enforcing promise on promissory estoppel theory depends in part on the extent to which "the evidentiary, cautionary, deterrent and channeling functions of form are met"); Ian Ayres & Robert Gertner, *Filling Gaps in Incomplete Contracts: An Economic Theory of Default Rules*, 99 Yale L.J. 87, 123–24 (1989) (characterizing Lon Fuller as justifying legal formalities by their evidentiary, cautionary, and channeling functions).

[41] *See* C. Douglas Miller, *Will Formality, Judicial Formalism, and Legislative Reform: An Examination of the New Uniform Probate Code "Harmless Error" Rule and the Movement Toward Amorphism*, 43 Fla. L. Rev. 167, 259–60 (1991) (discussing intent-verifying and ritual purposes of formality).

a particular case.[42] The cautionary function of formality induces deliberation and reflection before action.[43]

Technology can satisfy the evidentiary function very well. Indeed, EDI exchanges and public key encryption coupled with procedures defined through trading partner agreements meet evidentiary needs better than traditional formalities shoehorned into the electronic context. A properly authenticated digital signature is much better evidence of the source and integrity of a message than an electronic replica of a handwritten signature printed on hard copy output. Nevertheless, most computer-readable media are inherently malleable; it is more difficult to say that the contents of a computer file are the same as those of the file at an earlier time (if encryption is not used as an authentication technique) than it is to say that the contents of a paper record are the same as the contents of that paper record at an earlier time. This inherent malleability means that the forms of computer representations may serve the evidentiary function less well than contracts represented on paper. Trading partners cannot rely on the characteristics of the communication and storage media; they must give special attention to ensure that the evidentiary function is served appropriately.

Electronic contracting invites rethinking of the channeling function. A traditional contract is a single document that is self-contained within its "four corners." The parties and a court hearing a dispute over a claim of breach can determine contractual duties and privileges by referring to no more than the single document.[44] In electronic contracting practice, however, a collection of distinct messages and files make up the contractual obligation. Distributing a contract over multiple documents certainly is not unknown in conventional contracting; parties regularly make external references, include fine print on the back of a preprinted form, write purchase orders against a master agreement, and inferentially rely on trade custom to give meaning to their contractual obligations.[45] But the range of evidentiary artifacts that are candidates for inclusion in electronic contract is surely greater. Typical computer-to-computer communication is cryptic, necessitating reliance on external tables, code books, and documentation to give meaning to symbols.

Electronic contracting serves the channeling function as long as the channels are well designed by system architects. The architects must distinguish

---

[42] *Id.* at 269 (explaining channeling function of attestation clause in terms of standardizing will and routinizing probate).

[43] *Id.* at 261.

[44] Parties frequently put "integration clauses" in contracts to make sure that external references are not intended. *See generally* Restatement (Second) of Contracts § 210 (1981) ("A completely integrated contract is an integrated agreement adopted by the parties as a complete and exclusive statement of the terms of the agreement").

[45] See the discussion of course of performance, course of dealing, and usage of trade earlier in **§ 9.4.**

communicative acts intended to have legal effect from those not intended to
have legal effect. From a litigator's perspective, the problem is first to show the
set of information the parties were aware of, and then to show the subset they
intended to be a part of their mutual obligations.[46] One way to do that is to have
a system that flags legally effective messages differently from informal communications not intended to have legal effect. Alternatively, digital signature
techniques can be used as an automated integration clause.[47] All legally significant communications are collected into one or more files that are digitally
signed.

The cautionary and protective functions are more difficult to meet. A computer programmed to enter into EDI transactions does so automatically and will
do so virtually forever without any reflection on the part of the person being
contractually bound. Even when there is nominal human intervention, as in the
case of screens that disclose the terms of contracts and warn that proceeding past
that screen will have legal consequences, the warnings are easily ignored by
impatient users accustomed to moving from screen to screen as fast as they can.
The law may develop default rules to mitigate the danger of consumers and
small enterprises being overreached by automatic contractual obligations that
are relatively hard to undo.[48] It is difficult, however, to assess the need for
statutory, regulatory, or judicial intervention to police cautionary and protective
functions unless examples of abuse reach the courts or legislative bodies. The
author knows of no significant abuses at the present time.

The protective function can be enhanced by electronic contracting techniques.
These techniques easily can prevent a vulnerable actor from performing a
legally significant act without the knowledge and participation of another.
Features in electronic information services like America Online and Compu-
Serve that prevent children from accessing certain files and discussion areas
without parental consent are models of how the protective function can be
served.[49]

---

[46] *But see* W. David Slawson, *Standard Form Contracts and Democratic Control of Lawmaking
Power,* 84 Harv. L. Rev. 529 (1971). Recognizing that it is unrealistic in this day and age to
require standard form contracts to be uncoerced, informed agreements, the article attempts to
"construct an 'administrative law' of contracts, whereby the unilaterally drawn portions of
what we now call contracts could similarly be kept consistent with the parties' actual agreement and otherwise fair to both of them." *Id.* at 532–33.

[47] An *integration clause* in a contract is a clause that excludes all communications and documents
other than the document in which it appears as evidence of contract terms. "This document
represents the complete agreement of the parties," is a simple integration clause. See § **9.12**
for discussion of digital signature techniques.

[48] An example of the problem, although not an example of electronic contracting, is the arrangement for automatic deductions from a bank account or preauthorized automatic monthly bills to
a credit card account. Such authorizations are relatively easy to establish, but it may be difficult
to stop them without incurring higher transaction costs.

[49] See § **9.24** presenting the language of the AOL agreement.

§ 9.7   —Statute of Frauds: Signatures and Writings

The statute of frauds requires signatures and writings for certain types of contracts. One version of the statute of frauds is codified in § 2-201(1) of the Uniform Commercial Code: "[e]xcept as otherwise provided in this section a contract for the sale of goods for the price of $500 or more is not enforceable by way of action or defense unless there is some writing sufficient to indicate that a contract for sale has been made between the parties and signed by the party against whom enforcement is sought or by his authorized agent or broker." Similar requirements exist for letters of credit,[50] securities,[51] and security interests.[52]

The statute of frauds interacts with authentication requirements discussed in § 9.10. Suppose B has repudiated an alleged contractual obligation running in favor of A, in B's pleadings in a breach of contract action brought by A. A seeks to introduce evidence of the contract in the form of two plain language messages, one representing the offer, and the other representing the acceptance. A's authentication problem is to show that the messages produced in court are the messages exchanged between the parties. A's statute of frauds problem is that even if these are the messages exchanged between the parties, they may not give rise to a contractual obligation because they do not constitute writings and/or they are not signed.

As one of the formalities of contract formation, signatures play an important role in the evidentiary requirement for authentication, discussed in § 9.10. Conventional signatures also serve cautionary and channeling functions. Well-designed electronic contracting systems serve the evidentiary function of signatures by linking something associated with the signer to the thing signed. This may be accomplished by a password such as the personal identification number (PIN) associated with an electronic funds transfer or debit card, by the private key used to make a digital signature through public key encryption, or by swiping the magnetic strip on an electronic identification card. More simply, a person may be requested by a screen message: "If you wish to sign this request, please type your full name in the field below, intending that it be your signature." Any of these techniques should suffice as a *signature*, which usually is defined as any mark made with the intent that it be a signature.[53] The cautionary

---

[50] U.C.C. § 5-104(1) (1990) ("A credit must be in writing and signed by the issuer and a confirmation must be in writing and signed by the confirming bank. A modification of the terms of a credit or confirmation must be signed by the issuer or confirming bank.")

[51] *Id.* § 8-319 (explicity sets forth a statute of frauds requirement for contracts for the sale of securities).

[52] *Id.* § 9-203.

[53] *See* 1 U.S.C. § 1 ("In determining the meaning of any Act of Congress, unless context indicates otherwise, 'signature' . . . includes a mark when the person making the same intended it as such"). *See generally* Joseph Denunzio Fruit Co. v. Crane, 79 F. Supp. 117 (D.C. Cal. 1948) (explaining signature requirements).

and channelling functions are served by a system design that makes the signing "ceremony," such as the card swipe or PIN entry, distinct from the rest of the transaction.

The traditional writing requirement serves evidentiary, cautionary, and channeling purposes. Written communications are more reliable evidence of their content than the memories of witnesses of oral communications. Writing something down is a more serious act than talking about it and thus serves the cautionary function. Only written communications have contractual significance, not oral ones, and this serves the channeling function. Electronic representations of electronic communications differ from traditional writings only in their evidentiary value. The question is whether the electronic record, as it exists at the time of a dispute, is at least as good evidence of the communication as it occurred at the legally relevant time as would be a communication recorded on paper at the legally relevant time. The answer depends on the nature of the electronic system. The starting point should be to recognize that the requirement for a writing has been applied flexibly for a century or more.[54] Then one must focus on the reliability of the electronic system producing the evidence of the transaction,[55] essentially an evidentiary question, considered in **Chapter 12.** The probative character of a computer-stored and computer-generated writing is increased by the use of digital signature techniques, which ensure the detectability of an alteration, as explained in § **9.12.**

§ 9.8 —Attestation

Attestation is a formality beyond writing and signature requirements, traditionally associated with wills.[56] Attestation has evidentiary value because those attesting to a will are available to testify as to the fact that the will actually was signed by the person whose signature is purported to be on it. Attestation reinforces signature requirements, providing additional sources of evidence to associate a signature with a particular person, coupling the signature more tightly with the documents to which it is affixed, and further authenticating

---

[54] *See* Nationwide Resources Corp. v. Massabni, 658 P.2d 210 (Ariz. Ct. App. 1982) (acknowledging statute of frauds requirement, but finding "[t]he majority rule is that the contract must be signed by the party against whom it is sought to be enforced, but not by the party who seeks to enforce it and a written offer signed by the party sought to be changed, if orally accepted by the person to whom it was made, will be sufficient to satisfy the Statute of Frauds.") The court concluded by finding a mailgram to be sufficient to satisfy the statute of frauds. *Id.* at 215.

[55] John Robinson Thomas, *Legal Responses to Commercial Transactions Employing Novel Media,* 90 Mich. L. Rev. 1145 (1992) (reviewing cases involving statute of frauds questions over telegraphic communications, and concluding that electronic mail should satisfy requirements).

[56] Bruce H. Mann, *Formalities and Formalism in the Uniform Probate Code,* 142 U. Pa. L. Rev. 1033, 1041 (1994).

those documents. Attestation also serves cautionary, channeling, and protective purposes.[57] Attestation requirements serve cautionary functions because having witnesses to attest to a signature considerably increases the formality of the signing "ceremony." They also serve a channeling function because only those verbal acts channeled into the attested document have legal effect and all others can be disregarded. One commentator says that the presence of disinterested witnesses at the execution ceremony guards the testator against nefarious acts such as fraud or undue influence.[58] This is a protective function. Attestation also is used for documents other than wills, for example for drug test certificates.[59]

Attestation plays a role in electronic contracting only when there is an explicit legal requirement that an electronic record be attested. This might occur in the case of electronic wills, where video recording may be the best way to satisfy the requirement, or in the case of public records, considered in **Chapter 12** dealing with the rules of evidence.

§ 9.9   —Contracts under Seal

Contracts under seal were accorded preferred status in contract law because the seal was a particularly strong formality.[60] A seal could not be made without the use of a mechanical device closely controlled by the owner, thus enhancing the evidentiary purpose of this formality. Applying a seal was an unambiguous act with legal significance, thus serving channeling and cautionary functions. The electronic equivalent of using a seal is the use of a private key to enable a digital signature (see **§ 9.12**) or swiping the magnetic strip on a transaction card. The

---

[57] Kelly A. Hardin, *An Analysis of the Virginia Wills Act Formalities and the Need for a Dispensing Power Statute in Virginia,* 50 Wash. & Lee L. Rev. 1145, 1152–53 (1993) (explaining how attestation requirement and other formalities serve protective functions, also serve a cautionary or a ritual function because execution ceremony impresses upon testators the seriousness and importance of making testamentary disposition; serve to provide courts with reliable evidence that purported will is genuine).

[58] Bruce H. Mann, *Formalities and Formalism in the Uniform Probate Code,* 142 U. Pa. L. Rev. 1033, 1042 (1994).

[59] *See generally* Frere v. Commonwealth, 452 S.E.2d 682 (Va. Ct. App. 1995) (attestation implies more stringent requirements than mere signature, but is distinct from notarization; notary's official seal and signature attest only to genuineness of signature; attestation of drug certificate addresses genuineness and accuracy of certificate itself and its conclusions); *but see in re* Koziol, 603 N.E.2d 60, 63 (Ill. Ct. App. 1992) (notarization, like attestation, tends to prove authenticity of signatures and therefore could be substituted for strict compliance with attestation requirement for will); James Lindgren, *Abolishing the Attestation Requirement for Wills,* 68 N.C. L. Rev. 541, 554 (1990) (attestation serves all the purposes of other formalities, but particularly protects testator from fraud, duress, and undue influence).

[60] *See* Restatement (Second) of Contracts § 6(a) (1981) and accompanying comments (a contract under seal is one in a small list of contracts that are subject to special rules based on their formal characteristics).

likelihood of losing a card with a magnetic strip is about the same as the likelihood of losing one's seal. Although the legal significance of contracts under seal has diminished over the last century and a half, it may be that the concept is worth revitalizing for certain kinds of digitally authenticated electronic documents.

§ 9.10 —Authentication

As § 9.6 explains, one of the purposes of legal formalities is evidentiary. The traditional preference for signed writings was based on the proposition that such evidence is easier to authenticate. That means showing that a piece of evidence, such as a communication purporting to be an offer of a contract, is what it purports to be. Authentication as an evidentiary concept is explained in **Chapter 12.**

§ 9.11 —Notarization

Attestation by a notary public serves all of the requirements of attestation in general and some others as well. A notary public is licensed by the state[61] and typically is authorized to administer oaths. Thus, one who signs a false document and has it notarized may be liable for perjury. Regardless of that possibility, the existence of the notary's signature and stamp provides a reliable means of locating the witness to the signature, while the notary's log reinforces evidence that the purported signer actually signed the document on a particular date.[62]

As electronic commerce has matured, interest has grown in finding a place for the notary concept in the electronic information infrastructure. For example, the Science and Technology Section of the American Bar Association commissioned a special project to develop recommendations for electronic notaries.[63] More generally, using certificate authorities in systems of public key encryption, discussed in §§ **9.12** to **9.14,** are examples of using a trusted third party (akin to a notary) to authenticate legally significant transactions.

§ 9.12 Encryption and Digital Signatures

Contract-formation and contract-interpretation disputes can be significantly reduced by the use of certain encryption techniques. The same techniques satisfy

---

[61] Pa. Stat. Ann. tit. 57, §§ 31–168; Md. Ann. Code art. 68, §§ 1–10 (1957).

[62] *See generally* Peter N. Weiss, *Security Requirements and Evidentiary Issues in the Interchange of Electronic Documents: Steps Toward Developing a Security Policy,* 12 J. Marshall J. Computer & Info. L. 425 (1993) (discussing notorization in relation to computer transactions).

[63] *See* Theodore Sedgwick Barassi, *The CyberNotary: A New U.S. Legal Specialization for Facilitating Electronic Commerce,* A.B.A. Bull. of L., Sci. & Tech., Apr. 1995, at 5.

many or all requirements for formalities, such as signatures and writings. While these relatively sophisticated technological measures are not necessary in a wide range of electronic contract transactions,[64] they enable certain types of disputes to be resolved with great certainty. The most attractive encryption technology is public key encryption, described in § 9.13, because it is widely available in inexpensive software.

Public key encryption allows digital signatures to be affixed to electronic messages.[65] Digital signatures serve two functions: they make forgery and repudiation so difficult as to be impracticable; and they provide a means of detecting alterations and other tampering with the content of digitally signed documents.

Suppose an electronic publisher receives an electronic order for a copy of a valuable work, requesting that the copy be "shipped"[66] to a particular address. The electronic order is digitally signed by someone with whom the publisher has a long-standing relationship. The digital signature enables the publisher to reduce two risks ordinarily associated with electronic commerce. The first risk is that the order did not in fact come from the trusted customer, but from someone forging the customer's name to the order. The second risk is that the customer actually placed the order but will prove unworthy of trust and repudiate it by claiming, after the ordered material is received, that he did not place the order. Alternatively, the customer might admit placing the order but claim a much lower price was promised, or the customer might admit placing the order but deny instructions to ship it to the address used by the publisher.

A digital signature protects against the forgery and total repudiation risks because only the true customer has the code necessary to affix the digital signature. A forged signature would not match the corresponding code or key held by the publisher. Because forgery can be detected, so also can repudiation, as explained in § 9.2.

The risk of actual or falsely claimed alteration can be reduced by another feature inevitably used with digital signatures. This feature constructs a hash code for the message.[67] The *hash code* is a numerical quantity computed from the contents of the message. It is roughly analogous to a character count for a message. In contrast to a character count, however, the sophistication of the hash

---

[64] **Section 9.24** explains how the traditional legal requisites for contract formation and contract interpretation can be applied and adapted to relatively low technology arrangements.

[65] *See* Approval for Federal Information Processing Standards Publication 186, Digital Signature Standard, 59 Fed. Reg. 26,208 (May 19, 1994) (public key digital signature method). Other encryption techniques can be used for digital signatures as well. In fact most digital signature systems now in use, such as those employed in banking Automatic Teller Machines, use single-key systems. In these closed systems, maintaining security of the single key is not a problem.

[66] Shipment actually would occur by transferring a file containing the requested work over the Internet.

[67] Alternatively, the entire message could be encrypted, but most commercial systems do not do this because of performance penalties because of the length of time it takes to encrypt larger quantities of plain text.

code reduces nearly to zero the probability that two different message contents could produce the same hash code. The publisher has the same code algorithm the sender does and thus is able, by recomputing the hash code of the message actually received and comparing that computed code with the hash code sent along with the message, to determine if there have been any alterations. Because the publisher's key cannot encrypt a message so that it matches something sent by the customer, but only decrypt something actually sent by the customer, the combination of the encrypted message received by the publisher and the results of the decryption process unambiguously show that it came from the purported sender and was not tampered with.

The legal framework for encryption and digital signatures should be essentially that described in §§ **9.15** to **9.19** for electronic funds transfers. A contractual framework, either a trading partner agreement between two contracting parties or, more usefully, a master, multiparty contract resembling a clearinghouse agreement, specifies who bears the risk of loss if security arrangements (encryption and digital signatures) are available but not used appropriately. The basic concept is that a party failing to use available security arrangements, for example, failing to authenticate a digital signature, bears the risk of loss. On the other hand, a properly authenticated digital signature binds the owner of the private key unless notice has been given through predefined channels that the key has been compromised.

§ 9.13   Public Key Encryption

Section 9.12 noted that public key encryption is a particularly attractive technology for protecting against the risks of forgery and repudiation in electronic contracting. This section explains how public key encrpytion works and identifies some of the risks associated with public key encryption. Public key encryption involves mathematical algorithms that factor large numbers. Through the use of appropriate algorithms, it is possible to obtain two numbers, called *keys,* one of which creates an encrypted message from plain text, and the other of which recovers the plain text from the encrypted version. One of these keys is held by a user of the technique and not disclosed to anyone else. This is called that user's *private key.* The other number, a key associated with the private key, is disclosed publicly. This is that user's *public key.*

The public and private keys can be used together either to protect privacy in the content of a message, or to construct digital signatures like those discussed in § **9.12,** or both. Suppose the user wishes to send a private message to another, the addressee. The user uses the public key belonging to the addressee to encrypt the message.[68] While the message is in transit, and after it is received by anyone, its content cannot be determined because of the encryption. Only the intended

---

[68] For performance reasons, most commercial public key systems use public key encryption to encrypt a message-specific single key, which then is used to encrypt the message.

addressee can discern the contents by unlocking it (decrypting the message and restoring it to plain text) by using the addressee's private key.

Suppose the user wishes to affix a digital signature. This time the user uses his own private key to encrypt the message (or, more often, to encrypt only the hash code as explained in § 9.12) and sends it to the addressee. Now, the text of the message is not secret because anyone can decrypt it by using the sender's public key, but the intended function of the digital signature is realized because only the public key associated with the sender will decrypt the message. That uniquely associates it with the sender because only someone possessing the sender's private key could have sent that encrypted message.

If the sender wishes both privacy and a digital signature, he encrypts the message digest with his private key to obtain the digital signature function and then encrypts the digest and the message with the addressee's public key, to obtain the privacy result. The addressee first decrypts it with her private key, and then decrypts the result with the sender's public key.

Public key encryption is far superior to single key encryption[69] because it does not require the private exchange of secret keys. Thus, no code books need be exchanged and protected from falling into the wrong hands. While single-key encryption is faster than public key encryption, the need for secure channels to exchange the keys limits it to closed environments involving a relatively small number of interacting parties known to each other in advance.[70] Public key encryption offers the benefits of message privacy and digital signatures in open environments in which potential customers cannot be identified in advance yet want to make purchases on the spot. This of course describes the environment within which the largest volume of electronic commerce occurs.

There are, however, several risks and difficulties associated with public key encryption. One, considered in § 9.14, is the need for an infrastructure to manage the public keys. In the examples given in this section, the sender must have some reliable way of determining each addressee's public key, and each addressee must have some reliable way of determining each sender's public key. In the absence of such an infrastructure, a forger could falsely claim to be the customer and send her public key claiming it to be the public key belonging to the true customer. The most attractive public key management infrastructure is one utilizing a hierarchy of certificate authorities.

A second risk is that a participant in public key messaging would disclose her private key to an unauthorized person. If a forger has access to another's private key, the reliability of digital signatures in preventing forgery is eliminated. Also, a participant could falsely claim to have lost his private key, thus eliminating the utility of public key digital signatures in preventing repudiation, unless some

---

[69] Single-key encryption sometimes is called *private key encryption.*

[70] Single-key encryption typically is used to protect the integrity of electronic funds transfer messages. Given the closed environment in which electronic funds transfers occur, the single-key technique offers sufficient protection.

mechanism requires notification of a lost private key and shifts the risk of forgery to the loser of the key who fails to give notice.[71]

Two other difficulties with public key encryption are extrinsic to the technology. First, the most attractive implementation of public key encryption relies on two patented processes, and there is continuing controversy over the validity and boundaries of these patents. Thus, at least until the patents expire, there is the possibility that sellers of the patented public key encryption technology must pay royalties to the patent holders and if they do not, users of their products might be liable for patent infringement.

Second, the United States Department of Commerce has put certain public key encryption techniques on the list of munitions that may not be exported, for national security reasons.[72] These export restrictions do not prohibit the use of public key encryption with foreign trading partners, but they do prohibit the export of software containing the public key algorithms and certain key management procedures. There is strong pressure to modify these restrictions, and the vice president committed in mid-1994 to the development of a public key encryption system that would not involve export controls.[73]

§ 9.14 —Certification Authorities

Section 9.13 explained that one of the vulnerabilities of public key encryption is that, for both security and efficiency reasons, there must be a trusted source of public keys. The most satisfactory way of meeting this need is through a hierarchy of certificate authorities. This type of key management infrastructure is the one adopted by the Internet Engineering Task Force in its RFC 1422.[74] The concept involves trusted third parties as certification authorities or certificate authorities, who make available public keys for persons and entities known to them. The public keys are made available in "key certificates." The key certificates take the form of standardized records with identifying information about the public key holder, the value of the public key, the address of the holder, expiration dates, and certain optional information permitting a user of the certificate to determine the certainty with which the certificate authority has identified the purported owner of that key.

But one level of certificate authorities is not enough. A thief could set up a certificate authority that falsely would claim certain public keys to be associated

---

[71] *See* 15 U.S.C. § 1693(g) (1988), [Electronic Funds Transfer Act] (cardholder liable in excess of $50 for unauthorized transfers made between the time cardholder has knowledge of likelihood of unauthorized use and time cardholder notifies issuer).

[72] These export controls are considered more fully in **Ch. 14.**

[73] See **Ch. 3.**

[74] Privacy Enhancement for Internet Electronic Mail: Part II: Certificate-Based Key Management, RFC No. 1422 (1993) (available from Internet Engineering Task Force). http://www.ds.internic.net/ds

with honest persons, permitting forgers to send forged messages on behalf of those persons. So someone needs to vouch for the reliability of the certificate authority. This is where hierarchy is involved. Each certificate authority has a certificate authority above it that can provide a specialized certificate containing the public key of the lower level certificate authority and appropriate identifying information. This hierarchy can exist to arbitrary depth, and key holders may be vouched for by more than one certificate authority, as certificate authorities can be vouched for by more than one certificate authority above them. At the top is a national or international certificate authority that vouches for a limited number of regional or otherwise defined certificate authorities.

This kind of infrastructure facilitates a variety of other desirable features of electronic commerce. A certificate authority can serve as a source of credit or cybermoney, as discussed in **§§ 9.21** through **9.22.** A certificate authority inherently performs certain reliability-enhancing functions traditionally performed by a notary public, explained in **§ 9.11,** and a certificate authority also can perform additional time-stamping and logging functions helpful to the creation of audit trails.

In addition, certificate authorities can reduce the risk of lost private keys and of private keys falsely claimed to be lost. They are the natural instrumentality for handling notices of lost keys. Indeed, most proposals for implementing systems of certificate authorities provide for notices of key revocation, which are issued upon a notice of a lost key. In these systems, the owner of a private key that has become compromised remains responsible for messages signed with that private key unless and until she notifies certificate authorities maintaining the corresponding public key of the loss, permitting them to issue key revocation certificates. A major step toward rationalizing the legal infrastructure for public key encryption was taken when Utah enacted its Digital Signature Act,[75] which implements the Certificate Authority concept along the lines prescribed by RFC 1422, defines the duties of a CA, and makes digital signatures using public key encryption legally effective.

§ 9.15   Separate Trading Partner Agreements

As this chapter explains, the current state of law is such that electronic contracting can be carried on with reasonable confidence in the enforceability of contracts made electronically. Nevertheless, certainty can be increased, inevitable risks can be allocated, and a more precise framework for electronic commerce established through trading partner agreements. Trading partner agreements (TPAs) are contracts, usually written on paper, that mutually obligate the signatories to use defined electronic techniques for certain contractual

---

[75] 1995 Utah Laws ch. 61 §§ 1–27, codified at Utah Code Ann. § 46-3-101 to § 46-3-504.

transactions.[76] TPAs can be bilateral, as between two sophisticated corporations doing a considerable volume of repetitive transactions with each other. They can be multilateral as in credit card or check clearinghouse agreements, where each member of an association operates under the rules established by the TPA. They can be unilateral, as in the case of a bank depositor's agreement or a credit card agreement that defines how electronic transactions will occur.

A typical trading partner agreement specifies particular digital communications techniques and services and transaction sets and applications that may be used to effectuate binding obligations or waivers of rights. These specifications range from naming a particular service provider and software vendor to requiring simply that "commercially reasonable" methods be used. This aspect of TPAs defines a set of formalities that, when satisfied, ensure legal enforceability, notwithstanding other indications of intent.[77]

TPAs also typically allocate the risk of certain mishaps. Suppose, for example, that the TPA provides for digitally signed offers, acceptances, and orders. A forger allegedly sends an order with a digital signature that does not match that of an authorized party, but the party receiving the allegedly forged message does not check the digital signature. Who should bear the loss? Most TPAs would say the party—the receiver in this instance—who did not use the agreed-upon security procedures would bear the loss. Or, suppose the receiver did check the digital signature and it checked out as valid. Unfortunately, the sender had allowed its private key to be compromised, and the message actually came from a forger. Who should bear the loss here? Most TPAs would impose the loss on the party who allowed its private key to become compromised, thus undermining the intended effect of the agreed-upon security procedure.[78]

TPAs are not the final answer to all questions involving electronic contracting. For one thing, they require some kind of prior arrangement before they enable electronic commerce; complete strangers cannot do business with each other until they have entered into a TPA. Eventually, subscribing to a TPA might be done electronically in a manner that would make it almost simultaneous with the commencement of transacting business. But the length of most existing TPAs would make that intended simultaneity difficult to accomplish, if only

---

[76] Commission Recommendation of 19 October 1994 Relating to the Legal Aspects of Electronic Data Interchange, Doc. No. 394X0820, art. 1, Annex 1, 1994 O.J. (L 338) 98 [hereinafter EC EDI Recommendation] (recommending use of European model EDI agreement, attached as annex; describing nature and purpose of EDI agreement).

[77] In this respect they are analogous to the long-standing formalities imposed by the statute of frauds, except that they involve the exercise of party autonomy, and they focus on modern technology. *See generally* Bruce H. Mann, *Formalities and Formalism in the Uniform Probate Code,* 142 U. Pa. L. Rev. 1033, 1035 (1994) (explaining traditional role of formalities in the law of wills).

[78] Electronic Messaging Services Task Force, *The Commercial Use of Electronic Data Interchange—A Report and Model Trading Partner Agreement,* 45 Bus. Law. 1645 (1990).

because it would take the new signatory a considerable period of time to read and understand the terms of the TPA and, without such reading and understanding, the TPA might have uncertain effect.[79]

§ 9.16   Electronic Funds Transfer

Electronic funds transfers are a form of electronic contracting that is well established and for which the legal regime has crystallized. The initial part of the definition from the Federal Electronic Funds Transfer Act (EFTA)[80] is helpful:

> the term "electronic fund transfer" means any transfer of funds, other than a transaction originated by check, draft, or similar paper instrument, which is initiated through an electronic terminal, telephonic instrument, or computer or magnetic tape so as to order, instruct, or authorize a financial institution to debit or credit an account. Such term includes, but is not limited to, point of sale transfers, automated teller machine transactions, direct deposits or withdraws of funds, and transfers initiated by telephone.[81]

Such transactions are regulated by three different bodies of domestic law. The Electronic Funds Transfer Act regulates EFT transactions on behalf of consumers.[82] Article 4A of the U.C.C. covers "wholesale wire transfers, except for those covered by Federal Reserve regulations and operating circulars of Federal Reserve banks."[83] "If any part of a fund transfer is covered by EFTA, the entire funds transfer is excluded from Article 4A."[84] Federal Reserve regulation E elaborates the EFTA, while Federal Reserve Regulation J regulates funds transfer through FedWire. Electronic funds transfers with international components are covered by the model law on international credit transfers, adopted by the United Nations Commission on International Trade Law (UNCITRAL) in 1992.[85]

All of these statutory and regulatory regimes defer to terms expressed in contracts. Clearinghouse rules specify the details of commercial transactions, while depositor agreements specify the rules for consumer transactions.

---

[79] *See generally* David Slawson, *Standard Form Contracts and Democratic Control of Lawmaking Power,* 84 Harv. L. Rev. 529 (1971).

[80] 15 U.S.C. §§ 1693–1693q (1988).

[81] *Id.* § 1693a(6) (quotation omits exceptions and limitations).

[82] *Id.* § 1693a(6)(B) (excludes from the definition of electronic fund transfer any transfer of funds not designed primarily to transfer funds on behalf of a consumer).

[83] *Compare* U.C.C. § 4A-102 cmt. (Supp. 1994) (explaining subject matter of Article 4A) with U.C.C. § 4A-107 cmt. 1 (explaining Federal Reserve FedWire system and section that allows Federal Reserve regulations and circulars to supersede inconsistent provisions of Article 4A).

[84] U.C.C. art. 4A, pref. n. (Supp. 1994) (describing transactions covered by Article 4A).

[85] *Id.*

§ 9.17 —Uniform Commercial Code Article 4A

Article 4A of the Uniform Commercial Code regulates wholesale funds transfers. Article 4A recognizes that the terminology "funds transfer" is misleading
because no funds actually are transferred; rather, funds transfers are effected by
a series of payment orders. The following description of an electronic funds
transfer, drawn from the prefatory note to Article 4A, is a useful starting point
for understanding the legal framework for wholesale funds transfers:

> X, a debtor, wants to pay an obligation owed to Y. Instead of delivering to Y a
> negotiable instrument such as a check or some other writing such as a credit card
> slip that enables Y to obtain payment from a bank, X transmits an instruction to X's
> bank to credit a sum of money to the bank account of Y. In most cases X's bank
> and Y's bank are different banks. X's bank may carry out X's instruction by
> instructing Y's bank to credit Y's account in the amount that X requested. The
> instruction that X issues to its bank is a "payment order." X is the "sender" of the
> payment order and X's bank is the "receiving bank" with respect to X's order. Y is
> the "beneficiary" of X's order. When X's bank issues an instruction to Y's bank to
> carry out X's payment order, X's bank "executes" X's order. The instruction of X's
> bank to Y's bank is also a payment order. With respect to that order, X's bank is the
> sender, Y's bank is the receiving bank, and Y is the beneficiary. The entire series of
> transactions by which X pays Y is known as the "funds transfer." With respect to
> the funds transfer, X is the "originator," X's bank is the "originator's bank," Y is
> the "beneficiary" and Y's bank is the "beneficiary's bank." In more complex
> transactions there are one or more additional banks known as "intermediary banks"
> between X's bank and Y's bank. In the funds transfer the instruction contained in
> the payment order of X to its bank is carried out by a series of payment orders by
> each bank in the transmission chain to the next bank in the chain until Y's bank
> receives a payment order to make the credit to Y's account. In most cases, the
> payment order of each bank to the next bank in the chain is transmitted electroni-
> cally, and often the payment order of X to its bank is also transmitted electronically,
> but the means of transmission does not have any legal significance.[86]

As of January 15, 1994, 47 jurisdictions had enacted Article 4A,[87] which
completes the legal framework begun by regulation of certain aspects of wire
transfers under rules adopted by the various transfer and clearinghouse systems,
including FedWire, governed by Federal Reserve regulation J, and the CHIPS
rules.[88]

An important purpose of Article 4A was to allocate the risk of loss in a system
in which the prices for transactions are very low and in which the payment
orders are processed very quickly with funds frequently released to beneficiaries
before compensating payments are received through the transfer system. This

---

[86] U.C.C. art. 4A, pref. n. (Supp. 1994).

[87] U.C.C. § 4A, 4 U.L.A. 4A (Supp. 1994).

[88] U.C.C. art. 4A, pref. n. (explaining why Article 4A is needed in part because of only partial
coverage by clearinghouse and transfer-system rules).

payments clearing process has been characterized as a "high stakes game of hot potato."[89] In particular, Article 4A addresses insolvency of the bank obligated to make the compensating payment, failure to execute the payment order or late execution of a payment order, and errors in payment orders regarding the amount to be paid or identity of the person paid.[90]

The crucial legal transaction is when the beneficiary bank becomes legally obligated to pay the beneficiary, and this occurs when the beneficiary bank "accepts" the payment order issued to it by an intermediary bank.[91] Under Article 4A, the funds transfer is "completed when this debt is incurred."[92] Upstream, the initial bank, called the "receiving bank," is not obligated until it "accepts" the payment order from its customer. Acceptance and a duty to accept are matters of contract, supplemented by Article 4A. Under the statute, the receiving bank accepts its customer's payment order when it executes the order by itself issuing an order to an intermediary bank.[93] An electronic payment order may be stopped only in a manner that gives notice to the receiving bank at a time and in a manner such that it has a reasonable opportunity to act on the stop payment order before it accepts the preceding payment order.[94]

The beneficiary bank owes duties only to the beneficiary, and the initial receiving bank owes obligations only to its customer. On the other hand, intermediary banks owe obligations both to the originator and to the beneficiary, identified under U.C.C. § 4A-207.[95]

Uniform Commercial Code § 4A-302 expresses standards for the time and manner of executing payment orders. Sections 4A-303 and 4A-207 contain rules for determining rights and obligations when errors are made in the transfer process. Everyone in the chain benefits from a kind of "money back guarantee" effectuated by §§ 4A-402(c), 4A-406, and 4A-302. In general, Article 4 places

---

[89] Algemene Bank Nederland N.V. v. Federal Reserve Bank of N.Y., No. 89 Civ. 4946 (swk), 1991 WL 4513 (S.D.N.Y. Jan. 16, 1991) (quoting United States Fidelity & Guar. Co. v. Federal Reserve Bank of N.Y., 590 F. Supp. 486, 491 (S.D.N.Y. 1984)).

[90] U.C.C. art. 4A, pref. n. (Supp. 1994).

[91] Impulse Trading, Inc. v. Norwest Bank Minn., NA, 870 F. Supp. 954 (D. Minn. 1994) (beneficiary bank lost power to reverse credit to customer's account under Article 4A even though no "payment order" involved in complicated transaction involving transfer of funds through India begun by Russian bank of beneficiary's customer; acceptance under Article 4A determined whether beneficiary conversion theory against bank for reversing credit to account was meritorious).

[92] U.C.C. art. 4A, pref. n. (explaining concept) (Supp. 1994); *id.* § 4A-405 (rules for determining when obligation of beneficiary's bank to beneficiary has been paid).

[93] *Id.* art. 4A, pref. n.; *id.* § 4A-209(b) (explaining when receiving bank accepts order).

[94] Aleo Int'l, Ltd. v. Citibank, N.A., 612 N.Y.S.2d 540, 541 (Sup. Ct. 1994) (granting summary judgment against plaintiff on negligence claim against New York bank that sent stop payment order the morning after the payment order was sent to Germany).

[95] Donmar Enters., Inc. v. Southern Nat'l Bank of N.C., 828 F. Supp. 1230, 1239 (W.D.N.C. 1993) (rejecting argument that telex order that failed precisely and formally to identify beneficiary should have been rejected under § 4A-207; sender must have expected bank to identify beneficiary, and bank acted promptly as though identification was straightforward).

the loss on the "party in the best position to prevent it."[96] Section 4A-305 expresses the measure of damages for improper execution, ordinarily excluding consequential damages.[97]

Sections 4A-202 and 4A-203 allocate the risk of loss from forgery— unauthorized payment orders. When a receiving bank accepts an order and uses the agreed-upon security procedures, the customer is bound to pay the order even if it was not authorized, but only if the security procedure is judicially determined to be "commercially reasonable." If the bank accepts an unauthorized payment order without verifying compliance with security procedure, it bears the risk of loss. Importantly, if the originator can show that the unauthorized order was not initiated by its employee or another agent having access to confidential security information, or by a person obtaining the security information from the originator, the originator can shift the loss to the receiving bank.[98] Errors in transmission are the responsibility of the sender unless security procedures have been agreed to between sending and receiving banks and the receiving bank does not employ them.[99]

The risk of insolvency varies depending on the practice in the particular transfer system. In FedWire and in other systems in which the receiving bank can debit a funded account of the sender, the risk of insolvency loss is small. But in other systems, prominently including the New York Clearinghouse Interbank Payments Systems (CHIPS),[100] receiving banks frequently accept payment orders before receiving payment from sending banks. Payment occurs at the end of the day when settlements are made through the Federal Reserve system. "If the receiving bank is an intermediary bank, it will accept by issuing a payment order to another bank and the intermediary bank is obliged to pay that payment order."[101] Then, if the sending bank becomes insolvent before making its settlements at the end of the day, the downstream banks face a loss. The commentary to Article 4A encourages various means of reducing exposure, such

---

[96] Algemene Bank Nederland N.V. v. Federal Reserve Bank of N.Y., No. 89 Civ. 4946 (swk), 1991 WL 4513 (S.D.N.Y. 1991) (quoting United States Fidelity & Guar. Co. v. Federal Reserve Bank of N.Y., 620 F. Supp. 361, 371 (S.D.N.Y. 1985)).

[97] U.C.C. § 4A-305 cmt. 2 (Supp. 1994) (explaining rationale for limiting consequential damages).

[98] *See generally id.* § 4A-203 cmts. 1–7.

[99] *Id.* § 4A-205. *See* Banque Worms v. Bank Am. Int'l, 570 N.E.2d 189, 197–98, 568 N.Y.S.2d 541 (1991) (applying "discharge for value" rule and generally reviewing loss allocation rules of Article 4A to determine that bank that accepted payment order by crediting its depositor notwithstanding stop payment order it knew about was not entitled to recover amount from depositor).

[100] CHIPS handles 95% of the international transfers made in dollars, and transfers were made through participating banks located in New York because all CHIPS network members must maintain a regulated presence in New York. CHIPS is owned and operated by the New York Clearinghouse Association. *See* Banque Worms v. Bank Am. Int'l, 570 N.E.2d 189, 194 (N.Y. 1991) (describing CHIPS network).

[101] U.C.C. art. 4A, pref. n. (19) ("insolvency losses").

as a kind of insurance system established within the transfer systems.[102] In addition, §§ 4A-403(b) and (c) also address the problem by permitting setoffs of amounts owed to a failed bank against amounts owed by a failed bank.

A typical dispute is illustrated by *Sinclair Oil Corp. v. Sylvan State Bank.*[103] Sinclair Oil had sent electronic payment orders to Sylvan Bank to debit the account of a distributor in exchange for deliveries made by Sinclair to the distributor. Sylvan returned the payment orders because of insufficient funds in the distributor's account, but returned them late by mail instead of by E-mail. If national automated clearinghouse rules (NACHA rules) and Operating Letter 12 of the Federal Reserve Bank of Kansas City applied, Sylvan's late return would leave Sylvan obligated on the payment orders.[104] If the NACHA rules and operating letter did not apply, the Kansas version of U.C.C. § 4-104(a)(10) established a time limit that had been satisfied by Sylvan's return.[105] The bank argued that because Sinclair was not a financial institution, the NACHA rules and operating letter did not cover disputes between it and a financial institution.[106] The Kansas Supreme Court essentially ducked the core question by concluding that Article 4 of the Kansas Code did not apply to electronic fund transfers because they are not "items" under Article 4.[107] It thus concluded that it need not answer the questions regarding coverage by the clearinghouse rules and operating letter.[108]

§ 9.18   —Federal Reserve Regulations

Regulation J[109] regulates the clearance of financial items through the Federal Reserve system. One federal court has found that regulation J preempts common-law causes of action based on transactions within the scope of Regulation J.[110] In general, Regulation J obligates Federal Reserve banks to pay at par items received from Federal Reserve depository institutions and other institutions that maintain accounts at Federal Reserve banks.[111] It covers *items,* which

---

[102] *Id.*

[103] 869 P.2d 675 (Kan. 1994).

[104] *Id.* at 677 (explaining dispute and legal theories).

[105] *Id.* at 678.

[106] This is analogous to the argument that Article 4A does not apply to the transaction between a consumer-originator and an originating bank.

[107] 869 P.2d 675, 680–81 (Kan. 1994).

[108] *Id.* at 680.

[109] 12 C.F.R. §§ 210.1–210.32 & apps. A, B (1994).

[110] *See* Donmar Enters., Inc. v. Southern Nat'l Bank of N.C., 828 F. Supp. 1230, 1236 (W.D.N.C. 1993) (common-law claims for wrongful payment and negligence preempted by Regulation J and no violation of Regulation J for two-stage international currency transaction payment).

[111] 12 C.F.R. § 210.2(1) (1994) (defining sender to include depository institutions defined in 12 U.S.C. § 461(b) (1994) and other depositor institutions defined in 12 U.S.C. § 342, certain corporations in international organizations, and foreign banks as defined in 12 U.S.C. § 632 and 12 U.S.C. § 358).

are defined as instruments for the payment of money, whether negotiable or not, that are payable in a Federal Reserve district, and specifically includes cash and noncash items but excludes payment orders as defined in 12 C.F.R. § 210.26(i) and handled under subpart B.[112] Those payment orders are defined to be the same as those covered by U.C.C. Article 4A, except that they do not include ACH transfers or communications defined in Federal Reserve operating circulars as not being payment orders.[113]

Subpart B tracks Article 4A closely.[114] The commentary notes that subpart B incorporates the provisions of Article 4A, overriding only those provisions of 4A that are inconsistent with specific parts of subpart B itself.[115] Subpart B allows Federal Reserve banks to identify banks involved in fund transfers by identifying numbers on the payment order even if the payment order identifies other banks by name and the names and numbers are inconsistent.[116] Negligence standards govern the conduct of participants.[117] Reasonably strict compliance with clearinghouse rules for marking returned items is necessary.[118]

Federal Reserve system Regulation E covers electronic funds transfers by consumers. It expressly excludes from its coverage wire transfers through systems used primarily for transfers between financial institutions or businesses.[119] Telephone bill payment codes and telephone transfer orders are

---

[112] Subpart B is 12 C.F.R. §§ 210.25–210.32 (1994).

[113] 12 C.F.R. § 210.26(i) (1994).

[114] *See, e.g. id.* § 210.26(i) (defining payment order as that in Article 4A; *id.* § 210.26(d) (same definition of beneficiary bank as in Article 4A); *id.* § 210.32 (damages and payment of interest determined as under Article 4A).

[115] 12 C.F.R. § 210.25(b), app. A (1994).

[116] *Id.* § 210.27. *See* Restatement (Second) of Contracts § 26 cmt. b (1981) ("It is of course possible to make an offer by an advertisement directed to the general public, but there must ordinarily be some language of commitment or some invitation to take action without further communication.").

[117] Northwest Bank & Trust Co. v. First Westside Bank, 941 F.2d 722, 724 (8th Cir. 1991) (affirming judgment against paying bank that failed to exercise ordinary care in giving prompt notice of dishonor pursuant to Regulation J); Brothers Trading Co. v. Charleston Nat'l Bank, 972 F.2d 338 (4th Cir. 1992) (reversing district court and remanding for trial of claim that beneficiary bank negligently handled funds pursuant to mistaken electronic payment order sent to it by originating bank; common-law negligence principles supplement Regulation J); Lichtenstein v. Kidder Peabody & Co., 840 F. Supp. 374, 387 (W.D. Pa. 1993) (failure of depository institution to exercise reasonable care caused it to bear the loss of forged checks even though depositor failed to detect forgeries that might have been revealed by monthly statement; applying Articles 3 and 4 of U.C.C.).

[118] *See* Algemene Bank Nederland N.V. v. Federal Reserve Bank of N.Y., No. 89 Civ. 4946 (swk), 1991 WL 4513 (S.D.N.Y. Jan. 16, 1991) (imposing loss on participant in clearinghouse system that returned check without using stamps and marks or invalidating magnetic codes as required by clearinghouse rules incorporated into Regulation J).

[119] 12 C.F.R. § 205.3(b) (1994). "This Act and this regulation do not apply to the following: (b) wire transfers. Any wire transfer of funds for a consumer through the Federal Reserve Communications System or other similar network that is used primarily for transfers between financial institutions or between business."

included,[120] but payments and currency from an ATM are not.[121] Home PC equipment initiating transfers and point of sale terminals initiating transfers in conjunction with debit cards are covered.[122] ATM transactions forced by robbers are unauthorized.[123] When ACH wire transfers are followed by ATM transactions, any FedWire portion is exempt, but ACH transfers to employee accounts are covered.[124]

§ 9.19   —Electronic Funds Transfer Act

The Electronic Funds Transfer Act (EFTA) regulates consumer electronic funds transfers.[125] It is the authority for Federal Reserve Regulation E. The EFTA has important limitations on its scope, excluding for example the interbank parts of consumer funds transfers,[126] and telephonic transfer orders initiated by consumers in face-to-face instructions for wire transfers.[127] On the other hand, the statute requires the Federal Reserve Board by regulation to extend the protections of EFTA to electronic fund transfer services made available by nonbanks.[128]

The statute requires disclosure of EFT procedures to consumers, including an explanation of the consumer's right to stop payment of preauthorized EFTs and the right to receive documentation.[129] Transfers must be documented in writing.[130] In an appendix to Regulation E, the board has provided model disclosure clauses, but has delayed mandatory compliance until March 1, 1997.[131]

---

[120] 12 C.F.R. pt. 205, *in* Supp. II, § 205.2, 2-1Q (official staff interpretations) (1994).

[121] *Id.* 2-10Q.

[122] *Id.* 2-23Q, 2-24Q.

[123] *Id.* 2-28Q.

[124] *Id.* 3-3Q.

[125] 15 U.S.C. §§ 1693a–1693q (1994).

[126] Shawmut Worcester County Bank v. First Am. Bank & Trust, 731 F. Supp. 57, 61–62 (D. Mass. 1990) (claim by originating bank against receiving bank to reverse erroneous FedWire payment order 109 days later not covered by EFTA because bank-bank transaction not involving consumer directly; also rejecting conversion and agency theories against receiving bank that refused to reverse payment).

[127] 15 U.S.C. § 1693a(6)(E) (1988) (excluding transfers initiated by telephone conversation); Wachter v. Denver Nat'l Bank, 751 F. Supp. 906, 908 (D. Colo. 1990) (wire transfer made at request of customer who visited bank and paid for wire transfer with cash not within EFTA both because of personal contact rather than electronic device to initiate, and because no account of customer was debited or credited); Curde v. Tri-City Bank & Trust Co., 826 S.W.2d 911, 915 (Tenn. 1992) (deposit of check covered by EFTA because only face-to-face personal contacts removed check deposits from Act's coverage, but customer cancellation of attempted deposit via ATM machine removed it from EFTA).

[128] 15 U.S.C. § 1693b(d) (1988).

[129] *Id.* § 1693c(5) (stop payment), 1693c(6) (right to receive documentation).

[130] 15 U.S.C. § 1693d (1988).

[131] *See* 12 C.F.R. pt. 205, App. A (1994).

The statute requires financial institutions to investigate errors alleged by consumers within 60 days after documentation is sent and to report the results of their investigations and any determination thereon to the consumer within 10 business days.[132] If the financial institution determines that no error occurred, upon the consumer's request, it must deliver or mail to the consumer reproductions of all documents supporting its determination.[133] Oral reports do not comply.[134]

The statute limits consumer liability for unauthorized transfers to $50, except for unauthorized transfers made when the consumer fails to notify the financial institution of facts known to the consumer that suggest the likelihood of unauthorized transfers.[135] This limitation would not exonerate a consumer from transfers made by persons to whom the consumer has given a funds transfer card and disclosed the consumer's PIN. Negligence by a consumer, for example, writing the PIN on the ATM card, does not alter the allocation of risk of unauthorized transfers.[136] Financial institutions expressly are liable for failures to make EFTs correctly and in a timely manner subject to certain exceptions, such as insufficient funds, or unforeseeable technical malfunctions when the financial institution exercised reasonable care.[137] The burden of proof with respect to alleged unauthorized transfers is imposed on the financial institution to show that the transfer was in fact authorized.[138] The statute explicitly prohibits waiver of the statutory rights and causes of action created by the Act.[139] The statute creates private rights of action.[140] Bank regulatory agencies and the Federal Trade Commission also are given enforcement authority.[141] The statute preempts state laws only to the extent that they are inconsistent with EFTA,[142] but allows the Federal Reserve Board to exempt fund transfers from federal

---

[132] *Id.* § 1693f; *id.* § 1693f(e) (providing treble damages for certain violations of its provisions).

[133] *Id.* § 1693f(d).

[134] Bisbey v. D.C. Nat'l Bank, 793 F.2d 315 (D.C. Cir. 1986).

[135] 15 U.S.C. § 1693(g); *see also* Federal Reserve Regulation E, 12 C.F.R. § 205.2(*l*) (defining unauthorized electronic fund transfer to exclude transfer initiated by person furnished with access device unless consumer notifies financial institution that transfers by that person are no longer authorized). *See* Kruser v. Bank of Am. NT & SA, 281 Cal. Rptr. 463, 466 (Ct. App. 1991) (bank not obligated on $9,000 worth of unauthorized transfers because customers failed to report unauthorized $20 transfer approximately one year earlier on card they assumed had been destroyed).

[136] 12 C.F.R. pt. 205, *in* Supp. II, § 205.2, 2-1Q (official staff interpretations) (1994).

[137] 15 U.S.C. § 1693(h). *See generally* Feinman v. Bank of Del., 728 F. Supp. 1105 (D. Del.) (no liability for temporary denial due to security reasons), *aff'd,* 909 F.2d 1475 (3d Cir. 1990).

[138] 15 U.S.C. § 1693g(b).

[139] *Id.* § 1693*l* (preventing a waiver of rights, but explicity allowing agreements to provide greater protection to the consumer).

[140] *Id.* § 1693m.

[141] *Id.* § 1693o.

[142] *Id.* § 1693q.

regulation when it certifies that the fund transfers exempted are subject to state law requirements substantially similar to those imposed by the federal Act.[143]

§ 9.20   Article 8 and the Move Away from Document-Based Commercial Transaction Systems

The proposed redraft of Article 8 of the Uniform Commercial Code exemplifies commercial law's abandonment of paper as the central feature of commercial markets.[144]

Historically, corporate securities transactions, like many other property transactions, were paper-based. Sale and ownership of real property was evidenced by possession of a deed that named the purported owner as the grantee. Currency, negotiable instruments, and stock certificates all similarly memorialize the ownership of intangible personal property. Transfers were effected by transferring the piece of paper. But the availability of computer and improved communications technologies, coupled with growing volume on stock exchanges, made paper-based stock-transfer systems infeasible, and the securities markets moved to systems for transferring ownership electronically. Nevertheless, the law still required the transfer of a paper stock certificate, much as EFTA facilitates electronic funds transfers by consumers, while still requiring paper receipts and reports.[145]

The 1994 revision of Article 8 of the U.C.C. moves away from a theory of commercial transactions that is paper-based.[146] It abandons statutory concerns with "settlements," which are the ceremonies in which physical delivery takes place. Now, settlements between intermediaries explicitly may be done on a "net basis," which means that these intermediary transactions do not contain information about individual buyers and sellers. Now, the determinative event is posting a credit or debit on the account books of the broker with whom a buyer or seller of a security has an immediate relationship.[147] Under the new § 8-501,

---

[143] *Id.* § 1693r.

[144] U.C.C. art. 8 (revised Nov. 9, 1994). Article 8 revisions were approved by the National Conference of Commissioners on Uniform State Laws at its August 1994 meeting and by the American Law Institute in May 1994. Similar changes were being made to Article 5, covering letters of credit. *See Commercial Law,* 63 U.S.L.W. 2737 (May 30, 1995) (reporting on § 5-104 of discussion draft saying that a letter of credit may be issued "in any form that is a record," recognizing that letters of credit and other documents need not be in writing). *See also A.B.A., UCC Subcommittee Reports,* Commercial Law Newsletter, June 1995, at 8 (working group recommends that Article 9 redrafting effort redefine chattel paper as "chattel obligations" to include paperless transactions, and broaden possession concept to include concept of "control").

[145] 15 U.S.C. § 1693d (requiring electronic funds transfers to be documented in writing).

[146] U.C.C. art. 8, pref. n. (1994 rev.).

[147] This is an example of a general trend to break the link between chattels and intangibles. Tangible chattels still are transferred by transferring physical possession; increasingly, intangibles are transferred electronically and not by transferring a paper certificate of ownership.

the key event is one's own broker crediting one's account, not a transfer of something. The investor-issuer relationship has become legally insignificant; the important relationship is the customer-intermediary relationship. This philosophy builds on Article 4A's payment order concepts.

This fundamental change in the focus of Article 8 necessitated rethinking the idea of negotiability. The drafters came up with this solution: they forgot about negotiability as a distinct concept and simply sought to codify its purpose. Thus, under the new Article 8, an adverse claim, for example, one based on a theory of conversion or asserted in a replevin action against one with a security entitlement, may not be successfully asserted unless the entitled person had notice of the alleged wrongdoing. Thus, the obligee at the end of the transfer chain is insulated from challenges relating to the sequence of transactions leading up to his entitlement. The holder in due course doctrine now has been codified directly without relying on the concept of negotiability of a piece of paper.

This kind of legal development is helpful in removing barriers to the use of information technology. It does, however, present a risk from a public policy standpoint. As paper is eliminated, so also is eliminated a cheap and reliable means of proving commercial transactions. Especially from a historical standpoint, the possibility that one's ownership depends on the continued existence of a computer record in someone else's computer instead of a piece of paper and one's own possession is disconcerting. There are two conceptual ways for dealing with this risk. One is to revitalize the concept of a government registry for important information, one not based on paper records as in registrars of deeds, but one based on electronic records. Important transactions would be registered with the registrar, much as one might file a will or record a deed or mortgage. A second way of dealing with the risk is simply to impose the burden of proof on the party maintaining the records. Thus, if the party cannot come up with a record of an alleged transaction, that party would have to pay the alleged obligation. An obvious problem with this approach is that it would leave record keepers vulnerable to fraudulent claims of entitlements based on records that never existed.

§ 9.21   Digital Cash

Various proposals have been made and are just beginning to be tried out for digital cash, sometimes called "cybermoney." The common feature of all the digital cash proposals is that value could be exchanged in electronic networks in the form of an electronic token that would be a legally effective claim to payment and perhaps also constitute legal tender. Typically, the claim for redemption of a token would be asserted against the issuer of cybermoney, but it also could be the legal equivalent of a personal check, which represents the legal obligation only of the person offering it initially in payments until it is "accepted" by a third party.[148] Cybermoney works only if people to whom it is tendered have confidence that it will be redeemed. They can spend it or get credit for it in their bank accounts only to the extent that everyone in a chain of presenters and depositories[149] are virtually certain of eventual redemption.[150]

This certainty of redemption exists only if the issuer can be found, has a legal obligation to redeem with few possible defenses, and has sufficient assets to make redemption. These sound like the hallmarks of a banking system, but they can be satisfied outside traditional banking law. For example, American Express Travelers Checks are an extremely effective form of quasi currency even though American Express is not a bank. The reason for the effectiveness of American Express Travelers Checks is that American Express has a reputation, backed up by, but exceeding, legal obligations imposed by Article 3 of the U.C.C., for redeeming with few questions asked traveler's checks that have been properly signed and countersigned. Western Union and Seven-Eleven money orders are similarly effective for the same reasons.

Aside from these prerequisites for any system of money or near money, cybermoney requires an infrastructure like that for public key encryption, described in **§ 9.14.** Participants in a cybermoney system must be able to detect forgery and counterfeiting.[151]

§ 9.22   Credit Cards in the NII

The requisites of a cheap and pervasive electronic payment system could be satisfied by the existing credit card system, with relatively few modifications. Most of the credit card approval and authorization process between merchants and issuing banks is electronic, conducted in private networks run by banks and Visa and Mastercard Associations. For large merchants, the "deposit" of credit card records of charge with merchant banks is electronic, conducted in networks provided by the banks. There are two gaps to be filled in before this type of payment system can become seamlessly integrated into the NII. First, the basic purchase, presentment, and authorization transactions must occur in an open system like the Internet so that the availability of electronic payment does not depend upon subscription to any particular proprietary network. Second, the transaction between consumer and merchant must be electronic so that a physical credit card need not be presented and imprinted and a human being need not

---

[148] The accepting third party in the case of a personal check is the drawee bank.

[149] In the check clearance process, each transferor is known as a presenter, and each transferee is known as a depository.

[150] U.C.C. § 4-108. Two of the most active promoters of digital cash are CyberCash, Inc., http://www.cybercash.com, and DigiCash, http://digicash.com.

[151] Counterfeiting is arguably a type of forgery, but the separate word is used in the text to signify unauthorized duplication and use of a cybermoney token.

read aloud the numbers from the credit card over a voice telephone connection. All of the electronic communications must be appropriately secure, of course, to prevent acquisition of credit card numbers by criminals, leading to subsequent attempts at their unauthorized use.

As in a digital cash system, the efficacy of a completely electronic credit card system depends on the confidence of merchants and others in the present-ment/depository chain of eventual redemption of the record of charge (ROC) by the credit card issuer. The credit card issuer, of course, is willing to redeem only those ROCs representing bona fide charges by its cardholders. Existing credit card systems impose on the merchant the responsibility of making sure that cards are presented only by their holders and of obtaining authorization for charges over certain amounts.[152] The authorization process serves the merchant as well as the issuer because it is a way of authenticating the card and detecting the presentation of forged or counterfeit cards. These same needs must be met in a purely electronic credit card system. They can be met by deploying public key encryption discussed in § **9.13.** Digital signatures can ensure that payments are made only by the authorized holders of electronic credit cards. Digital signa-tures of issuers also can protect against counterfeit electronic credit cards. Public key encryption in the privacy mode ensures against unauthorized acquisi-tion of credit card numbers and other card and cardholder information.

§ 9.23   Offering Securities Through the NII

Some corporations and entrepreneurs have begun to seek investors through the NII. This raises the question whether such communication may constitute an offer of securities regulated by the Federal Securities and Exchange Commis-sion under the Securities Act of 1933, or by state securities regulators under state blue-sky laws. Whether these investment opportunities must be registered and subjected to regulatory review before they may be presented in NII communica-tions turns on whether the NII communications constitute "offers." Section 4(2) of the Securities Act of 1933[153] exempts from the registration and prospectus requirements of section 5 of that Act[154] "transactions by an issuer not involving any public offering." The SEC has interpreted the boundary between such private offerings and public offerings in its Regulation D, initially issued in 1982. In general, that regulation denies the private placement safe harbor to any person who directly or through an agent offers to sell securities by

---

[152] *See* Michigan Bankard Services, Merchant Agreement §§ 8, 9 (July 1992) (on file with the author). VISA has announced standards for Internet transactions. http://www.visa.com/visa-stt/ So has mastercard. http://www.mastercard.com.

[153] 15 U.S.C. § 77d (1988) ("The provisions of section 77c (§ 5) shall not apply to transactions by an issuer not involving any public offering.").

[154] *Id.* § 77e (detailing various prohibitions on interstate commerce).

any form of general solicitation or general advertising, including, but not limited to, the following:

(1) Any advertisement, article, notice or other communication published in any newspaper, magazine, or similar media or broadcast over television or radio; and

(2) Any seminar or meeting whose attendees have been invited by any general solicitation or general advertising.[155]

Small offerings made exclusively in and in accordance with the regulations of states may be promoted through publications and seminars notwithstanding Regulation D.[156]

Mailings constitute offers when the addressees were not persons with a preexisting relationship with the issuer.[157] Under this guidance, most forms of NII communication would constitute offers. The text of Regulation D refers to "other media," which surely would include E-mail broadcasts and newsgroup postings as well as the placement of a file on an anonymous FTP server, a Gopher server, or a World Wide Web server. The mass mailing cases reinforce this conclusion. There are, however, two circumstances under which NII communications about an issue of securities could qualify as a private offering. Those are E-mail communications between pre-acquainted electronic correspondents, and a limited discussion through a list serve or restricted newsgroup that permits participation only by sophisticated investors known to the issuer before the discussion occurs. The SEC issued policy guidance and proposed rules in October, 1995 to make it easier for issuers to give required notices electronically, through the Internet and otherwise.[158]

The "state" exception would not likely be applicable because of the virtual impossibility of confining NII communications to a single state. Moreover, the purpose of the registration requirement is to protect unsophisticated investors. There is no reason to suppose that communication through the NII would be limited to sophisticated investors. In most states, the private offering exemption is premised on section 402(b)(9) of the Uniform Securities Act of 1956. This section provides in material part that no more than 10 persons can be solicited within any 12 consecutive months.[159] States have added exemptions to the section 402(b)(9) exemption mostly through the Uniform Limited Offering Exemption (ULOE), which resembles SEC Regulation D.

---

[155] 17 C.F.R. § 230.502(b)(2)(vii)(c) (1994).

[156] *Id.* § 504(b)(1).

[157] *See* Kenman Corp., Securities Exchange Act Release No. 21,962 (Apr. 19, 1985) (finding relatively small mailing to be an offer).

[158] *See* Use of Electronic Media for Delivery Purposes, 60 Fed. Reg. 53458 (Oct. 13, 1995); Proposed Rules, Use of Electronic Media for Delivery Purposes, 60 Fed. Reg. 53468 (Oct. 13, 1995).

[159] Unif. Securities Act § 402(b)(9) (1956). *See generally* SEC v. Ralston Purina Co., 346 U.S. 119, 124–25 (1953) (summarizing purpose of registration requirement and interpreting requirement in terms of whether investors need protection).

§ 9.24   Draft Language for Electronic Offers
of Contracts

This section provides sample language for electronic contract offers in which human beings participate. Such language obviously is not needed when the transaction is completely automatic, as in the exchange of EDI transaction sets.

The following would be presented on a computer screen by the computer system making the offer or soliciting offers:

You are about to enter into a contract. By typing the words "I accept" in the space provided at the bottom of your screen, you accept our offer to connect you to the database containing housing code provisions for your state. You will be billed at a price of $20 per hour for your usage of this database, and by typing "I accept" at the bottom of this screen you agree to pay that charge and also acknowledge your use of the database according to records we will keep.

If you do not wish to enter into this contract at this time, simply press the enter or escape key and you will be returned to the preceding screen.

The following is a form of waiver of intellectual rights, and also illustrates a slightly different approach to the acceptance of terms:

You are about to enter a discussion area in which you are allowed to post messages and comments. By participating in this discussion group, you are entering into a contractual waiver of any intellectual property rights you may have in anything you post or upload or type. In other words, you are giving up any claim of copyright to your messages into this service.

There are two buttons shown at the bottom of your screen. If you agree to waive your intellectual property rights and to continue into the discussion group, select the button labeled "I agree to waive intellectual property rights." If you do not agree, select the button "I do not agree" or hit any key on your keyboard, and you will be returned to the preceding screen.

The following is from America Online terms of service:

Your use of the America Online service constitutes acceptance of our terms of service. The terms of service is comprised that the terms of service agreement and the rules of the road. The most common terms of service violations fall under the on-line conduct category, which appears as a separate icon below. We ask that you read these documents carefully. To contact the terms of service staff, select the right to terms of service staff icon below. [Four icons follow this text: "terms of service agreement" "rules of the road" "on line conduct," "right to terms of service staff"].

The terms of service icon leads to another set of icons that represent segments of the terms of service. They include:

1.3 By completing the enrollment process and using AOL service and AOL software (other than to read the TOS agreement and the rules of the road for the first time), you agree to be legally bound and to abide by the terms of service, just as if you had signed this agreement. If you do not wish to be bound by our TOS, you may not continue to use the AOL service and AOL software. In that case, you should immediately terminate your membership account and you are prohibited from using AOL software.

1.4 AOL Inc. may modify its TOS at any time and in any manner. Any modification is effective immediately upon either a posting on the AOL service, electronic mail, or conventional mail. If any modification to the TOS is unacceptable to you, you may immediately terminate your membership as provided in § 8 below. Your continued use of the AOL service following modification to the TOS shall be conclusively deemed as acceptance of such modification.

1.5 The terms of service agreement, rules of the road and the membership conditions together constitute the entire and only agreement between AOL Inc. and member with respect to the AOL service and AOL software. AOL Inc. may discontinue or alter any aspect of the AOL service, including, but not limited to, (i) restricting the time of availability, (ii) restricting the availability and/or scope of the AOL service for certain platforms (i.e., computer types and operating systems), (iii) restricting the amount of use permitted, and (iv) restricting or terminating any member's right to use the AOL service, at AOL Inc.'s sole discretion and without prior notice or liability. AOL Inc. reserves the right to change or add any fees or surcharges at any time effective upon thirty (30) days' prior notice.[160]

---

[160] As viewed on AOL terms of service screens, May 8, 1995 (notice concludes with "transmitted: 95-02-21 10:38 12 Est"). Copyright 1995 America Online, Inc. All Rights Reserved.

CHAPTER 10

INTELLECTUAL PROPERTY

§ 10.1   The Problem: Information As a Commodity

The NII can realize its potential only if it protects private property and makes it possible to offer something for sale or license in open networks like the Internet without it being misappropriated by a competitor. The law protects intellectual property because intellectual creativity is stunted if creators are unable to recover their investment in inventive or creative effort before competitors appropriate their authorship or inventions and get a free ride on the creative effort. The law affords protection in four conceptually distinct but overlapping forms: copyright, patent, trade secret, and trademark. All four protect the creator of value against competitive free riding by making available a limited monopoly over the subject matter. All four forms represent a balance between excluding users and new entrants from valuable information in order to protect pioneers, while allowing legitimate uses of information in a market environment.

Intellectual property law always has responded to new technologies. Copyright was invented as a response to the development of the printing press. Patent law was rationalized to enable the benefits of industrial inventions to be shared more widely. More recently, the widespread use of the photocopy machine refocused copyright concerns. In the 1960s and 1970s, intellectual property scholars and legislators struggled to fit computer programs into an appropriate intellectual property category. Now open, distributed architectures like the Internet pose further challenges.

High-speed digital environments permit unlimited proliferation of copyrighted works through perfect digital copies.[1] They permit partial extraction and sampling and thus raise the threat of uncontrolled derivative works. They permit scanning of printed works into electronic form. They also permit constant updating of textual materials, sometimes referred to as "plasticity," electronic contracting to make immediate binding contracts for transfer of electronic works, and automated billing and collection systems implemented through the same networks that are used for publishing.[2] These changes in the environments present concerns and opportunities not only for print publishers, but also for traditional on-line services, which no longer can assume that centralized databases will be the norm in providing information to network users.

In the seventeenth century the right to copy was equivalent to a right to vend because it was cheaper to buy an authorized original of the work than to copy it. Now, of course, with the photocopy machine, and even more with computer and

---

[1] *See generally* Joseph L. Ebersole, Protecting Intellectual Property Rights on the Information Super Highway (Information Industry Ass'n, Washington, D.C.) Mar., 1994 (inventorying problems posed by new technologies and suggesting requirements for intellectual property law).

[2] Electronic contracting and payments systems are considered in **Ch. 9.**

communications technologies, it may be cheaper to copy than to buy. Basic concepts of copyright protection must shift as the relative costs of the events affecting the creator's market position change. Despite print copyright's association with "fixing" expression on a tangible medium and "copying," other events accomplished through new technologies invite legal regulation. "Performance" or "transmission" may be a more natural event to delineate copyright in computer formats than "fixation" and "copying."[3] The intellectual basis for a copyright in television programming, for example, is common-law copyright for dramatic works—where fixation in a tangible medium of expression is less important than performance.

The disaggregation of production[4] makes it possible for the integrated work to come into existence only upon command of a user. Therefore, it may be more appropriate to focus legal protection on the publication event, now occurring on user demand, which looks more like performance than the reproduction of a work fixed in advance. The problem is that making every performance a potential infringement also makes every *use* a potential infringement—a profound reversal of the traditional approach to print copyright and inconsistent with a limited, utilitarian, information-enhancing understanding of copyright.

Copyright law protects computer programs. The challenge now is to adapt intellectual property principles to electronic publishing—not simply the production and distribution of computer programs, but the more interesting and difficult protection of computerized data that is created electronically, stored in conjunction with tags to facilitate computerized retrieval, retrieved via computer, and distributed via digital communication systems. In responding to that challenge, all four types of intellectual property protection have a role to play, even though much of the value expected to be exchanged through the NII is of the type either traditionally protected by copyright law or constituting computer programs currently protected by copyright law. Patent law plays an increasing role in protecting sophisticated processes important in the NII, such as encryption algorithms and devices, compression techniques, and graphical image representation algorithms. Trade secret and the more general concept of contractual protection are more flexible than statutory arrangements. Trademark and related issues of unfair competition can assure World Wide Web authors and publishers of identification as the source of information value.

Experienced practitioners of intellectual property law know that advocates and judges exhaust legal logic and analysis relatively early in the decision-making process. They must pay close attention to policy when they decide cases

---

[3] *See* L. Ray Patterson & Stanley W. Lindberg, The Nature of Copyright: A Law of Users' Rights (1991).

[4] **Chapter 1** explains how new network architectures similar to that of the Internet facilitate disaggregating production and unbundling the elements of value that make up an information product desired by a consumer.

under the intellectual property statutes and under claims of misappropriation. Thus, even the most real-world oriented practitioner must be concerned with policy issues. The intellectual property policy framework acknowledges that some free riding is inevitable in any publishing activity; the important question about systems for protecting intellectual property is whether *large scale* piracy by competing publishers can be deterred.

The character of the distributed network itself is some protection. It is relatively easy, through patent, trade secret, and access controls to protect novel *process* value in a high-speed digital network. The easiest way to get useful content in such a network is through such processes rather than by seeking it directly from content servers. Any user of the Internet would rather search for content through a NetScape, Mosaic, or Gopher interface rather than browse a large set of unfriendly anonymous file transfer protocol (ftp) servers. Authors and inventors of such finding and retrieval aids can protect their intellectual property by controlling access to the processes they embody, without worrying about pirates being able to copy the intellectual property representing the process itself. The distinction between these value-added features and the content is that the former need not be copied to be used. This protection through process reduces the load on the law and other technological features to protect the intellectual property in the content. The real protection for most content will be the quality assurance associated with authorized sources and planned obsolescence as new versions are released, much as frequent new versions in PC software mitigate piracy threats.

Current law provides substantial penalties for large-scale pirates when they are caught, and the nature of electronic publishing environments like the Internet can make it easier to catch pirates. More work is being done on collective licensing schemes, accompanied by the electronic copyright "police" that could detect abnormal traffic patterns associated with unauthorized access to publishers' servers. Such systems not only enhance detection; they greatly enhance proof in eventual litigation or prosecution.

Technologists understand the need to adapt standards and languages so that licensing cooperatives and other commercial arrangements can work with low transaction costs. For example, much of the current effort to redefine the hypertex transfer protocol (http) standards at the core of the World Wide Web, through http-ng ("next generation"), focuses on handling the terms for intellectual property exchange among intermediaries.[5] Economic analysis also plays an important role in defining intellectual property in the NII and resolving disputes over its use. **Section 10.2** provides an economic framework within which to address intellectual property legal concepts.

---

[5] *See* http://www.w3.org/hypertext/WWW/Protocols/HTTP-NG/http-ng-status.html; http://www.w3.org/hypertext/WWW/Protocols/HTTP-NG/http-ng-arch.html (summary of http-ng draft protocols).

§ 10.2 Economics of Intellectual Property

Intellectual property is necessary because intellectual property is a public good.[6] Economists define *public goods* as those that are nonappropriable and nonrival.[7] *Nonappropriable* means that the producer or other owner cannot practically exclude people from using the good. The light from a lighthouse is the traditional example. A lighthouse owner cannot block off its light from those who have not paid to use the lighthouse. *Nonrival* means that use of a good by one does not limit its use by another. Unlike a pair of shoes, an electronic information product can be used by multiple people at the same time, through copying or otherwise. Markets do not work to create incentives to produce public goods because their nonappropriability and nonrival characteristics mean that free riders can enjoy the benefits of a good just as much as someone who has paid; therefore, producers of public goods find it difficult or impossible to earn a return on their investment.

Information is a special category of public good. Unlike the light from a lighthouse, information is appropriable. One can limit the distribution or access only to someone who has paid for the information. The problem is the nonrival character of information; every customer becomes a potential competitor of the seller because possession of an information item gives the purchaser the capacity to reproduce it. That would not be a serious problem for sellers except that when a purchaser buys an information item and thereby gets the capacity to reproduce it, the purchaser also avoids any investment the original producer made in creating the information item in the first place. For example, if someone bought a copy of this chapter in electronic form, he could reproduce it and sell it (except for intellectual property law) without incurring the cost of writing it in the first place. For the most part, the free-riding potential is equivalent to the fixed costs of the original producer.[8]

---

[6] *See* William H. Landes & Richard A. Posner, *An Economic Analysis of Copyright Law,* 18 J. Legal Stud. 325 (1989); *see generally* L.H. Reichman, *Legal Hybrids Between the Patent and Copyright Problems,* 94 Colum. L. Rev. 2432, 2509 (1994); Ralph S. Brown, *Eligibility for Copyright Protection: A Search for Principled Standards,* 70 Minn. L. Rev. 579, 595 (1985) (critical analysis of economic view of copyright).

[7] Economist Fritz Machlup accomplished some of the most extensive analysis of the economics of information, beginning with his 1962 classic, *The Production and Distribution of Knowledge in the United States* [hereinafter Machlup, Production and Distribution]. He elaborated on this work in a multivolume treatise, the first part of which was published in 1980, and which was interrupted by his death. *See* 1 Fritz Machlup, Knowledge and Knowledge Production (1980) [hereinafter Machlup, Theory of Information]; 3 Fritz Machlup, The Economics of Information and Human Capital (1984) [hereinafter Machlup, Economics of Information]. The multivolume work is entitled Knowledge: Its Creation, Distribution and Economic Significance.

[8] This is not strictly true because only sunk costs incurred by the original producer cannot be recovered by selling the investment to someone else. B. Curtis Eaton & Richard G. Lipsey, *Capital, Commitment, and Entry Equilibrium,* 12 Bell J. Econ. 593, 594 (1981).

Some forms of intellectual property can be protected from free riders by keeping it secret, but then the society may not have full benefit of the knowledge kept secret. Both patent and copyright law work to encourage creators to make the fruits of their creativity available publicly without fear of misappropriation by free riders.

Associated with the intellectual property protection issue, although distinct from it conceptually, is the question of how works on the information super-highway will be priced. Too many people assume that the only alternatives are the traditional Internet approach of charging for connections but not charging for access to particular information objects; or the traditional on-line services approach, charging on an object-usage basis, usually by the minute. The National Information Infrastructure represents a richer spectrum of possibilities than those two alternatives encompass. It is worth recalling when early radio and television pioneers confronted the technological reality that it was infeasible to collect from consumers on a usage basis for radio and television program-ming. They adapted advertiser funding as a way of paying for authorship and production.

There are a wide variety of techniques for paying for authorship and produc-tion value on the NII, certainly including advertising. Another technique is subsidization of content production by value-adding intermediaries who recog-nize that the attractiveness of their intermediary services will be enhanced as richer content is available on the NII. It is important to recognize that intellec-tual property law must protect pricing arrangements as well as the underlying information product. In this regard, sellers may want to engage in price dis-crimination between different submarkets, and thus they will need to enforce prohibitions on reselling their product from one market into another.

Encryption is attractive as a way of reducing the free-riding potential without heavy reliance on intellectual property law, but there are important limitations on encryption as a solution. Encryption works only when encryption standards are adhered to by both producer and consumer of information. There is nothing in the history of developing standards for computer formats that suggests optimism about the feasibility of developing a truly universal standard for encryption.[9] Nor is it either feasible or desirable for the government to mandate adherence to such a standard. Such a mandate would put the government in the position of prohibiting expression except through the approved encryption standard, and that would raise insuperable First Amendment problems. There-fore, encryption as a solution to intellectual property challenges would mean a plethora of incompatible encryption systems. The result would not be a national information infrastructure, but a collection of technically isolated archipelagos, much as CompuServe, America Online, NEXIS, Dialog, Westlaw, and LEXIS were isolated from each other before the NII encouraged interconnections and gateways. Pricing models and technological protections are considered further in § **10.22.**

---

[9] See **Ch. 8** regarding the dynamics of private standard setting.

§ 10.3 Copyright

Federal copyright law is the principal form of intellectual property law for protecting computer programs and data. (State common-law copyright is considered in § 10.21.) Copyright extends to "original works of authorship fixed in any tangible medium of expression, now known or later developed, from which they can be perceived, reproduced or otherwise communicated, either directly or with the aid of machine or device."[10] This statutory scope obviously includes computer-readable media. Nevertheless, copyright protection does not extend to "any idea, procedure, process, system, method of operation, concept, principle, or discovery, regardless of the form in which it is described, explained, illustrated, or embodied in such work."[11] Copyright exists from the moment that a work is fixed,[12] but certain advantages, including the right to sue for infringement, accrue from registering the copyright with the United States Copyright Office. Copyright extends from the time of creation until 50 years after the author's death.[13]

Copyrightable works include:

(1) literary works;

(2) musical works, including any accompanying words;

(3) dramatic works, including any accompanying music;

(4) pantomimes and choreographic works;

(5) pictorial, graphic, and sculptural works;

(6) motion pictures and other audiovisual works;

(7) sound recordings; and

(8) architectural works.[14]

Computer programs usually are classified as literary works, although the advent of multimedia means that computer programs and associated data may also be audiovisual works, sound recordings, and musical works.

Copyright is a limited form of property, encompassing only certain enumerated rights, which are statutorily reserved to the copyright owner. These rights are

(1) to reproduce the copyrighted work in copies or phonorecords;

(2) to prepare derivative works based on the copyrighted works;

(3) to distribute copies or phonorecords of the copyrighted work to the public by sale or other transfer of ownership, or by rental, lease, or lending;

---

[10] 17 U.S.C. § 102(a) (1988).

[11] *Id.* § 102(b).

[12] *See id.* § 101 (definition of "created," noting that the portion of a work that is fixed in any particular time constitutes the work as of that time; where a work is prepared in different versions, each version constitutes a separate work).

[13] *Id.* § 302(a) (applicable to works created on or after January 1, 1978).

[14] *Id.* § 102(a).

(4) in the case of literary, musical, dramatic and choreographic works, panto-mimes and motion pictures and other audio visual works, to perform the copy-righted work publicly; and

(5) in the case of literary, musical, dramatic, and choreographic works, pan-tomimes and pictorial, graphic, or sculptural works, including the individual images of a motion picture or other audiovisual work, to display the copyrighted work publicly.[15]

The nature of computerized works engenders significant controversy over statutory concepts originally developed for paper, pictures, and plays. For example, there was some early uncertainty about when computer-recorded information is sufficiently fixed to be entitled to copyright protection. Although that controversy now mostly has ended, continuing uncertainty exists with respect to the boundary between copyrightable expression and unprotectible procedures, processes, and ideas, and between protectible original expression and unprotectible facts. In addition, there is some uncertainty about what constitutes conduct exclusively reserved to the copyright owner under 17 U.S.C. § 106. Finally, there is much debate over the appropriate scope of certain privileges, particularly the fair use privilege when information is exchanged and sold in Internet-like infrastructures.

§ 10.4 —Scope of Protection

The language of the Copyright Act[16] contains the seeds of major difficulties in defining the boundary of copyright protection for computer works. Although saying that copyright protection does not extend to a procedure, process, system, or method of operation, it suggests that "the form in which [the procedure, process, system, or method of operation] is described, explained, illustrated, or embodied" is protectible. Because computer programs are valuable precisely because they specify a procedure, process, system, or method of operation, they occupy an uncomfortable position in copyright law despite broad acceptance of

---

[15] *Id.* § 106. These rights belong to the author. When the author is an employee, and the work is prepared within the scope of employment, the rights presumptively vest in the employer under the work made for hire doctrine. 17 U.S.C. § 201(b) (1988). See Community for Creative Non-Violence v. Reid, 490 U.S. 730, 738–39 (1989) (adopting common-law rule for determin-ing existence of employment). When the author is an independent contractor, the copyright belongs to the person retaining the independent contractor only if there is an express agreement to that effect. *Id.* at 738, explaining requirements of 17 U.S.C. 101(2). In other situations, an independent contractor and the person retaining the contractor may be joint authors, if they intended that their contributions merge into inseparable or interdependent parts of a unitary whole. 490 U.S. at 752. The conditions of joint authorship are likely to be satisfied if someone making a speech or engaging in other creative oral conduct, hires another to record the oral work. See Easter Seal Society for Crippled Children and Adults v. Playboy Enterprises, 815 F.2d 323, 337 (5th Cir. 1987) (creator and filmer of production were joint authors).

[16] 17 U.S.C. § 102(b).

the idea that computer programs qualify as copyrightable works.[17] The result is a continuing effort to define the boundary between the unprotectible idea or concept of the procedure, process, or method of operation, and the protectible form of description, explanation, or illustration. This boundary is not new with computer works; it long has been necessary to distinguish between the protectible expression in a traditional literary work like a novel, and the unprotectible idea constituting the plot.[18]

In the late 1980s and early 1990s, several U.S. courts of appeals converged on a "filtration" technique enabling a systematic method for determining the protectible elements of computer programs. The filtration method initially was proposed by the *Altai* court[19] and is a refinement of the abstractions test first suggested by Judge Learned Hand a half-century ago. Important to filtration analysis is the precept that pervades all kinds of intellectual property law: that intellectual property law must not sweep so broadly that it removes material from the public domain needed by others to perform their own creative acts.

The reluctance to preempt public domain information is reinforced by the realization that the justification for copyright is to reward new contributions, not merely to increase the revenue for old contributions. By extending protection to the value-added elements—"original expression"—and no farther, copyright law conforms to its justification without sweeping too broadly. In filtration analysis of a computer program, this means asking at each level of abstraction, beginning from the most general idea or algorithm level, how many alternatives there are. If there is only one approach, that particular level of abstraction constitutes an idea or a procedure or process and is unprotectible. Protecting the only alternative takes it away from everyone else. As the filtration proceeds, a point will be encountered in which a multiplicity of alternatives exist, and the one chosen by the proponent of copyright protection is more or less arbitrary and therefore original with that author. At that point, the expressed technique is protectible. Protecting only one of several alternatives leaves plenty of room for creativity by others. Thus, the idea of a spreadsheet format for presenting numerical information is unprotectible, but a spreadsheet along with certain arrangements of commands and menu items is arbitrary, does not exhaust the alternative ways of presenting a spreadsheet and thus is protectible.[20]

---

[17] *See* Apple Computer, Inc. v. Franklin Computer Corp., 714 F.2d 1240 (3d Cir. 1983) (computer program code protectible); Legislative History of the 1976 Act; 17 U.S.C. § 117 note (limitations on exclusive rights and computer programs). Section 117 would hardly be necessary if computer programs did not qualify for protection at all. *See also* Manifesto at 2316 (computer works "behave," and this makes them an unusual copyright work).

[18] Nicholas v. Universal Pictures Corp., 45 F.2d 119 (2d Cir. 1930) (Hand, J.) ("abstractions" test).

[19] Computer Assocs. Int'l, Inc. v. Altai, Inc., 982 F.2d 693 (2d Cir. 1992).

[20] Lotus Dev. Corp. v. Paperback Software, 740 F. Supp. 37 (D. Mass. 1990) (menu command structure was copyrightable); Lotus Dev. Corp. v. Borland, Inc., 49 F.3d 807 (1st Cir. 1995).

The filtration approach encounters particular difficulties when the work as to which copyrightability is being assessed has been so successful in the market-place that competitors can succeed only by imitating certain of its features. In such a situation, the imitators plausibly argue that certain core features, like a command set[21] of a popular program, is the only commercially feasible alternative. Thus, they argue, in effect, that a particular look and feel might have been sufficiently arbitrary and nonexhaustive of alternatives to qualify for copyright protection when first adopted, but as it is more successful, it becomes the norm and thus squeezes out the alternatives that made it copyrightable in the first place.[22] From a policy standpoint, this shrinking base of protectible expression may be appropriate because it forces early innovators to find new types of value to add rather than resting on the laurels from an earlier contribution. On the other hand, it creates uncertainty because the scope of copyright protection for a particular work can diminish over time as more and more of the hierarchical elements of the work become unprotectible because they have in some sense become generic.[23]

In *Lotus Development Corp. v. Borland International, Inc.,*[24] the United States Court of Appeals for the First Circuit found the *Altai* filtration approach of more use when nonliteral copying is alleged than when literal copying is alleged.[25] In *Lotus,* Borland admitted that it literally had copied the menu and command hierarchy from Lotus 1-2-3. The First Circuit found that the menu command hierarchy was an unprotectible method of operation under § 102(b).[26] It made the following comparison in support of its conclusion:

> In many ways, the Lotus menu command hierarchy is like the buttons used to control, say, a video cassette recorder ("VCR"). Users operate VCRs by pressing a series of buttons that are typically labelled "Record, Play, Reverse, Fast Forward, Pause, Stop/Eject." That the buttons are arranged and labeled does not make them a "literary work," nor does it make them an "expression" of the abstract "method of operating" a VCR via a set of labeled buttons. Instead, the buttons are themselves the "method of operating" the VCR.

---

[21] A *command set* is the vocabulary and syntax of a computer programming language or the keystrokes and words used to perform tasks. Using the F1 key to obtain help is a trivial example.

[22] Indeed, Circuit Judge Boudin recognized this in his concurring opinion in Lotus Dev. Corp. v. Borland Int'l, Inc., 49 F.3d 807, 819 (1st Cir. 1995) (Boudin, J., concurring). He recognized that, "a new menu may be a creative work, but over time its importance may come to reside more in the investment that has been made by users in learning the menu and in building their own mini program macros in reliance on the menu." *Id.*

[23] Use of the word "generic" suggests a rough analogy between this aspect of copyright law and the scope of trademark protection, discussed in § **10.11.**

[24] 49 F.3d 807 (1st Cir. 1995) (reversing district court and finding no copyright infringement).

[25] *Id.* at 814–15 (citing Computer Assocs. Int'l, Inc. v. Altai, Inc., 982 F.2d 693 (2d Cir. 1993), and finding it misleading when literal copying of a potentially unprotectible command hierarchy is involved).

[26] *Id.* at 815.

When a Lotus 1-2-3 user chooses a command, either by highlighting it on the screen or by typing its first letter, he or she effectively pushes a button. Highlighting the "Print" command on the screen, or typing the letter "P," is analogous to pressing a VCR button labeled "Play."[27]

The First Circuit also hinted, without deciding, that the long prompts might be uncopyrightable because they merge with the underlying idea of explaining functions,[28] but it also suggested that the computer program code of Lotus 1-2-3 is copyrightable.[29]

Because *Lotus* disagrees with the Ninth Circuit approach,[30] further evolution of the competing approaches is likely, although the First Circuit's explanation of the need to leave methods of operation in the public domain is persuasive:

> [I]n most contexts, there is no need to "build" upon other people's expression, for the ideas conveyed by that expression can be conveyed by someone else without copying the first author's expression. In the context of methods of operation, however, "building" requires the use of the precise method of operation already employed; otherwise, "building" would require dismantling, too. Original developers are not the only people entitled to build on the methods of operation they create; anyone can. Thus, Borland may build on the method of operation that Lotus designed and may use the Lotus menu command hierarchy in doing so.[31]

Essentially the same legal problem of drawing boundaries around protectible expression exists with computer accessible data (as contrasted to computer programs). Here, the problem is not distinguishing between protectible expression and unprotectible process, procedure, or method of operation; the problem is distinguishing between protectible expression and unprotectible ideas or facts. The statute itself recognizes that one can obtain copyright protection by harvesting elements from the public domain into compilations and derivative works. The Copyright Act[32] expressly provides that copyright can extend to compilations and derivative works, but it excludes those parts of such a work that infringe another's copyright.[33] The Act also provides that the compilation or derivation copyright extends only to the new value contributed by the second author, as distinguished from the preexisting material.[34]

This distinction between new value and preexisting value is appropriate regardless of whether the preexisting value was copyrightable, subject to an existing copyright, or uncopyrightable fact or idea. If the preexisting material is

---

[27] *Id.* at 817.

[28] *Id.* at 816 n.9.

[29] *Id.* at 816 n.11.

[30] 49 F.3d 807, 818–19 (1st Cir. 1995).

[31] *Id.* at 818 (citations omitted).

[32] 17 U.S.C. § 103.

[33] *Id.* § 103(a).

[34] *Id.* § 103(b).

both copyrightable and subject to an existing copyright, the drawing of a boundary is necessary to sort out the rights belonging to the first and subsequent authors. This of course is important when copyrightable material is collected through the NII and formed into new works. Both the reproduction of the preexisting material and its adaptation may infringe rights exclusively belonging to the first author.[35]

In many cases, value in the National Information Infrastructure consists of compilations of largely factual information: news reports, databases of statutes, judicial opinions, records of property ownership and zoning categories, airline schedules, and telephone numbers and Internet addresses. Therefore, the boundary separates potentially protectible value added by the compiler and database vendor from unprotectible facts and ideas. This boundary achieved constitutional dimensions in the leading case of *Feist Publications, Inc. v. Rural Telephone Service Co.*[36] The *Feist* Court reasoned that the constitutional justification for the monopolies represented by copyright and patent protection is based on the need for economic incentives for certain kinds of inventor and author activity.[37] Unless a publisher or purported author has added some value to what was already there, the publisher or purported author has done nothing qualifying for an incentive. Thus, facts and raw ideas are part of the stock of public domain information and are not entitled to copyright protection.[38] Further, the Congress lacks the constitutional power to extend protection to such public domain information. In *Feist* itself, names and telephone numbers making up a white pages telephone book were not entitled to protection because they were mere facts.[39]

Beyond that, the contribution of the compiler is not entitled to protection unless it is "original." The Copyright Act extends copyright protection only to "original works of authorship."[40] The work of a compiler is not original unless there is something about the selection or arrangement of the facts making up the compilation that is creative. In *Feist,* the Supreme Court found that the alphabetical arrangement of a telephone book and the selection of its elements—the name, address, and telephone number—were dictated by its nature and thus constituted neither original arrangement nor selection.[41]

Although the *Feist* framework is sound as a matter of policy and avoids preempting ready sources of underlying factual and other public domain information under the now-rejected "sweat of the brow" approach to copyright,[42] it

---

[35] This implicates the reproduction and derivative work rights in 17 U.S.C. § 106.

[36] 499 U.S. 340 (1991).

[37] *Id.* at 349–50.

[38] *Id.* at 358.

[39] *Id.* at 361.

[40] 17 U.S.C. § 102(a).

[41] 499 U.S. 340, 361 (1991).

[42] *Id.* at 360.

has alarmed vendors and potential vendors of data in the NII because of the realization that the best way to make a database attractive is to make it global in the sense that it includes every instance of a particular category. This means trouble in satisfying the original-selection requirement of *Feist*. Moreover, databases are more useful when their arrangement is relatively obvious to the community interested in that type of information, and this makes it potentially difficult to satisfy the original-arrangement aspect of *Feist*. The difficulty in designing successful products that embody original arrangement is exacerbated as the distributed character of the Internet makes it more important to adhere to standards for organizing and representing information.

On the other hand, good database design depends on a complex interaction of structure,[43] table design, primary and secondary key selection, and index design.[44] Articulate expert witnesses and database designers should be able to satisfy the original-arrangement element of *Feist* by explaining what is unique and valuable about their particular organization.[45]

The Copyright Act[46] prohibits copyright in federal government information. This limitation on copyright protection is considered further in **Chapter 11.**

§ 10.5 —Fixation Requirement

Fixation is important in applying copyright law to the national information infrastructure in two respects. Fixation determines copyrightability because a work is only "created" when it is "fixed."[47] In addition, reproduction, one of the most important exclusive rights of the copyright owner, does not occur unless fixation in a copy has occurred.[48]

A work is "fixed" in a tangible medium of expression when its embodiment in a copy or phono record, by or under the authority of the author, is sufficiently permanent or stable to permit it to be perceived, reproduced, or otherwise communicated for a period of more than transitory duration. A work consisting of

---

[43] The database "schema."

[44] Most databases, especially full-text databases, depend for feasibility on user access via indexes that reduce search time. Once a desired term is found in the index, the full record is easily retrieved.

[45] *See generally* CCC Info. Servs., Inc. v. Maclean Hunter Mkt. Reports, Inc., 44 F.3d 61, 67 (2d Cir. 1994) (database of used car prices was sufficiently original to be protectible under *Feist;* did not lose protection merely because it responded logically to needs of market) (reversing summary judgment; expert testimony not referred to).

[46] 17 U.S.C. § 105.

[47] 17 U.S.C. § 101 (definition of "created").

[48] Community for Creative Non-Violence v. Reid, 490 U.S. 730 (1989); Sony Corp. v. Universal City Studios, Inc., 464 U.S. 417 (1984); CNN, Inc. v. Video Monitoring Servs. of Am., Inc., 940 F.2d 1471 (11th Cir. 1991).

sounds, images, or both, that are being transmitted, is "fixed" for purposes of this title if a fixation of the work is being made simultaneously with its transmission.[49]

Thus, someone who gives an extemporaneous lecture is not entitled to copyright protection in the lecture because there is no fixation, but if the lecturer causes someone to record the lecture as it is being given, the lecturer enjoys a copyright in the recording (and perhaps in the lecture itself). Moreover, if the lecture is being "transmitted" at the same time that it is recorded at the direction of the lecturer, both the recording and transmitted representation enjoy copyright protection. **Section 10.3** considers the work-for-hire and joint-authorship doctrines. **Section 10.21** considers the possibility of state copyright in oral expression.

In the NII context, the fixation requirement is met sufficiently to assure copyrightability because it now is well established that magnetic and optical representations of information constitute fixation. It is conceivable that a controversy might arise if someone typed or orally expressed something and a third party recorded it. Because the speaker or keyboard operator would not be controlling the recording, the definition of fixation is not satisfied. Then, the question is whether the third-party recording entitles the third party to a copyright. The answer probably is no because the third party has contributed no original expression of her own. Thus, the odd situation might exist in which no one owns the copyright in the recorded representation of the keystrokes or spoken words and they may be used by others without restriction.[50]

Of greater practical concern in the NII is the possibility that certain uses of copyrighted information might constitute reproductions or preparation of derivative works because fixation is involved. The final report of the working group on intellectual property rights, part of President Clinton's Information Infrastructure Task Force, popularly known as the "White Paper,"[51] expressed concern about whether transmission of a digital work would satisfy the fixation requirement. It acknowledged, however, that "electronic network transmissions from one computer to another, such as Email, may only reside on each computer in random access memory, but that has been found to be sufficient fixation."[52] This concern expressed in the White Paper is questionable and can be viewed

---

[49] 17 U.S.C. § 101 (definition of "fixed").

[50] Article 14, para. 1 of the TRIP (see § **10.8**) suggests that a performer might be able to prevent fixation of an unfixed performance. This is not provided for under the U. S. statute. *Accord* J.H. Reichman, *Legal Hybrids Between the Patent and Copyright Paradigms, Symposium: Toward a Third Intellectual Property Paradigm,* 94 Colum. L. Rev. 2308 n.379 (1994).

[51] Intellectual Property and the National Information Infrastructure: Report of the Working Group on Intellectual Property Rights, Bruce A. Lehman, Assistant Secretary of Commerce & Commissioner of Patents & Trademarks, Chair (1995) [hereinafter White Paper].

[52] White Paper § I(A) (citing Advanced Computer Servs., Inc. v. MAI Sys. Corp., 845 F. Supp. 356, 363 (E.D. Va. 1994) but expressing concern that delay between transmission and fixation on a receiving computer screen or RAM might disqualify the fixation from being "simultaneous").

as a justification for the White Paper's recommendation for statutory recognition of a distinct transmission right, exclusively reserved to the copyright owner.[53]

The main significance of controversy over computerized fixation is its use to justify the establishment of a new transmission right. Otherwise, one can be reasonably confident that most steps practically necessary in NII technologies either to create or to misappropriate a copyrighted work will satisfy the statutory fixation requirement.

§ 10.6 —Originator and Intermediary Liability

The NII involves a variety of new types of intermediaries between content originator and ultimate consumer. Dial-up electronic bulletin boards were one early example. Anonymous ftp, Gopher, and World Wide Web servers are the more recent example in the Internet context. The Gopher and World Wide Web technologies exemplify a technological context in which multiple intermediaries may interact to make it possible for a consumer to retrieve information directly from a content originator in a way that makes it appear that the content is being delivered by the first intermediary.[54] An information object allegedly infringing another's copyright may move through several intermediaries in this distribution system. The potential liability of the various intermediaries for copyright infringement is a matter of obvious interest both to the intermediaries and to the copyright owner alleging infringement, who may perceive the intermediaries as having deeper pockets or being more amenable to personal jurisdiction than the originator of the allegedly infringing object.

From the perspective of the person claiming infringement, it is relatively easy to establish violation of one of the exclusive 17 U.S.C. § 106 rights by the originator of the allegedly infringing item. That originator almost certainly has

---

[53] *See* White Paper § IV(A)(1) (proposing new transmission rights). The White Paper is considered further in § **10.23.**

[54] A World Wide Web server typically presents a user with highlighted "hyper media links" or menu items representing full-content text or images or sound or video files. A user retrieves the indicated item simply by selecting the menu item or highlighted hyper media pointer. That causes the server displaying the pointer to download to the user's computer a short computer executable pointer called a universal resource locator (URL). The user's computer, running World Wide Web client software, then automatically executes the URL to retrieve the information directly from the computer pointed to by the URL. The first computer that supplied the URL disconnects as soon as it is transmitted to the URL of the user. Thus, it appears to the user that the information item is being retrieved from the first computer while in fact it is being retrieved from another. It is common for the World Wide Web process to be replicated through a chain of intermediaries, the first web server pointing to another, and the second pointing to a third and so on, with each intermediary server simply sending URLs to the customer until finally the full content of the desired item is retrieved. Throughout the chain, a typical user perceives that everything is coming from the first web server computer.

reproduced the copyrighted work and also engaged in distributing it.[55] It is somewhat less clear whether the intermediaries have infringed any § 106 rights.

Consider the case of a dial-up electronic bulletin board, where any item retrieved actually resides in the form of a file on the bulletin board from which the user selects it.[56] In circumstances when the owner of the bulletin board cannot be shown to have placed the allegedly infringing item on her own computer, it may be difficult to show that the bulletin board operator has infringed the reproduction right, because—at least until the point of transmission to the requester—the bulletin board operator has not herself caused a copy to be made. Rather, the copy was made by the third person placing the item on the bulletin board. Nevertheless, in *Playboy Enterprises v. Frena*,[57] the district court found that the operator of the electronic bulletin board on which third parties placed digitized images of Playboy centerfolds infringed the distribution right.[58]

Beyond that is the possibility that the bulletin board operator is engaged in making a performance or public display when a user browses material on the bulletin board.[59] It is not necessary, assuming that the conduct falling within § 106 can be shown to have occurred, to establish intent or knowledge on the part of the intermediary. *Playboy Enterprises* is the strongest authority for this in the NII context: "It does not matter that defendant Frena may have been unaware of the copyright infringement. Intent to infringe is not needed to find copyright infringement."[60]

---

[55] This violates the reproduction right under 17 U.S.C. § 106(1), and the distribution right under 17 U.S.C. § 106(3) if the distribution is to the public.

[56] In other words, the computer ultimately transmitting the full-content item is the same computer that generates the interface made available to the requesting user—and indexes on the interface.

[57] 839 F. Supp. 1552 (M.D. Fla. 1993).

[58] *Id.* at 1556. *See also* Sega Enter. Ltd. v. Maphia, 857 F. Supp. 679 (N.D. Cal. 1994) (finding that uploading of copyrighted material by third party to bulletin board constituted making unauthorized copies attributable to the bulletin board operator).

[59] *See* White Paper §§ I(A) (noting that mere file transfer would not constitute performance, but suggesting that browsing of digitized Playboy images or other works would constitute a public display); "[V]irtually all NII uses would appear to fall within the law's current comprehension of 'public display.'" *Id.* n.22 (citing Columbia Pictures Indus. v. Redd Horne, Inc., 749 F.2d 154 (3d Cir. 1984) (video store operator liable for public performance for renting tapes to customers who viewed them in semi-private screening rooms); Columbia Pictures Indus. v. Aveco, Inc., 800 F.2d 59 (3d Cir. 1986) (same result where customers also rented rooms for viewing); On Command Video Corp. v. Columbia Pictures Indus., 777 F. Supp. 787 (N.D. Cal. 1991) (infringement from hotel guests in room selecting tapes to be played on remote control console in hotel basement with signals sent to rooms) as authority for proposition that public performance concept keeps pace with new technologies for allowing multiple persons to view stored material).

[60] 839 F. Supp. 1552, 1559 (M.D. Fla. 1993) (finding infringement based both on distribution and display rights).

The infringement case against intermediaries who provide anonymous ftp sites is essentially the same as the case against electronic bulletin board operators. On the other hand, the case against Gopher and World Wide Web servers is more tenuous. They never have possession of the requested item, and thus it is less plausible that they have reproduced, distributed, displayed, or performed it. Rather, they are more like providers of bibliographies to works, some of which may be infringing. Still, one can argue that the scope of the § 106 rights should be extended to these intermediaries as well because they constitute links in a chain that necessarily results in the conduct covered by § 106. Copyright infringement is a statutory tort, and the causation requirement in tort law long has been satisfied by the doing of an act intended to and substantially certain to result in the conduct constituting the tort.[61]

Moreover, even if Gopher and World Wide Web type services do not expose their providers to liability for direct infringement, as in the *Playboy Enterprises* case, they may expose their providers to liability for derivative or contributory infringement.[62] The leading case on contributory infringement is *Sony Corp. of America v. Universal City Studios, Inc.,*[63] in which the Supreme Court held 5-4 that manufacturers of videocassette recorders were not liable for contributory infringement of televised works recorded on their machines by consumers. There were two parts to the Court's analysis, one finding that the consumer conduct was fair use and therefore did not constitute infringement at all. If the ultimate use of the system was noninfringing, then there could be no vicarious liability. The second part of the analysis is of more immediate importance to assessing the possibility of contributory liability by intermediaries. The Court held that systems that are capable of substantial noninfringing uses cannot produce contributory infringement.[64] The most appropriate way to apply this to the Gopher or World Wide Web server context is to ask whether the particular server is set up to facilitate access to noninfringing information objects. If it is, the fact that the server may occasionally be used to retrieve infringing objects does not suffice to establish contributory infringement by the operator of the server. On the other hand, if the server is set up predominately for the purpose

---

[61] *See* McGanty v. Standenraus, 321 Or. 532, 901 P.2d 841 (1995) (quoting Restatement (Second) of Torts to support proposition that tortfeasor need only act with substantial certainty that tortious consequences will result.

[62] *See generally* Frank Music Corp. v. CompuServe, Inc., No. 93 Civ. 8153 (JFK) (S.D.N.Y. filed Nov. 29, 1993) (alleging contributory or other vicarious liability for copyright infringement by CompuServe because permitting and facilitating recording and storage of copyrighted works with subsequent retrieval from defendant's database). The White Paper suggests, without clearly supporting authority, that providing services or facilities with the knowledge that they may be used for infringement would expose the provider to vicarious liability. White Paper § I(A)(8).

[63] 464 U.S. 417 (1984).

[64] *Id.* at 440.

of facilitating access to infringing objects, the operator of the server should be liable for contributory infringement.

An important missing ingredient in the intermediary copyright infringement cases is First Amendment analysis. Although it is generally accepted that First Amendment considerations are internalized into copyright law through the fair use defense,[65] courts, like the *Playboy Enterprises* court, that impose no-fault liability for copyright infringement on intermediaries fail to consider the First Amendment at all. As noted in the defamation context in the NII in **Chapter 4,** exposing intermediaries to no-fault liability for information carried by them chills conduct necessary for a competitive and diverse National Information Infrastructure to exist.[66] The same chilling effect occurs regardless of whether no-fault liability is imposed for defamatory messages or for intellectual property infringement. The basic requirement that a plaintiff show knowledge or circumstances leading to a duty of inquiry by the intermediary is appropriate for intellectual property infringement as well as for other torts. The role of First Amendment law in copyright infringement litigation is considered in **Chapter 6. Chapter 4** considers intermediary liability in greater breadth.

§ 10.7 —Fair Use

The Copyright Act provides a number of privileges, expressed as "limitations," on the rights of copyright owners.[67] By far the most important privilege in the NII context is the fair use privilege, codified in § 107. This section was intended to codify decisional law rather than to expand or alter it.[68] It says that whether a particular use of a copyrighted work is fair use and thus noninfringing is to be determined by consideration of a number of factors:

> [T]he factors to be considered shall include—
>
> (1) the purpose and character of the use, including whether such use is of a commercial nature or as for non-profit educational purposes;
>
> (2) the nature of the copyrighted work;

---

[65] *See* Harper & Row, Publishers, Inc. v. Nation Enters., 471 U.S. 539, 559 (1985).

[66] *See* Cubby, Inc. v. CompuServe, Inc., 776 F. Supp. 135 (S.D.N.Y. 1991).

[67] *See* 17 U.S.C. § 108 (reproduction by libraries and archives); *id.* § 109 (effect of transfer of particular copy or phono record); *id.* § 110 (exemption of certain performances and displays); *id.* § 111 (secondary transmissions); *id.* § 112 (ephemeral recordings); *id.* § 116 (compulsory licenses for public performances by coin-operated phono record players); *id.* § 117 (computer programs); *id.* § 118 (use of certain works in noncommercial broadcasting); *id.* § 119 (secondary transmissions of super stations and network stations for private home viewing).

[68] Quinto v. Legal Times of Wash., D.C., Inc., 506 F. Supp. 554, 560 (D.D.C. 1981); Elsmere Music, Inc. v. NBC Co., 482 F. Supp. 741, 744 n.8 (S.D.N.Y. 1980).

(3) the amount and substantiality of the portion used in relation to the copyrighted work as a whole; and

(4) the effect of the use upon the potential market for or value of the copyrighted work.[69]

The Supreme Court in *Sony*[70] and *Acuff-Rose*[71] noted that the last factor—the market effect of the purported fair use—is the most important.[72]

Among other things, this means that activities in the NII, particularly including the provision of pointers, finding, and retrieval aids for copyrighted works, should qualify as fair use even if they also constitute prima facie infringement because they expand rather than diminish the market for the content to which they point.[73] Similarly, the use of computer-to-computer interfaces should be fair use even if it constitutes prima facie infringement[74] because the use of the interface expands the market for the predecessor work as much as it may appropriate speculative markets for derivative works. The only exception might be appropriation of an internal interface for a bundle of value-added items to permit competition with one part of the bundle. Then, the appropriator of the interface can be said to be interfering with part of the market for the total bundle.

§ 10.8 —GATT-TRIP

The GATT-TRIP[75] appendix protects copyright by requiring compliance with articles 1 through 21 and the appendix of the Berne Convention of 1971 except for article 6 Bis. of that convention. It expressly provides that copyright protection extends only to expressions and not ideas, procedures, methods of operation of mathematical concepts as such,"[76] and that computer programs whether in source or object code shall be protected as literary works under the Berne Convention.[77] The GATT appendix separately provides for compilations of data

---

[69] 17 U.S.C. § 107.

[70] Sony Corp. of Am. v. Universal City Studios, Inc., 464 U.S. 417 (1984).

[71] Campbell v. Acuff-Rose Music, Inc., 114 S. Ct. 1164 (1994).

[72] *Id.* at 1169.

[73] Caching is a particularly strong candidate for fair use, as explained in **§ 10.10.**

[74] *See* Henry H. Perritt, Jr., *Unbundling Value in Electronic Information Systems: Intellectual Property Protection for Machine Readable Interfaces,* 20 Rutgers Computer & Tech. L.J. 415 (1994).

[75] General Agreement on Tariffs and Trade: Agreement on Trade-Related Aspects of Intellectual Property Rights, Jan. 1994, 33 I.L.M. 81 [hereinafter GATT-TRIP].

[76] GATT-TRIP, art. 9, para. 2.

[77] *Id.,* art. 10, para. 1.

or other material which "by reason of the selection or arrangement of their contents constitute intellectual creations."[78]

§ 10.9 —Proposals for New Copyright Legislation

The so-called White Paper recommended adding a new transmission right to 17 U.S.C. § 106.[79] It recommended that the definition of *transmit* in § 101 be amended to clarify that reproductions as well as performances and displays can be transmitted.[80] It also recommended a new chapter 12 of title 17 to prohibit fraudulent removal of copyright management information and to prohibit providing fraudulent copyright management information.[81]

§ 10.10 —Caching and Copyright Protection

Caching refers to the automatic copying of material to improve performance of computer systems. It is used in wide area networks like the Internet to reduce the time required for second and subsequent access to World Wide Web files. Because caching involves copying, it raises particular concerns about potential copyright violations.

This section describes how caching works in currently popular software for World Wide Web applications on the Internet and suggests how a privilege might be created under copyright law so that caching does not result in prima facie direct copyright infringement.[82] The following example presumes that the supplier of information content has made it available on the World Wide Web through a "content server" (CS), a web server from which the content may be retrieved. It further assumes that this content supplier has imposed restrictions on the content thus published, permitting access for purposes of browsing and viewing, but not copying.[83]

---

[78] *Id.,* art. 10, Agreement on Trade Related Aspects of Intellectual Property Rights, Including Trade and Counterfeit Goods.

[79] The report recommends amending 17 U.S.C. § 106(3) to read: "(3) to distribute copies or phono records of the copyrighted work to the public by sale or other transfer of ownership, by rental, lease, or lending, or by transmission." White Paper app. 1. § 2(a). The European Union may follow suit. See Commission of the European Communities, Green Paper: Copyright and Related Rights in the Information Society, Com(95) 382 final (July 17, 1995) (suggesting possible need for transmission right).

[80] *Id.* app. 1 § 2(b).

[81] *Id.* app. 1 § 4 (proposing new 17 U.S.C. §§ 1201–1204.

[82] The approach discussed in this chapter involves defining the duplication rights so that it does not cover caching; an alternative approach would be to define a new privilege, or to amend the fair use privilege so that it covers caching.

[83] The content supplier might be tempted to permit viewing and browsing but not "downloading." The difficulty with this distinction is that downloading is necessary to permit browsing and viewing on the client computer.

Suppose there are three others involved in a World Wide Web transaction: an ultimate consumer, C; another Internet server that provides pointers on its web pages to the content server, PS; a firewall computer, F.

Suppose C initially establishes a session with PS to locate material of interest. C finds on PS a pointer to an item on CS. C clicks on this pointer. As a result, PS automatically uploads to C's computer the selected pointer (in the form of a URL).[84] Now, the web browser software running on C's computer automatically establishes a connection with CS and retrieves the web file pointed to by the pointer. C's web browser caches the file thus retrieved so that if C requests it again, the cache copy can be loaded in the browser rather than the browser having to fetch the file again over the Internet.

In the transaction just described, PS never had the requested file either before or after C requested it. Any downloading and caching occurred on C's web browser application running on C's client computer.

As a second example, suppose that C's computer is connected through a Local Area Network that in turn is connected to the Internet through a firewall computer. While there are a variety of firewall configurations, one common one would cause the firewall to serve as a "proxy" for C. The popular NetScape web browser software has a proxy option to accommodate such a firewall role. The proxy function is best defined by describing how it works in a World Wide Web transaction. Similar to the one used in Example 1, C seeks to establish a connection to PS. The connection request is forwarded to F, which duplicates the request. Any information returned by PS, including the pointer, is transferred to F, which then caches it and sends a copy along to C. When C's computer activates the pointer to CS, CS returns the requested file to F, which caches it, and sends a copy along to C, which also caches it because it is running the same web browser as in Example 1.

Some web browsers, such as Netscape, keep the cached material even after the browser is exited. The next time the browser is run, the cached files are available to it. How long a browser uses a cached version rather than reloading from the server from which the material originated is determined by an expiration date included in the files sent by CS and thus kept in the cached version. This expiration date is set by CS, although it can be changed by the recipient. See http://www.ics.uci.edu/pub/ietf/http/draft-ietf-http-v10-spec-00.txt. It thus is not factually correct to conceive of the browsers'—and the firewalls'—caching as being ephemeral or transitory.

As a third example, consider an information services provider such as CompuServe, Prodigy, or America Online. Such a service provider might want to provide World Wide Web access to its customers so that information retrieved through the web would be more or less indistinguishable from material retrieved from the provider's host computer. It would be natural for the provider to design its client software to include a web browser function that would work somewhat differently than the web browser software described in Examples 1 and 2. The provider's World Wide Web access system, while it might call for its client

---

[84] Actually, the page containing the pointer already had been uploaded into C's computer.

software to cache material whether retrieved through the web or from the provider host, almost certainly also would provide for the caching of material retrieved through the web on the provider's host so that if another subscriber wishes to retrieve the same material, the second subscriber could do so directly from the provider's host computer, without the host having to go out and fetch the material again across the Internet.

In all three examples, it seems appropriate to classify the caching as consistent with the assumed restrictions on use of the content. In other words, the caching described should not be considered to be prohibited copying. Avoidance of infringement for caching can be achieved by defining certain types of caching as fair use, or by concluding that there is an implied license to cache.

The problem is in how to describe such privileged caching. Limiting the privilege to ephemeral copies would be too narrow because of the way Netscape caches to disk and preserves cached files after a Netscape session is terminated. Extending the privilege to copies made merely to facilitate performance in retrieving the same material in the future might be overbroad because such a privilege could frustrate a content supplier's legitimate interest in restricting secondary copying. For example, the provider in the third example might find it convenient to allow its customers to obtain material from its host without paying for access to the material from CS. Or, C might pay once for an access to CS, but then obtain another copy from a cached version on the provider's host and make prohibited copies of that second cached copy, arguing that the restrictions applicable to the original accessed material do not apply to material accessed from the provider's host. It might be appropriate to condition any privilege on the cached version not being used intentionally or foreseeably to frustrate the restrictions imposed by the content supplier with respect to third parties. Another possible approach is to treat caching as privileged unless the originator sets the header of the work to prevent caching.

§ 10.11 Trademark and Unfair Competition

Trademark infringement is a branch of unfair competition law. The federal Lanham Act[85] partially federalizes the law of unfair competition while coexisting with state statutory and common-law unfair competition law. At its most general, unfair competition law protects a business from a competitor gaining a free ride on the goodwill of the first business. The trademark branch of unfair competition law deals with the kind of free riding that occurs when the first business associates a particular word, phrase, artistic design, or even a

---

[85] 15 U.S.C. §§ 1051–1127 (Supp. IV 1992).

distinctive color—the "mark"—with its product or service.[86] If a second business uses that phrase, design, or color, the second business is appropriating customer loyalty and goodwill that is connected with the mark.[87] In order for this kind of competitive injury to occur, the mark used by the second business must be the same or confusingly similar to the first. It also must be used for a product or service in a market such that its use by the second business tends to confuse consumers as to the actual source of the good or service. Unlike copyright and patent, there is no need for the mark to represent any particular added value in a utilitarian or artistic or literary sense. Indeed, product features that are purely utilitarian are disqualified from trademark protection.[88] Unlike trade secrets, trademarks need not be secret; obviously, their value depends upon their being widely known.

Federal trademark protection had a false start because the Supreme Court declared the first congressional trademark act unconstitutional, as unauthorized by the patents and copyright clauses of the Constitution.[89] Now trademark law is well within the ambit of the commerce clause.

Section 1114(1) of title 15, United States Code, was amended in 1992 to make it clear that states and municipalities do not enjoy Eleventh Amendment immunity from trademark infringement claims.[90]

---

[86] *See id.* § 1052 ("no trademark by which the goods of the applicant may be distinguished from the goods of others shall be refused registration on account of its nature unless . . ."; enumerating limited exclusions from trademark subject matter). *But see id.* § 1052(e)(1) (excluding merely descriptive or deceptively misdescriptive marks); *id.* § 1052(e)(2) (excluding descriptions of geographic origin); *id.* § 1052(e)(4) (excluding surnames). Section 1052(f) allows registration of marks otherwise disqualified if they have become distinctive of the applicants goods in commerce, and § 1053 makes service marks registrable under the same criteria as trademarks.

[87] Hanover Star Milling Co. v. Metcalf, 240 U.S. 403, 414 (1916) (trademark is a protection for the goodwill of an existing business).

[88] Harper House, Inc. v. Thomas Nelson, Inc., 889 F.2d 197 (9th Cir. 1989); Whelan Assocs. v. Jaslow Dental Lab., Inc., 979 F.2d 1222 (3d Cir. 1986); Brandir Int'l, Inc. v. Cascade Pac. Lumber Co., 834 F.2d 1142 (2d Cir. 1987).

[89] United States v. Steffens, 100 U.S. 82 (1879). The Court noted that the right to use a symbol or device to distinguish the goods or property made or sold by one person had long been protected by the common law. *Id.* at 92. It found, however, no power in the Congress under the patent and trademarks clause to legislate on the subject of trademark protection because "the ordinary trademark has no necessary relation to invention or discovery." While trademarks might constitute writings, the writings which were to be protected under the trademark and patent clause only were "the fruits of intellectual labor." *Id.* at 94. It suggested that if Congress wanted to justify trademark legislation as authorized by the commerce clause, it needed to refer to interstate commerce in the statute. *Id.* at 96–98.

[90] Pub. L. No. 102-542 § 3(a), adding definition of "any person" to include states, their instrumentalities, and employees acting in their official capacities.

Trademarks can arise under common law[91] as well as through registration with the United States Patent and Trademark Office. Damages for infringing trademarks are available in common-law actions[92] as well as in statutory actions under the Lanham Act.[93] Section 42(a) of the Lanham Act protects unregistered trademarks, but essentially the same requirements must be satisfied to qualify an unregistered mark as to register one.[94]

Beyond trademark law, unfair competition law protects against a wide variety of unfair competitive practices. These practices include not only trademark infringement, some aspects of trade secret misappropriation,[95] and some more general types of misappropriation resembling copyright infringement,[96] but also fraudulent misrepresentation regarding product capabilities.[97] Consistent with the theme of this chapter, this section only considers those aspects of unfair competition that relate to misrepresenting the origin of a product or service. That, obviously includes trademark infringement. Other types of misrepresentation are considered in **Chapter 4.**

Trademark protection, like all other forms of intellectual property law, must be limited lest it preempt the use of many kinds of knowledge, information, and language that must be freely available if the core purposes of intellectual property—increasing the creativity and variety of products available—are to be fulfilled. In trademark law, these limitations take the form of boundaries between marks qualifying for protection on the one hand and alleged product labels, names, or characteristics that are merely descriptive,[98] or functional,[99] or

---

[91] American Int'l Group, Inc. v. American Int'l Airways, Inc., 726 F. Supp. 1470, 1476 & n.2 (E.D. Pa. 1989) (identical standards governed service mark and trademark rights and infringement under Lanham Act and Pennsylvania common law; denying injunction against use of allegedly confusing mark); Tarin v. Pellonari, 625 N.E.2d 739, 745–46 (Ill. App. Ct. 1993) (applying traditional common-law standards for federal and state claims; affirming denial of injunction for alleged misappropriation of trademark).

[92] Computer Assocs. Int'l, Inc. v. Altai, Inc., 982 F.2d 693 (2d Cir. 1992); Bridge Publications, Inc. v. Vien, 827 F. Supp. 629 (S.D. Cal. 1993); Data Gen. Corp. v. Grumman Sys. Support Corp., 795 F. Supp. 501 (D. Mass. 1992).

[93] 15 U.S.C. § 1114 (remedies for infringement); id. § 1116 (injunctive relief); id. § 1117 (measures of damages); id. § 1118 (destruction of infringing articles). See also id. § 1121 (jurisdiction of federal courts).

[94] Two Pesos, Inc. v. Taco Cabana, Inc., 112 S. Ct. 2753, 2757 (1992).

[95] See Renee Beauty Salons, Inc. v. Blose-Venable, 652 A.2d 1345, 1347 (Pa. Super. Ct. 1995) (characterizing alleged trade secret misappropriation as type of unfair competition).

[96] The use of the "reverse passing off" doctrine of unfair competition law in Playboy Enters. Inc. v. Frena, 839 F. Supp. 1552, 1562 (M.D. Fla. 1993), to impose liability for, in effect, misappropriating copyrighted photographs, is an example. See also Roy Export Co. v. CBS, 503 F. Supp. 1137 (S.D.N.Y. 1985) (unfair competition for broadcasting films copyrighted by another).

[97] Nordale, Inc. v. Samco, Inc., 830 F. Supp. 1263 (D. Minn. 1993).

[98] Dranoff-Perlstein Assocs. v. Sklar, 967 F.2d 852 (3d Cir. 1992); Spraying Sys. Co. v. Delavan, Inc., 762 F. Supp. 772 (N.D. Ill. 1991).

[99] Duraco Prod. v. Joy Plastic Enter., Ltd., 40 F.3d 1431 (3d Cir. 1994); Sicilia Di R. Biebow & Co. v. Cox, 732 F.2d 417 (5th Cir. 1984).

generic[100] on the other. The purpose for this differentiation is this: If a business enterprise were entitled to trademark protection for the word "computer,"[101] everyone else making a computer would have to find a different word to call his products. If the first producer of a red fire truck were entitled to trademark protection for the color red, all other makers of fire trucks would have to paint their trucks a different color. Thus, as with all other forms of intellectual property law, the purpose is to permit the appropriation of a certain amount of information by the creator of some added value, while making sure that not too much of what should remain in the public domain is appropriated and thus removed from possible use by others.[102] The crucial distinction is whether consumers associate the alleged mark with a particular producer or with the product regardless of who makes it.[103]

In the computer software and network information fields, trademark protection has begun to emerge as a powerful form of protection. It is superior in many respects to copyright, which is limited by the *Feist* doctrine and is always an uncomfortable fit with the essentially utilitarian nature of computer programs and much computer database information. Trademark protection is often superior to patent, which is expensive and uncertain to acquire. In a collection of cases, the federal district courts have been sympathetic in using trademark and associated unfair representation concepts fairly broadly to protect against misrepresentation of product origin.[104] In some factual settings, the degree of protection afforded by trademark is nearly indistinguishable as a practical matter from the kind of protection afforded by copyright.[105] One who copies information from another's product and offers it as one's own not only copies, and thus potentially commits copyright infringement, but also misrepresents the origin and potentially commits trademark infringement or unfair competition.

Marks are often classified in categories of generally increasing distinctiveness, including (1) generic; (2) descriptive; (3) suggestive; (4) arbitrary; or (5) fanciful.[106] Marks that are merely descriptive of a product do not inherently qualify, but they may acquire the distinctiveness that causes them to represent

---

[100] A.J. Canfield Co. v. Honickman, 808 F.2d 291 (3d Cir. 1986); Lamb-Weston, Inc. v. McCain Foods, Inc., 818 F. Supp. 1376 (E.D. Wash. 1993).

[101] The word "computer" would be generic or merely descriptive when used with respect to a computer product, but arbitrary if used as the name of a variety of apple.

[102] Anti-Monopoly, Inc. v. General Mills Fun Group, 611 F.2d 296, 300 n.1 (9th Cir. 1979) (genericness doctrine of trademark law is analogous to copyright exclusion of business ideas and concepts from copyrightability).

[103] *Id.* at 305–06 (asking for Monopoly by name because "I would like a Parkers Brothers version of a real estate trading game because I like Parker Brothers products," or "I am interested in playing the game of Monopoly. I don't much care who makes it.").

[104] See § **10.12.**

[105] See § **10.12,** considering reverse passing offs.

[106] Two Pesos, Inc. v. Taco Cabana, Inc., 112 S. Ct. 2753, 2757 (1992) (explaining that the suggestive, arbitrary, and fanciful categories intrinsically serve to identify a particular source of a product and thus are deemed inherently distinctive and entitled to protection).

information about a particular source of a product by acquiring so-called secondary meaning.[107]

Investacorp, Inc. v. Arabian Investment Banking Corp. (Investcorp) E.C.[108] is a good example of the analysis used in trademark infringement and unfair competition cases. Investacorp, engaged in the investment banking and brokering business, began using the term "Investacorp" in 1978,[109] and five years later, Investcorp began using its term. After an initial skirmish before the Patent and Trademark Office, when Investcorp tried to register its name as a service mark, Investacorp sued for federal service mark infringement under section 43A of the Lanham Act,[110] Florida common-law service mark infringement, Florida common-law unfair competition, and violation of the Florida antidilution law.[111] The court of appeals determined that the federal service mark claim failed because the plaintiff had no proprietary interest in the "Investacorp" mark, and therefore the other claims failed as well.[112] The circuit court explained that "each time a business uses a mark, it enhances the customer recognition of the mark and its association with the service, thereby inuring to the business greater rights in the mark."[113] Nevertheless, proprietary rights in a mark depend not on mere use but exist only if the mark either is inherently distinctive or if the mark contains secondary meaning.[114] Reviewing the categories of distinctiveness, the court affirmed the district court conclusion that "Investacorp" is descriptive.[115] Because "Investacorp" is made up of the words "invest" and "corp," it bears a relationship to the type of services being offered and therefore cannot be arbitrary or fanciful. Based on the need to use the terms "invest" and "corp" (and actual use by competitors), they should not be classified as suggestive.[116] Thus, the only way the plaintiff could obtain service mark status was if "Investacorp" had acquired secondary meaning.[117] "Secondary meaning is the connection in the consumer's mind between the mark and the provider of service."[118] In determining whether secondary meaning has occurred, one must consider the following:

---

[107] *Id.* at 2757–58.

[108] 931 F.2d 1519 (11th Cir. 1991) (affirming summary judgment for defendant).

[109] *Id.* at 1525.

[110] 15 U.S.C. § 1125(a).

[111] Fla. Stat. Ann. § 495.151 (West 1988).

[112] 931 F.2d 1519, 1521 (11th Cir. 1991).

[113] *Id.* at 1522.

[114] *Id.*

[115] *Id.* at 1522–23 ("milk delivery" is generic; "barn Milk" is descriptive. "Barn barn" is suggestive, and "barn barn fish" is arbitrary and fanciful").

[116] *Id.* at 1523 (noting that the two terms are indispensable to the investment services industry and thus competitors would need to use the terms).

[117] *Id.* at 1524.

[118] 931 F.2d 1519, 1525 (11th Cir. 1991).

1. Length and manner of use

2. Nature and extent of advertising and promotion

3. Efforts made by the purported owner to promote conscious connection in the public's mind between the alleged mark and the plaintiff's business

4. Extent to which the public actually identifies the name with the plaintiff's service.[119]

The plaintiff had done little in the way of promotion, simply using the Investacorp mark on most of its transactional documents, and the plaintiff was unable to present much evidence that consumers associated the term with its business.[120]

Showtime/The Movie Channel, Inc. v. Covered Bridge Condominium Ass'n, Inc.,[121] illustrates trademark's power in the information services industry. Cable television companies and program originators sued a condominium association that received unauthorized feed of the plaintiffs' programming through a satellite dish antenna. In addition to claims under the Federal Communications Act for unlawful interception,[122] the plaintiffs also asserted claims under the Lanham Act and Florida statutory and common law.

The district court concluded that use of the plaintiffs' trademarks themselves usurped the plaintiffs' goodwill and therefore constituted trademark infringement.[123] The defendants apparently argued that no trademark infringement was involved because the condominium residents got the product actually produced by the trademark owners, but the district court disagreed because the reception through the satellite antenna might be inferior.[124] In addition, the court found that by falsely implying that the entertainment programming services delivered through the defendants' system were authorized by the originators, it violated the unfair competition provisions of the Lanham Act.[125]

Perhaps the most interesting use of trademark protection in the NII context occurred in *Playboy Enterprises, Inc. v. Frena*.[126] The defendant operated a subscription computer bulletin board service that distributed unauthorized copies of *Playboy* magazine photographs. Customers could browse digitized images and download those they wanted. They also could upload material to the bulletin board. In addition to finding copyright violations, the district court

---

[119] *Id.* (citing Conagra, Inc. v. Singleton, 743 F.2d 1508, 1513 (11th Cir. 1984)).

[120] *Id.* at 1525–26.

[121] 693 F. Supp. 1080 (S.D. Fla. 1988) (granting summary judgment and injunction to plaintiffs).

[122] 47 U.S.C. § 605.

[123] 693 F. Supp. 1080, 1089 (S.D. Fla. 1988) (distinguishing Home Box Office, Inc. v. Corinth Motel, Inc., 647 F. Supp. 1186 (N.D. Miss. 1986)).

[124] *Id.* (no trademark infringement because trademark owners had absolute control over quality and therefore no risk that consumers would get anything less then they expected because quality of signals received by satellite antenna might be diminished).

[125] *Id.* at 1090 (finding violation of 15 U.S.C. § 1125(a)).

[126] 839 F. Supp. 1552 (M.D. Fla. 1993) (granting partial summary judgment to plaintiff).

found first that "Playboy" and "Playmate" were entitled to a high degree of trademark protection because they are suggestive and have acquired great distinctiveness in the public mind.[127] It found the defendant's intent irrelevant because consumer conclusion can occur regardless of the infringer's intent.[128] It also found it unnecessary to find actual confusion among consumers; tendency to confuse is enough.[129] Because the defendant usurped the plaintiff's goodwill by using its exact marks, the court found trademark infringement.[130] Moreover, the court found unfair competition because the bulletin board operator made it appear that Playboy Enterprises had authorized its products.[131]

Beyond this, the district court also found unfair competition under the "reverse passing off" theory of section 43(a). Reverse passing off involves the defendant taking credit for the plaintiff's work by passing it off as its own. Of course, this theory applies only when the defendant has not modified the plaintiff's product so much that it really is a different product.[132] This reverse passing off theory is obviously quite powerful because it covers almost any kind of misappropriation even when the misappropriator conceals the origin of the product.

§ 10.12   —Reverse Passing Off

The Lanham Act section 43(a), prohibiting false designation of origin, is a particularly powerful form of federal unfair competition protection, having a long border with copyright protection. Section 43(a), amended in 1988,[133] was enacted by the Congress in 1946.[134] It replaced a much more limited protection under section 3 of the Trademark Act of 1920, which referred only to false designation of origin and was limited to articles of merchandise, thus excluding services. Moreover, section 3 required proof that a false designation of origin occurred willfully and with intent to deceive. Because of its limitations, it became virtually a dead letter.[135]

Early in its life, section 43's false description of representation encompassed two kinds of wrong: false advertising, and the common-law tort of "passing off." "False advertising meant representing that goods or services possess characteristics

---

[127] *Id.* at 1559.

[128] *Id.* at 1561.

[129] *Id.*

[130] *Id.*

[131] *Id.* at 1562.

[132] 839 F. Supp. 1552, 1562 (M.D. Fla. 1993) (explaining reverse passing off theory and citing cases).

[133] Trademark Law Revision Act of 1988, Pub. L. No. 100-667, 102 Stat. 3935.

[134] Lanham Act, ch. 540, 60 Stat. 427 (1946).

[135] Two Pesos, Inc. v. Taco Cabana, Inc., 112 S. Ct. 2753, 2762 n.2 (Stevens, J., concurring).

that they did not actually have and passing off meant representing one's goods as those of another."[136] Passing off had developed early in the nineteenth century as a derivative of the torts of fraud and deceit.[137] Over time, section 43 was broadened so that it created a general federal law of unfair competition.[138] In 1988 the Congress essentially codified the case law, broadly construing section 43(a).[139]

A particularly potent theory of unfair competition is "reverse passing off," indicating that goods actually originating with another originated with the accused unfair competitor. Reverse passing off obviously overlaps to some extent with copyright because it falsely indicates the originator of a product, which may include a work. The more traditional section 43(a) and unfair competition claims involve falsely claiming that one's own product was originated by someone else. Under the traditional theory, only appropriation of goodwill and name is involved and not appropriation of creative aspects of the product. Reverse passing off, therefore, overlaps copyright and patent to a much greater extent than trademark and traditional unfair competition. The Supreme Court has not embraced the reverse passing off theory.[140]

Reverse passing off literally violates section 43(a)[141] because it "is likely to cause confusion, or to cause a mistake, or to deceive as to the affiliation, connection, or association of [the alleged infringer] with another person or as to the origin, sponsorship, or approval of his or her goods, services, or commercial activities by another person."[142]

Two recent court of appeals cases consider use of the reverse passing off theory and circumstances that significantly overlap copyright. *Cleary v. News Corp.*[143] involved copyright, reverse passing off, and unfair competition claims by an author of a version of *Roberts Rules of Order* against a publisher. The author argued that removing his name from the title page after giving him credit for 20 years was reverse passing off.[144] The court of appeals questioned whether section 43 should create a duty of attribution when the author arguably had contracted away any right of attribution. But it did not resolve that question because the edition of *Roberts Rules of Order* from which the plaintiff's name had been omitted was not identical to the one he authored. Reverse passing off

---

[136] *Id.* at 2762 (Stevens, J., concurring).

[137] *Id.* at 2762 n.5 (Stevens, J., concurring) (describing history of passing off).

[138] *Id.* at 2763 (Stevens, J., concurring) (characterizing conclusions of United States Trade Association Trademark Review Commission).

[139] *Id.* at 2764–65 (Stevens, J., concurring).

[140] A Westlaw search of the Supreme Court database on May 25, 1995, revealed no cases using the phrase "reverse passing off."

[141] 15 U.S.C. § 1125(a).

[142] *Id.* § 1125(a)(1)(A).

[143] 30 F.3d 1255 (9th Cir. 1994) (affirming summary judgment for defendant).

[144] *Id.* at 1260.

requires "bodily appropriation."[145] The court approved dismissal of the state unfair competition claims because they were substantially congruent with the Lanham Act claims,[146] and dismissed the copyright claims because the work constituted a work for hire and thus belonged to the publisher rather than the author/plaintiff.[147]

In *Waldman Publishing Corp. v. Landoll, Inc.,*[148] both plaintiff and defendant published children's books that were adaptations of classical literary works like *Oliver Twist, The Merry Adventures of Robin Hood, Black Beauty,* and so on. The plaintiff claimed that the defendant's books were confusingly similar to the plaintiff's work and asserted Lanham Act section 43(a) and New York common-law and statutory claims. The court noted that a reverse passing off theory might be applied to written works if, for example, a second publisher were simply to tear the cover off a book and sell it with a false cover or simply reproduce a work and misrepresent its creator. "The misappropriation is of the artistic talent required to create the work, not of the manufacturing talent required for publication."[149] It found appropriate scope for a reverse passing off theory, distinct from copyright infringement theories, and borrowed from copyright law to determine whether the plaintiff added enough value to the public domain works to "constitute an origin which may be falsely designated."[150] Because it found sufficient added value to satisfy the originality test for a derivative work, it found that the plaintiff's works would have been entitled to copyright protection, and therefore could constitute an origin protectible by the reverse passing off theory.[151] Then, it questioned whether the defendant's works were sufficiently similar to the plaintiff's works to constitute reverse passing off. Here, it applied a more generous standard than the Ninth Circuit's bodily appropriation theory, finding that the "substantial similarity" standard used to show copyright infringement could constitute reverse passing off.[152] Although the court of appeals approved the district court's analysis on the merits of the reverse passing off theory necessary to decide probability of success on the merits, it found the scope of the injunction granted overbroad and thus reversed and remanded.[153]

Under *Landoll,* reverse passing off is an extremely powerful theory that could fill gaps and increase protection for sweat-of-the-brow left by *Feist.* Sweat-of-the-brow involves careful work in many cases, and it is reasonable to conclude

---

[145] *Id.* at 1261–62.

[146] *Id.* at 1262–63.

[147] *Id.* at 1259–60.

[148] 43 F.3d 775 (2d Cir. 1994) (vacating injunction against publishing or selling books, copying books of plaintiff).

[149] *Id.* at 781.

[150] *Id.* at 784–85.

[151] *Id.* at 782–83.

[152] *Id.* at 783. *See also id.* at 781 (rejecting bodily appropriation rule).

[153] *Id.* at 785.

that one harvesting material from the public domain seeks a reputation for quality in the harvesting. Even if the harvesting does not meet the originality test for selection and arrangement necessary to secure copyright protection, it may be a sufficient "origin" to qualify for protection against appropriation of goodwill under the reverse passing off theory. Because the *Feist* limitations are based on limitations of the copyright and patent clause, and because trademark protection and other protections afforded by the Lanham Act are based instead on the commerce clause, the *Feist* constitutional concerns do not limit reverse passing off. Of course, there may be limits imposed by the First Amendment under the *Cubby v. CompuServe* principle that channels of distribution must be reasonably free from the chilling effect of no-fault liability in order to serve First Amendment interests.

§ 10.13   —Trademarks under GATT-TRIP

Under the GATT-TRIP appendix, trademarks include the following:

> any sign, or any combination of signs, capable of distinguishing the goods or services of one undertaking from those of other undertakings, shall be capable of constituting a trademark. Such signs, and particular words including personal names, letters, numerals, figure developments and combinations of colors as well as any combination of such signs, shall be eligible for registration as trademarks. Where signs are not inherently capable of distinguishing the relevant goods or services, members may make registrability depend on distinctiveness inquired through use. Members may require, as a condition of registration, that signs be visually perceptible.[154]

The owner of a registered trademark

> shall have the exclusive right to prevent all third parties not having his consent from using in the course of trade identical of similar signs for goods or services which are identical or similar to those in respect of which the trademark is registered where such use would result in a likelihood of confusion. In case of the use of an identical sign for identical goods or services, a likelihood of confusion shall be presumed.[155]

GATT members are allowed to provide exceptions to the rights conferred by a trademark, such as fair use of descriptive terms, "provided that such exceptions take account of the legitimate interests of the owner of the trademark and of third parties."[156]

---

[154] GATT-TRIP, art. 15, para. 1.

[155] *Id.,* art. 16.

[156] *Id.,* art. 17.

§ 10.14 —Internet Addresses as Trademarks

A particular controversy is brewing over the application of trademark protection to Internet addresses.[157] The concern is that an Internet address assigned to A would contain words constituting B's trademark. If A is in an entirely different business from B, there is no trademark infringement problem because there is no possibility of consumer confusion. But A may be in the same business, in which case wide public exposure to A's Internet address could lead to consumer confusion and make consumers think that A is associated with B and that products from A originate with B. The basic problem is not entirely new. Efforts have been made to assert trademark to telephone numbers and to assert trademark infringement from the use of addresses resembling trademarks.[158]

Historically, the frequency of trademark infringement controversies has been constrained by geographic limits on markets and advertising. Thus, a seller of bread products in Germany using the name Stroehman would be unlikely to infringe a trademark owned by Stroehman's Bakery in Pennsylvania, simply because the consumers in the two markets are distinct and neither is likely to be exposed to the trademark used in the other market. Because sellers try to focus advertising on their actual or likely markets, the scope of advertising similarly has been limited. The Internet changes all that. Now, if the German bakery gets the Internet address stroehman.dnet.de, there is a real possibility of consumer confusion regarding the source of Stroehman's bread. Trademark law is not without solutions to this problem. There have been instances in which media circulation or penetration or product lines expanded, thus expanding the reach of advertisements carrying a product name or label that created the potential for consumer confusion about the origin of products that were nonexistent before the expansion and media reach.[159]

The other problem rises from more clearly blameworthy conduct. For example, C asks for assignment of an Internet address, intending that the address be confusingly similar to D's product or company name. The expectation apparently is that D will pay C not to use the name—or perhaps C will sell it to D, although it is not clear that Internet names and addresses can be transferred.[160]

---

[157] *See generally* Andre Brunel, *Billions Registered But No Rules: The Scope of Trademark Protection for Internet Domain Names,* 7 J. Proprietary Rts., No. 3, at 2 (1995) (reviewing particular controversies and concluding that Internet domain names qualify for trademark protection, partially by analogy with telephone number mnemonics).

[158] Feist Publications, Inc. v. Rural Tel. Serv. Co., 499 U.S. 340 (1991); Dial-A-Mattress v. Page, 880 F.2d 675 (2d Cir. 1959); MTV Networks, Inc. v. Curry, 867 F. Supp. 202 (S.D.N.Y. 1994); Exxon Corp. v. Humble Exploration Co., 524 F. Supp. 450 (N.D. Tex. 1981).

[159] Fisons Horticulture, Inc. v. Vigoro Indus., Inc., 30 F.3d 466, 474 (3d Cir. 1994) (recognizing role of expansion-of-market assessment in evaluating trademark claims).

[160] In any event the numerical address cannot simply be transferred because it indicates where in a more or less geographically based hierarchy a node is located.

§ 10.15 Trade Secret

Trade secrets are protected by common law, codified in about half the states under the Uniform Trade Secrets Act (UTSA).[161] To be within the scope of trade secret protection, information must afford its owner a competitive advantage by virtue of not generally being known. Derived from this basic definition are requirements for reasonable efforts to maintain secrecy and proof of competitive advantage resulting from the trade secret.[162]

Liability for trade secret misappropriation can be imposed on two types of misappropriators. The first kind of misappropriator learns the trade secret in the context of a special relationship.[163] The most common type of special relationship is an employment relationship. Even in the absence of an explicit contract obligating the employee to respect the employer's trade secrets, such an obligation is implied from the nature of the relationship.[164] Other special relationships exist with suppliers and commercial customers, although it is relatively unusual for an obligation to respect trade secrets to be implied simply from the relationship.[165] Rather, special relationships in the commercial supplier and customer setting usually require a nondisclosure agreement.[166]

A second kind of misappropriator is a third party who uses unreasonable methods to obtain access to a trade secret, or, under the UTSA,[167] who discovers the trade secret by accident or through the wrongful conduct of another and uses it with knowledge of its trade secret status. Wrongful methods subjecting a third party to liability for trade secret misappropriation include methods that are illegal, methods that are independently tortuous, and methods involving

---

[161] Unif. Trade Secrets Act, 12 U.L.A. 433 (1985).

[162] *See generally* Henry H. Perritt, Jr., Trade Secrets: A Practitioner's Guide (1994).

[163] UTSA § 1(2)(ii)(B)(II) (defining *misappropriation* to include disclosure or use by one who knows from circumstances she gained knowledge with a duty to maintain secrecy).

[164] Eaton Corp. v. Giere, 971 F.2d 136, 141 (8th Cir. 1992) (even if no contractual obligation, common-law fiduciary obligation existed supporting injunction and summary judgment for plaintiff's former employer).

[165] Burten v. Milton Bradley Co., 763 F.2d 461, 463 (1st Cir. 1985) (confidential relationship implied between inventor submitting game containing trade secrets and corporation receiving it); *see also* Phillips v. Frey, 20 F.3d 623 (5th Cir. 1994); Van Rensselear v. General Motors Corp., 223 F. Supp. 323, 331 (E.D. Mich. 1962), *aff'd,* 324 F.2d 354 (6th Cir. 1963).

[166] *See* RTE Corp. v. Coatings, Inc., 267 N.W.2d 226, 233 (Wis. 1978) (if trade secret is disclosed under circumstances not implying confidential relationship, a future attempt to create express confidentiality agreement does not create confidential relationship concerning previously disclosed trade secret); Wanberg v. Ocean Spray Cranberries, Inc., 194 U.S.P.Q. (BNA) 350, 352, 1977 WL 22790 (N.D. Ill. 1977) (confidential relationship cannot be predicated merely upon plaintiff's statement in unsolicited letter that idea has not been submitted to anyone else).

[167] UTSA § 1(2)(ii)(C) (accident).

deception which may not rise to the level of the tort of fraudulent misrepresentation.[168]

Trade secrets protection frequently is associated with covenants not to compete, but the two concepts are distinct. A covenant not to compete obligates the signatory not to engage in competitive activities without regard to whether the competitive activity makes use of trade secrets. Frequently, however, covenants not to compete extending beyond promises not to use trade secrets or other confidential commercial information are unenforceable except to the extent that they reinforce the tort-based obligation not to misappropriate trade secrets.[169]

Trade secret protection extends to data as well as procedural knowledge and also extends to knowledge harvested from the public domain with considerable effort.[170] The effort required, similar to the sweat-of-the-brow concept in copyright law, gives the entity that already has extended the effort a competitive advantage over its competitors who have not yet invested that effort.

Trade secret protection in the NII is an important safeguard for any aspect of a computer or communication system that can serve its purpose while still being hidden from others. This potentially extends to the workings of encryption algorithms, to the organization of data in any kind of database, and the combination of human and automated procedures used for marketing, integrity assurance, and data acquisition. Pricing information also is entitled to trade secret protection so long as it is not obvious.[171]

The scope of trade secret protection is limited by copyright and patent preemption (see § **10.21**) and by antitrust law concepts. The only reason that trade secret law is not preempted by copyright and patent law is that it protects distinguishable subject matter. If misappropriation law were to be extended beyond subject matter that is secret and confers a competitive advantage for that

---

[168] *See* Restatement (Third) of Unfair Competition § 43 & cmt. c (1995) (complete catalogue of improper means not possible); UTSA § 1 cmt. (offering a "partial listing" of improper means); *see also* Top Serv. Body Shop, Inc. v. Allstate Ins. Co., 582 P.2d 1365, 1371 n.11 (Or. 1978) ("commonly included among improper means are violence, threats, or other intimidation, deceit or misrepresentation, bribery, unfounded litigation, defamation, or disparaging falsehood"; intentional interference with contract claim); E.I. du Pont de Nemours & Co. v. Christopher, 431 F.2d 1012, 1017 (5th Cir. 1970) (airplane flight over plant under construction was improper means of acquiring information, whether or not flight complied with FAA regulations).

[169] See **Ch. 5,** analyzing restrictions on noncompetition agreements.

[170] Ecolab, Inc. v. Paolo, 753 F. Supp. 1100, 1112 (E.D.N.Y. 1991) (explaining how effort in collecting creates competitive advantage).

[171] Panther Sys. II v. Panther Computer Sys., 783 F. Supp. 53 (E.D.N.Y. 1991) (customer list including customer usage, needs, and prices they would pay was trade secret); Ecolab, Inc. v. Paolo, 753 F. Supp. 1100 (E.D.N.Y. 1991) (information regarding how much customers paid and how much they used was trade secret); Courtesy Temporary Serv. v. Camacho, 272 Cal. Rptr. 352 (Ct. App. 1990) (temporary employment services list of customers with key contacts, billing rates, and markup percentages was trade secret); Allan Dampf, P.C. v. Bloom, 512 N.Y.S.2d 116 (App. Div. 1987) (fees billed by dentist, among other information, photocopied by associate dentist was trade secret).

reason, then the likelihood of conflict with federal copyright and patent concepts increases. For example, protection of processes that are neither secret nor meet the patent novelty requirement goes further than the federal Constitution and patent statutes permit.[172] Extension of misappropriation law to protect expression that is not secret and that confers no competitive advantage intrudes into an area in which copyright law intends for information to be in the public domain.

Antitrust concepts circumscribe trade secret protection by limiting the scope of noncompetition agreements. A central feature of noncompetition agreement law is that the procompetitive policy of antitrust law gives way to the anticompetitive effect of such contracts only when enforcement of the contract is necessary to protect a legitimate business interest such as trade secrets.[173]

§ 10.16   —Trade Secrets under GATT-TRIP

The GATT-TRIP appendix recognizes trade secret protection in the following way:

> natural and legal persons shall have the possibility of preventing information lawfully within their control from being disclosed to, acquired by, or used by others without their consent in a manner contrary to honest commercial practices so long as such information:
>
> is secret in the sense that it is not, as a body or in the precise configuration and assembly of its components, generally known among or readily accessible to persons within the circles that normally deal with the kind of information in question;
>
> has commercial value because it is secret; and
>
> has been subject to reasonable steps under the circumstances, by the person lawfully in control of the information, to keep it secret.[174]

§ 10.17   Patent

The patent statutes of the United States entitle anyone to a patent who "invents or discovers any new and useful process, machine, manufacture, or composition of matter, or any new and useful improvement thereof."[175] A patent is not available, however, if the invention was known or used by others in the United States or patented or described in a printed publication in the United States or a foreign country before the invention by the applicant.[176] Nor is a patent available

---

[172] Bonito Boats, Inc. v. Thunder Craft Boats, Inc., 489 U.S. 141 (1989).

[173] See **Ch. 5,** discussing noncompetition agreements.

[174] GATT-TRIP, art. 29, para. 2.

[175] 35 U.S.C. § 101 (1988).

[176] *Id.* § 102(a).

for an invention that was in public use or on sale in the United States more than one year before the date of the application for a patent.[177] A patent is not available to an inventor who has abandoned the invention.[178]

Patents are unavailable for inventions patented in other countries on applications filed more than one year before a parallel application was filed in the United States.[179] Inventors may not obtain patents for inventions covered by applications for patents filed either in the United States or in an international application before the invention by the current applicant.[180] When two people have invented the same subject matter, the first person to invent who did not abandon, suppress, or conceal the invention is entitled to the patent.[181]

Even when the requirements of 35 U.S.C. § 101 as to subject matter are satisfied, a patent may not be obtained for an invention that is obvious. Section 103 negates patentability if the differences between the subject matter sought to be patented and the prior art are such that the subject matter as a whole would have been obvious at the time the invention was made to a person having ordinary skill in the art to which the subject matter pertains.[182]

Patents are issued in the United States by the United States Patent and Trademark Office after an examination and a determination that the statutory requirements have been satisfied. Applications typically are prepared by specialists in "patent prosecution" and are secret until the patent is granted. If it is denied, the application remains secret.[183] Patents must be applied for by the inventor personally.[184] In order to obtain a patent, one must file an application in the form prescribed by the United States Patent and Trademark Office (USPTO). The application must contain a "specification," including: "a written description of the invention, the manner and process of making and using it, in such full, clear, concise, and exact terms, as to enable any person skilled in the art, to make and use it, and must set forth the best mode contemplated by the inventor for carrying out his invention."[185] The specification must conclude with one or more "claims" "particularly pointing out and distinctly claiming the subject matter which the applicant regards as his invention."[186] The claims represent the metes and bounds of the invention. Typically, they are drafted in a kind of hierarchy

---

[177] *Id.* § 102(b).

[178] *Id.* § 102(c).

[179] *Id.* § 102(d).

[180] *Id.* § 102(e).

[181] 35 U.S.C. § 102(g) (providing also for consideration of diligence in reducing conception to practice). GATT-TRIP mandates a change to a first-to-file system.

[182] *Id.* § 103.

[183] *Id.* § 122. Despite debate, implementation of GATT-TRIP left this rule intact. *See* Pub. L. No. 465, §§ 531–534.

[184] 35 U.S.C. § 102(f) (excluding from patent entitlement one who "did not himself invent the subject matter sought to be patented").

[185] *Id.* § 112.

[186] *Id.*

with the most general claims put first and more particular or specific claims following. Skilled drafters of patent claims usually draft the more general claims to the limits of conceivable patentability.

During the prosecution of a patent application, the applicant and the assigned examiner from USPTO usually negotiate a narrowing and redrafting of the claims language. This negotiation process is recorded in a file called the "patent wrapper," and it constitutes a kind of legislative history that subsequently can be used to construe the language of the patent as it actually issues.

Once a patent issues, anyone who, without authority of the patent holder, "makes, uses, or sells any patented invention, within the United States during the term of the patent infringes it."[187] Anyone who actively induces infringement of a patent is also liable as an infringer.[188]

Thus patentability, unlike copyrightability, depends on novelty of subject matter, advance review by a government official, and a determination by that official that statutory requirements have been satisfied. A patent also includes a statement of metes and bounds for the intellectual property before it comes into existence. The rights of the owner of the intellectual property in a patent has a monopoly over use, unlike the owner of a copyright.

§ 10.18   —Patents under GATT-TRIP

The GATT Agreement on Trade Related Aspects of Intellectual Property Rights (TRIP) includes a section on patents.[189] Article 27 defines patentable subject matter and says that patent protection shall be available for any inventions, whether products or processes, in all fields of technology, provided that they are new, involve an inventive step, and are capable of industrial application.[190] It provides that patents must be available and patent rights enjoyable without discrimination as to the place of invention, the field of technology, and whether products are imported or locally produced.[191] The agreement provides that a patent shall confer on its owner the following exclusive rights: "making, using, offering for sale, selling, or importing for those purposes."[192] The patentee of a process may prevent third parties not having his consent from the acts of: "using the process, and from the acts of using, offering for sale, selling, or importing for these purposes at least the product obtained directly by that process."[193]

---

[187] *Id.* § 271.

[188] *Id.*

[189] GATT-TRIP, pt. II, § 5.

[190] *Id.,* art. 27, para. 1.

[191] *Id.,* art. 27, para. 1.

[192] *Id.,* art. 28, para. 1(a) (products).

[193] *Id.,* art. 28, para. 1(b) (process patent).

Unlike pre-GATT U.S. law, in some circumstances the GATT-TRIP provides for compulsory licenses to prevent the withholding of beneficial inventions from society. It entitles someone to compel issuance of a license who unsuccessfully has sought to obtain authorization from the patentee on reasonable commercial terms. GATT-TRIP requires that any such license be limited in scope and duration by its purpose,[194] that it be nonexclusive,[195] that it be nonassignable,[196] that it be predominantly for the domestic market,[197] that it be terminated if justification ceases,[198] and that the patentee be adequately compensated for the license.[199]

More generally, the GATT-TRIP provides for a patent term of 20 years counted from the filing date. Prior U.S. law provided for a term of 17 years counted from the date of issuance of the patent.[200] The GATT appendix defines *patentable subject matter* as "any inventions, whether products or processes, in all fields of technology, provided that they are new, involve an inventive step and are capable of industrial application.[201]

Signatories may require that patent applicants disclose the invention in a manner sufficiently clear and complete for the invention to be carried out by a persons skilled in the art and may require the applicant to indicate the best mode for carrying out the invention.[202]

§ 10.19 —Patents in the NII

Until relatively recently, patents played only a limited role in protecting additions to value in the NII. There were significant doubts about whether software could be patented,[203] and innovators thought the process of obtaining a patent too expensive and cumbersome. Now, however, patents are a powerful means of obtaining protection for a variety of specialized algorithms, including those for

---

[194] *Id.,* art. 31(c).

[195] GATT-TRIP, pt II, § 5, art. 31(d).

[196] *Id.,* art. 31(e).

[197] *Id.,* art. 31(f).

[198] *Id.,* art. 31(g).

[199] *Id.,* art. 31(h).

[200] This goes by the GATT proposition, art. 33 (term of protection).

[201] GATT-TRIP, pt II, § 5, art. 27.

[202] *Id.,* art. 29.

[203] *In re* Epstein, 32 F.3d 1559, 1567 (Fed. Cir. 1994) (affirming denial of claims for computerized warehousing system based on prior art; no suggestion that software per se is not patentable); *see also* Diamond v. Diehr, 450 U.S. 175 (1981) (process involving computer program was patentable); Dann v. Johnston, 425 U.S. 219 (1976) (computerized accounting system unpatentable on grounds of obviousness).

encryption systems,[204] for compression algorithms,[205] and for techniques for representing graphical images.[206] There also have been efforts to patent database retrieval techniques.[207]

A major process within the Clinton administration's Information Infrastructure Task Force has been consideration of the role that patents should play in protecting computer software.[208]

---

[204] U.S. Patent No. 4,405,829 (Sept. 20, 1983) (RSA encryption), inventor Rivest, Shamir & Adelman; U.S. Patent No. 4,200,770 (Apr. 29, 1980) (key exchange), Diffie, Hillman & Merkle.

[205] U.S. Patent No. 5,396,343 (Mar. 7, 1995) (image compresssion systems with optimized data access), Hanselman.

[206] U.S. Patent No. 5,428,741 (June 27, 1995) (high-speed image preprocessing system including a multipurpose buffer for storing digital image data and data cropping means for selectively cropping the digital image data), Ho; assignee NCR Corp.; U.S. Patent No. 5,428,462 (June 27, 1995) (facsimile apparatus having user name register with means for receiving image signals and for compressing and storing same so as to print identifier, logo, or trademark of sender with reduced storage means), Kim; assignee Goldstar Company. CompuServe's Graphics Interchange Format (GIF) incorporates Unisys' Lempel-Zev-Welch (LZW) algorithm, U.S. Patent No. 4,558,302 (Dec. 10, 1985), inventor Terry Welch; assigned to Sperry Corporation.

[207] *See* William A. Tanenbaum, *Current Multimedia Patent, Copyright, Work Made for Hire, and Rights Acquisition Issues,* (PLI Patent Course Handbook Series No. 383, 1994. One particularly controversial patent was issued for the database techniques involved in publishing an encyclopedia on CD-ROM. The uproar led to a reexamination. Tanenbaum states that the Commissioner gets his authority for reexamination from 37 C.F.R. § 1.520, which limits reexaminations to public policy questions where there are no interests by any other persons. Reexaminations are used to determine the validity of an issued patent in light of previously issued patents and preexisting printed publications (prior art). Prior art can give rise to substantive questions concerning the validity of a patent when there exists a substantive likelihood that a reasonable patent examiner would consider prior art important in making a determination. The Commissioner's order (Reexamination Control No. 90/003,270 (order date Dec. 14, 1993)—Patent No. 5,241,671, assigned to Michael Reed et al.) cited 12 prior art patents and publications that raised a substantial new question as to the patentability of the 41 claims of the '671 patent.

See generally Dan L. Burk, *Patents in Cyberspace: Territoriality and Infringement on Global Computer Networks,* 68 Tulane L. Rev. 1 (1993).

[208] In January and February of 1995, the Task Force held hearings regarding proposed changes in patent law as it pertains to computer software. The *Federal Register* invited comments in written and electronic form prior to the dates of the hearings. 58 Fed. Reg. 66,347 (Dec. 20, 1993). The hearings were held in San Jose (Jan. 26/27) and Arlington (Feb. 10). Many questions were posed prior to the hearings regarding the process for obtaining patents. Among these were questions as to whether there is needed a new form of protection. Questions were raised as to concerns over "prior art" (i.e., the standards of examiners and examiner procedures). Other questions related to the disclosure of software-related inventions on patents and other publications.

At the two hearings many people testified on various aspects of computer software patents. For example, William Ryan (intellectual property owners) spoke in support of continued strong patent protection for computer program subject matter. While, Jerry Fidler (Wind

§ 10.20 Compatibility as Infringement

In some limited circumstances, interoperability or computability can give rise to infringement of intellectual property rights.[209] The most prominent example of this possibility arose in the copyright infringement litigation brought by Lotus Development Corporation against Borland International. Borland had constructed its spreadsheet product Quattro so that it offered users the Lotus 1-2-3 command set and macros as an alternative to the Quattro command set and macros. Lotus claimed that this compatibility infringed copyrighted elements of its Lotus 1-2-3 program. The district court agreed with Lotus, finding that the Quattro compatibility had been achieved by copying certain data structures, that these data structures were protectible expression under the Copyright Act, and that Borland's copying did not constitute fair use.[210] The United States Court of Appeals disagreed and reversed the district court, finding that aspects of the Lotus 1-2-3 program for which Lotus sought protection were unprotectible methods of operation.[211]

There are a number of circumstances under which compatibility and interoperability could be accused of infringing, although many copyright holders able to make such arguments are unlikely to do so because compatibility increases the market for their products. Although the matter is not entirely clear,[212] the First Circuit analysis is the appropriate one. Most compatibility can

---

River Systems) argued for an end to the issuing of any software patents, stating that they are not necessary to creation of software and that issuing patents will only impede their creation/advancement. Robert Kohn (Borland Int'l) spoke on the proper scope of intellectual property protection. He sought to distinguish between strong enforcement on the one hand and the scope of enforcement on the other. He said that just because strong enforcement promotes innovation does not mean that a broader scope of intellectual property protection will also. Steven Henry (Wolf, Greenfield and Sack, P.C.—"a large intellectual property law firm") addressed the problems with the current system as it now stands. He questioned the examiners and reexaminations. Joseph Grace (Tetrasoft—a starting up company) raised a constitutional challenge on the basis of art. 1, § 8 cl. 8, stating that when patents stop promoting growth they become unconstitutional. So there was varied assortments of perspectives at the two hearings covering (what seems to be) the gammit of questions related to the future of the PTO and its relation to computer software patents and also patents in general.

[209] See Interactive, Inc. v. NTN Communications, Inc., 875 F. Supp. 1398, 1405 (N.D. Cal. 1995) (characterizing argument of plaintiff that infringement occurred because of similarity of ordering and structure of data fields, but insufficient proof of similarity in data feed structures to support claim).

[210] Lotus Dev. Corp. v. Borland Int'l, Inc., 799 F. Supp. 203, 217–18 (D. Mass. 1992) (holding that the copied elements of the "menu command" and "menu structure" contained expressive aspects separable from the two and that they were an integral part of the program).

[211] Lotus Dev. Corp. v. Borland Int'l, Inc., 49 F.3d 807, 819 (1st Cir. 1995). The Lotus case is discussed more extensively in § 10.4.

[212] See Henry H. Perritt, Jr., Unbundling Value in Electronic Information Products: Intellectual Property Protection for Machine Readable Interfaces, 20 Rutgers Comp. & Tech. L.J. 415 (1994).

be achieved by copying no more than methods of operation. Even when copying involves arguably expressive material, some such copying still should not produce liability. As long as no more reproduction has occurred than is necessary to achieve compatibility, either there has been no infringement of protected expression because the bare compatibility elements are unprotectible under the merger doctrine, or else sufficient copying to achieve mere compatibility or interoperability is fair use.[213]

§ 10.21 Preemption

Two traditional types of intellectual property law—copyright and patent—are almost exclusively federal. One type—trademark and unfair competition—is concurrently state and federal, while the fourth type—trade secret protection— is exclusively state. All four forms overlap to a considerable extent; different aspects of one product may enjoy protection under some or all four types of intellectual property law. This possibility has created a challenge for working out the framework for federal preemption of copyright and patent. Two 1964 Supreme Court cases set the basic ground rules for preemption of state law: *Sears, Roebuck & Co. v. Stiffel Co.*[214] and *Comp Co. v. Day-Brite Lighting, Inc.*[215] The cases invalidated a broad form of state unfair competition that protected unpatented product designs. The two cases were read by many commentators in lower courts as standing for the proposition that the patents and copyrights clause of the United States Constitution[216] automatically preempts state protection of any subject matter within the scope of the constitutional clause left unprotected by federal statutes. This interpretation was based on two propositions: first, that by limiting the scope of statutory protection, the Congress impliedly expressed an intent that everything outside that scope should be unprotected; and second, that the limited scope of the patent and copyrights clause itself evidences an intent by drafters of the Constitution that everything outside that scope must remain unprotected by the states as well as by the Congress as a matter of constitutional law.

These broad preemption theories were, however, dashed in *Goldstein v. California.*[217] In that case, although the Supreme Court did not overrule *Sears* and *Comp Co.,*[218] it rejected the idea that the patent and copyrights clause

---

[213] In addition, there are many cases in which the quantity of expression copied to achieve compatibility would be so small as not to qualify for protectibility under the originality doctrine of *Feist*.

[214] 376 U.S. 225 (1964).

[215] 376 U.S. 234 (1964).

[216] U.S. Const. art. I, § 8, cl. 8.

[217] 412 U.S. 546 (1973).

[218] *Id.* at 571.

conferred exclusive authority on the federal government to protect intellectual property.[219] Thus, in subsequent cases, such as *Kewanee Oil Co. v. Bicron Corp.*,[220] the Supreme Court found preemption only when the state law represents some conflict with statutory provisions. *Bonito Boats, Inc. v. Thunder Craft Boats, Inc.*,[221] is such a case. There, the Court found a Florida statute preempted by federal patent law. The Florida statute prohibited the use of a molding process to make boats. The Court reasoned that the subject matter was covered by the patent statute, but no patent had been obtained. The state law thus tended to frustrate national uniformity intended by Congress.[222] On the other hand, in *Aronson v. Quick Point Pencil Co.*,[223] the Court emphasized that a royalty contract that extended beyond the time a patent for the design was denied was not made unenforceable by federal preemption: "The states are free to regulate the use of intellectual property in any manner not inconsistent with federal law."[224] The possibility that contract enforcement ordinarily escapes preemption, even though a state statute with the same content would be preempted, enjoys support from the Supreme Court's analysis in *American Airlines, Inc. v. Wolens*.[225] There, the Supreme Court suggested that state common law of contract enforcement operates on a different plane from state statutes or other positive law when claims of federal preemption are made.[226]

Nevertheless, the *Kewanee Oil* Court and dozens of lower federal and state courts have worked out an analytical framework for preemption of trade secret misappropriation claims that emphasizes the traditional elements of trade secret, particularly including secrecy as the reasons why trade secret protection is not preempted by copyright law.[227] Accordingly, a contract that purports to limit uses of factual information outside of copyright protection under *Feist,* or public information outside of copyright protection under § 105 or First Amendment

---

[219] *Id.* at 553–54 (referring to The Federalist No. 32, at 241 (B. Wright ed., 1961)).

[220] 416 U.S. 470 (1974).

[221] 489 U.S. 141 (1989).

[222] *Id.* at 162.

[223] 440 U.S. 257 (1979).

[224] *Id.* at 262 (noting that enforcement of the royalty contract did not prevent anyone from copying the unpatented idea and thus did not conflict with federal patent law).

[225] 115 S. Ct. 817, 824 (1995) (suggesting that state law enforcing contract is less vulnerable to preemption than state positive law).

[226] *Id.* at 824–25.

[227] *See* Computer Assocs. Int'l, Inc. v. Altai, Inc., 982 F.2d 693 (2d Cir. 1992) (restating copyright preemption law as it pertains to misappropriation law); Roboserve, Ltd. v. Tom's Food, Inc., 940 F.2d 1441 (11th Cir. 1991) (reversing denial of judgment n.o.v. because trade secret protection for information in the public domain is preempted); Boeing Co. v. Sierracin Corp., 738 P.2d 665, 674 (Wash. 1987) (explaining that copyright and trade secret protect different elements; trade secret protects ideas possessing some novelty that are undisclosed and for those reasons escape preemption); Balboa Ins. Co. v. Trans Global Equities, 218 Cal. App. 3d 1327, 267 Cal. Rptr. 787 (1990) (common-law misappropriation claim preempted but not trade secret claim in violation of confidential relationship claim).

analysis, as explained in **Chapter 11,** well might be preempted because it enjoys none of the features that have exempted trade secret protection from preemption: secrecy and breach of a confidential relationship.

The prevailing view is that contracts imposing restrictions on redissemination of *Feist* material are enforceable because they do not directly address rights addressed by copyright, and because preemption analysis allows more room for state enforcement of contractual rights than state statutory law.[228] But this is not necessarily the correct conclusion. Contractual restrictions on redissemination are covenants not to compete, and they should be scrutinized under the same standards used for traditional covenants not to compete.[229] Covenants not to compete are enforceable only when they seek to protect legitimate interests of the beneficiary, for example an interest in protecting trade secrets, and when the scope and duration of their restraints are reasonable. Otherwise, they are unenforceable because they violate public policy. Thus, any redissemination restriction should be analyzed to determine whether it relates to genuinely proprietary information and whether its restraints are reasonable. When the information as to which redissemination is prohibited is public information, the first test fails. It is unnecessary to proceed to the other criteria.

Before enactment of the Copyright Act of 1976, there were two types of copyright protection: a common-law copyright, which arose upon the creation of the work and continued until its publication; and a statutory copyright, which essentially replaced the common-law copyright when the work was published and the statutory formalities then applicable, such as registration and notice affixation, complied with.[230]

The preemption provisions of the 1976 Act[231] eclipsed common-law copyright except for three situations: with respect to subject matter not within statutory subject matter, "including works of authorship not fixed in any tangible medium of expression";[232] causes of action arising from undertakings commenced before January 1, 1978;[233] and activities violating legal and equitable rights not equivalent to those specified in 17 U.S.C. § 106.[234]

This leaves a fair amount of elbowroom for state claims, especially for those involving unfixed expression such as speeches, or dramatic performances.

---

[228] *See* American Airlines, Inc. v. Wolens, 115 S. Ct. 817, 824 (1995) (suggesting that state law enforcing contract is less vulnerable to preemption than state positive law).

[229] See **Ch. 5.**

[230] *See* Jim Henson Prods., Inc. v. John T. Brady & Assocs., 867 F. Supp. 175, 184 (S.D.N.Y. 1994) (describing role of common-law copyright).

[231] 17 U.S.C. § 301.

[232] *Id.* § 301(b)(1). *See* Baltimore Orioles, Inc. v. Major League Baseball Players Ass'n, 805 F.2d 663, 675 (7th Cir. 1986) (recognizing possibility of unpreempted common-law copyright in unrecorded performance such as baseball game, but finding that rights in game merged into statutory copyright because game was recorded simultaneously with being played, and thus any state common-law claim was preempted).

[233] 17 U.S.C. § 301(b)(2).

[234] *Id.* § 301(b)(3).

§ 10.22   Alternative Protection Methods

There are more than a dozen ways, shown in **Table 10–1,** in which creators of content and added value can protect themselves against free riding without relying exclusively on copyright law. Some of these were introduced in §§ **10.1** and **10.2** introducing this chapter and explaining the economics of intellectual property. Electronic publishing techniques in the NII, while they may make it easier for some types of free riding to occur and make certain types of infringement of intellectual property rights more difficult to detect, also offer new possibilities for protecting entrepreneurial effort.[235]

Table 10–1

Protecting Intellectual Property Without Copyright

Technique	Analogy	Electronic Example
1. planned obsolescence	supplemented professional books	frequent updates of material
2. finer granularity		small http- or gopher-retrievable files
3. addition of presentation markup		HTML tagging
4. subsidies of content producers by producers of downstream value		Web server subsidizes suppliers of content on other servers
5. third-party subsidy	advertising	
6. system access controls		Westlaw, LEXIS passwords
7. content encryption		CNI/Library of Congress test bed

---

[235] *See generally* Eric Schlachter, *Generating Revenues from Websites,* Boardwatch, July 1995, at 60 (suggesting subscription model for relying on revenue streams generated from end users; shopping mall model for generating revenues from fixed fee plus performance incentives; advertising model; computer services model for generating revenues from providing storage space, html markup, and design and consulting); Mark Nollinger, *America Online,* Wired, Sept. 1995, at 158, 200 (reporting that America Online's partners are paid 10 to 20 percent of revenues, but Microsoft plans to pay 70 percent).

Technique	Analogy	Electronic Example
8. giving content away to attract consumers to electronic markets	newspaper	
9. bundling vulnerable material to less vulnerable value-added elements		embedding content in CD-ROM software; Westlaw, LEXIS, CompuServe
10. bond, or open-ended credit card authorization, from customers to ensure compliance with license		
11. extremely low-transaction-cost payment systems linked with chunks that it is not worthwhile to steal		
12. "global" license by creator in exchange for share of revenues determined per some aggregate formula	collective licensing schemes	
13. concentrating investment on value-added features other than content		
14. contract protection		Westlaw, LEXIS, Lexis Counsel Connect
15. trademark protection	branded software	
16. trade secret protection		applies only to procedures, not to content

One of the most obvious examples is the protection available to vendors of remotely accessible databases. Even though there are significant doubts about the protectibility of the content in such databases,[236] vendors of such databases have relatively little to worry about in terms of free riding. They can ensure that no database access is permitted unless payment or payment arrangements have been made. While they lack technical control over reuse and redissemination of material retrieved from their databases, as a practical matter, the granularity of such databases is such that a pirate would face such large transaction costs to download the entire content that she would not gain any particular advantage, compared with gathering the information on her own. Moreover, such massive downloading would be relatively easy to detect. Thus, the more added value in the database, the less the risk of piracy because the added value in most conventional database technologies results in finer granularity and additional markup tags distributed throughout the information.

In addition, most such databases are useful only because they are continuously updated. The state of the database at any particular point in time would begin to lose value as soon as it was pirated. Thus, planned obsolescence also plays an important role in protecting the competitive position of the originator.

Newer search and retrieval technologies, including Z39.50, Gopher, and World Wide Web, do not detract from the protective effect of finer granularity and planned obsolescence. Indeed, they enhance it because not only are all the elements of the particular database finally grained, but they are distributed across the NII and thus more difficult and more expensive to assemble.[237] Also, in distributed databases controlled by a multiplicity of sponsors, more than content becomes obsolete; the pointers themselves need continual maintenance in order to point to real sources.

Equally important is the fact that much of the value in electronic publishing is not in the content but in the processes used to retrieve desired content. Process is easier to protect from piracy than content because one need not give the process to someone in order for him to use it; a user does not get the means of replication when he uses process as opposed to content. At least, this is true when the process is used through a network rather than being used locally. When one accesses information from a remote host,[238] one runs a computer program but does not have a copy of the computer program. No matter how many times one uses the program, one never gets the means of replicating it or a free ride on the investment of the person who wrote the program. Thus any added value that

---

[236] **Section 10.4** explains why factual content is unprotectible under the Supreme Court's *Feist* decision, and also explains that the selection and arrangement of components of comprehensive databases, such as those containing all the statutes of a particular jurisdiction, may be unprotectible because they are obvious.

[237] On the other hand, a pirate can extract value from the distributed grains simply by pointing to them and thus, at relatively little cost, set himself up in competition with those originators of the database views represented by collections of pointers.

[238] This is true regardless of whether the architecture is post and dumb terminal or client server.

permits user execution without having its procedures and algorithms disclosed to the user is inherently protected from misappropriation.

Because process is easier to protect than content, an information infrastructure that combines process and content—as all conceivable electronic publishing ventures in the NII will do—invites income transfer from vendors of process to vendors of content. The value of any of the value-added processes, beginning with chunking and tagging and ranging all the way through billing and collection services, is proportional to the content to which they facilitate access. Thus, if pure content providers are confronted with less than compensatory prices because of the threat of free riding, and process producers do not face such a threat, the process producers have an incentive to make payments to content producers in order to induce the production of more content. One obvious way to do this is simply to make grants to content producers to produce content and place it in the NII for access through the World Wide Web and similar architectures. Even though the content is then available for exploitation by those who have not paid the subsidy as well as by those who have, giving the nonpayers a kind of free ride on the backs of process producers and subsidizers, the subsidizers nevertheless have a head start for some period of time. They know about the content and its location, and their potential competitors not involved in the subsidization lack such knowledge. Also, there are other forms of subsidy, including training, and the use of content preparation tools that may cost the subsidizer relatively little and yet be of proportionately greater benefit to the content producer receiving the subsidy. Nevertheless, subsidizers will worry about the threat of free riding on the fruits of their subsidy.

Subsidized content in a scheme described in this paragraph is an archetypal public good because others not paying for it are nevertheless excluded from its benefits.[239] Because of this concern, subsidizers will have a strong incentive to build some kind of fence around the content they subsidize. They can do this in several ways. The most obvious way is simply to buy the content and hide it behind their own processes. That is what existing electronic information vendors have done—CompuServe, Westlaw, LEXIS, and Dialog.[240] To the extent that this is the way subsidization occurs,[241] the NII will not look like the World Wide Web; it will look like a modest elaboration of the pre-Internet information architecture: many proprietary islands.

There are, however, other ways of building fences, including combinations of subsidy by producers of downstream value with licensing collectives[242]

---

[239] See § 10.2 for an analysis of the public good concept.

[240] This is an example of "bundling vulnerable material to less vulnerable value-added elements."

[241] The subsidy process works the same way that it does in conventional book publishing. Publishers pay authors either on a flat-fee or royalty basis to produce content that is exclusively reserved for sale by that subsidizing publisher.

[242] See generally Stanley M. Besen et al., An Economic Analysis of Copyright Collectives, 78 Va. L. Rev. 383 (1992) (reviewing economic conditions in which collective licensing arrangements can be sustained, and synthesizing legal principles pursuant to which they are allowed). Justice Department and EC guidelines on intellectual property licenses are reviewed in **Ch. 5.**

reinforced by copyright law and contract or trademark; and subsidy cooperatives reinforced by technological means of detecting free riding. Such cooperatives may be economically efficient because each participant could share the cost of content production by splitting the subsidy with other members of the cooperative.

The advertising model represents yet another form of subsidy for content production. An advertiser has no reason to build fences around the subsidized content because the more people who use and redisseminate the content the greater the benefit to the advertiser—as long as the advertisement is not stripped off the content it subsidizes. World Wide Web technologies open up a variety of new techniques for associating advertisements with content, ranging from simple notices of sponsorship through more elaborate techniques for requiring that a buyer of content actually read or download the advertisement before gaining access to the desired content. In addition, the NII opens up the possibility that an advertisement may also be a gateway to an electronic market, which may be valuable in its own right. As noted in another position in **Table 10–1,** another way that content may be subsidized is to subsidize it and give it away to induce people to come to the threshold of an electronic market, somewhat as a newspaper or magazine delivers content frequently below cost in order to induce readers to enter the marketplace represented by classified advertisements.

Content encryption is a way of extending technical protection beyond value-added processes to the content itself. There are a variety of proposals for digital libraries that would rely on encrypted content in order to make the otherwise public good excludable.[243] All of them rely on the basic concept that one could decrypt the desired information content only by using a key for which one would have to pay. Encryption technologies permit the deployment of systems that would limit the number of times encrypted content could be accessed and that also would permit certain types of use while excluding other types, such as replication. The same technologies permit one to determine with high reliability whether content has been altered, including the removal of various notices and advertisements.[244]

As electronic payment systems become more sophisticated,[245] it becomes easier to require some or all of the users of electronic publishing systems to post a kind of bond to ensure compliance with limitations on their use of material

---

[243] Karen Frank & Michael Higgins, *Fair Use: In the Courts and Out of Control* (PLI Patent Course Handbook Series No. 411, 1995).

[244] Marvin A. Sirbu, *Internet Billing Service Design and Prototype Implementation, in* 1 Proceedings Technological Strategies for Protecting Intellectual Property in the Networked Multimedia Environment 67 (Interactive Multimedia Ass'n 1994); Robert E. Kahn, *Deposit Registration and Recordation in an Electronic Copyright Management System, in* 1 Proceedings Technological Strategies for Protecting Intellectual Property in the Networked Multimedia Environment 111 (Interactive Multimedia Ass'n 1994).

[245] See **Ch. 9.**

obtained through the system. Thus, while it might not be feasible technically to prevent someone from replicating and redisseminating material, the cost of imposing sanctions for such activities could be reduced through a security bond. This might be little more than a credit card number with an accompanying contractual authorization to charge the credit card in the event of breach of a license agreement.

New payment systems facilitate protecting intellectual property in another way. If payment systems can be deployed that have extremely low transaction costs for buying small amounts of information—say five cents worth—relatively large revenue streams can be directed to content suppliers while maintaining a price for any grain of information lower than the cost of stealing it.

The notion of a "global" license by content creators in exchange for a share of revenues from downstream process vendors is not completely unlike the Shareware approach, although it depends on other aspects shown in **Table 10–1** for success.[246] It also must be recognized that weaknesses in protecting content will tend to focus investment on value-added features other than content. This phenomenon is evident in the present NII, which has a relatively rich set of products associated with public information, where the content is freely available and produced by government agencies with tax revenues, thus eliminating the need to find a way to direct revenue to content producers. Even if the NII is biased in this fashion toward public information and away from privately authored content, it still would be of significant value. Of course what also may happen is that a relatively open NII would be associated with public information, while a collection of more closed islands would be associated with privately authored content.

Several types of legal protection in addition to copyright protection play an important role, as this chapter explains. The predominant means of protecting value-added features in the present NII is contract. **Chapter 9** explains how the enforceability of contracts made in the NII can be enhanced, and there is little reason to suppose that the typical limitations in information licensing agreements would be preempted.[247] Trade secret protection and patent protection reinforce technical protections for processes. Because there is no need for the details of a process to be disclosed in order for it to be used by the consuming public, the requisite elements of trade secret protection can exist.[248] In addition, trademark and unfair competition law can be quite valuable because it protects the investment of an originator in goodwill and the fruits of its advertising. Trademark is a good way to protect and enhance the lead time available to first inference in an electronic information market.

---

[246] *See generally* Stanley M. Besen et al., *An Economic Analysis of Copyright Collectives,* 78 Va. L. Rev. 383 (1992) (reviewing economic conditions in which collective licensing arrangements can be sustained, and synthesizing legal principles pursuant to which they are allowed). *See also* 37 C.F.R. § 201.26 (1994) (rules for computer shareware).

[247] But see § **10.21.**

[248] See § **10.15.**

Finally, although the purpose of this section was to focus attention on means of protection other than copyright, copyright plays an important role in protecting content. As long as content producers and vendors make it clear that they are not impliedly licensing all use and redissemination and are not placing their content in the public domain, copyright gives them a powerful legal remedy against large-scale piracy once it is detected. The threat of a copyright infringement lawsuit with associated damages enters into the economic calculus of a potential pirate.[249]

Chapter 1 explains that much of the concern about protecting intellectual property through new statutes and elaborate encryption structures is overblown. As with other threats to property and personal interests through the NII, a combination of existing law and effective entrepreneurial mobilization of the particular attributes of new technologies should suffice to strike a reasonable balance between competing interests.

As the NII matures, the advantages of closed networks for protecting intellectual property and discouraging tortious and criminal content will lead to a merger of the open and closed architectures. Although some role may remain for the original closed networks like pre-1993 CompuServe, America Online, Westlaw, and LEXIS, it is more likely that new Internet technologies will permit certain features of those approaches to exist alongside traditional open architectures in the Internet, for example, secure payment systems that deny access to certain Internet resources until appropriate payment arrangements have been made. That is already possible now with a combination of NetScape CG-bin scripts and public key encryption. Access to a particular set of web pages or newsgroups can be denied without an account name and password associated with that particular set of resources. Public key encryption permits either the private transmission of credit card numbers or authentication of an account holder's identity.

Suppliers of intellectual property will be drawn to this and away from completely autonomous closed systems because of the flexibility of Internet-based tools like the web and NetScape, and because of the much larger potential market available through the Internet as contrasted with independent services, each of which must convince people to subscribe.

§ 10.23 Proposed Legal Initiatives

In an extensive article published by the *Columbia Law Review,*[250] a number of intellectual property scholars proposed a new system of protection for computer works. They started from the proposition that computer programs "behave." The

---

[249] W.M. Landes & R.A. Posner, *An Economic Analysis of Copyright Law,* 18 J. Legal Stud. 325 (1989).

[250] Pamela Samuelson et al., *A Manifesto Concerning the Legal Protection of Computer Programs,* 94 Colum. L. Rev. 2308 (1994) [hereinafter Manifesto].

behavior constitutes a process and thus makes copyright protection uncomfortable for computer programs because of the exclusion of processes and procedures from copyrightability.[251] Many different expressions produce the same behavior, and thus conceiving of copyright protection as focusing on the expression contained in the text of a computer program is underinclusive to some extent. On the other hand, innovation in computer works is incremental, and each significant increment may not satisfy the requirements of patentability either because it is not novel or because the increment fails to satisfy the nonobviousness requirement.[252]

The Manifesto authors proposed as a solution a three-year[253] blockage period for clones. The blocking period could differ for different types of original work in clones. It would allow development but not distribution during the blocking period. A system of registration could extend the blocking period. This would be a "light" registration system, more like copyright than patent, in that there would be no examination. The Manifesto authors acknowledge a problem with a registration system for their type of value: there is no clear artifact to register for a computer program, unlike the mask for a semiconductor work that can be registered under the Semiconductor Chip Protection Act.[254] The Manifesto considers but rejects the possibility of a privilege for imitations that also improve the state of the art, on the grounds that defining such a privilege would be too difficult. On the other hand, it proposes somewhat vaguely an electronic repository of information about the art, but is wildly optimistic about pattern matching capabilities necessary to make such a repository useful.

In the same volume, a number of other commentators not coauthoring the Manifesto offered other perspectives. Professor Gordon characterized the Manifesto as providing a "well-lit playing field" for intellectual property. The proposal by Professor Reichman constitutes a more flexible regime, although both recognize the dangers of overprotection. He notes that the Manifesto is minimalist and proposes something quite different from a property regime.

Professor Reichman proposes a hybrid solution, working from a background of the two great international conventions that define the subject matter of intellectual property: the Paris Convention, which focused on industrial property,[255] and the Berne Convention, which focused on artistic works.[256] He finds appealing the concepts of trade secret law, but acknowledges that trade secret protection is sometimes arbitrary and that the amount of protection available for a trade secret basically depends on how easy reverse engineering is. When reverse engineering is easy, trade secret is underprotective. When it is difficult,

---

[251] 17 U.S.C. § 102(b).

[252] *See* 35 U.S.C. § 101 (novelty requirement); *id.* § 103 (nonobviousness requirement).

[253] The authors were somewhat ambiguous as to the length of the blocking period.

[254] Protection of Semiconductor Chip Products, (as codified in 17 U.S.C. § 902 (1988)).

[255] Convention of the Union of Paris, Mar. 20, 1883, 53 Stat. 1748.

[256] Berne Convention for the Protection of Literary and Artistic Works, *opened for signature,* Sept. 9, 1886, Doc. No. 27, 99th Cong., 2d Sess. (1986), 828 U.N.T.S. 221.

trade secret is overprotective.[257] Professor Reichman begins with the proposition that the key goal is adequate lead time for the inventor to recover his investment. Professor Reichman proposes adapting trade secret concepts to compensate originators while allowing socially desirable derivatives. He emphasizes that property rights are not the right concept.

Professor Ginsberg was critical of the Manifesto proposal. She observes that it is too soon, in the sense that there is no demonstrated problem with traditional intellectual property law categories; but it also is too late, because the traditional categories have been codified into international law under GATT-TRIP. She finds the manifesto too optimistic regarding the common-law misappropriation approach, and too pessimistic about copyright capacity to provide appropriate levels of protection for computer works.

Professor Goldstein emphasizes practical considerations such as congressional politics, which completely constrain any legislative initiative, and the difficulty of implementing indeterminate concepts such as those found in abundance in the Manifesto. He also notes that international considerations receive too little attention in the Manifesto.

§ 10.24   Checklist for Intellectual Property in the NII

This section reviews several questions about intellectual property rights. These are the questions that arise most frequently as owners and users of intellectual property employ new technologies.

Q. Who owns the copyright on messages posted to a bulletin board or Internet newsgroup?

A. A copyright exists in any message from the moment it is entered on a keyboard. As **§ 10.3** explains, copyright exists from the moment an expression is fixed into a form from which it can be retrieved or perceived. No copyright notice or registration with the copyright office is necessary for a copyright to exist.

Q. Aren't certain messages and postings in the public domain and free for anyone to exploit?

A. A copyright owner can place her copyright into the public domain. Whether this has occurred depends on the intent of the originator of the expression. In addition, certain information starts out in the public domain and cannot be appropriated through copyright. This is the teaching of the Supreme Court's *Feist* case, analyzed in **§ 10.4.** Thus, purely factual information and procedures and processes are not subject to copyright, although processes may be eligible for patent if they satisfy the requirements explained in **§ 10.17.** Therefore, if the circumstances support an inference that the originator of a

---

[257] See **§ 10.15** (explaining how trade secret law allows reverse engineering in most circumstances).

message or file intended to place it in the public domain by putting it in a particular place on the NII, or if the content of the message or file is purely factual or purely procedural, it is plausible that the material is in the public domain. The problem with placing too much reliance on this assumption is that a deeper inquiry into the intent of the originator may negate the requisite intent for public domain status, although intent has nothing to do with factual or procedural material.

Q. What uses can be made of another's intellectual property?

A. No use may be made of another's patent without permission of the patent holder. Copyrighted material may, however, be used without infringing any of the exclusive rights granted to the copyright holder, (see **§ 10.3**). The most obvious example is that one may read a copyrighted book without infringing any copyright. In the NII, defining the scope of permissible use is tricky because most of the ways in which the technology permits human use of material also involve conduct that constitutes reproduction, distribution to the public, preparation of a derivative work, performance, or display, which are the exclusive prerogatives of the copyright owner.

The legal basis for acceptable uses depends on express or implied license and the copyright fair use doctrine. As an example of an *implied license,* if I send you a message, asking you to forward it to a third person, I have impliedly licensed you to do the copying and distribution necessary to send the message on to the third person. Likewise, it may be reasonable to infer that contributing to a newsgroup that has been established for the purpose of gathering commentary for a collection to be published elsewhere, constitutes an implied license to reuse the posting in the eventual publication. On the other hand, implied license, like public domain status, depends on the intent of the originator, who may defeat the implied license conclusion by explicitly prohibiting uses that might otherwise appear to be within an implied license.

Fair use does not depend on the intent of the originator. Its boundaries, reasonably well understood in the abstract, as explained in **§ 10.7,** are indistinct in the NII. One clear example is in the area of caching (see **§ 10.7**). Although it surely is reasonable to suppose that the copying of a universal resource locator (URL) incident to retrieving material pointed to from a World Wide Web page is fair use (if not within an implied license), it is less clear that caching is fair use when it permits avoidance of further transactions with the originator and reduces revenue to the originator.

Q. What are the respective rights of the originator of content and a repackager or other intermediary?

A. This question arises frequently when governmental information, like judicial opinions and statutes, are published electronically. Then, the public domain character of the underlying content deprives that governmental entity of any copyright, although there is room for argument about the entitlement of state and municipal entities to copyright (see **Chapter 11**). The question under *Feist,* considered in **§ 10.4,** is whether the intermediary has added enough value in the form of original selection and arrangement to be entitled to a copyright on that added value. In no event does the intermediary gain a copyright on the underlying content by packaging or distributing it.

When the underlying content is eligible for copyright, the analysis is somewhat more complicated, likely to result in the conclusion that the originator has a copyright in the content, but not in the value added by the intermediary, and the intermediary has the copyright in its added value, but not in the underlying content. Alternatively, if the two have collaborated, they may be found to be joint authors. Like tenants in common, either has all of the rights with respect to the entire joint work.

The most complicated version of this question arises when the originator of the content did not fix it, as when one makes a speech or plays an athletic event. This presents several possibilities: the speaker or player may own nothing, and the person who records the speech or athletic event may own a copyright in the entire work. The speaker or player may own a copyright in the entire work that springs into being as soon as the fixation occurs through the recording by a second party, and the recorder owns nothing because he added no value and thus failed the originality test of *Feist* (see **§ 10.4**). The two may also be considered as joint owners of the work.

Q. What role do trade secret and trademark play in the NII?

A. Trade secret is an important source of protection for computer programs and other procedures and processes, as well as data (for example, the Internet addresses associated with an anonymous remailer). It operates whenever the information can serve its purpose while remaining secret. See **§ 10.15.**

Trademark and associated unfair competition concepts are growing in importance as creators and entrepreneurs recognize that trademark may protect the goodwill they build up through their creativity and marketing efforts. Copyright protection may not because of the factual character of the content with which they work or because the nature of their distribution channels make copyright enforcement questionable.

Q. What are the respective rights if more than one person is involved in creating the original work?

A. One possibility is that the employer owns the work, under the work-for-hire doctrine, considered in **§ 10.3.** That would be the case if the person actually preparing the work is the common law employee of the other and prepares the work within the scope of employment. If an independent contractor relationship is involved, no work-for-hire treatment exists unless there is an express agreement that the work is a work for hire.

Q. What happens in the case of oral expression?

A. If the person uttering the oral expression (or otherwise performing) may have a federal copyright if someone else, legally an agent, causes fixation to occur as by recording or transcribing the performance or utterance. If the second person is not the agent of the first, a joint work may be involved, as explained in **§ 10.3,** or there might be a state copyright in the oral expression, as explained in **§ 10.21.**

CHAPTER 11

PUBLIC INFORMATION

§ 11.1 Introduction and Description of the Problem

Some of the earliest electronic publishing and information retrieval successes of the NII involved public information, available through commercial services like Westlaw and LEXIS. Public information, especially legal information, is an attractive raw material for exploitation in the NII both because it generally is not encumbered by intellectual property, and because of a high demand. In order for the full potential of the NII as a conduit for public information to be realized, however, private sector electronic publishers and individual citizens must have access to basic governmental data collected by public entities, particularly

469

including primary legal information. This does not mean that public entities must give away their data without any means of recovering the cost of dissemination. It does mean that they must not set up monopolies to enable themselves or favored contractors to finance particular value-added elements at the expense of competitive access to those elements.

Public and private sector publishers long have earned a return by selling public information.[1] Public information policy is tricky, however. On the one hand, government monopolies and restrictions on redissemination restrict access to the raw material of government. On the other hand, if the government gives away public information or sells it below cost, it may undermine market opportunities for private sector vendors of public information. Either approach is undesirable because any conceivable system of dissemination of public information depends to some degree on private sector channels. If the government eliminates competing sources of public information, it not only raises the price; it also creates the possibility of governmental control over what the people are allowed to know about their governmental operations.

The temptations are the same and the legal issues similar at federal, state, and municipal levels of government in the United States and, indeed, in Europe.[2] This chapter synthesizes public information policies showing that equal access must be the centerpiece of an information policy at federal, state, and local levels. It analyzes a variety of legal obligations that force agencies to provide access to electronic formats and explains why agencies are not legally entitled to copyright such information collected at taxpayer expense or to arrange for their contractors to copyright it.[3]

The law reinforces policies encouraging access to electronic information formats through a diversity of channels and sources.[4] The recently enacted federal Paperwork Reduction Act[5] explicitly obligates federal agencies to avoid exclusive arrangements and to encourage diversity of sources.[6] Freedom

---

[1] A number of colonial printers, including Benjamin Franklin, got their starts by contracting to print the laws of provincial assemblies.

[2] *See* Henry H. Perritt, Jr., *Commercialization of Government Information: Comparisons between the European Community and the United States,* 4 Internet Res. 7 (Meckler, Summer 1994).

[3] Parts of the legal analysis initially were developed in Henry H. Perritt, Jr., *Sources of Right to Access Public Information,* 4 Wm. & Mary Bill of Rts. J. 179 (Summer 1995) and Henry H. Perritt, Jr., *Should Local Governments Sell Local Spatial Databases Through State Monopolies?,* 35 Jurimetrics J. 449 (1995).

[4] The strongest statement of the principle of diversity is found in the dissemination provisions of the Paperwork Reduction Act of 1995: "Each agency shall . . . encourag[e] a diversity of public and private sources for information based on government public information." 44 U.S.C. § 3506(d)(1)(A) (Supp. 1995).

[5] 44 U.S.C. § 3506 (d), *amended by* the Paperwork Reduction Act of 1995, Pub. L. No. 104-13, 109 Stat. 163 (May 22, 1995).

[6] See § **11.2.**

of Information Acts[7] entitle everyone to electronic formats when they exist and contravene exclusive arrangements. Intellectual property law does not permit copyrights in basic public information. The First Amendment invalidates most restrictions on competitive publishing. Antitrust law is suspicious of state monopolies. Substantive due process and dormant commerce clause analysis, reviewed more generally in **Chapter 6,** subjects exclusive arrangements to close scrutiny.

When raw governmental information is accessible to all producers of value-added products through the NII, the economics of publishing change dramatically from the traditional print publishing baseline, leading to a more competitive marketplace with lower barriers to entry. With Internet World Wide Web technology, a would-be publisher needs only enough capital to establish a server that adds a particular type of value, without having to have the capacity to own the content and all the other types of value—or to provide a full range of subject matter.[8] The Internet thus provides demand economies of scope.[9] A good example of the attractiveness of Internet technology is the "Thomas" system, established by the Library of Congress to make congressional materials available in full text.[10] Thomas uses World Wide Web technology on the Internet and was established in a matter of weeks. It is free, contrasted with a more limited service established over a period of years by the Government Printing Office using mostly dial-up access.[11]

Government decision makers are, however, subject to temptations that tend to frustrate this technological possibility. Public information in electronic form is valuable. Government agencies charged with creating, collecting, and

---

[7] 5 U.S.C. § 552 (1994). *See* Henry H. Perritt, Jr., *Format & Content Standards for the Electronic Exchange of Legal Information,* 33 Jurimetrics J. 265 (Winter 1993).

[8] **Chapter 1** explains the different types of added value.

[9] *Economies of scope* exist when the per unit cost is lower when a greater variety of unit types are available from the same supplier. *Demand economies of scope* exist when economies of scope exist from the purchaser's perspective. In other words, in traditional publishing, demand economies of scope exist for a bookstore because a user faces lower per unit transaction cost by buying from a bookstore that has a wide variety of materials instead of having to go to one bookstore for the *New York Times,* another for the *Washington Post,* and another for *Newsweek* magazine. *See* F. Scherer & D. Ross, Industrial Market Structure and Economic Performance 100–02 (3d ed. 1990) (explaining economies of scope); *see generally* Teece, *Economies of Scope and the Scope of the Enterprise,* 1 J. Econ. Behav. & Organization 223 (1980) (enterprise scope determined by transaction costs and realization of economies associated with simultaneous supply of inputs common to processes for producting distinct outputs); Teece, *Towards an Economic Theory of the Multiproduct Firm,* 3 J. Econ. Behav. & Organization 39 (1982) (exploring economies of scope for different inputs).

[10] Thomas is reachable through the World Wide Web at http://thomas.loc.gov/, or indirectly through the Villanova Federal Web Locator, http://www.law.vill.edu/fedwebloc.html.

[11] *See generally Gingrich Inaugurates Thomas: Republicans to Rethink Access to Government Info,* 5 Electronic Pub. Info. Newsl., Jan. 13, 1995, at 1–3 (describing Thomas system, running on an RISC-chip Unix platform operating through a T1 connection to the Internet).

maintaining information like statutes, judicial opinions, administrative agency decisions, land records, and survey information face stringent budget constraints. In this economic context, it is natural for public agency decision makers to suppose that they can ease their budget pressures and serve their publics better by appropriating some of the revenue stream potentially available from sale of their information directly to the public or through "partnerships" entered into with private sector entities.

It is but a short step from aspirations to raise revenue through selling public information to imposing restrictions on what other venders and distribution channels can do. Most public agencies charged with responsibility for basic public information have either a natural or de jure monopoly on the information. Monopolists perceive that they can increase their total revenue stream by setting prices higher than they would be in a competitive market.[12] Monopolists also are tempted to extend their monopolies into downstream markets. Thus, public agency decision makers, behaving like rational monopolists in the private sector, implement their partnership aspiration by prohibiting private sector competition with their chosen partners; a state monopoly is formed.[13] The vice of such an arrangement is that it limits economic and technological benefits

---

[12] *See* Edwin Mansfield, Microeconomics: Theory and Application 270 (2d ed. 1975) (monopolist maximizes its profit by setting price above marginal costs, and thus higher than the competitive price).

[13] Strategies for public finance that depend on selling franchises to perform public functions are not new. One of the main ways that King Charles I of Britain financed his government without seeking parliamentary approval of taxes was through franchises. Pauline Gregg, King Charles I, at 215 (1981) (King Charles's granting of monopoly rights of production, sale, or management in return for fee or rent had become a scandal earlier (leading to Monopoly's Act of 1624 in the reign of King James), allowing many exceptions which King Charles exploited in "an amazing series of projects"). Some of the revolutionary fervor both for the English revolution and the American one more than a century later came from reaction to perceived corruption associated with the grant of franchises. *See generally* T.H. Breen, Tobacco Culture: The Mentality of the Great Tide Water Planters on the Eve of Revolution 184–203 (1985) (reviewing calls from Patrick Henry, George Washington, and others for the planter class in the southern colonies to reduce their need for luxuries, coupled in part to a belief that the merchant culture in England was corrupt). The reaction to exclusive franchises in England preceding the execution of King Charles and the establishment of Cromwell's Commonwealth was not so much based on a perception of corruption as it was on the exclusion of the parliament from public finance decisions. Theoretically, franchises fell into disfavor because they deprive the public of the benefits of competition. *See* Richard W. Painter, *The Moral Interdependence of Corporate Lawyers and Their Clients,* 67 S. Cal. L. Rev. 507, 521 n.48 (1994) (citing Adam Smith, The Wealth of Nations, 703, 712–16 (Edwin Cannan ed., The Modern Library, 5th ed. 1937) (1789) (south sea company is example of type of parliamentary-sponsored monopoly that should be replaced from independent free enterprise)); Neil Netanel, *Alienability Restrictions and the Enhancement of Author Autonomy in United States and Continental Copyright Law,* 12 Cardozo Arts & Ent. L.J. 1 & n.40 (1992) (characterizing Adam Smith as being critical of monopoly privileges but approving temporary monopolies granted to authors and their assigns under the Statute of Anne as an efficient means of stimulating book production); Mark F. Grady & Jay I. Alexander, *Patent Law and Rent Dissipation,* 78 Va. L. Rev. 305, 310–11 (1992) (same).

otherwise available to a broad range of potential distributors of the public information, and as the monopolies are extended downstream by exclusive "partnerships," they block participation in a variety of rapidly changing and diverse markets for value-added information products.

While some monopolies may be efficient in the microeconomic sense,[14] the incidence of such situations is low.[15] The pace of technological change and the fragmentation of the market[16] make it far more likely that the best market structure is one with many vendors specializing in products for particular market segments. There is no reason to suppose that public decision makers are better than consumers and entrepreneurs in picking technologies and product design; yet that is exactly what they must do when they set up exclusive arrangements. The best market structure is one in which everyone is allowed to follow his or her instincts in commercializing new technologies and developing markets. The best information policy is one with a diversity of channels and sources for geographic information. Fortunately, that information policy is one that coincides with legal entitlements to access.

The analytical framework for access to public information is more coherent if one begins with two policy propositions. First, federal, state, and local governments must make electronic formats available when they exist. Second, they must allow and promote a diversity of channels and sources of public information.[17]

The first principle, that electronic formats should be made available, is consistent with a policy statement adopted by the American Bar Association in 1990,[18] recommendations adopted by the Administrative Conference of the

---

[14] Alaska Airlines, Inc. v. United Airlines, Inc., 948 F.2d 536, 548 (9th Cir. 1991) (antitrust law tolerates efficient monopolies and natural monopolies; rejecting monopoly leveraging attack on computerized airlines reservation); Rudolph J. Peritz, *A Counter-History of Antitrust Law,* 1990 Duke L.J. 263, 304 (allowing efficient monopoly as a policy choice); Todd Marcus Young, Comment, *Unestablished Businesses and Treble Damage Recovery under Section Four of the Clayton Act,* 49 U. Chi. L. Rev. 1076, 1087 n.55 (1982) (explaining that efficient monopolies are those that can set prices lower than they would be set in competitive markets).

[15] *See* Thomas W. Hazlett, *Duopolistic Competition in Cable Television: Implications for Public Policy,* 7 Yale J. on Reg. 65, 117 (1990) (transaction costs of identifying efficient monopoly are high, especially because of the "moral hazard" of franchising agents eager to justify exclusive arrangements).

[16] The fragmentation of the market is a natural result of the possibility of unbundling in new technological environments.

[17] *See generally* Henry H. Perritt, Jr., Public Information in the National Information Infrastructure, Report to the Regulatory Information Service Center, General Services Administration, and to the Administrator of the Office of Information and Regulatory Affairs, Office of Management and Budget (May 20, 1994) (commissioned, but not necessarily endorsed, by the recipients).

[18] ABA Recommendation No. 102, adopted by A.B.A. House of Delegates, Aug. 1990 (guidelines for applying Freedom of Information Act to electronic formats); ABA Recommendation No. 109C, adopted by A.B.A. House of Delegates, Aug. 1991 (guidelines for federal and state agency dissemination of public information in electronic form). Both ABA recommendations are available in full text for viewing or downloading from the World Wide Web at http://www.law.vill.edu/Aba/adminlaw.html.

United States,[19] policies adopted by the President's Office of Management and Budget (OMB),[20] and legislation passed by the Senate in 1994[21] and reintroduced in the 104th Congress in 1995. To deny public access to electronic formats denies the public the benefits of public record formats paid for with public funds, and also significantly impairs public accessibility to public information by increasing the cost of search and retrieval. Indeed, the impairment is so great that denial of access makes some records practically unavailable.

The need for a diversity of sources and channels of information, endorsed by the ABA,[22] the Administrative Conference, OMB, and now by the Congress,[23] is based on the reality that no one supplier can design modern information products to suit the needs of all users. The diversity principle is inimical to any state-maintained or state-granted monopoly over public information.[24]

Sometimes, public sector decision makers are concerned about an information policy that seems to subsidize private sector activities. In evaluating this concern, it is important to distinguish between making information and value-added features already developed with taxpayer money for pursuit of agency missions available, and using new money to finance things of use only to particular private sector vendors. The first is not subsidization; it is allowing the public access to something they already have paid for. The second is subsidization and is reasonable to avoid.

---

[19] *Federal Agency Use of Computers in Acquiring and Releasing Information,* 1 C.F.R. § 305.88-10 (1993) (recommendations by Administrative Conference of the United States); *see also* Henry H. Perritt, Jr., *Electronic Acquisition and Release of Federal Agency Information: An Analysis of ACUS Recommendations,* 41 Admin. L. Rev. 253 (1989) (explanation of Recommendation 88-10 by its principal author); Henry H. Perritt, Jr., *Federal Electronic Information Policy,* 63 Temp. L. Rev. 201 (1990) (elaboration of Freedom of Information Act concepts developed in Recommendation 88-10).

[20] 58 Fed. Reg. 36,068 (July 2, 1993). In late 1994 OMB released draft guidelines for applying FOIA to electronic formats.

[21] S. 1782, 103d Cong., 2d Sess. (1994) to amend title 5, U.S.C., to provide for public access to information in an electronic format, passed the Senate, Aug. 25, 1994. 140 Cong. Rec. D1046-02 (daily ed. Aug. 25, 1994).

[22] ABA Recommendation No. 109C, adopted by A.B.A. House of Delegates, Aug. 1991 (guidelines for federal and state agency dissemination of public information in electronic form), available through the World Wide Web on the Internet at http://www.law.vill.edu/Aba/adminlaw.html.

[23] 44 U.S.C. § 3506 (d), *amended by* the Paperwork Reduction Act of 1995, Pub. L. No. 104-13, 109 Stat. 163 (May 22, 1995), requires that agencies act so as to encourage a diversity of sources and channels, as explained in § **11.1.**

[24] *See* House Comm. on Government Operations, Electronic Collection and Dissemination of Information by Federal Agencies: A Policy Overview, H.R. Rep. No. 560, 99th Cong., 2d Sess. 2 (1986) (criticizing exclusive arrangements preventing access to government information in electronic form; the report's principal author was Robert M. Gellman, Counsel to the Subcommittee on Information); Robert M. Gellman, *Twin Evils: Government Copyright and Copyright-Like Controls over Government Information,* 45 Syracuse L. Rev. 999 (1995).

The Government Information Locator System (GILS), adopted by the executive branch of the federal government in December 1994, is a good model for how public agencies should participate in the National Information Infrastructure. GILS is built on top of an international standard known as Z39.50 and colloquially referred to as Wide Area Information Service (WAIS).[25] This standard makes it possible for a supplier of information to describe it in a kind of standard header. The information content and its header are made available on servers connected to the Internet. Then, any potential user of the information can search all Z39.50 compliant information servers throughout the Internet, selecting only those items of interest. The Z39.50 standard by itself does not represent a database schema, but it comfortably accommodates database schemas as a part of the associated information product.[26]

§ 11.2 Dissemination Duties

Few jurisdictions had explicit statutory statements of electronic dissemination policy until 1995, when the Congress enacted dissemination policy into the Paperwork Reduction Act. The language reflects a consensus that had been developing over a number of years, reflected in ABA policy statements, and in OMB circulars summarized in § 11.1:

With respect to information dissemination, each agency shall—

(1) ensure that the public has timely and equitable access to the agency's public information, including ensuring such access through—

(A) encouraging a diversity of public and private sources for information based on government public information;

(B) in cases in which the agency provides public information maintained in electronic format, providing timely and equitable access to the underlying data (in whole or in part); and

(C) agency dissemination of public information in an efficient, effective, and economical manner;

(2) regularly solicit and consider public input on the agency's information dissemination activities;

(3) provide adequate notice when initiating, substantially modifying, or terminating significant information dissemination products; and

(4) not, except where specifically authorized by statute—

---

[25] Actually WAIS is a proprietary name claimed by certain entrepreneurs originally associated with Thinking Machines Corporation, most prominently including Brewster Kahle.

[26] Elliot Christian of USGS was the principal architect and component of the GILS approach finally adopted. USGS has made available for free or at very low prices a variety of videotapes and other training materials on the Internet and on GILS.

(A) establish an exclusive, restricted, or other distribution arrangement that interferes with timely and equitable availability of public information to the public;

(B) restrict or regulate the use, resale, or redissemination of public information by the public;

(C) charge fees or royalties for resale or redissemination of public information; or

(D) establish user fees for public information that exceed the cost of dissemination.[27]

Figure 11–1 shows how these principles operate when an agency decides to offer its own complete bundle of value-added information. Rather than cutting off access to discrete elements of its content, at point 1, or to its added value, at points 2, 3, and 4, the diversity principle requires the agency to make access available so that competing sources and channels, shown as A, B, C, and D, can get preexisting taxpayer-funded information in a form that meets their product concepts and production needs.

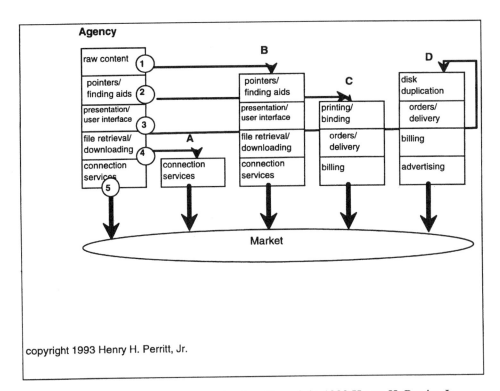

Figure 11–1. Access to agency-owned value. Copyright 1993 Henry H. Perritt, Jr.

---

[27] 44 U.S.C. § 3506 (d), *amended by* the Paperwork Reduction Act of 1995, Pub. L. No. 104-13, 109 Stat. 163 (May 22, 1995).

§ 11.3   Access Rights: Freedom of Information Acts

Freedom of Information Acts[28] grant a right to obtain and copy records held by governmental entities. Properly interpreted, they are the most important protection against state-established monopolies over public information and are the central source of right for electronic publishers to gain access to public information.

§ 11.4   —Federal FOIA

At the federal level, the Freedom of Information Act extends to virtually all records held by federal agencies outside the judicial and legislative branches of government, including electronic formats. FOIA is interpreted broadly, and its exemptions narrowly.[29] The purpose for which one requests an agency record under FOIA is irrelevant.[30] Thus, FOIA is an instrument of the diversity principle. It undercuts efforts to establish information monopolies because it grants private sector redisseminators an entitlement to public information notwithstanding agency efforts to block access in order to support exclusive distribution arrangements.

Application of federal FOIA to ensure access to federal information in electronic form is not free from controversy, however. For example, contracts can be structured so that an agency lacks control over some or all of the electronic information. When that occurs, is an "agency record" involved within the meaning of FOIA? Suppose a federal contractor adds proprietary features to the basic federal information, making it difficult to access the raw content without also accessing the proprietary features. Which prevails, copyright protection for the proprietary features or FOIA access rights? Both of these issues are presented in the *Tax Analysts v. United States Department of Justice* case presently pending in the United States District Court for the District of Columbia. In this case, Tax Analysts, a nonprofit publisher of public information, seeks access to JURIS, a comprehensive database of federal judicial

---

[28] Terminology differs from state to state. For convenience, this article refers to *federal FOIA* and similar state statutes as *FOI statutes.*

[29] *See* John Doe Agency v. John Doe Corp., 493 U.S. 146, 151–52 (1989) (reiterating basic principle but finding that records requested by defense contractor were properly withheld because within law enforcement exemption even though not originally created for law enforcement purposes); United States Dep't of Justice v. Tax Analysts, 492 U.S. 136, 142 n.3 (1989) (burden on agency to show that requested records not within FOIA); Assembly v. United States Dep't of Commerce, 968 F.2d 916, 920 (9th Cir. 1992) (reiterating prodisclosure policy of FOIA and affirming order that Commerce Department disclose computer tapes with census figures).

[30] 5 U.S.C. § 552(a)(4)(a)(ii) (Supp. 1994) (providing that agency regulations must develop fees schedules for both commercial and private use).

opinions, statutes, and agency materials compiled partially by public agencies and partially by West Publishing Company. The Justice Department took the position that those aspects of the JURIS database that are subject to claims of intellectual property by West Publishing Company do not constitute agency records[31] or, alternatively, are privileged from disclosure by § 552(b)(4) of FOIA.

Another problem when FOIA is used to compel publisher access to basic legal information is whether the availability of the information from other sources makes a difference. The Supreme Court said the answer to this question is no. In *United States Department of Justice v. Tax Analysts,*[32] the Supreme Court forced the Justice Department to make available district court tax opinions and final orders, even though those materials were available from the courts that wrote them. Tax Analysts wanted those materials to facilitate its publication of paper and electronic databases containing judicial opinions.

The Supreme Court *Tax Analysts* case undercuts any argument that an agency can avoid a duty to disclose electronic formats merely because the same content is available in paper formats. That case also suggests that the existence of commercial motivation does not make electronic formats any less available under FOIA. Justice Blackmun, the lone dissenter, thought that FOIA was not the appropriate vehicle for a commercial enterprise to obtain access to its raw material.[33] The rejection of Justice Blackmun's views strengthens the inference that FOIA is an appropriate vehicle for private publishers to obtain access to basic content for their publications.

Obviously, access to an electronic database of public information greatly reduces the cost to the requester of meaningful access to the information, compared with having to contact a multiplicity of sources and then to convert paper information. The Ohio Supreme Court made this point especially clearly in the *Margolius* case, discussed in § **11.5**. In *Petroleum Information Corp. v. United States Department of the Interior,*[34] the D.C. Circuit rejected an argument by the Department of the Interior that it need not provide a magnetic tape containing a preliminary version of a comprehensive database of land records for certain states on the grounds that the material was available in paper form from other sources and from the agency itself.[35] In litigation involving records preservation statutes other than FOIA,[36] the United States Court of Appeals for

---

[31] 5 U.S.C. § 552(b)(3) (1988).

[32] 492 U.S. 136 (1989) (requiring Department of Justice to make available under FOIA copies of district court decisions in its possession).

[33] *Id.* at 156, 157 (Blackmun, J., dissenting).

[34] 976 F.2d 1429 (D.C. Cir. 1992) (affirming order that agency disclose legal land description computer database file).

[35] *Id.* at 1437.

[36] The Supreme Court in *Tax Analysts* recognized the appropriateness of borrowing definitional language from records preservation statutes for interpreting the FOIA. United States Dep't of Justice v. Tax Analysts, 492 U.S. 136, 145 (1989) (quoting 44 U.S.C. § 3301).

the D.C. Circuit rejected the argument that paper printouts of electronic communication systems are acceptable legal substitutes for the electronic records themselves.[37] It is but a small step from this conclusion to a conclusion that the greater utility of electronic formats and the greater accessibility justifies obligating agencies under FOIA to disclose them when requesters prefer them to paper versions,[38] a derivative conclusion developed further by many state courts.

§ 11.5   —State Freedom of Information Law

State public records laws are not identical to FOIA; nor is state court interpretation of similar language in such state statutes necessarily the same as federal court interpretation of FOIA. Nevertheless, there is broad agreement on the basic propositions. There is virtually unanimous agreement among state courts that electronic formats are covered by state FOIA acts.[39] There also is strong authority for the proposition that requestors can specify computer-readable formats when an agency has both paper and computer-readable formats available.

---

[37] Armstrong v. Executive Office of the President, 1 F.3d 1274, 1282–84 (D.C. Cir. 1993) (electronic versions were not merely extra copies of paper versions because electronic records contained certain additional data); *id.* at 1286–87 (same).

[38] *Cf.* Armstrong v. Executive Office of the President, 810 F. Supp. 335, 341 (D.D.C.) (enumerating features of electronic records not present in paper printouts of same records), *aff'd,* 1 F.3d 1274 (D.C. Cir. 1993).

[39] *See, e.g.,* Jersawitz v. Hicks, 448 S.E.2d 352, 353 (Ga. 1994) (real estate deed records on computer tape were public record under Open Records Act, Ga. Code Ann. § 50-18-70(a)); Maher v. Freedom of Info. Comm'n, 472 A.2d 321, 325 (Conn. 1984) (state Freedom of Information Commission had power to compel agency to disclose computer tapes when requester paid the cost of production, notwithstanding statutory language that referred to disclosure of "printouts"); State *ex rel.* Stephan v. Harder, 641 P.2d 366, 374 (Kan. 1982) (magnetic tapes were public records and requester was entitled to disclosure of computer file listing names of physicians and amount of public funds paid for abortions); Szikzay v. Buelow, 436 N.Y.S.2d 558, 563 (Sup. Ct. 1981) (county assessment rolls in computer tape format must be disclosed under Freedom of Information law); Minnesota Medical Ass'n v. State, 274 N.W.2d 84, 88 (Minn. 1978) (rejecting argument that computer tapes containing abortion data were not public records). *See also* Brownstone Publishers, Inc. v. New York City Dep't of Bldgs., 560 N.Y.S.2d 642, 643 (App. Div. 1990) (publisher intending to sell computer database on subscription basis entitled to computer formats with statistical information on every parcel of real property in New York City; noting undesirability of agency's proposed printing of a million sheets of paper at a cost of $10,000 for the paper, taking five or six weeks, and necessitating reconversion of data into computer-usable form at a cost of hundreds of thousands of dollars). The trial court opinion, 550 N.Y.S.2d 564, 565 (Sup. Ct. 1990), noted that the record supported the requester's position that a hard copy would not provide reasonable access to the information, and declined to follow Dismukes v. Department of Interior, 603 F. Supp. 760 (D.C. 1984) (holding that, under FOIA, agency had no obligation to accommodate requester's preference of format).

In *State ex rel. Margolius v. City of Cleveland,* the Ohio Supreme Court emphasized that "a set of public records stored in an organized fashion on a magnetic medium also contains an added value that inherently is a part of the public record. . . . [T]he added value is not only the organization of the data, but also the compression of the data into a form that allows greater ease of public access."[40] The court reached its conclusion that computer-readable versions of public data must be disclosed by analogy:

> Consider two sets of identical public records kept on paper—one set organized in a file cabinet, and another kept as a random set of papers stacked on the floor. Certainly we would not permit an agency to discharge its responsibility by providing access to the random set while precluding the disclosure of the organized set, even though both sets are "readable" as required by the statute.[41]

Later, the Ohio Court of Appeals, relying on *Margolius,* aptly put it this way in *Athens County Property Owners Ass'n:*

> The basic tenet . . . is that a person does not come—like a serf—hat in hand, seeking permission of the lord to have access to public records. Access to public records is a matter of right. The question in this case is not so much whether the medium should be hard copy of [sic] diskette. Rather, the question is: Can a government agency, which is obligated to supply public records, impede those who oppose its policies by denying the value-added benefit of computerization?[42]

Most of the state statutes, like the federal FOIA, do not allow for balancing or assessing the reason for which a requester wants access. Under such statutes, the only occasion for considering the commercial nature of a requester's motivation is when access rights must be balanced against privacy rights under a privacy exemption to access duties, considered in § **11.6.**

Nevertheless, a few courts persist in downgrading the legitimacy of FOI requests by electronic publishers. For example, in *Kestenbaum v. Michigan State University,*[43] the court held that the legislature's purpose in enacting FOI statutes was not to provide a channel between the government and commercial publishers.[44] That proposition overlaps to a considerable extent the proposition that mandating disclosure of public information to private publishers would

---

[40] 584 N.E.2d 665, 669 (Ohio 1992).

[41] *Id.*

[42] State ex rel. Athens County Property Owners Ass'n, Inc. v. City of Athens, 619 N.E.2d 437, 439 (Ohio Ct. App. 1992).

[43] 294 N.W.2d 228, 235–36 (Mich. Ct. App. 1980) (existence of commercial purpose negates entitlement to computer tape containing student records both because commercial purpose must be weighed against privacy invasion in order to apply "clearly unwarranted" test, and also because public funds may not be used to support a private purpose; mandating access to commercially valuable private information would violate that principle).

[44] *Id.* at 236.

constitute the use of public funds for private purposes, also a concern of the *Kestenbaum* court. Both propositions are flawed. The mere fact that an individual or entity may obtain income from an activity that serves a public purpose does not negate the public nature of the activity. When a commercial publisher disseminates public information, it is serving a public purpose, the same purpose that is the central justification for enactment of Freedom of Information statutes: increasing access to government information.

This illusory conflict between public and private purposes is implicated in a 1994 amendment to the New Jersey public records law that could be interpreted to eliminate any statutory right to obtain public information in electronic formats. The New Jersey attorney general took the position in litigation before the New Jersey Supreme Court[45] that this amendment does deny access to electronic formats and that such denial is good public policy in order to prevent private exploitation of materials developed at public expense. The author of this book participated as an *amicus curiae* in the presentation of an opposing position to the New Jersey Supreme Court, which allowed access to the electronic format.[46]

In addition to statutory entitlements to public information, many states recognize a common-law entitlement. Such a common-law entitlement was used by the Supreme Court of New Jersey to reverse a trial court and grant access to electronic versions of tax assessment records.[47] Such common-law doctrines usually are uncertain in their scope both with respect to the kinds of information to which they give an access right, and the kinds of request or interests that justify access. Unlike FOIA, these common-law doctrines balance the interest of the requester in obtaining access against the interest of the public entity in denying access.[48]

The policy principles identified in § **11.1** support enactment and interpretation of state records access laws broadly so that they, like the federal FOIA, extend to all electronic formats and also present a counterpoise to public agency efforts to set up information monopolies. In other words, state records access statutes should be written and applied consistently with the 1990 ABA policy statement, cited in § **11.1,** a consistency expressed by most of the recent state FOI judicial decisions.

---

[45] *See* Petition for Certification on Behalf of Defendant-Respondent Essex County Board of Taxation, Supreme Court of New Jersey, No. 39,333 (Nov. 23, 1994) (seeking review of Higg-a-Rella, Inc. v. County of Essex, 647 A.2d 862 (N.J. Super. App. Div. 1994)).

[46] Higg-a-Rella, Inc., t/a State Info. Serv. v. County of Essex, No. 39,333, Motion and Application for Leave to Appear and Brief of Amicus Curiae Henry H. Perritt, Jr. (N.J. filed Apr. 28, 1995), *decided in* 660 A.2d 1163 (N.J. 1995).

[47] Higg-a-Rella, Inc. v. County of Essex, 660 A.2d 1163 (N.J. 1995).

[48] *See* Henry H. Perritt, Jr. & James A. Wilkinson, *The Federal Advisory Committee Act After Five Years,* 63 Geo. L.J. 725 (1975) (explaining decline in role of assessing requestor interest in public access law), *cited in* Public Citizen v. United States Dep't of Justice, 491 U.S. 440, 456 (1989).

§ 11.6 —FOI Privacy Considerations

The scope of the privacy exemptions to FOI statutes usually depends on whether the invasion of privacy is "unreasonable" or "unwarranted." To apply this standard, decision makers must consider the interests of the requester to determine whether they should override the interests of the subject.[49]

Some cases like *Kestenbaum,*[50] purportedly limiting FOIA rights on other grounds, actually involved privacy concerns.[51] In other, more recent cases, however, state courts have recognized that technology can help strike a balance between personal privacy and public access.[52] In many instances, agencies use privacy concerns as a subterfuge for denying general access to computer format when the real motive is to protect monopoly electronic publishing arrangements. Therefore, privacy claims as justifications for declining access to electronic information should be scrutinized closely. When the information already is accessible in paper formats, the agencies should have a heavy burden to demonstrate how electronic access raises privacy concerns that nonelectronic access does not.

§ 11.7. Intellectual Property and Exclusivity

Unlike British Commonwealth countries, and like most other developed nations, the United States does not recognize Crown Copyright.[53] The United States

---

[49] *See* United States Dep't of Defense v. Federal Labor Relations Auth., 114 S. Ct. 1006, 1012 (1994) (to decide whether a record is exempt from FOIA disclosure under Exemption 6, court must "balance the public interest in disclosure against the interest Congress intended the exemption to protect" in order to decide whether the invasion of privacy would be "unwarranted") (quoting United States Dep't of Justice v. Reporters Comm. for Freedom of Press, 489 U.S. 749, 773 (1989)); United States Dep't of State v. Ray, 502 U.S. 164, 178, 112 S. Ct. 541, 549 (1991) (balancing privacy against basic policy of FOIA; official information that sheds light on an agency's performance of its statutory duties falls squarely within FOIA's purpose); United States Dep't of Justice v. Reporters Comm. for Freedom of Press, 489 U.S. 749, 771–72 (1989) (whether invasion of privacy is warranted cannot turn on purposes for which the request for information is made, but whether disclosure of private document under Exemption 7(C) is warranted must turn on nature of requested document and its relationship to "basic purpose of FOIA; basic purpose not served by disclosure of information about private citizens accumulated in various government files that reveals little or nothing about agency's own conduct); Minnesota Medical Ass'n v. State, 274 N.W.2d 84 (Minn. 1978) (data requested by publishing company regarding abortions performed for medical assistance recipients not exempt for privacy reasons); State *ex rel.* Stephan v. Harder, 641 P.2d 366 (Kan. 1982) (disclosure of information on abortions performed by physicians receiving public funds did not threaten physician privacy rights).

[50] Kestenbaum v. Michigan State Univ., 294 N.W.2d 228 (Mich. Ct. App. 1980).

[51] *Id.* at 236 (purpose of FOIA could be achieved "without invading the privacy of the individual students").

[52] *See* Hamer v. Lentz, 547 N.E.2d 191, 195 (Ill. 1989) (state agency could be compelled to write computer program to separate exempt information from nonexempt information).

[53] Crown Copyright is the claim of the government to a copyright in all public information. Copyright, Designs and Patents Act, 1988, ch. 48 § 163 (Eng.).

Copyright Act disables federal agencies from obtaining a copyright in public information.[54] This express disability does not extend, however, to state or local agencies. Thus, from the literal text of the Copyright Act, state and municipal governments can copyright their public information resources if such resources otherwise qualify as copyrightable works. There are arguments based on the Copyright Act itself and on the copyright and patents clause of the United States Constitution, however, that limit state or local copyrights in public information.[55]

Under the Copyright Act,[56] copyright does not extend to factual information. Moreover, Congress lacks the power under the patents and copyrights clause of the United States Constitution to extend copyright protection beyond that necessary to provide incentives for creative efforts. In *Feist Publications v. Rural Telephone Co.,*[57] the Supreme Court of the United States eliminated the possibility of copyright protection for "sweat of the brow"— the effort in assembling factual information—except when the selection and arrangement of such information involves nontrivial creative contributions. In no event can copyright extend to the underlying factual information. The logic of *Feist* excludes state or local copyright in the memorialization of physical realities and verbal conduct constituting lawmaking. For example, *Feist* does not permit a copyright in survey information or basic records of land ownership,[58] or in the text of statutes, judicial opinions, or agency rules or orders.

---

[54] 17 U.S.C. § 105 (1988).

[55] L. Ray Patterson & Craig Joyce, *Monopolizing the Law: The Scope of Copyright Protection for Law Reports and Statutory Compilations,* 36 UCLA L. Rev. 719 (1989).

[56] *Id.* § 102. Section 102(a) allows copyright in "original works of authorship." Facts are outside the scope of this phrase because no original effort is involved with respect to preexisting facts. To remove any doubt, § 102(b) says that copyright protection does not extend to "any idea, procedure, process, system, method of operation, concept, principle, or discovery."

[57] 499 U.S. 340 (1991).

[58] *See* Mason v. Montgomery Data, Inc., 765 F. Supp. 353, 355 (S.D. Tex. 1991) (factual matters such as the abstract, tract boundaries and ownership name and tract size are not copyrightable). The court of appeals reversed, 967 F.2d 135 (5th Cir. 1992), holding that the district court had erroneously found that the merger doctrine barred copyright of the plaintiff's maps. The district court found that the maps were the only pictorial presentation that could result from a correct interpretation of the legal description and other uncopyrightable facts. 967 F.2d at 138 (characterizing district court conclusion). The court of appeals disagreed, finding that the underlying data could be portrayed in a variety of ways. 967 F.2d at 139. Thus, under the merger doctrine, the plaintiff's portrayal in its maps could be protected without preempting free use of the underlying facts. 967 F.2d at 139 (explaining motivation for merger doctrine and noting how competing maps differ in selection of sources, interpretation of sources, discretion in reconciling inconsistencies and skill and judgment in depicting information). The court, disagreeing with the defendants, found that *Feist's* standards for selection, coordination and arrangement pertain to application of the merger doctrine, as well as to the threshold question of originality. 967 F.2d at 140 n.7. The court went on also to find that the plaintiff's added value satisfied the requirements for originality. 967 F.2d at 141.

The *Feist* analysis[59] proceeds from the proposition that facts may not be copyrighted because they lack the originality component that is constitutionally mandated as a prerequisite for copyright.[60] The patents and copyright clause gives power to the Congress to grant limited monopolies only to create incentives for original expression by authors, and more generally to provide incentives for discovery and other creative effort. Such incentives are entirely unnecessary for public entities who have a statutorily mandated duty to collect, organize, and disseminate information, such as that represented in spatial databases. Absent the incentive justification, Congress lacks the power to extend copyright protection to these expressions. The courts of appeals routinely have recognized this centrality of economic incentive as the justification for copyright.[61] When the incentive is not needed, as when the authors in question are legally obligated to perform their creative effort, the patents and copyright clause does not authorize a copyright.

Of course, this statutory and constitutional copyright argument does not eliminate the possibility of extending copyright protection to value-added enhancements to public information as long as they are not supplied in the performance of a public duty. But even when incentive may seem an appropriate justification for copyright protection, the *Feist* Court specifically rejected the idea that originality can result simply from gathering facts. It rejected "sweat of the brow" justification for copyright. Moreover, even copyrighted compilations are copyrightable only to the extent of their original selection or arrangement: "[A] subsequent compiler remains free to use the facts contained in another's publication to aid in preparing a competing work, so long as the competing work does not feature the same selection and arrangement."[62]

Several cases support the proposition that states may not assert a copyright in some public materials even though copyright statutes seem to permit it.[63] The newer cases build on a cluster of cases decided in the nineteenth century.[64]

---

[59] The *Feist court* did not elaborate on the logic of limiting copyrightability of factual information except to point out that the facts must be available for exploitation by others. There is, however, another component to the *Feist* logic, developed in the text.

[60] 499 U.S. 340, 347–48 (1991).

[61] *See* National Rifle Ass'n v. Hand Gun Control Fed'n, 15 F.3d 559, 561 (6th Cir. 1994) (use of mailing list was fair use; noting that scope of prima facie copyright protection is limited to uses of a work that would undermine the incentive for creation). *See also* Sony Corp. of Am. v. Universal City Studios, Inc., 464 U.S. 417, 429 (1984) (discussing goals and incentives of copyright protection); Twentieth Century Music Corp. v. Aiken, 422 U.S. 151, 156 (1975) ("ultimate aim is, by this incentive [securing a fair return for author's creative labor], to stimulate artistic creativity for the general public good").

[62] 499 U.S. 340, 349 (1991).

[63] The author appreciates research assistance on this section from his law clerk, Thomas Thistle, Villanova University School of Law, Class of 1996.

[64] Rand McNally & Co. v. Fleet Management Sys., Inc., 591 F. Supp. 726, 735–36 (N.D. Ill. 1983) (citing nineteenth century cases).

In *Building Officials & Code Administration v. Code Technology, Inc.*[65] the court of appeals doubted whether a model code, developed by a private entity but subsequently adopted by the Commonwealth of Massachusetts, could qualify for copyright. Synthesizing from the early case law, the First Circuit reasoned that the public "owns the law" not just because it pays the salaries of those who write the statutes and judicial opinions, but because "each citizen is a ruler, a law-maker," and therefore "the citizens are the authors of the law."[66] Beyond that, the court found, due process guarantees access because it requires notice of legal obligations.[67] It found these principles irreconcilable with limiting access under the copyright law, and with a situation in which a copyright holder would decide for itself when, where, and how the code was to be reproduced and made publicly available.[68]

Not all governmental adoptions of privately copyrighted material vitiate continued copyright protection, however. In *Practice Management Information Corp. v. American Medical Ass'n,*[69] the district court rejected the argument that a system of codes for medical procedures lost its copyright protection when it was adopted by the federal Health Care Financing Administration and made mandatory.[70]

Georgia v. Harrison Co.[71] directly brought into play the possibility of a copyright by the state; the early cases involved assertion of copyright by state contractors. *Harrison Co.* cited 17 U.S.C. § 105, which specifically provides that copyright protection is not available for any work of the U.S. government, and argued that if Congress had wanted to preclude states from having copyright protection it should have so provided in the Copyright Act. The court concluded that § 105 leaves states free to copyright some information, but not what is in the public domain.[72] The court denied a preliminary injunction against a competing publisher: "The courts of this country have long held that neither judicial opinions or statutes can be copyrighted."[73] "A state's 'ownership' of its statutes does not preclude anyone from publishing those statutes."[74] The rationale for prohibiting copyright in such materials applied, the court found, regardless of whether the state itself or a private citizen asserts copyright.[75] "The public must

---

[65] 628 F.2d 730 (1st Cir. 1980).

[66] *Id.* at 734 (quoting Banks v. West, 27 F. 50, 57 (C.C.D. Minn. 1886)).

[67] *Id.*

[68] *Id.*

[69] 877 F. Supp. 1386 (C.D. Cal. 1994).

[70] *Id.* at 1391–92 (citing cases).

[71] 548 F. Supp. 110 (1982), *vacated,* 559 F. Supp. 37 (N.D. Ga. 1983) (on unanimous request of parties after settlement).

[72] *Id.* at 114.

[73] *Id.* at 113 (citing early cases).

[74] *Id.* at 114.

[75] *Id.*

have free access to the state laws, unhampered by any claim of copyright, whether that claim be made by an individual or the state itself."[76]

The recent decisions build on basic principles established in the 1800s.[77] In *Wheaton v. Peters,*[78] the Supreme Court stated (without offering much analytical support), "no reporter has or can have any copyright in the written opinions delivered by this court, and ... these judges thereof cannot confer on any reporter any such right."[79]

Later, *Banks v. Manchester*[80] invalidated a state law that purported to allow an official reporter to obtain a copyright on the opinions of the Ohio Supreme Court. The reporter could not claim authorship of the opinions, and the state was not a "citizen or resident" under copyright law[81] and could not obtain a copyright for itself. The court stated that "the whole work done by judges constitutes the authentic exposition and interpretation of the law ... [and] is free for publication to all."[82]

In *Nash v. Lathrop,*[83] the Massachusetts Supreme Judicial Court ordered the reporter of decisions to permit a competing publisher to examine and copy opinions in the reporter's custody. The court stated:

> Every citizen is presumed to know the law thus declared, and it needs no argument to show that justice requires that all should have free access to the opinions, and that it is against sound public policy to prevent this, or to suppress and keep from the earliest knowledge of the public the statutes or the decisions and opinions of the justices.[84]

It avoided deciding whether the state itself could hold a copyright in the opinions, deciding only that the state had not granted an exclusive right to Little, Brown & Co., the reporter.[85] The court also stated that the publisher had the right to make reasonable regulations to prevent damage or disruption to the orderly management of his official papers.[86]

---

[76] *Id.*

[77] Building Officials & Code Admin. v. Code Technology, Inc., 628 F.2d 730, 733–34 (1st Cir. 1980).

[78] 33 U.S. (8 Pet.) 591 (1834).

[79] *Id.* at 668.

[80] 128 U.S. 244 (1888).

[81] There is room for a similar argument under present 17 U.S.C. § 104(b)(1), which allows copyright only to a "national or domiciliary of the United States, or ... a national, domiciliary, or sovereign authority of a foreign nation." The language pertaining to U.S. authors excludes institutional authors, while the language pertaining to foreign authors appears to allow governments to be statutory authors.

[82] 128 U.S. 244, 253 (1888).

[83] 6 N.E. 559 (1886).

[84] *Id.* at 560.

[85] *Id.* at 563. Most of the court's analysis focused on the state statute authorizing the contract with Little, Brown & Co.

[86] *Id.*

Two other early cases, *Davidson v. Wheelock*[87] and *Howell v. Miller*,[88] held that although the reporter could obtain a valid copyright on his compilation and analysis, anyone could freely copy the laws themselves.[89] "[N]o one can obtain the exclusive right to publish the laws of a state in a book prepared by him."[90] If one cuts from another's book the general laws of a state and uses the pages thus cut and nothing more from the first work to prepare a competing compilation, there would be no copyright infringement.[91]

In *In re Gould & Co.*[92] the Connecticut Supreme Court held that the reporter of opinions was not entitled by its copyright or by the exclusive franchise granted it by the secretary of state to withhold slip opinions from competing publishers. Among other things, the court noted that the reporter's duty is to allow the public to make copies without inquiry as to the requester's purpose.[93] It suggested however, in dictum, that the state could copyright the text of judicial opinions through legislation.

It may be that, while some public information is uncopyrightable under the rationale of the cases reviewed in this chapter, other public information does not involve the same core values. In other words, perhaps only basic legal information should be excluded from copyright. The problem with this argument is that it may inappropriately define basic legal information. For example, databases of land records are the same as statutes and judicial opinions in all legally relevant respects. One limitation on copyright in public materials is based on a concern that the basic data for the legal system must be freely accessible and not controlled by any exclusive arrangements. To apply this rule, one must ask whether the information in question is pertinent to the operation of the legal system. Must citizens have access to it in order to understand their rights and obligations? The answer is yes with respect to land records. One cannot adhere to zoning regulation unless one knows the classification of particular areas of land. One cannot enjoy the privileges of property ownership and avoid trespassing on others' property unless one knows the boundaries of parcels of land and easements. One cannot participate meaningfully in legislative debates and judicial proceedings concerning land and land use unless one has access to the facts that will determine the outcome of such proceedings.

---

[87] 27 F. 61, 62 (C.C.D. Minn. 1866) (refusing an injunction against competing publication of legislative materials because no copying of marginal notes or references; only text of law, which is "open to the world"). The copyright in the statutory compilation was "awarded" to the plaintiff as the low bidder. *Id.*

[88] 91 F. 129 (6th Cir. 1898) (affirming denial of injunction against competing publisher of state code). Much of the opinion evaluated and rejected the defendants' argument that they could not be enjoined from publication because they had been ordered by the state to publish their compilation.

[89] Building Officials & Code Admin. v. Code Technology, Inc., 628 F.2d 730, 734 (1st Cir. 1980) (analyzing earlier cases).

[90] Howell v. Miller, 91 F. 129, 137 (6th Cir. 1898).

[91] *Id.*

[92] 2 A. 886 (Conn. 1885).

[93] *Id.* at 890.

§ 11.8 —Trademark Protection

If copyright is not an appropriate way to manage the dissemination of public information, another type of intellectual property is potentially useful. Trademark, reviewed more extensively in **Chapter 10,** is potentially available to all three levels of government, and it also raises fewer problems in realizing the policy precepts, identified in **§ 11.1.** Trademark is aimed at protecting the reputation for quality associated with particular suppliers of goods and services. It does this by reducing the likelihood of consumer confusion about the origin of similar products and services.[94] Thus, assuming other statutory criteria are satisfied, a public agency could obtain a trademark for its information products and limit the use of the trademark to those with a license from the public agency.[95] Conceivably, a local government could obtain a trademark for the "official version" of a land records database and deny use of the trademark to unofficial sources. This form of intellectual property permits public agencies to reduce risks of poor quality information that might endanger the public, while also permitting a diversity of channels and sources to exist. If over time the consuming public prefers an unofficial source, it would have that source available and would be perfectly free to reject the trademarked official source.

§ 11.9 Public Contracting

Public contracting law affects access to public information in two respects. It guarantees a measure of competition in the establishment of contractual arrangements between agencies possessing public information and private entities that may provide value-added enhancements and/or distribution channels. On the other hand, as a general matter, public contracting law authorizes agencies that follow competitive bidding practices to enter into exclusive arrangements with the successful bidder. It is thus appropriate to consider whether this power to establish exclusive arrangements for dissemination of public information overrides freedom of information and copyright principles that otherwise ensure access. Although public contracting law allows exclusive arrangements for the procurement of goods and most kinds of services, it does not allow exclusive

---

[94] Nebraska Irrigation, Inc. v. Koch, 523 N.W.2d 676, 679–81 (Neb. 1994) (holding no infringement of trade name because no likelihood of public confusion; plaintiff must show likelihood public would do business with one and believe they were doing business with another).

[95] Smokey Bear is a kind of statutory trademark. *See* 18 U.S.C. § 711 (1988); 19 Op. Att'y Gen. 361–62 (1889) (United States appropriated figure of eagle with letters U.S. under it, and may prevent private manufacturers from using it). *Cf.* Vuitton Et Fils S.A. v. J. Young Enters., 644 F.2d 769, 775 (9th Cir. 1981) (symbol that is not a national insignia unprotectible); Geo. Washington Mint, Inc. v. Washington Mint, Inc., 349 F. Supp. 255, 262 (S.D.N.Y. 1972) (trademark of doubtful validity because might mislead customers into thinking they were doing business with government); *In re* Application of Gorham Mfg. Co., 41 App. D.C. 263 (1913) (affirming denial of registration of mark that looked like official seal of British government agency).

arrangements for dissemination of public information. The cases limiting copyright and copyright-like controls over public information, reviewed in § **11.7,** the cases relying on the First Amendment to guarantee the privilege of disseminating public information, reviewed in § **11.10,** and the relationship between FOIA and public contracting law all make it clear that public contracts cannot override basic copyright, Freedom of Information Act, and First Amendment concepts.

§ 11.10   First Amendment Role

Even if the Copyright Act were interpreted to extend to public information at the state and local level, and even if section 105 of the Copyright Act were amended to allow federal government copyright, the First Amendment to the United States Constitution and similar state constitutional grants of privileges and immunities with respect to communication and expression would limit the assertion of such copyright. The same First Amendment and state constitutional doctrines would limit the assertion of information monopolies supported by any other source of law. The First Amendment enters the access controversy in two ways: as a limitation on direct restrictions on access and publication, and as a limitation on copyright.

When a monopoly is granted or asserted with respect to public information, the monopoly is enforced by denying access to the underlying public information within the scope of the monopoly and also by imposing a duty not to publish or disseminate that public information. The duty not to publish or disseminate directly collides with the First Amendment's protection of publishing and speaking. Denial of the right to access indirectly collides with the First Amendment's free speech and free press protections. The Supreme Court for many years has recognized that access to information is an essential part of the kind of democratic political system the First Amendment seeks to protect.[96]

The Second Circuit accepted the general proposition that the First Amendment can entitle a publisher to electronic formats of state legislative material in *Legi-Tech, Inc. v. Keiper.*[97] Legi-Tech sought to enjoin New York state officials from denying it access to a state-owned computerized database that contained legislative information and was available through subscription to the general public.[98] Legi-Tech marketed a computerized information retrieval service that summarized pending legislation, votes on bills, attendance and voting records of legislators, and campaign contributions of the New York and California legislators.[99] The district court found statutory restrictions on Legi-Tech's access to

---

[96] Turner Broadcasting Sys., Inc. v. FCC, 114 S. Ct. 2445, 2469–70 (1994) (recognizing relationship between access to information and the First Amendment).

[97] 766 F.2d 728 (2d Cir. 1985).

[98] *Id.* at 730.

[99] *Id.* at 731.

the governmental database, Legislative Retrieval Service (LRS), reasonable because the state only sought to protect its natural monopoly on computer-supplied legislative information. LRS would be driven out of business if competitors were not restricted and could retransmit the state's data at lower prices.[100] The Second Circuit disagreed with the district court's legal theories and remanded for further findings. The court of appeals noted that information about legislative proceedings is vital to the functioning of government and the exercise of political speech, which is at the core of the First Amendment.[101] Denying the private press access to such information on an equal basis with individual citizens and the preferred state publisher was an exercise of censorship that allowed the government to control the form and content of the information reaching the public.[102] There was nothing natural about a monopoly that arose out of a combination of LRS's special access to information and Chapter 257's prohibition on competitors having access to LRS's database.[103] The court of appeals also rejected New York's claim of a privilege to discriminate against republishers to prevent competitors from getting a free ride on its costly investment,[104] although it suggested that a price that would negate free riding would be permissible.[105]

When copyright is the basis for access or publication restrictions, the First Amendment plays a background role. "Copyright law incorporates First Amendment goals by ensuring that copyright protection extends only to the forms in which ideas and information are expressed and not to the ideas and information themselves."[106] First Amendment considerations also shape determinations of fair use under the Copyright Act.[107]

The First Amendment is concerned with public debate.[108] Certain content is closer to the core of that concern than other content. It is arguable that First Amendment protection of access to public information should be limited to legislative, judicial, and administrative agency decisional information and not

---

[100] *Id.* at 732.

[101] *Id.*

[102] *Id.* at 733.

[103] 766 F.2d 728, 733 (2d Cir. 1985).

[104] *Id.* at 735.

[105] *Id.* at 735–36. Legi-Tech stipulated that it would be willing to pay a higher price than the general public, and the court speculated that this might encompass a price that would reflect lost revenue to LRS.

[106] Los Angeles News Serv. v. Tullo, 973 F.2d 791, 795 (9th Cir. 1992).

[107] *Id.* (noting, however, that Nimmer suggests that idea-expression dichotomy in fair use doctrine may not adequately protect First Amendment interest). *See also* Twin Peaks Prod., Inc. v. Publications Int'l, Ltd., 996 F.2d 1366, 1378 (2d Cir. 1993) ("except perhaps in an extraordinary case, 'the fair use doctrine encompasses all claims of First Amendment in the copyright field'"; citing numerous cases).

[108] *But see* Eberhardt v. O'Malley, 17 F.3d 1023, 1026 (7th Cir. 1994) (holding that the First Amendment protects entertainment as well as "matters of public concern").

extended to more utilitarian content like that involved in spatial databases. Nevertheless, even geographic information pertains directly to property ownership and the use of public ways. Not only is enjoyment of property—a core interest protected by the United States and state constitutions—tied up in this type of information, but also much political debate surrounds ownership and use of property. It would be hard for a public entity to sustain the position that one can participate effectively in a debate about a zoning ordinance without access to the zoning map, even though it is arguably utilitarian rather than expressive in the usual First Amendment sense.

§ 11.11   Antitrust Arguments

The federal antitrust laws favor competition and thus provide legal support for the information policy diversity precepts.[109] Someone suffering antitrust injury[110] caused by a monopoly of public information can collect damages and obtain injunctions against maintenance of the monopoly. An explicit establishment or grant of an information monopoly, absent legal justification, would violate section 2 of the Sherman Act.[111] If contracts between legally separate entities were involved, section 1 of the Sherman Act also would be violated.[112]

Any justification for public information monopolies would have to arise from its procompetitive effects or the infeasibility of using other, less restrictive, arrangements. Such conditions are unlikely unless the market is so small that the market for whatever the downstream supplier does is a natural monopoly. For example, a very small municipality might be able to establish as a matter of fact the absence of sufficient demand for its ordinances to induce more than one supplier of electronic publishing value, like chunking and tagging, pointers, and location and distribution. The difficulty with this defense is that the presence of a plaintiff challenging an exclusive arrangement with the purported natural monopolist belies the argument that there is room for only one producer.

State action immunity also might shield some exclusive arrangements for dissemination of state or local information.[113] States and municipalities regularly

---

[109] **Chapter 2** considers the role of antitrust law as a source of access rights more generally, regardless of whether public information is involved.

[110] Consumers are the primary intended beneficiaries of the antitrust laws. Thus, consumers are more likely to have standing to litigate violations of the Sherman Act than competitors of those engaging in the alleged illegal conduct.

[111] Sherman Act, at 15 U.S.C. § 2, prohibits monopolization.

[112] Sherman Act, at 15 U.S.C. § 1, prohibits combinations or conspiracies that restrain trade, thus focusing on contracts that fix prices or limit output.

[113] *See* Capital Tel. Co. v. New York Tel. Co., 750 F.2d 1154, 1159–60 (2d Cir. 1984) (reviewing history of state action immunity and applying two-part test to find both affirmative state policy and active supervision over pricing of telephone service, thus requiring dismissal of antitrust claim).

grant franchises and set prices for products and services. Similarly, a state monopoly with respect to public information might qualify for the "state action" exemption to the antitrust laws.[114] Many state regulatory programs are immunized from antitrust liability even though they limit competition because of the need to allow some elbowroom for state regulatory power.

In the mid-1980s, the Supreme Court relaxed federal antitrust scrutiny of municipal anticompetitive arrangements,[115] imposing two requirements: state legislative contemplation of municipal anticompetitive activity, and general supervision of the municipal activity. The legislative contemplation element is satisfied if anticompetitive conduct was the foreseeable or logical result of the legislation.[116] Active supervision of the municipality by the state is not required when the municipality sanctions private anticompetitive conduct;[117] general and potential oversight is sufficient.[118] One respected commentator, Philip Areeda, suggested that proprietary activities by municipal governments, by which he meant "public activities that compete directly with private firms in the open market and that differ from them only in stockholder identity," might be subject to greater antitrust scrutiny, although he expressed concern that drawing the distinction between proprietary and nonproprietary activities always has proven troublesome.[119]

Conversely, one could argue that states and municipalities should be entitled to grant exclusive franchises to private entities to perform services that otherwise would be performed by government itself. Because governments historically have a natural or de jure monopoly on performance of public services exempt from antitrust liability, the argument would go, they should be able

---

[114] *See* Federal Trade Comm'n v. Hospital Bd. of Directors, 38 F.3d 1184 (11th Cir. 1984) (state action requirement shielded purchase by county hospital board of private hospital because powers granted to political subdivision by state contemplated anticompetitive effect); Continental Bus Sys. Inc. v. City of Dallas, 386 F. Supp. 359, 363 (N.D. Tex. 1974) (state action doctrine prevented city-granted exclusivity to bus lines serving airport from giving rise to antitrust liability).

[115] *See generally* Thomas M. Jorde, *Antitrust and the New State Action Doctrine: A Return to Deferential Economic Federalism,* 75 Cal. L. Rev. 227, 228 (1987) (explaining that trilogy of cases substantially clarified application of state action doctrine to municipalities; discussing Hoover v. Ronwin, 466 U.S. 558 (1984); Town of Hallie v. City of Eau Claire, 471 U.S. 34 (1985); Southern Motor Carriers Rate Conference v. United States, 471 U.S. 48 (1985)).

[116] *Id.* at 242 (citing *Hallie,* 471 U.S. at 42). Anticompetitive action under the authority of a general home rule grant would not qualify, however, because the legislative direction is not specific enough. *Id.* (citing Community Communications Co. v. City of Boulder, 455 U.S. 40 (1982); *Hallie,* 471 U.S. at 43).

[117] *Id.* at 245 (discussing *Hallie,* 471 U.S. at 46 & n.10).

[118] *Id.* (discussing *Southern Motor Carriers,* 471 U.S. at 51, 61 nn.23 & 66).

[119] *Antitrust Immunity for State Action after Lafayette,* 95 Harv. L. Rev. 435, 443 (1981) (suggesting that waste disposal, water service, municipal transport, and public parks probably should not be included in the proprietary category and that mere regulation of zoning, cable television, and other public franchises would not be proprietary).

to delegate this immunity to their contractors. Winning with this argument, however, should depend on sustaining the proposition that competition for the privatized service would harm essential public interests. Because public information policy benefits from a multiplicity of sources and channels, the opposite is true. Monopoly position is contrary to the public interest rather than supporting it.

§ 11.12   International Issues

Markets for public information are not limited by national boundaries. Lawyers and others in the United States have a need to know the content of European Union and national law from Britain and Japan, just as persons in other countries have a need to know the law of California. Because of the limited role that copyright plays in public information, the possibility of international movement of public information raises interesting legal questions. Ordinarily, under the Berne treaty[120] and the intellectual property appendix to the 1994 amendments to GATT,[121] signatories must respect one another's intellectual property. There is, however, an exception for public information. The general concept is that Berne treaty signatories are allowed to make their own rules for copyrights and public information, but when they provide for copyright, other signatories need not respect it. Thus, public information copyrights fairly easily can be avoided by moving the public information to another country and disseminating it through the Internet from there.

GATT-TRIP raises some questions about the permissibility of a signatory allowing copyrighted public information from another signatory to be routed through its country and thus to evade the copyright imposed by the source country. TRIP generally is intended to provide "national treatment": the same treatment in a signatory country for foreign copyrighted information as for copyrighted information of domestic origin, but obligates signatories to conform to the Berne Convention for elaboration of copyright rights. Because the Berne Convention allows public information to be copyrighted as a matter of national law (Article 2(4)), GATT-TRIP could be read to extend this protection throughout all nations covered by TRIP—although this would go beyond the national treatment concept. Otherwise, the placing of public information in the public domain as soon as it crosses a border would have the same effect as the lack of international copyright protection for private sector works that GATT was intended to remedy.

---

[120] Berne Convention for the Protection of Literary and Artistic Works, *opened for signature* Sept. 9, 1986, art. 2(4), S. Treaty Doc. Nos. 27, 38, 99th Cong., 2d Sess. (1986), 828 U.N.T.S. 221, 229.

[121] General Agreement on Tariffs and Trade, Multilateral Trade Negotiations (the Uruguay Round), Agreement on Trade-Related Aspects of Intellectual Property Rights, Including Trade and Counterfeit Goods, 33 I.L.M. 81, 83, 87 (1994).

§ 11.13 Burdens on Interstate Commerce

Because of the likelihood that a diversity of channels and sources for public information would involve interstate commerce, a state-sanctioned monopoly on such information adversely affects interstate commerce. Such an effect is permissible but only if it is justified by pursuit of a legitimate state interest, a criterion that is difficult to satisfy, under the analytical principles provided in **Chapter 6.**

§ 11.14 Substantive Due Process and Equal Protection

Substantive due process under the Fourteenth Amendment of the United States Constitution immunizes persons from deprivation of life, liberty, or property except when the deprivation is justified by a legitimate state interest. Equal protection analysis is similar.[122] A state-established monopoly on electronic publishing adversely affects First Amendment interests, which are a fundamental right, and therefore should trigger strict scrutiny under the equal protection clause of the Fourteenth Amendment[123] and similar scrutiny under substantive due process doctrine. It would be difficult for a state or municipality to show how an information monopoly is necessary to promote a legitimate state interest. There is little authority for the proposition that making money is a legitimate state interest, justifying interference with private entrepreneurial interests. It also would be difficult to justify information monopolies on the grounds of ensuring an accurate flow of public information because the less restrictive trademark approach is available to protect any interest in avoiding errors in public information. Thus, state monopolies on public information could be vulnerable to attack under 42 U.S.C. § 1983 and 42 U.S.C. § 1985(3) when they are established at the state and local level, and to challenges as constitutional torts when they are established at the federal level.

§ 11.15 Pricing Public Information

Pricing arguments have much to do with cost accounting: whether prices for public access to public information may reflect a portion of the fixed costs of

---

[122] Bray v. Alexandria Women's Health Clinic, 113 S. Ct. 753, 777 (1993) (Souter, J., concurring in part and dissenting in part) (noting that civil rights conspiracy claim could be evaluated similarly under substantive due process or equal protection tests). *But see* Nollan v. California Coastal Comm'n, 483 U.S. 825, 835 n.3 (1987) (questioning whether equal protection and substantive due process standards are the same in property-taking cases).

[123] *See* Arkansas Writers' Project, Inc. v. Ragland, 481 U.S. 221, 230 (1987) (state sales tax targeting general interest magazines, while exempting other publications, violated First Amendment rights).

agency information systems, perhaps including systems designed to collect public information. Most policy guidelines addressing cost accounting say that only the direct costs of providing public access should be recoverable. The Paperwork Reduction Act of 1995 reiterates this principle:

> [An agency shall not:]
>
> (B) restrict or regulate the use, resale, or redissemination of public information by the public;
>
> (C) charge fees or royalties for resale or redissemination of public information; or
>
> (D) establish user fees for public information that exceed the cost of dissemination.[124]

Even when this is the law or policy, however, determining direct cost is not simple. Automated information systems usually have a relatively high proportion of fixed costs for capital goods—hardware and software and communications facilities—that produce a variety of output streams. When one of these streams is public access, how much of the fixed and joint cost should be allocated to that stream as opposed to others presents an essentially indeterminate question.

The basic policy on pricing of public information should be that the price should reflect the incremental or marginal cost of providing public access; an agency should not be permitted to recover the fixed costs of its information systems developed for internal agency purposes. On the other hand, costs for modems or Internet connections are directly attributable to public access, and it should be permissible to recover those costs unless the legislature determines that the public interest justifies the use of appropriated funds, as it traditionally has for printed access to certain public information. **Table 11–1** provides informal rules of thumb for treatment of costs.[125]

Historically, pricing public information at marginal cost threatened private publishers because they priced to cover their fixed costs as well as their marginal costs. Conventional publishing has high fixed costs compared to variable costs (printing presses and binderies cost more money than the labor and paper to print a significant press run), while Internet architectures with their easy duplication, cheap routing, and distributed production possibilities, change the relationship between fixed and variable costs. Newer technologies for providing public access to public information reduce the risk that marginal cost pricing will threaten the viability of nonsubsidized publishers.[126]

---

[124] 44 U.S.C. § 3506(d)(4), *amended by* the Paperwork Reduction Act of 1995, Pub. L. No. 104-13, 109 Stat. 163 (May 22, 1995).

[125] Peter N. Weiss of the Office of Management and Budget suggested the concepts summarized in the table.

[126] Even in the absence of government prices at marginal cost, microeconomic theory says that competition will force prices to a level close to marginal cost. Edwin Mansfield, Microeconomics: Theory and Applications 241 (2d ed. 1975) ("at the equilibrium price, price will equal marginal cost for all firms that choose to produce, rather than shut down their plants"). The existence of high fixed costs increases the challenge of staying in business because marginal cost pricing means that fixed costs may not be covered. *Id.* ("Price may be above or below average total cost, since there is no necessity that profits be zero or that fixed costs be covered in the short run.").

Table 11–1

Cost Accounting

Not recovered	Amortized (indirect) Logically identifiable with dissemination context	Direct recovery
Non-dissemination costs		"Incremental"
		Telecommunications Access costs CPU time Customer service Duplication Software licensing
Database development	Database modification for dissemination	
Hardware	Hardware enhancements for dissemination: capacity ports	
Value-added for gov't use	Value-added for dissemination: software enhancements advertising mastering and pre-mastering	
Creation/collection Data maintenance Archiving		
	"The gray area where informed discretion must prevail"	

Pricing at marginal cost for access to the basic content presents no threat to private sector publishers because agencies have a natural monopoly for the raw information,[127] which is the raw material for private publishers. What is essential is that *all* private sector competitors get the benefit of the public investment at cost. As long as that is true, taxpayer subsidy of agency activities does not pose a threat to private sector activity aimed at adding additional added value.

Any private sector adders of value can obtain access to the agency-produced baseline at a price reflecting marginal cost to the agency and can put whatever value-added features on top of it they wish, protected by intellectual property in

---

[127] This natural monopoly does not mean that private sector entities are prohibited from collecting the information; it just means that it would not pay them to do so.

their value-added component. This arrangement is summarized in **Figure 11–1** in **§ 11.2.** Then, the only risk of free riding is the risk of undetected or unpunished intellectual property infringement and the risk of free riding on sweat of the brow. Public policy can lower the threat of that kind of free riding by making little sweat of the brow necessary, by things like Internet distribution and GILS finding aids.

§ 11.16   Strategies for Private Sector Publishers

Governmental entities should not establish monopolies, but private sector publishers may use intellectual property to protect themselves against free riding from competitors. This section reviews strategies that private sector publishers can use to protect their intellectual property, assuming that information value components supplied by governmental entities are not entitled to legal protection and are freely accessible by anyone, including competitors.

First, it is appropriate to make a preliminary observation. Ready accessibility of publicly supplied information value benefits private sector providers because this means that they can get their raw material without having to get permission from their competitors or to pay royalties to their competitors.

There is no question that private sector publishers are entitled to copyright protection for their computer programs and for selection and arrangement of publicly supplied information that meets the relatively low-originality standards of *Feist*. Beyond that, trade secret protection may be useful for certain formats and computer program codes. In addition, the growing acceptability of patent protection for computer procedures may be useful for graphical image manipulation algorithms.[128] Finally, trademark protection is regularly and appropriately used to prevent competitors from appropriating the good name and goodwill of a private sector publisher, although it does not protect the underlying value-added elements like computer programs, formats, and selection and arrangement.[129]

Perhaps the most important form of legal protection is contractual. A private sector publisher can impose on persons purchasing directly from it whatever contractual duties it desires, limiting redissemination and use, subject to broad limits imposed by copyright preemption and the antitrust laws.[130]

---

[128] For example, CompuServe's Graphics Interchange Format (GIF) incorporates Unisys's Lempel-Zev-Welch (LZW) algorithm, Patent No. 4,558,302, Terry Welch, Dec. 10, 1985.

[129] An interesting but entirely speculative possibility is that certain look and feel aspects of computer products might be entitled to trade dress protection. *See* Two Pesos, Inc. v. Taco Cabana, Inc., 112 S. Ct. 2753, 2757 (1992) (holding that trade dress that is inherently distinctive is protectible under the Lanham Act § 43 without a showing of secondary meaning).

[130] Bonito Boats, Inc. v. Thunder Craft Boats, Inc., 489 U.S. 141 (1989) (holding that federal patent law preempts state statute granting patent-like protection to unpatented goods already available to the public); Kaiser Steel Corp. v. Mullins, 455 U.S. 72 (1982) (holding that illegal contractual promises in cases controlled by federal law are unenforceable on public policy grounds). *See also* Continental Wallpaper Co. v. Louis Vioght & Sons Co., 212 U.S. 227 (1909) (refusing to enforce promise based on an illegal bargain under federal antitrust laws).

All of this, however, still leaves a private sector publisher vulnerable to certain kinds of piracy and free-riding competition. A pirate lacking privity of contract still would have the legal privilege to extract publicly supplied information value from the private sector publisher's products and reuse it in competition with that publisher as long as the pirate does not use patented procedures, represent his product as coming from the publisher, or reproduce or distribute copyrighted components of value added by the private sector publisher. There are, however, some product design and technological protections that can substantially eliminate the risk.

Desktop computer software publishers discovered relatively early in the life of that industry that planned obsolescence can reduce their exposure to piracy. Frequent updates and supplements, like later editions of print products, can render worthless the materials that a pirate has obtained and is publishing in competition with the originator. Usually, it is not worth it to a user to ascertain the differences between the updated product and the earlier product. Thus, most users simply elect to buy the newest version from the originator rather than buying a lower-priced pirated earlier version.

Granularity of information (how big the retrievable pieces are) also protects against piracy. If an originator chunks content so that the content elements are finally grained in the product as received by an intended customer, the transaction costs are increased for a pirate. The pirate must extract each grain and then reassemble the grains into a larger quantity of information in order to set itself up in competition. Thus, as a private sector publisher adds value to make its product attractive to consumers, it also is likely to establish more and more grain boundaries that will get in the way of a pirate.

§ 11.17   Draft Principles for Public Information Policy

The following guidelines are synthesized from ABA recommendations and from the author's experience in advising federal and state governments and European Union institutions on public information policy:

1. Information maintained by or under the authority of a public agency in electronic form constitutes agency records available under Freedom of Information Acts. The nature of the format should not change the availability of the information, but information in electronic form is subject to the same exemptions that would justify withholding information in paper formats.

2. The fact that a requester of information under a Freedom of Information Act intends commercial publication of the information accessed should not diminish the entitlement to information.

3. In responding to freedom of information requests, government entities should release electronic information in the format in which it is requested, as long as the requested format already exists or may be generated by the agency with reasonable effort using available software and equipment.

4. Agencies should adopt affirmative programs of electronic public information dissemination.

5. Agencies should ensure that electronic information and value-added features developed with public funds are available to the public.

6. When agencies contract with private entities to develop new electronic information products, agencies should insist on contractual terms that put both the data and the appropriate retrieval software to obtain access to that data in the public domain.

7. Agencies should anticipate public requests for electronic information and should build features into their electronic information systems so that information most likely to be requested by the public may be actively released, thereby reducing the cost to agencies and requesters.

8. Agencies should encourage development and distribution of multiple electronic information products serving the same market and containing the same public information so that consumers will have choices among particular value-added product features.

9. Agencies should not hold copyrights in public information, nor should they establish or maintain exclusive arrangements for access to public information.

10. When agencies offer value-added information products, they should make available versions of the same information with less value added when that is requested by an entity seeking to provide an alternative means of access to the information.

11. Agencies should make their information content available on the Internet without restrictions on access to the raw content.

12. Agencies should set prices no higher than necessary to recover the direct costs of dissemination. Direct costs do not include the costs of collection, the development of value-added features for internal agency use, or fixed costs not directly attributable to the public access channel.

CHAPTER 12

CIVIL DISPUTE RESOLUTION AND PROCEDURE

§ 12.1   Overview

Conduct with potentially serious legal consequences is difficult for traditional sovereigns to control in the NII because it is ephemeral and invisible and crosses geographic boundaries easily. This chapter explores how the legal system deals with information technology procedurally, beginning with well-recognized problems of jurisdiction and exploring closely associated problems in choice of law. Then it explains how the law of evidence is accommodating the special characteristics of electronic formats as repositories of legally significant facts.

At several points, the chapter provides model forms, for example, model clauses on forum selection and choice of law to reduce uncertainty with respect to personal jurisdiction and choice of law. In addition to these practice-oriented materials, the chapter also offers historical and basic conceptual material on procedural issues. An understanding of core concepts and of historical foundations is important to a sound practical understanding of the potential for existing procedural doctrines to evolve to accommodate the peculiar characteristics of the NII technologies.

§ 12.2   Civil Procedure Issues

Four procedural issues interact in circumscribing the power of a particular court to decide a controversy according to particular substantive rules: personal jurisdiction, notice by service of process or otherwise, choice of law, and venue. A fifth doctrine encompasses all of the other four: enforcement of judgments. The res judicata effect of a judgment and therefore its enforceability[1] depends

---

[1] There may be other limitations on enforceability, based, for example, on the absence of a procedural scheme for enforcing foreign judgments (see Sweden), but a threshold requirement for enforcing foreign judgments is recognition, and recognition is available only for final judgments, i.e., those with res judicata effect.

on the court rendering the judgment having personal jurisdiction, being the appropriate venue, and giving appropriate notice to those bound by the judgment. Inappropriate choice of law also is a basis for challenging the efficacy of a judgment, albeit a much weaker one.

The four doctrines were not particularly distinct in early English procedure, but then they diverged in nineteenth century and early twentieth century American jurisprudence. Now, they are beginning to converge again.[2] The fair play and substantial justice test for personal jurisdiction[3] requires interest analysis similar to that used to resolve choice of law disputes.[4] That test also overlaps considerably with forum non conveniens analysis used to determine venue. More flexible rules for personal jurisdiction necessitate an expansion of the types of the notice that are acceptable.[5] Venue rules also interact with choice of law rules. In the federal system where forum non conveniens analysis may result in transfer of a case to another district court, under 28 U.S.C. § 1404, the choice of law rule of the original court must be used by the transferee court.[6]

As commerce and therefore litigation become more international in character, American personal jurisdiction, venue, choice of law, and notice rules must be reassessed and perhaps harmonized with corresponding rules in other countries.[7] The expansion and improvement in the use of information infrastructure makes it easier for commercial and political transactions to be international in character. This reinforces the internationalization phenomenon, while also introducing new types of contact with forum states and new techniques for giving notice that also require rethinking some of the rules. Analysis would be simplified if the convergence eventually results in the atrophy of independent

---

[2] *See generally* Harold G. Maier & Thomas R. McCoy, *A Unifying Theory for Judicial Jurisdiction and Choice of Law,* 2 Am. J. Comp. L. 249, 280–90 (1991) (constitutional limits on personal jurisdiction can also serve as appropriate limits on choice of law, but only if general jurisdiction is abolished).

[3] See § **12.4.**

[4] See § **12.11.**

[5] When the limits of jurisdiction are the physical boundaries of a sovereign entity, notice can be confined to in-hand service of process. When the limits of personal jurisdiction cross the physical boundaries, mail service and constructive service by publication become necessary. See §§ **12.4** and **12.6** discussing long-arm statutes and service-by-mail rules.

[6] *See* Ferens v. John Deere Co., 494 U.S. 516 (1990) (extending § 1404 rule to transfer initiated by plaintiff).

[7] *See generally* Linda J. Silberman, *Developments in Jurisdiction and Forum Non Conveniens in International Litigation: Thoughts on Reform and a Proposal for a Uniform Standard,* 28 Tex. Int'l L.J. 501 (1993) (noting that procedural idiosyncrasies attract international litigants to U.S. courts, and substantive rules in the antitrust and products liability areas attract plaintiffs, requiring frequent application of personal jurisdiction and choice of law rules in marginal cases, and also challenging judgment enforcement rules except when foreign defendants have assets in the United States).

personal jurisdiction inquiry, replaced by stronger forum non conveniens rules and clearer limitations on choice of law.[8]

§ 12.3 —Historical Relationship among Jurisdiction, Venue, Choice of Law

The prospects for unifying personal jurisdiction, venue, and choice of law rules are influenced by the historical separation of the rules and their historical links to private international law concepts. Historically, venue rules were the most prominent means for determining where suit might be brought and what law would be applied. Until *Pennoyer v. Neff*,[9] territorial limitations were imposed by state venue statutes. Venue, in turn, depended on whether the cause of action was "local" or "transitory." Local causes of action had only one acceptable venue, while transitory causes of action might have several. Choice of law meanwhile was hardly an issue in the earliest cases. It was assumed that any court would apply its own substantive law; choice of forum thus determined choice of law.[10]

One of the best explanations of the original relationship among venue, personal jurisdiction, and enforcement is found in *Livingston v. Jefferson*.[11] In that case, an action for trespass was brought against Thomas Jefferson. The alleged trespass occurred in New Orleans, and Jefferson was found in Virginia. The circuit court dismissed the action, finding that it was local and therefore could be brought only where the trespass occurred. Jefferson was not found in that district and therefore could not be sued there. Apparently, he could not be sued anywhere. Both Judge Tyler and Circuit Justice Marshall agreed that the rule was long established that trespass actions were local rather than transitory.[12]

---

[8] *See* Linda J. Silberman, *Reflections on* Burnham v. Superior Court: *Toward Presumptive Rules of Jurisdiction and Implications for Choice of Law,* 22 Rutgers L.J. 569, 584–90 & nn.74–101 (1991) (acknowledging proposals and implementation in Australia, citing Weintraub and objective basis for rejecting transient jurisdiction, 22 Rutgers L.J. 611 (1991), but expressing concern that limited review of venue decisions and lack of clear constitutional restraints on choice of law would make nationwide service of process undesirable).

[9] 95 U.S. 714 (1877) (constitutionalized personal jurisdiction by making it clear that the United States Constitution imposes territorial limits on the exercise of judicial power by state courts).

[10] *See* A.E. Anton & P.R. Beaumont, Private International Law 18 (2d ed. 1990) (assumption that choice of judge determined law had to be relaxed as trade spanned boundaries of traditional sovereigns, but intellectual justifications had to be developed for applying foreign law).

[11] 15 F. Cas. 660 (C.C.D. Va. 1811).

[12] *See* Reasor-Hill Corp. v. Harrison, 249 S.W.2d 994, 995–96 (Ark. 1952) (reviewing rationale for *Livingston v. Jefferson* and concluding that basis for distinguishing local and transitory actions no longer made any sense, in part because courts easily could obtain knowledge of the legal rules applicable in jurisdictions where land lies). Tax claims were another prominent example of purely local claims. The courts in England would not entertain a claim by France for taxes due in France. But by the mid-1950s, the rule had begun to erode, at least with respect to interstate jurisdiction within the United States. *See* Oklahoma v. Neely, 282 S.W.2d 150, 152 (Ark. 1955) (explaining why rule originally may have made sense but no longer). But see Her Majesty the Queen v. Gilbertson, 597 F.2d 1161 (9th Cir. 1979) (declining to enforce Canadian judgment for taxes).

As important as the holding is the explanation offered by Chief Justice Marshall. In trespass actions, the title and bounds of land might come into question, and only a jury from the vicinage of the land could appropriately determine such facts.[13] (This factor is analogous to the convenience factors in the doctrine of forum non conveniens.) Second, Judge Tyler reasoned that a judgment for the plaintiff would potentially necessitate execution by the sheriff and his posse to remove the trespasser, if necessary. "And suppose the sheriff and jury should deny the power of the court, could they be coerced?" In other words, the power of the court should be coterminous with the court's power over the officer who must execute the court's judgment.[14] If execution could be had only in one place, then only the court of that place had the power to try the case.[15]

Transitory actions were different. As to them, venue existed more or less wherever the defendant could be found. Contract was the archetypal transitory action, based on a legal and moral obligation in the person to perform the contracts he promised to perform. Such actions thus were not tied to any particular place.[16] There was a loose correspondence between real actions and local actions, and between personal actions and transitory actions. When enforcement required doing something with respect to a res, only the local sheriff could do it. Conversely, when enforcement involved a person who might move around (as for imprisonment for debt, or simply through a *capias ad satisfaciendum*[17] or *capias ad respondendum*[18]) enforcement could occur wherever the person was found.

These limitations, however, were purely common-law limitations.[19] The distinction between real and personal actions achieved constitutional status in *Pennoyer v. Neff,*[20] some 66 years later when an action proceeded as though it were personal when the remedy sought was in rem.[21] In *Pennoyer,* the Supreme

---

[13] Early juries used their own knowledge of the facts as well as testimony adduced from witnesses.

[14] Similar issues of control arise in the extradistrict enforcement of injunctions, considered in **§ 12.10.**

[15] Livingston v. Jefferson, 15 F. Cas. 660, 662 (C.C.D. Va. 1811) (describing two factors).

[16] *Id. Accord* 15 F. Cas. at 664 (Marshall, J.).

[17] A writ of execution calling for the arrest of a judgment debtor in order to compel him to satisfy the judgment.

[18] A judicial writ directing the sheriff to arrest the defendant and bring him into court to answer a complaint filed against him. *See* Vermont Nat'l Bank v. Taylor, 445 A.2d 1122, 1124 (N.H. 1982) (quashing ex parte capias procedure used to initiate civil contempt proceeding).

[19] Livingston v. Jefferson, 15 F. Cas. 660, 663–65 (C.C.D. Va. 1811) (emphasizing role of English common law in Virginia).

[20] 95 U.S. 714 (1877).

[21] The property here in controversy sold under the judgment rendered was not attached, nor in any way brought under the jurisdiction of the court. Its first connection with the case was caused by a levy of the execution. It was not, therefore, disposed of pursuant to any adjudication, but only in enforcement of a personal judgment, having no relation to the property, rendered against a nonresident without service of process upon him in the action or his appearance therein.

Id. at 720.

Court reasoned that the separate states are like nation states in the territorial limits on the power of their courts. If a sovereign purported to decide a personal action when it lacked the power to serve process on the person of the defendant, its judgments were not entitled to recognition or enforcement in other states. Conversely, the same court could exercise power over a real action because it had de facto power over the res located within its territorial limits.[22] Of course, an important feature of this distinction was that an in rem judgment could be enforced only to the limits of the value of the thing.[23] The *Pennoyer* Court went further and held that purporting to decide cases against persons not within the personal jurisdiction of the court violated due process under the Fourteenth Amendment.[24]

The distinctions between personal and real actions and between local and transitory actions have largely disappeared from personal jurisdiction analysis. The inherently nonlocal nature of information technology might seem to make the distinction entirely irrelevant in analyzing civil procedure issues for the NII. That is not so. The traditional distinction between local and transitory actions appropriately sought to conform doctrine to practical limits on judicial power. The rationale used by Judge Tyler in *Livingston v. Jefferson* is a good example. Now even though interests analysis is the centerpiece of the law of personal jurisdiction[25] and choice of law analysis,[26] the power dimension, along with an assessment of efficiency and convenience, becomes more important in deciding as a practical matter where a lawsuit over electronic conduct should be litigated and where judgments resulting from such a lawsuit can be enforced practicably. The simple answer, as in *Jefferson* and *Pennoyer,* is that judicial power may be exercised over the NII wherever a human being may be found and wherever some assets are located. The NII may span geographic boundaries, but its human actors are present in some traditional jurisdiction. The hardware, software, and financial assets used to operate each part of the NII are located in some traditional jurisdiction. Lawsuits will be effective in those jurisdictions. The practical interaction between judicial power and electronic actors appropriately guides application of modern personal jurisdiction, choice of law, venue, and enforcement doctrines considered in the next several sections.

§ 12.4 Personal Jurisdiction

Personal jurisdiction of an American court, state or federal, depends on the interaction of an affirmative statutory or common-law source of jurisdiction,

---

[22] *Id.* at 730–31.

[23] *Id.* at 731–32 (judgment and action for jurisdiction were obtained by attachment of bedstead could not exceed value of bedstead).

[24] *Id.* at 733. *But see id.* at 735 (exempting status decisions such as divorce and requirements that nonresidents consent to jurisdiction and appoint agents for service of process).

[25] See § **12.4.**

[26] See § **12.11.**

and limitations imposed by constitutional due process. Traditionally, state courts asserted jurisdiction over persons physically present within their territorial boundaries and served with process while they were there, and asserted jurisdiction over things found within their territorial boundaries and attached while they were there.[27] Under the Supreme Court's decision in *Burnham v. Superior Court*,[28] the traditional character of these two types of jurisdiction is enough to make them satisfy due process.[29]

States also typically assert jurisdiction in other cases under long-arm statutes. Typical of long-arm statutes are the provisions of the Uniform Interstate and International Procedure Act:[30]

§ 1.02. [Personal Jurisdiction Based upon Enduring Relationship]

A court may exercise personal jurisdiction over a person domiciled in, organized under the laws of, or maintaining his or its principal place of business in, this state as to any [cause of action] [claim for relief].

§ 1.03. [Personal Jurisdiction Based upon Conduct]

(a) A court may exercise personal jurisdiction over a person, who acts directly or by an agent, as to a [cause of action] [claim for relief] arising from the person's

(1) transacting any business in this state;

(2) contracting to supply services or things in this state;

(3) causing tortious injury by an act or omission in this state;

(4) causing tortious injury in this state by an act or omission outside this state if he regularly does or solicits business, or engages in any other persistent course of conduct, or derives substantial revenue from goods used or consumed or services rendered, in this state;[31] [or]

---

[27] 15 Joseph Story, Commentaries on the Conflict of Laws §§ 532–38, at 900–05 (4th ed. 1852) (personal jurisdiction in Roman law was limited to domicile of defendant except for in rem actions, which could be brought where personal or real property was situated; civil law also allowed place where contract was made or was to be fulfilled if defendant or his property could be found there, even though it was not the place of his domicile). "Considered in an international point of view, jurisdiction, to be rightfully exercised, must be founded either upon the person being within the territory, or upon the thing being within the territory; for, otherwise, there can be no sovereignty exerted upon the known maxim." *Id.* at 905. Story noted questions about quasi in rem jurisdiction. Proceeding against nonresidents by attaching property found within the jurisdiction is not personally binding on the party as a judgment in personam; it only binds the property seized or attached, "and is in no just sense a decree or judgment, binding upon him beyond that property. In other countries, it is uniformly so treated, and is justly considered as having no extraterritorial force or obligation." *Id.* § 549 at 921–22. *See also* 28 U.S.C. § 1655 (federal in rem jurisdiction); Colo. R. Civ. P. 4 (personal jurisdiction); Colo. R. Civ. P. 4(f)(3) (in rem jurisdiction); Iowa R. Civ. P. 56.1 (personal jurisdiction).

[28] 495 U.S. 604 (1990).

[29] There is some doubt about the effect of *Burnham* because the rationale stated in the text was embraced by only four justices. 495 U.S. at 604.

[30] Uniform Interstate and International Procedure Act, 13 U.L.A. 355 (1986) (adopted by Arkansas, District of Columbia, Massachusetts, Michigan, Pennsylvania, and Virgin Islands).

[31] The Uniform Act has two different provisions applicable to tort: Item (3) "causing tortious injury by an act or omission in this state," allows personal jurisdiction even when the injury

(5) having an interest in, using, or possessing real property in this state[; or

(6) contracting to insure any person, property, or risk located within this state at the time of contracting].

(b) When jurisdiction over a person is based solely upon this section, only a [cause of action] [claim for relief] arising from acts enumerated in this section may be asserted against him.

Long-arm statutes typically reflect the constitutional analysis[32] of a line of Supreme Court cases beginning with *International Shoe Co. v. Washington.*[33] Under this line of cases, jurisdiction over a person or a corporation not found and served with process within the jurisdiction is permissible, but only when the defendant has minimum contacts with the forum state, and only when the assertion of jurisdiction satisfies considerations of fair play and substantial justice.[34] When a defendant is a nonresident and is not physically present in the jurisdiction, personal jurisdiction may be obtained over a defendant if a court finds that the defendant has established "certain minimum contacts with [the forum] such that the maintenance of the suit does not offend 'traditional notions of fair play and substantial justice.' "[35] This two-part analysis begins with an assessment of the defendant's minimum contacts with the forum. In determining minimum contacts, a court properly focuses on "the relationship among the defendant, the forum, and the litigation."[36] The second part of the analysis

---

occurs somewhere else; item (4) covers tortious injury in the forum state caused by an act or omission out of state, but only if the defendant regularly does or solicits business, or engages in any other persistent course of conduct or derives substantial revenue from good used or consumed for services rendered in the forum state.

[32] The Constitution is a limit on personal jurisdiction, while long-arm statutes affirmatively grant jurisdiction. The Constitution influences drafters of long-arm statutes because they want to draft a statute that does not go beyond what the Constitution allows thus making it vulnerable to constitutional attack.

[33] International Shoe Co. v. Washington, Office of Unemployment Compensation & Placement, 326 U.S. 310 (1945).

[34] *See* Asahi Metal Indus. Co. v. Superior Court, 480 U.S. 102 (1987) (explaining interaction of minimum contacts and fair play and substantial justice). The best way to combine two considerations is to realize that when minimum contacts analysis results in a close question, fair-play and substantial-justice factors should play greater weight. The fair-play and substantial-justice part of the inquiry sometimes is called the "Gestalt" inquiry. It considers five factors:

1. Burden on the defendant

2. Forum state's interest in adjudicating the dispute

3. The plaintiff's interest in obtaining most efficient resolution of the controversy

4. The interstate judicial system's interest in most efficient resolution

5. The shared interest of the several states in furthering fundamental substantive social policies.

Burger King v. Rudzewicz, 471 U.S. 462 (1985) (identifying factors).

[35] International Shoe Co. v. Washington, Office of Unemployment Compensation & Placement, 326 U.S. 310, 316 (1945) (quoting Milliken v. Meyer, 311 U.S. 457, 463 (1940)).

[36] Shaffer v. Heitner, 433 U.S. 186, 204 (1977).

focuses on the contacts "in light of other factors to decide whether the assertion of personal jurisdiction would comport with 'fair play and substantial justice.'"[37]

Within this analytical framework, contacts such as sending goods into the forum state and permitting instrumentalities that cause injury to enter the forum state count as minimum contacts only if they are purposeful; mere foreseeability of contact with the forum state is not enough.[38] Also, entering into a contract with someone in the forum state may satisfy minimum contacts requirements, when the contract provides for a repetitive series of transactions with the forum state.[39]

Personal jurisdiction concepts in Europe place less emphasis on service of process while a defendant is physically present, and greater emphasis on factors that fit comfortably within the minimum contacts concept in American jurisprudence.[40] Thus, a defendant always may be sued where he lives, and nonresident defendants also may be sued when they have intentionally engaged in transactions with someone in the forum state.[41] Beyond that, some European countries assert what is known as "exorbitant bases of jurisdiction." France and Scotland are examples. One exorbitant basis permits courts in the plaintiff's place of residence to hear suit against nonresident defendants, at least when the claim has some relationship to the jurisdiction. Another allows what Americans would call *quasi in rem jurisdiction.* A third allows jurisdiction over anyone served with process while temporarily present within the forum—so-called tag jurisdiction.[42]

§ 12.5   —Obtaining Personal Jurisdiction over Publications

A number of cases apply the minimum contacts and fair-play and substantial-justice factors to print publications.[43] These cases are helpful in applying

---

[37] Madara v. Hall, 916 F.2d 1510,1517 (11th Cir. 1990) (quoting Burger King v. Rudzewicz, 471 U.S. 462, 476 (1985)). These other factors include "the burden on the defendant in defending the lawsuit, the forum state's interest in adjudicating the dispute, the plaintiff's interest in obtaining convenient and effective relief, the interstate judicial system's interest in obtaining the most efficient resolution of controversies and the shared interest of the states in furthering fundamental substantive policies." *Id.* at 1517.

[38] *See* World-Wide Volkswagen Corp. v. Woodson, 444 U.S. 286 (1980); Asahi Metal Indus. Co. v. Superior Court, 480 U.S. 102 (1987).

[39] *See* Burger King v. Rudzewicz, 471 U.S. 462 (1985).

[40] *See generally* Friedrich Juenger, *Judicial Jurisdiction in the United States and in the European Communities: A Comparison,* 82 Mich. L. Rev. 1195 (1984).

[41] The Brussels Convention binds signatory states—the members of the European Union—to rules for jurisdiction and enforcement roughly corresponding to the rules under *International Shoe* and its progeny. *See* Paul R. Beaumont, Anton & Beaumont's Civil Jurisdiction in Scotland, ch. 5, at 90–124 (1995) (explaining bases of jurisdiction under convention).

[42] Paul R. Beaumont, Anton & Beaumont's Civil Jurisdiction in Scotland § 1.10, at 6–7 (1995) (explaining exorbitant bases of jurisdiction with examples).

[43] The research and initial drafting of this section was done by Andrew J. Vella, Villanova Law School Class of 1996, law clerk to the author.

personal jurisdiction doctrine to the NII because print publications, like electronic ones, spread out and come in contact with a multiplicity of jurisdictions, based on conduct that is concentrated at the place of the author or publisher. A publication usually satisfies the minimum contacts analysis if it has a substantial circulation in the jurisdiction[44] or if the defendant-publisher intended to cause injury in the jurisdiction.[45]

Circulation

In *Keeton v. Hustler Magazine, Inc.,*[46] a resident of New York brought a libel action against an Ohio corporation, in the United States District Court for the District of New Hampshire.[47] The Supreme Court upheld New Hampshire's jurisdiction over Hustler based on minimum contacts via circulation in New Hampshire and that state's interest in adjudicating the dispute.

In examining Hustler's contacts with New Hampshire, the Court focused on Hustler's circulation of magazines within the state,[48] consisting "of the sale of some 10 to 15,000 copies of Hustler magazine in that State each month."[49] The Court held that Hustler's "regular circulation of magazines in the forum State [was] sufficient to support an assertion of jurisdiction in a libel action based on the contents of the magazine."[50]

The circulation gave New Hampshire a substantial interest in the dispute:

[a] state has an especial interest in exercising judicial jurisdiction over those who commit torts within its territory. This is because torts involve wrongful conduct which a state seeks to deter, and against which it attempts to afford protection, by providing that a tortfeasor shall be liable for damages which are the proximate result of his tort. . . . This interest extends to libel actions brought by nonresidents. False statements of fact harm both the subject of the falsehood and the readers of the statement. New Hampshire may rightly employ its libel laws to discourage the deception of its citizens.[51]

---

[44] *See* Keeton v. Hustler Magazine, Inc., 465 U.S. 770, 781 (1984) (holding that defendant "continuously and deliberately exploited the New Hampshire market" by circulating its magazine in that jurisdiction).

[45] *See* Calder v. Jones, 465 U.S. 783 (1984) (holding California's exercise of jurisdiction was proper over Florida defendants in a libel action arising out of an article written and edited by defendants in Florida, which caused injury to plaintiff in California).

[46] 465 U.S. 770 (1984).

[47] *Id.* at 772.

[48] *Id.* at 773.

[49] *Id.*

[50] *Id.*

[51] *Id.* at 776 (quoting Leeper v. Leeper, 319 A.2d 626, 629 (N.H. 1974)).

Intentional Conduct Directed at the Forum State

Calder v. Jones[52] accompanied *Keeton v. Hustler Magazine, Inc.* In *Calder,* the plaintiff, a California resident, brought a libel action against the defendants, both residents of Florida and both employed by the *National Enquirer.*[53] The defendants wrote and edited the allegedly libelous article in Florida that was later published in the *National Enquirer* and circulated within California.[54]

The Supreme Court had to decide whether the defendants had established sufficient minimum contacts with California to warrant personal jurisdiction over them. While the Court did address the issue of the *National Enquirer's* circulation in California,[55] that was not the focal point of the minimum contacts analysis. Instead, the Court focused its inquiry on the activities of the defendants rather than the activities of their employer.[56] Eschewing an inquiry into the defendants' actual contacts with California,[57] the Court instead examined their actions that were "expressly aimed at California."[58]

The defendants wrote and edited "an article that they knew would have a potentially devastating impact upon [Shirley Jones]. And they knew that the brunt of that inquiry would be felt by [Shirley Jones] in the State in which she lives and works and in which the National Enquirer has its largest circulation."[59] Based on these facts, the Court found that the defendants had established minimum contacts with California, stating, "petitioners are primary participants in an alleged wrongdoing intentionally directed at a California resident, and jurisdiction is proper over them on that basis."[60]

"Traditional notions of fair play and substantial justice"[61] also supported the exercise of jurisdiction in California. In light of the circumstances, the defendants "'must reasonably anticipate being haled into court [in California]' to answer for the truth of the statements made in their article."[62]

---

[52] 465 U.S. 783 (1984).

[53] *Id.* at 785.

[54] *Id.* at 785–86.

[55] The Court pointed out that the *National Enquirer* had a weekly circulation of approximately 600,000 copies in California. *Id.* at 785.

[56] *Id.* at 789–90.

[57] The Court found that both of the petitioners had been to California on various occasions (some relating to *National Enquirer* business matters) but did not place any significance on this fact. *Id.* at 785–86.

[58] 465 U.S. 783, 789 (1984).

[59] *Id.* at 789–90.

[60] *Id.* at 790.

[61] International Shoe Co. v. Washington, Office of Unemployment Compensation & Placement, 326 U.S. 310, 316 (1945).

[62] 465 U.S. 783, 790 (1984) (quoting World-Wide Volkswagen Corp. v. Woodson, 444 U.S. 286, 297 (1980)).

Similar minimum contacts analysis applies when the defendant makes an allegedly tortious statement that is later published by another, although the maker of the statement may have less responsibility for where circulation occurs. In *Madara v. Hall*,[63] the plaintiff, a California resident, brought suit in a Florida district court against the defendant for allegedly libelous statements made by the defendant in California during a telephone interview with a magazine reporter.[64] The statements were later published in a magazine that was circulated in Florida.[65] The United States Court of Appeals for the Eleventh Circuit applied the traditional minimum contacts analysis in considering whether the defendant had sufficient contacts with Florida to warrant personal jurisdiction over him.

The court of appeals[66] distinguished *Keeton* in determining whether asserting personal jurisdiction over Hall would comport with "traditional notions of fair play and substantial justice:" "[s]imply giving an interview to a reporter is not enough to cause Hall to anticipate being haled into court in Florida. Hall was not the magazine's publisher and did not control its circulation and distribution; thus, he is in a qualitatively different position than the defendant in Keeton."[67]

The court also found that the other factors that determine the reasonableness of jurisdiction were not sufficient to warrant assertion of jurisdiction over the defendant. First, the forum was not convenient to either of the parties.[68] Second, Florida had little interest in adjudicating the dispute because neither party resided in the state.[69] Finally the court concluded that "neither the interstate judicial system's interest in obtaining the most efficient resolution of controversies nor the interest of the states in furthering fundamental social policies would be served by subjecting Hall to the jurisdiction of Florida courts."[70]

In *Ticketmaster-New York, Inc. v. Alioto*,[71] the plaintiff brought a defamation action in Massachusetts district court against the defendant, a California resident,

---

[63] 916 F.2d 1510 (11th Cir. 1990).

[64] *Id.* at 1513.

[65] *Id.*

[66] In the first part of the analysis the court rejected the argument that the defendant had relevant contact with Florida. Although the defendant had contact with Florida, these contacts did not relate to the tortious statement. First, he had performed in Florida a total of seven times between 1985 and 1988. Second, "[h]is musical recordings are widely distributed throughout Florida." Finally, the court of appeals found that Hall was a "partner in a partnership that itself owns limited partnership interests in partnerships that own property in Miami and Jacksonville." Based on these facts, the court of appeals concluded that "Hall did not purposefully establish minimum contacts with Florida so that he should reasonably anticipate being haled into court there." *Id.* at 1517.

[67] *Id.* at 1519.

[68] *Id.*

[69] 916 F.2d 1510, 1519 (11 Cir. 1990).

[70] *Id.*

[71] 26 F.3d 201 (1st Cir. 1994).

for statements he made during a telephone interview that were later published in a Massachusetts newspaper. The court of appeals framed the issue in terms of "whether an individual who merely answers a telephone call, but, having done, so, knowingly directs his comments into the forum state, may be said to have purposefully availed himself of the privilege of conducting activities in the state."[72] The court of appeals identified two factors as determinative in assessing purposeful availment: foreseeability and voluntariness.[73] If "the source of an allegedly defamatory remark did not initiate the pivotal contact, and the in-forum injury is not reasonably foreseeable, jurisdiction may not be asserted over the source based on the comment."[74] The court of appeals found that the defendant did not make the initial contact, but the in-forum injury was foreseeable.[75] At this point the court of appeals "evaluate[d] the fairness of assessing jurisdiction in the totality of circumstances"[76] and found that it would be fundamentally unfair to assert personal jurisdiction over the defendant.[77] The court's inquiry into the fairness of asserting personal jurisdiction focused on the Gestalt factors announced by the Supreme Court in *Burger King v. Rudzewicz*.[78] The analysis hinged on the factor regarding the burden of appearance on the defendant. The court of appeals stated that requiring "a California resident to appear in a Massachusetts court is onerous in terms of distance, and there are no mitigating factors to cushion that burdensomeness here."[79] The Court concluded that it would not be fair "on the strength of a single remark uttered in the course of a single unsolicited telephone call from a Massachusetts-based journalist, to compel a California resident to defend a tort suit in a court 3000 miles away."[80]

The touchstones of personal jurisdiction analysis drawn from print publication cases are appropriate for NII cases. An electronic publisher should be subject to personal jurisdiction in any place to which the electronic publisher intentionally sends its publication. Thus, subscription-based commercial systems like CompuServe or America Online should be subject to personal

---

[72] *Id.* at 207.

[73] *Id.*

[74] *Id.* at 208.

[75] *Id.*

[76] *Id.* at 209.

[77] 26 F.3d 210, 210 (1st Cir. 1994). A similar case in the Third Circuit adopted a different rationale. In Dion v. Kiev, 566 F. Supp. 1387 (E.D. Pa. 1983), the defendant was contacted by a *Philadelphia Inquirer* reporter and gave statements to that reporter during a telephone interview. The district court asserted personal jurisdiction over a defendant reasoning that: "the defendant was fully aware that the reporter was from the Philadelphia Inquirer and that it was a major metropolitan newspaper in Pennsylvania with a major distribution in the Philadelphia area. It was readily foreseeable to [the defendant] that his statement about plaintiff could be published in the Philadelphia area and result in harm to plaintiff." 566 F. Supp. at 1390.

[78] 471 U.S. 462 (1985). The factors are listed in footnotes in § **12.4.**

[79] Ticketmaster-N.Y., Inc. v. Alioto, 26 F.3d 201, 210 (1st Cir. 1994).

[80] *Id.* at 212.

jurisdiction in places where significant numbers of their subscribers reside. The residence of subscribers is known to these services, they derive revenue from those subscriptions, and there is little reason to distinguish between the electronic subscriber and the print subscriber. If an electronic publisher (including an individual poster) publishes a statement intended to injure someone, the publisher should be subject to personal jurisdiction in the place where the injured party is located, under the precedent represented by *Calder v. Jones,* although the Gestalt factors might be brought into play and lead to a different result, as in *Madara v. Hall.*

There are many conceivable NII cases in which publication does not support the exercise of personal jurisdiction so strongly. For example, one might post a message to a list. The list causes dissemination to all those subscribed to the list. But the poster usually has no knowledge of the extent of the list, and thus the dissemination of his posting to a particular person is usually neither purposeful nor foreseeable, unless other facts indicate specific knowledge of a particular recipient of messages posted to that list. Absent such special facts, the exercise of personal jurisdiction is not appropriate merely based on the dissemination of messages through the list. An even weaker case for the assertion of personal jurisdiction arises from placement of material on servers connected to the Internet or Internet-like open architectures. Then, the act resulting in the receipt of the message in a particular place is the act, not of the publisher, but of the retriever. Publication in these circumstances should not subject the publisher to personal jurisdiction in places where the information is retrieved, under the rationale of *Hansen v. Denckla.*[81]

§ 12.6   Service of Process

Service of process performs two functions in Anglo-American civil procedure: it represents assertion of judicial power of the forum state over the person of the defendant; and it is the formal means of providing notice to the defendant so that he may defend the lawsuit.[82] **Section 12.4** considers the power dimension of personal jurisdiction. This section considers the notice requirement of procedural due process in the civil litigation context.

---

[81] 357 U.S. 235 (1958) (unilateral acts of others cannot subject a defendant to personal jurisdiction based on minimum contacts). The only basis for personal jurisdiction would be a stream-of-commerce theory similar to the one rejected by a plurality in Asahi Metal Indus. Co. v. Superior Court, 480 U.S. 102, 111 (1987). Four justices would have recognized the stream of commerce theory. 480 U.S. at 116 (Brennan, J., concurring, joined by White, Marshall, Blackmun, J.J.).

[82] *See* Mullane v. Central Hanover Bank & Trust Co., 339 U.S. 306, 313–14 (1950) (distinguishing between service of process as means of exercising power and service of process as constitutionally sufficient means of giving notice).

In early Anglo-American procedure, a defendant subjected to personal jurisdiction was entitled to notice except for claims involving breach of the peace or
malice, in which case personal jurisdiction could be asserted by arresting the
defendant under a writ of capias ad respondendum. Even when no breach of the
peace or malice was involved, capias would issue if the defendant did not
respond to the initial notice. Real claims—those involving what later came to be
known as in rem jurisdiction—always could be commenced simply by attaching
or otherwise levying on the property itself, regardless of whether separate notice
was given to the person entitled to possession. Now, constitutional due process
entitlements prohibit significant deprivation of liberty or property interests until
notice is given. Thus capias and commencement of an action by attachment are
reserved for exigent circumstances. Exigent circumstances involve a risk that
the defendant will abscond or dispose of property before notice can be given.[83]

"Personal service of written notice within the jurisdiction is the classic form
of notice always adequate in any type of proceeding."[84] Other forms of notice
may be constitutionally adequate when reasonably calculated under the circumstances to give actual notice.[85] Of course constitutional adequacy is not enough;
the method of notice also must be authorized by some affirmative source of law
representing the service process rules of the forum. Service of process must
occur within time limits set by civil procedural rules, although extensions can be
granted by the court.[86] The growing use of digital information technologies
introduces the possibility of electronic service of process, including telex, fax,
and E-mail,[87] although these methods of service are not yet countenanced
widely.[88]

---

[83] *See* Fuentes v. Shevin, 407 U.S. 67 (1972) (prejudgment attachment unconstitutional in the
absence of exigent circumstances and safeguards for property interests of person attached);
North Ga. Finishing Co. v. DiChem, 419 U.S. 601 (1975) (invalidating prejudgment garnishment under *Fuentes*); Connecticut v. Doehr, 501 U.S. 1 (1991) (invalidating lien on real estate
imposed based on five-sentence affidavit; risk of erroneous deprivation of property interest too
great); Vermont Nat'l Bank v. Taylor, 445 A.2d 1122, 1124 (N.H. 1982) (quashing ex parte
capias procedure used to initiate civil contempt proceeding).

[84] Mullane v. Central Hanover Bank & Trust Co., 339 U.S. 306, 313 (1950).

[85] *See id;* Greene v. Lindsey, 456 U.S. 444 (1982) (invalidating service of process by posting
notice on door of low-income housing project).

[86] Petrucelli v. Bohringer & Ratzinger 46 F.3d 1298 (3d Cir. 1995) (remanding denial of extension of time to serve process and dismissal of complaint against products liability defendant;
revised Rule 4(m) mandates abuse-of-discretion standard of review, plaintiff made inexcusable
errors by relying on verbal [oral?] assurance of service of unknown person in Secretary of
State's Office, failing to inquire when notice of acknowledgment was not returned, claiming
that mailing to Texas would be fruitless, and failing to inquire whether corporation was in good
standing with Secretary of State's Office).

[87] In addition, there is the conceptual possibility that service by publication might be accomplished by electronic publication in an appropriately public forum.

[88] But see the changes to Fed. R. Civ. P. 4(d)(2)(B) adopted in 1995; Fed. R. App. P. 25(a).

Despite the practical feasibility and attractiveness of electronic service of process, authorization for electronic service is thin. On occasion, that form of service has been authorized in particular cases.[89] Some commentators have urged authorization of service by facsimile,[90] but most jurisdictions only authorize the use of facsimile for service of process after the initial service of summons and complaint.[91] Some older state rules authorize telegraphic service.[92] Fax service has the advantage that fax machines automatically produce an acknowledgment, thus providing a form of proof of service.

The federal rules authorize service of process pursuant to the law of the forum state or the law of the state in which service is effected,[93] and by the law of foreign countries in which service is to be made or under international treaty means reasonably calculated to give notice.[94] However, the explicit implications of the federal rules provide only modest possibilities for electronic service under the failure of service provisions that permit notice of the commencement of an action and a request that the defendant waive service of the summons, which can be "dispatched through first class mail or other reliable means."[95] The appellate rules permit individual courts of appeals to permit papers to be filed "by facsimile or other electronic means."[96] Few state rules permit electronic service.[97] The Federal Rules of Civil and Appellate Procedure now permit electronic service of notices for waiver of formal service.[98] A few administrative agencies are beginning to authorize electronic service.[99]

---

[89] *See* New England Merchants Nat'l Bank v. Iran Power Generation & Transmission Co., 495 F. Supp. 73, 81 (S.D.N.Y. 1980) (authorizing service on Iranian defendants in Farsi and English by telex, followed by personal service on counsel and copies by mail, under Fed. R. Civ. P. 4(i)(1)(E) as it then existed).

[90] *See* David A. Sokasits, *The Long Arm of the Fax: Service of Process Using Fax Machines,* 16 Rutgers Computer & Tech. L.J. 531 (1990).

[91] *See id.* at 547–49 & nn.93–105 (reviewing New York and Oregon roles).

[92] *Id.* at 549 & nn.106–08 (citing Idaho R. Civ. P. 4(c)(3); Mont. Code Ann. § 25-3-501; Utah R. Civ. P. 4(1)).

[93] Fed. R. Civ. P. 4(e)(1).

[94] Fed. R. Civ. P. 4(f).

[95] Fed. R. Civ. P. 4(d)(2)(B).

[96] Fed. R. App. P. 25(a) (requiring, however, that local rules be consistent with standards established by the Judicial Conference of the United States).

[97] A Westlaw search on Oct. 3, 1995, of all state statutes under "facsimile or "electronic" within the same sentence as "service of process," turned up only Va. Code Ann. § 13.1-637 (Michie 1991), permitting corporations to authorize service by fax.

[98] *See* amendments to Fed. R. Civ. P. 4(d)(2)(B); Fed. R. App. P. 25(a) advisory committee's notes.

[99] See SEC's EDGAR rules providing for service of certain notices by placing in electronic mailbox of filer, 58 Fed. Reg. 14,628, 14,655 (Mar. 8, 1993).

§ 12.7   —Model Service of Process Rule

The model rule in **Form 12–1** can be incorporated not only into the standing rules of a court or agency, but also could be incorporated into an order authorizing service by this means in a particular case.

FORM 12–1
SERVICE OF PROCESS RULE

Process may be served by facsimile on any individual by sending a copy of the summons and complaint to the facsimile machine at a number assigned to the individual. If service through this means is challenged, the electronic confirmation produced by the receiving facsimile machine shall be presumptive evidence that service was completed.

Process may be served on a corporation by sending a copy of the summons and complaint through a facsimile machine answering a telephone number assigned to the corporate headquarters or another office likely to be concerned with the general affairs of the corporation and likely to notify appropriate corporate authority of the facsimile message. Proof of service and challenges to service shall be resolved in the same manner provided for facsimile service on individuals.

Process may be served by other electronic means by sending a copy of the summons and complaint to an electronic mailbox assigned to the person or entity to be served. Service by this means is not complete unless the party serving obtains an electronic receipt indicating not only that the message was placed in the electronic mailbox, but also that it was received from that mailbox by the person to whom the mailbox was assigned. Alternatively, the person seeking service through this means may prove by other reliable extrinsic evidence that the person to be served actually retrieved the message from the mailbox.

§ 12.8   Venue

Civil actions in federal court based on diversity jurisdiction may be brought in a judicial district where any defendant resides, where a substantial part of the events or omissions giving rise to the claim occurred, or where a substantial part of the property that is the subject if the claim is situated. Or civil actions may be brought in a judicial district in which "the defendants are subject to personal jurisdiction at the time the action is commenced, if there is no district in which the action otherwise may be brought."[100] The rules for actions based on federal question jurisdiction are the same except that the catchall allows litigation in "a

---

[100] 28 U.S.C. § 1391(a).

judicial district in which any defendant may be found," as opposed to one in which the defendant is "subject to personal jurisdiction."[101] These venue rules are typical; most state rules are similar.

Reuber v. United States[102] provides some interesting guidance on venue in a case involving electronic conduct. Reuber filed a Federal Tort Claims Act (FTCA) action, for which venue is governed by 28 U.S.C. § 1402. Section 1402 authorizes venue only in the judicial district where the plaintiff resides or "wherein the act or omission complained of occurred."[103] The language limiting venue is a more restrictive version of the "in which a substantial part of the events or omissions giving rise to the claim occurred" in language from the general federal venue statute.[104] The plaintiff filed one suit in the United States District Court for the District of Columbia, and another against a codefendant in Maryland state court, which was removed to the United States District Court for the District of Maryland. The D.C. action was also transferred to Maryland.[105]

The United States claimed improper venue. The court of appeals distinguished a case involving an FTCA suit over an air traffic controller transmission from Utah to a pilot flying over Montana causing that pilot to crash.[106] It found that the radio transmission was directed specifically to the pilot in Montana and thus the situs of the act in that case could reasonably be perceived as including the place where the tortuous radio transmission was targeted and where the foreseeable harm would occur.[107] But in Reuber's case, the allegedly tortuous conduct involved disclosure and dissemination of a letter critical of him, and the court of appeals found that even though some communication occurred in Maryland, the tortuous act was complete upon the release, which occurred in the District of Columbia.

Forum non conveniens is a doctrine that permits dismissal of cases on the grounds that the venue is inconvenient. It depends on a showing that venue lies in another, more convenient place.[108] Forum non conveniens dismissals are less

---

[101] *Compare id.* § 1391(b) (federal question jurisdiction) *with id.* § 1391(a).

[102] 750 F.2d 1039 (D.C. Cir. 1985).

[103] 28 U.S.C. § 1402(b).

[104] *Compare id.* (FTCA venue) *with id.* § 1391(a) & (b) (venue for diversity jurisdiction in federal question jurisdiction cases).

[105] Reuber v. United States, 750 F.2d 1039, 1046 n.8 (D.C. Cir. 1985).

[106] *Id.* at 1047 (analyzing and distinguishing Forest v. United States, 539 F. Supp. 171 (D. Mont. 1982)).

[107] *Id.*

[108] *Compare* Piper Aircraft Co. v. Reyno, 454 U.S. 235 (1981) (approving dismissal of case brought by Scottish plaintiff as a result of air crash in Scotland) *with* Dow Chem. Co. v. Castro Alfaro, 786 S.W.2d 674 (Tex. 1990) (reversing dismissal of suit by foreign employees of American company) *and* Picketts v. International Playtex, Inc., 576 A.2d 518 (Conn. 1990) (reversing dismissal of suit by Canadian plaintiffs on forum non conveniens grounds) (video-tape depositions make it more difficult for defendant to satisfy burden of showing inconvenience). *But see* Myers v. Boeing Co., 794 P.2d 1272 (Wash. 1990) (affirming dismissal of damage claims by foreign plane crash victims); Stangvik v. Shiley, Inc., 819 P.2d 14, 1 Cal. Rptr. 2d 556 (Cal. 1991) (affirming forum non conveniens dismissal and adopting rationale of *Piper*).

common in federal than in state courts because transfer to a more convenient forum is straightforward.[109] "For the convenience of parties and witnesses, in the interest of justice, a district court may transfer any civil action to any other district or division where it might have been brought."[110] In addition, the multidistrict litigation procedure allows cases involving one or more common questions of fact pending in different districts to be consolidated for pretrial proceedings based on an application to the judicial panel on multidistrict litigation.[111] Pressure is growing to unify forum non conveniens doctrines with the closely related fair-play and substantial-justice analysis of personal jurisdiction, considered in § 12.4, and to rationalize application of venue concepts to foreign plaintiffs.[112]

Forum selection clauses are an important determinant of venue. Historically, such clauses were not favored, but in a series of cases, beginning with *Bremen v. Zapata Off-Shore Co.,*[113] the Supreme Court has been increasingly hospitable to such clauses. In *Stewart Organization, Inc. v. RICOH Corp.,*[114] the Supreme Court held that federal law rather than state law governs the enforceability of a forum selection clause in a contract within the diversity jurisdiction of the federal district court.[115] Justices Kennedy and O'Connor wrote a concurring opinion explaining that enforcement of forum selection clauses protects party expectations and furthers vital interests of the justice system, thus extending the rationale of *Bremen* to federal courts sitting in diversity.[116]

In *Carnival Cruise Lines, Inc. v. Shute,*[117] the Supreme Court made it more difficult to avoid forum selection clauses even when they are not actually negotiated but rather are contained in form contracts.[118] The Court acknowledged that forum selection clauses are subject to judicial scrutiny for fundamental

---

[109] *See* 28 U.S.C. § 1404 (district court may transfer any civil action for convenience). *But see* Creative Technology, Ltd. v. Aztech Sys. PTE, Ltd., 61 F.3d 696 (9th Cir. 1995) (affirming dismissal on forum nonconveniens grounds; copyright action brought by foreign corporation).

[110] *Id.* § 1404(a).

[111] *Id.* § 1407.

[112] *See generally* Linda J. Silberman, *Developments in Jurisdiction and Forum Non Conveniens in International Litigation: Thoughts on Reform and a Proposal for a Uniform Standard,* 28 Tex. Int'l L.J. 501 (1993) (proposing federal legislation to govern jurisdiction over alien defendants and access to U.S. courts by foreign plaintiffs).

[113] 407 U.S.1 (1972).

[114] 487 U.S. 22 (1988).

[115] *Id.* at 27–28 (concluding that federal law, 28 U.S.C. § 1404(a), governed under application of the *Erie* doctrine). In Erie R.R. v. Tomkins, 304 U.S. 64 (1938), the Supreme Court held that state law must be applied in diversity cases unless a federal statute or constitutional provision governs. *See also* Hannah v. Plumer, 380 U.S. 460 (1965) (federal law must be applied when a valid federal rule of civil procedure governs the issue).

[116] 487 U.S. 22, 33 (1988) (Kennedy, J., concurring).

[117] 499 U.S. 585 (1991) (reversing court of appeals).

[118] *Id.* at 593 (noting that contract was "purely routine and doubtless nearly identical to every commercial passage contract issued by petitioner and most other cruise lines"). "Common sense dictates that a ticket of this kind will be a form contract the terms of which are not subject to negotiation, and that an individual purchasing the ticket will not have bargaining parody with the cruise lines." *Id.*

fairness. It suggested that they are unenforceable if there is evidence of their inclusion for the purpose of discouraging parties from pursuing legitimate claims by assigning litigation to a remote and alien forum, by proof that resisting parties lacked notice of the clause, or evidence of fraud or other over reaching.[119] Nevertheless, the Court extolled the virtues of such clauses as ways of dispelling confusion about where suits for breach of contract might be brought and defended "sparing litigants the time and expense of pretrial motions to determine the correct forum and conserving judicial resources that otherwise would be devoted to deciding those motions."[120] In addition, the facts of the case made the forum designated by the clause, Florida, entirely appropriate and did not support the court of appeal's conclusion of inconvenience to the consumer.[121] Although *Carnival Cruise Lines* was an admiralty case, there is no suggestion in the opinion or its analytical underpinnings that diversity or federal question cases would be treated any differently. The presumption in favor of enforcing forum selection clauses extends to clauses in international contracts that provide for litigation in the forums of other countries.[122]

The forum selection clause cases have important implications for electronic commerce. They permit reduction of the uncertainty with respect to the place of litigation, and they also reduce uncertainty about the methods of binding the user of an electronic service to a forum selection clause. Forum selection clauses not only resolve venue issues; they also resolve personal jurisdiction issues because a valid forum selection clause constitutes consent to personal jurisdiction in the forum selected. *Carnival Cruise Lines* reduces the likelihood that a participant in electronic commerce could avoid a forum selection clause on the grounds that there was not negotiation over it. It should be enough to show that the resisting party had notice of the clause and that the forum selected by the clause was reasonable in light of the nature of the contract. The types of notice suggested in **Chapter 9** should suffice. Sample forum selection clause language is provided in § **12.15.**

§ 12.9 Enforcement of Judgments

Section 12.3 explains that personal jurisdiction, venue, choice of law, and judgment enforcement are interrelated. Thus, one should consider the analysis of judgment enforcement in this section along with the analysis of the related issues in §§ **12.2, 12.8,** and **12.11.** The NII produces few interesting problems

---

[119] *Id.* at 595.

[120] *Id.* at 594.

[121] *Id.* at 594–95.

[122] *See* Bonny v. Society of Lloyd's, 3 F.3d 156, 160–61 (7th Cir. 1993) (rejecting arguments that clause requiring litigation in English courts imposed sufficient financial hardship to justify not enforcing it, and concluding that English remedies adequately would vindicate plaintiff's substantive rights under securities laws).

when a dispute and a resulting civil judgment are entirely local; the victor—the judgment creditor—simply gets a writ of execution under local procedure and has the sheriff levy on such personal or real property of the judgment debtor as can be found.[123] The problems of turning a judgment into liquid assets become more difficult when the judgment comes from another state or from another country. Thus, a plaintiff may have obtained a judgment against an Internet service provider in an Alabama circuit court but may find assets worthy of executing against only in Virginia. Execution thus must be sought in a Virginia court based on the "foreign judgment" from Alabama. Or, an author in Sweden may obtain a judgment in a Swedish court for copyright infringement resulting from an act by the operator of an Internet server in Massachusetts. In order to obtain monetary relief, the victim must enforce the Swedish judgment against assets held by the server operator in Massachusetts.

In both of these situations, the first step conceptually is to obtain recognition of the judgment. When the foreign judgment is from another American state, the full faith and credit clause of the United States Constitution obligates the enforcing state to recognize it. When the foreign judgment is from another country, either state statutory law, the Uniform Foreign Money Judgments Recognition Act in about half the states,[124] or comity[125] prescribes the criteria for recognition. Basically, these sources of law require recognition unless the party opposing recognition can show violations of procedural due process, lack of personal jurisdiction by the rendering court,[126] or in rare instances, violations of public policy in the recognition state.[127]

Regardless of the path to recognition, the effect and scope of a judgment afforded recognition is determined by concepts of preclusion (res judicata and collateral estoppel) under the preclusion law of the rendering state. Thus, discrete decisions on fact or law issues may have collateral estoppel effect, depending on the rules of issue preclusion of the rendering state. Transactionally related claims that might have been brought in the foreign lawsuit may be foreclosed by res judicata, depending on the claim preclusion rules of the rendering state.[128]

---

[123] *See* Fed. R. Civ. P. 69 (incorporating state judgment execution procedure); Ill. R. Civ. P. art. 12 (West 1995) (enforcing judgments); Iowa R. Civ. P. div. X (West 1995) (same); Kan. R. Civ. P. art. 24 (West 1995) (executions and order of sale).

[124] Uniform Foreign Money Judgments Recognition Act, 13 U.L.A. 261 (1962).

[125] *See* de la Mata v. American Life Ins. Co., 771 F. Supp. 1375 (D. Del. 1991).

[126] 15 Joseph Story, Commentaries on the Conflict of Laws § 586, at 978 (4th ed. 1852) (universally accepted that foreign judgment not supported by jurisdiction is treated as a mere nullity, entitled to no respect). The personal jurisdiction and procedural due process standards are essentially American in character.

[127] *See* Matusevitch v. Telnikoff, 877 F. Supp. 1 (D.D.C. 1995) (declining to recognize and enforce British libel judgment under Maryland's Uniform Foreign Money Judgments Recognition Act because British libel law lacked constitutional protections applied in United States).

[128] Authority for collateral estoppel and res judicate effect of recognized judgment being determined by preclusion law of rendering state.

If the foreign judgment is recognized, then it must be enforced as a procedural matter. This occurs either under a state statute like the Uniform Enforcement of Foreign Judgments Act,[129] or by bringing a new lawsuit in the state of enforcement on the debt represented by the recognized foreign judgment.[130] The Uniform Enforcement Act allows the judgment creditor simply to file the foreign judgment with the clerk and obtain a writ of execution. The new-lawsuit approach results in a new judgment that supports a writ of execution. The Brussels Convention, binding members of the European Union, provides for summary enforcement of covered foreign judgments under procedures similar to those of the Uniform Enforcement Act.[131] Recognition and enforcement are not two separate proceedings. Rather, recognition is a substantive decision within the enforcement proceeding.[132]

The other interesting judgment execution question in the NII context is what assets are subject to execution. Clearly, hardware and computer programs are subject to execution. But what about software as to which the judgment debtor has only a license? And what about obligations owing to the judgment creditor. How feasible is garnishment when these obligations run from persons all over the world?

When a judgment debtor has a license on software, execution could include obtaining rights to any income from the license or possibly transferring the license from the judgment debtor. Garnishment of obligations from persons around the world may not be feasible because the garnishee is not within the physical reach of execution process, and foreign garnishment would be too time-consuming. Writs of garnishment against local debtors of the judgment debtor, however, would be attractive and entirely practicable.

§ 12.10   —Geographic Scope of Injunctions

The ineffectiveness of territorial limitations on the law of electronic communications invites consideration of the geographic scope of an injunction. Suppose a court in jurisdiction A issues a valid injunction against C1, prohibiting certain exchanges of files through the Internet. As long as C1 remains within

---

[129] 13 U.L.A. 152 (1964).

[130] In such a lawsuit, the plaintiff should be entitled to summary judgment based on recognition of the foreign judgment.

[131] Paul R. Beaumont, Anton & Beaumont's Civil Jurisdiction in Scotland §§ 1.28–1.30, at 14–16 (1995) (overview of convention's summary enforcement procedures).

[132] See Don Docksteader Motors, Ltd. v. Patal Enters., Ltd., 794 S.W.2d 760, 760 (Tex. 1990) (constitutional entitlement to challenge recognition within the judgment enforcement process; Texas version of uniform recognition act met requirements). If a new lawsuit is brought on the debt represented by a foreign judgment, the recognition issue would arise in adjudication of the plaintiff's summary judgment motion. If recognition is denied, of course, the plaintiff would have to retry the merits.

the jurisdiction, its noncompliance may be punished by contempt.[133] But suppose C1 leaves the jurisdiction and violates the terms of the order elsewhere? Or suppose C2 who has never been inside the jurisdiction cooperates with C1 to violate the order? What power does the court issuing the injunction then have to punish either C1 or C2?

The answers are clear when a federal court has issued the injunction. By being served with process and participating in the lawsuit giving rise to the injunction, C1 is subject to the enforcement jurisdiction of the issuing court wherever he goes, anywhere in the country. "The decree . . . bound the respondent personally. It was a decree which operated continuously and perpetually upon the respondent in relation to the prohibited conduct. The decree was binding upon the respondent, not simply within the district of Massachusetts, but throughout the United States."[134]

The second question is whether a nonparty to the original proceeding who remains outside the district in which the injunction is issued can nevertheless be punished by contempt for aiding and abetting a named party in violating the injunction. The United States Court of Appeals for the Fifth Circuit answered this question in the affirmative in *Waffenschmidt v. McKay,* a securities fraud case.[135] The district court issued a TRO and preliminary injunction against McKay, ordering him not to transfer the proceeds of an alleged security fraud. McKay nevertheless transferred money to three persons in Texas. The court issuing the injunction and McKay were located in the northern district of Mississippi. When the Texas actors were confronted with contempt orders, they challenged the jurisdiction of the district court. The district court held, and the court of appeals agreed, that the mandate of an injunction issued by a federal court runs nationwide,[136] that enforcement through a contempt proceeding must

---

[133] The steps in civil contempt are the service of a notice of contempt, a hearing in which the court makes a factual determination whether contempt is occurring, issuance of a contempt order in which sanctions for further noncompliance are specified, and reduction of the sanctions to judgment if further noncompliance occurs. The steps in criminal contempt are the issuance of a notice, the opportunity for bail if arrest occurs, a hearing at which criminal standards of proof apply, and a conviction or acquittal.

[134] Lehman v. Krentler-Arnold Hinge Last Co., 284 U.S. 448, 451 (1932) (reversing court of appeals and reinstating contempt order of district court against defendant in patent infringement suit who engaged in violation of Massachusetts injunction in Michigan after participating in lawsuit in Massachusetts); *see* Messner, *The Jurisdiction of a Court of Equity Over Persons to Compel the Doing of Acts Outside the Territorial Limits of the State,* 14 Minn. L. Rev. 494, 514–29 (1930) (citing cases and other authority); Phelps v. McDonald, 99 U.S. 298, 308 (1878) (when necessary parties are before a court of equity, immaterial that res of controversy is beyond territorial jurisdiction of tribunal); French v. Hay, 89 U.S. (22 Wall.) 231 (1874) (court with in personam jurisdiction has power to require defendants to act outside limits of territorial jurisdiction). *But see* People v. Central R.R., 42 N.Y. 283 (1870) (New York court lacks jurisdiction to order abatement of nuisance in New Jersey).

[135] 763 F.2d 711 (5th Cir. 1985).

[136] *Id.* at 716.

occur in the issuing jurisdiction "because contempt is an affront to the court issuing the order,"[137] that the issuing court may "therefore hold an enjoined party in contempt, regardless of the state in which the person violates the court's orders,"[138] that an injunction binds not only the parties named therein but also nonparties who act with the enjoined party,[139] and therefore that "the nationwide scope of an injunction carries with it the concomitant [nation-wide] power of the court to reach out to nonparties who knowingly violate its orders."[140] The court of appeals thought defendant McKay's actions a paradigm of how a named defendant can enlist the assistance of out-of-state persons to frustrate an injunction.[141]

The court found no problem with personal jurisdiction, concluding first that the acts of aiding and abetting placed the actors within the personal jurisdiction of the district court.[142] The due process requirements of *International Shoe* were not violated because a district court has inherent power to enforce its orders, and the purposefulness contacts requirements of *International Shoe* and *Worldwide Volkswagen* were satisfied by the intentional assistance given the named enjoined party.[143]

That left the problem of service of process under Federal Rule of Civil Procedure 4, as it then existed. Because then Rule 4(f) and (e) allowed extra-territorial service of process when permitted by state law, and Mississippi allowed service on nonresidents committing acts outside the state with foresee-able effects resulting within the state, service of the injunction on the Texas actors was permissible.[144] Subsequently, the federal rules were amended to add Rule 4.1:

> an order of civil commitment of a person held to be in contempt of a decree or injunction issued to enforce the laws of the United States may be served and enforced in any district. Other orders in civil contempt proceedings shall be served in the state in which the court issuing the order to be enforced is located or elsewhere within the United States if not more than 100 miles from place at which the order to be enforced was issued.[145]

The Advisory Committee notes make it clear that nationwide service of con-tempt papers is contemplated only when the injunction enforces federal law. For

---

[137] *Id.*

[138] *Id.* (citing *Lehman,* 284 U.S. 448 (1932)). This is the circumstance of defendant C1 in the textual hypothetical.

[139] 763 F.2d at 717; *see* Fed R. Civ. P. 65(d).

[140] 763 F.2d at 717 (citing *In re* Lennon, 166 U.S. 548, 555 (1897); Alemite Mfg. Corp. v. Staff, 42 F.2d 832 (2d Cir. 1930)).

[141] *Id.*

[142] *Id.* at 718.

[143] *Id.* at 723; *see* § **12.4.**

[144] 763 F.2d at 720.

[145] Fed. R. Civ. P. 4.1(b).

injunctions that enforce state law, the more limited 100-mile rule applies. Rule 4.1 was intended to conform civil contempt service to the service permissible for criminal contempt. 28 U.S.C. § 3041 permits criminal contempt enforcement against a contemner wherever the contemner may be found.[146]

Thus, service of contempt papers from federal court no longer depend on state service of process rules unless it is state law that is being enforced. It is important, however, to recognize that the rationale of *Waffenschmidt* extends only to nonparties who knowingly aid and abet a named enjoined party. The court of appeals extensively reviewed the evidence supporting knowledge and complicity on the part of the Texas actors.[147]

Moreover, a federal court lacks the power to enforce an injunction against an out-of-district person who is not subjected to the personal jurisdiction of the court. Thus, a plaintiff in Massachusetts could not enforce an injunction against someone in Oregon simply by naming the Oregon party in a complaint and the injunction without ever bothering to obtain personal jurisdiction over the Oregon party. An issuing court does not automatically acquire personal jurisdiction over anyone who may be helpful to the enforcement of the injunction. In *Lynch v. Rank*,[148] the district court distinguished *Waffenschmidt* and held that it did not have personal jurisdiction over an Oregon welfare official sufficient to hold him in contempt for failing to effectuate an injunction issued in a nation-wide class action relating to Social Security benefits. The district court quoted Judge Learned Hand for the general rule: "No court can make a decree which will bind anyone but a party; a court of equity is as much so limited as a court of law; it cannot lawfully enjoin the world at large, no matter how broadly it words its decree."[149] The court found the Oregon official outside its personal jurisdiction based on the minimum contacts framework of *International Shoe* because the Oregon official lacked the commonality of incentives and motivations with named defendants necessary to find that they were acting in concert or participating with each other.[150] It thought the facts of *Waffenschmidt*, showing a common scheme to launder illegally obtained proceeds, entirely distinct.[151]

Another district court in *Reebok International, Ltd. v. McLaughlin*,[152] aligned itself with *Waffenschmidt* and distinguished *Lynch*, finding that a bank in Luxembourg could be held in contempt for releasing funds within the scope of an earlier-issued injunction. The court noted that "the basis of personal jurisdiction, if it exists, evolves out of the allegations that make out the contempt."[153]

---

[146] Fed. R. Civ. P. 4.1 advisory committee's notes.

[147] *See* Waffenschmidt v. McKay, 763 F.2d 711, 723–27 (5th Cir. 1985).

[148] 639 F. Supp. 69 (N.D. Cal. 1985).

[149] *Id.* at 72 (quoting Alemite Mfg. Corp. v. Staff, 42 F.2d 832 (2d Cir. 1930)).

[150] *Id.* at 71–72.

[151] Id. at 74 (distinguishing facts of Waffenschmidt v. McKay, 763 F.2d 711 (5th Cir. 1985)).

[152] 827 F. Supp. 622 (S.D. Cal. 1993).

[153] *Id.* at 624 n.1.

The court of appeals reversed.[154] It accepted the district court's analytical framework, applying the specific jurisdiction branch of *International Shoe's* tests for personal jurisdiction.[155] It found, however, that the district court's reliance on *Waffenschmidt* was misplaced, because *Waffenschmidt* logically built on the nationwide jurisdiction of federal courts.[156] The court of appeals thought that the analysis "begins to crumble when a district court seeks to reach out across the Atlantic in an attempt to impose conflicting duties on another country's nationals within its own borders.[157] Because the TRO had not been registered in Luxembourg—apparently because the Luxembourg courts thought it did not qualify as a judgment or a claim that was certain and due—it was not an enforceable order in Luxembourg.[158] Thus, conduct by the Luxembourg bank inconsistent with the terms of the order could not be contempt. Because it had not engaged in contempt, it could not be said that it purposefully directed its activities toward the United States.[159] From a policy perspective, the court of appeals reasoned, "We do not agree that when a national of a foreign country follows the law of that country in that country it can be dragged half way around the world to answer contempt charges arising out of a foreign court's ineffective order."[160]

The reasoning of *Waffenschmidt* remains intact for enforcement of injunctions throughout the United States: conscious aiding and abetting can constitute the purposeful contact with the forum state necessary to satisfy the requirements of *International Shoe*. The Ninth Circuit *Reebok* opinion also leaves open the possibility that if an American injunction is appropriately registered in a foreign country or otherwise attains legal status in that country, violation of that injunction might create personal jurisdiction in the American court issuing the injunction under the theory of *Waffenschmidt*. The problem in *Reebok* was that the injunction never attained that status in the foreign country.

On the other hand, as to persons already parties, or when TROs are issued ex parte, or as to persons expected to act in concert with parties, what counts is notice and not the formalities of service.[161]

---

[154] Reebok Int'l, Ltd. v. McLaughlin, 49 F.3d 1387 (9th Cir. 1995).

[155] *Id.* at 1391–92. See § **12.4.**

[156] 49 F.3d 1387, 1391–92 (9th Cir. 1995).

[157] *Id.* at 1392–93 (citing Restatement (Third) of the Foreign Relations Law of the United States § 441(1)(a)).

[158] *Id.*

[159] *Id.* at 1394.

[160] *Id.* at 1393. Accord, Kilbarr Corp. v. Business Systems Inc., 990 F.2d 83 (3d Cir. 1993) (reviewing history of case involving contempt penalties against foreign bankruptcy trustee).

[161] SEC v. Current Fin. Servs., Inc., 798 F. Supp. 802, 806 n.11 (D.D.C. 1992) (notice to parties is presumed; must prove notice, but not formal service, on nonparties); *see also* United States v. Hochschild, 977 F.2d 208, 212 (6th Cir. 1992) (actual notice avoids need for formal service of process for civil contempt, acknowledging I.A.M. Nat'l Pension Fund v. Wakefield Indus., Inc., 699 F.2d 1254, 1260 (D.C. Cir. 1983) (mail service of contempt motion on nonparty insufficient), to the contrary); Environmental Defense Fund, Inc. v. Environmental Protection

In the international context, the same principles apply. A person originally within the personal jurisdiction of the issuing court is bound by an injunction wherever in the world she may go. A person not originally within the personal jurisdiction of the court or not named as a party and served with process may fall within the personal jurisdiction of a court issuing an injunction by aiding and abetting a named party's violation of an injunction. The difficulty in both of these situations would be practical enforcement of the injunction extraterritorially. Judgment recognition statutes generally exclude equitable remedies,[162] and thus it is unlikely that a foreign jurisdiction would make its courts and judicial officers available to enforce an American injunction. Thus, incarceration is not likely to be available as a contempt penalty. Nevertheless, monetary penalties could be enforced against assets of the contemner located in the United States. In addition, civil contempt penalties could be reduced to judgment in the United States. Then the resulting money judgment could be subjected to recognition and enforcement in other countries that recognize American money judgments, although the moving party likely would be confronted with an argument that such a judgment represents a penal sanction and thus is outside the scope of both treaty-based and comity-based international judgment recognition.[163]

§ 12.11 Choice of Law

As §§ 12.2 and 12.3 explain, choice of law is related to personal jurisdiction, venue, and enforcement of judgments. Nevertheless, it is a distinct inquiry. A forum may have personal jurisdiction and venue and nevertheless be obligated by its choice of law rules, perhaps reinforced by the constitution, to apply the substantive law of another jurisdiction. Historically, choice of law was driven by formal rules such as *lex locus contractu,* which required the forum to apply the substantive law of the place of contracting to a contracts dispute, and *lex locus delicti,* which obligated the forum to apply the substantive law of the place of the wrong to a tort claim.

Although these rules were applied by American courts virtually universally, they had their origin in seventeenth and eighteenth century private international law, which adapted itself well to the American federal system with the states

---

Agency, 485 F.2d 780, 784 & n.2 (D.C. Cir. 1973) (nonparties with actual notice bound by temporary restraining order even though not formally served; citing early cases); Select Creations, Inc. v. Paliafito Am., Inc., 852 F. Supp. 740, 778–80 (E.D. Wis. 1994) (reviewing *Reebok* and other, earlier, cases and holding that nonparty may be subjected to contempt as an aider or abettor only when that party has notice of injunction and notice that acting in concert with certain persons would subject them to contempt proceedings, but need not have formal service; evidence showed lack of notice, thus no contempt permissible because jurisdiction lacking); Fed. R. Civ. P. 4.1 advisory committee notes (service of process not required to notify party of decree, injunction, or show cause order for contempt).

[162] See § 12.9.

[163] *Id.*

as independent sovereigns.[164] Joseph Story's 1834 treatise on conflict of laws was the first effort to synthesize conflicts of laws, and his preface notes the importance of the subject for trade between foreign states and between the different states of the American union. It also noted that much of the learning on the subject derived from the work of continental European civil law commentators.[165]

Despite their unambiguous expression, the traditional rules required considerable interpretation. For example, the place of contracting might be the place of making a contract, or it might be the place of performance.[166] The place of wrong in a tort claim might be the place where the defendant acted, or the place where the injury occurred.[167] By the latter third of the twentieth century, most courts and commentators agreed on a more flexible "interests analysis" approach to resolving choice of law questions. In many cases the traditional rule produces the same results as the interest analysis.[168]

The analysis for tort claims—such as an NII defamation claim—requires determining the state with the most significant relationship to the occurrence and the parties. This includes consideration of the place where the injury occurred; the place where the conduct causing the injury occurred; the domicile, residence, nationality, place of incorporation and place of business of the parties; and the place where any relationship between the parties is centered.[169] Contracts cases are adjudicated according to the law chosen by the parties or, in the absence of any such chosen law, by the law of the state that has the most significant relationship to the transactions and the parties with respect to a

---

[164] See A.E. Anton & Paul R. Beaumont, Private International Law 12 (2d ed. 1990) (noting utility of well-developed American choice-of-law doctrine as a basis for private international law, because issues are the same).

[165] 15 Joseph Story, Commentaries on the Conflict of Laws (4th ed. 1852).

[166] Id. § 233, at 353–55 (explaining differing views on whether the place of making or the place of execution should govern a contract).

[167] Joseph Story put lex locus delicti this way:

> the doctrine of the common law is so fully established on this point, that it would be useless to do more than to state the universal principle, which it has promulgated; that is to say, that in regard to the merits and rights involved in actions, the law of the place where they originated, is to govern ... but the forms of remedies and the order of judicial proceedings are to be according to the law of the place where the action is instituted, without any regard to the domicile of the parties, the origin of the right, or the country of the act.

Id. § 558, at 934.

[168] See Levine v. CNP Publications, Inc., 738 F.2d 660, 667 (5th Cir. 1984) (Restatement § 150(2) law of plaintiff's domicile usually governs defamation actions; most significant relationship test leads to same conclusion on facts); Laxalt v. C.K. McCatchy, 116 F.R.D. 438, 449–51 (D. Nev. 1987) (opinion on motion to disclose; Nevada shield law applied both under traditional place of wrong and under interest analysis because virtually entire distribution occurred in Nevada and no printing occurred in California).

[169] Restatement (Second) of Conflict of Laws § 145 (1971).

particular issue.[170] The most significant relationship is determined based on the place of contracting; the place of negotiation of the contract; the place of performance; the location of the subject matter of the contract; and the domicile, residence, nationality, place of incorporation and place of business of the parties.[171] "If the place of negotiating the contract and the place of performance are in the same state, the local law of this state will usually be applied."[172]

There are limitations on choice of law by the parties. The general rule is that their choice will govern "if the particular issue is one which the parties could have resolved by an explicit provision in their agreement directed to that issue."[173] In other words, if the parties could explicitly provide detailed ground rules for determining whether performance met the requirements of the contract, they could choose the law of a state to decide whether performance was sufficient. Even if they could not have explicitly governed the issue, they could choose law unless the chosen state has no reasonable relationship to the parties or the transaction and there is no other reasonable basis for the parties' choice, or if application of the law of the chosen state would contravene a fundamental public policy of a state that has a materially greater interest in determination of the particular issue.[174] Despite one of the limitations of the traditional formulation, the *Restatement* specifically contemplates the possibility of parties' choice of the law of a jurisdiction well known to them even though that state has no relationship to the contract:

> When contracting in countries whose legal systems are strange to them as well as relatively immature, the parties should be able to choose a law on the ground that they know it well and that it is sufficiently developed. For only in this way could they be sure of knowing accurately the extent of their rights and duties under the contract.[175]

The language of the *Restatement* apparently contemplates that the only law eligible for choosing is law of a particular state,[176] thus excluding the possibility of the parties choosing general legal principles such as those Unidroit (see **Chapter 14**) or lex mercatoria (see **§ 12.12**).

Constitutional due process requirements constrain choice of law to some extent, but Supreme Court jurisprudence on the relationship between due process and choice of law is in an uncertain state. In *Sun Oil Co. v. Wortman*,[177] five justices

---

[170] *Id.* § 186 (1971) (general rule); *id.* § 187 (law of the state chosen by the parties); *id.* § 188 (law governing in absence of effective choice by the parties).

[171] *Id.* § 188 (1971).

[172] *Id.* § 188(3).

[173] Restatement (Second) of Conflict of Laws § 187(1) (1971).

[174] *Id.* § 187(2).

[175] *Id.* § 187 cmt. f.

[176] *Id.* § 187(1) says, "the law of the state chosen by the parties".

[177] 486 U.S. 717 (1988).

agreed on the soundness of the doctrine that the Constitution does not bar application of the forum state statute of limitations to claims that in their substance are governed by the law of a different state.[178] The full faith and credit clause does not compel a state to substitute the statute of another state for its own statutes dealing with a subject matter concerning which it is competent to legislate.[179]

Procedural rules of its courts are matters on which a state is competent to legislate. Thus, a state may apply its own procedural rules to actions litigated in its courts. A statute of limitations is procedural; therefore, a state court may apply its own statute of limitations.[180] The issue on which controversy exists is whether a statute of limitations should be considered procedural for this purpose.[181] The early cases, looking to international law, uniformly held that the forum statute of limitations governed.[182] The majority rejected the argument that *Guaranty Trust v. New York*,[183] treating statute of limitations as substantive for *Erie* purposes, should govern.[184] Because of long-standing tradition under the full faith and credit clause, a due process challenge similarly must fail.[185] Justice Brennan reached the same result through interest analysis:

> [g]iven the complex of interests underlying statutes of limitations, I conclude that the contact a State has with a claim simply by virtue of being the forum creates a sufficient procedural interest to make the application of its limitations period to wholly out-of-state claims consistent with the Full Faith and Credit Clause. This is clearest when the forum State's limitations period is shorter than that of the claim State.[186]

On the other hand, when, as in the case before him, the forum state's limitation period was longer, the interests of the forum state were less clear. Because the various choice of law arguments were fairly balanced and somewhat ambiguous, Justice Brennan concluded that the Constitution permitted the choice that the forum state made to apply its own limitations period.[187] The balance of the case involved disagreement over whether Kansas correctly interpreted the substantive laws of Texas, Oklahoma, and Louisiana.[188]

---

[178] *Id.* at 722.

[179] *Id.* (quoting Pacific Employers Ins. Co. v. Industrial Accident Comm'n, 306 U.S. 493, 501 (1939)).

[180] *Id.*

[181] *Id.* at 722–23.

[182] *Id.* at 724–25.

[183] 326 U.S. 99 (1945).

[184] 486 U.S. 717, 726–27 (1988).

[185] *Id.* at 729–30.

[186] *Id.* at 737.

[187] *Id.* at 739. Justice Brennan essentially disagreed with the majority reliance on long-established constitutional tradition. *Id.* at 740.

[188] *Compare* 486 U.S. at 730–34 (majority; explaining why law of all four states permitted conclusion drawn) *with* 486 U.S. at 743–44 (O'Connor, J., dissenting in material part) (explaining why Kansas misconstrued laws of other states).

Three years earlier, in *Phillips Petroleum Co. v. Shutts,*[189] the U.S. Supreme Court reviewed a case in which the Kansas courts applied Kansas law to a class action, notwithstanding that over 99 percent of the gas leases involved in the case and 97 percent of the plaintiffs had no connection with the state of Kansas except for the lawsuit.[190] The Court began by noting that in *Allstate Insurance Co. v. Hague,*[191] a plurality recognized that the due process clause and the full faith and credit clause provide only modest restrictions on the application of forum law: "for a state's substantive law to be selected in a constitutionally permissible manner, that state must have a significant contact or significant aggregation of contacts, creating state interest, so much that choice of its law is neither arbitrary nor fundamentally unfair."[192] Applying this standard, the Court thought the fact that the defendant owned property and conducted substantial business in the state, and the fact that none of the plaintiffs had opted out of the class action both too tenuous to support application of Kansas law. Fairness, it held, depends importantly on expectations of the parties, and "there is no indication that when the leases involving land and royalty owners outside of Kansas were executed, the parties had any idea that Kansas law would control."[193] It declined the Kansas Supreme Court's suggestion that more relaxed standards should apply to nationwide class actions.[194] Justice Stevens would have affirmed because he saw no real conflict among the laws of the various states having significant contact.[195]

Because NII transactions frequently permit actor, intermediary, and victim to be widely separated geographically, interest analysis requires careful scrutiny of the technology and the facts of a particular transaction. Consider a hypothetical situation in which an Internet server in California makes available material that users in Tennessee find offensive. In a lawsuit filed by the Tennessee users against the California server operator, for example, for intentional infliction of emotional distress, the choice of law question would be whether Tennessee or California law should apply. Assuming there is a difference between the substantive law of the intentional infliction tort in the two states, Tennessee may have the most significant interests. It seeks to protect its residents against extreme emotional distress intentionally inflicted by others. California, of course, also has interests: seeing its citizens free to publish material that would

---

[189] 472 U.S. 797 (1985).

[190] *Id.* at 815–16 (characterizing contacts).

[191] *Id.* at 818 (citing Allstate Ins. Co. v. Hague, 449 U.S. 302 (1981) (declining to invalidate choice of law on constitutional grounds)).

[192] *Id.* (quoting Allstate Ins. Co. v. Hague, 449 U.S. at 312–13). This is a summary of the requirements for jurisdiction to prescribe.

[193] *Id.* at 823.

[194] *Id.* at 820–21.

[195] 472 U.S. at 823–24, 834 (questionable construction by forum of the laws of the sister state is not violation of full faith and credit clause).

not under California standards be tortious. But under the Supreme Court's tests, there would be sufficient Tennessee interest to allow the application of Tennessee law and the refusal of a Tennessee court to apply California law.

Cases involving defamation claims against interstate publishers offer some analogies to NII activities.[196] The rule that the most significant interest is where the sting was felt usually leads to application of the law of the domicile of the plaintiff in defamation cases.[197] Many courts apply a nine-factor test in defamation cases involving more than one state:

1. State of plaintiff's domicile
2. State of plaintiff's principal activity to which the defamation relates
3. State where plaintiff suffered greatest harm
4. State of publisher's domicile or incorporation
5. State where defendant's main publishing office is located
6. State of principal circulation
7. State of emanation
8. State where libel was first seen
9. State of forum.[198]

Hoffman v. Roberto[199] involved a defamation claim arising from union officials' statements in telex messages sent to various states claiming that the plaintiff diverted funds of an employer. Because of the multiple states of publication, the district court looked to the place of conduct, the residences or

---

[196] Jean v. Dugan, 20 F.3d 255, 261 (7th Cir. 1994) (affirming district court choice of Indiana law; Indiana had the most significant contacts to defamation; reputational injury occurred in Indiana although publication occurred both in Indiana and Illinois; defamatory article originated in Illinois); Vineland v. Hurst Corp., 862 F. Supp. 622, 627 (Mass. 1994) (Massachusetts had most significant relationship to defamation claim based on broadcast that originated in Massachusetts and was shown in Massachusetts and surrounding states; plaintiff apparently lived in Texas); *but see* Chevalier v. Animal Rehabilitation Ctr., Inc., 839 F. Supp. 1224, 1229 (N.D. Tex. 1993) (place of injury deemphasized in multistate defamation cases under Restatement (Second) of Conflicts of Laws § 145 cmt. e (1971); party relationship centered in Texas, Texas was place of injury, many defendants resided in Texas and others injected themselves into Texas activities, and most conduct occurred in Texas, Texas has most significant relationships).

[197] Buckley v. McGraw-Hill, Inc., 782 F. Supp. 1042, 1047 (W.D. Pa. 1991) (ordinarily law of domicile of plaintiff represents most significant contacts with defamation claim, but stipulation by parties that New York law should be applied was honored because New York also had interest in dispute).

[198] Zerman v. Sullivan & Cromwell, 677 F. Supp. 1316, 1318–19 (S.D.N.Y. 1988) (enumerating nine factors and determining that none of them usually overshadowed contacts in state of plaintiff's domicile).

[199] 578 N.E.2d 701 (Ind. Ct. App. 1991) (affirming dismissal of lawsuit by president of corporation against union).

places of business of the parties, and the place where the relationship was centered.[200] Because none of those inquiries was determinative, it concluded that Michigan law, where the employment relationship was centered, should be applied.[201] Privilege is determined by the law of state with the most significant contacts.[202]

The defamation choice of law cases mean that the likelihood is great that the law of the place where the injured plaintiff is domiciled will govern defamation actions arising in the NII. Invasion of privacy claims, like defamation claims, are centered where the plaintiff lives and conducts her affairs because that is where the privacy interest exists. The same thing is true of emotional distress claims. The same result is appropriate for intellectual property infringement actions,[203] unless the party arguing for the choice of different law can show that adversely affected markets are located somewhere else. Intellectual property claims primarily involve injuries to markets, and where the markets are located should drive the interest analysis.

§ 12.12 —Adoption of Specialized Legal Principles for the NII

Choice of law includes more possibilities than the law of different states or nations; increasingly, contracting parties, litigants, and courts recognize that other, private, bodies of law are worthy of consideration in choice of law analysis. This is particularly true in international arbitration. Regardless of the degree of self-governance allowed private institutions within the NII,[204] legal disputes arising in the NII almost certainly will involve specialized substantive legal principles.

There are a variety of ways in which these principles can be brought to bear in cases decided by arbitrators and judges. Perhaps the most general way is through *lex mercatoria*.[205] The lex mercatoria (the Law Merchant) has its roots

---

[200] *Id.* at 705.

[201] *Id.* at 705–06. Actually, the first two factors were indeterminative; the third factor, where the relationship was centered, was determinative.

[202] Washington Nat'l Ins. Co. v. Administrators, 2 F.3d 192, 195–96 (7th Cir. 1993) (Easterbrook, J.) ("sting" of defamation was felt in Iowa and thus Iowa law determined privilege of Illinois defendant).

[203] Of course choice of law is less important in patent and copyright claims because federal law applies. It may be important, however, in trademark, unfair competition and trade secrets claims.

[204] See **Ch. 7.**

[205] *See* Okezie Chukwumerije, Choice of Law in International Commercial Arbitration 110–14 (1994) [hereinafter Chukwumerije] (evolution of lex mercatoria from middle ages to the present).

in the fourteenth and fifteenth centuries in Europe, representing the customary law of the trade fair. In recent years, after a period of diminished legitimacy,[206] lex mercatoria has again become attractive as a body of general commercial law to be applied to international disputes, especially in disputes heard by arbitrators.[207] Despite the lower probability that lex mercatoria explicitly would be applied by an American court hearing a purely domestic dispute or by an arbitrator hearing a purely domestic dispute, the doctrine illustrates generally the variety of sources of customary law, including treaties, at least when they have been ratified by most nations; model statutes, at least when they have been widely adopted by legislatures; and standards of good practice adopted by trade bodies.[208] Beyond that, expert testimony can flesh out what the custom actually is.

Thus, lex mercatoria is not conceptually all that different from the use of trade custom to interpret contract provisions. Uniform Commercial Code § 1-103 specifically allows the use of trade custom and the law merchant to interpret commercial contracts. Lex mercatoria also is recognized as a source of commercial law transcending narrower national concepts.[209] It is well recognized that almost any legal text requires some interpretation when it is being applied, and that extrinsic evidence is useful in the interpretation process.

For those interested in developing specialized rules for the NII, much can be done by getting interested persons together and writing model statutes and codes of good practice. Existing mechanisms like the Commissioners on Uniform State Laws can be used, or ad hoc forums can be assembled. Such efforts must, however, manage a variety of tensions successfully if they are to influence dispute resolution. First, the broader the scope of the group that agrees to a set

---

[206] There are both English and American cases that limit lex mercatoria. *See* National Metropolitan Bank v. United States, 323 U.S. 454 (1945) (federal statutes supersede law of merchant); Manhattan Co. v. Morgan, 150 N.E. 594 (N.Y. 1926) (applicable statutes for negotiable instruments override the law of merchants); Pan Atl. Ins. Co. Ltd. v. Pine Top Ins. Co. Ltd., 3 All E.R. 581 (H.L. 1994) (stating 1906 statute supplants law of merchants); Container Transport Int'l, Inc. v. Oceanus Mut. Underwriting Ass'n, [1984] 1 Lloyd's Rep. 476 (C.A.) (statutes may supersede law of merchants).

[207] Chukwumerije at 114–15.

[208] *Id.* at 112–13 (explaining sources of customs, usages, and uniform law of international trade).

[209] One of the best examples is Alaska Textile Co. v. Chase Manhattan Bank, 982 F.2d 813, 816 (2d Cir. 1992), in which the court of appeals explained the concept of a letter of credit and its origins in the lex mercatoria as internalized into English common law by Lord Mansfield. The relations between the beneficiary and issuer of letters of credit are to be determined largely by lex mercatoria as expressed in the "uniform customs and practices for documentary credits (UCP) even though it is not "law." *See also* Pribus v. Bush, 173 Cal. Rptr. 747, 749 (Ct. App. 1981) (relying on the law merchant to fill in gaps in the UCC as to whether an endorsement of a promissory note effectuated on a separate piece of paper was effective to negotiate the note); 173 Cal. Rptr. at 749 n.5 (reviewing history and role of lex mercatoria or common law of merchants); Mirabile v. Udoh, 399 N.Y.S.2d 869, 870–71 (Civ. Ct. 1977) (relying on lex mercatoria to enforce payment of money order by issuing bank even though payment had been stopped and maker's money refunded).

of rules or principles, the more influential the rules or principles are likely to be. But the broader the group, the more difficult forming consensus will be. Second, the more specific the rules or policies, the more likely they will be outcome determinative. Yet the more specific the rules or principles, the more likely that a particular dispute will be outside their scope and the more difficult forming a consensus will be. Nevertheless, struggling with these tensions is something that legislators and mediators do all the time, and thus the effort may be worthwhile if there is widespread concern about the inappropriateness of existing legal doctrine or about uncertainty because the only legal doctrine on point is very general.

§ 12.13   Factual Example of Procedural Issues

One international banking system exemplifies the kind of information infrastructure that gives rise to challenging personal jurisdiction, choice of law, and judgment enforcement questions. Inter Bank On-line Systems (IBOS) is a consortium of European banks offering international funds transfer services.[210] Under the arrangement, an American bank, for example, can offer to its customers the capability of transferring funds from an account in a European bank by using a computer terminal. Thus, a Philadelphia enterprise with a relationship with First Fidelity Bank in Philadelphia, which is a member of this consortium, could use a computer in Philadelphia to access its account in a bank in Madrid. Now, suppose something goes wrong. There is no difficulty with personal jurisdiction over First Fidelity; it clearly is present in Pennsylvania. To the extent that First Fidelity engaged in wrongful conduct, Pennsylvania substantive law would seem a strong possibility under choice of law rules discussed in § 12.11. Nor would there be any difficulty in enforcing a judgment against First Fidelity, which has many assets in Pennsylvania. Suppose, however, that the fault lay with the Spanish bank.

It would be in the interest of the Philadelphia enterprise to litigate in a Pennsylvania court, state or federal, against the Spanish bank. But that would necessitate the Pennsylvania court having personal jurisdiction. One possibility is that the consortium agreement contains forum selection and choice of law clauses, which under *Carnival Cruise Line* would govern.[211] Another possibility is that *Burger King* would justify asserting jurisdiction over the Spanish bank merely because it entered into the contract with First Fidelity. As in *Burger King,* the Spanish bank, by entering into the contract with Fidelity, has established a substantial connection with Pennsylvania, intending through the contract to derive substantial benefits from a long-term relationship with a significant

---

[210] Andrew Cassel, *First Fidelity Joining World Wide Bank Group,* Phila. Inquirer, Feb. 16, 1995, at C1.

[211] Carnival Cruise Lines, Inc. v. Shute, 499 U.S. 585 (1991).

organization. The relationship between the Spanish bank and Fidelity, like the contact between Burger King and its franchisee, can hardly be described as "random, fortuitous, or attenuated."[212] On the other hand, the interdependence between the Spanish bank and Fidelity is less than the interdependence between Burger King and its franchisee. The Spanish bank, unlike the franchisee, hardly can be said to take its direction from Fidelity, nor must notices and payments be sent to Fidelity. Moreover, the Spanish bank's relationship with Fidelity, unlike the franchisee's relationship with Burger King, is nonexclusive. To the extent that transmissions were initiated only in Pennsylvania and none in Spain, personal jurisdiction in Pennsylvania over the Spanish bank would be unlikely under *World Wide Volkswagen*[213] and *Hansen v. Denckla*.[214] The Spanish defendant has done nothing to deal with Pennsylvania; it has merely received communications initiated by another. Indeed, as the scope of the banking network grows, the relationship between banking transactions conducted with any particular member of the network begins to look more like a product placed in the stream of commerce than a purposeful contact.[215]

Nevertheless, the scope of networks like that one joined by Fidelity is defined by membership. Admitting a new member from a particular country or state is the kind of conscious decision to enter into a continuing relationship that constitutes availing of the benefits of the state in which the new member is located. Thus, it seems appropriate to subject all of the members of the network to jurisdiction in the state of each member for harm any of them does in that jurisdiction arising out of the network. If such diverse jurisdictional possibilities are not acceptable to the network members, they easily can write their network agreement to include a forum selection clause.

§ 12.14 Arbitration

Arbitration is a dispute resolution process in which a binding decision is made by one or more private individuals under an agreement entered into by the

---

[212] Burger King v. Rudzewicz, 471 U.S. 462, 480 (1985).

[213] World Wide Volkswagen Corp. v. Woodson, 444 U.S. 286 (1980) (due process does not permit personal jurisdiction to be exercised over New York automobile dealership merely because consumer drove automobile to Oklahoma).

[214] 357 U.S. 235 (1958) (contacts due solely to conduct of plaintiff or third party are not attributable to defendant and thus do not justify the exercise of personal jurisdiction over defendant).

[215] *See* Asahi Metal Indus. Co. v. Superior Court, 480 U.S. 102, 108–13 (1987) (merely placing a product in the stream of commerce coupled with awareness or foreseeability that it may reach the forum state is insufficient to justify assertion of personal jurisdiction under the Fourteenth Amendment due process clause) (Part II(A) (plurality opinion); *id.* at 113–16 (Part II(B) (assertion of personal jurisdiction over Japanese valve manufacturer would not comport with fair play and substantial justice because inconvenience for defendant of defending in California court would be large; California has only a weak sovereignty interest in litigating a case against a nonresident defendant; other nations have an interest against exercise of jurisdiction).

disputants. The availability of arbitration thus depends upon the existence of an arbitration agreement, either entered into in advance for a class of disputes, or entered into after a particular dispute has arisen, limited to that dispute.

The legal effectiveness of arbitration depends on the willingness of regular courts to channel disputes to the arbitration forum when one of the parties tries to present them to another forum, and on the willingness of the regular courts to enforce an arbitration award.[216] The first type of relationship between arbitration and the regular courts is frequently referred to as enforcement of the arbitration agreement or "compelling arbitration."[217] The criteria for compelling arbitration and for enforcing arbitration awards are similar because award enforcement is a subset of arbitration agreement enforcement; when one enters into an arbitration agreement one agrees either expressly or impliedly to comply with the award.

Because the power of an arbitrator is contractual, parties are obligated to arbitrate and obligated to obey arbitration awards only when the dispute is within the scope of a valid agreement. Deciding whether a dispute is within a valid arbitration agreement presents the question of substantive arbitrability.[218] Conceptually, there is no doubt that the question of substantive arbitrability is, in the end, for a regular court to decide,[219] although courts must defer to arbitral decisions on questions of substantive arbitrability when the agreement contemplates arbitrator decisions on those questions.[220]

If a dispute is substantively arbitrable, the parties to the arbitration agreement are obligated to use the arbitration process and through that agreement are considered to have waived any power to present the dispute to a regular court instead of arbitration.[221] Once disputes have been arbitrated and the arbitrator has issued an award, that award is enforceable, either in a breach of contract action seeking specific performance of the arbitration agreement or in a

---

[216] An arbitration award is the decision of an arbitrator.

[217] *See generally* Merrill Lynch, Pierce, Fenner & Smith, Inc. v. Lauer, 49 F.3d 323 (7th Cir. 1995) (cannot seek to narrow arbitration by suing in district other than district where arbitration is occurring; applying § 4 of the Federal Arbitration Act and generally reviewing law under which one sues to compel arbitration).

[218] Procedural arbitrability is the question whether appropriate procedures have been followed in presenting the dispute to the arbitrator.

[219] AT&T Technologies, Inc. v. Communications Workers, 475 U.S. 643 (1986) (courts have the ultimate say on whether a dispute is substantively arbitrable).

[220] First Options v. Kaplan, 115 S. Ct. 1920 (1995).

[221] 9 U.S.C. § 4 (federal court has power to compel arbitration); UAA § 2, 7 U.L.A. 5, 68 (1985) (same power in state court under Uniform State Act); United Nations Convention on the Recognition and Enforcement of Foreign Arbitrable Awards [hereinafter "New York Arbitration Convention"] art. II, § 3 (1958) (requiring courts of contracting states to refer arbitrable agreement to arbitration as long as they find arbitration agreements to be valid). *See* Howard Fields & Assocs. v. Grand Wailea Co., 848 F. Supp. 890 (D. Haw. 1993) (staying federal court litigation pending arbitration; explaining relationship between Federal Arbitration Act and state arbitration law, acknowledging that Volt Info. Sciences, Inc. v. Board of Trustees, 489 U.S. 468 (1989), allows choice of law provision in arbitration agreement to apply state arbitration law rather than federal arbitration agreement law).

summary proceeding under an arbitration award enforcement statute.[222] As the citations in this section indicate, the basic legal framework for arbitration is the same regardless of whether the arbitration is purely domestic or whether it is international.[223]

Until recently, certain statutory claims were not arbitrable as a matter of public policy in the United States, but the Supreme Court has significantly relaxed this doctrine. Now, it is reasonable to presume that almost any subject matter can be arbitrable, at least if the arbitration agreement clearly manifests an intent to make it arbitrable.[224]

Assuming that there are no artificial limitations on the types of claims that may be arbitrated, arbitration offers important advantages in the NII context. One advantage is that arbitrators can be selected and arbitration procedures and choice of law can be specified in the arbitration agreement to suit the nature of claims arising in the NII better than regular judicial procedure and generalist judges. A second advantage, given the transnational character of many NII transactions, is that the New York Arbitration Convention provides greater certainty as to the enforceability of international arbitration awards than is available with respect to the enforceability of the judgments of regular courts under the treaty framework considered in § **12.9.**

---

[222] *See* 9 U.S.C. § 9 (authorizing federal court enforcement of award if the parties have so provided in their agreement and requiring enforcement unless it can be shown that the award was procured by corruption, fraud, or undue means; there was evident partiality or corruption in the arbitrators; where the arbitrators were guilty of misconduct in refusing to postpone the hearing or in refusing to hear pertinent evidence; where the arbitrators exceeded their power); UAA §§ 8, 12 (similar power and criteria for state courts); New York Arbitration Convention art. III (1958) (providing for enforcement of arbitration awards); New York Arbitration Convention art. V, § 1 (allowing for refusal of enforcement of arbitration award only if agreement was invalid; party seeking to avoid enforcement was not given appropriate notice; award is outside the scope of arbitration agreement; composition of the arbitral body was in violation of the agreement or the law of the country where the arbitration took place; award has not yet become binding or has been set aside by competent authority where the award was made); New York Arbitration Convention § 2 (allowing for refusal of enforcement if law of country where enforcement is sought does not allow that type of dispute to be arbitrated; enforcement would be contrary to public policy of that country).

[223] *Accord* 9 U.S.C. §§ 201–208 (providing for enforcement of arbitration agreements and awards under New York Convention in accordance with criteria and procedures generally applicable to domestic arbitration).

[224] Scherk v. Alberto-Culver Co., 417 U.S. 506 (1974) (international arbitration agreement may provide for binding arbitration of statutory securities law claim); Gilmer v. Interstate/Johnson Lane Corp., 500 U.S. 20, 26–27, 111 S. Ct. 1647, 1652 (1991) (allowing arbitration of age discrimination claims under individual employment agreement); Mitsubishi Motors Corp. v. Soler Chrysler-Plymouth, Inc., 473 U.S. 614, 625 (1985) (rejecting presumption against arbitration of statutory claims; contrary presumption applies in international arbitration; finding antitrust disputes to be arbitrable). *But see* Wolf v. Gruntal & Co., 45 F.3d 524 (1st Cir. 1995) (arbitrator lacked jurisdiction over federal securities law claim because not explicitly submitted in writing and therefore award had no res judicata effect in subsequent court litigation).

Realizing the advantages of arbitration requires the parties to understand and specify appropriate procedure and choice of substantive law for their arbitrations. In general, arbitration procedure is entirely a creature of the arbitration agreement. Thus, whether discovery is permitted, whether fact or notice pleading is to be utilized, and whether the different rules of evidence are applicable are matters to be defined by the parties in their arbitration agreement. They may incorporate by reference rules of procedure issued by various bodies sponsoring arbitration, such as the American Arbitration Association, the International Chamber of Commerce, or the UN Commission on International Trade Law (UNCITRAL).[225] Choice of substantive law historically has been a bit trickier, although there is early authority for party autonomy in this regard: the notion that the party should be entirely free to choose the substantive law to be applied.[226] Indeed, there is a growing trend to allow arbitrators to refer to a general commercial law without the necessity of finding any roots in the issuances of national legal institutions, as § **12.11** explains. This is an endorsement of lex mercatoria in the arbitration context.[227] The only reason that an express reference to lex mercatoria or any other source of private law should not be permissible is a positivist theory of law, denying the efficacy of any source of law other than a conventional legislature or court. Arbitrators usually can be given authority to award a variety of remedies, including punitive damages.[228]

§ 12.15   Model Forum Selection and Choice of Law Clauses

This section contains several choice of law, forum selection, and arbitration clauses that have been validated in court (**Forms 12–2** through **12–10**). They

---

[225] American Arbitration Ass'n Arbitration Rules art. 20 (1995) (evidence); American Arbitration Ass'n Arbitration Rules art. 24 (1995) (default provision); UNCITRAL Arbitration Rules art. 24–25 (1976) (evidence and hearings); UNCITRAL Arbitration Rules art. 28 (1976) (default); International Chamber of Commerce art. 24 (1975) (finality and enforceability of award).

[226] *See generally* Chukwumerije at 107–08; *but see* Vita Food Prods. v. Unus Shipping Co., [1939] App. Cas. 277, 290 (P.C.) (choice of law may be disregarded if choice is not bona fide where there is public policy ground for avoiding it although party choice accepted in this case.).

[227] *See* Chukwumerije at 110–17 (discussing sources of law within lex mercatoria, including those of UNCITRAL and International Institute for the Unification of International Private Law (UNIDROIT); Hutton v. Warren, [1835–1842] All E.R. 151 (Ex. Ch. 1836) (endorsing use of extrinsic evidence of custom and usage in disputes over commercial transactions).

[228] *See* Mastrobuono v. Shearson Lehman Hutton, Inc., 115 S. Ct. 1212, 1217–19 (1995) (contract allowed arbitrator of dispute between securities brokerage and customers to award punitive damages; choice of law provision pointing to New York law did not require application of New York doctrine against punitive damages by arbitrator because that was procedural and conflicted with the Federal Arbitration Act).

easily can be adapted to the needs of NII service providers by selecting the appropriate source of law or the choice of law clauses, an appropriate tribunal for the forum selection clauses, and the appropriate body of arbitration rules to be used in conjunction with the arbitration clauses. Ordinarily it would not be a good idea to define the location of the forum or of the substantive law to be applied indirectly, in terms of the location of a particular server, for example. Usually, drafters of choice of law clauses pick the law to be applied based on its content. Typically, they pick the location of the forum based on its convenience to the drafter, with the attractiveness of its procedure as a secondary consideration.[229] The rules to be applied under an arbitration clause typically are selected for their familiarity. As specialized rules for electronic commerce or global information infrastructure arbitration become available, they would be an obvious candidate.

FORM 12–2
CHOICE OF LAW CLAUSE

"Hawaii law will govern . . . remedies for breach or any other claims related to this Agreement."[230]

FORM 12–3
CHOICE OF LAW CLAUSE

"This Agreement, with respect to all portions of the CMA Service, including interest charges on loans you may make to me, will be governed by and interpreted under the laws of the state of New York. The terms of my agreement with MLB & T, including those relating to the issuance of the Card, are governed by Federal and New Jersey law. The terms of my agreement with MLNF, including those relating to finance charges, are governed by Federal law and, except to the extent my state law explicitly applies, Utah law."[231]

FORM 12–4
FORUM SELECTION CLAUSE

"8. It is agreed by and between the passenger and the Carrier that all disputes and matters whatsoever arising under, in connection with or incident to this Contract shall be litigated, if at all, in and before a Court located in the State of Florida, U.S.A., to the exclusion of the Courts of any other state or country."[232]

---

[229] Typically, a forum applies its own procedure and uses a choice of law clause or choice of law rules to select the substantive law to be applied. See § **12.11.**

[230] Howard Fields & Assocs. v. Grand Wailea Co., 848 F. Supp. 890, 892 (D. Haw. 1993) (quoting dispute resolution and choice of law clauses found to be binding).

[231] Merrill Lynch, Pierce, Fenner & Smith, Inc. v. Lauer, 49 F.3d 323, 324 n.2 (7th Cir. 1995) (noting lack of clarity of quoted choice of law clause).

[232] Carnival Cruise Lines, Inc. v. Shute, 499 U.S. 585, 587–88 (1991) (quoting forum selection clause found to be enforceable).

FORM 12-5
FORUM SELECTION CLAUSE

"Dealer and Ricoh agree that any appropriate state or federal district court located in the Borough of Manhattan, New York City, New York, shall have exclusive jurisdiction over any case or controversy arising under or in connection with this Agreement and shall be a proper forum in which to adjudicate such case or controversy."[233]

FORM 12-6
ARBITRATION CLAUSE

"The parties are waiving their right to seek remedies in Court. . . . [A]ll controversies which may arise between us, including but not limited to those involving any transaction or the construction, performance, or breach of this or any other agreement between us whether entered into prior, on or subsequent to the date hereof shall be determined by arbitration."[234]

FORM 12-7
INTERNATIONAL ARBITRATION CLAUSE

"ARBITRATION OF CERTAIN MATTERS

"All disputes, controversies or differences which may arise between MMC and BUYER out of or in relation to Articles I-B through V of this Agreement or for the breach thereof, shall be finally settled by arbitration in Japan in accordance with the rules and regulations of the Japan Commercial Arbitration Association."[235]

FORM 12-8
MEDIATION AND ARBITRATION CLAUSE

"Owner and Consultant recognize that it is in their mutual best interests to resolve and settle any claims or disputes between them in a cooperative and expeditious manner. Accordingly, Owner and Consultant hereby agree to meet promptly to negotiate, mediate, or arbitrate any claim, dispute, or other matter in question arising out of or relating to this Agreement."[236]

---

[233] Steward Org., Inc. v. Ricoh, 487 U.S. 22, 24 (1988) (quoting forum selection clause found to be government by federal, rather than state, law and thus enforceable).

[234] Merrill Lynch, Pierce, Fenner & Smith, Inc. v. Lauer, 49 F.3d 323, 324 n.1 (7th Cir. 1995) (quoting arbitration clause and holding that suit to limit arbitration must be filed in district of arbitration).

[235] Mitsubishi Motors Corp. v. Soler Chrysler-Plymouth, Inc., 473 U.S. 614, 643 (1985) (Stevens, J., dissenting) (quoting arbitration clause found by the majority to compel arbitration of international antitrust claims).

[236] Howard Fields & Assocs. v. Grand Wailea Co., 848 F. Supp. 890, 891 (D. Haw. 1993) (granting stay pending arbitration).

FORM 12–9
INTERNATIONAL CHOICE OF LAW CLAUSE, WITH SEPARATE
INTERNATIONAL FORUM SELECTION CLAUSE

"2.1 The rights and obligations of the parties arising out of or relating to the Member's membership of, and/or underwriting of insurance business at, Lloyd's and any other matter referred to in this Undertaking shall be governed by and construed in accordance with the laws of England.

"2.2 Each party hereto irrevocably agrees that the courts of England shall have exclusive jurisdiction to settle any dispute and/or controversy of whatsoever nature arising out of or relating to the Member's membership of, and/or underwriting of insurance business at, Lloyd's."[237]

FORM 12–10
CHOICE OF LAW AND FORUM SELECTION CLAUSE

"This agreement shall inure to the benefit of your successors and assigns, shall be binding on the undersigned, my heirs, executors, administrators and assigns, and shall be governed by the laws of the State of [state]. Unless unenforceable due to federal or state law, any controversy arising out of or relating to my accounts, to transactions with you, your officers, directors, agents and/or employees for me or to this agreement or the breach thereof, shall be settled by arbitration in accordance with the rules then in effect, of the National Association of Securities Dealers, Inc. or the Boards of Directors of the New York Stock Exchange, Inc. and/or the American Stock Exchange, Inc. as I may elect. If I do not make such election by registered mail addressed to you at your main office within 5 days after demand by you that I make such election, then you may make such election. Judgment upon any award rendered by the arbitrators may be entered in any court having jurisdiction thereof. This agreement to arbitrate does not apply to future disputes arising under certain of the federal securities laws to the extent it has been determined as a matter of law that I cannot be compelled to arbitrate such claims."[238]

§ 12.16　Discovery of Electronic Formats

As more and more of the information maintained by any modern entity is kept in electronic form, litigators must be sure that their civil discovery activities adequately probe electronic as well as nonelectronic sources of information. The following sections propose language for the basic types of civil discovery

---

[237] Bonny v. Society of Lloyd's, 3 F.3d 156, 158 (7th Cir. 1993) (quoting choice of law clause found to be binding in international contract).

[238] Mastrobuono v. Shearson Lehman Hutton, Inc., 115 S. Ct. 1212, 1217 n.2 (1995) (quoting arbitration and choice of law clauses; arbitration clause allowed award of punitive damages by arbitrator despite rule against punitive damages under law referred to by choice of law clause).

documents to ensure that electronic formats are not overlooked. The model language is intended to be used along with language tailored for the issues in a particular case. The model language should not be used as is, but should be reviewed carefully and combined with language drafted by counsel to cover other forms of information and to relate the request or demand to the context.[239]

§ 12.17 —Model Request for Production of Electronic Records

The likelihood is great that information pertinent to a claim is maintained in whole or in part in electronic form. **Form 12–11** in this section suggests language to be included in combined requests for production of documents and things and interrogatories that address electronic records. The questions and demands can be adapted for deposition questions and for subpoenas duces tecum for depositions. Obviously, the language should be tailored to the type of discovery request involved as well as being tailored to the type of claim."

FORM 12–11
REQUEST FOR PRODUCTION OF ELECTRONIC RECORDS

1. "Record" includes any medium from which information can retrieved in a form perceivable by a human being, including but not limited to magnetic disks, diskettes, cartridges, and tape; and optical or magneto optical disks.

2. "Document" includes any form of record or systems of records.

3. Please provide copies of any software or computer programs necessary to read and interpret records covered by other paragraphs of this request.

4. Please identify all systems of records maintained by you or containing information disclosed by you that may contain information about or provided by the plaintiff.

5. Please describe these systems of records in terms of each major step in the process from information acquisition to subsequent retrieval, identifying the organizational entities and persons responsible for each step.

6. Please describe any methods used for verifying the accuracy of information in each system of records, including measures aimed at discovering data entry errors and errors made in computer recording or translation.

7. Please describe methods for controlling disclosure of information from each system of records.

---

[239] The author acknowledges good work by his law clerk, Eugene Schriver IV, Villanova Law School, Class of 1994, in developing the model language.

8. Please describe the criteria pursuant to which information is disclosed.

9. Please describe each class of persons to whom disclosure is made.

10. Please describe the record formats and the software used or useful to interpret and provide human-readable output from each system of records.

11. Please provide any public or private keys, key rings, or decryption software necessary to decrypt and read messages or files that may contain information pertinent to this action or lead to information pertinent to this action.

§ 12.18   Definitions for Discovery of Electronic Information

FORM 12–12
ELECTRONIC DEFINITIONS

magnetic tape cartridges - tapes used to store electronic data on a magnetic medium in an analog or digital form. Cartridges are removal media enclosing a tape medium.

magnetic disk cartridges - magnetic disks used to store electronic data on a magnetic medium in an analog or digital form and enclosed within a case.

flash memory cartridges (or cards) - non-volatile random access memory enclosed within a case, which may be removed.

CD-I - interactive optical disks.

PCMCIA - any medium using a PCMCIA computer interface.

DDS - digital data storage.

DAT - digital audio tape.

floptical disks (magnetic-optical disks) - diskettes using dual medium involving both magnetic and optical storage techniques.

§ 12.19   Model Request for Production

This request for production (**Form 12–13**) is intended for use under Federal Rules of Civil Procedure 34(b) and 37(a).[240] It should be used in conjunction with definitions such as those provided in **Forms 12–11** and **12–12.**

---

[240] Rule 37(a)(2)(b) requires that the movant has in good faith conferred with or attempted to confer with the person or party failing to make discovery so that the information may be obtained without court action. Further, Rule 37(a)(2)(b) requires that a certification that such

FORM 12–13
REQUEST FOR PRODUCTION (ORDER TO COMPEL)

[*Title of court*]

[*Caption*]

[*Requesting party*], by her attorney, requests an Order from this Court, pursuant to Rule 37(a) of the Federal Rules of Civil Procedure, directing [*Opposing party*] to permit the inspection and copying of [*Describe each document*] that is stored on magnetic tape cartridges, magnetic disk cartridges, flash memory cartridges, magnetic disks (including, but not limited to fixed disk systems, portable or removable disk systems, floppy diskettes, and magnetic-optical disks), optical disks (including, but not limited to CD-ROM, CD-I, laser disks, floptical diskettes, WORM, and other rewritable optical media), non-volatile RAM (including, but not limited to programmable ROM, PCMCIA flash memory cards, and PCMCIA hard drive cards), computer tape (including, but not limited to 9 track magnetic tape, 1/4 inch magnetic tape, DDS cartridge tapes, 8mm magnetic tape, 4mm magnetic tape, DAT magnetic tape, and standard audio tape), and punch cards and punch tape. This motion is based on the grounds that the requested information is the proper object of discovery and that [*Opposing party*] has, although having been properly requested to do so, refused to permit the inspection and copying of such electronically stored information. [*Requesting party*] has in good faith [Conferred *or* attempted to confer] with [*Opposing party*] in an effort to secure the disclosure without court action, but such effort was unproductive, as is more fully shown by the attached affidavit of _____.

[*Requesting party*] further moves, pursuant to Rule 37(a)(4), Federal Rules of Civil Procedure, that [*Opposing party*] be required to pay to [*Party*] the reasonable expenses, including attorney's fees incurred by [*Requesting party*] in bringing this motion.

Dated:_____.

[*Signature and address*]

CERTIFICATE OF COMPLIANCE WITH RULE 37(a)

OF THE FEDERAL RULES OF CIVIL PROCEDURE

_____, counsel for [*Moving party*], hereby certifies that he has conferred with counsel for [*Opposing party*] in a good faith effort to resolve the issues raised by the foregoing motion to compel production and that he and counsel for [*Opposing party*] have been unable to resolve the dispute.

Dated:_____.

[*Signature and address*]

---

action has been taken be attached to the motion. Therefore, this request for production by court order must be premised on a rejection of a prior request for production between the parties.

NOTICE OF MOTION

To:_____, Attorney for [*Opposing party*]

[*address*]

Please take notice that on [*date*] at _____o'clock ___.M., or as soon thereafter as counsel can be heard, in Room _____, United States Court House, [*address*], the undersigned will bring the above motion on for hearing.

Dated:_____.

[*Signature and address*]

§ 12.20 —Model Subpoena Duces Tecum Language

Form 12–14 is intended for use under Federal Rule of Civil Procedure 45(d)(1). It should be used in conjunction with the definitions provided in **Forms 12–11** and **12–12.**

FORM 12–14
SUBPOENA DUCES TECUM

[*Title of court and cause*]

To [*Name of witness*],

All business and excuses being laid aside, we command you to appear and attend before [*Name and title of officer*], at [*Room and street address*], in the City of _____, County of _____, and State of _____, on the _____ day of _____, 19____, at _____o'clock in the _____(A.M. or P.M.), to testify and give evidence by deposition pursuant to Rule 30 of the Federal Rules of Civil Procedure in a certain action now pending undetermined in the [*Title of court*], between [Plaintiff] and [Defendant] [On the part of the plaintiff *or* defendant] and that you bring with you and produce at the time and place aforesaid all information stored on magnetic tape cartridges, magnetic disk cartridges, flash memory cartridges, magnetic disks (including, but not limited to fixed disk systems, portable or removable disk systems, floppy diskettes, and magnetic-optical disks), optical disks (including, but not limited to CD-ROM, CD-I, laser disks, floptical diskettes, WORM, and other rewrittable optical media), non-volatile RAM (including, but not limited to programmable ROM, PCMCIA flash memory cards, and PCMCIA hard drive cards), computer tape (including, but not limited to 9 track magnetic tape, 1/4 inch magnetic tape, DDS cartridge tapes, 8mm magnetic tape, 4mm magnetic tape, DAT magnetic tape, and standard audio tape), and punch cards and punch tape regarding [clearly define informational category sought], and permit the inspection and copying thereof, and this you do under penalty of law.

Please provide any public or private keys, key rings, or decryption software necessary to decrypt and read messages or files that may contain information pertinent to this action or lead to information pertinent to this action.

Witness, Honorable _____, Judge of the United States District Court at the City of _____, the _____ day of _____, in the year of our Lord one thousand nine hundred and _____. [*Seal*]

_____

Clerk of the United States

District Court for the _____ District of _____.

§ 12.21 —Model Request to Permit Entry on Land

Form 12–15 is intended for use under Federal Rule of Civil Procedure 34. It should be used in conjunction with the definitions provided in **Forms 12–11** and **12–12.**

FORM 12–15
REQUEST TO PERMIT ENTRY ON LAND

[*Title of court*]

[*Caption*]

To: [*Name*], [*Party*], and [*Name*], counsel

You are requested pursuant to Rule 34(a) of the Federal Rules of Civil Procedure to permit [*Party*] to enter on [*Describe real property, including designation by street and number if possible*] to inspect, test, copy, and sample the following forms of electronically stored information: [Use any of the following: magnetic tape cartridges, magnetic disk cartridges, flash memory cartridges, magnetic disks (including, but not limited to fixed disk systems, portable or removable disk systems, floppy diskettes, and magnetic-optical disks), optical disks (including, but not limited to CD-ROM, CD-I, laser disks, floptical diskettes, WORM, and other rewrittable optical media), non-volatile RAM (including, but not limited to programmable ROM, PCMCIA flash memory cards, and PCMCIA hard drive cards), computer tape (including, but not limited to 9 track magnetic tape, 1/4 inch magnetic tape, DDS cartridge tapes, 8mm magnetic tape, 4mm magnetic tape, DAT magnetic tape, and standard audio tape), and punch cards and punch tape].

The time for making such entry shall be [Date]. The proposed manner of conducting the acts mentioned above are as follows: [Indicate manner of conduct].

Service of a written response to the foregoing request is due from you within 30 days of the date of service of this request.

Dated:_____.

[Signature and address]

§ 12.22 —Model Motion to Quash

Form 12–16 is intended for use under Federal Rule of Civil Procedure 45(b)

FORM 12–16
MOTION TO QUASH

[Title of court]

[Caption]

[Moving party], by his attorney, moves this Court to quash the subpoena duces tecum issued against him under Rule 45(b) of the Federal Rules of Civil Procedure at the request of [Opposing party] for the following reasons:

The items requested are [State reasons for undue burden, e.g., matters of public record are readily available to opposing party in other formats, to produce information stored on hard drive or on mainframe would require disproportionate expense and inconvenience, the items being sought are of a confidential nature and their confidentiality is vital to the health of the company, the information being sought would require the setup of huge sums of electronic equipment in the courtroom that would greatly inconvenience the court, the moving party has already provided all portions of information relevant to the issues at trial to the opposing party.]

[Moving party] prays that said subpoena duces tecum be quashed and held void by this Court and that [Moving party] recover its costs and attorney's fees upon this motion and be given such other relief as he may be entitled.

Dated:_____.

[Signature and address]

§ 12.23   —Model Protective Order

Form 12–17 is intended to be used under Federal Rule of Civil Procedure 26(c)(7). It should be used in conjunction with definitions provided in **Forms 12–11** and **12–12.**

FORM 12–17
PROTECTIVE ORDER

[*Title of court*]

[*Caption*]

It is hereby ORDERED that:

1. All confidential information produced in the course of this Litigation shall be disclosed to qualified recipients only, and those recipients shall use such information solely for the purpose of this Litigation.

2. "QUALIFIED RECIPIENT" as used herein means, so long as such persons or entities are obligated to use covered information only for purposes of this litigation:

    (a) Plaintiff, _____, Defendant, _____, and Third Parties _____, and _____.

    (b) An attorney of record in this action.

    (c) A member of the paralegal, secretarial, clerical, data entry or data processing, or information systems staff retained by a receiving party or its attorneys of record while assisting in connection with this action.

    (d) A technical consultant employed or retained by the receiving party or its attorneys of record while assisting in connection with this action.

    (e) A court reporter retained or employed by a party holding a deposition to transcribe the testimony in the deposition.

3. "CONFIDENTIAL INFORMATION" as used herein means all information or material stored in electronic format that is produced for or disclosed to a party, that the producing party in good faith believes is proprietary. Further, the producing party must mark or note each item of confidential information as CONFIDENTIAL-PROTECTED BY COURT ORDER, and must clearly indicate the Civil Action Number. The marking may occur by marking the outside of a diskette or tape or cartridge. It also may occur by such other means as to which the parties agree. Any item so designated shall be treated in accordance with this Order.

4. "RESTRICTED INFORMATION" as used herein means all information and material stored in electronic format which the producing party in good faith believes to contain trade secrets or confidential research, development, or commercial information. Further, the producing party must mark or note each item of restricted information as RESTRICTED-FOR COUNSEL ONLY-BY COURT ORDER, as specified in paragraph 3, and must clearly indicate the Civil Action Number. Any item so designated shall be treated in accordance with this Order.

5. During the preparation or trial of this action, if a receiving party deems it necessary to disclose CONFIDENTIAL or RESTRICTED INFORMATION to another party that is not a QUALIFIED RECIPIENT, the receiving party shall give notice to the party that produced the information. The notice shall include the person or persons to whom disclosure is to be made as well as a description of the specific items that may include magnetic disk cartridges, flash memory cartridges, magnetic disks (including, but not limited to fixed disk systems, portable or removable disk systems, floppy diskettes, and magnetic-optical disks), optical disks (including, but not limited to CD-ROM, CD-I, laser disks, floptical diskettes, WORM, and other rewrittable optical media), non-volatile RAM (including, but not limited to programmable ROM, PCMCIA flash memory cards, and PCMCIA hard drive cards), computer tape (including, but not limited to 9 track magnetic tape, 1/4 inch magnetic tape, DDS cartridge tapes, 8mm magnetic tape, 4mm magnetic tape, DAT magnetic tape, and standard audio tape), and punch cards and punch tape to be disclosed to each person. Further, the notice must also include from each party that is not a QUALIFIED RECIPIENT to whom disclosure is to be made a written acknowledgement that she has read and understands this Order and agrees to be bound to its terms. If the producing party objects to the proposed disclosure, it shall do so in writing and shall include its reasons therefor within ten days of receiving notice. Upon objection by the producing party, the disclosure shall not be made unless further ordered by this Court.

6. CONFIDENTIAL or RESTRICTED INFORMATION shall not be reproduced in any way by a receiving party unless it is being transmitted to a QUALIFIED RECIPIENT, or unless it is being stored in any other format by a QUALIFIED RECIPIENT for use by a QUALIFIED RECIPIENT.

7. If a party wishes to use or refer to any CONFIDENTIAL INFORMATION in any affidavits, briefs, memoranda of law, or other papers filed in this Court for this Litigation, such CONFIDENTIAL INFORMATION used shall be maintained under seal by this Court.

8. Inadvertent disclosure by the producing party does not constitute waiver of that party's claim of confidentiality, regarding either particular information that is disclosed or the whole of the item containing that particular information.

9. Within sixty (60) days of the conclusion of this Litigation, all original items or reproductions of the information contained therein that are subject to this Order shall be returned to the producing party. Reproductions of such information stored in any format, as well as other information objects containing or referring to such information, shall be destroyed by the receiving party. Use of any information protected by

this Order will continue to be protected after the conclusion of this Litigation, except that there shall be no restriction on the use of information that becomes a part of the public record, and except that a party may seek subsequent modification of this Order or receive express permission from the producing party regarding disclosure.

10. Nothing herein shall be construed as an agreement or admission by any party other than the party seeking protection that any information is in fact CONFIDENTIAL INFORMATION, or that such information is relevant or material. Further, neither the entry of this Order nor denotation of an item as CONFIDENTIAL INFORMATION or RESTRICTED INFORMATION shall constitute evidence with respect to any issue in this Litigation.

11. This Order is entered without prejudice to right of any party to apply to the Court at any time for additional protection, or to modify any of the terms of this Order.

Dated:_____.

United States District Judge

§ 12.24   Evidence

The admissibility of evidence proffered in electronic form depends on the interaction of a number of evidentiary concepts. It does not, as laypersons sometimes suggest, depend on a specific rule, statute, or case approving any particular form of evidence. The authentication requirement of Federal Rule of Evidence 901[241] conceptually overlaps at least two other rules of evidence: the original documents or "best evidence rule," and the exclusion of hearsay. Under the traditional best evidence rule, copies of documents were excluded because of a concern that they would be unreliable evidence of the contents of and characteristics of the original. The best evidence rule thus functioned as a kind of per se or presumptive nonauthentication rule. A modern view, expressed in Rules 1002 and 1003, is that copies are sufficiently reliable evidence of the contents and characteristics of their originals to be admitted unless the opponent raises some question of reliability.[242]

The hearsay rule[243] similarly is linked with authentication. Out-of-court statements are thought to be unreliable evidence of the matters asserted in them because cross-examination is unavailable to test their reliability. Thus, the hearsay rule functions as a kind of per se or presumptive nonauthentication rule

---

[241] The text addresses the Federal Rules of Evidence, which have become the model for rules of evidence in many states.

[242] Fed. R. Evid. 1003 (duplicates admissible to same extent as original unless genuine question is raised as to authenticity of original or other circumstances make it unfair to admit duplicate).

[243] *See* Fed. R. Evid. 802 (excluding hearsay unless admissible under other rule or statute).

for the contents of hearsay offered to prove the facts asserted by those contents. Just as authentication requires a showing that the thing offered in court is what it purports to be,[244] exceptions to the hearsay rule qualify certain types of hearsay as admissible evidence because circumstances increase the likelihood that the out-of-court statement is probative of what its contents report.

§ 12.25 —Admissibility of Electronic Information

Electronically stored documents are admissible if the systems storing and producing them are shown to be reliable and capable of producing authentic copies of originals. The law abounds with requirements for reliability in documentary evidence. Under traditional legal rules generally understood to require particular media for recording, storing, and reporting on legally significant conduct, the factual disputes almost always resolve themselves into disputes about the reliability of underlying systems rather than the merits of particular physical media. The real responsibility for admissibility of optical records thus rests with system designers more than with legislators, judges, and counsel.

§ 12.26 —Authentication in General

In *State v. Johnson*,[245] the intermediate Arizona court, in a careful opinion, rejected the argument that a computer-printed certification on motor vehicle division records made those records self-authenticating under a state public record certification statute. It noted the illogic of permitting a computer to certify the accuracy of its own record simply because it had been programmed automatically to do so. This analysis and conclusion are sound.

But the court also concluded that testimony by the record custodian as to identifying characteristics on the record showing that it came from the public records system laid sufficient foundation to admit the records under Arizona Rule 901(b), apparently under a paragraph similar to Federal Rule of Evidence 901(b)(7), permitting authentication of records as to which foundational evidence shows that "a writing authorized by law to be recorded or filed and in fact recorded or filed in a public office, or a purported public record, report, statement, or data compilation, and any form, is from the public office where items of this nature are kept."[246]

---

[244] Fed. R. Evid. 901(a).

[245] No. 1 CA-CV 93-0162, 1994 WL 464862 (Ariz. Ct. App. Aug. 30, 1994) (reversing exclusion of motor vehicle division records showing traffic violations).

[246] Fed. R. Evid. 901(b)(7) (illustration of how public records can be authenticated).

§ 12.27   Statute of Frauds

The *statute of frauds* is an evidentiary rule that permits important contracts to be enforced only when there is evidence of the contract in the form of a signed writing. The purpose is to prefer the reliability of written evidence of contract rather than the fallibility of memory of oral statements. The purpose of the rule is satisfied by computer "writings" and "signatures." Historical application of statutes of frauds indicates that there is flexibility in the meaning of "writing" and "signature." A signature is any mark made with the intent that it be a signature.[247] Thus an illiterate person can "sign" by making an "X," and the signature is legally effective. Another person may sign a document by using a signature stamp. Someone else may authorize an agent to sign his name or to use the signature stamp. In all three cases the signature is legally effective. There may of course be arguments about who made the X, or whether the person applying the signature stamp was the signer or his authorized agent, but these are questions going to the reliability of the underlying system, not arguments about hard and fast admissibility issues.

Under the generally accepted legal definition of a signature, there is no legal reason why the "mark" may not be made by a computer printer (including a laser raster imaging output device), or for that matter by the write head on a computer disk drive, magnetic or optical, taking the form of a digital signature.[248] The authorization to the computer agent to make the mark may be given by entering a PIN (personal identification number) on a keyboard. To extend the logic, there is no conceptual reason to doubt the legal efficacy of authority to make a mark if the signer writes a computer program authorizing the application of a PIN upon the existence of certain conditions that can be tested by the program. The resulting authority is analogous to a signature pen that can be operated only with a mechanical key attached to somebody's key ring, coupled with instructions to the possessor of the key.

Which of these various methods should be selected for particular types of transactions does not depend on what the law requires, because the law permits any of these methods. Rather, it depends on the underlying purposes of the legal requirement and which method best serves those purposes.

---

[247] Michael S. Baum & Henry H. Perritt, Jr., Electronic Contracting, Publishing and EDI Law, ch. 6 (John Wiley & Sons, Inc., 1991) (contract, evidence, and agency issues) [hereinafter Baum & Perritt]. *Accord Signature Requirements Under EDGAR,* Memorandum from D. Goelzer, Office of the General Counsel, SEC, to Kenneth A. Fogash, Deputy Executive Director, SEC (Jan. 13, 1986) (statutory and nonstatutory requirements for "signatures" may be satisfied by means other than manual writing on paper in the hand of the signatory." In fact, the electronic transmission of an individual's name may legally serve as that person's signature, providing it is transmitted with the present intention to authenticate.").

[248] See **Ch. 9.**

The real issue is how to prove that a particular party made the mark. This issue implicates not only the admissibility requirements considered in §§ **12.24** and **12.25**; it also involves foundational and supporting evidence that increases the credibility of digital formats to the fact finder.

Authority is skimpier on how flexible the "writing" requirement is. The best approach is to borrow the fixation idea from the copyright statute and conclude that a writing is "embodiment in a copy . . . sufficiently permanent or stable to permit it to be perceived, reproduced, or otherwise communicated for a period of more than transitory duration."[249]

The most important thing conceptually is to understand the purpose of the writing and signature requirements. Signature requirements, like requirements for writings and for original documents, have an essentially evidentiary purpose.[250] If there is a dispute later, they specify what kind of evidence is probative of certain disputed issues, like "who made this statement and for what purpose?" The legal requirements set a threshold of probativeness.

Fulfillment of the evidentiary purpose depends on the reliability of the information retained by the computer systems. Such systems must be designed to permit the proponent of contract formation to establish the following propositions if the other party to the purported contract attempts to repudiate it.

1.   It came from computer X.

2.   It accurately represents what is in computer X^{251} now.[252]

3.   What is in computer X now is what was in computer X at the time of the transaction.

---

[249] 17 U.S.C. § 101. For copyright purposes, a work is created, and therefore capable of protection, when it is fixed for the first time. "[I]t makes no difference what the form, manner, or medium of fixation may be—whether it is in words, numbers, notes, sounds, pictures, or any other graphic or symbolic indicia, whether embodied in a physical object in written, printed, photographic, sculptural, punched, magnetic, or any other stable form, and whether it is capable of perception directly or by means of any machine or device 'now known or later developed.'" *Id., reprinted in* 1976 U.S.C.C.A.N. 5659, 5665.

[250] They also serve a consciousness-raising or awareness purpose to assure that a person making a legally binding contract knows what she is doing. *See* **Ch. 9;** Baum & Perritt, ch. 6 (discussing "awareness").

[251] Or, more likely, what is on the computer medium read by computer X, such as an optical or magneto-optical disk used for archival records. Further references in the textual discussion to "what is in computer X now" should be understood to include such computer-readable media.

[252] *Cf.* R. Peritz, *Computer Data and Reliability: A Call for Authentication of Business Records Under the Federal Rules of Evidence,* 80 Nw. U. L. Rev. 956, 980 (1986) [hereinafter Peritz] (proof that a printout accurately reflects what is in the computer is too limited a basis for authentication of computer records).

4.   What was in computer X at the time of the transaction is what was received from the input channel.[253]

5.   What was received from the input channel is what was (a) sent, (b) by computer Y or perceived by the actor.[254]

Factual propositions 1 through 4 can be established by testimony as to how information is written to and from input channel processors, primary storage, and secondary storage. Factual proposition 5 requires testimony as to the accuracy of the input channel and characteristics of the message that associate it with computer Y. Only the last proposition (number 5) relates to signatures because signature requirements associate the message with its source.[255] The other propositions necessitate testimony as to how the basic message and database management system works. It is instructive to compare these propositions with the kinds of propositions that must be established under the business records exception to the hearsay rule when it is applied to computer information.

   Those propositions may be supported with nontechnical evidence, presented by nonprogrammers. A witness can lay a foundation for admission of computer records simply by testifying that the records are generated automatically and routinely in the ordinary course of business. The more inflexible the routine, and the less human intervention in the details of the computer's management of the database, the better the evidence.[256] The ultimate question is trustworthiness, and if the computer methods are apparently reliable, the information should be

---

[253] In some cases, the electronic transaction will be accomplished by means of a physical transfer of computer-readable media. In such a case, this step in the proof would involve proving what was received physically.

[254] Computer Y could be the offeror's computer. The "actor" may be the recipient of an offer, or she may be a medical professional who observes an injury. Two other questions relate to matters other than the authenticity of the message: (6) Computer Y was the agent of B; (7) The message content expresses the content of the contract (or more narrowly, the offer or the acceptance). *See generally* Peritz at 979 (citing as examples of authentication Ford Motor Credit Co. v. Swarens, 447 S.W.2d 53 (Ky. 1969) (authentication by establishing relationship between computer-generated monthly summary of account activity and the customer reported on); Ed Guth Realty, Inc. v. Gingold, 34 N.Y.2d 440, 315 N.E.2d 441, 358 N.Y.S.2d 367 (1974) (authentication of summary of taxpayer liability and the taxpayer)).

[255] Of course, a paper document signed at the end also is probative of the fact that no alterations have been made. In this sense, a signature requirement telescopes several steps in the inquiry outlined in the text.

[256] *See* United States v. Linn, 880 F.2d 209, 216 (9th Cir. 1989) (computer printout showing time of hotel room telephone call admissible in narcotics prosecution). *See also* United States v. Miller, 771 F.2d 1219, 1237 (9th Cir. 1985) (computer-generated toll and billing records in price-fixing prosecution based on testimony by billing supervisor although he had no technical knowledge of system that operated from another office; no need for programmer to testify; sufficient because witness testified that he was familiar with the methods by which the computer system recorded information).

admitted unless the opponent of admissibility can raise some reasonable factual question undercutting trustworthiness.[257]

§ 12.28　Original Documents Rule

Sometimes known as the "best evidence rule," this rule traditionally required that someone offering documents offer the original rather than a copy when the original existed. Its modern version, in Federal Rules of Evidence 1002 to 1003, allows duplicates to be admitted on the same footing as originals unless there is some reason to question the reliability of the duplicate.[258]

Electronic technology does not distinguish between originals and copies. Every original is a copy, in the sense that each digital representation is a copy of a digital representation that existed somewhere else. Even an old-fashioned application of the best evidence rule permits admitting a copy of a message when the original is unavailable, and also permits admitting, as an original, any computer output "readable by sight, shown to reflect the data accurately."[259] One court has suggested that normal output from a computer system is the best evidence of what is stored in the computer.[260] When original electronic records have been destroyed in the ordinary course of business, transcripts or other summaries may be admitted in their stead.[261]

---

[257] *See* United States v. Hutson, 821 F.2d 1015, 1020 (5th Cir. 1987) (remanding embezzlement conviction on other grounds; computer records were admissible under business records exception, despite trustworthiness challenge based on fact that defendant embezzled by altering computer files; access to files offered in evidence was restricted by special code).

[258] *See also* Fed. R. Evid. 1001(3) (defining original to include printout or other output readable by sight known to reflect data stored in the computer or similar device accurately); Fed. R. Evid. 1001(4) (providing for admissibility of duplicate that includes counterpart produced by mechanical or electronic rerecording, which accurately reproduces the original); Fed. R. Evid. 1005 (permitting introduction of copy of official records certified by a witness who has compared it with the original).

[259] Fed. R. Evid. 1001(3).

[260] King v. State, 222 So. 2d 393 (Miss. 1969) (computer records are admissible if proponent shows that hardware was standard, without testimony by those who made entries if entries are made in regular course of business at or reasonably near time of happening of event recorded, and court satisfied that sources of information, method, and time of preparation indicate trustworthiness). "Records stored on magnetic tape by data processing machines are unavailable and useless except by means of the print-out sheets such as those admitted in evidence in this case. In admitting the print-out sheets reflecting the record stored on the tape, the Court is actually following the best evidence rule." *Id.* at 398.

[261] United States v. Ross, 33 F.3d 1507, 1513–14 (11th Cir. 1994) (affirming drug distribution conviction; transcripts of Spanish wiretaps properly admitted even though original audio recordings had been destroyed; requirements of Fed. R. Evid. 1004 and Foreign Business Records Act, 18 U.S.C. § 3505 were satisfied). The court heard evidence of a participant in the transcribed conversations who testified that the transcripts accurately matched his recollection of the telephonic conversations. *Id.* at 1525–26 (Black, J., concurring) (noting also that defense counsel had opportunity to examine Spanish police officers of transcript procedure and noting that such evidence and opportunity should be required before transcript could be admitted).

§ 12.29   Business Records Exception to the Hearsay Rule

The motivation for the hearsay rule is to include unreliable evidence. Because of the role of cross-examination in the adversary system of exposing evidence that may be unreliable, the hearsay rule establishes a presumption against admitting out-of-court statements offered to prove what their makers may assert because the makers of such statements are not available for cross-examination. Consider, for example, a computerized log file offered to prove that an electronic payment order was sent to a particular address. If the issue as to which the log file is material is whether an electronic payment order was sent to the computer address, then the computer log file is being admitted to prove the truth of the matter asserted therein. The log file represents out-of-court statements: one made by a combination of the person who wrote the computer program creating the log files and the computer executing the program. The evidentiary problem is that the maker of the statement cannot be cross-examined. Nevertheless, the business records exception of the hearsay rule may permit the log file to be admitted as long as certain prerequisites are met:

Records of regularly conducted activity

A memorandum, report, record, or data compilation, in any form, of acts, events, conditions, opinions, or diagnoses, made at or near the time by, or from information transmitted by, a person with knowledge, if kept in the course of a regularly conducted business activity, and if it was the regular practice of that business activity to make the memorandum, report, record, or data compilation, all as shown by the testimony of the custodian or other qualified witness, unless the source of information or the method or circumstances of preparation indicate lack of trustworthiness. The term "business" as used in this paragraph includes business, institution, association, profession, occupation, and calling of every kind, whether or not conducted for profit.[262]

Traditional evidence law permits computer records to be introduced in evidence when they satisfy the requirements of the business records exception: basically that they are made in the ordinary course of business, that they are relied on for the performance of regular business activities, and that there is no independent reason for questioning their reliability.[263]

The business records exception shares with the authentication concept, the statute of frauds, and the parol evidence rule a common concern with reliability.[264] The same procedural guarantees and established practices that ensure reliability for hearsay purposes also ensure reliability for the other purposes.

---

[262] Fed. R. Evid. 803(6).

[263] *Id.* (excluding business records from inadmissibility as hearsay); 28 U.S.C. § 1732 (Business Records Act, permitting destruction of paper copies of government information reliably recorded by any means and allowing admission of remaining reliable record).

[264] *See* Peritz at 978–80, 984–85 (noting body of commentator opinion saying that business records exception and authentication are parallel ways of establishing reliability).

Under the business records exception, the proponent must identify the source of a record, through testimony by one familiar with a signature on the record, or circumstantially.[265] The steps in qualifying a business record under the common law, relaxed under the Federal Rules of Evidence, were

- Proving that the record is an original entry made in the routine course of business
- Proving that the entries were made upon the personal knowledge of the proponent/witness or someone reporting to him
- Proving that the entries were made at or near the time of the transaction
- Proving that the recorder and his informant are unavailable.[266]

These specific requirements are easier to understand and to adapt to electronic records systems by understanding the rationale for the business records exception. The hearsay rule excludes out-of-court statements because they are inherently unreliable, primarily because the statement maker's demeanor cannot be observed by the jury and because the maker of the statement is not subject to cross-examination. On the other hand, there are some out-of-court statements that have other guarantees of reliability. Business records are one example. If a continuing enterprise finds the records sufficiently reliable to use them in the ordinary course of business, they should be reliable enough for a court.[267] The criteria for the business records exception all aim at ensuring that the records really are relied upon by the business to conduct its ordinary affairs.

The Manual for Multidistrict Litigation[268] suggests steps for qualifying computer information under the business records exception:

1. The document is a business record.
2. The document has probative value.
3. The computer equipment used is reliable.
4. Reliable data processing techniques were used.

The key to adapting the business records exception to digitally stored documents is evidence of system reliability.[269] Establishing these propositions and

---

[265] *See* Fed. R. Evid. 901(b)(4) (appearance, contents, substance, internal patterns, as examples of allowable authentication techniques).

[266] Peritz at 963–64 (identifying steps and trends resulting in Fed. R. Evid.).

[267] Premier Bank v. H.A.G. Partnership, 647 So. 2d 636, 639 (La. Ct. App. 1994) (reversing dismissal of claim by bank on promissory note proven by computer printout of payment history properly admitted into evidence under state version of business records exception to hearsay rule; no analysis of evidence rule).

[268] Federal Judicial Center, Manual for Complex Litigation § 21.446 (2d ed. 1985).

[269] Fawer, Brian, Hardy & Zatzkis v. Howes, 639 So. 2d 329, 331–33 (La. Ct. App. 1994) (reviewing detailed testimony of attorneys about how computerized billing system worked, and concluding that requirements of business records exception to the hearsay rule similar in its requirements to federal rule were satisfied).

the evidentiary propositions set forth elsewhere in this chapter requires expert testimony. The burden may be on the party objecting rather than on the proponent, however.[270] Any designer of a digital records system must consult with counsel and understand what testimony an expert would give to establish these propositions. Going through that exercise will influence system design.

In *McDonald v. State*,[271] the Wyoming Supreme Court addressed the following questions:

> whether a driver's record, maintained in an electronic database, then reproduced on paper in the form of an abstract and certified by the custodian as such, is admissible . . . as a record kept in the usual course of business for purposes of the business records exception to the hearsay rule, or as a public record for purposes of the public records exception to the hearsay rule.[272]

The court, with no analysis of testimony, but noting that the opponent of the records did not assert any inaccuracies or any problems in the record-keeping system, noted that "this is the kind of evidence commonly relied upon by reasonably prudent men in the conduct of their serious affairs," and that "it is exactly the sort of document which is now utilized throughout our society for the smallest businesses to the largest governmental departments and agencies."[273] The case reinforces the essentiality of some focused objection to a computer record raising some particular doubt about the reliability of the system that produced it. The only way that an opponent usually can raise such a doubt is to have done a good job in discovery of scrutinizing the operation of the system and its possible shortcomings.

§ 12.30   —Sample Direct and Cross-Examination Questions for Witness Authenticating Electronic Records

This section presents sample questions for direct and cross-examination of a witness whose testimony is intended to authenticate electronic records offered under Federal Rule of Evidence 802(6) (**Forms 12–18** and **12–19**). The strategy of the proponent of the records is to show that the system is reliable and that it

---

[270] *See* United States v. Layne, 23 F.3d 409 (6th Cir. 1994) (per curium) (no foundational requirement under Fed. R. Evid. 803(6) for affirmative testimony that hardware functioned accurately and reliably nor for evidence of procedures for input control in the absence of any evidence that the computer system was malfunctioning). The *Layne* analysis in effect establishes a presumption of reliable functioning as long as no objection is made. The weight of the *Layne* opinion may be minimal because apparently no objection of any kind was made to the admissibility of the computer records in the case.

[271] 846 P.2d 694 (Wyo. 1993) (affirming suspension of driver's license based on printout of abstract maintained in electronic database).

[272] *Id.* at 695.

[273] *Id.* at 697.

satisfies the elements of Rule 802(6). The strategy for the opponent of the records is to introduce doubt about both the reliability and the nature of the records as business records. Even if the records are admitted, good cross-examination questions will plant seeds of doubt that will reduce their weight and credibility.

FORM 12–18
QUESTIONS FOR WITNESS AUTHENTICATING ELECTRONIC RECORDS

1. Please state your name.

2. What is your technical background?

3. What responsibilities did you have for the establishment of the system that produced Exhibit X?

4. What responsibilities do you have in supervising the ongoing operations of the system that produced Exhibit X?

5. How is Exhibit X typical or atypical of the outputs produced by this system?

6. What other outputs are produced?

7. How are these outputs used by the corporation?

8. What measures, if any, do you follow to ensure the accuracy of data in the system?

9. Are audits performed to determine whether employees are following procedures?

10. Are audits performed to determine whether the data in the system accurately reflect reality?

11. Are you familiar with the practices in the information systems management profession generally to assure accuracy and reliability of data processing systems?

12. How do the practices used by the corporation compare with the industry practices?

13. If an intruder were to access the system without authorization would any trail be left?

14. What is it?

15. Have you checked the log file to determine if any intruders accessed the system?

16. If someone altered a record, would any trail be left? What is it?

17. Have you checked the log file that would record any alterations? With what result?

FORM 12–19
CROSS-EXAMINATION QUESTIONS

1. You do not have a degree in computer science, do you?

2. In fact, you do not have a college degree in any technical field, do you?

3. Isn't this the first job you have ever had working with sophisticated database management systems?

4. You didn't write the computer programs that are used by the database management system that produced Exhibit X, did you?

5. You have never watched data entry personnel actually enter data for any significant period of time, have you?

6. Isn't it possible that someone who understood the program could alter the program to bypass your security procedures?

7. Isn't it true that the following persons have an incentive to alter data in the system?

8. Isn't it true that you were instructed to make sure that the system contained data that could be useful in defending lawsuits? Isn't it true that there is no other reason to have these data elements and the procedures used in connection with them in the system?

9. Wasn't it exactly those procedures that produced Exhibit X?

10. Isn't it true that encryption techniques exist to protect data in computers like yours?

11. Did you use those encryption techniques?

In discovery, the opponent of the record should have asked for information about any instances of unauthorized access or errors or malfunctions in the information processing system. If any such mishaps were revealed in discovery, the witness should be confronted with those in further questions on cross-examination.

§ 12.31 Video Depositions

A video deposition proceeds as a conventional deposition, but the record of the deposition is made on videotape rather than on a stenographic transcript. Video depositions are widely accepted.[274] The New York requirements for video depositions are typical:

1. The deposition begins by an on-camera announcement of the operator's name and address; the name and address of the operator's employer; the date, time, and place of the deposition; and the party on whose behalf the deposition is taken

2. On-camera swearing of the witness

3. Inclusion of an automatic time-date generator record showing the hours, minutes, and seconds permanently recorded on the tape

4. A privilege afforded any party to have a conventional stenographic transcription made of the deposition at his or her own expense

5. Certification of accuracy by the officer before whom the video deposition was taken, and an opportunity for the deponent to view the videotape and make objections to its accuracy.[275]

Under the New York rule, if objections are filed, the court must rule on those objections and provide instructions for editing of the deposition.[276]

One commentator[277] urges that video depositions be covered by stipulations stating that the deposition officer has exclusive control over (1) the video

---

[274] *See, e.g.,* Fed. R. Civ. P. 30(b(2) (as amended through Dec. 1, 1993); U.S. Dist. Ct. R., S.D. Tex., Rule 5 (1993) (granting leave for videotape depositions in civil cases when the notice or subpoena so indicates); N.Y. Ct. Rules § 202.15 (1992) (allowing video depositions conforming to technical, notice, and record-keeping requirements of rule). Steven W. Quattlebaum cites a number of statutes and rules: Cal. Civ. Proc. Code § 2019 (West 1983 & Supp.1995); Ill. Sup. Ct. R. 206(a)(2); Mich. Ct. R. 2.315 (1995); Mo. R. Civ. P. S7.03(c); Neb. Rev. Stat. §§ 25–1240, 25-1242 (1989); N.J. Civ. Prac. R. 4:14-9; N.Y. Civ. Prac. L. & R. § 3113(b) (McKinney 1970 & Supp. 1994); N.C. R. Civ. P. 30(b)(4) (1995); Ohio R. Civ. P. 30(b)(3) (1995); Pa. R. Civ. P. S4017.1; Tenn. Code Ann. §§ 24-9-121, 24-9-125 (1980); Tenn. R. Civ. P. 30.02 (1994); Tex. R. Civ. P. 202 (1995); Va. Sup. Ct. R. 4:5; Va. Rule 4(7)(a); Wis. Stat. Ann. §§ 885.40-.47 (West Supp.1994). Some rules permit video depositions only by stipulation of all parties. Others, like the federal rule, permit the noticing party unilaterally to specify video tape recording. *See* Steven W. Quattlebaum, *Effective Video Presentations at Trial: Put on a Good Show But Cut to the Chase* (pt. 2), 27 Ark. L. 56 (1993) (available on Westlaw) (analyzing Rule 30(b)(4) of the [former] federal and Arkansas Rules of Civil Procedure, and comparing with Uniform Audio-Visual Act, 12 U.L.A. 13 (Supp. 1992), and arguing in favor of unilateral designation).

[275] N.Y. Ct. R. § 202.15(c) (notice); *id.* § 202.15(d) (beginning announcement, time-date generator, opportunity for witness to review), *id.* § 202.15(f) (certification).

[276] N.Y. Ct. R. § 202.15(f)(3).

[277] Steven W. Quattlebaum, *Effective Video Presentations at Trial: Put on a Good Show But Cut to the Chase* (pt. 2), 27 Ark. L. 56 (1993) (available on Westlaw) (draft stipulation for video deposition) [hereinafter Quattlebaum].

equipment—camera angles and zoom shots; (2) the procedure for going off-the-record; and (3) obtaining on-camera oath by the video operator that he will record the deposition accurately and apply with the stipulated procedures, procedures for objecting, and certification.[278] The commentator also urges that objections be made off the video record on a conventional stenographic transcript to avoid encumbering the video record with objections that must be edited out prior to trial.[279]

Witness preparation for video depositions is somewhat different from preparation for conventional depositions. Counsel and witnesses should be aware of the exaggerated effect of facial expressions, the distracting effect of hand gestures, and the effect of unnecessary movement like rocking or swiveling in a chair. They should also be aware of the desirability of answering questions looking directly into the camera.[280]

The principal motivation for using videotape methods for depositions is the potential for use of the resulting videotape at trial. The main problem with trial use of video depositions—as with conventional deposition transcripts—is the rule against hearsay. It is increasingly possible to avoid the hearsay problems if there has been an adequate opportunity for cross-examination as the deposition was taken. That presupposes adequate notice of the possibility that the deposition might be used at trial.

Use of video depositions at trial is governed by the usual rules allowing use of depositions at trial.[281] In fact, the revised Federal Rules express a preference for videotaped depositions in jury trials over stenographic records of depositions.[282] Under the Federal Rules, the deposition of a witness may be used at trial by any party for any purpose if

1. The witness is dead

2. The witness is more than 100 miles from the place of trial or hearing or is outside the country

3. The witness is unable to attend or testify because of age, illness, infirmity, or imprisonment

---

[278] Quattlebaum at 63.

[279] *Id.; compare id. with* N.Y. Ct. R. § 202.15(g)(2).

[280] Quattlebaum at 62.

[281] Angelo v. Armstrong World Indus., Inc., 11 F.3d 957, 963 (10th Cir. 1993) (denying trial use of deposition testimony by physician because of insufficient efforts by plaintiff to enforce subpoena; thus witness did not meet unavailability criterion of Rule 32(a)(3)(E)). *See, e.g.,* N.Y. Ct. R. § 202.15(i); W. Va. Local R. for Kanawha County Civ. Ct. 12 (allowing presentation of video depositions to the jury with leave of court). *See also* Reber v. General Motors Corp., 669 F. Supp. 717, 720 (E.D. Pa. 1987); Commonwealth v. Stasko, 370 A.2d 350, 355 (Pa. 1977) (accepting video deposition testimony as almost as good as live testimony); Mark A. Dombroff, Dombroff on Demonstrative Evidence §§ 6.1–6.26 (John Wiley & Sons, Inc., 1983 & Supp. 1990) (videotape depositions and day in the life presentations); Richard J. Leighton, *The Use and Effectiveness of Demonstrative Evidence and Other Illustrative Materials in Federal Agency Proceedings,* 42 Admin. L. Rev. 35 (1990).

[282] Fed. R. Civ. P. 32(c).

4. The party offering the deposition has been unable to procure the attendance of the witness by subpoena, or

5. Exceptional circumstances exist.[283]

Criterion 2 is inapplicable if the absence of the witness is caused by the party offering the deposition. Depositions taken early without leave of court in which objecting parties were not represented and depositions taken subject to a pending motion for a protective order may not be used.[284] Of course, deposition testimony can be used at trial in any situation where the parties so stipulate as a part of the pretrial process.

Costs typically are borne by the party noticing the video deposition,[285] and in New York, at least, those costs are taxable.[286] Typically, also, a conventional transcript of any video deposition must be made part of the record on appeal.[287]

---

[283] Fed. R. Civ. P. 32(a). *Compare* General Motors Corp. v. Moseley, 447 S.E.2d 302, 308 (Ga. Ct. App. 1994) (error to admit video deposition from another case, no incentive to cross-examine witness on point for which video deposition testimony was admitted) *with* Verdict v. State, 868 S.W.2d 443 (Ark. 1993) (video deposition of medical expert validly admitted at murder trial because expert was unavailable in London; affirming conviction). In Miller v. Solaglas Cal., Inc., 870 P.2d 559 (Colo. Ct. App. 1993), the defendants unsuccessfully argued on appeal that the trial court erred in refusing to grant a new trial based upon the admission of a video deposition in lieu of live testimony, the rejection of certain objections to the showing of the video, and the trial judge's leaving the bench in the courthouse during the jury's viewing of the video deposition. The use of the deposition was authorized by the Colorado rules and, more importantly, the plaintiff had listed his intention to use the video deposition in lieu of live testimony in his "trial data certificate" and the defendant failed to object timely. 870 P.2d at 569–70. On the other point, the defendants had stipulated that the trial judge's presence during the playing of the videotape was unnecessary. *See also* Web v. Thomas, 837 S.W.2d 875, 878 (Ark. 1992) (no prejudice shown from refusal to admit transcript of videotape deposition in addition to videotape deposition itself); State v. Vaughn, 786 P.2d 1051, 1056 (Ariz. Ct. App. 1989) (affirming conviction; videotape testimony of witness who was on vacation at time of trial validly admitted because witness was under oath and was cross-examined during videotaping). *But see* Carter v. Sowders, 5 F.3d 975, 979 (6th Cir. 1993) (overturning conviction; only evidence was video deposition improperly admitted because refusal of defendant's counsel to participate in videotaping; use of videotape deposition violated confrontation clause).

[284] Fed. R. Civ. P. 32(a)(3).

[285] *See* Miller v. National R.R. Passenger Corp., 157 F.R.D. 145, 146 (D. Mass. 1994) (denying costs of video deposition because saved no time and otherwise unnecessary because medical expert witness was available to testify in person; disagreeing with Commercial Credit Equip. Corp. v. Stamps, 920 F.2d 1361, 1368 (7th Cir. 1990)); Kirby v. Ahmad, 635 N.E.2d 98 (Ohio C.P. 1994) (expert witness fees of $750 per hour for video deposition was unreasonable; fee request reduced to $250 per hour for all depositions).

[286] N.Y. Ct. R. § 202.15(k).

[287] *Id.* § 202.15(*l*) (videotapes remain part of the original record and are transmitted to the court of appeals, but audio depositions must be transcribed in the same way as other testimony and transcripts). *But see* Cal. R. of Ct. 203.5 (1993) (court reporter need not transcribe electronic recording admitted into evidence).

A trial, especially a jury trial, is in part a dramatic event.[288] Effective drama requires movement at the right pace. This is particularly true with videotape presentations because the format resembles television with which virtually all jurors and judges have grown up. They are accustomed to professionally produced video, which does not require them to watch "talking head" shots for extended periods. One commentator urges that when video depositions—at least talking heads—are used at trial, they be used in segments shorter than 15 minutes. Videotapes of key portions of documents, of computer animation, of surgery, and of days in the life of can be very effective at trial.[289] Witness shots in the deposition should be accompanied by on-camera use of enlarged documents, photographs, models, video segments, computer graphics, and X-ray films and action or demonstrations by the witnesses to avoid juror boredom.[290]

§ 12.32   Demonstrative Evidence

Using prerecorded demonstrative evidence at trial is not a new idea. Personal injury litigators have been offering day-in-the-life movies and videotapes for a long time.

Demonstrative evidence on videotape raises different legal issues compared with video depositions. The problem with demonstrative evidence is not so much hearsay as it is relevancy. A recent First Circuit case[291] summarizes the problem very well: "The test track replication shown on the tape was vivid and pertinent. One sees in a way that no words could capture the tie wheel slip out of alignment and the tire then dragging on the track." A lay juror asked whether a look at the tapes would be helpful would likely answer yes.[292]

If it is so good then why keep it out? The court of appeals continues:

> The concern lies not with the use of tape or film. The issue would be largely the
> same if the jurors were taken to the test track for a live demonstration. But the

---

[288] "[P]ersuasive techniques are the same whether a judge or jury is deciding . . . indeed the theory and skill of persuasion may usefully be mastered by those in disciplines other than law practice. Historically, the study of rational and nonrational persuasion was the work of philosophers and dramatists before it became the province of lawyers." Michael E. Tigar, Examining Witnesses XII–XIII (1993). "Edward Bennett Williams wisely likened trials to dramatic presentations, in which the lawyer is producer, director, actor, and stage manager, but all within the quite demanding constraints of the evidence in the law." *Id.* at 1.

[289] Quattlebaum at 65; Ronald K.L. Collins & David M. Skovar, *Paratexts,* 44 Stan. L. Rev. 509, 544–45 & nn.185–90 (1992).

[290] Quattlebaum at 64 (noting that witness must use visual aids effectively). The Quattlebaum article contains a useful bibliography of articles on videotape depositions and video trial materials, mostly from the 1970s and early 1980s.

[291] Fusco v. General Motors Corp., 11 F.3d 259, 263–64 (1st Cir. 1993).

[292] *Id.* at 263–64.

problem lies with the deliberate re-creation of an event under staged conditions that may not match up sufficiently with the actual conditions.[293]

The problem was not with hearsay but with Federal Rule of Evidence 403, the relevancy rule in which the probativeness of the evidence needs to be balanced against its prejudicial danger.[294]

When either video deposition or prerecorded demonstrative evidence is used at trial, counsel must have ready access to videotape counter readings where selected portions of testimony are recorded so that the appropriate portion of the tape can be located readily at trial.

§ 12.33   Video Trials

The legal system has growing experience with the use of information technology to eliminate the need for everyone to be present at the same place for a trial or other factual hearing.[295] For the most part, these experiences have involved the giving of notice, planning conferences, and the presentation of legal arguments rather than presentation of factual evidence. Undoubtedly, the desire for demeanor information has discouraged the use of remote appearances for fact-finding.

But, as the use of video technology in the deposition context increases and as the use of video transcripts increases, counsel and courts should become more comfortable with the utility of basic video recording and display technology in fact-finding. As this occurs, prerecorded trials become a realistic possibility. For example, here is what one state trial judge had to say recently in an electronic discussion group on the future of courts: "As a Philadelphia judge, I have conducted video arraignments and mandated and conducted 'Prerecorded Videotape Trials' in asbestos cases, where all the testimony had to be presented on videotape, and only opening statements and closing arguments were live."[296]

---

[293] *Id.*

[294] *Compare id.* (videotape of simulated automobile component failure and resulting accident properly excluded because dramatic effect of videotape would likely override jury's awareness that simulated conditions did not correspond to accident conditions) *with* Walls v. Armour Pharmaceutical Co., 832 F. Supp. 1505, 1508–09 (M.D. Fla. 1993) (denying motion for new trial; videotape deposition of child who later died of AIDS was admissible as deposition of declarant unable to be present or testify; pretrial review by judge resulted in editing out portions that went solely to child's pain and suffering).

[295] The possibility of assembling the demonstrative evidence before trial. Recording it on videotape and then showing the videotape to the fact finder is increasingly attractive to litigators and judges on efficiency grounds. There is ample authority under the Federal Rules of Evidence and the Federal Rules of Civil Procedure for that kind of trial presentation. *See* Henry H. Perritt, Jr., *Video Depositions, Transcripts and Trials,* 43 Emory L.J. 1071 (1994).

[296] Judge Richard Klein, Philadelphia Common Pleas Judge from @PUCC.PRINCETON.EDU: OWNER-FUTUREL@VM.TEMPLE.EDU (Mon. Mar. 7 19:48 EST 1994).

In the future, the pretrial and trial process can work like this: a comprehensive pretrial order, similar to the initial pretrial order under present Rule 16, will schedule the deposition of all witnesses either party wishes to call, subject to control by the court under the same standards used to control the actual trial process to promote efficiency and reduce repetition. These witnesses will be deposed on videotape. Objections, of whatever form, will be made as the deposition proceeds and be part of the video record. The depositions would differ from present practice only in the attention given by counsel "sponsoring" a witness to effectiveness on-camera, and to the greater intensity of cross-examination by opposing counsel, somewhat as occurs now for "trial depositions" as opposed to "discovery depositions."

At the final pretrial hearing, the trial judge (or other judicial officer supervising the pretrial process) will hear argument and resolve objections to admissibility, producing a final pretrial order that will designate those portions of the videotape depositions that are inadmissible. The legal process at this point, except for its focus on the video record and further video production activities, will be exactly like ruling on a series of motions in limine.

After the final pretrial hearing, counsel working with appropriate video production and editing personnel will produce the trial program, weaving together the admissible segments of the videotaped depositions. Although this final production stage is not dependent on any particular technology, it is likely that a desktop computer executable trial script, keyed to portions of the raw video record, will selectively present the video signal from portions of a videotape or video disk format to video display devices. Each counsel would have broad discretion within the final pretrial order to arrange the presentation of that counsel's case in the manner desired. If disputes arise during the final production stage, they can be resolved by the trial judge on an ad hoc basis.

Pretrial video productions are not limited to witness testimony. They also can include a variety of simulations, other demonstrative evidence, and views of actual facilities and phenomena. The video-program approach to trials will enhance the possibility of the fact finder seeing evidence that is closer to the actual events giving rise to the controversy, rather than depending on indirect witness recollections and descriptions of reality. The fact finder—jury, administrative law judge, or trial judge—will simply watch the program and make a decision. Counsel and other representative and judicial personnel need be present only to monitor the viewing.

Merely because it is possible to move virtually all of the fact-gathering and fact-presenting activity from the trial to the pretrial stages by the use of video technology does not mean that it is desirable to do so. Analysis of the desirability, however, should focus on real problems and not illusory ones. For example, the security of the video trial program against tampering is not a problem in this context, although it may be a problem for other applications of electronic formats. Because of the adversarial character of the pretrial and trial process, material alterations are likely to be readily detected and objected to appropriately.

CHAPTER 13

CRIMINAL LAW

§ 13.1   Introduction and Nature of Issues

Electronic information technologies create a variety of challenges for criminal law and procedure. They make it possible for wrongdoers to appropriate value that has been created by others—by copying their assets without permission, by obtaining their services without paying, and by accessing their resources without permission either for malicious purposes or for invading the commercial or personal privacy of others. These possibilities raise questions about the applicability of traditional criminal statutes, such as those defining theft and forgery. In addition, a variety of new statutes criminalizing certain kinds of computer fraud and abuse have been enacted, and their application to various kinds of conduct in the NII is worth exploring. Perhaps most prominent in the public awareness is the application to NII participants of criminal laws prohibiting pornography, stalking, and harassment.

Procedurally, also, the growing use of digital information technologies raises challenges for the criminal justice system. For example, as a number of other chapters in this work have noted, the NII links suppliers and users of electronic resources around the world, making it more difficult to localize wrongdoing for purposes of criminal or civil litigation. The same lack of localization makes it difficult to enforce judgments of criminal and civil courts. Also, the nature of electronic resources raises new questions about the interaction between the tools of criminal investigation, especially search warrants and subpoenas, on the one hand, and countervailing privacy and property interests on the other.

§ 13.2   Substantive Crimes

Computers may be involved in criminal activity with respect to storage, communications, and publishing. Computers also may be the target of an offense, the tool of an offense, or incidental to the offense.[1]

The FBI characterizes the following statute sections as most important in prosecuting computer crimes: 18 U.S.C. §§ 2701 (ECPA), 1030 (Computer Fraud and Abuse Act), 641 (embezzlement or theft of public money property or records), 793 (espionage), 798 (espionage), 1341 (mail fraud), and 1343 (wire fraud). Most of those statutes and some others are considered in the following sections.

---

[1] The incidental category includes computers used for record-keeping purposes for drug transactions. Because a single computer system may be used both for criminal purposes and for legitimate purposes, the minimalization requirement, considered in § 13.20, with respect to search warrants is important. 42 U.S.C. § 2000aa also imposes minimalization requirements when a computer is used for publishing purposes. For example, a drug dealer's computer might be used to keep records on the drug transactions and also be used to publish a newsletter. Thus, a warrant should be limited solely to the criminal use of the computer.

One of the problems in prosecuting computer crimes is that the definition of computer in 18 U.S.C. § 1030(e)(1) is broad enough to include microwave ovens with microprocessors, and most advanced telephone systems.[2]

§ 13.3 —Wire Fraud

In 1872[3] the mail fraud statute was enacted as part of a recodification of the postal laws.[4] The statute contained a general proscription against using the mails to initiate correspondence in furtherance of "any scheme or artifice to defraud,"[5] now expressed in 18 U.S.C. § 1341,[6] to prevent the post office from being used to execute fraudulent schemes.[7] Section 1341 represents congressional power to forbid any mailing in furtherance of a scheme that Congress regards as contrary to public policy, even if it does not possess the power to regulate the underlying fraud (the power is reserved for the states).[8] Hence, the federal mail fraud statute

---

[2] Presentation by Scott Charney, Chief, Computer Crime Unit, Criminal Division, U.S. Dep't of Justice, & Hal Hendershot, Supervisory Special Agent, Economic Crime Unit, F.B.I., before Council of A.B.A. Section on Administrative Law and Regulatory Practice (Feb. 5, 1994).

[3] The research and initial drafting for this section was done by William Harrington, Villanova Law School, Class of 1996, law clerk to the author.

[4] *See* McNally v. United States, 483 U.S. 350 (1987) (holding that the mail fraud statute does not prohibit schemes to defraud people of intangible rights). This holding has essentially been overturned by the congressional enactment of 18 U.S.C. § 1346, which includes under the wire and mail fraud statutes schemes to defraud of intangible rights to honest services.

[5] Cong. Globe, 41st Cong., 3d Sess., 35 (1870). "The sponsor of the recodification stated, . . . that measures were needed to prevent the frauds which are mostly gotten up in the large cities . . . by thieves, forgers, and rapscallions."

[6] 18 U.S.C. § 1341 (1995):

Whoever, having devised or intending to devise any scheme or artifice to defraud, or for obtaining money or property by means of false or fraudulent pretenses, representations, or promises, or to sell, dispose of, loan, exchange, alter, give away, distribute, supply, or furnish or procure for unlawful use any counterfeit or spurious coin, obligation, security, or other article for the purpose of executing such scheme or artifice or attempting so to do, places in any post offices or authorized depository for mail matter, any matter or thing whatever to be sent or delivered by the Postal Service, or deposits or causes to be deposited any matter or thing whatever to be sent or delivered by any private or commercial interstate carrier, or takes or receives therefrom, any such matter or thing, or knowingly causes to be delivered by mail or such carrier according to the direction thereon, or at the place at which it is directed to be delivered by the person to whom it is addressed, any such matter or thing, shall be fined under this title or imprisoned not more than five years, or both. If the violation affects a financial institution, such person shall be fined not more than $1,000,000 or imprisoned not more than 30 years, or both.

[7] *See* Durland v. United States, 161 U.S. 306 (1896) (holding defendant liable for mail fraud for using the mails to engage in the sale of bonds with no intent to pay at maturity).

[8] United States v. Lopez, 115 S. Ct. 1624 (1995) (Gun-Free School Zones Act exceeded congressional power under commerce clause); Parr v. United States, 363 U.S. 370 (1960) (quoting Badders v. United States, 240 U.S. 391) (1916)).

does not attempt to reach all frauds, just those involving use of the mails as a part of the execution of the fraud, leaving all other cases to be dealt with under state law.[9]

The wire fraud statute was enacted to complement the mail fraud statute[10] by expanding the jurisdiction of federal prosecutors to include wire transmissions.[11] Therefore, the wire fraud statute uses the same language in relevant part as the mail fraud statute, and violations of both statutes are subject to the same analysis.[12] Congress adopted the wire fraud provisions, § 1343,[13] as part of the 1952 amendments to the Communications Act of 1934.[14] Although the 1952 amendments dealt largely with the regulatory powers of the FCC, nothing in the scope of § 1343 suggests that it is limited to frauds committed by use of interstate wires regulated by the FCC. "On the contrary the legislative history suggests that Congress wished to prohibit as much wire fraud as it could constitutionally make unlawful, limited only by the desire to avoid Federal intrusion upon the police power of the states."[15]

A criminal prosecution under the mail and wire fraud statutes involves a two-pronged analysis: first, the government must prove the formation of a

---

[9] Kann v. United States, 323 U.S. 88, 95 (1944) (holding that the mailing must be for the purpose of executing the fraud, that this purpose was lacking in mailing of checks in this case).

[10] "The wire fraud statute was enacted to cure a jurisdictional defect . . . created by the growth of [new communications technologies]." United States v. LaMacchia, 871 F. Supp. 535, 540 (D. Mass. 1994) (holding defendant not guilty of wire fraud for pirating software and placing it on an internet bulletin board); *see, e.g.,* United States v. Mann, 884 F.2d 532 (10th Cir. 1989) (holding transmission of radio broadcast outside the scope of wire fraud act because the specific advertisement failed to promote the defendant's scheme to defraud); United States v. Andreadis, 366 F.2d 423 (2d Cir. 1966) (holding defendant liable for wire fraud for transmitting false information about weight-loss product in television broadcast). Criminal conduct arising from fraudulent activity carried out in complete reliance upon the use of radio and wire facilities was not within the reach of the then current mail fraud statute. United States v. LaMacchia, 871 F. Supp. at 541 (citing H.R. Rep. No. 388, 82d Cong., 1st Sess. 102 (1951)).

[11] United States v. LaMacchia, 871 F. Supp. 535 (D. Mass. 1994).

[12] Carpenter v. United States, 484 U.S. 19, 25 n.6 (1987) (holding a reporter for a financial newspaper and a stockbroker guilty of both wire and mail fraud for their participation in an insider trading scheme).

[13] 18 U.S.C. § 1343 (1984):

> Whoever, having devised of intending to devise any scheme or artifice to defraud, or for obtaining money or property by means of false or fraudulent pretenses, representations, or promises, transmits or causes to be transmitted by means of wire, radio, or television communication in interstate or foreign commerce, any writings, signs, signals, pictures, or sounds for the purpose of executing such scheme or artifice, shall be fined under this title or imprisoned not more than five years or both. If the violation affects a financial institution, such person shall be fined not more than $1,000,000 or imprisoned not more than 30 years, or both.

[14] *See* United States v. Giovengo, 637 F.2d 941 (3d Cir. 1980) (holding defendant guilty of violating § 1343 for defrauding his employer Trans World Airlines of money paid in cash by passengers for tickets).

[15] *Id.* at 943 (quoting H.R. Rep. No. 388, 82d Cong. 1st Sess. 102 (1951)).

scheme with the intent to defraud; second the government must prove that the defendant used the mails or wires in furthering the fraudulent scheme.[16]

Establishing a Scheme

The first prong, the formation of a scheme with the intent to defraud, requires the government to establish three elements: (1) the existence of a scheme to defraud; (2) accompanied by an intent to do harm; and (3) potential or actual deprivation of property, money, or an intangible right.

When establishing a scheme to defraud, the phrase *to defraud* is defined as it is commonly understood, essentially amounting to dishonest methods or schemes that deprive someone of value by trick or deceit.[17] In *Carpenter v. United States*,[18] the scheme to defraud involved "tipping," giving others confidential stock information held by the *Wall Street Journal*. A reporter at the Journal wrote a column entitled, "Heard on the Street," which evaluated the purchase of certain stocks or groups of stocks. The policy at the Journal was that prior to publication the contents of the column were the Journal's confidential information. The reporter violated this policy by giving others this information before the column was published.[19] Unauthorized release of the information deprived the Journal of its right to exclusive use of the information, thus satisfying the "property" component of the mail fraud statute.[20]

Other schemes to defraud involved the dissemination of files garnered through unauthorized access into a corporation's computer files. In *United States v. Riggs*,[21] the defendant acquired Bell South's emergency 911 text file by accessing its computer system without authorization. The defendant's cohort furthered this fraudulent scheme by editing the file, so that their scheme would not be detected.[22] The defendants then published the edited version of the text file in a newsletter for readers to view and to copy. The property element of wire fraud was based on the telephone company's intangible interest in the confidentiality of the file.[23]

The second element of a scheme to defraud requires the government to establish a specific intent to defraud by showing that the defendant intended for harm to result from his deceit. This does not require showing that the intended victim was actually harmed; only that there was an intent to harm. For example,

---

[16] *See* United States v. Shavin, 287 F.2d 647 (7th Cir. 1961).

[17] Carpenter v. United States, 484 U.S. 19, 27 (1987).

[18] *Id.* at 23.

[19] *Id.*

[20] *Id.* at 26.

[21] 739 F. Supp. 414 (N.D. Ill. 1990) (holding defendant guilty of violating wire fraud statute for illegally accessing corporate computer files).

[22] *Id.* at 417.

[23] *Id.* at 419 n.7.

in *United States v. Loney,*[24] the defendant engaged in a scheme in which she added thousands of unearned frequent flyer miles to accounts of friends and relatives. The defendant argued that there was no evidence that the airlines suffered any financial loss from this scheme because there was no proof that the beneficiaries of the scheme used tickets that displaced fare-paying passengers or that these beneficiaries would have otherwise purchased these tickets. The court dismissed these arguments, stating that the government only had to demonstrate an intent to harm the airline, not that the harm actually resulted.[25]

The third element of a scheme to defraud, establishing an envisioned deprivation of value, is the most controversial aspect of the mail wire fraud analysis. The statute criminalizes deprivations of money,[26] tangible and intangible property,[27] and other intangible rights.[28] Recent litigation has focused in large part on what constitutes property. Courts have taken a broad view of what constitutes *property,* including in that definition computer text files, confidential business information, and frequent flyer miles. In *United States v. Mullens,*[29] mileage credits fraudulently acquired from the airlines were deemed property because the airline books a liability when these mileage credits are issued.

Use of the Mails or Wires in Furthering the Scheme

In the second prong of the mail and wire fraud analysis, the government must prove that the mails and/or wire were used in furthering the scheme. To do so, the government must prove that the use of the mails (wire) was essential to carrying out the scheme. Next, the government must prove that the use of the mails (wire) was reasonably foreseeable to the party engaged in the fraudulent scheme. The government's burden is to establish the use of the mails (wire) as incidental to an essential part of the scheme. Therefore, even if the mails (wire) are not used directly in the scheme to defraud, if they are necessary in effectuating the scheme, the defendant's conduct is covered by mail and wire fraud statute.

---

[24] 959 F.2d 1332 (5th Cir. 1992) (affirming defendants' wire fraud conviction for adding unearned frequent flyer miles to accounts).

[25] *Id.*

[26] *Id.* (holding financial loss actionable under the statute).

[27] Carpenter v. United States, 484 U.S. 19 (1987) (holding that confidential information owned by the newspaper was a protected property interest).

[28] 18 U.S.C. § 1346 (effectively overturns McNally v. United States, 483 U.S. 350 (1987), because it extends property to intangible rights. *McNally* holds that property only addressed property rights not intangible rights such as a politician's fiduciary duty to his constituents.).

[29] 992 F.2d 1472 (9th Cir. 1993). The court in *Mullens* held mileage credits, fraudulently obtained from airline, to be property. This conclusion was based on the fact that the airline corporation owes a liability when it enters mileage credits on its books.

For example, the defendant in *Schmuck v. United States*[30] defrauded retail automobile customers by selling automobiles with altered odometers. Subsequent to buying these automobiles, the purchasers would receive title documents through the mail.[31] Although the mailings did not directly contribute to the fraud, they were essential to the passage of title, which was essential to carrying the scheme to fruition.[32] A mailing that is incident to an essential part of a scheme satisfies the mailing element of the mail fraud offense.[33] Here, the mailing was essential because it made the transaction complete.[34]

In credit card schemes, mailing can be incidental to the fraud but not an essential part of the scheme. In *United States v. Maze,*[35] the defendant used another's credit card to defraud hotels and restaurants of their goods and services. Here, the mailing of the credit invoices to the bank in exchange for payment was incident to the scheme but did not further an essential element of the scheme.[36] The scheme came to fruition at the time the defendant received the goods,[37] and the mailing to the bank actually detracted from the scheme because it increased the chances of being detected.[38]

Using the mails in furtherance of a scheme does not require that the mailing (use of the wire) be accomplished or completed by the defendant. It is a violation of the mail (wire) fraud statute if the defendant caused the mailing to be done. If the defendant did not complete the mailing himself, the use of the mails (wire) must have been known or reasonably foreseeable to the defendant in the ordinary course of business.[39]

The defendant in *United States v. Bentz,*[40] was prosecuted for defrauding a scrap metal broker by misrepresenting the metal he was selling as stainless steel. The defendant violated the wire fraud statute because he was paid for the scrap metal via computer-generated checks, from data transmitted over interstate wires.[41] The court held that the defendant did not violate § 1343 because there was no proof that he knew that the checks were transmitted over interstate wires, nor was it reasonably foreseeable that the checks would be transmitted in this fashion.[42]

---

[30] 489 U.S. 705 (1989).

[31] *Id.* at 707.

[32] *Id.* at 712.

[33] *Id.* at 712–15.

[34] *Id.* at 714.

[35] 414 U.S. 395 (1973).

[36] *Id.* at 402–03.

[37] *Id.* at 403.

[38] *Id.* at 395.

[39] *Id.*

[40] 21 F.3d 37 (3d Cir. 1994).

[41] *Id.* at 37.

[42] *Id.*

In contrast, in *Pereira v. United States*,[43] the defendant tricked a victim into loaning him money to invest in a nonexistent hotel. The defendant secured the victim's trust by marrying her. Then he tricked her into loaning him the money.[44] While the defendant in this case did not directly use the mails to carry out the scheme, the money loaned to the defendant was paid to the defendant in check form mailed from an out-of-state bank.[45] The defendant violated the mail fraud statute because he knew that the check was going to be mailed.[46]

§ 13.4   —Copyright Infringement as Wire Fraud

"The issue is whether the bundle of rights conferred by copyright is unique and distinguishable from the indisputably broad range of property interests protected by the mail and wire fraud statutes."[47] The court in *United States v. LaMacchia* held that copyrights are unique and prosecution of copyright violations under the mail fraud statute is not allowable absent a clear indication of congressional intent.[48] The court declined to allow the government to "subvert the carefully calculated penalties of the Copyright Act by selectively bringing some prosecutions under the more generous penalties of the mail and wire fraud statutes."[49]

In *United States v. LaMacchia,* the government argued that the defendant violated the wire fraud statute by making available pirated software on the Internet for others to download.[50] The object of the scheme was facilitation of illegal copying and distribution of copyrighted software without payment of licensing fees and royalties to the software manufacturers.[51] The court concluded that the defendant did not commit a criminal act under the copyright statute because he did not profit monetarily or commercially from his conduct.[52] Further, the court noted that if the defendant could be prosecuted for his actions under the wire fraud statute, the conduct of the vast number of home computer

---

[43] 347 U.S. 1, 4 (1954).

[44] *Id.* at 4–5.

[45] *Id.* at 5.

[46] *Id.* at 12.

[47] United States v. LaMacchia, 871 F. Supp. 535, 543 (D. Mass. 1994).

[48] *Id.* at 535. Infringing a copyright "willfully and for purposes of commercial advantage or private financial gain" is a crime. 17 U.S.C. § 506(a). The crime extends to fraudulent removal of copyright notices. 17 U.S.C. § 506(d). The commercial gain element does not necessitate realization at a profit. United States v. Cross, 816 F.2d 297, 301 (7th Cir. 1987). Penalties for violation of these provisions may reach five years incarceration depending on the magnitude of the infringement. 18 U.S.C. § 2319.

[49] United States v. LaMacchia, 871 F. Supp. 535, 544 (D. Mass. 1994).

[50] *Id.* at 545.

[51] *Id.* at 544.

[52] *Id.* at 536.

users who copy only a single software program for private use would be criminalized as well.[53] The court stated that if Congress intended to reach this activity it would need to revise the copyright act; "it is the legislature, not the court which is to define a crime and ordain its punishment."[54]

The court distinguished *LaMacchia* from its antecedent *Dowling v. United States*.[55] In *Dowling,* the defendant had an affirmative duty to notify copyright owners of the intention to distribute audio recordings. The defendant in *Dowling* sold bootleg Elvis Presley albums by soliciting catalogue orders from post office boxes.[56] Nondisclosure with an intent to deprive the copyright owners of their royalties in *Dowling* served as an obvious means of furthering a scheme to defraud.[57]

Nevertheless, infringing a copyright "willfully and for purposes of commercial advantage or private financial gain" is a crime.[58] The crime extends to fraudulent removal of copyright notices.[59] The commercial gain element does not necessitate realization of a profit.[60] Penalties range to five years incarceration depending on the magnitude of the infringement.[61]

§ 13.5   —Computer Fraud and Abuse

The Computer Fraud and Abuse Act[62] makes it a crime to access certain computers without authorization or in excess of authorization and thereby to cause certain results.[63] Violations are punishable by up to 10 years imprisonment and up to 20 years for a repeat offense.[64] The Secret Service has authority to investigate offenses.[65] Computers covered by the Act include computers used by financial institutions or the United States government and any computer "which

---

[53] *Id.* at 545.

[54] 871 F. Supp. at 545 (quoting Dowling v. United States, 473 U.S. 207, 214 (1985)).

[55] 473 U.S. 207 (1985).

[56] *Id.* at 209–11.

[57] *Id.* at 228.

[58] 17 U.S.C. § 506(a) (1995). *See generally* United States v. LaMacchia, 871 F. Supp. 535 (D. Mass. 1994) (dismissing indictment under wire fraud statute for facilitating distribution of infringing articles via Internet server in part because no intent for private financial gain and thus no violation of criminal copyright section).

[59] 17 U.S.C. § 506(d).

[60] United States v. Cross, 816 F.2d 297, 301 (7th Cir. 1987) (it is purpose that counts).

[61] *See* 18 U.S.C. § 2319 (providing penalties for criminal copyright infringement).

[62] 18 U.S.C. § 1030.

[63] *Id.* § 1030(a).

[64] *Id.* § 1030(c).

[65] *Id.* § 1030(d).

is one of two or more computers used in committing the offense, not all of which are located in the same state."[66] Thus, an interstate access is subject to the Act. The following offenses are criminalized by the statute:

1. Obtaining classified information pertaining to national defense or foreign relations or restricted atomic energy data with intent or reason to believe that the information so obtained is to be used to the injury of the United States or to the advantage of any foreign nation[67]

2. Obtaining information contained in a financial record of a financial institution, of a credit card issuer, or of a consumer reporting agency relating to a consumer[68]

3. Accessing a computer of a department or agency of the United States and adversely affecting the government's use of such computer[69]

4. Furthering an intended fraud by accessing a covered computer unless the fraud consists only of the use of the computer[70]

5. Transmitting program, information, code, or command intending that it will damage a computer system, data, or program or delay or deny the use of such program if such conduct causes loss or damage aggregating more than $1,000 during any one-year period[71] or

6. Transmitting data, information, code, or program that actually or potentially modifies or impairs medical information[72]

7. Transmitting program, information, code, or command with reckless disregard of a substantial and unjustifiable risk that the transmission will damage the operation of computer system, information, data, or program or deny or delay the use of a computer system and thereby cause more than $1,000 aggregate damage during a one-year period, or modify or impair medical information[73] or

8. Knowingly and with intent to defraud, trafficking in any computer access passwords.[74]

Intentional access is sufficient; the government need not prove intent to cause damage or injury.[75] Also, using a computer system to which one has authorized access for an unauthorized purpose satisfies the unauthorized access element.[76]

---

[66] Id. § 1030(e)(2)(D).

[67] Id. § 1030(a)(1).

[68] 18 U.S.C. § 1030(a)(2).

[69] Id. § 1030(a)(3).

[70] Id. § 1030(a)(4).

[71] Id. § 1030(a)(5)(A).

[72] Id.

[73] Id. § 1030(a)(5)(B).

[74] 18 U.S.C. § 1030(a)(6).

[75] United States v. Morris, 928 F.2d 504, 505 (2d Cir. 1991) (affirming conviction of computer science graduate student who introduced worm, a damaging "virus-like" program, into Internet).

[76] Id. at 509–510.

Increasingly, expert systems have become useful in detecting unusual system access that might signal the activities of an intruder. The Next Generation Intruder Detection Expert System (NGIDES), for example, detects sign-ons made outside the normal pattern. A user may sign on at 9:30 A.M. every day. The NGIDES would alert the system administrator to a sign-on with that user name at 8:00 A.M.

§ 13.6 —Unauthorized Access and Disclosure

The Electronic Communications Privacy Act (ECPA) is used to prosecute unauthorized access and certain disclosures. Anyone who intentionally accesses without authorization a facility through which an electronic communication service is provided or intentionally exceeds an authorization to access that facility and "thereby obtains, alters, or prevents authorized access to a wire or electronic communication while it is in electronic storage of such system" is subject of a fine of up to $250,000 (under 18 U.S.C. § 3571(b)(3)) and imprisonment for up to one year for a first offense if the offense is committed for purposes of commercial advantage, malicious destruction or damage, or private commercial gain.[77] The maximum term of incarceration increases to two years for subsequent offenses.[78] When the criminal intent requirements are not satisfied, the fine drops to $5,000 and the imprisonment term drops to six months.[79]

Intentional interception or disclosure of electronic communication streams is subject to imprisonment for up to five years.[80] Of course, it is not an offense to disclose pursuant to a warrant or other judicial process, discussed in § **13.15**.[81] Interception and disclosure of electronic communication streams is discussed further in **Chapter 3.**

§ 13.7 —Pornography

Federal pornography statutes focus on child pornography.[82] One who "knowingly makes, prints, or publishes, or causes to be made, printed, or published" advertisements seeking to receive, exchange, buy, produce, display, distribute, or reproduce any visual depiction involving the use of a minor in sexually explicit conduct is subject to imprisonment for up to 10 years.[83] The predicate mental state is knowing or having reason to know that the notice or advertisement will be transported in interstate or foreign commerce "by any means

---

[77] 18 U.S.C. § 2701.

[78] *Id.* § 2701(b)(1)(b).

[79] *Id.* § 2701(b)(2).

[80] 18 U.S.C. § 2511(4).

[81] ECPA is discussed further in **Ch. 3.**

[82] 18 U.S.C. § 2251.

[83] *Id.* § 2251(c).

including by computer, or if the notice or advertisement actually is transported in interstate or foreign commerce by any means including by computer."[84] The "causes to be made, printed, or published" language is broad enough to include establishing a pointer on a web server to a notice or advertisement located on another server.

Many state statutes prohibit similar conduct[85] while other state statutes are much broader.[86] For example, Illinois provides, "A person commits obscenity when, with knowledge of the nature or content thereof, or recklessly failing to exercise reasonable inspection which would have disclosed the nature or content thereof, he sells, delivers or provides, . . . publishes, exhibits or otherwise makes available anything obscene."[87] Under the Illinois statute, any property used in any manner to commit the offense of obscenity is subject to forfeiture.[88] A separate hearing after conviction for obscenity focuses on whether the property is subject to forfeiture, for which the state has the burden of proof.[89]

New York's forfeiture statute is somewhat narrower, covering only "equipment used in the photographic, filming, printing, producing, manufacturing or projecting of pornographic still or motion pictures."[90]

The Missouri statute criminalizes only pornography aimed at minors or possession of obscene material for the purpose of pecuniary gain.[91]

The Oregon statute focuses on causing material to be brought into the state: "A person commits the crime of transporting child pornography into Oregon if the person knowingly brings into this state, or causes to be brought or sent into this state, for sale or distribution" material depicting sexually explicit conduct involving a child.[92]

---

[84] *Id.* § 2251(c)(2). United States v. Chapman, 60 F.3d 894 (1st Cir. 1995) (vacating sentence imposed for violation of 18 U.S.C. § 2252(a)(l) for transmitting child pornography via America Online); United States v. Maxwell, 42 M.J. 568 (A.F. Crim. App. 1995) (affirming court martial conviction of air force officer for exchanging child pornography via America Online in violation of 18 U.S.C. § 2252).

[85] Alaska Stat. § 11.61.125 (distribution of child pornography by possessing, preparing, publishing, or printing with intent to distribute defined material).

[86] *See* Ala. Code § 13A-12-200.2 (1994) (possessing with intent to distribute obscene material for pecuniary value); Ariz. Rev. Stat. Ann. § 13-3502 (transporting or transmitting in interstate commerce for commercial distribution any obscene item); Cal. Penal Code § 311.1 (west) (causing to be brought into the state for sale or distribution or possessing within the state with intent to distribute child obscenity); Fla. Stat. Ann. § 847.06 (West 1994) (knowingly transporting into the state for purpose of sale or distribution any matter of obscene character); Md. Ann. Code. art. 27 (crimes and punishments), § 418 (1994) (knowingly sending or causing to be sent or brought into the state for sale or distribution or distributing within the state obscene matter).

[87] Ill. Rev. Stat. ch. 720, para. 5/11-20 (Supp. 1995).

[88] *Id.* para. 5/11-20(g)(3)(ii).

[89] *Id.* para. 5/11-20(g)(4).

[90] N.Y. Penal Law § 410.00(1) (McKinney 1994).

[91] Mo. Rev. Stat. § 573.030 (1994) (based on New York Penal Law § 235.05).

[92] Or. Rev. Stat. § 163.677(1) (1993).

The California statute explicitly exempts telephone companies from liability for transmitting messages described in the section.[93]

A Michigan statute permits the chief executive or legal officer of any municipality to obtain an injunction against further sale or distribution of any

> book, magazine, pamphlet, comic book, story paper, writing, paper, picture, drawing, photograph, figure or image of any written or printed matter of any indecent character, which is obscene, lewd, lascivious, filthy, indecent, or disgusting or which contains an article instrument of indecent or immoral use or purports to be for indecent or immoral use or a purpose.[94]

Another Michigan statute criminalizes knowing distribution of obscene matter to minors.[95]

New Jersey statute criminalizing obscenity for minors defines *knowingly* as "having knowledge of the character and content of the material or film . . . or having failed to exercise reasonable inspection which would disclose its character and content."[96]

The Pennsylvania statute defines *knowingly* as "having general knowledge of, or reason to know or a belief or ground for belief which warrants further inspection or inquiry of, the character and content of any material or performance described therein which is reasonably susceptible of examination by the defendant."[97] The "reasonably susceptible of examination" language is an appropriate proviso with respect to technologies like the World Wide Web.

The Texas statute takes a somewhat different approach to the mental state: "A person commits an offense if he intentionally or knowingly displays or distributes an obscene photograph, drawing, or similar visual representation or other obscene material and is reckless about whether a person is present who will be offended or alarmed by the display or distribution."[98] This might include the operator of a web server who failed to post appropriate warnings around potentially offensive material.

Virginia prohibits possession of obscene items with intent to distribute.[99] *Distribute* is defined to include "any other means by which obscene items . . . may pass from one person . . . to another."[100]

In *United States v. X-Citement Video, Inc.,*[101] the Supreme Court held, in a somewhat strained linguistic interpretation of 18 U.S.C. § 2252, that the federal

---

[93] Cal. Penal Code § 311.2(g) (West 1994).

[94] Mich. Comp. Laws § 600.2938(1) (1994).

[95] *Id.* § 722.675.

[96] N.J. Rev. Stat. § 2(C):34-3(a)(5) (1994).

[97] 18 Pa. Cons. Stat. § 5903(b) (1994).

[98] Tex. Penal Code Ann. § 43.22(a) (West 1995).

[99] Va. Code Ann. § 18.2-374 (Michie 1994).

[100] *Id.* § 18.2-374(4).

[101] 115 S. Ct. 464 (1994) (adopting tortured interpretation of statute criminalizing distribution of child pornography in order to find a knowledge element with respect to the age of the performer and thus avoid First Amendment problems that would result from no-fault criminal liability).

child pornography statute is constitutional only because the knowingly element applies to knowledge of the content of the accused material.[102]

§ 13.8 —Transportation of Stolen Property

Section 2314 of Title 18 provides:

> Whoever transports, transmits, or transfers in interstate or foreign commerce any goods, wares, merchandise, securities or money, of the value of $5,000 or more, knowing the same to have been stolen, converted or taken by fraud . . . shall be fined not more than $10,000 or imprisoned not more than 10 years, or both."

United States v. Riggs[103] concerned a prosecution for interstate transportation of stolen property, among others, and for stealing proprietary information contained in 911 computer text files and publishing that information. The district court in *Riggs* characterized as an issue of first impression whether the electronic nature of the business information moving from one computer to another across state lines defeated the "goods, wares, merchandise, securities or money" element of § 2314. The defendant argued that § 2314 was not violated because the only thing he caused to be transferred across state lines was electronic impulses. The district court rejected that argument, finding a number of cases involving fraudulent transmission of money across state lines through electronic impulses.[104] It thus found that the proprietary information contained in the telephone company's 911 text file constituted a "good . . . or merchandise" within the statute, based on the proprietary nature of the information.[105] It did recognize, however, that some courts have taken the position that a "thing" is never transferred within contemplation of § 2314 when the thing never takes tangible form.[106] The Tenth Circuit disagreed with Riggs, however, in *United States v. Brown*,[107] finding that the tangibility requirement of the stolen property statute is essential.[108]

§ 13.9 —Threatening Communications

On February 9, 1995, a University of Michigan student was charged in a criminal complaint with transmitting threatening communications in interstate

---

[102] *Id.* at 469.

[103] 739 F. Supp. 414 (N.D. Ill. 1990).

[104] *Id.* at 420.

[105] *Id.*

[106] *Id.* at 421 (citing cases).

[107] 925 F.2d 1301 (10th Cir. 1991) (affirming dismissal of indictment for alleged theft of computer program and source code).

[108] *Id.* 1308–09.

commerce in violation of 18 U.S.C. § 875(c). The threatening communications were a combination of postings to a newsgroup and private E-mail communications fantasizing about kidnapping and torturing a fellow student.[109] The district court subsequently dismissed the indictment, based on First Amendment protections.[110]

§ 13.10   —Crimes under RICO

Series of computer crimes potentially implicate the Racketeer Influenced and Corrupt Organizations Act (RICO). However, not all common computer crimes constitute "predicate crimes" in order to be within RICO's scope. RICO dates from 1970, when, following more than 10 years of struggle,[111] Congress passed the Organized Crime Control Act (OCCA),[112] of which RICO is a part.[113]

RICO consists of eight subsections in Title 18 of the United States Code, containing civil and criminal provisions. Section 1961 contains the definitions for critical terms used in RICO, such as "racketeering activity,"[114]

---

[109] *See generally* United States v. Alkhabaz, No. 95-1184 (6th Cir.) (Brief for the United States, filed Feb. 22, 1995).

[110] United States v. Baker, 890 F. Supp. 1375 (E.D. Mich. 1995).

[111] In November 1957, a force of New York State police troopers stumbled upon a dinner meeting of 75 Sicilian men. Many of the men were suspected heads of crime families from all parts of the country. The dinner attendees had 223 collective arrests and convictions, and the government had its long sought-after proof of the existence of what it called the Mafia, an intricately organized criminal alliance. The discovery led to massive investigations by federal, state, and local authorities and a push for federal legislation that would assist in the prosecution of organized crime. Judge Gerard L. Goettel, Foreword to Paul A. Batista, Civil RICO Practice Manual at vii (John Wiley & Sons, 1987).

[112] Pub. L. No. 91-452, 84 Stat. 941 (1970).

[113] *Id.* tit. IX (codified as amended at 18 U.S.C. §§ 1961–1968 (1988 & Supp. V 1993)). "The original purpose of RICO was to afford federal law enforcement a broad and far-reaching tool to root out organized crime from legitimate business and to prevent the infiltration of legitimate business by organized crime." Stephen D. Brown & Alan M. Lieberman, RICO Basics: A Primer, 35 Vill. L. Rev. 865 (1990) (citing United States v. Turkette, 452 U.S. 576, 591 (1981)).

[114] 18 U.S.C. § 1961(1). *Racketeering activity* is defined as

(A) any act or threat involving murder, kidnaping, gambling, arson, robbery, bribery, extortion, dealing in obscene matter, or dealing in narcotic or other dangerous drugs, which is chargeable under State law and punishable by imprisonment for more than one year; (B) any act which is indictable under any of the following provisions of title 18, ... (C) any act which is indictable under title 29, United States Code, section 186 (dealing with restrictions on payments and loans to labor organizations) or section 501(c) (relating to embezzlement from union funds), (D) any offense involving fraud connected with a case under title 11, fraud in the sale of securities, or the felonious manufacture, importation, receiving, concealment, buying, selling, or otherwise dealing in narcotic or other dangerous drugs, punishable under any law of the United States, or (E) any act which is indictable under the Currency and Foreign Transactions Reporting Act.

"enterprise,"[115] and "pattern of racketeering activity."[116] Section 1962 enumerates the activities made unlawful by RICO. Sections 1963 and 1964 establish the criminal penalties and civil remedies, respectively, available for any violation of RICO. Finally, the last four sections comprise the procedural framework for the statute.[117]

Each of the substantive RICO crimes[118] revolves around the acquisition or operation of an "enterprise," and a "pattern" of "racketeering activity" with respect to that enterprise.[119] In order to understand RICO, it is important to understand how the statute defines each term and how the courts have interpreted them.

An *enterprise* under RICO is an umbrella term covering any association of individual persons or groups of people, including legal organizations, like partnerships and corporations, and nonlegal organizations, where an association may be found "in fact."[120] Congress defined "enterprise" broadly, encompassing corporations, loose and mixed associations, and individual criminals.[121] "Enterprise" includes legitimate and illegitimate associations,[122] and a RICO enterprise need not be "economically motivated."[123]

Computer fraud, a federal crime under 18 U.S.C. § 1030, has not yet been included as a predicate racketeering activity contemplated by RICO § 1961(1). *See id.* (Significantly, it is not included within the specified provisions of title 18 listed in subpart (B).). Section 1030 was enacted in 1984 in the Comprehensive Crime Control Act to make unlawful the unauthorized use of computers for improper means. Pub. L. No. 98-473, 98 Stat. 1837, 2190–91 (1984), *reprinted in* 1984 U.S.C.C.A.N. 1837, 2190–92. Congress has amended RICO several times, including in the Comprehensive Crime Control Act of 1984, but has not included § 1030 within the definition of racketeering activity.

[115] 18 U.S.C. § 1961(4). *Enterprise,* under RICO, "includes any individual, partnership, corporation, association, or other legal entity, and any union or group of individuals associated in fact although not a legal entity."

[116] *Id.* § 1961(5). *Pattern of racketeering activity* is defined as requiring "at least two acts of racketeering activity, one of which occurred after the effective date of this chapter and the last of which occurred within ten years (excluding any period of imprisonment) after the commission of a prior act of racketeering activity."

[117] *Id.* § 1965 ("Venue and process"); *id.* § 1966 ("Expedition of actions"); *id.* § 1967 ("Evidence"); *id.* § 1968 ("Civil investigative demand").

[118] 18 U.S.C. §§ 1962(a)–(d).

[119] *Id.*

[120] *Id.* § 1961(4). "The number of persons making up an enterprise is irrelevant, however, in that even a single individual may be considered an 'enterprise' under the statutory definition." United States v. Elliott, 571 F.2d 880, 898 n.18 (5th Cir. 1978).

[121] George E. Lynch, *A Conceptual, Practical, and Political Guide to RICO Reform,* 43 Vand. L. Rev. 769, 771 (1990). Congress chose not to encumber "enterprise" with an exact definition, using instead a list of illustrative examples, indicating by the use of the word "includes," that the list was not all-encompassing. *Id.* at n.3.

[122] United States v. Turkette, 452 U.S. 576, 580–81 (1981).

[123] National Org. for Women, Inc. v. Scheidler, 114 S. Ct. 798, 805 (1994). The defendants, a coalition of antiabortion organizations and individuals, argued and the district court agreed that in order to be considered an enterprise under RICO, an association must be engaged in

Initially, RICO was enacted with "gangsters" in mind, so the acts considered "racketeering" were those that made gangsters infamous, such as murder, extortion, and the drug trade.[124] However, Congress made sure that the defined acts were broad enough to take into account the notion that "the mob . . . would try anything for a profit."[125] Concurrently with the expanded use of RICO,[126] Congress expanded the scope of conduct considered to be racketeering activities.[127] Presently RICO "racketeering activity" consists of five broad categories of conduct.[128] The first category includes actual or threatened state crimes of murder, kidnapping, gambling, arson, robbery, bribery, extortion, and dealing in obscene matter or drugs.[129] The second category includes mail and wire fraud, money laundering, interstate transportation of stolen property, and white slave trafficking under Title 18 of the United States Code.[130] The third category addresses associations with labor organizations and embezzlement from union funds in violation of Title 29.[131] The fourth category includes Title 11 fraud,

---

racketeering activities at least partly for the purpose of generating income. *Id.* at 802. The Supreme Court rejected this argument by pointing out that the language of § 1962(c) includes enterprises that "affect" interstate commerce, which the Court held to mean: have a "detrimental influence on." *Id.* at 804 (quoting Webster's Third New International Dictionary 35 (1969)). The Court concluded that, "An enterprise surely can have a detrimental influence on interstate or foreign commerce without having its own profit-seeking motives." *Id.*

[124] *See* H.J. Inc. v. Northwestern Bell Tel. Co., 492 U.S. 229, 245 (1989); Russello v. United States, 464 U.S. 16, 26 (1983); United States v. Turkette, 452 U.S. 576, 591 (1981). "Congress focused on, and the examples used in the debates and reports to illustrate the Act's operation concern, the predations of mobsters. Organized crime was without a doubt Congress's major target." *H.J. Inc.,* 492 U.S. at 245.

[125] George E. Lynch, *A Conceptual, Practical, and Political Guide to RICO Reform,* 43 Vand. L. Rev., 769, 773 (1990).

[126] *See* Stephen D. Brown & Alan M. Lieberman, *RICO Basics: A Primer,* 35 Vill. L. Rev. 865, 865 (1990).

> It has been used in wrongful discharge cases [Shearin v. E.F. Hutton Group, Inc., 885 F.2d 1162 (3d Cir. 1989)], against pro-life activists [Northeast Women's Center, Inc. v. McMonagle, 868 F.2d 1342 (3d Cir. 1989)], in securities cases [Sheridan v. Weinberger, 687 F. Supp. 152 (M.D. Pa. 1987); Gilbert v. Prudential-Bache Sec., Inc., 643 F. Supp. 107 (E.D. Pa. 1986)], and virtually every other area of litigation [including commercial bribery, ERISA, and breach of contract].

Id. at 865 & nn.4–7.

[127] *See, e.g.,* amendments to RICO § 1961(1): Pub. L. No. 101-73, 103 Stat. 183 (1989) (added § 1344 relating to financial institution fraud); Pub. L. No. 99-646, 100 Stat. 3592 (1986) (added §§ 1512 & 1513 relating to witness tampering and retaliation); Pub. L. No. 98-473, 98 Stat. 1837, 2136, 2143 (1984) (added violations of the Currency and Foreign Transactions Reporting Act and §§ 1461–1465 relating to obscene matter).

[128] 18 U.S.C. § 1961(1)(A)–(E).

[129] *Id.* § 1961(1)(A). Crimes under the first category must carry a prison sentence of more than one year.

[130] *Id.* § 1961(1)(B).

[131] *Id.* § 1961(1)(C).

securities fraud, and federal drug offenses.[132] The fifth category includes any act indictable under the Currency and Foreign Transactions Reporting Act.[133]

The definition of *pattern of racketeering activity* requires that at least two racketeering activities be committed, and that they occur within 10 years of each other,[134] an extremely broad scope.[135] The definition merely "place[d] an outer limit on the concept of a pattern of racketeering,"[136] however, while the legislative history indicates that the predicate acts must be related and "amount to . . . a threat of continued criminal activity."[137]

The Supreme Court looked to Title X of the OCCA to help define the relation necessary for a pattern of racketeering activities to exist under RICO.[138] The majority of the Court agreed that Congress intended criminal conduct to form a pattern under RICO "if [the conduct] embraces criminal acts that have the same or similar purposes, results, participants, victims, or methods of commission, or otherwise are interrelated by distinguishing characteristics and are not isolated events."[139]

---

[132] *Id.* § 1961(1)(D).

[133] *Id.* § 1961(1)(E). This statute is addressed in **Ch. 14.**

[134] 18 U.S.C. § 1961(5). These racketeering activities are commonly referred to as "predicate crimes."

[135] The Supreme Court in Sedima, S.P.R.L. v. Imrex Co., 473 U.S. 479 (1985), "suggested" that the seemingly limitless construction of the pattern requirement was one of the major reasons of the breadth of RICO's reach. *See* H.J. Inc. v. Northwestern Bell Tel. Co., 492 U.S. 229, 236 (1989) (citing *Sedima,* 473 U.S. at 500 and *id.* at 501–02 (Marshall, J., dissenting)). The Court attempted to guide the lower courts in their analyses of "pattern of racketeering activity" by advancing four "clues":

> First, we stated that the statutory definition of the term in 18 U.S.C. § 1961(5) implies "that while two act are necessary, they may not be sufficient." Second, we pointed out that "two isolated acts of racketeering activity," "sporadic activity," and "proof of two acts of racketeering activity, without more" would not be enough to constitute a pattern. Third, we quoted a snippet from the legislative history stating "[i]t is this factor of continuity plus relationship which combines to produce a pattern." Finally, we directed lower courts' attention to 18 U.S.C. § 3575(e), which defined the term "pattern of conduct which was criminal" used in a different title of the same Act, and instructed them that "[t]his language may be useful in interpreting other sections of the Act."

492 U.S. at 251 (Scalia, J., concurring in the judgment) (emphasis omitted) (citations omitted). However, Congress did not respond with any clarification.

[136] H.J. Inc. v. Northwestern Bell Tel. Co., 492 U.S. 229, 237 (1989).

[137] *Id.* at 239. The Court relied heavily on the statements of RICO's principal sponsor, Senator McClellan, such as, "It is this factor of continuity plus relationship which combines to produce a pattern." *Id.* (emphasis omitted).

[138] *Id.* at 239–40.

[139] *Id.* at 240 (quoting 18 U.S.C. § 3575(e)). The concurrence, however, found fault in the majority's conclusion. *Id.* at 251–56. (Scalia, J., concurring in the judgment). Justice Scalia not only found the § 3575(e) definition "utterly uninformative," but stated,

> [I]f normal (and sensible) rules of statutory construction were followed, the existence of § 3575(e)—which is the definition contained in another title of the Act that was

But merely because a series of predicate acts are shown to be related is not sufficient.[140] The prosecution must show that the acts indicate a continuing threat of racketeering activity.[141] Continuity can be established if the predicate acts themselves evidence an implicit or explicit threat of "long-term racketeering activity," or if they are activities normally undertaken by the offending enterprise.[142]

The crimes constituting violations of RICO are divided into three substantive prohibitions and a conspiracy provision.[143] The first two prohibitions, which punish the acquisition of an enterprise involved in interstate commerce through the use of income gained from a pattern of racketeering activity[144] and the acquisition of an enterprise by racketeering activities,[145] are not as widely used as the third.[146] A person[147] is prohibited from investing any money obtained from a pattern of racketeering activity[148] in the acquisition and operation of an enterprise involved in interstate commerce.[149] Likewise, it is unlawful for a person to obtain an enterprise engaged in interstate commerce directly by means of activities that add up to a pattern of racketeering.[150] In other words, the first two prohibitions make it illegal to invest in businesses with racketeering profits or to use fraud or strong-arm tactics to acquire a business.

The third prohibition, § 1962 (c), is the broadest and is the basis for a large percentage of both civil and criminal RICO cases.[151] It makes it a crime to operate an enterprise by a pattern of racketeering,[152] regardless of how the

---

explicitly *not* rendered applicable to RICO—suggests that *whatever* "pattern" might mean in RICO, it assuredly *does not* mean that. . . . "[W]here Congress includes particular language in one section of the same Act, it is generally presumed that Congress act intentionally and purposely in the disparate inclusion or exclusion."

[140] 492 U.S. 229, 239–40 (1989). Although this is a separate element from relatedness, the Court acknowledged that "in practice their proof will often overlap." *Id.*

[141] *Id.*

[142] *Id.* at 243.

[143] 18 U.S.C. § 1962(a)–(d). The conspiracy provision prohibits the conspiracy to violate any of the first three provisions. *Id.* § 1962(d).

[144] *Id.* § 1962(a).

[145] *Id.* § 1962(b).

[146] George E. Lynch, *A Conceptual, Practical, and Political Guide to RICO Reform,* 43 Vand. L. Rev. 769, 770 (1990).

[147] A *person* under RICO "includes any individual or entity capable of holding a legal or beneficial interest in property." 18 U.S.C. § 1961(3).

[148] Prohibitions under each form of RICO violation include "through collection of an unlawful debt" in addition to through a pattern of racketeering. *See id.* § 1962(a)–(d).

[149] *Id.* § 1962(a).

[150] *Id.* § 1962(b).

[151] George E. Lynch, *A Conceptual, Practical, and Political Guide to RICO Reform,* 43 Vand. L. Rev., 769, 774 (1990) (An "overwhelming majority of RICO cases . . . are predicated on subsection (c)").

[152] 18 U.S.C. § 1962(c).

enterprise was obtained. Therefore, a civil or criminal action can be brought against anyone in a legitimate business or association, or the organization of a criminal "family," whose activities in the course of managing the enterprise's affairs include a pattern of racketeering.[153]

RICO is both a criminal[154] and civil statute.[155] As a criminal statute, RICO provides the government with a tool to punish "the crime of being a criminal."[156] A criminal RICO violator can face fines and/or prison[157] and forfeiture of property and interests related to the conviction.[158] A civil action may be brought by the government[159] or through a private action by an individual injured as a result of the RICO violation.[160] For an individual seeking compensation from the defendant, RICO permits recovery of treble damages and reasonable attorneys' fees and costs.[161] Other civil remedies available to a court under RICO include restricting and even divesting an individual's interests in an enterprise and forcing the dissolution or reorganization of an enterprise.[162]

In understanding RICO and its potential impact on computer-related legal issues, it is helpful to consider why the defendant in *LaMacchia* could not have been prosecuted under RICO.[163] In order to prosecute under RICO, the government must establish "'(1) conduct (2) of an enterprise (3) through a pattern (4) of racketeering activity.'"[164] The fourth requirement, "racketeering activity," is not present in the facts of *LaMacchia* (discussed in § **13.4**). While wire fraud is a predicate act under RICO,[165] the court held that the defendant did not violate § 1343.[166] Moreover, the court determined that he did not violate the

---

[153] George E. Lynch, *A Conceptual, Practical, and Political Guide to RICO Reform*, 43 Vand. L. Rev. 769, 774 (1990).

[154] 18 U.S.C. § 1963.

[155] *Id.* § 1964.

[156] George E. Lynch, *RICO: The Crime of Being a Criminal*, 87 Colum. L. Rev. 661 (1987).

[157] 18 U.S.C. § 1963(a). The maximum sentence is 20 years unless the violation is based on an underlying racketeering activity that carries a maximum life term, in which case the maximum penalty for the RICO count is also life.

[158] *Id.*

[159] *Id.* § 1963(b).

[160] *Id.* § 1963(c).

[161] *Id.*

[162] *Id.* § 1964(a).

[163] *See* United States v. LaMacchia, 871 F. Supp. 535 (D. Mass. 1994).

[164] Azrielli v. Cohen Law Offices, 21 F.3d 512, 520 (2d Cir. 1994) (quoting Sedima S.P.R.L. v. Imrex Co., 473 U.S. 479, 105 S. Ct. 3275, 3285 (1985)).

[165] 18 U.S.C. § 1961(1)(B) ("any act which is indictable under any of the following provisions of title 18 . . . section 1343 (relating to wire fraud)").

[166] 871 F. Supp 535, 542 (D. Mass. 1994). The court determined that where the allegation of wire fraud is based on nondisclosure of information such as "conceal[ment of] . . . activities from the copyright holders with the intent to deprive them of their royalties," it is only actionable

copyright statute; but even if it did find a violation, a violation of the Copyright Act is not included among the predicate acts listed under the definition of racketeering activities of RICO.[167]

While the facts of *LaMacchia* precluded a RICO prosecution, one can easily envision computer-facilitated conduct, such as money laundering, in which the underlying conduct would fall within RICO.

§ 13.11   —State Crimes

A number of states have statutes similar to the Computer Fraud and Abuse Act[168] and ECPA.[169] The crime of terroristic threat could be committed by sending a message threatening to commit a crime of violence with a purpose to terrorize someone or cause public inconvenience.[170] One who threatens to expose a secret tending to subject a person to hatred, contempt, or ridicule or to impair credit or business reputation constitutes the crime of criminal coercion.[171] It is possible that one who puts in motion a chain of events that could completely disrupt the operation of communication systems or financial systems could commit the crime of causing or risking a catastrophe, which is defined as including release of "harmful or destructive force or substance," or "by any other means of causing potentially widespread injury and damage."[172]

Conceivably, the crime of burglary could occur if electronic entry could be said to constitute "entry."[173] The same is true of criminal trespass.[174] The case law, however, suggests that entry occurs only when some part of the body breaks the close.[175]

---

when the defendant had and breached an independent affirmative duty to disclose that information. Id. (quoting United States v. Dowling, 739 F.2d 1445, 1449 (9th Cir. 1984)). The court determined that LaMacchia did not have an independent duty.

[167] 18 U.S.C. § 1961(1).

[168] *See* Synernergistic Technologies, Inc. v. IDB Mobile Communications, Inc., 871 F. Supp. 24, 33 (D.D.C. 1994) (denying summary judgment on counterclaim for violation of Virginia Computer Crimes Act, based on allegations that vendor of satellite data switching system was only entity with password and therefore must have been the entity that deleted source code from system without authority).

[169] 18 Pa. Cons. Stat. § 5741 (1994) (statute penalizes unlawful access of stored electronic communications). Other state statutes related to unauthorized access are considered in **Ch. 3.**

[170] Model Penal Code § 211.3 (1994).

[171] *Id.* § 212.5.

[172] *Id.* § 220.2.

[173] *Id.* § 221.1.

[174] *Id.* § 221.2.

[175] Commonwealth v. Gordon, 477 A.2d 1342, 1348 (Pa. Super. Ct. 1984).

Because property is defined to include anything of value, including intangible personal property,[176] one who deprives another of intellectual property or intangible interests associated with the operation of computer systems, such as files or computing resources, should be liable for their various theft offenses.[177] Because "writing" is defined to include any method of recording information, one altering a computer record with intent to defraud or injure someone should be guilty of forgery;[178] one who falsifies, destroys, removes, or conceals computer records should be guilty of the crime of tampering with records.[179] On the supply side, one who makes a false or misleading statement for the purpose of promoting the purchase or sale of property or services or for the purpose of obtaining property or credit commits the crime of deceptive business practices.[180] **Chapter 3** contains a table summarizing other state statutes that criminalize certain conduct relating to access to or disclosure of computer data.

§ 13.12 Procedure

A number of criminal procedure issues arise when substantive criminal law is applied to conduct occurring in the NII, including issues relating to jurisdiction, venue, domestic computer searches, and foreign searches.

§ 13.13 —Jurisdiction and Venue

A vexing procedural problem arises from the difficulty in determining *where* a computer crime was committed. A criminal defendant is entitled constitutionally and statutorily to be tried in the place where he allegedly committed the crime. Article III, Section 2 of the United States Constitution guarantees a defendant a trial in the state where the crimes were committed.[181] The Sixth Amendment entitles criminal defendants to trial in "the state and district wherein the crime shall have been committed."[182] Federal Rule of Criminal Procedure 18 states

---

[176] Model Penal Code § 223.0(6) (1994) (specifically mentioning electric or other power).

[177] *See id.* §§ 223.1–223.9. *See also* Ga. Code Ann. § 16-9-93 (Michie 1992) (computer theft); Iowa Code Ann. § 716A.9 (West 1993) (computer theft defined); Minn. Stat. Ann. § 609.89 (West 1987) (computer theft); R.I. Gen. Laws § 11-52-4 (Michie 1994) (computer theft).

[178] *Id.* § 224.1.

[179] *Id.* § 224.4.

[180] *Id.* § 224.7.

[181] U.S. Const. art. III, § 2, cl. 3. Trial of crimes committed outside the country must be at such place or places as the Congress directs by statute.

[182] U.S. Const. Amend. VI; *see* Travis v. United States, 364 U.S. 631, 633 (1961) (citing 18 U.S.C. § 3237(a)) (finding appropriate revenue to lie in the jurisdiction where the offense was begun).

that "except as otherwise permitted by statute or by these rules, the prosecution shall be had in a district in which the offense was committed."[183] These criminal venue guarantees do not apply to the states.[184]

Many federal criminal statutes provide for venue, but when they do not, the prevailing practice is to apply the "verb test," to determine the nature of the crime alleged and the location of the act or acts constituting it. Under this test, the court looks to the verbs defining the proscribed act and determines where the conduct specified by those verbs actually occurred. That becomes the place of the crime and the place for prosecution.[185] As mentioned previously, Article 3, Section 2, Clause 3 of the United States Constitution and the Sixth Amendment of the Constitution entitle a criminal defendant to prosecution in the state and district in which the crime was committed. This does not mean that there is a single proper situs for trial in the case of a crime that affects more than one district; several districts may be permissible venue.[186] The verb test properly takes into account a number of factors: "the site of the defendant's acts, the elements and nature of the crime, the locus of the effect of the criminal conduct, and the suitability of each district for accurate factfinding."[187] Usually, the site of the defendant's acts provides proper venue, but other factors may give another venue equal standing.[188] In particular, the place where the effects of the crime are felt may be an appropriate venue.[189]

Virtually all states have adopted the Uniform Criminal Extradition Act.[190] Under the Act, the governor of one state has a duty to arrest and deliver to the

---

[183] See United States v. Kibler, 667 F.2d 452, 454 (4th Cir. 1982); *see also* United States v. Cofield, 11 F.3d 413, 416 (4th Cir. 1993) (reviewing "verb rule," but concluding that witness intimidation offense should be tried by the court in which underlying proceeding was pending because it was that court's authority that was jeopardized by the witness intimidation).

[184] Caudill v. Scott, 857 F.2d 344, 345 (6th Cir. 1988) (affirming denial of habeas corpus based on inapplicability of Sixth Amendment to state prosecution; noting that due process does place some limits on trying a state defendant in a distant place); Zicarelli v. Dietz, 633 F.2d 312, 325 (3d Cir. 1980) (affirming denial of habeas corpus; extensive review of history and purpose of Sixth Amendment venue clause shows that it should not be applied to the states, despite general applicability of some of the jury provisions of Sixth Amendment).

[185] United States v. Cofield, 11 F.3d 413, 417 (4th Cir. 1993) (reviewing verb test but concluding that witness intimidation prosecution should occur before court in which the intimidated witness would appear).

[186] United States v. Reed, 773 F.2d 477, 480 (2d Cir. 1985) (reviewing constitutional concept of venue).

[187] *Id.* at 481 (enumerating factors).

[188] *Id.*

[189] *Id.* at 481–82 (finding perjury permitted in California could be tried in Southern District of New York because deposition in which perjury occurred was ancillary to proceeding in Southern District of New York; venue for obstruction of justice charge also lay in that district).

[190] Introductory Note to Uniform Criminal Extradition Act, 11 U.L.A. 38 (1994 Supp.). The Uniform Act implements the extradition clause of the United States Constitution. U.S. Const. art. IV, § 2, cl. 2; 18 U.S.C. §§ 3182, 3194, 3195.

executive authority of any other state any person charged with a crime in the other state who is found in the first state.[191] Demands for extradition must be in writing and allege that the accused was present in the demanding state at the time of the commission of the alleged crime and thereafter fled from the state.[192] The writing requirement apparently has not been construed to include or exclude a computer message.[193] If the receiving governor "decides that the demand should be complied with," he issues a warrant of arrest directed to any peace officer "or any other person whom he may think fit to entrust with the execution thereof."[194] Although the governor has a nondiscretionary duty to honor an extradition request, apparently there are no means of compelling him to honor it.[195] No person may be returned after an arrest on an extradition warrant without being afforded the opportunity to challenge the legality of the arrest under a writ of habeas corpus or otherwise.[196] The statute also allows for arrest without a warrant upon reasonable information that the accused is charged in the courts of any state with a capital crime or a serious felony.[197] In the event of such a warrantless arrest, the arrestee may be confined for not to exceed 30 days while the governor is given time to issue a warrant under section 6 of the Act.[198] The warrantless arrest authority adequately covers situations in which the request for extradition or a less formal request to arrest a fugitive is communicated electronically.

§ 13.14   Enforcement of Foreign Criminal Law

Choice of law, considered in **Chapter 12,** does not function in the criminal arena the way it does in the civil arena because virtually all crimes are local instead of transitory. Nevertheless, there are circumstances under which criminal laws conflict. That may occur when venue is appropriate in different jurisdictions, as explained in **§ 13.13.** That in turn may occur when the criminal laws of various jurisdictions are given extraterritorial effect, thus overlapping geographically. This section considers the ground rules for determining when extraterritorial application of criminal law is appropriate, and the closely related question, when is it appropriate for the courts of one jurisdiction to apply the criminal laws of another?

---

[191] Uniform Criminal Extradition Act § 2, 11 U.L.A. 61 (1974).

[192] *Id.* § 3, 11 U.L.A. at 92 (also requiring that demand be accompanied by copy of indictment, information, affidavit, and warrant or judgment of conviction or sentence).

[193] No citations found for § 3 n.4 "writing requirement" in main volume or 1994 supplement.

[194] Uniform Criminal Extradition Act § 7, 11 U.L.A. 296 (1995).

[195] *In re* Lucas, 343 A.2d 845 (N.J. Super. Ct.), *aff'd,* 346 A.2d 624 (N.J. Super. Ct. 1975); Allen v. Leach, 626 P.2d 1141 (Colo. 1981).

[196] Uniform Criminal Extradition Act § 10, 11 U.L.A. 337 (1995).

[197] *Id.* § 14, 11 U.L.A. 406.

[198] *Id.* § 15, 11 U.L.A. 411.

In general, there is no constitutional bar to the extraterritorial application of U.S. penal law.[199] Extraterritoriality is determined by looking to congressional intent, presuming that Congress does not want to violate international law.[200] Thus, unless Congress explicitly directs otherwise, extraterritoriality is limited to what international law permits.[201] Choice of law does not arise in criminal cases in the same way that it arises in civil cases.[202] The basic reason for this is that crimes were never thought to be transitory,[203] and thus the only inquiry was whether a court had jurisdiction. When a court had jurisdiction, it applied its own law.[204] Nevertheless, a wide range of extraterritorial conduct may be a crime.[205] Thus, one could be criminally liable in state A for computer-triggered conduct in state B that caused injury in state A as long as state A expressly prohibited extraterritorial conduct of that character and the actor knew or should have known of the adverse effect in state A.[206]

Application of the criminal law of another sovereign, however, is much less likely. "A court in the United States may try a person only for violation of United States law, not for violation of the penal law of a foreign state."[207] The

---

[199] United States v. Vasquez-Velasco, 15 F.3d 833 (9th Cir. 1994) (affirming conviction of Mexican citizen and resident under U.S. statute prohibiting violent crimes committed in aid of racketeering enterprise).

[200] *Id.* at 839–40.

[201] *Id.* at 840.

[202] See **Ch. 12.**

[203] Transitory causes of action, as distinguished from local causes of action, were a kind of property that traveled with the plaintiff. The plaintiff could assert the claim representing this species of property wherever he happened to be—assuming the court in which the plaintiff filed had personal jurisdiction over the defendant.

[204] *See* Restatement (Second) of Conflict of Laws § 89 (1969) ("no action will be entertained on a foreign penal cause of action").

[205] *See* Model Penal Code § 1.03 (1994) (allowing conviction "in this state" committed by conduct occurring within the state or conduct occurring outside the state sufficient to constitute an attempt, conspiracy, an extraterritorial omission to perform a legal duty imposed by domestic law with respect to a person, thing, or transaction in the state, or when extraterritorial conduct is expressly prohibited by a domestic statute when the conduct bears a reasonable relation to a legitimate interest of the state and the actor knows or should know that his conduct is likely to affect that interest). Of course the physical presence of the defendant must be procured before she may be tried. See Crosley v. United States, 113 S. Ct. 748, 751 (1993) (describing rule against trials in absentia); United States v. Alvarez-Machain, 504 U.S. 655 (1992) (reviewing extradition and extra-legal means of obtaining defendant's presence).

[206] *Id.* § 1.03(1)(f).

[207] Restatement (Third) of Foreign Relations § 422(1) (1986). *See generally* United States v. Hudson & Goodwin, 11 U.S. (7 Cranch) 32 (1812). In *United States v. Hudson & Goodwin,* the Supreme Court held that federal courts may not convict for common-law crimes, but only for crimes for which jurisdiction is vested by statute. The rationale was that federal government institutions are institutions of limited jurisdiction. The rationale precludes federal court jurisdiction over crimes defined by foreign states because that jurisdiction has not been given to the courts by Congress. Of course, the rationale permits Congress to define a foreign crime as a U.S. crime within the jurisdiction of a United States federal court.

commentary to § 422 of the *Restatement (Third) of Foreign Relations,* on the other hand, notes that some civil law countries try persons whom they cannot extradite for crimes committed in other countries. This constitutes a kind of "transitory" criminal action.

One can argue that a state court would have the power to try an actor for the foreign crime because state courts are not limited by the federal Constitution. Of course, the state in which the court sits may impose its own limits on judicial power, but there are at least some states in which common-law crimes exist, albeit mostly in theory. In such a state, the courts are not bound only to those crimes declared expressly to be so by statute, and they would have the power to apply foreign criminal definitions, unless some overriding constitutional privilege would be infringed by doing do. This would, of course, be a revolutionary idea; the linkage between territorial sovereigns and substantive criminal law is very strong.[208]

There still would need to be an affirmative basis for the criminal proscription for which the defendant is prosecuted. It surely would violate procedural due process to prosecute for a crime that was not defined as such when the defendant acted.[209] So the prosecution would need to establish either a sufficient connection between the defendant's conduct and the foreign jurisdiction whose criminal law is being relied on or else a basis in international law, as might be the case with terrorism, possibly including computer terrorism.[210]

§ 13.15 Search Warrants

Search warrant law is important to participants in the NII. Materials stored in electronic form are an increasingly common target of searches and seizure, and digital electronic communications techniques can be used to apply for and to execute searches and seizures. The following sections begin with some basic information about search and seizure law, explaining the practical difference between a warrant and a subpoena and exploring the possibility of providing

---

[208] United States v. Gecas, 50 F.3d 1549 (11th Cir. 1995) (reversing district court; Fifth Amendment privilege against self-incrimination extended to prosecution under laws of foreign country), illustrates the depth of sovereign-specificity of criminal law, even while recognizing a privilege under the U. S. Constitution when foreign prosecution is shown to be likely. By requiring the asserter of the privilege to demonstrate probability of extradition, the doctrine acknowledges the safety from prosecution under the laws of country A of one physically in country B, absent a possibility of extradition. The court's analysis also acknowledged the traditional concerns that the criminal law of A might offend the policy of B, and the difficulty of B keeping track of the criminal laws of all the As in the world.

[209] Marks v. United States, 430 U.S. 188, 192 (1977) (declining to give retroactive effect to standards articulated in Supreme Court opinion because that would violate due process by criminalizing conduct not criminal when it occurred).

[210] United States v. Layton, 855 F.2d 1388, 1396–97 (9th Cir. 1988).

information in support of a search warrant by electronic means. Then, §§ **13.20** and **13.21** explore the procedure for electronic surveillance, including electronic surveillance of stored electronic information under the Electronics Communications Privacy Act (ECPA).

As Justice Stevens explained in his dissenting opinion in *Zurcher v. Stanford Daily News*,[211] the incidence of conflict between governmental interests and custodial interests increased significantly when the Supreme Court decided in *Warden v. Hayden*[212] that the Fourth Amendment permits "mere evidence" of crimes to be seized as well as fruits and instrumentalities of crimes and contraband.[213] While innocent third parties are relatively unlikely to possess fruits or instrumentalities of crimes, and they are not innocent if they possess contraband, they are highly likely to possess information constituting evidence of crime. Thus, when law enforcement authorities are empowered by the Fourth Amendment to seek "mere" evidence, they are much more likely to want information possessed by innocent custodians.

In reviewing constitutional cases, however, it is important to remember that the Constitution protects only against governmental conduct, "state action," and not against private conduct.[214]

§ 13.16   —Searches and Seizures of Papers and Information

Search and seizure law always has been especially respectful of books and papers and other forms of information. *Ex parte Jackson*[215] started with the proposition, decided by the Senate in 1836, that a statute excluding from the mails printed material tending to incite slave insurrections would be unconstitutional because it would violate the First Amendment freedom of the press.[216] The Supreme Court observed that regulations lawfully excluding matter from the mail "cannot be enforced in a way which would require or permit an examination into letters, or sealed packages subject to letter postage, without warrant.[217]

---

[211] 436 U.S. 547 (1978) (rejecting argument that innocent third party must be served with subpoena rather than search warrant).

[212] 387 U.S. 294 (1967).

[213] 436 U.S. at 577 (Stevens, J., dissenting).

[214] Reporters Comm. for Freedom of the Press v. American Tel. & Tel. Co., 593 F.2d 1030, 1041 & n.21 (D.C. Cir. 1978) (declining to decide whether telephone company so enmeshed in government request for toll records as to be state actor).

[215] 96 U.S. 727 (1877) (Fourth Amendment warrant requirements covered sealed letter in the United States mails and thus relaxed the narrow property concept of Fourth Amendment protection).

[216] *Id.* at 733–34.

[217] *Id.* at 735.

But, inasmuch as the cases before it involved no challenge to the way in which evidence was obtained, the Court affirmed a conviction for violation of a statute excluding lottery materials from the mails.[218]

Boyd v. United States[219] involved an effort to condemn plate glass imported in violation of the customs laws. A conviction was obtained based on an invoice subpoenaed from the defendants, and the basis for the appeal was that the subpoena violated the Fifth Amendment. The government claimed that a subpoena cannot violate the Fourth or Fifth Amendments, but the Supreme Court disagreed. The Supreme Court referred to the issue as one "involving the personal security, and privileges and immunities of the citizen."[220] Because the statute mandated an adverse presumption against the defendant upon a failure to respond to a subpoena, the court found it tantamount to compelling production of the papers.[221] The compulsory production was within the Fourth Amendment limitations even though it did not involve "certain aggravating incidents of actual search and seizure, such as forcible entry into a man's house and searching among his papers."[222] The Court distinguished searches for contraband from searches for private books and papers: "In the one case [contraband], the government is entitled to possession of the property; in the other [private books and papers] it is not."[223] When contraband is involved, attachment or execution is not limited by the Fourth or Fifth Amendments because someone else (the government) has a superior property interest.[224] The competing property interest lessens the subject's right against governmental intrusion.

The special position of books and papers in search and seizure law is evident from the Court's lengthy discussion of the English suit for trespass by John Wilks against the King's messengers and the Secretary of State who issued a warrant for a search of Wilks's personal books and papers.[225] The Supreme Court thought that the language of Lord Camden was likely to have been in the minds of the drafters of the Fourth and Fifth Amendments and thus construed those Amendments as protecting the same interests recognized by Lord Camden.[226] Papers not only are

---

[218] *Id.* at 737.

[219] 116 U.S. 616 (1886) (citing Entick v. Carrington, 9 Howell State Trials 1029 (1762) and emphasizing privacy more than security of property as the interests protected by the Fourth Amendment).

[220] *Id.* at 618.

[221] *Id.* at 622.

[222] *Id.*

[223] *Id.* at 623.

[224] *Id.* at 624.

[225] 116 U.S. 616, 626–27 (1886) (describing Entick v. Carrington, 19 Howell State Trials 1029 (1762)).

[226] *Id.* at 630.

the owner's goods and chattels; they are his dearest property, and are so far from enduring a seizure, that they will hardly bear an inspection; and though the eye cannot by the laws of England be guilty of a trespass, yet where private papers are removed and carried away the secret nature of those goods will be an aggravation of the trespass, and demand more considerable damages in that respect.[227]

This passage captures the conflict between a privacy and a property view of the Fourth Amendment. The eye cannot commit a trespass because inspecting something is not necessarily an interference with property interest. Nevertheless, papers are special because they are private, and once the threshold of the property-associated tort of trespass has been crossed, the privacy interest should increase the damages available. Though there was not yet a willingness to recognize an independent cause of action for invasion of privacy, there was recognition of the legitimacy of the privacy interest.

Moreover, the Court looked to section 15 of the Judiciary Act of 1789.[228] This Act "introduced a great improvement in the law of procedure," by authorizing compulsory production of books or writings in the possession of a party to an action at law "where they might be compelled to produce the same by the ordinary rules of proceedings in chancery."[229] Chancery had long declined to decree discovery that might tend to convict the party of a crime or lead to forfeiture of his property. Thus, the Court thought the subpoena section of the Judiciary Act necessarily incorporated the limitations of the Fifth Amendment.

The final step in the Court's logic was to conclude that the Fourth and Fifth Amendments are intimately related and that the Fourth Amendment should not be read to authorize searches and seizures for information that are prohibited by the Fifth.[230] The law authorizing the notice to produce the invoice was unconstitutional and void. Thus, the notice was void and the inspection of the invoice and its subsequent admission in court was erroneous and unconstitutional.[231] Consequently, a new trial was awarded.

So, by the beginning of the twentieth century, private letters in the United States mails were protected by the Fourth Amendment against inspection without a warrant, and individuals were protected by the Fourth and Fifth Amendments from being compelled to disclose their own records even with process when those records would tend to incriminate them. But in *Olmstead v. United States*,[232] the Supreme Court declined to extend Fourth and Fifth Amendment

---

[227] *Id.* at 627–28 (quoting Lord Camdon in *Entick v. Carrington*).

[228] Rev. Stat. § 724.

[229] 116 U.S. 616, 631 (1886).

[230] *Id.* at 633.

[231] *Id.* at 638.

[232] 277 U.S. 438 (1928) (Brandeis, J., dissenting) (Fourth Amendment should protect against intrusions using new technologies; disagreeing with majority conclusion that telephone conversations were outside Fourth Amendment protection).

protection to telephone conversations. The defendants were convicted of conspiracy to violate the prohibition laws based on private telephone conversations intercepted by means of wiretaps. "The [wiretaps] were made without trespass upon any property of the defendants. They were made in the basement of the large office building. The taps from house lines were made in the streets near houses."[233] The majority thought that two aspects of the eavesdropping took it outside the limitation of the Fourth Amendment. First, voluntary conversations were secretly overheard; there was no compelled communication.[234] Second, there was no search or seizure of material things.[235] Even though a statute in the state of Washington forbids interception of telephone and telegraph communications, the majority thought that violation of this statute did not justify excluding the evidence.[236]

The dissent of Justice Brandeis now, of course, is much more famous than the majority opinion.[237] "The progress of science in furnishing the government with means of espionage is not likely to stop with wiretapping . . . . To Lord Camden a far slighter intrusion seemed subversive of all the comforts of society. Can it be that the constitution affords no protection against such invasions of individual security?"[238] Justice Brandeis thought both *Boyd* and *Jackson* compelled exclusion of the wiretap evidence. By the time that *Olmstead* was decided, Justice Brandeis was able to identify 24 state statutes making it a crime to intercept telegraph or telephone messages,[239] and a number of other state statutes making it a crime for telephone or telegraph company employees to disclose messages.[240]

In *Katz v. United States*,[241] the Supreme Court explicitly held that the Fourth Amendment is concerned with privacy interests as well as property interests. Therefore, the Court held that interception of a telephone conversation in a public telephone booth constituted a search and seizure for Fourth Amendment

---

[233] *Id.* at 457.

[234] *Id.* at 464. The Supreme Court distinguished *Boyd* because there was no compulsion for the defendants to talk on the telephone. *Id.* at 462 (distinguishing *Boyd,* and other cases, including Weeks v. United States, 232 U.S. 383, 34 S. Ct. 341 (1914) (excluding papers and articles seized after arrest without a warrant)).

[235] *Id.* at 464. It distinguished *Jackson* on the grounds that the letter was in the custody of the government, but the telephone conversations were not. "The intervening [telephone] wires are not a part of his house or office, any more than are the highways along which they are stretched." *Id.* at 465.

[236] 277 U.S. 438, 468–69 (1928) (applying common-law rule that admissibility of evidence is unaffected by the means used to obtain it).

[237] *Id.* at 471 (Brandeis, J., dissenting).

[238] *Id.* at 474.

[239] *Id.* at 479 n.13.

[240] *Id.*

[241] 389 U.S. 347 (1967) (replacing trespass requirement of Fourth Amendment with reasonable expectation of privacy as threshold inquiry).

purposes.[242] That the eavesdropping device did not penetrate the wall of the booth was irrelevant. The Court declined a Fourth Amendment formulation based on constitutionally protected areas,[243] but it also declined to translate the Fourth Amendment into a general constitutional right to privacy.[244]

The Court expressly disavowed the trespass doctrine of *Olmstead*.[245] Instead, it stated the Fourth Amendment "protects individual privacy against certain kinds of governmental intrusion," but others of its protections have nothing to do with privacy.[246] The Court would have Fourth Amendment protection turn on distinguishing what an individual "knowingly exposes to the public even in his own home or office" (no protection),[247] from "what he seeks to preserve as private, even in an area accessible to the public" (protected).[248] The Court went on to review the reasonableness branch of Fourth Amendment protection of electronic communications, working from the basic principle that "no greater invasion of privacy [should be] permitted than [is] necessary under the circumstances."[249] This is a minimization requirement, but the Court declined to find the eavesdropping reasonable in the absence of a warrant no matter that it may have satisfied the minimalization requirement.

The Court observed that unlike a traditional warrant, an electronic eavesdropping authorization is unlikely to give notice to the subject of the warrant.[250] The Court found it essential that the estimate of probable cause be presented for detached scrutiny by a neutral magistrate in advance, that the search itself be confined within precise limits established in advance by a specific court order, and that the search be followed by notification to the authorizing magistrate listing exactly what had been seized.[251] It found it difficult to imagine how any of the exceptions justifying warrantless searches could ever apply to electronic surveillance.[252]

---

[242] *See also* Berger v. New York, 388 U.S. 41, 58–59, 87 S. Ct. 1873 (1967) (extending Fourth Amendment to electronic eavesdropping, and invalidating New York statute authorizing eavesdropping warrants without specifying conversations to be intercepted).

[243] Katz v. United States, 389 U.S. 347, 350 (1967).

[244] *Id.*

[245] *Id.* at 353.

[246] *Id.* at 350.

[247] *See* United States v. White, 401 U.S. 745, 750, 91 S. Ct. 1122 (1971) (eavesdropping with permission of one party to conversation was not an intrusion requiring a Fourth Amendment warrant; *Katz* distinguished because no consent involved).

[248] Katz v. United States, 389 U.S. 347, 351 (1967).

[249] *Id.* at 355.

[250] *Id.* at 356 (noting that exigent circumstances may justify exceptions to the notice requirement for search warrants).

[251] *Id.*

[252] *Id.* at 357–58 (ruling out incident to arrest, hot pursuit, and consent exceptions).

Reliance on a Fourth Amendment search and seizure characterization may not be necessary for constitutional protection. In *York v. Story,*[253] the Ninth Circuit found that privacy is protected against arbitrary intrusions by the police by the due process clause of the Fourteenth Amendment, without necessitating a conclusion of Fourth Amendment coverage.[254] The validity of this conclusion in the NII context depends on whether conversational privacy is a constitutionally protected liberty interest. The Fourteenth and Fifth Amendments ensure due process only when life, liberty, or property deprivations are involved. Despite the controversy over the scope of penumbral privacy protection,[255] it appears safe to conclude that if a penumbral right to privacy exists under the Constitution, it extends to conversational privacy—and, more generally, to information content privacy.

The important distinction in electronic communications and records search and seizure between message content and transactional records derives from *Smith v. Maryland,*[256] which used *Katz* as its "lodestar,"[257] but held that transactional records are not protected against monitoring. The Court found no reasonable expectation of privacy in the numbers dialed from the subject's telephone. First, the Court doubted subjective expectation of privacy because people know that they must communicate the telephone numbers they dial to the telephone company and that the phone company records the numbers for the purposes of making out bills and for detecting harassing telephone calls.[258] But even if there were a subjective expectation of privacy, society would not regard it as reasonable. In reaching this conclusion, the Court emphasized that the disclosure to third parties (the telephone company) was analogous to the disclosure of bank deposit information to banks (which defeated an expectation of privacy in *United States v. Miller*).[259] Because the subject voluntarily disclosed the numbers to the third party phone company, it "assumed the risk that the information would be divulged to police."[260]

Miller[261] involved the subpoena of bank records that resulted in evidence of illegal manufacture and distribution of liquor without paying taxes. After the

---

[253] 324 F.2d 450, 454 (9th Cir. 1963) (42 U.S.C. § 1983 claim for police taking and distributing photographs, based on constitutional protection; Fourth Amendment did not extend to distribution of photographs).

[254] *Id.* at 455.

[255] *Compare* Planned Parenthood v. Casey, 112 S. Ct. 2791, 2805 (1992) (finding abortion to fall within the penumbra of personal privacy thus warranting constitutional protection) *with* Bowers v. Hardwick, 478 U.S. 186 (1986) (holding constitutional privacy protection not to extend to private consensual homosexual conduct).

[256] 442 U.S. 735, 99 S. Ct. 2577 220 (1979) (pen register not a Fourth Amendment search).

[257] 442 U.S. at 739.

[258] *Id.* at 742.

[259] 425 U.S. 435, 442–44 (1976).

[260] 442 U.S. 735, 745 (1979).

[261] United States v. Miller, 425 U.S. 435, 96 S. Ct. 1619 (1976) (Fourth Amendment does not extend to bank records).

subpoenas were served on the banks, the banks produced the records without informing the subjects and eventual defendants.[262] The Supreme Court rejected application of *Boyd,* concluding that the subpoenaed documents did not fall within a zone where there is a reasonable expectation of privacy: "The documents subpoenaed here are not respondent's 'private papers.'"[263] The records belong to the banks.[264] The Court thought that the compulsion embodied in the Bank Secrecy Act, which required the bank to keep the records, did not change the conclusion. This was so, it thought, because the underlying records, checks, and deposit slips were not clothed with a legitimate expectation of privacy as being confidential communications.[265] Moreover, by disclosing the records to the banks, the subjects took the risk that the banks would disclose them to law enforcement officials.[266]

Smith Court dissenting Justices Stewart and Brennan quite appropriately criticized *Smith's* third-party disclosure theory because it is impossible to make a telephone call without disclosure to the telephone company. In this respect, *Smith* was no different from *Katz* because the conversation in *Katz* also had to be disclosed to the telephone company.[267] Dissenting Justices Marshall and Brennan argued that "whether privacy expectations are legitimate within the meaning of *Katz* depends not on the risks an individual can be presumed to accept when imparting information to third parties, but on the risk he should be forced to assume in a free and open society."[268]

State courts have not followed *Smith* when state constitutional protections are involved. *State v. Hunt*[269] involved a conviction for bookmaking based on telephone toll billing records. The toll records resulted in placement of a pen register pursuant to court order and subsequent wiretaps pursuant to court order. The New Jersey Supreme Court reviewed *Katz* and *Smith* because "the expectation of privacy in a pen register, both subjectively and objectively, is substantially similar to that in toll billing records."[270] It declined to defer to the federal analysis, however, preferring to extend protection to toll records under the state constitution.[271] The New Jersey Supreme Court explained that the list of local or long distance numbers called involved private information because it "easily could reveal the identities of the persons and the places called, and thus reveal

---

[262] 425 U.S. at 438.

[263] *Id.* at 440.

[264] This is straightforward property analysis.

[265] 425 U.S. 435, 442 (1976).

[266] *Id.* at 442–43.

[267] Smith v. Maryland, 442 U.S. 735, 746 (1979).

[268] *Id.* at 750.

[269] 450 A.2d 952 (N.J. 1982) (toll billing records would not be protected by federal Constitution but are protected by state constitution).

[270] *Id.* at 954 (noting that federal courts that have considered toll billing records have concluded they are not entitled to Fourth Amendment protection).

[271] *Id.* at 955 (noting independent role that state constitutional protection plays).

the most intimate details of a person's life."[272] It makes no difference that the numbers have been disclosed to the telephone company. That disclosure is necessitated because of the nature of the instrumentality and for only a limited business purpose and not for release to other persons for other reasons.[273] Similarly, *Burrows v. Superior Court*[274] concluded that the California constitution protects bank records because there is a reasonable expectation of privacy in those records.[275] *Suburban Trust Co. v. Waller*[276] involved a common-law claim for invasion of privacy resulting from disclosure of bank records by the bank to the police. "If it is true that a man is known by the company he keeps, then his soul is almost laid bare to the examiner of his checking account."[277] Most of the Maryland court's analysis was based on a duty of secrecy implied from the relationship between depositor and bank.[278] It affirmed a judgment for the plaintiff on liability, but remanded for retrial of damages.

When mere evidence is searched for, the Supreme Court and lower federal courts recognize the risk that a general rummaging through records and information will intrude upon matters not associated with any state interest in detecting or preventing crime. As a matter of Fourth Amendment law, this concern is dealt with by requiring the issuing authority to particularize the things to be searched.[279]

---

[272] *Id.* at 956.

[273] *Id.* at 956–57 (citing Colorado, California, and Pennsylvania cases and distinguishing Indiana, Maine, and Wyoming cases).

[274] 529 P.2d 590, 118 Cal. Rptr. 166 (1974) (voluntary disclosure of bank records violated state constitution).

[275] *Id.* at 595.

[276] 408 A.2d 758 (Md. Ct. Spec. App. 1979) (bank had common-law duty to keep bank records confidential). *Suburban Trust* generally is considered as resting on a fiduciary duty to keep certain records confidential. This notion is reflected in the Right to Financial Privacy Act of 1978, 12 U.S.C. §§ 3401–3422.

[277] 408 A.2d at 762 (quoting Justice Douglas's dissent in California Bankers Ass'n v. Schultz, 416 U.S. 21, 94 S. Ct. 1494 (1974)).

[278] *Id.* at 762–65.

[279] Zurcher v. Stanford Daily News, 436 U.S. 547, 564 (1978) (characterizing Stanford v. Texas, 379 U.S. 476, 482 (1965)). *See* Reporters Comm. for Freedom of the Press v. American Tel. & Tel. Co., 593 F.2d 1030, 1096 (D.C. Cir. 1978) (Wright, J., dissenting) (emphasizing essentiality of judicial scrutiny of warrants and subpoenas to ensure that records search is no greater in scope than necessary); *see also* United States v. Conley, 4 F.3d 1200, 1208 (3d Cir. 1993) (warrant authorizing search for "all" records in video game parlor not illegal general warrant because limitation on records to be searched could be inferred from context of crime alleged); Vonderahe v. Howland, 508 F.2d 364, 366 (9th Cir. 1975) (search warrant authorizing indiscriminate seizure of all records including personal documents was violative of Fourth Amendment as "general warrant" but question of evidence suppression was premature).

§ 13.17   —Privacy Protection Act

The Privacy Protection Act[280] provides:

> Notwithstanding any other law, it shall be unlawful for a government officer or employee, in connection with the investigation . . . of a criminal offense to search for or seize any work product materials possessed by a person reasonably believed to have a purpose to disseminate to the public a newspaper, broadcast, or other similar form of public communication.[281]

The legislative history suggests an objective measure for officers encountering work product that might be used for publishing. The work product must be possessed by someone "reasonably believed" to have a purpose to communicate to the public.[282]

§ 13.18   Distinction Between Warrants and Subpoenas

It is important to understand the basic differences between subpoenas and warrants as sources of authority to obtain access to private places or information.[283] A warrant authorizes greater intrusion because there is no notice before the property or information must be given up, and the law enforcement officer

---

[280] 42 U.S.C. § 2000aa (1994).

[281] *Id.* § 2000aa(a).

[282] Steve Jackson Games, Inc. v. United States Secret Serv., 816 F. Supp. 432, 440 (W.D. Tex. 1993), *aff'd,* 36 F.3d 457 (5th Cir. 1994) (awarding damages for violation of Privacy Protection Act for seizure of computer bulletin board materials) (citing S. Rep. No. 874, 96th Cong., 2d Sess. 10 (1980), *reprinted in* 1980 U.S.C.C.A.N. 3950, 3957).

[283] The differences between subpoenas and warrants were thoroughly considered in Zurcher v. Stanford Daily News, 436 U.S. 547 (1978). The Supreme Court reversed a lower court conclusion that search warrants ordinarily should not be issued to obtain records or other information in the possession of innocent third parties, but that subpoenas ordinarily should be used instead. The Court emphasized that "the critical element in a reasonable search is not that the owner of the property is suspected of crime but that there is reasonable cause to believe that the specific 'things' to be searched for and seized are located on the property to which entry is sought." *Id.* at 556. "Search warrants are not directed at persons; they authorize the search of 'places' and the seizure of 'things' and as a constitutional matter they need not even name the person from whom the things will be seized." *Id.* at 555. Only two conclusions are necessary to support the probable cause for a warrant. First, the items sought must in fact be seizable by virtue of being connected with criminal activity. Second, the items must be found in the place to be searched. *Id.* at 557.

Nevertheless, search warrants involving the risk of a generalized combing through of personal papers and records must be minimized by particularization. *Id.* at 564 (characterizing Stanford v. Texas, 379 U.S. 476, 482 (1965)).

executing the warrant decides what property or information is within the scope of the warrant. The law enforcement officer then takes custody of the property or information identified. Conversely, a subpoena gives notice in advance of the time when the property or information must be produced.[284] The person responding to the subpoena decides initially what is within its scope. The person responding maintains custody of the property or information. Because of these differences, the requirements for obtaining a warrant are more stringent. For one thing, the prior commission of a crime must be alleged in order to justify issuance of a warrant.[285] Even though, under *Zurcher v. Stanford Daily News,*[286] a search warrant may issue without evidence that the person responsible for the premise to be searched is engaged in criminal activity, there nevertheless must be probable cause to believe that someone has engaged or is engaging in criminal activity.[287] Finally, a neutral and detached magistrate must make the decision to issue a warrant, while a subpoena is issued more or less routinely and subject to challenge only after it is served.

When warrants are used, officers executing the warrant typically take away (seize) property belonging to the person searched. That person obviously has an interest in recovering the property as soon as possible. Rule 41(e)[288] provides for an evidentiary hearing and a motion for return of unlawfully seized property. Denial of such a motion is appealable, although when it is coupled with a motion to suppress in an ongoing criminal proceeding, the appeal must be delayed until after conclusion of the criminal prosecution.[289]

§ 13.19   Obtaining Search Warrants Through Electronic Means

The Federal Rule of Criminal Procedure 41(c)(2)(A) states: "If the circumstances make it reasonable to dispense, in whole or in part, with a written

---

[284] *See* Zurcher v. Stanford Daily News, 436 U.S. 547, 573 (1978) (Stuart, J., dissenting) (search warrant allows police officers to ransack files while subpoena would permit newspaper itself to produce only specific documents requested). *Id.* at 576 (Stuart, J., dissenting) (subpoena allows adversary hearing through motion to quash, but search warrant does not until after information has been reviewed and seized).

[285] United States v. Rundle, 327 F.2d 153, 162–63 (3d Cir. 1964) (search warrant may be issued only based on allegation of preexisting or current crime, not on speculation that crime may be committed in future).

[286] 436 U.S. 547 (1978).

[287] *See* United States v. Conley, 4 F.3d 1200, 1206–07 (3d Cir. 1993) (reversing district court suppression and finding warrant supported by probable cause, noting that even if operator of video game parlor was not involved in illegal activity, there was probable cause to believe his records would indicate illegal use of machines by others).

[288] Fed. R. Crim. P. 41(e).

[289] Church of Scientology v. United States, 591 F.2d 533, 537 (9th Cir. 1979) (dismissing interlocutory appeal of motion to return 20,000 seized records).

affidavit, a federal magistrate judge may issue a warrant based upon sworn testimony communicated by telephone or other appropriate means, including facsimile transmission."[290] The phrase "other appropriate means" allows for the possibility of obtaining the information necessary to support issuance of a warrant by E-mail or other computer communications. In that case, the applicant must prepare a "duplicate original warrant" and must "read" such duplicate original warrant verbatim to the federal magistrate judge. The reference to "read" presumably could be satisfied by transmitting a verbatim copy. The magistrate judge must either record all of the call after being informed that the purpose is to request a warrant by a "voice recording device," or have a stenographic or long-hand verbatim record made.[291] If the magistrate determines that the warrant should be issued, the magistrate signs the original warrant, entering the exact time when the warrant was ordered to be issued. The applicant must sign the duplicate original warrant in the name of the magistrate judge at the same time.[292]

There is some authority for harmless error under this rule.[293] A variety of technical deviations from Rule 41's requirements for telephone warrants are tolerated.[294] This flexibility has extended to telephonic warrant applications made by persons not qualifying as law enforcement officers and use of tape-recorded affidavits.[295] Despite the usual rule that criminal statutes and rules are construed strictly, there probably is sufficient flexibility to adapt the language of the rule to use of a variety of digital communications technologies.

---

[290] Fed. R. Crim. P. 41(c)(2)(A) (1995) (emphasis added).

[291] *Id.* 41(c)(2)(D).

[292] *Id.* 41(c)(2)(C).

[293] *See* United States v. Hawthorne, 45 F.3d 428 (4th Cir. 1995).

[294] *See* United States v. Richardson, 943 F.2d 547, 549 (5th Cir. 1991) (failure of recording equipment to work and vagueness as to whether oath was administered violated Rule 41, but search fell within good-faith exception to exclusionary rule); United States v. Stefanson, 648 F.2d 1231, 1235 (9th Cir. 1981) (failure to record entire telephone conversation and administration of oath after statement was given did not invalidate telephone warrant); United States v. Rome, 809 F.2d 665, 667–68 (10th Cir. 1987) (failure of applicant to read from actual duplicate original, failure to sign original warrant immediately, not authorizing final list of things to be seized, and participating in one or more unrecorded telephone conversations did not justify invalidating warrant and search); United States v. Johnson, 641 F.2d 652, 656 (9th Cir. 1980) (a variety of technical violations of Rule 41 did not invalidate telephone search warrant); United States v. Ritter, 752 F.2d 435, 440–41 (9th Cir. 1985) (allowing telephonic warrant authorized by state judge even though Rule 41 authorizes only federal judicial officers to issue telephone warrants); United States v. Small, 664 F. Supp. 1357, 1362–63 (N.D. Cal. 1987) (finding Rule 41 satisfied even though applicant did not read verbatim from duplicate original warrant); United States v. Allen, 586 F. Supp. 825, 829–30 (N.D. Ill. 1984) (blank tape of telephonic application transaction did not necessitate invalidating warrant).

[295] United States v. Luk, 859 F.2d 667, 670–71 (9th Cir. 1988) (referring to tape-recorded affidavit); *id.* at 672 (referring to issuance of warrant on written application by state justice of the peace); *id.* at 673 (application by one not a law enforcement officer).

§ 13.20   ECPA Procedures for Interception

The Electronic Communications Privacy Act (ECPA)[296] provides comprehensive procedures for interception, search, and seizure of both electronic
communication streams and stored electronic messages. Law enforcement
authorities may compel access to communications and electronic messages and
files by obtaining warrants under the provisions of the Act.[297] A warrant must
particularly describe the things to be searched and seized.[298] This has been
translated into a minimization requirement for electronic interception warrants.[299] Section 2518(5) of 18 U.S.C. limits interception pursuant to court order
to a 30-day period commencing on the later of the beginning of the interception
or 10 days after the order issues. If the intercepted communications are in
code or a foreign language, the 30-day rule is relaxed to permit obtaining a
translator or decoder.

Warrants for interception of electronic communications may be obtained by
defined officers in the Justice Department or state and county prosecuting

---

[296] The Electronic Communications Privacy Act of 1986 (ECPA) consists of 18 U.S.C. §§ 1367,
2101–2710, 3117, 3121–3126, 2236, 2511–2513, and 2516–2520.

[297] 18 U.S.C. § 2703 (stored communications); *id.* § 2516 (authorization for interception of
wire, oral, and electronic communications). *See* Steve Jackson Games, Inc. v. United States
Secret Serv., 816 F. Supp. 432 (W.D. Tex. 1993) (assessing statutory damages against Secret
Service for violating Stored Wire and Electronic Communications and Transactional Records
Access Act).

[298] *See generally* Burrows v. Superior Court, 529 P.2d 590, 597–99 118 Cal. Rptr. 166 (1974)
(invalidating search because it extended beyond the terms of the warrant and thus was
impermissible under state constitution).

[299] The minimization requirement is expressed in 18 U.S.C. § 2518(5). The leading case is Scott
v. United States, 436 U.S. 128, 98 S. Ct. 1717 (1978) (minimization requires only good-faith
effort to minimize irrelevant conversations intercepted). Not all interceptions of nonrelevant
communications are prohibited, but the methods used to minimize the incidence of such
overbroad interception must be judged by the nature of the communications channel and the
identity of the users. 436 U.S. at 140, 98 S. Ct. at 1724. *See* Williams v. Philadelphia Housing
Auth., 826 F. Supp. 952, 954 (E.D. Pa. 1993) (denying leave to amend wrongful termination
complaint to add Fourth Amendment claim for seizure and review of personal computer disk;
review of computer disk found in desk drawer was reasonably incident to supervision of
work; and scope of "search" was not unreasonable because it was necessary to look at
personal items on disk in order to find work-related items). *See also* United States v. Cafero,
473 F.2d 489 (3d Cir. 1973) (court of appeals disagreed with a district court opinion in
another case finding the particularization requirements of the statute to violate the Fourth
Amendment; 473 F.2d at 494–96 (reviewing constitutional arguments and rejecting them). In
particular, the court found that the virtually unlimited interceptions during a fixed time period
condemned in *Berger* had been remedied by the statutory requirement for judicial scrutiny,
the possibility of sua sponte judicial review at any time after surveillance begins, and the
automatic expiration of statutory authority to continue the surveillance once the objective has
been achieved. 437 F.2d at 496 (summarizing statutory protections against overbroad continuing surveillance).

attorneys for the investigation of enumerated crimes[300] under special procedure.[301] These procedures require presentation by the government and a finding
by the judge issuing the warrant that normal investigative procedures are
impracticable. The procedures further require limitations in the warrant to
communications involving particular persons, through particular communications facilities, involving particular contents over an authorized period of time.
No warrant may authorize interception for longer than 30 days. Emergency
interceptions also are authorized if application for a warrant is made within 48
hours after the interception has occurred.[302] Intercepted communications must
be taped or otherwise recorded,[303] and notice must be given to the parties to the
intercepted communications within 90 days.[304] Upon request, the judge issuing
the warrant may make the intercepted contents available to the parties to the
communication.[305] The notice and content disclosure provisions are important
protections because traditional searches usually were not secrets. The person
whose privacy was affected by the search knew about it when the search warrant
was executed.[306] Nevertheless, traditional search warrant practice permits some
delay in providing notice and an inventory, and the application of the statutory
period for giving notice under ECPA Title I is constitutional depending on a
reasonableness assessment.[307]

Wire and electronic communications are treated differently. The statutory
exclusionary rule[308] applies to the interception of wire communications, including such communications while they are in electronic storage,[309] but not to the
interception of electronic communications.[310] Also, the types of crimes that may
be investigated by means of surveillance directed at electronic communications[311] are not as limited as those that may be investigated by means of

---

[300] 18 U.S.C. § 2516.

[301] *Id.* § 2518.

[302] *Id.* § 2518(7).

[303] *Id.* § 2518(8)(a).

[304] *Id.* § 2518(8)(d). The statute thus strikes a compromise between the situation with a traditional search warrant, where notice typically occurs when the warrant is executed, and the
technological possibility with electronic interceptions that the subject would never have
notice of an interception.

[305] *Id.*

[306] United States v. Cafero, 473 F.2d 489, 498 (3d Cir. 1973) (considering problem posed by
secret search, which did not typically occur in the heritage of the Fourth Amendment).

[307] *Id.* at 500 (delay in giving notice to be judged by reasonableness standard; 90-day period in
statute not per se unreasonable).

[308] 18 U.S.C. § 2515.

[309] *See id.* § 2510(1).

[310] *See id.* § 2518(10)(a); United States v. Meriwether, 917 F.2d 955, 960 (6th Cir. 1990); S.
Rep. No. 541, 99th Cong., 2d Sess. 23 (1986), *reprinted in* 1986 U.S.C.C.A.N. 3555, 3577.

[311] 18 U.S.C. § 2516(3) ("any federal felony").

surveillance directed at wire or oral communications.[312] Additionally, the minimization requirements applicable to interception of streams does not apply to acquisition of stored electronic communications.[313] Further, the duration requirements are different.[314] Acquisition of E-mail messages before they are read by the addressee does not constitute interception of an electronic communication stream under Title I, although it obviously does constitute acquisition of stored electronic communications under Title II.[315]

The procedures for intercepting stored communications and for accessing remote computing facilities are more flexible because the Fourth Amendment does not limit access to records kept by third parties. The ECPA[316] addresses searches and seizures of three different types of stored communications. Stored communications may be accessed pursuant to either federal or state warrants; or for information stored for more than 180 days; or with notice to the subscriber or customer under an administrative, grand jury, or trial subpoena; or a court order based on a governmental showing that the information sought is "relevant to a legitimate law enforcement inquiry."[317]

Electronic communications in electronic storage must be disclosed to a governmental entity only pursuant to a federal or state warrant, unless the contents have been in storage for more than 180 days. In that case they must be disclosed under any of the methods applicable to contents in a remote computing service.[318]

Governmental entities may compel disclosure of the contents of electronic communications in a remote computing service in three ways. First, they may obtain a federal or state search warrant, in which case they need not give notice to the subscriber or customer whose contents they are accessing.[319] Second, they may, with prior notice to the subscriber or customer, use an administrative subpoena from a federal or state administrative agency or federal state grand jury or trial court.[320] Finally, they may obtain a court order based on a finding that the governmental entity has reason to believe that the contents "are relevant

---

[312] *See id.* § 2516(1) (specifically listing felonies). *See also* Steve Jackson Games, Inc., v. United States Secret Serv., 36 F.3d 457, 461 n.6 (5th Cir. 1994) (comparing treatment of wire and electronic communications), *aff'g* 816 F. Supp. 432 (W.D. Tex. 1993).

[313] Steve Jackson Games Inc., v. United States Secret Serv., 36 F.3d at 463.

[314] *Id.*

[315] *Id.* at 464 (affirming district court conclusion that Title II, but not Title I, applied to seizure of stored E-mail messages).

[316] 18 U.S.C. § 2703.

[317] 18 U.S.C. § 2703(b); *see* Steve Jackson Games, Inc. v. United States Secret Serv., 816 F. Supp. 432 (W.D. Tex. 1993) (awarding damages for violation of ECPA stored communications provisions but finding no Title I interception).

[318] *Id.* § 2703(a).

[319] *Id.* § 2703(b)(2)(A).

[320] *Id.* § 2703(b)(2)(B)(i).

to a legitimate law enforcement inquiry."[321] When the third method is used, notice to the customer or subscriber may be delayed for up to 90 days, based on a judicial determination that an adverse result might occur if immediate notice was given. Adverse results include flight from prosecution, destruction of or tampering with evidence, intimidation of potential witnesses, and "otherwise seriously jeopardizing an investigation or unduly delaying a trial."[322] The delayed notice is available for subpoenas as well as the legitimate law enforcement inquiry order.[323] Transactional records may be obtained pursuant to federal or state warrant or subpoena or relevant law enforcement inquiry order or with the consent of the subscriber or customer, and notice need not be given in the event of such disclosure.[324] Moreover, the privilege of a provider to disclose transaction records to those other than law enforcement entities is preserved.[325]

When a subpoena or legitimate law enforcement inquiry order so provides, a provider must make backup copies of designated records.[326] The backup copy must be made before notice is given.[327] The backup copy must be released to the requesting governmental entity if the customer or subscriber has not challenged the governmental entity's request within 14 days.[328] Except for telephone toll records and telephone listings, the government must reimburse providers for reasonably necessary costs directly incurred in searching for, assembling, reproducing, or otherwise providing information pursuant to warrants, subpoenas, and legitimate law enforcement inquiry orders.[329]

The procedure for accessing information stored for more than 180 days is similar to what the custodian in *Stanford Daily News* unsuccessfully asked for.[330] A backup copy of the requested information is created before notice is given to the subject.[331] The backup is released to the governmental requestor no sooner than 14 days after the notice is given, unless the subject challenges the legitimacy of releasing it.[332] On the other hand, for information kept more than 180 days, the probable cause required for a warrant is not necessary. Providers

---

[321] *Id.* §§ 2703(b)(2)(B)(ii), 2703(d).

[322] *Id.* § 2705.

[323] 18 U.S.C. § 2703(b)(2)(B) (last clause).

[324] *Id.* § 2703(c).

[325] *Id.* § 2703(c)(1)(A).

[326] *Id.* § 2704(a) (also providing for notice to subscriber or customer within three days unless delayed notice is authorized).

[327] *Id.* § 2704(a)(1).

[328] *Id.* § 2704(a)(4). Section 2704(b) provides a procedure for customer or subscriber challenges to backup orders.

[329] 18 U.S.C. § 2706.

[330] *See generally* Zurcher v. Stanford Daily News, 436 U.S. 547 (1978).

[331] 18 U.S.C. § 2704.

[332] *Id.* § 2704(a)(4).

disclosing pursuant to court orders, warrants, subpoenas, or certifications are immunized from civil liability.[333]

Subpoenas or orders may require the provider to make a backup copy of the contents of the stored communications sought.[334] The purpose of this is to prevent the owner of the information, who is entitled to notice, from erasing it and thus depriving the government of access to it.

If Judge Posner is correct that federal (and perhaps state) courts have the power both under Federal Rule of Criminal Procedure 41 and inherently to issue search warrants for electronic eavesdropping, then the language in ECPA Title II, which suggests that the order for access to stored communications can be executed only by requiring the provider to make the communications available, is not exclusive. A search warrant could be issued entitling law enforcement authorities physically to enter and to seize the computing systems containing the desired information, as long as the basic requirements for particularization and probable cause under the Fourth Amendment are satisfied.

Pen registers and trap and trace devices[335] must be authorized by application to a government attorney who certifies that the requested surveillance is "relevant to an ongoing criminal investigation being conducted by that agency."[336] The authorization order must identify the telephone number to be monitored, must be limited in time to 60 days, and must be sealed.[337] The statute does not provide for notifying the target.

Magistrate judges are not authorized to decide applications for wiretaps under Title I or II of ECPA, although they are so authorized under Title III pertaining to pen registers and similar devices.[338] Intercepted communications may not be used as evidence in state or federal court unless parties against whom the evidence is offered are given copies of the order authorizing interception.[339]

Section 2703 of 18 U.S.C. was amended by the digital telephony legislation of 1994. It obligates a provider of electronic communications service or remote computing service to disclose to a government entity

> the name, address, telephone toll billing records, telephone number or other subscriber number of identity, and length of service of a subscriber to or customer

---

[333] *Id.* § 2703(e).

[334] *Id.* § 2702.

[335] *Id.* § 3123 states, "shall issue an ex parte order" when the applicant certifies as to the requirements of the statute. It does not require that the judge make findings. But see Brown v. Waddell, 50 F.3d 285, 293 (4th Cir. 1995) (use of clone pager to monitor numerical pager messages subject to more stringent procedures for electronic communications under ECPA, rather than pen-register procedures).

[336] *Id.* § 3122.

[337] 18 U.S.C. § 2723.

[338] *In re* United States, 10 F.3d 931, 936 (2d Cir. 1993) (granting mandamus against district judge's delegation of wiretap application to magistrate judge).

[339] 18 U.S.C. § 2518(9).

of such service and the types of services the subscriber or customer utilized, when the governmental entity uses an administrative subpoena authorized by federal or state statute or federal or state grand jury or trial subpoena or any other means available under subparagraph (B).[340]

§ 13.21   Foreign Intelligence Surveillance Act

As has been observed so often in this book, NII traffic is inherently international in character; thus, search and seizure powers relating to foreign instrumentalities are especially relevant in the NII context. The Foreign Intelligence Surveillance Act (FISA)[341] regulates electronic surveillance of foreign powers and agents. It was enacted in 1978 and represented the first statutory regulation of presidential power in the foreign intelligence surveillance field.[342] The legislation resulted from controversy over presidential use of wiretaps and uncertain guidance from the courts under the Supreme Court's "Keiff" case[343] and conflicting courts of appeals decisions regarding national security surveillance.[344]

FISA sets up a special court comprised of seven district judges who hear and determine applications for electronic surveillance warrants[345] under the Act.[346] The statute allows warrantless electronic acquisition of communications exclusively between foreign powers not involving substantial likelihood that the surveillance will acquire the contents of any communication to which a "United

---

[340] Pub. L. No. 103-414, 108 Stat. 4279, § 207 amending 18 U.S.C. § 2703 to add new subparagraph (C) to subsection (c)(1).

[341] 50 U.S.C. §§ 1801–1808.

[342] *See generally* S. Rep. No. 604(I), 95th Cong., 1st Sess. (1977), *reprinted in* 1978 U.S.C.C.A.N. 3904.

[343] United States v. United States Dist. Court, 407 U.S. 297 (1972) (recognizing limited executive power to engage in warrantless electronic surveillance for domestic security surveillance but imposing warrant requirement in certain circumstances).

[344] *See* S. Rep. No. 604(I), 95th Cong., 1st Sess. 14–16 & nn. 25–28 (1977) (citing and discussing United States v. Brown, 484 F.2d 418 (5th Cir. 1973) (allowing warrantless foreign intelligence wiretap); United States v. Butenko, 494 F.2d 593 (3d Cir. 1974) (en banc) (allowing warrantless electronic surveillance for primary purpose of obtaining foreign intelligence); Zweibon v. Mitchell, 516 F.2d 594 (D.C. Cir. 1975) (requiring warrant before wiretapping domestic organization that is neither agent nor collaborator of foreign power and questioning existence of national security exception to warrant requirement)).

[345] Although the statute uses the term "court order" instead of "warrant," the two terms are synonymous. *See* United States v. Megahey, 553 F. Supp. 1180, 1190 (E.D.N.Y. 1982) (FISA order is a warrant within the meaning of Fourth Amendment), *aff'd without opinion,* 729 F.2d 1444 (2d Cir. 1983).

[346] 50 U.S.C. § 1803(a) (1991). The Act also establishes a court of review, comprised of three United States district judges or circuit judges who have jurisdiction to review denial of any application made to the seven-judge court, with the possibility of certiorari review by the Supreme Court. *Id.* § 1803(b).

States person" is a party, and the acquisition of technical intelligence other than the spoken communications of individuals from property or premises under the open and exclusive control of a foreign power.[347] *United States person* is defined to include United States citizens, resident aliens, unincorporated associations involving substantial U.S. membership, and corporations incorporated in the United States, but excludes corporations controlled by foreign governments.[348]

These types of surveillance are permitted only upon certification by the attorney general, which must be filed under seal with the special court established by the Act.[349] These surveillances may not exceed one year in duration.[350] FISA court orders are available only on application by a federal officer supported by an attorney general finding of compliance with the criteria of the Act.[351] The application must disclose the facts and circumstances justifying the applicant's belief that the target is a foreign power or agent of a foreign power, the facilities or places at which the surveillance is directed are being used or are about to be used by a foreign power or agent of a foreign power, a description of the nature of the information sought, and the type of communications or activities to be subjected to the surveillance.[352] In addition, the application must include a certification by the assistant to the president for national security affairs or another executive branch official designated by the president supporting the application, including a certification that the information sought "cannot reasonably be obtained by normal investigative techniques,[353] and a statement of the proposed "minimization procedures."[354] A judge of the special court is required to issue an ex parte order upon finding that the application requirements have been satisfied.[355]

In emergency situations, the attorney general may authorize the commencement of surveillance, followed by an application for a court order within

---

[347] 50 U.S.C. § 1802 (1982).

[348] *Id.* § 1801(i) (1991).

[349] *Id.* § 1802(a) (certification by attorney general); *id.* § 1802(a)(2) (filing requirement).

[350] *Id.* § 1802(a)(1).

[351] *Id.* § 1804(a) (1991). *See* United States v. Megahey, 553 F. Supp. 1180, 1194–95 (E.D.N.Y. 1982) (FISA requirements and procedures satisfied by surveillance order for home telephone), *aff'd without opinion,* 729 F.2d 1444 (2d Cir. 1983)

[352] 50 U.S.C. §§ 1804(a)(4), (6). *See* United States v. Cavanagh, 807 F.2d 787, 791 (9th Cir. 1987) (nature of foreign intelligence information makes it impossible to provide detailed description of the nature of information sought; no Fourth Amendment violation from absence of detailed description of targeted information).

[353] 50 U.S.C. § 1804(a)(7)(C).

[354] *Id.* § 1804(a)(5). *Minimization procedures* are defined in 50 U.S.C. § 1801(h) as meaning specific procedures to minimize the acquisition, retention, and dissemination of nonpublic information concerning unconsenting United States persons. *See* United States v. Megahey, 553 F. Supp. 1180, 1195 (E.D.N.Y. 1982) (approving minimization), *aff'd without opinion,* 729 F.2d 1444 (2d Cir. 1983).

[355] 50 U.S.C. § 1805.

24 hours.[356] When information obtained under the Act is to be used as evidence in any judicial or administrative proceeding, the government must notify the person against whom it is to be used, and that person may move to suppress the evidence on the grounds that it was unlawfully acquired or that the surveillance producing it did not conform with an order under the statute.[357]

The scope of the statute is determined by its definition of *electronic surveillance*,[358] which includes the nonconsensual acquisition of the contents of any wire communication within the United States by means of an electronic, mechanical, or other surveillance device,[359] and the intentional acquisition by the same means of any wire or radio communication sent by or intended to be received by a particular, known United States person who is in the United States if that person is targeted and has a reasonable expectation of privacy and a warrant would be required for law enforcement purposes.[360] Radio communications are included when both sender and all intended recipients are located within the United States, a reasonable expectation of privacy exists, and a warrant would be required for law enforcement purposes.[361] Monitoring by the same means "to acquire information, other than from a wire or radio communication" is covered under circumstances in which a person has a reasonable expectation of privacy and a warrant would be required for law enforcement purposes.[362] This part of the definition is broad enough to include stored electronic communications and electronic communications streams as they are defined in the Electronic Communications Privacy Act.[363]

The nature of the information targeted by a FISA warrant must relate to foreign intelligence and not criminal conduct. However, this subject matter requirement has been construed broadly to include almost any basic information about the nature of contacts between United States citizens and foreign powers or agents.[364] There is some overlap between FISA and domestic warrants and ECPA orders, particularly for terrorist activities.[365]

---

[356] *Id.* § 1805(e).

[357] *Id.* § 1806. *See* United States v. Thomson, 752 F. Supp. 75, 76 (W.D.N.Y. 1990) (denying motion for disclosure of FISA information that government did not intend to use).

[358] 50 U.S.C. § 1801(f).

[359] *Id.* § 1801(f)(2).

[360] *Id.* § 1801(f)(1).

[361] *Id.* § 1801(f)(3).

[362] *Id.* § 1801(f)(4).

[363] See § **13.20** and **Ch. 3.**

[364] United States v. Thomson, 752 F. Supp. 75, 82 (W.D.N.Y. 1990) (rejecting argument that FISA requirements had not been met because information could not have related directly to terrorism, foreign defense, or diplomatic matters).

[365] United States v. Sarkissian, 841 F.2d 959, 964 (9th Cir. 1988) (wiretap connected with investigation of international terrorism in United States properly sought under FISA rather than Title III even though activities were criminal offenses punishable under federal law).

It is in the nature of FISA information that a FISA warrant cannot be supported solely by probable cause of criminal activity, but the absence of this element does not violate the Fourth Amendment.[366] In general, the probable cause necessary to justify national security surveillance is different from that necessary to criminal investigations.[367]

§ 13.22   Model Search Warrant Language

"To any police officer: you are hereby commanded to search the premises at [*Address*] for and to seize any:

*   *   *

"computer hardware and computer software and documents relating to the use of the computer system and financial documents and licensing documentation relative to the computer programs and equipment at said address which constitute evidence of federal crimes.

*   *   *

"you are commanded and authorized to read information stored and contained on the above described computer and computer system."[368]

§ 13.23   Foreign Searches

One of the most common electronic search and seizure problems is that presented in *The Cuckoo's Egg*.[369] A computer system operator in California, victimized by an intruder, obtained a search warrant from a California state court authorizing a tap by the telephone company. The tracing of the data communication, however, led to Virginia, and the C&P Telephone Company in Virginia declined to disclose the necessary information to trace the call further based on the California warrant. A warrant could not be obtained in Virginia because no crime had been committed in Virginia. Thus, the investigation of the intrusion was effectively blocked. The same problem occurred when the trail led to Germany. No crime had been committed in Germany, and the German courts would not issue compulsory process compelling the searches necessary to

---

[366] United States v. Cavanagh, 807 F.2d 787, 791 (9th Cir. 1987) (rejecting argument to suppress fruits of FISA warrant because of Fourth Amendment violation due to absence of likelihood of uncovering evidence of crime).

[367] *Id.* at 790 (characterizing United States v. United States Dist. Court, 407 U.S. 297, 322 (1972)).

[368] Based on warrant language in Steve Jackson Games, Inc. v. United States Secret Serv., 36 F.3d 457, 459 (5th Cir. 1994).

[369] Clifford Stoll, The Cuckoo's Egg: Tracking a Spy Through the Maze of Computer Espionage (1989).

further the investigation. Eventually, requests under legal assistance agreements between the United States and Germany allowed the investigation to proceed.

The issue of foreign searches involving NII material is likely to grow in importance and difficulty. It is thus appropriate to identify some alternative ways of dealing with the problem. Understanding the possible solutions to this type of NII problem requires understanding the present state of the law with respect to searches and seizures conducted in one country incident to criminal prosecution in another country. Traditionally, coercive power to obtain evidence was purely territorial. Traditional American and European procedure began with the principle that criminal jurisdiction is territorial and that exercise of power by one state on the territory of another is prohibited.[370] The procedure for obtaining evidence in a foreign country involved letters rogatory, which encompassed search warrants and requests for seizure.[371]

The letter rogatory procedure rarely is satisfactory for criminal investigations because it is slow and usually provides for advance notice and participation by opposing parties. Criminal justice authorities almost always prefer ex parte procedures contemplated by American search warrants, subpoenas, and warrant-less searches.

In understanding the legal framework for transnational search warrants and subpoenas, one should think about two basic scenarios: The first is when suspected criminal activity or intended criminal prosecution in the United States motivates a search and seizure or production of evidence in another country; the second is when criminal activity or potential criminal prosecution in another country motivates search and seizure or production of evidence in the United States. Then, it is appropriate to understand the implications of a search not authorized within this framework. Finally, this section identifies alternative policy initiatives to rationalize transnational search and seizure according to U.S. concepts of the appropriate balance between investigative and prosecutorial interests on the one hand and personal privacy and autonomy interests on the other.

U.S. Crime, Foreign Search

The first scenario involves criminal activity or intended criminal prosecution in the United States and the desire to obtain evidence located in a foreign country pertinent to that U.S. investigation and prosecution. To simplify the analysis,

---

[370] Dionysios D. Spinellis, *A European Perspective, in* 2 M. Cherif Bassiouni, International Criminal Law: Procedure 351 (1986) [hereinafter Spinellis].

[371] Spinellis at 366–37 (noting that European Convention provides for search and seizure in Article 5); Convention on Mutual Assistance in Criminal Matters, Europ. T.S. No. 30, art. 5 (reservation of right to make execution of letters rogatory for search or seizure of property dependent upon condition that offense motivating letter rogatory is punishable under both the law of the requesting part and the law of the requested party). This convention was adopted by the Council of Europe, Mar. 17, 1978.

this discussion assumes that prosecution occurs in the same place where the criminal activity occurred.[372] When criminal activity or an intended criminal prosecution in the United States suggests that evidence exists in a foreign country, the legal framework for compulsory access to that evidence is defined by two basic concepts. First, the Fourth Amendment to the United States Constitution has, at most, limited application to foreign searches conducted by either foreign or U.S. officials. Second, the assertion of official U.S. law enforcement power in a foreign country may offend the sovereignty of that foreign country. Of course, the foreign country may agree to various forms of cooperation, or the foreign country may be unable to prevent an affront to its sovereignty, as a practical matter.

It long has been recognized that the Fourth Amendment is a limitation only on official conduct by federal officers or, pursuant to its incorporation into the Fourteenth Amendment, state officers. It thus has no application to searches or seizures conducted by officers of foreign states. For Fourth Amendment purposes, they are like private citizens whose searches and seizures are not constrained by the Fourth Amendment (although they may be subject to common-law damages actions). Until 1990 the major unresolved transnational Fourth Amendment question was whether the Amendment covered searches by U.S. officers outside the territorial limits of the United States.

In *United States v. Verdugo-Urquidez,*[373] the United States Supreme Court decided that the Fourth Amendment does not apply to search and seizures by United States agents of property owned by a nonresident alien and located in a foreign country. It distinguished earlier cases involving the constitutional rights of American citizens subjected to adverse treatment abroad.[374] The case arose after the defendant Verdugo-Urquidez was apprehended by Mexican police in Mexico, transported to a United States Border Patrol station, and there arrested by United States marshals. After the arrest, American DEA agents searched the defendant's Mexican residences for evidence of narcotics trafficking and involvement in the kidnapping and torture murder of a DEA special agent. The director general of the Mexican federal judicial police authorized the search, which then was carried out by DEA agents working together with Mexican federal judicial police officers.[375]

The Supreme Court majority reasoned that nonresident aliens are not within the class protected by the Fourth Amendment[376] and that Fourth Amendment

---

[372] When the criminal activity occurred in the same place where the investigation occurs, even though the prosecution occurs in another country, the country in which the investigation occurs has a stronger interest in facilitating the prosecution.

[373] 494 U.S. 259 (1990).

[374] *Id.* at 270 (distinguishing Reid v. Covert, 354 U.S. 1 (1957) (wives of American servicemen could not be tried by court marshall because certain constitutional privileges apply outside the territorial limits of United States).

[375] *Id.* at 262.

[376] *Id.* at 265–66.

protections generally were not intended to apply beyond the borders of the United States.[377] Justice Kennedy, writing separately, noted that it would be impracticable to apply the Fourth Amendment abroad because of "the absence of local judges or magistrates available to issue warrants, the differing and perhaps unascertainable conceptions of reasonableness and privacy that prevail abroad, and the need to cooperate with foreign officials."[378]

Justice Stevens thought the reasonableness clause of the Fourth Amendment applied, but not the warrant clause.[379] Justice Brennan thought the Fourth Amendment protections should have as much reach as the authority of federal law enforcement officials.[380] Justice Blackmun argued that the Fourth Amendment applied, except that the warrant clause was inapplicable because an American magistrate would lack the power to authorize a search abroad.[381]

Regardless of whether the Fourth Amendment applies at all to foreign searches, however, it remains true that a foreign search by U.S. officers potentially offends the sovereignty of the foreign state in which it occurs, thus potentially subjecting the United States and its citizens to retaliation and the officials performing the search and seizure to punishment by the foreign country. Accordingly, the normal practice contemplates some formal legal channel for authorizing the foreign search.

The *U.S. Attorneys' Manual* identifies three ways of obtaining evidence located in foreign countries: formal requests under mutual legal assistance treaties, letters rogatory in the absence of a treaty or executive agreement, and subpoenas directed to U.S. citizens and permanent residents of the United States located abroad.[382]

One might be tempted to suppose that the appropriate way to conduct a foreign search is simply for judicial process to authorize U.S. officers to conduct a search or to compel a third party to produce the desired evidence. There are two conceptual problems with this approach: the affront to foreign sovereignty,[383] and the likelihood that U.S. judicial power stops at the borders. Otherwise, the fact that criminal activity occurred within the district of the court issuing the process would support its issuance. There is a limited set of circumstances under which foreign subpoenas are authorized: when the person subject

---

[377] *Id.* at 266–68 (Justice Brennan characterizes the majority conclusion as turning only on the identity of the defendant and not on territoriality).

[378] *Id.* at 278 (Kennedy, J., concurring).

[379] 494 U.S. 259, 279 (1990) (Stevens, J., concurring in the judgment).

[380] *Id.* at 284–86 (Brennan, J., dissenting).

[381] *Id.* at 279 (Blackmun, J., dissenting).

[382] United States Attorneys' Manual §§ 9-13.520 to 9-13.525, at 13–18 (1988).

[383] State v. Mathews, No. 20154, 1994 WL 376131 (Idaho July 18, 1994) (reversing denial of suppression; state search warrant executed within Indian reservation was invalid because invaded Indian national sovereignty); Buenrostro v. Collazo, 973 F.2d 39, 43 (1st Cir. 1992) (warrantless home arrest and search in Virgin Islands could not be legitimated by New York law enforcement request, which was not equivalent to warrant).

to the subpoena is a U.S. citizen or resident alien, and when there is some means of enforcing the subpoena within the United States.[384]

The foreign sovereignty problem is avoided when the local law of the foreign jurisdiction authorizes the search and seizure or otherwise compels the production of the desired evidence. In many cases the standards for issuance of such foreign process are different from American standards for search warrants and subpoenas.[385] Conversely, in the absence of a treaty commitment, foreign courts and agencies may be unwilling to authorize or compel obtaining evidence to support a U.S. criminal investigation. Because no local crime can be established in the foreign country, foreign law may not authorize a search or compulsory process. This is the converse of the proposition in some American jurisdictions that local searches can occur only with respect to local crimes. When local law of the foreign jurisdiction authorizes the search or seizure, there is little doubt that any Fourth Amendment reasonableness concerns are satisfied.[386]

Currently, U.S. law enforcement authorities obtain evidence located in foreign countries pursuant to a variety of informal and formal techniques. Formal methods include mutual legal assistance treaties with approximately 17 countries, including Belgium, Canada, Italy, Mexico, the Netherlands, Spain, Turkey, and the United Kingdom.[387] Informal methods include letters rogatory.[388]

"Every United States mutual assistance treaty in criminal matters contains a provision obligating a requested country to conduct searches and seizures on behalf of a requested [*sic;* "requesting"] country if the request includes information justifying such action under the laws of the requested country."[389] Although

---

[384] 28 U.S.C. § 1783 (1994) (authorizing subpoena of national or resident of the United States if in a foreign country); *id.* § 1784 (authorizing contempt proceeding to enforce subpoena served in a foreign country and authorizing seizure of property within the United States pursuant to such contempt finding).

[385] Richard S. Frase, *Comparative Criminal Justice as a Guide to American Law Reform: How Do the French Do It, How Can We Find Out and Why Should We Care?,* 78 Cal. L. Rev. 539, 574–81 (1990) (French law does not require warrants or probable cause, but does permit rogatory commissions to be executed only by the federal police official or judge, and residential searches must be witnessed by resident or by two independent persons).

[386] *See* United States v. Inigo, 925 F.2d 641, 656 (3d Cir. 1991) (summarily rejecting argument that evidence seized by Swiss police incident to Swiss arrest should be suppressed in U.S. prosecution for extortion; based on *Verdugo-Urquidez*); United States v. Juda, 797 F. Supp. 774, 782–83 (N.D. Cal. 1992) (Fourth Amendment applied to placement of beeper on seagoing vessel in Australia because American citizen was involved, but no Fourth Amendment violation because American authorities relied in good faith on advice from Australian officials that no warrant was required under Australian law), *aff'd,* 46 F.3d 961 (9th Cir. 1995).

[387] Eric Bentley, Jr., *Toward an International Fourth Amendment: Rethinking Searches and Seizures Abroad After* Verdugo-Urquidez, 27 Vand. J. Transnat'l L. 329, nn.169–70 (1994).

[388] *See id.* at n.160 (referring to United States Attorneys' Manual § 9-13.500 (1988)).

[389] 3 Michael Abbell & Bruno A. Ristau, International Judicial Assistance: Criminal § 12-4-4(7), at 114 (1990). *See* Treaty Between the United States of America and the Commonwealth of the Bahamas on Mutual Assistance in Criminal Matters, June 12–Aug. 18, 1987, art. 1, § 2(c), Hein's No. KAV 55 (requiring assistance in "executing request for searches and seizures"); *id.* art. 1, § 4 (requests under treaty shall be executed in accordance with the law

the treaties require that allegations of treaty violation be presented only to the executive authority of the requesting country and not to its courts, persons adversely affected by warrant equivalents or subpoenas do have recourse to the courts of the requested country to the extent that those courts are involved in obtaining the information.[390] Because many other treaty partners lack a process equivalent to a subpoena duces tecum, the standards applicable to warrants are used for such countries.[391] Efforts in the United States to suppress evidence obtained in foreign countries uniformly have been unsuccessful on the rationale that the purpose of the exclusionary rule would not be served by excluding evidence because of the purported conduct of foreign law enforcement officers.[392]

---

of a requested state). The scope of the treaty is determined by the definition of "offense," which includes conduct punishable as a crime under the laws of both jurisdictions, and under the laws only of the requesting state when they involve illegal narcotics or drug activity, theft, crime of violence, fraud, or currency or financial transactions and are punishable by one-year imprisonment or more. *Id.,* art. 2, § 1. A requested state may deny compliance if "the request has not established that there are reasonable grounds for believing: (i) that the criminal offense specified in the request has been committed; and (ii) that the information sought relates to the offense and is located in the territory of the requested state." *Id.,* art. 3, § 1(e). Further, a request for search, seizure, and delivery of any article "shall be executed if it includes the information justifying such action under the laws of the requested state." *Id.,* art. 15, § 1. *Accord* Treaty Between the United States of America and Kingdom of Belgium on Mutual Legal Assistance and Criminal Matters, Jan. 28, 1988, art. 7, 27 U.S.T. 1966 (executing request for search and seizure); Treaty Between the Government of the United States of America and the Government of Canada on Mutual Legal Assistance in Criminal Matters, Mar. 18, 1985, art. XVI, 24 I.L.M. 1092 (search and seizure request to be executed in accordance with requirements of the law of the requested state); Treaty on Cooperation Between the United States of America and the United Mexican States for Mutual Legal Assistance, Dec. 9, 1987, art. 12, Hein's No. KAV 1324 (request for search, seizure, and delivery of any object shall be executed if it includes the information justifying such action under the laws of the requested party); Treaty Between the United States of America and the Kingdom of the Netherlands on Mutual Assistance in Criminal Matters, June 12, 1981, art. 6, 1359 U.N.T.S. 209 (requested states shall execute request for search and seizure in accordance with its laws and practices if subject offense is punishable under laws of both parties by deprivation of liberty for period exceeding one year or, if law is specified in annex;

> offense shall be deemed punishable under the laws of the requested state if the acts or omissions alleged, occurring in similar circumstances in the requested state, would constitute a criminal offense under the laws of that state. For purposes of this paragraph, purely jurisdictional elements of United States federal offenses, such as the use of the mails or interstate commerce, shall not be considered as essential elements of these offenses. . . . A request to the United States for a search and seizure shall be accompanied by a statement made under oath before, or by a judge in the Kingdom of the Netherlands, which shall establish good cause to believe that an offense has taken place or is about to take place and that evidence of the offense is to be found on the persons or the premise to be searched, and shall provide a precise description of the person or premises to be searched. Such a statement shall be considered in the United States in lieu of an affidavit sworn before a United States judicial officer.).

[390] 3 Michael Abbell & Bruno A. Ristau, International Judicial Assistance: Criminal § 12-4-7(1), at 135 (1990).

[391] *Id.* § 12-2-2(3), at 28.

[392] *Id.* § 12-2-1(3), at 26–28 (citing Powell v. Zuckert, 366 F.2d 634 (D.C. Cir. 1966); United States v. Heller, 625 F.2d 594, 599–600 (5th Cir. 1980) and other cases).

U.S. Search, Foreign Crime

The second scenario helpful in exploring the legal framework for transnational search warrants and subpoenas is suspected criminal activity or a potential criminal prosecution in a foreign country leading to a desire to search for and seize evidence in the United States. Except when treaty commitments, already reviewed in connection with foreign searches incident to U.S. crimes, obligate the United States to conduct searches on behalf of foreign authority, the legal authority for such U.S. searches is uncertain. Explicit federal authority is not very helpful, being limited to depositions,[393] more or less based on the letters rogatory concept under 28 U.S.C. § 1782 providing for appointment of commissioners to conduct examinations.

Beyond that, there may be authority for a state or federal magistrate to issue a search warrant based on a foreign request. Obviously, if a U.S. warrant can be obtained based on a foreign request for evidence, the problem is solved from the perspective of foreign law enforcement authorities. Any sovereignty and power concerns are averted because state and federal magistrates uniformly have the power to authorize searches and seizures within their districts, as long as the criteria for warrants are satisfied. The problem is that the absence of a local crime may defeat probable cause.

There is general agreement on the proposition that probable cause for a search warrant necessitates the existence of two elements: the commission of a crime, and property related to the crime being located in the district of the issuing magistrate.[394] The second scenario envisions location of property within the district. Thus the question is whether the crime, the commission of which must be established, must be local as well. There is some authority suggesting that a local crime must be established.[395] On the other hand, informal conversations with state magistrates in Pennsylvania reveal that search warrants regularly are issued based on affidavits by law enforcement officers from other states saying that the warrant is needed in connection with investigation of a crime committed in the other state.[396]

Unless issuance of a search warrant based on a foreign crime is mandated by the full faith and credit clause of the United States Constitution, which

---

[393] U.S. Attorneys' Manual § 9-13.540, at 21–22 (1988).

[394] United States v. Rakowski, 714 F. Supp. 1324, 1329–30 (D. Vt. 1987) (probable cause for search warrant must be based on two propositions: (1) a crime was committed; and (2) evidence of such crime is at the location to be searched) (citing United States v. Travisano, 724 F.2d 341, 345 (2d Cir. 1983)).

[395] Commonwealth v. Nation, 598 A.2d 306, 310 (Pa. Super. Ct. 1991) (vacating conviction; being a fugitive does not constitute a crime in Pennsylvania and therefore could not serve as basis for search warrant).

[396] See United States v. Paroutian, 299 F.2d 486, 488 (2d Cir. 1962) (reversing conviction on illegally obtained evidence; suggesting that a letter from out-of-state law enforcement authorities might have been sufficient basis to obtain search warrant).

ordinarily has only limited criminal-law application and would have no application to a foreign request, this practice, if legal, suggests that evidence of a crime in a foreign country also would support issuance of a search warrant by a federal or state magistrate. Of course a foreign warrant or subpoena would have no effect in the United States for the same reasons discussed earlier that a U.S. warrant or subpoena would have no effect in a foreign country.[397]

Impact of Search Not Being Authorized

It is not enough to conclude in the abstract that a search and seizure is illegal. One must understand the consequences of the illegality. There are three pertinent consequences: exclusion in any subsequent criminal prosecution, under the exclusionary rule, of the evidence seized illegally; criminal prosecution of or a private damages action against the searching and seizing officials; and a simple privilege by the person holding custody of the desired property to refuse the search and seizure.

Verdugo-Urquidez establishes the proposition that evidence seized in a foreign country is not subject to the Fourth Amendment exclusionary rule in a federal criminal prosecution. Whether evidence seized in the United States would be excluded in a foreign prosecution depends on whether the foreign country has an exclusionary rule. That leaves open the possibility that evidence seized in a foreign country might be excluded from a U.S. prosecution for some reason other than the Fourth Amendment. The answer probably is no, based on the rationale articulated by the New Jersey Supreme Court in *State v. Mollica.*[398]

In *Mollica,* the court reasoned that constitutional limitations of one sovereign apply only to activities of that sovereign's officers. The court determined that its own constitutional search and seizure protections did not limit the activities of the federal agents who obtained telephone toll records in a manner complying with federal requirements but not complying with New Jersey requirements. It found the federal-state question analogous to treatment accorded officers of a foreign country, "who, in the exercise of their own government's authority, are not subject to the federal Constitution."[399] State constitutional limitations that are not applied to private citizens are not applied to officers of a foreign jurisdiction.[400] The "silver platter" doctrine, used to implicate American constitutional standards when foreign agents seize information abroad under the

---

[397] The earlier discussion did explain that a foreign subpoena might be effective against a foreign citizen in the United States at least to the extent it could be enforced against property located in the issuing jurisdiction. Many foreign nations object to this practice, however.

[398] 554 A.2d 1315 (N.J. 1989).

[399] *Id.* at 1325 (citing cases).

[400] *Id.*

direction of American authorities, is based on the presence of agency between officers of the two sovereigns.[401]

> In determining the validity of a search and seizure conducted by officers of another jurisdiction, the critical assumption that obviates the application of the state constitution is that the state's constitutional goals will not thereby be compromised . . . . None of these constitutional values, however, is genuinely threatened by a search and seizure of evidence, conducted by the officers of another jurisdiction under the authority and in conformity with the law of their own jurisdiction, that is totally independent of our own government officers. Thus, in that context, no purpose of deterrence relating to the conduct of state officials is frustrated, because it is only the conduct of another jurisdiction's officials that is involved. Judicial integrity is not imperiled because there has been no misuse or perversion of judicial process.[402]

The New Jersey court did find some cases, however, suggesting application of choice of law factors in deciding whether the forum state should apply the other state's search and seizure law.[403]

Whether a U.S. officer could be prosecuted by a foreign country for conducting an unauthorized search and seizure there depends on the criminal law of that country. Whether a foreign private-damages action could succeed against the U.S. officer depends on the civil or common law of that country. It also is conceivable that the foreign person harmed by such a search could successfully maintain an action under 43 U.S.C. § 1983 against the U.S. officer, brought in an American court. Whether such an action could succeed depends on whether a federal right can be shown to have been violated, and whether the foreign person would have standing under § 1983. Both propositions are questionable under *Verdugo-Urquidez,* which undercuts the two elements of a § 1983 action by undercutting the Fourth Amendment protection in such a situation.

Whether an American common-law action for damages—trespass or conversion, and possibly invasion of privacy—could be maintained depends on personal jurisdiction and choice of law. If the search were conducted in a foreign country by a U.S. officer, the person victimized by the search should have little difficulty filing suit in a U.S. court, and the U.S. court should have little difficulty obtaining personal jurisdiction over the U.S. officer conducting the search. On the other hand, it might be quite difficult for a U.S. citizen victimized

---

[401] *Id.* at 1326 (citing People v. Touhy, 197 N.E. 849, 857 (Ill. 1935) (denying suppression of evidence seized by Wisconsin police); Young v. Commonwealth, 313 S.W.2d 580, 581 (Ky. 1958) (admitting evidence in Kentucky seized by Missouri officers even though seizure contravened both Kentucky and Missouri constitutions)).

[402] *Id.* at 1328(citations omitted).

[403] *Id.* at 1326 n.6.

by a foreign search to obtain personal jurisdiction in a U.S. court over the foreign officers conducting the search. Sovereign immunity should not be a problem because the assumption is that the search was unauthorized and thus outside the scope of any sovereign immunity.[404]

Assuming personal jurisdiction could be obtained, whether an American common-law damages doctrine would apply depends on choice of law rules. All of the pertinent legal theories for damages are tort theories. The traditional choice of law rule for torts is *lex locus delicti*. Application of this traditional rule would mean that the law of the place where the search occurred would be applied. That means U.S. law in the case of the U.S. search, but foreign law in the case of a foreign search. Modern choice of law rules engage a more flexible interests analysis. Interest analysis is likely to focus on the law of the place where the search occurred, significantly mitigated by the interest of the other jurisdiction in successfully prosecuting crimes committed there.

Someone confronted with an apparently unlawful demand for evidence can simply refuse the demand. Then, the questions become ones of physical power and subsequent prosecution or suit of the person refusing the demand, who essentially does so at his peril. This protection against unlawful search and seizure depends frequently on the will of the person presented with the demand for access to the evidence.

§ 13.24 —Solutions

One must, of course, recall that there are two interests embodied in American search and seizure concepts: the interest of law enforcement agencies in obtaining evidence to facilitate prosecution, and the interests of private persons in not being exposed to intrusive inquiries. The most obvious way of extending the U.S. balance between these two interests is to negotiate additional treaties, along the lines of the judicial assistance treaties reviewed earlier in this chapter, to countries not presently covered by those. To the extent necessary, new treaties and amendments to existing treaties could be written so as to refer specifically to databases of escrowed keys and other electronic material. This alternative would provide the greatest certainty and the clearest channels for exercise of search and seizure authority. On the other hand, the international treaty negotiation process is slow and, because of differing positions of foreign countries, likely to have spotty effect.

---

[404] Of course a good-faith exception might extend the immunity beyond the scope of actual authority.

Exert raw power abroad; leave foreign states adrift when they need U.S. search. This alternative is conceivable theoretically,[405] but represents bad foreign policy and leaves it to law enforcement authorities to decide what searches are appropriate.

Interpret Human Rights Convention and Fourth Amendment to limit foreign searches. In the absence of, or pending the adoption of, appropriate judicial assistance treaties, the Fourth Amendment could be applied to foreign searches to exclude evidence obtained in violation of a combination of U.S. and foreign legal concepts.[406] There is some authority in the *Verdugo-Urquidez* opinions and in some state decisions making the exclusion of evidence turn on the reasonableness of a foreign search, measured by its compliance with the law of the location in which the search occurred. [407]

§ 13.25 Damages Actions under 42 U.S.C. § 1983 for Misuse of Criminal Justice Powers

Privacy invasions by federal officials are remediable under an implied private right of action for constitutional violations.[408] Similar invasions by state and municipal officials are remediable under 42 U.S.C. § 1983, which creates a private right of action for damages against officials acting under color of state law and infringing federal rights. Neither prosecutors[409] nor law enforcement

---

[405] While this approach might seem absurd, the Supreme Court has validated kidnapping of suspects in foreign territory, which represents a comparable extension of U.S. power into the borders of a foreign sovereign. *See generally* Elizabeth McJimsey, United States v. Alvarez-Machain: *International Governmental Abductions,* 41 U. Kan. L. Rev. 119 (1993) (discussing governmental abductions of criminal suspects in Canada and Mexico, and reviewing implications of United States v. Alvarez-Machain, 504 U.S. 655 (1992) (district court had jurisdiction to try Mexican national who was kidnapped and brought to the United States; extradition treaty did not provide exclusive procedure).

[406] Eric Bentley, Jr., *Toward an International Fourth Amendment: Rethinking Searches and Seizures Abroad After* Verfugo-Urquidez, 27 Vand. J. Transnat'l L. 329 (1994) (evaluating competing approaches from opinions in *Verdugo-Urquidez* and suggesting a new "international Fourth Amendment" based on combination of Fourth Amendment reasonableness standard and Article 17 and 9(1) of International Covenant on Civil and Political Rights).

[407] Dillon v. State, 844 S.W.2d 139, 143–44 (Tenn. 1992) (Tennessee search and seizure constitutional provision satisfied as long as Florida search conformed to Florida law).

[408] *See* Bivens v. Six Unknown Narcotics Agents, 403 U.S. 388, 91 S. Ct. 1999 (1971) (recognizing implied private right of action under Constitution for federal officer conduct violating constitutional rights).

[409] *See generally* Pinard v. County of Suffolk, 52 F. 3d 1139 (2d Cir. 1995) (prosecutorial immunity under § 1983 is absolute only with respect to acts "within the scope of [their] duties in initiating and pursuing a criminal prosecution"); Liffiton v. Keuker, 850 F.2d 73, 76 (2d Cir. 1988) (no absolute immunity of state prosecutor for improper access to financial records because those activities were not intimately associated with judicial phase of criminal

officers[410] have absolute immunity for intercepting electronic communications without probable cause. The availability of relief under ECPA does not prevent an independent § 1983 or *Bivens* claim for constitutional violations.[411]

Private entities are liable under § 1983 when they put in motion the judicial process.[412] For example, private officials of the American Society for the Prevention of Cruelty to Animals were held potentially liable under § 1983 for breaking through a building where a cat was trapped, without seeking to obtain a warrant.[413] Conversely, another Humane Society agent escaped § 1983 liability because statements given to obtain a search warrant were sufficient to give rise to probable cause and thus failed to satisfy the test that knowingly or recklessly providing false information in support of a warrant application triggers § 1983 liability. They were entitled to judgment notwithstanding a $50,000 verdict against them.[414]

While a provider of electronic information services would not be exposed to § 1983 liability merely for responding to judicial process under ECPA or otherwise, § 1983 becomes a consideration when the service provider takes the initiative and makes a report to criminal justice authorities or directly to a magistrate seeking judicial process. Then, reckless or knowingly false statements can subject the service provider to liability under § 1983 or to

---

process; further development of record necessary to apply conditional privilege); Houston v. Partee, 978 F.2d 362, 365 (7th Cir. 1992) (prosecutors have only qualified immunity when they authorize warrantless wiretaps; citing Burns v. Reed, 500 U.S. 478, 480 (1991) (absolute immunity for prosecutor participation in probable cause warrant hearing, but not deciding degree of immunity for bad-faith seeking of warrant or other conduct outside courtroom; rejecting absolute immunity for prosecutors giving legal advice) and Mitchell v. Forsyth, 472 U.S. 511, 520 (1985) (no absolute immunity for authorizing national security wiretaps)).

[410] Malley v. Briggs, 475 U.S. 335, 340 n.2, 344 n.6 (1986) (law enforcement officer individually liable under § 1983 or *Bivens* for successful application for search or arrest warrant if facts presented would not have led reasonably competent officer to believe probable cause existed).

[411] PBA Local 38 v. Woodbridge Police Dep't, 832 F. Supp. 808, 825 (D.N.J. 1993) (ECPA no bar to § 1983 relief although covers municipal agencies and officers, because § 1983 claim independently premised on Fourth, Ninth, and Fourteenth Amendment rights); Amati v. City of Woodstock, 829 F. Supp. 998, 1004–05 (N.D. Ill. 1993) (ECPA does not preempt § 1983 action based on Fourth Amendment, in part because no ECPA Title 1 liability for municipal police officer).

[412] Wyatt v. Cole, 504 U.S. 158 (1992) (reversing court of appeals and holding that private citizens who invoke state replevin statute may be liable under § 1983 but they are not entitled to immunity; remanding for findings whether particular plaintiffs acted under color of state law within meaning of Lugar v. Edmondson Oil Co., 457 U.S. 922 (1982)).

[413] Suss v. American Soc'y for the Prevention of Cruelty to Animals, 823 F. Supp. 181, 186 (S.D.N.Y. 1993) (ASPCA was state actor because its services involved governmental functions and break-in was done under assumption of sovereign powers of compulsion; denying motions for summary judgment).

[414] Hartzler v. Licking County Humane Soc'y, 740 F. Supp. 470, 477 (S.D. Ohio 1990).

common-law liability for malicious prosecution[415] or for abuse of process.[416] Analysis of privileges under § 1983 is closely related to the analysis of privileges and immunities under the common-law actions.[417] Section 1983 actions can be brought in state as well as federal court.[418]

---

[415] Restatement (Second) of Torts § 653 (1977) (private person who initiates or procures institution of criminal proceeding liable if he acted without probable cause and primarily for a purpose other than bringing the offender to justice and criminal proceedings terminated in favor of accused).

[416] *Id.* § 674 (one who initiates, continues, or procures civil proceedings liable if he acts without probable cause and primarily for purpose other than securing proper adjudication of claim and proceedings have terminated in favor of person against whom they were brought).

[417] Wyatt v. Cole, 112 S. Ct. 1827, 1831 (1992) (immunities under § 1983 depend an important part on immunities under common-law actions for malicious prosecution and abuse of process).

[418] Allen v. McCurry, 449 U.S. 90, 100 (1980) (collateral estoppel and res judicata relitigation of § 1983 claim in federal court); Charchenko v. City of Stillwater, 821 F. Supp. 1284, 1286 (D. Minn. 1993) (well settled that state courts have concurrent jurisdiction to hear § 1983 claims); State *ex rel.* Carter v. Schotten, 637 N.E.2d 306, 309 (Ohio 1994) (state courts have concurrent jurisdictions with federal courts over § 1983 claims).

CHAPTER 14

INTERNATIONAL LAW AND TRADE

§ 14.1 Introduction and Overview

The National Information Infrastructure (NII) is perhaps more appropriately referred to as the Global Information Infrastructure (GII). There is little about GII activities that respects national boundaries. A message sent from California goes as easily to an addressee in the Netherlands as to one in California or Massachusetts. A defamatory document located on a server in Sweden can be retrieved as easily from a client machine in Virginia as from one in Israel.

It is possible usually to determine after the fact where a message or a request to retrieve information came from. It also is possible to configure routers so they will not accept messages or requests from a particular country. Both the origin-detection capability and the national suppression capability have major limitations. The origin-detection capability can detect only the node immediately before the node doing the checking. In many cases, even perfectly innocent messages come indirectly through one or more intermediate nodes, in which case the origin-detection capability would only detect the penultimate node and not the actual origin. Moreover, a variety of "anonymous servers" exist for the purpose of concealing the origin of traffic. The national suppression capability is subject to avoidance by all of the techniques useful to defeat firewalls and to spoof addresses.

Moreover, one of the attractive features of the Internet is that it is an open system and rarely has involved either post hoc investigation as to the source of traffic or a priori blockages on traffic origins. The result is an inherently international technological regime within which conduct occurs, one that does not conform naturally to inherently national systems of law. The Internet encourages people to engage in conduct aimed at other countries. As people do that they need to know something about the international context of law.[1] Even if one intends only to use the National Information Infrastructure within the United States, the ease with which conduct aimed nationally has effects internationally necessitates some consideration of private international law principles as well.

The international character of the Internet and other parts of the GII influence almost all of the chapters of this book, not just this one. Accordingly, much of the basic analytical treatment of privacy, procedure, and jurisdiction included attention to international aspects. When international aspects have been treated in depth in other chapters, the analysis is not repeated in this chapter. Rather, a brief recap of the international dimensions is presented here, along with cross-references to the other chapters containing deeper analytical treatment.

This chapter provides some basic background on international institutions, recognizing that many American lawyers are unfamiliar with the structure of the government of the European Union, for example, and the ways in which UN-sponsored bodies developed substantive commercial law principles.

§ 14.2   Institutional Arrangements

This section provides an overview of the institutional structures and powers of supranational organizations through which the law pertinent to the information infrastructure is developed. Substantive transnational legal principles are dealt with in other sections of this chapter.

International organizations are particularly active in developing commercial principles that apply to transnational transactions. The International Law

---

[1] It is perhaps more appropriate to think about the analysis in this chapter as involving private international law or "transnational" law rather than public international law, which is what some people mean when they use the phrase "international law."

Association (ILA) was founded in Brussels in October 1873 and developed rules for adjusting maritime disputes between owners and insurers of vessels and owners and insurers of cargo, a system of law that became known as the "general average."[2] The ILA subsequently developed the York-Antwerp Rules of 1877, resulting in standard language for maritime agreements.[3] But the progress on developing ILA principles was slow, and the international community developed a competing organization, the Comite Maritime International (CMI) in 1877. The CMI functioned through 13 international conferences until 1979, resulting in six international conventions governing collision, salvage, limitation of ship owner liability, bills of lading, maritime liens and mortgages, and immunity of state-owned ships before the Second World War. The CMI covered civil jurisdiction in matters of collision, penal jurisdiction in matter of collision, arrests of seagoing ships, limitation of liability of ship owners, stowaways, carriage of passengers, liability of operators of nuclear ships, vessels under construction, passenger luggage, protocols amending the 1924 convention of bills and lading, and maritime liens and mortgages.[4] By 1968, however, support for the CMI process had eroded because the CMI worked primarily through conferences of private interests, while CMI conventions required adoption by international political bodies.[5]

The International Labor Organization has functioned since 1919, publishing some 150 conventions governing hours of work and minimum labor standards for the maritime industry.[6]

UNIDROIT,[7] the International Institute for the Unification of Private Law, was established in 1926 by its intergovernmental agreement, the Statute of UNIDROIT. It is headquartered in Rome.[8] UNIDROIT was preserved by the Italian government and its constituent member states since the end of the Second World War and is devoted to the science of comparative law.[9] UNIDROIT now works in conjunction with organs of the United Nations in the preparation of draft texts harmonizing significant aspects of international commercial law, such as its work on relations between principals and agents, international commercial contracts, franchising, carriage of dangerous goods, financial leasing, and factoring.[10]

---

[2] Joseph C. Sweeney, *From Columbus to Cooperation: Trade and Shipping Policies from 1492 to 1992,* 13 Fordham Int'l L.J. 481, 494 & n.44 (1989–1990) [hereinafter Sweeney].

[3] Sweeney at 494.

[4] *Id.* at 496–98.

[5] *Id.* at 498–99.

[6] *Id.* at 499–501.

[7] Tom Thistle, Villanova University School of Law, Class of 1996 and law clerk to the author, did research and some drafting in connection with this section.

[8] Sweeney at 504 n.94.

[9] *Id.* at 504.

[10] The status of UNIDROIT projects can be obtained from the following address: International Institute for the Unification of Private Law (UNIDROIT); Via Panisperna 28; 00184 Rome; Italy; (06) 678-31-89 Fax: (06) 678-13-94

A number of UNIDROIT documents are pertinent to harmonizing international electronic transactions. Others, while not directly applicable, show trends in the development of substantive principles of private international law. In 1983 the Geneva Convention on Agency in the International Sale of Goods was adopted.[11] The convention was prepared because it was commonly recognized that international sales contracts are concluded through agents rather than directly by the principals.[12] As of April 3, 1991, the following four countries were parties to the convention: France, Italy, Mexico, and South Africa.[13]

In May 1988 the UNIDROIT Convention on International Financial Leasing was adopted.[14] The convention was designed to remove certain legal impediments to the international financial leasing of equipment while maintaining a fair balance of interests between the parties to the transaction.[15] This convention applies when the lessor and lessee have their places of business in different states and either

1. Those states and the state in which the equipment supplier has its place of business are contracting states, or
2. Both the supply agreement and the leasing agreement are governed by the law of a contracting state.[16]

Because this convention requires so many of the states involved in any transaction to be contracting states, it may not affect many transactions until it becomes widely ratified.[17] Presently there are no parties to the convention,[18] but the following countries have signed the convention: Belgium, Czechoslovakia, Finland, France, Ghana, Guinea, Italy, Morocco, Nigeria, Panama, Philippines, Tanzania, and the United States.[19]

During the same diplomatic conference at which the UNIDROIT Convention on International Financial Leasing was prepared, the UNIDROIT Convention on International Factoring was prepared.[20] Factors provide financing to merchants by purchasing their accounts receivable at a discount.[21]

---

[11] Houston Putnam Lowry, *UNIDROIT Convention on Agency in the International Sale of Goods,* International Commercial Law and Arbitration § 9.1 (1991) [hereinafter Lowry].

[12] Lowry § 9.1.

[13] *Id.* § 9.3.

[14] *Id.* § 4.1.

[15] *Id.*

[16] *Id.* § 4.2.

[17] *Id.*

[18] Party status depends on ratification under procedures of the signatory country.

[19] Lowry § 4.3.

[20] *Id.* § 5.1.

[21] *Id.* at n.1.

This convention applies to receivables from contracts for sale of goods only if

1. The supplier and debtor have places of business in different states, and
2. Those states and the state in which the factor has its place of business are contracting states, or
3. Both the contract of sales of goods and the factoring contract are governed by the law of the contracting state.[22]

As with the leasing convention a restrictive application clause in the factoring convention limits application of this convention until more states become parties to it.[23] At the time of printing there were no parties to the convention, but the following countries have signed the convention: Belgium, Czechoslovakia, Finland, France, Germany, Ghana, Guinea, Italy, Morocco, Nigeria, Philippines, Tanzania, United Kingdom of Great Britain, Northern Ireland, and the United States.[24] In May 1994 the Governing Council gave its formal approval to the UNIDROIT Principles of International Commercial Contracts and recommended its widest possible distribution in practice.[25]

In 1986 UNIDROIT initiated an attempt to adopt uniform laws throughout all states regarding cultural property.[26] The intent was to enhance the effectiveness of the UNESCO[27] Convention by ensuring that all states, civil and common-law jurisdictions alike, apply a uniform body of cultural property law.[28] The UNIDROIT Convention on the Prevention of the Illicit Import, Export, and Transfer of Ownership of Cultural Objects was still in the draft stages with its provisions subject to vigorous debate.

The General Agreement on Tariffs and Trade (GATT) and its new executive and dispute resolution organization, the World Trade Organization (WTO), are of increasing importance because of the role the import and export controls play in extending domestic regulation. The Trade Related International Property (TRIP) appendix, discussed in **Chapter 10,** resulting from the Uruguay Round of GATT negotiation,[29] largely restates American intellectual

---

[22] *Id.* § 5.2.

[23] *Id.*

[24] *Id.* § 5.3.

[25] Michael J. Bonell, An International Restatement of Contract Law: The UNIDROIT Principles of International Commercial Contracts 24 (1994).

[26] Comment, *The UNIDROIT Draft Convention on Cultural Objects: An Examination of the Need for a Uniform Legal Framework for Controlling the Illicit Movement of Cultural Property,* 7 Emory Int'l L. Rev. 457, 461 (Fall 1993).

[27] United Nations Educational, Scientific, and Cultural Organization.

[28] Comment, *The UNIDROIT Draft Convention on Cultural Objects,* 7 Emory Int'l L. Rev. 457, 461 (Fall 1993).

[29] Sweeney at 510–11 (describing Uruguay Round as having been in progress since 1986). The Uruguay Round was concluded in 1992, and ratified by the United States Congress early in 1995. *See* 19 U.S.C. § 3511 (Supp. 1995) (approving trade agreements and statement of administrative action, and authorizing president to implement the WTO agreement when he determines that a sufficient number of foreign countries have accepted its obligation).

property law, with some notable exceptions considered in **Chapter 10,** and is likely to have the effect of harmonizing basic intellectual property law principles internationally. GATT and WTO are considered more extensively in §§ **14.4** and **14.5.**

The United Nations Commission on International Trade Law (UNCITRAL) was created in 1966 and has 36 members elected by the General Assembly of the UN.[30] UNCITRAL has issued voluntary arbitration and conciliation rules (1976), a Convention on the International Sale of Goods (1980), a Convention on International Negotiable Instruments (1990), and other documents pertaining to industrial plans and shipping rules.[31] UNCITRAL now is working on government procurement contracts, "counter trade" (trades made in kind rather than in cash), standby letters of credit, and electronic funds transfers.[32]

The European Union (EU) and the North American Free Trade Agreement (NAFTA) are significant regional organizations. The European Union grew out of the European Iron and Steel Community, the European Atomic Energy Community, and the European Economic Community formed in the early 1950s under leadership from the French Minister of Finance, seeking to form economic bridges that would prevent another European war.[33] By 1990 it had evolved into a virtual economic and political federation in Europe, with significant legal authority exercised by a European Parliament accompanied by a European Council of Ministers, a European Commission, a European Court of Justice. The European Union is significant not only in terms of the law of information infrastructure in Europe, but also internationally because its adoption of law pertaining to data protection and intellectual property in electronic databases represents models that shape the American debate and, in some cases, as explained in § **14.9,** necessitate the extension of their legal duties into non-European territory. The North American Free Trade Agreement is significant because it extends U.S. intellectual property principles on the one hand, but also subjects American activities to potential scrutiny by supranational organizations set up to administer the treaty. Because of their importance, NAFTA and EU are considered separately in §§ **14.6** and **14.7.**

The International Court of Justice is actually an arbitration body, whose jurisdiction is limited to disputes between nations. Some scholars have suggested initiatives to improve its institutional framework for dealing with

---

[30] Sweeney at 516.

[31] *Id.* at 517.

[32] *Id.* at 520.

[33] P.J.G. Kapteyn & P. Verloren Van Themaat, Introduction to the Law of the European Communities 1 (1990) (describing motivation of Robert Schuman, French Foreign Minister in making May 9, 1950, announcement that he would seek to place German and French iron and steel industry under a common high authority)

international legal disputes.[34] An International Criminal Court is being discussed under UN auspices.[35]

§ 14.3   Relationship Between International Law and Domestic Law

International law and international agreements of the United States are federal law and thus supreme over state law.[36] This includes "customary international law."[37] The relationship between an international agreement and federal law depends on whether the international agreement is "self-executing." A self-executing treaty is equivalent to a legislative act in its legal effect; a non-self-executing treaty requires subsequent legislation to be effective.[38]

An international agreement thus is not superior to federal law, although when possible federal statutes are interpreted so as not to conflict with international

---

[34] *See* John H. Barton & Barry E. Carter, *International Law and Institutions for a New Age,* 81 Geo. L.J. 535 (1993) (suggesting consideration of GATT Antitrust Code, *id.* at 550; binding arbitration in NAFTA, *id.* at 560; making the judgments of the International Court of Justice enforceable in domestic courts as are arbitration awards under New York Convention, *id.* at 560; more flexible procedures for the I.C.J., *id.* at 560; further elaboration of an international common law, *id.* at 561; acceptance by United States that rights recognized by U.S. Constitution or International Human Rights Convention govern U.S. government when it acts abroad, *id.* at 561; acceptance by United States that international treaties and executive agreements can be enforced by U.S. domestic courts, *id.* at 561).

[35] *See* Virginia Morris & M-Christaine Bourloyannis-Vrailas, *The Work of the Sixth Committee at the Forty-Ninth Session of the UN General Assembly,* 89 Am. J. Int'l L. 607, 613 (1995) (reporting on discussions of recommendation for an international criminal court and suggesting that concept might be ripe now for negotiation of a treaty establishing such a court); Madeline K. Albright, *International Law Approaches the Twenty-First Century: A U.S. Perspective on Enforcement,* 18 Fordham Int'l L.J. 1595 (1995) (reporting Clinton administration interest in International criminal court proposal); Jelena Pejic, *The International Criminal Court: Issues of Law and Political Will,* 18 Fordham Int'l L.J. 1762 (1995) (suggesting that international conference of plenipotentiaries may be convened to draft convention on establishing an international criminal court in late 1995); James Crawford, *The ILC Adopts a Statute for an International Criminal Court,* 89 Am. J. Int'l L. 404 (1995) (reporting on basic parameters for a draft statute developed by International Law Commission); Paul D. Marquardt, *Law Without Borders: The Constitutionality of an International Criminal Court,* 33 Colum. J. Transnat'l L. 73 (1995); American Bar Association, *American Bar Association Task Force on an International Criminal Court Final Report,* 28 Int'l Law. 475 (1994).

[36] Restatement (Third) of Foreign Relations Law of the United States § 111(1) (1986).

[37] *Id.* § 111 reporters note 2 (1986) (characterizing Banco Nacional de Cuba v. Sabbatino, 376 U.S. 398 (1964)).

[38] *Id.* § 111 reports note 5 (1986) (explaining difference between executing and non-self-executing agreements). *See also* United States v. Postal, 589 F.2d 862, 875–77 (5th Cir. 1979) (finding 1958 convention on the high seas was not self-executing; reviewing distinction).

law or with an international agreement of the United States.[39] Sometimes, of course, a federal statute or the federal Constitution and an international document cannot be reconciled. In such case:

> "[A]n act of Congress supersedes an earlier rule of international law or a provision of an international agreement as law of the United States if the purpose of the act to supersede the earlier rule and provision is clear and if the act and the earlier rule or provision cannot be fairly reconciled"[40]

> "[A] provision of a treaty of the United States that becomes effective as law of the United States supersedes as domestic law any inconsistent pre-existing provision of a law or treaty of the United States"[41]

> Nevertheless, "a rule of international law or a provision of an international agreement of the United States will not be given effect as law in the United States if it is inconsistent with the United States Constitution."[42]

A sole executive agreement made by the president has the same status as a treaty as long as it is within his authority.[43]

§ 14.4 —GATT and WTO

The Uruguay Round of Multilateral Trade Negotiations produced "the broadest, most comprehensive trade agreements in history," of particular importance to the United States, which is the world's largest trading nation.[44] The Uruguay Round was begun by President Reagan in September 1986 and resulted in a final agreement, signed by 111 nations on April 15, 1994. An executive agreement, rather than a treaty,[45] the agreement required implementing legislation, but not a two-thirds vote in the Senate.

---

[39] Restatement (Third) of Foreign Relations of the United States § 114 (1986).

[40] *Id.* § 115(1)(a). *See* United States v. Palestine Liberation Org., 695 F. Supp. 1456, 1465 (S.D.N.Y. 1988) (U.N. Headquarters Agreement was not superseded by Anti-Terrorism Act, and thus United States could not force closure of PLO mission under Act).

[41] Restatement (Third) of Foreign Relations of the United States § 115(2) (1986).

[42] *Id.* § 115(3). *Compare* Cherokee Tobacco, 78 U.S. (11 Wall.) 616 (1871) (later statute prevails) *with* Cook v. United States, 288 U.S. 102 (1933) (later treaty prevailed).

[43] Restatement (Third) of Foreign Relations of the United States § 115 reporters note 5 (1986) (citing United States v. Belmont, 301 U.S. 324 (1937)); *but see* United States v. Guide W. Capps, Inc., 204 F.2d 655 (4th Cir. 1953), *aff'd on other grounds,* 348 U.S. 296 (1955) (executive agreement bypassing congressionally prescribed procedures did not override inconsistent statute). *See also* Dames & Moore v. Regan, 453 U.S. 654, 657 (1981) (presidential action not inconsistent with Foreign Sovereign Immunities Act and thus finally settled international claim).

[44] Message from the President of the United States, H.R. Doc. No. 103-316, 140 Cong. Rec. H9882 (daily ed. Sept. 27, 1994).

[45] 140 Cong. Rec. S15,271, S15,275 (daily ed. Dec. 1, 1994) (remarks of Senator Domenici, explaining why Uruguay Round agreements to GATT is not a treaty).

Under the agreement, a new World Trade Organization (WTO) replaces the General Agreement on Tariffs and Trade (GATT) as an institution. On the other hand, the 1994 agreement (GATT 1994) is legally distinct from the 1947 General Agreement on Tariffs and Trade (GATT 1947) and does not succeed it as a substantive legal matter.[46] The agreements themselves were signed by the United States Trade Representative under authority granted by § 1102 of the Omnibus Trade and Competitiveness Act of 1988. The Congress approved the Uruguay Round agreements and enacted implementing legislation in late 1994.[47]

The text of the trade agreements themselves does not supersede U.S. law.[48] State laws conflicting with provisions of the Uruguay Round agreements may be declared invalid only in an action brought by the United States for the purpose of declaring such law or application invalid.[49] Private rights of action to assert any cause of action or defense "under any of the Uruguay Round agreements or by virtue of Congressional approval of such an agreement" are explicitly denied by the legislation.[50]

Under Article III of the Uruguay Round agreement, the WTO has oversight responsibility. It provides the framework within which member governments conduct their trade relations under the agreements and the framework for future negotiations on trade matters under Article III of the agreement. In addition, the WTO administers the Trade Policy Review Mechanism (TPRM) and the rules and procedures governing the settlement of disputes.[51] The top level of the WTO is the Ministerial Conference, which, under Article IV, consists of representatives of all WTO governments that convene every other year. When the Ministerial Conference is not in session, its functions are carried out by a general council, also composed of representatives of WTO-member governments. When

---

[46] The Uruguay Round Agreements Act, Administrative Action Statement, H.R. Doc. No. 316, 103d Cong., 2d Sess. 792 (1994), at 3, *reprinted in* 1994 U.S.C.C.A.N. 4040, 4042–43 (explaining basic structure of WTO and relationship between GATT 1947 and GATT 1994) [hereinafter Administrative Action Statement]. The Administrative Action Statement was submitted to the Congress to comply with § 1103 of the Omnibus Trade and Competitiveness Act of 1988 and accompanied the implementing bill for the Uruguay Round agreements.

[47] 19 U.S.C. § 3511 (Supp. 1995) (approving trade agreements and statement of administrative action, and authorizing president to implement the WTO agreement when he determines that a sufficient number of foreign countries have accepted its obligation). The president made such a finding on December 23, 1994. 60 Fed. Reg. 1003 (Dec. 23, 1994), *reprinted in* 19 U.S.C. § 3511 note (Supp. 1995).

[48] 19 U.S.C. § 3512 (Supp. 1995).

[49] *Id.* § 3512(b)(2)(A). Procedures for such challenges are prescribed in *id.*, para. B.

[50] *Id.* § 3512(c). The administrative action statement accompanying the implementing legislation emphasized that the legislation "precludes any private right of action or remedy—including an action or remedy sought by a foreign government—against a federal, state, or local government, or against a private party, based on the provisions of the Uruguay Round agreements." Administrative Action Statement, Agreement Establishing the World Trade Organization § B(1)(f), *reprinted in* 1994 U.S.C.C.A.N. 4040, 4054–55.

[51] Administrative Action Statement, *reprinted in* 1994 U.S.C.C.A.N. at 4043.

the dispute settlement mechanisms are applied, the council convenes as the Dispute Settlement Body (DSB).[52] Article VI provides for a WTO secretariat, headed by a director general, who is selected by the Ministerial Conference. "Like other multilateral organizations, the staff of the secretariat is required to be impartial and member governments may not seek to influence staff actions."[53] The Ministerial Conference of the General Council are authorized to issue authoritative, binding interpretations of the WTO agreement.[54] A government may withdraw from the WTO agreement upon giving six-months notice.[55] Article IX:1 of the WTO agreement requires the WTO to continue the practice of decision making by consensus on policy matters, rather than by formal votes.[56]

The dispute settlement procedures reflect U.S. pressure to improve the effectiveness of rights dispute resolution under the agreement. The United States used the GATT dispute settlement mechanism more often than any other country, and was frequently frustrated by its possibilities for delay.[57] The Dispute Settlement Understanding (DSU) imposes stringent time limits for each stage of the dispute settlement process, creates an appellate body to review panel interpretations, provides for automatic adoption of panel or appellate body reports and requests for retaliation in the absence of a consensus at the higher level, and provides automatic authority for complaining parties to retaliate if panel recommendations are not implemented and there is no other mutually satisfactory solution. The new dispute settlement system does not, however, override national law: "If a panel finds that a country has not lived up to its commitments, all the panel may do is recommend that the country begin observing its obligations. It is then up to the disputing countries to decide how they will settle their differences."[58]

The Dispute Settlement Body, established by Article II, establishes panels, adopts panel and appellate body reports, oversees the implementation of panel recommendations adopted by the DSB, and authorizes retaliation. The DSB must make all decisions by consensus, "meaning that no member formally objects to the proposal under consideration."[59] Panels are composed of three persons selected from lists maintained by the secretariat. Potential panelists must be drawn from either the public or private sector and be well qualified based on past participation in DSU procedures, representation of a government

---

[52] *Id.*

[53] *Id.* § A(5), *reprinted in* 1994 U.S.C.C.A.N. at 4044.

[54] *Id.* § A(8), *reprinted in* 1994 U.S.C.C.A.N. at 4044–45.

[55] *Id.* § A(13), *reprinted in* 1994 U.S.C.C.A.N. at 4047.

[56] *Id.* § B(1)(h), *reprinted in* 1994 U.S.C.C.A.N. at 4056 (explaining Uruguay Round agreement provision and corresponding provision of implementing legislation, § 122).

[57] Administrative Action Statement, Understanding on Rules and Procedures Governing the Settlement of Dispute § A(1), *reprinted in* 1994 U.S.C.C.A.N. at 4300.

[58] *Id.*

[59] *Id.* § A(3), *reprinted in* 1994 U.S.C.C.A.N. at 4301.

in the WTO or GATT, service with the secretariat, having taught or published in the international trade field, or having served as a senior trade policy official. Panels generally must act within six months.[60] Article XVII authorizes the establishment of a seven-member appellate body, from which three-person appellate panels are drawn. The appellate body is authorized to uphold, modify, or reverse the legal findings and conclusions of one of its three-member panels, which is authorized to review the legal issues presented in any first-level panel report.[61] The DSU procedures are exclusive, under Article XXIII, except that arbitration may be used, pursuant to Article XXV. The implementing legislation requires presidential review of the WTO panel roster and reports to congressional committees on actual panel use.[62] Whenever the United States is a party to a dispute settlement panel, the special trade representative must publish a notice in the *Federal Register* and provide access to most documents presented to the dispute settlement panel, except for proprietary information or information treated as confidential by a foreign government.[63]

§ 14.5   —Substantive WTO Provisions

Substantively, the Uruguay Round agreements affect global information infrastructure activities mainly through the following:

1. The agreement on trade-related aspects of intellectual property rights (TRIP)[64]
2. The general agreement on trade and services
3. The agreement on government procurement
4. The agreement on trade-related investment measures
5. The agreement on technical barriers to trade.

TRIP is the most significant of these. One knowledgeable commentator characterized TRIP as largely implementing what the United States had tried to do unilaterally by extraterritorial application of its antitrust laws and application of its intellectual property laws through import restrictions.[65] TRIP and implementing legislation are considered more fully in **Chapter 10.**

---

[60] *Id.* § A(6)(c)–(e), *reprinted in* 1994 U.S.C.C.A.N. at 4302–04.

[61] *Id.* § A(7), *reprinted in* 1994 U.S.C.C.A.N. at 4304–05.

[62] 19 U.S.C. § 3533 (Supp. 1995) (added by § 123, Pub. L. No. 103-465).

[63] *Id.* § 3537; *id.* § 3537(c) (access to documents).

[64] The TRIP provisions are discussed in more detail in **Ch. 10.**

[65] Scott Fairley, *Extraterritorial Assertions of Intellectual Property Rights in International Trade, in* George R. Stewart et al., International Trade and Intellectual Property: The Search for a Balanced System 141 (1994). Mr. Fairley is president of the Canadian Council on International Law and a barrister in Canada. He cites United States v. Imperial Chem. Indus.,

The general agreement on trade and services "is the first multilateral, legally enforceable agreement covering trade and investment in the services sector."[66] In general, member governments must treat services and service suppliers from other WTO countries in a manner that is "no less favorable" than the manner in which they treat services and service suppliers from any other member country, although certain exceptions are provided for in Article II of the general agreement on trade and services.[67] While Article VIII permits WTO governments to designate sole providers in a particular services market, they must ensure that these designated monopolists do not abuse their monopoly positions "through action in nonmonopolized markets that are inconsistent with any specific commitments made by the government in respect of that market."[68] Article XVI, however, allows six types of limitations on competition and new entry, depending on commitments made by member governments.[69]

The annex on telecommunication services ensures that service providers have reasonable and nondiscriminatory access to, and use of, basic telecommunication services in member countries and specifically provides that services may be used for intracorporate communications and to provide service to customers in covered countries. It also provides that services firms may attach the equipment of their choice to the telecommunications networks, interconnect to other private networks, and use proprietary protocols. It allows telecommunications authorities to regulate use of basic telecommunication services as necessary "to ensure universal service, to protect the technical integrity of the network, and to prevent the provision of unauthorized service." Nondiscrimination duties are suspended pending further negotiations.[70] Those negotiations are to be concluded by April 30, 1996, intending to cover local, long distance, and international basic telecommunication services.[71]

The agreement on government procurement generally provides for nondiscriminatory procurement procedures and standards and specifically provides for electronic tendering as a means of adding flexibility.[72]

---

100 F. Supp. 504 (S.D.N.Y. 1951), supplemental op., 105 F. Supp. 215 (S.D.N.Y. 1952); British Nylon Spinners v. Imperial Chem. Indus., [1953] 1 Crim. App. ch. 19 (1952), made permanent [1955] 1 Crim. App. ch. 37 (1954), as representing aggressive U.S. assertion of extraterritorial power, and British reactions. He cites the Supreme Court's decision in EEOC v. Arabian Am. Oil Co., 111 S. Ct. 1227 (1991), as retreating somewhat from the aggressive stands. Nevertheless, Hartford Fire Ins. v. California, 113 S. Ct. 2891 (1993), reasserts extraterritorial effect of U.S. antitrust law.

[66] Administrative Action Statement, The General Agreement on Trade and Services § A, *reprinted in* 1994 U.S.C.C.A.N. 4269.

[67] *Id.* § A(2), *reprinted in* 1994 U.S.C.C.A.N. at 4269.

[68] *Id.* § A(2)(g), *reprinted in* 1994 U.S.C.C.A.N. at 4271.

[69] *Id.* § A(3), *reprinted in* 1994 U.S.C.C.A.N. at 4273.

[70] *Id.* § A(7)(c), *reprinted in* 1994 U.S.C.C.A.N. at 4275–76.

[71] *Id.* § B(2)(a), *reprinted in* 1994 U.S.C.C.A.N. at 4277.

[72] Administrative Action Statement, Agreement on Government Procurement § A, *reprinted in* 1994 U.S.C.C.A.N. at 4321–22.

The agreement on trade-related investment measures seeks to eliminate requirements for purchase of local goods or limitations on imports as a precondition to investment.[73]

The agreement on technical barriers to trade recognizes that governments and the private sector have a legitimate need for standards and procedures for assessing product conformity with standards, while guarding against the unjustified use of standards and standard-implementation procedures to protect a domestic industry.[74] Legitimate objectives under the agreement include national security requirements; prevention of consumer deception; and protection of human health or safety, animal or plant life or health, or the environment. It explicitly excludes protecting domestic production.[75] In general, Article 2.4 requires governments to use relevant international standards as basis for their own technical regulations except when there is a legitimate reason not to do so.[76] Suppliers from other WTO countries must be provided access to conformity assessment procedures that do not discriminate.[77] Under Article XIV of the Technical Barriers to Trade Agreement, all disputes arising under it are to be settled under the provisions of the WTO DSU.[78]

The relationship between the Uruguay Round agreement and the European Union is uncertain.[79] The EU itself has authority to negotiate matters of commercial policy and thus, theoretically, is more significantly involved in trade negotiations than the individual EU member countries. In reality, this is not always the case. The principal legal context for the EU-WTO relationship is found in Article XXIV of GATT, which allows a customs union exemption from most-favored-nation clauses, but also requires that on the whole its common external trade barriers not be higher than experienced by the rest of the world from the member states of the customs union prior to its formation.[80]

§ 14.6 —NAFTA

The North American Free Trade Agreement (NAFTA) eliminates all bilateral tariffs and most nontariff trade barriers between the United States and Canada,

---

[73] Administrative Action Statement, Agreement on Trade Related Investment Measures, *reprinted in* 1994 U.S.C.C.A.N. at 4149–50.

[74] Administrative Action Statement, Agreement on Technical Barriers to Trade § A, *reprinted in* 1994 USCCAN at 4127–28.

[75] *Id.* § A(7), *reprinted in* 1994 U.S.C.C.A.N. at 4130.

[76] *Id., reprinted in* 1994 U.S.C.C.A.N. at 4131.

[77] *Id.* § A(9)(a), *reprinted in* 1994 U.S.C.C.A.N. at 4134.

[78] *Id.* § A(11), *reprinted in* 1994 U.S.C.C.A.N. at 4135.

[79] *See generally* John H. Jackson, The European Community and World Trade: The Commercial Policy Dimension in Singular Europe: Economy and Policy of the European Community After 1992. at 321, 326 (William J. Adams ed. 1995) ("the EC and GATT: Troubled Relationship?").

[80] *See id.* at 328 (describing impact of GATT Article XXIV).

and between the United States and Mexico by 1998. NAFTA builds on the success of the US-Canada Free Trade Agreement (CFTA) effective since January 1, 1989. NAFTA was concluded on December 17, 1992, and approved by the Congress on March 7, 1995.[81] The agreement became operative on December 27, 1993.[82]

The Implementation Act makes it clear that NAFTA does not override federal law.[83] The Act provides for a consultation process to review state law,[84] but provides that no person other than the United States may challenge any action by a state or political subdivision on the ground that such action is inconsistent with NAFTA.[85] State laws may be declared invalid as inconsistent with NAFTA only in actions brought by the United States.[86] The Act expressly negates the possibility of a private right of action under NAFTA.[87] The agreement generally is administered by a secretariat within the Department of Commerce,[88] and the president accepted in advance panel and committee decisions under the Tariff Act of 1930 related to NAFTA.[89]

NAFTA is the first trade agreement that provides a mechanism for resolving private commercial disputes. It commits the United States, Canada, and Mexico to encourage arbitration and other alternative dispute resolution techniques for settling international commercial disputes between private parties involving free trade. In particular, it requires Mexico to provide procedures to ensure recognition and enforcement of arbitration agreements and awards. It establishes an advisory committee on private commercial disputes through the NAFTA commission to make further recommendations on arbitration and other procedures.[90] NAFTA establishes a Free Trade Commission with general oversight responsibility, which may create bilateral or trilateral panels of private sector experts to resolve disputes involving interpretation of the NAFTA text.

When consultations through the Free Trade Commission are unsuccessful, the agreement provides for arbitration between the governments involved.[91] Awards

---

[81] NAFTA, Pub. L. No. 103-182, 107 Stat. 2057, approved Dec. 8, 1993 (codified in 19 U.S.C. § 3311 (Supp. 1995)).

[82] Exec. Order No. 12,889, 58 Fed. Reg. 69,681, 3 C.F.R. 707 (Dec. 27, 1993).

[83] 19 U.S.C. § 3312(a) (Supp. 1995).

[84] Id. § 3312(b)(1).

[85] Id. § 3312(c)(2).

[86] Id. § 3312(b)(2).

[87] "No person other than the United States shall have any cause of action or defense under the agreement or by virtue of congressional approval therefore." Id. § 3312(c)(1).

[88] Exec. Order No. 12,889, § 1, 58 Fed. Reg. 69,681, 3 C.F.R. 707,708 (Dec. 27, 1993) (establishing United States section of NAFTA secretariat within the Department of Commerce).

[89] Id. § 2 (referring to 19 U.S.C. § 1516(a)(g)(7)(B) panel and committee decisions).

[90] Administrative Action Statement, Statement as to How the NAFTA Serves the Interest of the United States Commerce § 7(b), 1993 WL 561219.

[91] NAFTA, art. 2008.

of these public arbitration panels are potentially enforceable by suspension of NAFTA benefits.[92] On the other hand, no country may provide a right of action in its domestic courts to challenge the consistency of another government's actions under the agreement.[93] Under the textually separate labor "side agreement," a more binding form of dispute resolution is provided against a signatory that fails or refuses to enforce adequate labor standards and to permit collective bargaining. These dispute resolution awards are enforceable against a $20 million fund established for that purpose.[94]

NAFTA imposes procedural transparency obligations on the signatories, requiring prompt publication of laws, regulations, procedures, and administrative rulings concerning subjects covered by NAFTA and requiring appropriate opportunity to comment on them.[95] Firms and individuals also must be given the opportunity to participate in specific types of administrative proceedings affecting matters covered by the agreement.[96] A provision similar to a provision of GATT[97] requires establishment and maintenance of independent administrative or judicial review procedures: "These appeal rights must include a reasonable opportunity to present arguments and to obtain a decision based on evidence in the administrative record."[98]

If a signatory has a claim that could be initiated under either GATT or NAFTA, the complaining signatory may choose either forum. The forum chosen shall then be used to the exclusion of the other.

Substantively, in areas of particular interest to NII service providers, NAFTA makes major changes in trade relations respecting intellectual property, telecommunications, services, investment, government procurement, technical standards, and competition policy. Chapter 17 covers intellectual property. It requires each government to apply the substantive provisions of the Paris,[99] Berne,[100] and Geneva[101] Conventions, excepting Article 6 Bis. of the Berne Convention[102]

---

[92] *Id.*, art. 2019.

[93] *Id.*, art. 2021.

[94] *See generally* Earl V. Brown, *Principal Features of the North American Free Trade Side Agreement on Labor Cooperation, in* Henry H. Perritt, Jr., 1995 Wiley Employment Law Update 219 (John Wiley & Sons, Inc., 1995) (reviewing GATT labor agreement enforcement procedures).

[95] NAFTA, art. 1801.

[96] *Id.*, art. 1804.

[97] *Id.*, art. 1805 (similar to GATT, art. X.3(b)).

[98] Administrative Action Statement, Ch. 18: Publication, Notification and Administration of Laws § A, 1993 WL 561174.

[99] Paris Convention for the Protection of Industrial Property, Mar. 20, 1883, 21 U.S.T. 1583, 828 U.N.T.S. 305.

[100] Berne Convention for the Protection of Literary and Artistic Works, Sept. 9, 1986, revised in Paris, July 24, 1971, 828 U.N.T.S. 221.

[101] The Geneva Convention for the Protection of Producers of Phonograms Against Unauthorized Duplication of Their Phonogram, Oct. 29, 1971, 25 U.S.T. 309, 866 U.N.T.S. 67.

[102] Article 6bis refers to an author's moral rights of authorship and integrity.

with respect to the United States. It requires each NAFTA country to give nationals from other NAFTA countries treatment that is no less favorable than the treatment it gives to its own nationals and prohibits requirements such as local fixation.[103] It confirms that computer programs are literary works under the Berne Convention and requires signatories to protect them, also requiring copyright protection for compilations of data or other material that by reason of the selection or arrangement of the material are original.[104] Copyright holders must be accorded exclusive rights with respect to importation, communication to the public, and first public distribution, and they must be allowed to transfer their rights by contract without the possibility of discrimination against contract grantees.[105]

The agreement generally extends U.S. style trademark,[106] patent,[107] and integrated circuit layout design protection[108] throughout the free trade area. NAFTA is the first international agreement to include detailed provisions regarding protection of trade secrets.[109] Signatories must provide effective intellectual property enforcement procedures, including access by intellectual property rights holders to effective judicial proceedings or quasi-judicial administrative enforcement proceedings,[110] injunctive relief,[111] and criminal sanctions for willful copyright piracy and trademark counterfeiting on a commercial scale.[112] Procedures for seizure of pirated and counterfeit goods at the border must be provided.[113] Relatively few changes in U.S. law were required, limited to covering inventive activity in other NAFTA countries for purposes of establishing the date of patent invention, rental rights in computer programs and sound recordings, registrability of misleading geographic indications under trademark law, copyright protection for certain motion pictures not in the public domain and the United States, and compulsory licensing and government use of patents.[114]

Chapter 13 opens up telecommunications markets.[115] Firms from other NAFTA countries must be allowed to purchase, lease, and attach terminal or

---

[103] NAFTA, art. 1703.

[104] *Id.*, art. 1705.

[105] *Id.*

[106] *Id.*, art. 1706.

[107] *Id.*, art. 1709.

[108] *Id.*, art. 1710.

[109] NAFTA, art. 1711.

[110] *Id.*, arts. 1714–15.

[111] *Id.*, art. 1716.

[112] *Id.*, art. 1717.

[113] *Id.*, art. 1718.

[114] Administrative Action Statement, Ch. 17: Intellectual Property § B (summarizing necessary changes in U.S. law), 1993 WL 561170.

[115] *See generally* Administrative Action Statement, Ch. 13: Telecommunications, 1993 WL 561161.

other equipment to public networks; interconnect leased channels for domestic or cross-border use with other public networks or private networks; perform switching, signaling, and processing functions; and use operating protocols of their choice.[116] Firms operating public networks must price so as to reflect economic cost directly related to the provision of services and must make leased circuits available at flat rates, independent of usage, although cross-subsidization is not prohibited for the purpose of assuring universal service.[117] Firms must be able to move information freely over domestic public networks both domestically and cross-border, including movement of information over intracorporate networks and access to databases and other information stored in machine-readable form.[118] Governments may take appropriate action to ensure security and confidentiality and to protect subscriber privacy.[119] This privilege allows the restrictions imposed by the EU data protection directive,[120] notwithstanding the GATT entitlement to move information across borders.[121] Regulatory obligations of enhanced services providers such as credit card validation systems, electronic mail, on-line databases, and computer services (including remote data processing over a country's basic telephone network) are limited. They may not be required to fulfill common carrier obligations such as providing services to the public generally or filing tariffs, except to remedy a particular case of anticompetitive conduct or if the provider of enhanced services is a monopoly public telecommunications operator.[122] The signatories are obligated to promote standards for global compatibility and interoperability through the International Telecommunications Union and the International Organization for Standardization.[123]

With respect to standards, NAFTA prohibits use of standards for trade restrictive purposes[124] and obligates each signatory to use relevant international standards as the basis for its standards-related measures except when use of such standards would be ineffective or inappropriate ways to fulfill legitimate national objectives.[125] Conformity testing bodies of each signatory must be accredited, approved, and licensed on a nondiscriminatory basis by the other signatories.[126]

---

[116] NAFTA, art. 1302.

[117] *Id.* para. 3.

[118] *Id.* para. 4.

[119] *Id.* para. 5.

[120] See § **14.9** and **Ch. 3.**

[121] NAFTA, art. 1302, para. 4.

[122] *Id.,* art. 1303.

[123] *Id.,* art. 1308.

[124] *Id.,* art. 904(3), (4).

[125] *Id.,* art. 905.

[126] *Id.,* art. 908(1).

The agreement liberalizes trade in services except under explicit national reservations.[127] It promotes cross-border investment by providing four basic protections to investors from other signatories: nondiscriminatory treatment; freedom from "performance requirements"; free transfer of funds related to investments; and expropriation in conformity with international law.[128] NAFTA builds on the GATT agreement on government procurement, extending it to Mexico, which is not a party to the GATT code. It gives U.S. products and services guaranteed access to procurement by Mexican government agencies, on a staged basis.[129] More generally, it obligates the signatories to eliminate national restrictions on the majority of non-defense-related purchases by their federal governments.

With respect to competition, the agreement obligates all three countries to adopt or maintain effective antitrust measures, backed up by cooperative law enforcement policy, mutual legal assistance, notification, consultation, and exchange of relevant information.[130] Government owned and controlled enterprises must not discriminate against foreign owned enterprises, and such enterprises generally must act consistent with NAFTA's provisions.[131]

§ 14.7　—European Union

The European Union[132] grew out of a proposal initially made in 1950 by Robert Schuman, the French Foreign Minister, to place the whole of the French and German coal and steel output under a "high authority."[133] The result was a treaty establishing the European Coal and Steel Community, signed in Paris in 1951,[134] followed soon thereafter by the European Economic Community (EEC) and the European Atomic Energy Community.[135] This is the "Treaty of Rome," looked upon as the foundation document for the constitution of the European Union. The EEC was based from the beginning on a customs union, unlike the European

---

[127] *See* Administrative Action Statement, Ch. 12: Cross Border Trade and Services, 1993 WL 561160.

[128] Administrative Action Statement, Ch. 11: Investment, 1993 WL 561159.

[129] NAFTA, Annex 1001.2a; Administrative Action Statement, Ch. 10: Government Procurement, 1993 WL 561158.

[130] NAFTA, art. 1501; Administrative Action Statement, Ch. 15: Competition Policy, Monopolies and State Enterprises, 1993 WL 561163.

[131] NAFTA, arts. 1502–03.

[132] The usage changed from "European Community" to "European Union" after the Maastricht Treaty was negotiated.

[133] P.J.G. Kapteyn & P. Verloren Van Themaat, Introduction to the Law of the European Communities 1 (Laurence Gormley ed., 2d ed. 1989).

[134] *Id.* at 7.

[135] *Id.* at 13–17 (European Economic Community and European Atomic Energy Community signed in Rome in 1957).

Coal and Steel Community, which provided for no common external tariff.[136] From the outset, the three communities shared a common set of institutions: the European Parliament, the Council of Ministers, and the European Commission.[137] The Single European Act, which became effective in 1987, codified the role of the European Council—a consultive body composed of the heads of the governments of members of the union—and committed Europe to a single internal market by 1992.[138] The Maastricht Treaty,[139] agreed to in 1992, reallocated power among the Council of Ministers, the Parliament, and the Commission; established a plan for eventual monetary union within the union; and established the principle of subsidiarity—requiring deference to national and local institutions. The community is recognized as a distinct legal order, significantly different from mere international law relations among independent states.[140]

Some of the institutional changes made by the Maastricht Agreement are best understood if one understands the basic responsibilities of the three main nonjudicial institutions: the European Commission, the Council of Ministers, and the European Parliament (the European Court of Justice is an important institution in its own right, as explained later). Those who like American analogies compare the Council of Ministers to the United States Senate, the Commission to the American Presidency, and the European Parliament to the United States House of Representatives.

The European Commission is a kind of executive branch. It is composed of 17 commissioners, two from each of the five larger countries (France, Germany, Italy, Spain, and the United Kingdom), and one from each of the seven smaller countries. The president of the Commission is selected by the member states, after consulting the European Parliament. Then, the governments of the member states, consulting with the nominee for president, nominate the other person whom they intend to appoint as members of the Commission. The entire body of the Commission is subject to a vote of approval by the European Parliament.[141]

---

[136] *Id.* at 30 (describing two elements in a customs union: abolition of internal barriers to trade, and creation of common customs tariff toward rest of world; free trade areas distinguished by the absence of the second element).

[137] *Id.* at 33 (reviewing effect of the merger treaty of Apr. 8, 1965).

[138] *Id.* at 27.

[139] The treaty on European Union, formerly signed by the foreign and finance ministers at a summit in Maastricht, the Netherlands, in Feb. 1992, commonly is referred to as the "Maastricht Agreement."

[140] P.J.G. Kapteyn & P. Verloren Van Themaat, Introduction to the Law of the European Communities 38–39 (Laurence Gormley ed., 2d ed. 1989) (citing case 26/62, NV Algemene Transport en Expeditie Onderneming Van Gend en Loos v. Nederlandse admininistratie der belastingen, [1963] E.C.R. 1, 12; case 6/64, Costa v. ENEL, [1964] E.C.R. 585, 593).

[141] Neill Nugent, The Government and Politics of the European Union 85–86 (3d ed. 1994) (reviewing Article 158 of amended treaty) [hereinafter Nugent].

Commissioners are not supposed to be national representatives but are supposed to act in the common interest of the community, and they must not seek nor take instructions from any government. Each commissioner has a personal staff called a "cabinet." The permanent staff comprised slightly less than 20,000 as of 1993.[142] Each commissioner has responsibility for one or more directorates general. Directorates general (DG) include the following:

1. Competition (DG IV)
2. Internal market and industrial affairs (DG III)
3. Science, research, and development (DG XII)
4. Telecommunications, information technologies, and industries (DG XIII)
5. Audiovisual information, communication, and culture (DG X).[143]

Commission decisions originate as drafts developed at a middle ranking "A grade level" in the appropriate DG. The drafts are reviewed by the drafter's superiors, the cabinets of commissioners, and in weekly meetings of the chefs du cabinet.[144] Eventually, they reach a meeting of the commissioners.

The Commission is the principal initiator of opinions, recommendations, and legislation. It has a relatively free hand because of the absence of anything like a prime minister or parliamentary cabinet to give it political direction.[145] In theory, the Commission is obliged to respond to request by the Council of Ministers for policy initiation, but the practical initiative actually rests with the Commission.[146] This relatively weak role of the Council of Ministers has been intensified by the tendency of major policy initiatives to be dealt with by the European Council—a collection of heads of government—rather than by the Council of Ministers. The Commission also has important executive functions, including rule making.[147] Imposing the U.S. distinction between administrative rules and legislation is somewhat misleading inasmuch as some of the Commission's rule-making powers are subject only to "consultations with the Council of Ministers."[148] The Commission's powers are somewhat circumscribed by

---

[142] Nugent at 89.

[143] *Id.* at 92 (Table 4.1 directorates general and special units of the commission).

[144] The chefs du cabinet are the chiefs of staff to the commissioners; the weekly chefs du cabinet meeting is like a deputy group

[145] Nugent at 98–99. The Parliament's power to confirm Commission members has not ripened into real political control.

[146] *Id.* at 99.

[147] *Id.* at 103 (reporting 6000 to 7000 commission legislative instruments per year including directives, regulations, and decisions—distinguished from "recommendations" and "opinions" that do not have legislative force).

[148] *Id.* at 104 (noting breadth of commission's authority under Articles 58 (production quotas), 61 (allocation of production and minimum prices for steel), and 85 (clarification and development of position on restrictive practices)).

a system of management and regulatory committees, generally composed of governmental representatives from member states.[149]

The Commission also has standing to seek review of certain activities before the European Court of Justice, and acts as an external representative of the union.[150] The Commission became something of a lightning rod for criticism in the later 1980s, particularly from Britain. Many commentators perceive its role as having been diminished since the high-water mark of about 1990 when Jacques Delors was especially powerful as Commission president.[151] The struggle for primacy between the Commission and the Council of Ministers and the European Council looks to this American observer, however, rather like the continuing struggle between executive and independent agencies in the American system of government and the Congress.

The Council of Ministers is formally the main decision-making institution of the EU. This theoretical power is limited by two requirements: that the Council act on the basis of proposals made to it by the Commission, and that, under the co-decision procedure, it act only after receiving advice from the European Parliament. Nevertheless, the Council has made effective use of Article 152 to guide Commission initiative by the adoption of opinions, resolutions, agreements, and recommendations and by an increasingly developed bureaucracy.[152] The presidency of the council rotates among member states on a six-month basis and involves little more than the power to persuade and mediate.

The European Parliament clearly is the weakest of the several formal institutions, although its power has increased by several amendments to the constitutional documents. Its most important power lever is that its views must be sought in connection with important legislation.[153] There also are a variety of opportunities to influence policy development less formally and to adopt nonbinding initiative reports.[154] The Maastricht Treaty introduced the co-decision procedure, which prevents the Council from taking final action when the European Parliament disagrees and the matter cannot be resolved through a conciliation committee—which looks remarkably like a conference committee between the U.S. House and Senate.[155]

Until 1979 members of the European Parliament were nominated by national parliaments from among their members. Direct elections, authorized by Article 138 of the EEC Treaty, did not begin until 1979. Since then, direct elections of the European Parliament have increased the federal flavor of the European

---

[149] *Id.* at 109–12.

[150] *Id.* at 112, 118.

[151] Nugent at 122 (generally noting perceived decline and commission's power vis-à-vis European Council and the Council of Ministers).

[152] *Id.* at 124.

[153] *Id.* at 175 (referring to isoglucose 1980 ruling by ECJ).

[154] *Id.* at 174–75.

[155] *Id.* at 177 (explaining co-decision procedure).

Union and have reinforced pressure to make Parliament a more meaningful institution.[156]

The Court of Justice of the European Communities (E.C.J.), established and regulated by Articles 164 through 188 of the Treaty of Rome, enjoys significant powers. The court sits in Luxembourg and has responsibility for deciding questions of European law referred to it by national courts;[157] for reviewing and, if appropriate, invalidating acts of the Council and the Commission in actions brought by a member state, the Council, or the Commission or by a natural or legal person adversely affected by the challenged act;[158] for adjudicating damages actions against the EU institutions;[159] and for deciding whether a member state has fulfilled its obligations under EU law.[160] A Court of First Instance is authorized by Article 168(a), added by Article 11 of the Single European Act, and was established by the Council of Ministers in 1988.[161] The Court of First Instance hears cases brought by natural or legal persons, subject to appeal on points of law to the E.C.J.

The E.C.J. is composed of 13 judges,[162] assisted by six advocates general,[163] and a registrar.[164] The court sits in plenary session and also in panels called "chambers.[165] The advocates general play a particularly important role, a role not known in American judicial procedure.[166] After a case is submitted, the advocate general prepares a reasoned opinion and presents it in open court.[167] While the court also writes opinions justifying its decisions, often the opinion of the advocate general is more analytical and provides a better guide to the basis for decisions.

---

[156] *Id.* Nugent at 205–06 (considering whether "the EP is becoming a proper parliament," but concluding that in some ways the European Parliament, despite its weak constitutional powers, is more powerful in practice than national parliaments dominated by their executives).

[157] Treaty of Rome, art. 177. Article 177 is modeled on the Italian order of reference. References from national courts constitute the most significant part of the court's case load. *See* Nugent at 228.

[158] Treaty of Rome, art. 173 (review of legality of acts of council and commission), art. 175 (failure to act). Article 173 is modeled on French judicial review.

[159] Treaty of Rome, art. 178 (jurisdiction in disputes relating to compensation for damage authorized in art. 215, para. 2).

[160] *Id.,* art. 169 (actions by commission), art. 170 (actions by member state against other member state).

[161] The Court of First Instance of the European Communities was established by Council Decision of 24 Oct. 1988. *See* 1988. O.J. (L 319) 25.

[162] Treaty of Rome, art. 165.

[163] *Id.,* article 166 (describing duties and authorizing Council to increase number of advocates general upon request of E.C.J.).

[164] *Id.,* art. 168.

[165] *Id.,* art. 165 (also authorizing Council to increase number of judges upon request of the E.C.J.).

[166] *Id.,* art. 166 (the role of advocate general is derived from French criminal law).

[167] *Id.,* art. 166 (describing functions of advocates general).

Judgments of the E.C.J. are enforceable under the rules of civil procedure of the nation in which enforcement is sought.[168] E.C.J. procedures are prescribed in a separate protocol to the Treaty of Rome:[169]

> The procedure before the court shall consist of two parts: written and oral.
>
> The written procedure shall consist of the communication to the parties and to the institutions of the community whose decisions are in dispute, of applications, statements of case, defenses and observations, and of replies, if any, as well as of all papers and documents and support or of certified copies of them.
>
> Communications shall be made by the registrar in the order and within the time laid down and the rules of procedure.
>
> The oral procedure shall consist of the reading of the report presented by a judge acting as rapporteur, the hearing by the court of agents, advisors and lawyers entitled to practice before a court of a member state and of the submissions of the advocate general, as well as the hearing, if any, of witnesses and experts.[170]

The court may require parties to produce all documents and to supply all information that the court considers desirable,[171] and may order that a witness or expert be heard by the judicial authority of his place of permanent residence.[172] Judgments must be read in open court.[173] The procedure before the court of first instance is the same as that before the E.C.J.[174] Appeals from the court of first instance to the E.C.J. are limited to points of law,[175] and must be filed within two months of the appealed decisions.[176]

---

[168] Treaty of Rome, art. 187 (judgments of E.C.J. enforceable "under the conditions laid down in Article 192"). Article 192 provides for enforcement of Council and Commission pecuniary obligations under the

> Rules of Civil Procedure in force in the state and the territory of which it is carried out. The order for its enforcement shall be appended to the decision, without other formality than verification of the authenticity of the decision, by the national authority which the government of each member state shall designate for this purpose and shall make known to the commission and to the court of justice. When these formalities have been completed on application by the party concerned, the latter may proceed to enforcement in accordance with the national law, by bringing the matter directly before the competent authority.

Id., art. 192.

[169] Id., art. 188 (providing for "statute of the court of justice to be laid down in separate protocol"). The protocol is contained in Appendix I to the Treaty of Rome. A case is brought before the court by "a written application addressed to the registrar," containing the applicant's name and address, the name of the party against whom application is made, the subject matter of the dispute, the submissions, and a brief statement of the grounds on which the application is based. Id., app. I, art. 19.

[170] Id., app. I, art. 18.

[171] Id., art. 21.

[172] Treaty of Rome, app. I, art. 26.

[173] Id., art. 34.

[174] Id., art. 46.

[175] Id., art. 51.

[176] Id., art. 49.

Substantively, the E.C.J. has issued several landmark decisions. In *Costa v. ENEL,*[177] the court of justice decided that EU law constitutes an autonomous legal system, supervening sovereign powers of the member states who gave up some of their sovereignty by entering into the EU.

In *Van Gend Enloos,*[178] the court initially established the principle that some provisions of EU law may confer rights or impose obligations on individuals that national courts must recognize and enforce. Although there is no explicit supremacy clause in the Treaty of Rome or other constitutional documents of the EU, the E.C.J. early held that EU law is supreme. National courts must apply it in the event of conflict, even if domestic law is part of the national constitution.[179] The court also has been vigilant in enforcing what Americans would call separation of powers principles in the EU.[180] In October 1988 the court held that community institutions may take legal actions against non-EU companies.[181]

In addition to these institutions of the European Union, there is an overlapping set of institutions under the European Convention on Human Rights, which functions through the European Court of Human Rights and through the European Commission of Human Rights. The European Commission has proposed that the European Union accede to the European Convention on Human Rights, and the European Court of Justice has approached but not yet embraced the idea that the substance of the European Convention on Human Rights is part of European Union law.[182] The European Convention has been used in the information infrastructure context to invalidate national measures that infringe rights of free expression and the press.[183]

§ 14.8   Export Controls

Export controls imposed by the United States government have a significant influence on international trade, computer software, and certain network communications. Strong encryption is barred from export when it allows for encryption of data, text, or other media rather than being limited to data authentication

---

[177] Case 6/64, [1964] E.C.R. 585.

[178] Case 26/62 [1963] E.C.R. 1.

[179] Nugent at 219 (quoting from Simmenthal v. Commission (case 92/78)).

[180] *See* Isoglucose case (case 138/79) (Oct. 1980) (council may not adopt legislation until after receiving Parliament's opinion).

[181] Wood Pulp cases (joined cases 89, 104, 114–117, 125–129/85) (upholding fines imposed by Commission on American and Canadian finished producers of wood pulp based on their consorted practices affecting prices).

[182] P.J.G. Kapteyn & P. VerLoren van Themaat, Introduction to the Law of the European Communities after the Coming into Force of the Single European Act 166–67 (2d ed. 1990).

[183] Brind, [1991] 1 App. Cas. 759–62; Dudgeon v. United Kingdom, 4 Eur. Ct. H.R. Rep. 149 (1981). *See* P. Van Dijk & G.J.H. Van Hoof, Theory and Practice of the European Convention on Human Rights 10–18 (1984).

and digital signatures. These export controls have discouraged mass market software vendors from putting strong encryption into their products and thus have deterred wide use of such technologies, even though a special procedure was established to deal with mass-marketed software.

The Arms Export Control Act (AECA)[184] authorizes the president "to control the import and the export of defense articles and defense services."[185] The president delegated his functions to designate items and services subject to control to the secretary of state, with the concurrence of the secretary of defense.[186] Pursuant to the AECA, the secretary of state promulgated the International Traffic in Arms Regulations (ITAR).[187] ITAR lists controlled "defense articles," which is called the United States Munitions List.[188]

In addition to the "defense articles" specifically included on the Munitions List, ITAR defines "defense services" as (1) "[T]he furnishing of assistance (including training) to foreign persons" with respect to a "defense article," and (2) "[t]he furnishing to foreign persons of any technical data controlled under this subchapter, whether in the U.S. or abroad."[189] Encryption systems, software, and algorithms are included as "defense articles" on the Munitions List. Category XIII paragraph (b) includes the following:

(b) Information Security Systems and equipment, cryptographic devices, software, and components specifically designed or modified therefor, including:

(1) Cryptographic (including key management) systems, equipment, assemblies, modules, integrated circuits, components or software with the capability of maintaining secrecy or confidentiality of information or information systems, except cryptographic equipment and software as follows:

(i) Restricted to decryption functions specifically designed to allow the execution of copy protected software, provided the decryption functions are not user-accessible.

(ii) Specially designed, developed or modified for use in machines for banking or money transactions, and restricted to use only in such transactions. Machines for banking or money transactions include automatic teller machines, self-service statement printers, point of sale terminals or equipment for the encryption of interbanking transactions.

(iii) Employing only analog techniques to provide the cryptographic processing that ensures information security in the following applications:

(A) Fixed (defined below) band scrambling not exceeding 8 bands and in which the transpositions change not more frequently than once every second;

---

[184] 22 U.S.C. §§ 2751–2796d.

[185] *Id.* § 2778(a)(1).

[186] Exec. Order No. 11,958 § 1(l)(1) 42 Fed. Reg. 4311, 22 U.S.C. § 2751 n (Jan. 18, 1977). The secretary of commerce has enforcement authority. *Id.* § 1(l)(2).

[187] 22 C.F.R. pts. 120–130 (1994).

[188] *Id.* § 121.1.

[189] *Id.* § 120.9(1), (2).

(B) Fixed (defined below) band scrambling exceeding 8 bands and in which the transpositions change not more frequently than once every ten seconds;

(C) Fixed (defined below) frequency inversion and in which the transpositions change not more frequently than once every second;

(D) Facsimile equipment;

(E) Restricted audience broadcast equipment;

(F) Civil television equipment.

Note: Special Definition. For purposes of this subparagraph, fixed means that the coding or compression algorithm cannot accept externally supplied parameters (e.g., cryptographic or key variables) and cannot be modified by the user.

(iv) Personalized smart cards using cryptography restricted for use only in equipment or systems exempted from the controls of the USML.

(v) Limited to access control, such as automatic teller machines, self-service statement printers or point of sale terminals, which protects password or personal identification numbers (PIN) or similar data to prevent unauthorized access to facilities but does not allow for encryption of files or text, except as directly related to the password of PIN protection.

(vi) Limited to data authentication which calculates a Message Authentication Code (MAC) or similar result to ensure no alteration of text has taken place, or to authenticate users, but does not allow for encryption of data, text or other media other than that needed for the authentication.

(vii) Restricted to fixed data compression or coding techniques.

(viii) Limited to receiving for radio broadcast, pay television or similar restricted audience television of the consumer type, without digital encryption and where digital decryption is limited to the video, audio or management functions.

(ix) Software designed or modified to protect against malicious computer damage, (e.g., viruses).

Note: A procedure has been established to facilitate the expeditious transfer to the Commodity Control List of mass market software products with encryption that meet specified criteria regarding encryption for the privacy of data and the associated key management. Requests to transfer commodity jurisdiction of mass market software products designed to meet the specified criteria may be submitted in accordance with the commodity jurisdiction provisions of § 120.4. Questions regarding the specified criteria or the commodity jurisdiction process should be addressed to the Office of Defense Trade Controls. All mass market software products with cryptography that were previously granted transfers of commodity jurisdiction will remain under Department of Commerce control. Mass market software governed by this note is software that is generally available to the public by being sold from stock at retail selling points, without restriction, by means of over the counter transactions, mail order transactions, or telephone call transactions; and designed for installation by the user without further substantial support by the supplier.

(2) Cryptographic (including key management) systems, equipment, assemblies, modules, integrated circuits, components or software which have the capability of generating spreading or hopping codes for spread spectrum systems or equipment.

(3) Cryptanalytic systems, equipment, assemblies, modules, integrated circuits, components or software.

(4) Systems, equipment, assemblies, modules, integrated circuits, components or software providing certified or certifiable multi-level security or user isolation exceeding class B2 of the Trusted Computer System Evaluation Criteria (TCSEC) and software to certify such systems, equipment or software.

(5) Ancillary equipment specifically designed or modified for paragraphs (b) (1), (2), (3), (4) and (5) of this category.[190]

Cryptography and speech about cryptography are also included as "defense services" because they "furnish assistance" with respect to defense articles. They also qualify as "technical data" because they are "software directly related to" defense articles.[191]

ITAR § 121.8(f) defines *software* as follows: "Software includes but is not limited to the system functional design, logic flow, algorithms, application programs, operating systems and support software for design, implementation, test, operation, diagnosis and repair."

"Information in the public domain" is excluded from the controls,[192] but information related to cryptography is excluded from the public domain exception by ITAR XIII(k), because cryptographic information has been interpreted as included in the definition of a "defense service" on the grounds that it could give "assistance" to or furnish "technical data" to a foreign person with respect to a defense article under ITAR § 120.9. In effect, any information that gives "assistance" to a foreign person with respect to a defense article or that is information "directly related to defense articles" cannot be subject to the public domain exception. Thus, publication or public discussion of any such information is always prohibited under the ITAR.

Prohibitions on the export of data do not violate the First Amendment as long as they are narrowly construed to apply only to data with a clear relationship to prohibited items.[193] Public availability of the information in the United States is not a defense.[194] In *United States v. Johnson,*[195] the district court rejected a First Amendment challenge to the prohibition on knowing and willful possession of

---

[190] *Id.* § 121.1.

[191] *Id.* § 120.10(4).

[192] *Id.* § 125.1.

[193] United States v. Edler Indus., 579 F.2d 516, 520–21 (9th Cir. 1978) (reversing conviction for exporting technical data).

[194] *Id.* at 522. *See also* United States v. Posey, 864 F.2d 1487, 1492–93 (9th Cir. 1989) (no constitutional barrier to conviction for exporting technical aerospace data to South Africa merely because data was in the public domain and was available under the Freedom of Information Act). The court noted that making export control enforcement depend on the unavailability of information domestically would put the government in the position of suppressing domestic dissemination in order to enforce export controls. 864 F.2d at 1496–97.

[195] 738 F. Supp. 594 (D. Mass. 1990).

property and papers used or designed or intended for use in violating the statute.[196]

No person may export articles or services on the list without a license under the statute and regulations.[197] Willful violation of the AECA or the ITAR is a criminal offense, punishable by a fine of up to $1 million, imprisonment of up to 10 years, or both.[198] To be criminally liable, a defendant must be proven to have known that she had a legal duty not to export the items or services in question, but need not be shown to have known that the particular item or service was on the list.[199] A civil penalty may also be imposed under ITAR § 127.10.[200] The term "export," includes sending out of the United States and "[d]isclosing (including oral or visual disclosure) or transferring technical data to a foreign person,[201] whether in the United States or abroad."[202] Thus, publication in any form or any public discussion could result in "export" as defined in the ITAR, since each inherently presents a situation in which the speaker or publisher does not know all potential recipients of the information and a recipient might be a foreign person.

The regulatory ITAR scheme imposes four requirements. ITAR § 120.4 provides for requests to the Office of Defense Trade Controls (ODTC), within the State Department's Bureau of Politico-Military Affairs, to see if a license is required for a particular item or service. This is called a Commodity Jurisdiction Request (CJ Request). If ODTC determines that a license is required, a person must register with ODTC as an arms dealer.[203] If the registration is approved, the

---

[196] *Id.* at 597 (the fact that defendants were charged with possessing a laboratory workshop intended to aid terrorism made the constitutional decision easy).

[197] 22 U.S.C. § 2778(b)(2). *See* 22 C.F.R. § 127.1(a)(1), which states: "It is unlawful to export or attempt to export from the United States any defense article or technical data or to furnish any defense service for which a license or written approval is required by this subchapter without first obtaining the required license or written approval from the Office of Defense Trade Controls."

[198] 22 U.S.C. 2778(c): 22 C.F.R. § 127.3.

[199] United States v. Murphy, 852 F.2d 1, 7 (1st Cir. 1988) (conviction of exporting arms to Ireland sustained based on showing that defendants knew it was illegal to export weapons); United States v. Lizarraga-Lizarraga, 541 F.2d 826, 828 (9th Cir. 1976) (suggesting that when items exported could be on the list or could be permissible exports, the government must prove specific knowledge of illegality of export; reversing conviction of willfully attempting to export ammunition into Mexico).

[200] 22 U.S.C. 2778(c) provides for criminal penalties for those who "willfully" violate the statute or regulations. No such requirement of "willfulness" is included in AECA or ITAR provisions that allow civil penalties.

[201] *Foreign person* is defined at 22 C.F.R. § 120.16 as anyone who is not a lawful permanent resident under 8 U.S.C. 1101(a)(20), or who is not a "protected individual" under 8 U.S.C. 1324b(a)(3). This section defines "protected individual" to include U.S. citizens and certain lawfully admitted aliens.

[202] 22 C.F.R. § 120.17.

[203] 22 U.S.C. § 2778(b)(1)(A); 22 C.F.R. § 122.1.

person must then apply for and obtain a license. Thereafter, the person must seek advance approval from the State Department (in consultation with the other defendant agencies) for each license.[204] The filer of a CJ Request is entitled to a preliminary response within 10 days and a final CJ determination within 45 days.[205] An appeal of a CJ Request shall be determined within "30 days of receipt of the appeal."[206]

The Act purports to limit judicial review.[207] Nevertheless, precluding all review of agency decisions under the Act and regulation is unlikely to be constitutional under general principles of administrative law.[208]

§ 14.9 Transnational Data Flow Regulations

Chapter 3 reviews the European Commission's proposed data protection directive and the statute actually in force in Great Britain that may be imitated in other countries of the European Union. Any data privacy regime can be effective only to the extent that it addresses successfully flow of data across national boundaries. If data relating to persons in jurisdiction A with significant data privacy protection can flow across the border to jurisdiction B that lacks such protection, the privacy of individuals in jurisdiction A can be invaded by disclosure in jurisdiction B, and also by reimporting the data from jurisdiction B to jurisdiction A. The European approach basically deals with this problem by prohibiting the export of data except to jurisdictions that have comparable levels of protection. Such an approach puts either enforcement authorities or entities maintaining data or both in the position of having to assess the privacy law of other jurisdictions, which many cannot do effectively. The tendency therefore is to respond to the transnational data flow restrictions simply by imposing

---

[204] 22 C.F.R. § 123.9.

[205] *Id.* §§ 120.4(e), (g).

[206] *Id.* § 120.4(g).

[207] 22 U.S.C. § 2778(h) precludes judicial review of executive designations of items as "defense articles and defense services" by stating: "The designation by the President (or by an official to whom the President's functions under subsection (a) of this section have been duly delegated), in regulations issued under this section, of items as defense articles or defense services for purposes of this section shall not be subject to judicial review." ITAR § 128.1 purports to extend the preclusion of judicial review to any review under the Administrative Procedures Act, stating: "The administration of the Arms Export Control Act is a foreign affairs function and is thus encompassed within the meaning of the military and foreign affairs exclusion of the Administrative Procedure Act and is thereby expressly exempt from various provisions of that Act. Because the exercising of the foreign affairs function, including the decisions required to implement the Arms Export Control Act, is highly discretionary, it is excluded from review under the Administrative Procedure Act."

[208] *See generally* Johnson v. Robison, 415 U.S. 361, 373 (1974).

contractual obligations on recipients of data to maintain protections equivalent to those in effect in the transferor jurisdiction.

§ 14.10   International Electronic Money Transfer

As **Chapter 9** explains, electronic payment systems[209] and electronic banking are growing rapidly as methods of conducting business.[210] Some banks have taken electronic banking one step further by forming networks to allow worldwide banking from computer terminals.[211] The recently formed Inter Bank On-Line System (IBOS) is an example of such a network.[212] The IBOS allows bank customers to conduct monetary transactions in Europe via computer terminals in the United States.[213] Congress, recognizing the widespread use of such systems, has enacted statutes to control electronic transfers.[214]

When assessing these new forms of income transfer, the relevant reporting requirements must be considered, specifically the Currency and Foreign Transaction Reporting Act (CFTRA).[215] While these statutes were implemented to assist the government in criminal investigations,[216] there has been a substantial

---

[209] *See also* Commission Recommendation of 19 October 1994 Relating to the Legal Aspects of Electronic Data Interchange, Doc. No. 394X0820, Annex 1, art. 1, 1994 O.J. (L 338) 98, [hereinafter EC EDI Recommendation] (recommending use of European model EDI agreement, attached as annex; describing nature and purpose of EDI agreement). This section is based on research and initial drafting by Sean P. Lugg, Villanova Law School Class of 1996, law clerk to the author.

[210] This is evidenced by the widespread use of MAC machines and electronic wire transfers to accomplish low-scale financial dealings. Such systems reduce the time spent making transactions and allow customers to engage in transactions at their convenience, while at the same time enabling banks to more closely monitor financial dealings.

[211] *See* Andrew Cassel, *First Fidelity Joining World Wide Bank Group,* Phila. Inquirer, Feb. 16, 1995, at C-1.

[212] *Id.*

[213] *Id.*

[214] *See, e.g.,* Electronic Funds Transfer Act (EFTA), 15 U.S.C. § 1693 (1982). Recognizing the unique characteristics of electronic funds transfers, the legislature declared that "[i]t is the purpose of this subchapter to provide a basic framework establishing the rights, liabilities, and responsibilities of participants in electronic fund transfer systems. The primary objective of this subchapter, however is the provision of individual consumer rights." 15 U.S.C.A. § 1693(b) (West 1982).

[215] 31 U.S.C. §§ 5311–5325 (Supp. V 1993). These sections set forth the reporting requirements for domestic and international monetary dealings.

[216] *Id.* § 5311. The declaration of purpose states that the "purpose of this subchapter [is] to require certain reports or records where they have a high degree of usefulness in criminal, tax, or regulatory investigations or proceedings." *See also* Charles W. Blau et al., United States

impact on customers not engaged in criminal activity.[217] Due to the strict requirements these statutes place on otherwise innocent actors, one engaged in money transfer, specifically internationally, must proceed carefully.[218]

Congress enacted the Currency and Foreign Transaction and Reporting Act with the express intent of combating international money laundering.[219] The Act requires that reports be filed "[w]hen a domestic financial institution is involved in a transaction for the payment, receipt, or transfer of United States coins or currency."[220] These reports must comply with the format prescribed by the secretary of the treasury.[221] The Act also mandates that reports be

Department of the Treasury, Internal Revenue Service, Investigation and Prosecution of Illegal Money Laundering: A Guide to the Bank Secrecy Act (1984). This Report notes the difficulties incurred by the government in tracing funds that were directed through foreign countries, such as Switzerland, the Bahamas, the Cayman Islands, Liechtenstein, and Indonesia, with strict banking secrecy laws. *Id.* at 3, n.5. Responding to these difficulties, Congress enacted foreign financial transaction reporting requirements. *Id.* at 7. "Congress believed that by requiring the disclosure of certain information, law enforcement officials would be able to successfully trace transactions between United States residents and foreign banks in secrecy jurisdictions, thus eliminating the need for information from secret foreign bank accounts." *Id.* at 8. The statute has been effective in accomplishing its objective. *See* United States v. Goulding, 26 F.3d 656 (7th Cir. 1994). The defendants in *Goulding* were prosecuted under 31 U.S.C. §§ 5316(a) and 5322 when they transported $130,000 from the United States to the Cayman Islands. The court found that defendants knew that they had an obligation to report such a transaction and, moreover, that they "made clear in advance that they were not planning to comply with the reporting requirement." 26 F.3d at 666.

[217] *See* Sarah N. Welling, *Smurfs, Money Laundering, and the Federal Criminal Law: The Crime of Structuring Transactions,* 41 Fla. L. Rev. 287 (1989) (analyzing the 1986 enactment of the offense of structuring, referred to as the anti-smurfing statute). *See also* John K. Villa, *A Critical View of Bank Secrecy Act Enforcement and the Money Laundering Statutes,* 37 Cath. U. L. Rev. 489 (1988) (examining the application of the statute to a financial institution which failed to file a report, and how this criminal prosecution will impact the banking community) [hereinafter Villa].

[218] *See* 31 U.S.C. §§ 5314, 5315 (Supp. V 1993) (setting forth the reporting requirements for financial agency transactions and foreign currency transactions).

[219] *See* 132 Cong. Rec. E1142 (daily ed. Apr. 15, 1986) (statement of Rep. Pickle).

[220] 31 U.S.C. § 5313 (Supp. V 1993).

[221] *Id.* The act provides that the secretary is to prescribe the "amount, denomination, or amount and denomination" to be reported. Furthermore, the secretary may prescribe what institutions are covered. The form and content required of the report, Currency Transaction Report (CTR), is set forth in 31 C.F.R. § 103.22.:

Each financial institution . . . shall file a report of each deposit, withdrawal, exchange or currency or other payment or transfer, by, through, or to such financial institution which involves a transaction in currency or more than $10,000. Multiple currency transactions shall be treated as a single transaction if the financial institution has knowledge that they are by or on behalf of any person and result in either cash in or cash out totalling more that $10,000 during any one business day. Deposits made at night or over a weekend or holiday shall be treated as if received on the next business day following the deposit.

31 C.F.R. § 103.22(a)(1).

filed for both foreign financial agency transactions,[222] and foreign currency transactions.[223]

Realizing the pervasive use of wire transfers, the Department of the Treasury issued regulations regarding record-keeping requirements for funds transfers and transmittals.[224] Financial institutions must record any funds transfer[225] for an amount equal to or greater that $3,000.[226] Furthermore, these records must be maintained for a period of five years.[227] The amendment also mandates that transmittal orders from the United States to a foreign financial agency, or from a foreign financial agency to the United States, must be reported.[228]

The CFTRA provides substantial penalties for those who violate the relevant reporting requirements.[229] Although the statute was enacted in 1971, it was not

---

[222] 31 U.S.C. § 5314 (Supp. V 1993). This section requires reports to be filed or records to be kept when a "resident, citizen, [of the United States] or person [doing business in the United States] makes a transaction or maintains a relation for any person with a foreign agency. *Id.* § 5314(a). While this section is more flexible—the secretary may only require records to be kept, rather than demanding reports to be filed—it covers a broader range of activity. Not only are currency transactions recordable, so too are any other transactions with foreign financial agencies.

[223] *Id.* § 5315. This section requires "reports on foreign currency transactions conducted by a United States person or a foreign person controlled by a United States person." *Id.* § 5313(c). Congress supported this requirement by finding that "moving capital can have a significant impact on the proper functioning of the international monetary system." *Id.* § 5313(a)(1). Furthermore, reports are required to be filed if one "knowingly transports or has transported monetary instruments of more than $10,000 at one time from a place in the United States to or through a place outside the United States; or to a place in the United States from or through a place outside the United States." *Id.* § 5316(a).

[224] *See* 60 Fed. Reg. 220 (1995) (to be codified at 31 C.F.R. § 103). "The Financial Crimes Enforcement Network (group receiving delegation of authority from the Secretary of the Treasury to administer the Bank Secrecy Act) and the Board of Governors of the Federal Reserve System jointly have adopted a final rule that requires enhanced recordkeeping related to certain wire transfers." *Id.* The amendment is to go into effect on January 1, 1996.

[225] 60 Fed. Reg. 228 (1995) (to be codified at 31 C.F.R. § 103.11(q)). *Funds transfer* means "[t]he series of transactions, beginning with the originator's payment order, made for the purpose of making payment to the beneficiary of the order." *Id.*

[226] *Id.*

[227] *Id.*

[228] 60 Fed. Reg. 229 (1995) (to be codified at 31 C.F.R. § 103.25(b)(2)):

A regulation promulgated pursuant to paragraph (a) [promulgation of reporting require-ments] of this section shall designate one or more of the following categories of information to be reported . . . (2) transmittal orders received by a respondent financial institution from a foreign financial agency or sent by respondent financial institution to a foreign financial agency, including all information maintained by that institution pursuant to § 103.33.

[229] *See* U.S.S.G. § 2S et seq. (West 1994). This section of the Sentencing Guidelines provides the penalties for Money Laundering and Monetary Transaction Reporting violations. The relevant section for the purposes of this chapter is § 2S1.3, *Structuring Transactions to Evade Reporting Requirements; Failure to Report Cash or Monetary Transactions; Failure to File Currency and Monetary Instrument Report; Knowingly Filing False Reports.* U.S.S.G. § 2S1.3 (West 1995) at 206. This section sets the base offense level at 6. As an example of the application of the guidelines, one who has violated any of the applicable provisions of 31 U.S.C. §§ 5313 (domestic reporting), 5314, 5316 (foreign currency reporting), or 5324 (structuring transactions), and who falls in the second (II) criminal history category, faces a

until the mid-1980s that significant application began.[230] Such prosecutions forced financial agencies to change their institutional practices to ensure compliance with the reporting statutes. Not only were banks and financial institutions wary of criminal prosecution, they feared the publicity of being identified as a non-complying party.[231] Most banks currently keep records and file reports above and beyond what the statute mandates, and amended regulations increase obligations.[232]

It remains to be seen how these provisions will impact international electronic wire transfers, and commentators seem to be split as to the need and/or desire for such requirements.[233] Some feel that the reporting requirements substantially interfere with traditional theories of banking secrecy,[234] while admittedly furthering the purposes of preventing money laundering and assisting the government in investigating financial crimes.[235]

§ 14.11   Competition Regulation

Competition regulation, including American antitrust law, operates worldwide. For example, Articles 85 and 86 of the Treaty of Rome prohibit cartels and "abuse of dominant position" (monopolization) within the European Community and authorize the European Commission to act to prevent violations.[236] The United

---

mandatory sentence of one to seven months. *See* U.S.S.G. sentencing table—back cover. The applicable sentence increases based on the offender's criminal history.

[230] *See* Villa at 489 (The criminal prosecution of the Bank of Boston in 1985 "heralded a new chapter in the enforcement of the BSA [Bank Secrecy Act] against federally insured financial institutions.").

[231] *See generally id.*

[232] *See* 60 Fed. Reg. 220 (1995) (to be codified at 31 C.F.R. § 103). The Financial Crimes Enforcement Network and the Board of Governors acknowledge that the imposition of the new wire transaction reporting requirements will burden various agencies. *Id.* at 220–21. However, "[b]ased on the comments received, the Treasury and the Board have modified the proposed rule to reduce the burden associated with the rule, while maintaining the usefulness of the rule to law enforcement agencies." *Id.* at 221.

[233] *See generally* Villa at 489 (illustrating the history of the reporting requirements and the accompanying concerns in the banking field); 60 Fed. Reg. 220 (1995) (to be codified at 31 C.F.R. § 103) (discussing the various concerns expressed by commentators during the adoption process of the new regulations).

[234] *See* Villa at 491 (citing Note, *The Bank Secrecy Act: Conflict Between Government Access to Bank Records and the Right of Privacy,* 37 Alb. L. Rev. 566, 578 (1973)). "The BSA (Bank Secrecy Act) was controversial because it infringed on the traditional confidential relationship between the bank and the customer." *Id.*

[235] *See generally* Sarah N. Welling, *Smurfs, Money Laundering, and the Federal Criminal Law: The Crime of Structuring Transactions,* 41 Fla. L. Rev. 287 (1989) (explaining the impact the reporting requirements were intended to have on the money laundering "industry" and presenting an analysis of the relatively new crime of structuring monetary transactions to avoid the reporting requirements). *See also* Ratzlaf v. United States, 114 S. Ct. 655 (1994) (the most recent judicial interpretation of the structuring statute (31 U.S.C. § 5324)).

[236] Treaty establishing the European Economic Community, Mar. 25, 1957, arts. 85, 86, 298 U.N.T.S. 11.

States long has applied its antitrust laws extraterritorially, often to the detriment of foreign relations.[237]

In recent years, the U.S. government has sought bilateral arrangements with major trading partners to rationalize and harmonize the application of competition law. In 1994 the Department of Justice and the Federal Trade Commission published proposed antitrust enforcement guidelines for international operations[238] that summarize the state of these efforts. The guidelines establish the basic proposition that U.S. enforcement authorities do not discriminate based on the nationality of firms; they apply the same substantive antitrust rules to all, regardless of whether they operate within the United States or outside the United States.[239] The guidelines note that the "effects doctrine" for determining jurisdiction over antitrust violations has been adopted widely, not only in the United States.[240]

The guidelines analyze a number of hypothetical situations in terms of the likelihood of antitrust liability. A cartel agreement among foreign companies not having any U.S. production nor any U.S. subsidiaries that intentionally raises the price of a particular product subsequently sold into the United States violates the U.S. antitrust laws.[241] Under the Foreign Trade Antitrust Improvement Acts of 1982,[242] agreements between two foreign producers not to deal in the products of a U.S. company in order to prevent the U.S. company from entering their market also could violate U.S. antitrust law, as long as there is a substantial effect on U.S. exports.[243]

More generally, enforcement action against foreign companies engaging in such anticompetitive conduct depends on (1) the conduct having a direct, substantial, and reasonably foreseeable effect on exports from the United States, and (2) the United States courts obtaining jurisdiction over the foreign persons or corporations engaged in such conduct.[244] Enforcement agencies also consider international comity and, more particularly, whether significant interests of any foreign sovereign would be affected by a U.S. enforcement action.

---

[237] *See* Roger P. Alford, *The Extraterritorial Application of Antitrust Laws: The United States and European Community Approaches,* 33 Va. J. Int'l L. 1 (1992); Daniela Levarda, *A Comparative Study of U.S. and British Approaches to Discovery Conflicts: Achieving a Uniform System of Extraterritorial Discovery,* 18 Fordham Int'l L.J. 1340 (1995).

[238] Guidelines, 59 Fed. Reg. 52,810 (Oct. 19, 1994).

[239] *Id.* at 52,811.

[240] *Id.* at 52,815 (citing case 89/85, Ahlstrom v. Comm'n ("wood pulp"), 1988 E.C.R. 5193, 4 C.M.L.R. 901 (1988); characterizing the merger laws of the European Union, Canada, Germany, France, Australia, and the Czech and Slovak Republics as taking an approach similar to the effects doctrine).

[241] *Id.* at 52,816 (illustrative example A).

[242] *Id.* at 52,816 (citing and quoting 15 U.S.C. §§ 6(a), 45(a)(3)).

[243] *Id.* at 52,816 (illustrative example C).

[244] Guidelines, 59 Fed. Reg. 52,810 52,817 (Oct. 19, 1994).

In performing a comity analysis, the agencies take into account all relevant factors. Among others, these may include: (1) the relative significance to the alleged violation of conduct within the United States as compared to conduct abroad, (2) the nationality of the person involved in or affected by the conduct; (3) the presence or absence of a purpose to affect U.S. consumers, markets, or exporters; (4) the relative significance and foreseeability of the effects of the conduct on the United States as compared to the effects abroad; (5) the existence of reasonable expectations that would be furthered or defeated by the action; (6) the degree of conflict with foreign law or articulated foreign economic policies; (7) the effect on foreign enforcement; and (8) the effectiveness of foreign enforcement.[245]

When the person subject to regulation can comply with the laws of two states, there is no conflict with foreign law.[246]

The guidelines also explain that "the agencies have developed close bilateral relationships with antitrust and competition policy officials of many different countries."[247] In particular, formal written bilateral arrangements exist between the United States and Germany, Australia, and Canada. Cooperation also can occur through mutual legal assistance treaties in force with nearly 20 foreign countries, although only the agreement with Canada has been used to cover antitrust offenses so far.[248] The guidelines note close cooperation between U.S. antitrust authorities and those of the European Commission and the 25 member countries of the OECD.[249] The International Antitrust Enforcement Assistance Act of 1994,[250] specifically authorizes the attorney general and the Federal Trade Commission to provide antitrust evidence to foreign antitrust authorities when there is an antitrust mutual assistance agreement in effect.[251]

§ 14.12 Enforcing Judgments in Other Countries

For an American lawyer, enforcing judgments across national boundaries raises two questions. First, under what circumstances may a judgment rendered by a court in a foreign country be enforced in the United States? Second, under what circumstances may a judgment rendered by an American court be enforced abroad?

---

[245] *Id.* at 52,818.

[246] *Id.* (citing Hartford Fire Ins. Co. v. California, 113 S. Ct. 2891, 2910 (1993).

[247] *Id.* at 52,815.

[248] *Id.*

[249] *Id.* at 52,815 & nn.40, 43.

[250] Pub. L. No. 103-438, 108 Stat. 4597 (Nov. 2, 1994) (codified in part of 15 U.S.C. § 6201).

[251] Assistance in subject to 15 U.S.C. §§ 6204, 6207.

The answers to both questions depend conceptually on a body of private international law worked out over several centuries. These basic international law principles are expressed in the *Restatement (Second) of Judgments* provisions dealing with the enforcement of foreign judgments,[252] summarizing the doctrine of comity.[253] A (1) valid judgment rendered in a foreign nation, (2) after a fair trial in a contested proceeding will be recognized in the United States, (3) so far as the immediate parties and the underlying cause of action are concerned.[254] When the conditions are met, the effect to be accorded foreign judgments is the same as is required under the full faith and credit clause.[255] Qualifying foreign judgments may be enforced.[256] Equitable decrees from foreign courts also generally are enforceable in the United States as long as they meet the basic requirements set forth in *Restatement* § 98.[257]

Overlaid on the comity doctrine are positive law enactments, such as the Uniform Recognition of Foreign Money Judgments Act, adopted in about half the states. This legislation provides a framework for U.S. recognition of judgments from foreign countries, performing essentially the same function—though under slightly different criteria—that the full faith and credit clause of the United States Constitution performs with respect to judgments from sister states.[258] Within the European Community, the Brussels and Lugano conventions[259] rationalize recognition of judgments among members of the European Union and the European Free Trade Area. There is no truly international civil judgment enforcement convention to which the United States is a party.

The Uniform Recognition Act applies to "any foreign judgment that is final and conclusive[260] and enforceable where rendered even though an appeal therefrom is pending or it is subject to appeal."[261] *Foreign judgment* is defined as

---

[252] Restatement (Second) of Judgments §§ 81, 82 (1980).

[253] *See* de la Mata v. American Life Ins. Co., 771 F. Supp. 1375, 1380 (D. Del 1991); Restatement (Third) of Foreign Relations § 481 & cmt. c (1986).

[254] Restatement (Second) of Conflict of Laws § 98 (1969).

[255] *Id.* § 98 cmt. b.

[256] *Id.* § 100 cmt. d.

[257] *Id.* § 102 cmt. g.

[258] Full faith and credit requires that, absent a violation of due process, states must respect judgments from sister states as if they were their own. *See* Parsons Steel Inc. v. First Ala. Bank, 474 U.S. 518 (1986); Marrese v. American Academy of Orthopaedic Surgeons, 470 U.S. 373 (1985); Migra v. Warren City Sch. Dist. Bd. of Educ., 465 U.S. 75 (1984).

[259] Brussels Convention and Jurisdiction and Enforcement of Judgments in Civil and Commercial Matters, Sept. 27, 1968, 1968 O.J. (L 299) 32, *reprinted in* 29 I.L.M. 1413 (1990); Lugano Convention on Jurisdiction and the Enforcement of Judgments in Civil and Commercial Matters, Sept. 16, 1988, 1988 O.J. (L 319) 1, *reprinted in* 28 I.L.M. 620.

[260] Cerezo v. Babson Bros. Co., 1992 WL 18875 (N.D. Ill. Jan. 24, 1992) (prejudgment attachment issued by Spanish court not entitled to recognition under Illinois Uniform Foreign Money Judgments Recognition Act because not final and conclusive, and no notice to defendant).

[261] Uniform Foreign Money Judgments Recognition Act § 2, 13 U.L.A. 261, 264 (1986).

"any judgment of a *foreign state* granting or denying recovery of a sum of money, other than a judgment for taxes, a fine or other penalty, or a judgment for support in matrimonial or family matters."[262] *Foreign state* is defined as any governmental unit other than the federal government, a state, or a U.S. possession.[263] The heart of the Act grants full faith and credit status to a foreign judgment "to the extent that it grants or denies recovery of a sum of money,"[264] subject to certain exceptions. Three of the exceptions deprive the judgment of its status as a judgment if

(1) The judgment was rendered under a system which does not provide impartial tribunals or procedures compatible with the requirements of due process of law;

(2) The foreign court did not have personal jurisdiction over the defendant;

(3) The foreign court did not have jurisdiction over the subject matter.[265]

The remaining exceptions support discretionary nonrecognition:

(1) The defendant in the proceedings in the foreign court did not receive notice of the proceedings in sufficient time to enable him to defend;

(2) The judgment was obtained by fraud;

(3) The cause of action or a claim for relief on which the judgment is based is repugnant to the public policy of this state;

(4) The judgment conflicts with another final and conclusive judgment;

(5) The proceeding in the foreign court was contrary to an agreement between the parties under which the dispute in question was to be settled otherwise than by proceedings in that court;

(6) In the case of jurisdiction based only on personal service, the foreign court was a seriously inconvenient forum for the trial of the action.[266]

Ground (5) permits nonrecognition of a judgment resulting from litigation evading an agreement to arbitrate. With the exception of that ground, the basis for nonrecognition under the Uniform Act is essentially the same as the basis for nonrecognition under the doctrine of comity.[267]

The following states and territories have adopted the Uniform Recognition of Foreign Judgments Act, and Minnesota and North Dakota have judicially incorporated its provisions:[268]

---

[262] *Id.* § 1(2), 13 U.L.A. at 263.

[263] *Id.* § 1(1), 13 U.L.A. at 263.

[264] *Id.* § 3, 13 U.L.A. at 265.

[265] *Id.* § 4(a), 13 U.L.A. at 268.

[266] *Id.* § 4(b), 13 U.L.A. at 268.

[267] *See* Guiness PLC v. Ward, 955 F.2d 875, 884 (4th Cir. 1992).

[268] *See* de la Mata v. American Life Ins. Co., 771 F. Supp. 1375, 1382 (D. Del. 1991) (also noting that Texas, Massachusetts, and Georgia have versions of the Uniform Act. Texas, Massachusetts and Georgia require reciprocity in some form).

Alaska[269]

California[270]

Colorado[271]

Connecticut[272]

Georgia[273]

Idaho[274]

Illinois[275]

Iowa[276]

Maryland[277]

Massachusetts[278]

Michigan[279]

Minnesota[280]

Missouri[281]

Montana[282]

New Mexico[283]

New York[284]

North Carolina[285]

Ohio[286]

---

[269] Alaska Stat. §§ 09.30.100 to 09.30.180.

[270] Cal. Civ. Proc. Code §§ 1713 to 1713.8 (West).

[271] Colo. Rev. Stat. Ann. §§ 13-62-101 to 13-62-109 (West).

[272] Conn. Gen. Stat. Ann. §§ 52-610 to 52-618 (West).

[273] Ga. Code Ann. §§ 9-12-110 to 9-12-117.

[274] Idaho Code §§ 10-1401 to 10-1409.

[275] Ill. Ann. stat. ch. 735, 5/12-618 (Smith-Hurd).

[276] Iowa Code Ann. §§ 626B.1 to 626B.8 (West).

[277] Md. Code Ann., Cts. & Jud. Proc. §§ 10-701 to 10-709.

[278] Mass. Gen. Laws Ann. ch. 235, § 23A (West).

[279] Mich. Comp. Laws Ann. §§ 691.1151 to 691.1159 (West).

[280] Minn. Stat. Ann. § 548.35 (West).

[281] Mo. Ann. Stat. §§ 511.770 to 511.787 (Vernon).

[282] Mont. Code Ann. §§ 25-9-601 to 25-9-609.

[283] N.M. Stat. Ann. 1978, §§ 39-4B-1 to 39-4B-9 (Michie).

[284] N.Y. Civ. Prac. L. & R. 5301 to 5309 (McKinney).

[285] N.C. Gen. Stat. §§ 1C-1800 to 1C-1808.

[286] Ohio Rev. Code Ann. §§ 2329.90 to 2329.94.

Oklahoma[287]

Oregon[288]

Pennsylvania[289]

Texas[290]

Virginia[291]

Virgin Islands[292]

Washington[293]

The preparatory note to the uniform act makes it clear that one of the motivations for enactment of the Act is to provide for reciprocity with European states that will enforce U.S. judgments only if reciprocity exists. A comment to § 3 provides that the method of enforcing foreign judgments is the same as that provided in the Uniform Enforcement of Foreign Judgments Acts of 1948, which explicitly applies only to judgments of sister state courts.[294] Some U.S. courts have required a plenary hearing on the issue of recognition before a non-U.S. judgment can be enforced like a sister state judgment.[295]

In *Nipponemo-Trans Co. v. EMO-Trans, Inc.*,[296] the district court found probable that it would recognize a Japanese judgment under the New York

---

[287] Okla. Stat. Ann. tit. 12, §§ 710 to 718.

[288] Or. Rev. Stat. §§ 24.200 to 24.255.

[289] 42 Pa. Cons. Stat. §§ 22001 to 22009.

[290] Tex. Civ. Prac. & Rem. Code Ann. §§ 36.001 to 36.008.

[291] Va. Code 1950, §§ 8.01-465.6 to 8.01-465.13.

[292] V.I. Code Ann. tit. 5, §§ 561 to 569.

[293] Wash. Rev. Code Ann. §§ 6.40.010 to 6.40.915 (West).

[294] UFMJRA § 3 cmt., 13 U.L.A. at 265 (1986). *See* Bvan Kooten v. Dumarco Corp., 670 F. Supp. 227, 228 (N.D. Ill. 1987) (Uniform Foreign Money-Judgments Recognition Act, rather than Uniform Enforcement of Foreign Judgments Act governs enforceability of foreign judgments).

[295] Hennessey v. Marshall, 682 S.W.2d 340, 343–44 (Tex. Ct. App. 1984) (granting mandamus against post-judgment discovery order; English default judgment could not be recognized without a hearing on whether the criteria of § 5 and § 6 of the Uniform Recognition Act had been met; judgment not entitled to full faith and credit until hearing had been completed). *But see* Plastics Eng'g, Inc. v. Diamond Plastics Corp., 764 S.W.2d 924, 927 (Tex. Ct. App. 1989) (refusing to engraft hearing procedure on Recognition Act; failure explicitly to provide for hearing on statutory factors for recognition means Act is unconstitutional). *Plastics Engineering* was disapproved by the Texas Supreme Court in Don Docksteader Motors, Ltd. v. Patal Enters., Ltd., 794 S.W.2d 760, 761 (Tex. 1990) (failure to provide procedure for asserting nonrecognition grounds—subsequently remedied by Texas legislature—did not make Act unconstitutional because specific case involved bringing a common-law suit to enforce the judgment which allowed for notice and hearing; legislative amendment eliminates problem with "shortcut" procedure).

[296] 744 F. Supp. 1215 (E.D.N.Y. 1990).

Uniform Foreign Money Judgments Recognition Act but refused to allow for its enforcement until the Japanese appeal process was completed. The defendant, an American company, contested personal jurisdiction over it in the Japanese court, but that court found that it had jurisdiction. The U.S. federal court found that the foreign court's determination of the jurisdictional challenge was not entitled to preclusive effect.[297] The Tokyo court had based its assertion of jurisdiction on two factors: the obligation of the defendant to make payments to the plaintiff in Japan, and the existence of a Japanese affiliate of the defendant— bases of jurisdiction that would not support jurisdiction under New York law.[298] Nevertheless, the federal court found that under federal constitutional law standards for personal jurisdiction, the Tokyo court validly could assert jurisdiction.[299] The federal court found probable cause that the Japanese judgment was entitled to recognition, although it denied interim attachment sought by the judgment creditor.[300]

Under the Uniform Enforcement of Foreign Judgments Act, which applies by its terms only to judgments in sister states but is incorporated by reference into the Uniform Enforcement of Foreign Money Judgments Act, a foreign judgment may be enforced in one of two ways.[301] The judgment creditor can file a new action to enforce the judgment as though the Act did not exist. Or, under the Act, the judgment creditor may file an authenticated foreign judgment with the clerk of the local court. The Act requires the clerk then to treat the foreign judgment

> in the same manner as a judgment of the court of this state. A judgment so filed has the same effect and is subject to the same procedures, defenses and proceedings for reopening, vacating, or staying as a judgment of a court of this state and may be enforced or satisfied in like manner.[302]

The Act requires the clerk to give notice to the judgment debtor and requires the local court to stay enforcement of the foreign judgment until any appeal of the foreign judgment is completed as long as the judgment debtor shows that he has furnished security for the satisfaction of the judgment required by the state in which it was rendered.[303]

In a state that has adopted both uniform acts, a party wishing to enforce a judgment from a foreign country registers the judgment under the Execution Act, and then seeks recognition pursuant to the Recognition Act, probably by petition or motion, depending on local procedure. If the court with which the

---

[297] *Id.* at 1221.

[298] *Id.* at 1230.

[299] *Id.* at 1231, 1233.

[300] *Id.* at 1233.

[301] UEFJA § 6, 13 U.L.A. 152 (Master ed. 1986) (preserving the right of judgment creditor to bring an action to enforce judgment instead of preceding under Act).

[302] *Id.* § 2, 13 U.L.A. at 149.

[303] *Id.* § 4 (notice of filing); *id.* § 4 (stay).

judgment is registered recognizes it under the Recognition Act, the party then proceeds to enforce it pursuant to the Enforcement Act. In a sense, the Enforcement Act is procedural, and the Recognition Act is substantive. Canadian judgment recognition rules are similar to U.S. judgment recognition rules.[304]

The European Community lacks an explicit full faith and credit clause in its constitutional documents. The Brussels Convention on Jurisdiction and the Enforcement of Judgments in Civil and Commercial Matters, a multilateral European Treaty, combines a long-arm statute with a full faith and credit clause. It also disavows British and Irish "tag" practices and the asset-based jurisdiction of various other countries against common market domiciliaries.[305]

The Brussels and Lugano Conventions provide for recognition without any special procedures like the Deibazione in Italy, and the Exequatur in France, Belgium, and Luxembourg. A judgment supported by personal jurisdiction is entitled to recognition, which means it has the same authority and effectiveness as in the state of origin. Moreover, it is entitled to res judicata effect.[306] The enforcement procedure involves registering the judgment and is intended to be expeditious and of an ex parte nature.[307]

The United States has found it difficult to negotiate judgment recognition treaties with other countries. Such efforts so far have failed with the United Kingdom because of British reluctance to enforce large American jury verdicts in products liability and antitrust cases, and the difficulty of accommodating international practice to the particulars of American constitutional personal jurisdiction limitations.[308] Nevertheless, the Organization of American States succeeded in negotiating a treaty covering enforcement of support obligations.[309] Efforts continue, within the Hague Conference on Private

---

[304] *See* Hans Smit, *Dispute Resolution in Europe,* 17 Canada-U.S. L.J. 281, 291 (1991).

[305] Friedrich Juenger, *American Jurisdiction: A Story of Comparative Neglect,* 65 U. Colo. L. Rev. 1, 17–18 (citing Brussels Convention regarding jurisdiction and the enforcement of judgments, 1968 O.J. (L 299) 32, *reprinted in* 29 I.L.M. 1413 (1990)). The Brussels Convention concepts were extended to EFTA countries (Austria, Finland, Iceland, Norway, Sweden, and Switzerland) in the Lugano Convention. *Id.* (citing Convention on Jurisdiction and Enforcement of Judgments in Civil and Commercial Matters, Sept. 16, 1988, 1988 O.J. (L 319) 1, *reprinted in* 28 I.L.M. 620 (1989) (Lugano Convention)).

[306] Paul R. Beaumont, Civil Jurisdiction in Scotland: Brussels and Lugano Conventions §§ 8.9–8.10, at 183–84 (2d ed. 1995) (discussing recognition rules and citing DeWolf v. Cox, Case 42/76, [1976] E.C.R. 1759).

[307] *Id.* § 8.44, at 202.

[308] Friedrich Juenger, *American Jurisdiction: A Story of Comparative Neglect,* 65 U. Colo. L. Rev. 1, 21–22 & nn.152–59 (describing difficulties and citing Peter Hay & Robert J. Walker, *The Proposed Recognition-of-Judgments Convention Between the United States and the United Kingdom,* 11 Tex. Int'l L.J. 421, 452–59 (1976) (providing text of proposed draft)).

[309] *Id.* at 23 n.159 (citing Fourth Inter-American Specialized Conference on Private International Law in Montevideo, July 15, 1989, 29 I.L.M. 73 (1990); Carol S. Bruch, *The 1989 Inter-American Convention on Support Obligations,* 40 Am. J. Comp. L. 817 (1993)).

International Law, to work out a multilateral treaty on jurisdiction in judgment recognition.[310]

In Japan, recognition of foreign judgments is subject to satisfying four requirements:

1. Japanese law must not refuse to recognize the jurisdiction of the rendering court

2. If the judgment debtor is Japanese, that party receives notice of the action by means other than publication

3. The judgment of the foreign court must not be contrary "to public order or good morals in Japan" and

4. Reciprocity must be accorded Japanese judgments in the foreign jurisdiction.[311]

Punitive damages awards are especially suspect under the public order and good morals test.[312] The Japanese procedure for recognition involves a declaratory judgment action, somewhat more elaborate than mere registration under the Brussels Convention.[313]

§ 14.13   International Arbitration

The analysis of arbitration as a dispute resolution mechanism in **Chapter 12** included analysis of arbitration in an international context. When disputes cross national boundaries, arbitration is superior to litigation in national courts as a way of dealing with the dispute. The legal status of an arbitration award is greater than the legal status of a court decision in another country because of the existence of an international agreement providing for the enforcement of international arbitration awards.[314] There is no similar convention on the recognition and enforcement of judicial decisions. In addition, as **Chapter 12** explains, an international arbitrator or arbitration panel has greater flexibility to choose substantive law that fits the dispute, not being bound by national choice of law rules, and probably not being limited to national sources of law.

---

[310] *Id.* at 21 & nn.152–53 (citing 57 Fed. Reg. 54,439 (1992)).

[311] Takonobu Takehara, Japan in Enforcement of Foreign Judgments Worldwide 54, 55 (Charles Platto & William G. Horten eds., 2d ed. 1993).

[312] *Id.* at 58.

[313] *Id.* at 60.

[314] Convention on the Recognition and Enforcement of Foreign Arbitral Awards, June 10, 1958, 21 U.S.T. 2517, 330 U.N.T.S. 38.

The particular set of rules that apply to an international arbitration is determined by the written agreement to arbitrate.[315] Some of these rules, like those of the American Arbitration Association (AAA), are issued by a body that performs administrative services in connection with the arbitration. Others, like those issued by UNCITRAL,[316] allow the parties to select the body to provide administrative services.[317]

Under the UNCITRAL rules, a three-arbitrator panel is selected by each party appointing one arbitrator, and the two arbitrators thus selected picking a third, who acts as the chairperson.[318] The AAA rules provide for appointment under any procedure mutually agreed on.[319] If the parties are unable to agree on appointment of arbitrators, the arbitrators are appointed by the administrator of the AAA,[320] or by the secretary general of the Permanent Court of Arbitration at the Hague, who designates an appointing authority.[321] Under both the AAA and the UNCITRAL rules, the arbitration panel has discretion to conduct the arbitration in whatever manner it considers appropriate, subject to a general requirement that the parties be treated with equality and that each party be heard and given an opportunity to present its case. The only difference is that the AAA rules require a "fair opportunity to present a case,"[322] while the UNCITRAL rules refer to a "full opportunity of presenting his case."[323] The UNCITRAL rules also explicitly require oral argument if either party so requests at any stage of the proceedings.[324] The AAA rules have no such provision.

Both rules allow the arbitration panel to decide on the place of arbitration in the absence of party agreement and to meet at any place that it deems appropriate to hear witnesses or to inspect property or documents.[325] The AAA rules

---

[315] *Compare* AAA Int'l Arbitration Rules, art. 1 *with* UNCITRAL Rules art. 1. *See generally* John Y. Gotanda, *Awarding Interest in International Arbitration,* 90 Am. J. Int'l L. (forthcoming Jan. 1996).

[316] See § **14.2** for a description of UNCITRAL.

[317] *See also* Rules of Procedure of the Inter-American Commercial Arbitration Commission (1988), *reprinted in* 1991 WL 537102 (A.A.A.), at *2 (substantive rules are those of UNCITRAL, adapted for institutional requirements of Inter-American Commercial Arbitration Commission, established by the Inter-American Convention on International Commercial Arbitration, signed in Panama on Jan. 30, 1975, at the Inter-American Specialized Conference on Private International Law).

[318] UNCITRAL Rules, art. 7.

[319] AAA Int'l Rules, art. 6.

[320] *Id.,* art. 6(3).

[321] UNCITRAL Rules, art. 7(2).

[322] AAA Int'l Rules, art. 16(1).

[323] UNCITRAL Rules, art. 15(1).

[324] *Id.,* art. 15(2).

[325] *Compare* AAA Int'l Rules, art. 13 *with* UNCITRAL Rules, art. 16.

provide that the language of the arbitration in the absence of party agreement shall be the language of the documents containing the arbitration agreement unless the arbitration panel concludes otherwise.[326] The UNCITRAL rules contemplate a determination by the arbitral tribunal of the language to be used.[327] Both rules contemplate a requirement by the arbitrators that documents be accompanied by translations.[328]

Pleadings include a statement of claim or notice of arbitration, a statement of defense and counterclaims, amendments, and pleas to jurisdiction.[329] The AAA rules require somewhat more detailed reference to the arbitration agreement than the UNCITRAL rules,[330] while the UNCITRAL rules but not the AAA rules require "a statement of facts supporting the claim" and "the points at issue."[331] UNCITRAL statements of defense must reply to the particulars of facts, points at issue, and relief or remedy, but the AAA statement of defense need not.[332] Both sets of rules allow for counterclaims or setoffs within the same arbitration agreement.[333]

Under both sets of rules, the arbitration tribunal has jurisdiction to rule on its own jurisdiction, including the existence and validity of the arbitration clause or separate arbitration agreement.[334] Pleas to jurisdiction must be raised no later than 45 days after the commencement of the arbitration under the AAA rules,[335] and no later than the statement of defense under the UNCITRAL rules.[336] The arbitration panel may provide for further written statements by the parties under both sets of rules.[337]

In the hearings themselves, both sets of rules place the burden of proof on each party of "proving the facts relied on to support its claim or defense."[338] Both require the parties to provide an advance summary of documents and other evidence the party intends to rely on in support of a claim, if the panel so orders,[339] and to produce such documents, exhibits, or other evidence ordered by the arbitral tribunal.[340] Parties must give each other and the tribunal 15 days

---

[326] AAA Int'l Rules, art. 14.

[327] UNCITRAL Rules, art. 17.

[328] *Compare* AAA Int'l Rules, art. 14 *with* UNCITRAL Rules, art. 17.

[329] *Compare* AAA Int'l Rules, arts. 2–4, 15, 17 *with* UNCITRAL Rules, arts. 18–20.

[330] AAA Int'l Rules, art. 2(3).

[331] UNCITRAL Rules, art. 18(2).

[332] *Compare* AAA Int'l Rules, art. 3(1) *with* UNCITRAL Rules, art. 19(2).

[333] *Compare* AAA Int'l Rules, art. 3(2) *with* UNCITRAL Rules, art. 19(3).

[334] *Compare* AAA Int'l Rules, art. 15 *with* UNCITRAL Rules, art. 21.

[335] AAA Int'l Rules, art. 15(3).

[336] UNCITRAL Rules, art. 21(3).

[337] *Compare* AAA Int'l Rules, art. 17 *with* UNCITRAL Rules, art. 22.

[338] AAA Int'l Rules, art. 20(1); UNCITRAL Rules, art. 24(1).

[339] AAA Int'l Rules, art. 20(2); UNCITRAL Rules, art. 24(2).

[340] AAA Int'l Rules, art. 20(3); UNCITRAL Rules, art. 24(3).

notice of witnesses they intend to present at oral hearings.[341] The arbitration tribunal determines admissibility, relevance, materiality, and weight of evidence offered, under both sets of rules.[342]

Both sets of rules allow the arbitration tribunal to appoint one or more experts to report on specific issues based on relevant information the parties must provide the expert. The parties are entitled to an opportunity to comment on the expert's report and to examine the expert at a hearing.[343] The arbitrators may make interim orders, and seeking judicial enforcement of such an order is not a waiver of the agreement to arbitrate.[344]

Arbitration panels have broad authority under both sets of rules with respect to choice of law:

> "The tribunals shall apply the substantive law or laws designated by the parties as applicable to the dispute. Failing such a designation by the parties, the tribunal shall apply such law or laws as it deems to be appropriate.[345]

> "In arbitrations involving the application of contracts, the tribunal shall decide in accordance with the terms of the contract and shall take into account usages of the trade applicable to the contract."[346]

> "The arbitral tribunal shall apply the law designated by the parties as applicable to the substance of the dispute. Failing such designation by the parties, the arbitral tribunals shall apply the law determined by the conflict of the laws rules which it considers applicable."[347]

> "In all cases the arbitral tribunal shall decide in accordance with the terms of the contract and shall take into account the usages of the trade applicable to the transaction."[348]

The AAA choice of law rule may be somewhat broader because it does not limit the tribunal to "conflict of laws rules."

Arbitral awards shall be effective if signed by a majority of the arbitrators,[349] shall not be made public except with the consent of the parties,[350] must be in writing,[351] and must state the reasons on which the award is based unless

---

[341] AAA Int'l Rules, art. 21(2); UNCITRAL Rules, art. 25(2).

[342] AAA Int'l Rules, art. 21(6); UNCITRAL Rules, art. 25(6).

[343] AAA Int'l Rules, art. 23; UNCITRAL Rules, art. 27.

[344] AAA Int'l Rules, art. 22; UNCITRAL Rules, art. 26.

[345] AAA Int'l Rules, art. 29(1).

[346] *Id.,* art. 29(2).

[347] UNCITRAL Rules, art. 33(1).

[348] *Id.,* art. 33(3).

[349] AAA Int'l Rules, art. 28(3); UNCITRAL Rules, art. 32(4).

[350] AAA Int'l Rules, art. 28(4); UNCITRAL Rules, art. 32(5).

[351] AAA Int'l Rules, art. 28(1); UNCITRAL Rules, art. 32(1).

the parties have agreed that no reasons need be given.[352] Costs are apportioned by the arbitration panel and include expert fees and attorneys' fees.[353] One distinguished commentator, recognizing the advantages of institutional arbitration, as under the Court of Arbitration of the International Chamber of Commerce in Paris, suggests the establishment of a single worldwide institution, privately created and administered, that would improve institutional international arbitration.[354]

§ 14.14   Model International Arbitration Clause

"MODEL ARBITRATION CLAUSE

Any dispute, controversy or claim arising out of or relating to this contract, or the breach, termination or invalidity thereof, shall be settled by arbitration in accordance with the UNCITRAL Arbitration Rules as at present in force.

NOTE-parties might wish to consider adding: (a) The appointing authority shall be . . . (name of institution or person); (b) The number of arbitrators shall be . . . (one or three); (c) The place of arbitration shall be . . . (town or country); (d) The language(s) to be used in the arbitral proceedings shall be . . . ."[355]

§ 14.15   Access to Infrastructure in Other Countries

The globalization of trade affects the NII most significantly in the opening up of communications and information infrastructures in other countries to U.S. connections and entry. The specific provisions of NAFTA and Uruguay Round of the GATT negotiations, reviewed in §§ 14.5 and 14.6 exemplify this kind of opening up by their requirements that signatories not deny connections to foreign firms. Much remains to be done, however, with respect to allowing entry by foreign telecommunications firms into markets that historically were monopolized by state PTTs (postal, telephone, and telegraph) or were state-regulated monopolies. The evolution of the German telecommunications market, beginning in 1995, is particularly significant in that regard.[356] European

---

[352] AAA Int'l Rules, art. 28(2); UNCITRAL Rules, art. 32(3).

[353] AAA Int'l Rules, art. 32; UNCITRAL Rules, art. 38.

[354] Hans Smit, *The Future of International Commercial Arbitration: A Single Trans National Institution?*, 25 Colum. J. Transnat'l L. 9 (1986).

[355] AAA reprint of UNCITRAL arbitration rules, 1991 WL 537102.

[356] *Germany Privatizing Phone Service in '98*, N.Y. Times, Mar. 28, 1995, at D10; Greg Steinmetz, *Union Raises Objections to Deregulation of German Telecommunications Market*, Wall St. J., Apr. 25, 1995, at A17; Michael Lindemann, *Deutsch Telekom attacks market reform plan*, Fin. Times, Apr. 25, 1995, at 3.

telecommunications markets in general are being opened up under a 1990 directive of the European Commission,[357] providing for competition in general, and under a 1992 open network directive.[358]

---

[357] Commission Directive of 28 June 1990 on Competition in the Markets for Telecommunications Services, Doc. No. 390L0388, 1990 O.J. (L 192) 10.

[358] Council Directive 92/44/EEC of 5 June 1992 on the Application of Open Network Provision to Leased Lines, Doc. No. 392L0044, 1992 O.J. (L 165) 27 (applying to transparent transmission capacity between network termination points, but excluding switched services).

TABLE OF CASES

Case	*Book §*
Cooper v. California, 386 U.S. 58 (1967)	§ 6.12
Cooperative Communications, Inc. v. AT&T Corp., 867 F. Supp. 1511 (D. Utah 1994)	§§ 5.17, 7.16
Cornelius v. NAACP Legal Defense & Educ. Fund, 473 U.S. 788 (1984)	§ 6.12
Courtesy Temporary Serv. v. Camacho, 272 Cal. Rptr. 352 (Ct. App. 1990)	§ 10.15
Cowden v. Pacific Coast Steamship Co., 94 Cal. 470 (1892)	§ 2.8
Cox Cable Communications, Inc. v. United States, 866 F. Supp. 553 (M.D. Ga. 1994)	§ 7.12
Cox Cable Communications, Inc. v. United States, 992 F.2d 1178 (11th Cir. 1993)	§ 7.12
Crawford v. Williams, 375 S.E.2d 223 (Ga. 1989)	§ 5.14
Creative Technology, Ltd. v. Aztech Sys. PTE, Ltd., 61 F.3d 696 (9th Cir. 1995)	§ 12.8
Credit Data v. Arizona, 602 F.2d 195 (9th Cir. 1979)	§ 3.17
Crosley v. United States, 113 S. Ct. 748 (1993)	§ 13.14
Crump v. Beckley Newspapers, Inc., 320 S.E.2d 70 (W. Va. 1984)	§ 3.5
Cubby, Inc. v. Compuserve, Inc., 776 F. Supp. 135 (S.D.N.Y. 1991)	§§ 3.31, 4.2, 4.5, 6.6, 6.9, 10.6
Curde v. Tri City Bank & Trust Co., 826 S.W.2d 911 (Tenn. 1992)	§ 9.19
CVD, Inc. v. Raytheon, 769 F.2d 842 (1st Cir. 1985)	§ 2.22
Dalehite v. United States, 346 U.S. 15 (1953)	§ 4.28
Dames & Moore v. Regan, 453 U.S. 654 (1981)	§ 14.3
Dann v. Johnston, 425 U.S. 219 (1976)	§ 10.19
Data Gen. Corp. v. Grumman Sys. Support Corp., 36 F.3d 1147 (1st Cir. 1994)	§ 2.24
Data Gen. Corp. v. Grumman Sys. Support Corp., 795 F. Supp. 501 (D. Mass. 1992)	§ 10.11
Davidson v. Wheelock, 27 F. 61 (C.C.D. Minn. 1866)	§ 11.7
Davis v. Black, 591 N.E.2d 11 (Ohio Ct. App. 1991)	§ 4.6
Davis v. Odell, 729 P.2d 1117 (Kan. 1986)	§ 7.17
Davis v. Richmond, 512 F.2d 201 (1st Cir. 1975)	§ 7.17
Davis v. South Cent. Bell Tel. Co., 480 F. Supp. 826 (S.D. Miss. 1979)	§ 6.15
Dawson Chem. Co. v. Rohm & Haas Co., 448 U.S. 176 (1980)	§ 5.8
de la Mata v. American Life Ins. Co., 771 F. Supp. 1375 (D. Del. 1991)	§§ 12.9, 14.12
Deal v. Spears, 980 F.2d 1153 (8th Cir. 1992)	§ 3.8
Delaware & Hudson Ry. v. Consolidated Rail Corp., 902 F.2d 174 (2d Cir. 1990)	§ 2.20
Delorise Brown, M.D., Inc. v. Allio, 620 N.E.2d 1020 (Ohio Ct. App. 1993)	§ 5.13
DeMay v. Roberts, 9 N.W. 146 (Mich. 1881)	§ 3.5
Destination Ventures, Ltd. v. Federal Communications Comm'n, 46 F.3d 54 (9th Cir. 1995)	§ 6.4
DeWolf v. Cox, Case 42/76, [1976] E.C.R. 1759	§ 14.12
Dial-A-Mattress v. Page, 880 F.2d 675 (2d Cir. 1959)	§ 10.14
Diamond v. Diehr, 450 U.S. 175 (1981)	§ 10.19
Diamond Shamrock Ref. & Mktg. Co. v. Mendez, 844 S.W.2d 198 (Tex. 1992)	§ 3.5

Case	*Book §*
First Options v. Kaplan, 115 S. Ct. 1920 (1995)	§ 12.14
Fisons Horticulture, Inc. v. Vigoro Indus., Inc., 30 F.3d 466 (3d Cir. 1994)	§ 10.14
Flagg Bros. v. Brooks, 436 U.S. 149 (1978)	§§ 4.25, 6.3, 6.6, 7.17
Florida Star v. BJF, 491 U.S. 524 (1989)	§§ 3.17, 6.4
Flynn v. Reinke, 225 N.W. 742 (Wis. 1929)	§ 4.3
Ford Motor Credit Co. v. Swarens, 447 S.W.2d 53 (Ky. 1969)	§ 12.27
Forest v. United States, 539 F. Supp. 171 (D. Mont. 1982)	§ 12.8
Forsyth v. Barr, 19 F.3d 1527 (5th Cir. 1994)	§ 3.8
Foundation Software Labs., Inc. v. Digital Equip. Corp., 807 F. Supp. 1195 (D. Md. 1992)	§ 5.14
Fowler v. Southern Bell Tel. & Tel. Co., 343 F.2d 150 (5th Cir. 1965)	§ 3.5
Frank Music Corp. v. CompuServe, Inc., No. 93 Civ. 8153 (JFK) (S.D.N.Y. filed Nov. 29, 1993)	§ 10.6
French v. Hay, 89 U.S. (22 Wall.) 231 (1874)	§ 12.10
Frere v. Commonwealth, 452 S.E.2d 682 (Va. Ct. App. 1995)	§ 9.8
Frontier Broadcasting Co. v. FCC, 24 F.C.C. 251 (1958)	§ 2.6
Fuentes v. Shevin, 407 U.S. 67 (1972)	§ 12.6
Furniture Consultants, Inc. v. Datatel Mini Computer Co., No. 85 Civ. 8518, (R.L.C.) 1986 WL 7792 (S.D.N.Y. July 10, 1986)	§ 5.15
Fusco v. General Motors Corp., 11 F.3d 259 (1st Cir. 1993)	§ 12.32
Futurevision Cable Sys., Inc. v. Multivision Cable TV Corp., 789 F. Supp. 760 (S.D. Miss. 1992)	§§ 2.3, 2.18, 5.8
Garber v. Harris Trust & Sav. Bank, 432 N.E.2d 1309 (Ill. App. Ct. 1982)	§§ 2.13, 9.3
Garcia v. Andrews, 867 S.W.2d 409 (Tex. Ct. App. 1993)	§ 4.6
Garratt v. Dailey, 279 P.2d 1091 (Wash. 1955)	§ 4.7
General Motors Corp. v. Moseley, 447 S.E.2d 302 (Ga. Ct. App. 1994)	§ 12.31
Genin Trudeau & Co. v. Integra Dev. Int'l, 845 F. Supp. 611 (N.D. Ill. 1994)	§ 5.6
Geo. Washington Mint, Inc. v. Washington Mint, Inc., 349 F. Supp. 255 (S.D.N.Y. 1972)	§ 11.8
Georgia v. Harrison Co., 548 F. Supp. 110 (1982), *vacated,* 559 F. Supp. 37 (N.D. Ga. 1983)	§ 11.7
Gertz v. Welch, 418 U.S. 323 (1974)	§§ 4.5, 4.13
Gibbons v. Ogden, 22 U.S. (1 Wheat) 1 (1824)	§ 6.14
Giboney v. Empire Storage & Ice Co., 336 U.S. 490 (1949)	§ 6.6
Gilmer v. Interstate/Johnson Lane Corp., 500 U.S. 20, 111 S. Ct. 1647 (1991)	§ 12.14
Ginsburg v. New York, 390 U.S. 629 (1968)	§ 6.2
Gitlow v. New York, 268 U.S. 652 (1925)	§ 6.2
Goldstein v. California, 412 U.S. 546 (1973)	§ 10.21
Gould & Co., *In re,* 2 A. 886 (Conn. 1885)	§ 11.7
Grand Jury Proceedings, *In re,* 587 F. Supp. 1210 (E.D. Cal. 1984)	§ 3.18
Graphnet Sys., Inc., 73 F.C.C.2d 283 (1979)	§ 7.5
Gray v. American Express Co., 743 F.2d 10 (D.C. Cir. 1984)	§§ 2.13, 9.3

Case	*Book §*
Raikos v. Bloomfield State Bank, 703 F. Supp. 1365 (S.D. Ind. 1989)	§ 3.18
Rand McNally & Co. v. Fleet Management Sys., Inc., 591 F. Supp. 726 (N.D. Ill. 1983)	§ 11.7
Raritan River Steel Co. v. Cherry, Bekaert & Holland, 322 N.C. 200, 367 S.E.2d 609 (1988)	§§ 4.8, 5.9
Raskin v. Swann, 454 S.E.2d 809 (Ga. Ct. App. 1995)	§ 4.6
Rasor v. Retail Credit Co., 554 P.2d 1041 (Wash. 1976)	§§ 3.17, 4.22
Ratzlaf v. United States, 114 S. Ct. 655 (1994)	§ 14.10
R.A.V. v. City of St. Paul, 112 S. Ct. 2538 (1992)	§ 6.7
RCA Global Communications, Inc. v. FCC, 758 F.2d 722 (D.C. Cir. 1985)	§ 2.6
Reasor-Hill Corp. v. Harrison, 249 S.W.2d 994 (Ark. 1952)	§ 12.3
Reber v. General Motors Corp., 669 F. Supp. 717 (E.D. Pa. 1987)	§ 12.31
Red Baron-Franklin Park, Inc. v. Taito Corp., 883 F.2d 275 (4th Cir. 1989)	§ 5.7
Red Lion Broadcasting Co. v. FCC, 395 U.S. 367 (1969)	§§ 1.7, 6.1
Red Lobster Inns v. Lawyers Title Ins. Co., 492 F. Supp. 933 (E.D. Ark. 1980)	§ 5.9
Reebok Int'l, Ltd. v. McLaughlin, 49 F.3d 1387 (9th Cir. 1995)	§ 12.10
Reebok Int'l, Ltd. v. McLaughlin, 827 F. Supp. 622 (S.D. Cal. 1993)	§ 12.10
Reid v. Covert, 354 U.S. 1 (1957)	§ 13.23
Renee Beauty Salons, Inc. v. Blose-Venable, 652 A.2d 1345 (Pa. Super. Ct. 1995)	§ 10.11
Reporters Comm. for Freedom of the Press v. American Tel. & Tel. Co., 593 F.2d 1030 (D.C. Cir. 1978)	§§ 3.9, 13.15, 13.16
Request for Int'l Judicial Assistance, *In re,* 700 F. Supp. 723 (S.D.N.Y. 1988)	§ 3.18
Retail Credit Co. v. Dade County, 393 F. Supp. 577 (S.D. Fla. 1975)	§ 3.17
Retherford v. AT&T Communications, 844 P.2d 949 (Mont. 1992)	§ 4.6
Reuber v. United States, 750 F.2d 1039 (D.C. Cir. 1985)	§ 12.8
Rhodes v. Graham, 37 S.W.2d 46 (Ky. 1931)	§ 3.5
Ridgley v. Merchants State Bank, 699 F. Supp. 100 (N.D. Tex. 1988)	§ 3.18
Rindge Co. v. Los Angeles, 262 U.S. 700 (1923)	§ 6.15
Ritchie Enters. v. Honeywell Bull, Inc., 730 F. Supp. 1041 (D. Kan. 1990)	§§ 5.5, 5.13, 5.14
Roach v. Harper, 105 S.E.2d 564 (W. Va. 1958)	§ 3.5
Robins v. Pruneyard Shopping Ctr., 592 P.2d 341 (Cal. 1979)	§ 6.12
Roboserve, Ltd. v. Tom's Food, Inc., 940 F.2d 1441 (11th Cir. 1991)	§ 10.21
Rogers Radio Communications Servs., Inc. v. FCC, 751 F.2d 408 (D.C. Cir. 1985)	§§ 2.6, 2.8
Rosemont Enters., Inc. v. McGraw-Hill Book Co., 380 N.Y.S.2d 839 (Sup. Ct. 1975)	§ 6.10
Roth v. United States, 354 U.S. 476 (1957)	§ 7.12
Roy Export Co. v. Columbia Broadcasting Sys., Inc., 672 F.2d 1095 (2d Cir. 1982)	§ 6.10

TABLE OF REGULATORY DETERMINATIONS

INDEX